DATE DUE

			PRINTED IN U.S.A.

REFERENCE SOURCES IN SCIENCE, ENGINEERING, MEDICINE, AND AGRICULTURE

REFERENCE SOURCES IN SCIENCE, ENGINEERING, MEDICINE, AND AGRICULTURE

H. Robert Malinowsky

ORYX PRESS
1994

The rare Arabian Oryx is believed to have inspired the myth of the unicorn. This desert antelope became virtually extinct in the early 1960s. At that time several groups of international conservationists arranged to have 9 animals sent to the Phoenix Zoo to be the nucleus of a captive breeding herd. Today the Oryx population is nearly 800, and over 400 have been returned to reserves in the Middle East.

Copyright© 1994 by The Oryx Press
4041 North Central at Indian School Road
Phoenix, Arizona 85012-3397

Published simultaneously in Canada

Printed and Bound in the United States of America

☉ The paper used in this publication meets the minimum requirements of American National Standard for Information Science—Permanence of Paper for Printed Library Materials, ANSI Z39.48, 1984.

Library of Congress Cataloging-in-Publication Data

Malinowsky, H. Robert (Harold Robert), 1933–
    Reference sources in science, engineering, medicine, and
agriculture / by H. Robert Malinowsky.
    Includes bibliographical references and index.
    ISBN 0-89774-742-9. —ISBN 0-89774-745-3 (pbk.)
    1. Reference books—Science. 2. Science—Bibliography.
3. Reference books—Engineering. 4. Engineering—Bibliography.
5. Reference books—Medicine. 6. Medicine—Bibliography.
7. Reference books—Agriculture. 8. Agriculture—Bibliography.
I. Title.
Z7401.M278 1994
[Q158.5]
026.6—dc20
                                                    94-16133
                                                    CIP

Contents

Preface

Reference Sources in Science, Engineering, Medicine, and Agriculture is a bibliographic guide to over 2,400 titles in those disciplines. Most guides cover only science and engineering, or a single discipline such as chemistry, physics, engineering, or medicine. To cover four broad areas in one book without producing a volume the size of an encyclopedia was a challenge. As a result, this guide is selective but still representative. It covers those resources that are considered to be the most important, including some classics. The majority of selected titles are currently in print, with a few of the classic titles out of print.

Numerous guides and bibliographic works, as well as the reference collections in several libraries, were scanned for possible titles. Newly published works were identified in book reviewing journals and from notification slips from approval book vendors. After the initial selection, each title was searched for full bibliographic information. If the book was not available, a review or a publisher's advertisement was used to determine whether the book was appropriate. Many titles were rejected at this point, and others were combined so that the annotation for one entry may refer to other related titles. Recency was the goal, and entries had to be revised constantly because newer editions appeared or a better title was published. Even though every effort was made to be as up to date as possible, some new editions may have been overlooked, and some new titles may have been missed.

This book has several intended uses and audiences. First, it is a collection development tool for libraries. Librarians can use this book to assess and add to their reference collections and to determine whether they have newer titles or the latest editions of particular reference works. Prices have been included to help in selection. Second, researchers and students who need to access information but who are unfamiliar with the particular discipline in which they are working can use this book as a starting point. Third, reference librarians can use this guide to locate sources to help answer specific reference questions. Finally, the guide can be used as a text for information science students learning about the literature in these disciplines. The first four chapters of this book are designed specifically for these students.

LIBRARY SCIENCE CHAPTERS

Chapters 1 and 2 are contributed chapters that provide insight into serials pricing (chapter 1) and into how scientists communicate (chapter 2). It is important that the current pricing structure for journals be understood by students and librarians, because money that librarians spend on journals often takes away from what is spent on reference materials. Both chapters alert readers to important topics for building collections in science, engineering, medicine and agriculture. Chapter 3 discusses the various sources in which reference materials can be found, while chapter 4 outlines the formats in which reference materials may appear.

BIBLIOGRAPHIC CHAPTERS

Chapters 5 through 9 are bibliographic, and are the core of this book. Each entry in these sections is briefly annotated but not formally reviewed.

Chapter 5, "Multidisciplinary," covers those materials that contain information pertaining to more than one of the four main disciplines found in chapters 6 to 9.

Chapter 6, "Science," is further subdivided into these subchapters:

- General Science
- Astronomy
- Biology
- Botany
- Chemistry
- Computer Science
- Earth Sciences
- Mathematics
- Physics
- Zoology

Chapter 7, "Engineering/Technology," is further subdivided into these subchapters:

- General Engineering/Technology
- Civil Engineering, Building, Construction
- Electrical and Electronics Engineering
- Energy, Mining, and Natural Resources
- Environmental Engineering
- Industry and Manufacturing
- Mechanical Engineering
- Transportation

Chapter 8, "Medicine," is further subdivided into these subchapters:

- General Medicine
- Nursing
- Pharmacy, Pharmacology
- Special Areas

Chapter 9, "Agriculture," is further subdivided into these subchapters:

- General Agriculture
- Animal and Veterinary Science
- Food Science, Nutrition
- Plant Science, Agronomy, Horticulture

Because of today's complex research topics and overlapping disciplines, it can be difficult to categorize specific subjects. It is, therefore, important to use the subject index to locate topics. (See "Indexing" on the next page.)

Types of Reference Sources

Each subchapter is further subdivided by type of reference source:

- Abstracts/Indexes
- Atlases
- Bibliographies
- Biographical Sources
- Catalogs
- Dictionaries/Glossaries/Thesauri
- Directories
- Encyclopedias
- Guides/Manuals/Field Books
- Guides to the Literature
- Handbooks
- Histories
- Standards
- Tables
- Treatises
- Yearbooks/Annuals/Almanacs

Not every reference type is represented within every discipline, however.

Journals

At the end of each subchapter, selected journal titles for that discipline are listed. With the tens of thousands of titles to choose from, these journal lists are truly selective. They are intended to be the titles that one can expect to find in a library that covers that discipline. These journal entries are not annotated.

Entries

Books are listed alphabetically under each reference type by title. For each entry, some or all of the following information is included:

- Title and subtitle if appropriate
- Edition
- Authors, Editors, or Compilers
- Date of publication
- Place of publication
- State or province of publisher
- Publisher
- Country if other than the United States
- Distributor
- City of distributor
- State of distributor
- Pagination
- Price
- Series if numbered
- ISBN or ISSN number
- Annotation

If no price is available and the book is still in print, the note "price not available" appears. If the title is out of print, this is indicated. For multivolume sets where each volume is priced differently, a note states, "price varies per volume." If a paperback edition is available, the price and ISBN are given. If a title is published in volumes and not complete as of 1993, an open date is given with a frequency of irregular stated.

Annotations

This book is not a reviewing source, and so the annotations have been kept as brief as possible. Many annotations include references to other related works that are not included among the entries in this book. Some are older works that are still useful, while others are newer works that have not been seen or evaluated but appear to be useful based on their author's or publisher's reputation. Occasionally a reference is made to another entry, but this practice is not common. Those titles that are cross-referenced can be identified easily because they do not have date and publisher information following their titles. Annotations for indexing and abstracting sources indicate electronic availability.

Titles of books usually do not change from edition to edition, but authors, editors, and compilers do change. If a book has alternate titles, the annotation will note that fact, and the index will list both titles. In fact, all titles mentioned in the annotations are listed in the title index. (See "Indexing" below.) The annotation will also alert the user to whether the book is a translation.

Some people may feel that including a price adds little to the entry since prices change from year to year. There are reasons for including the price. First, it gives a library collections development person a ballpark idea of price range and a quick way to say yes or no to a title when funds are limited. Second, it is an excellent way to show just how expensive a reference collection can be, which is important when it comes to defending a budget.

Indexing

This volume is indexed by author, title, and subject. The Author Index includes authors, editors, compilers, and corporate names, including acronyms. All authors mentioned in the annotations are listed in the Author Index. The Title Index includes all main entry titles plus the added

alternate titles, original title of translations, and titles mentioned in the annotations. The Subject Index includes both broad terms, to include categories for entire sub-chapters, as well as specific terms pertaining to one or more entries. Collection development librarians could use the title index to check each entry against their holdings to determine the strength and recency of their collections.

It is hoped that this will be a useful reference guide, providing needed information for all researchers. If a title has been omitted, the author will welcome being informed at the University of Illinois at Chicago Library, PO Box 8198, Chicago, IL 60680. The author will be collecting new titles and plans to consider publishing a new edition in a timely manner.

ACKNOWLEDGMENTS

This book is the result of my dedication to the bibliographic documentation of science/technology reference sources. I have spent a great part of my professional life working in science and engineering, writing about the reference literature, and producing guides and reviewing sources in this area.

I began thinking about this book when I was editing the *Science and Technology Annual Reference Review*. It began to fall into place in 1991 and is now finally a reality. This book has been a labor of love, and I hope that it will be a useful addition to the professional literature.

I want to thank the University of Illinois at Chicago Library, and especially the director, Sharon Hogan, for giving me the support, encouragement, and time to work on the book; to Oryx Press, especially Sean Tape, for giving me both technical support and gentle nudges to try to keep me on a schedule; and to Charles Crumet who has been patient in helping me master a new personal computer with new software. Without them, I would still be working away without an end in sight.

PART 1
Introduction to Scientific Reference Sources

Chapter 1: Academic Library Responses to Serial Price Increase

N. Bernard Basch and Judy McQueen[1]

Escalating serial prices are not new. For decades serial prices have been increasing at a rate faster than inflation. The increases, and concern about the increases, are well documented. What is new is the way managers in college and university libraries are reacting to the price increases, and the impact of their actions on subscription agencies.

PRICE INCREASES

Serial prices have increased, are increasing, and will continue to increase. Over the past 17 years the average price of U.S. journals purchased by academic libraries rose from $31.79 in 1974 to $167.45 in 1991, an increase of $135.66 or 527 percent. (Compilations of periodical pricing data prepared by the Faxon Company have been published annually since 1974. The surveys for 1974 through 1980 appeared in *Library Journal*; those for 1981 through 1990 were published in *The Serials Librarian*. The 1991 update, "Periodical prices, 1989-1991" appeared in *Library Acquisitions: Practice & Theory*, v.16, no.1, 1992, pp.3-19.) In the same period, the average price of the foreign subscriptions maintained by academic libraries rose from $48.60 to $330.40, an increase of $281.80 or 680 percent. As demonstrated by the journals covered by major indexing services, the pattern is consistent across subject areas:

	1974	1991[2]	
Art Index	$16.68	$91.43	+548%
Biological Abstracts	$36.61	$263.18	+719%
Education Index	$14.07	$85.47	+607%
Engineering Index	$42.71	$358.10	+838%
Index Medicus	$42.26	$283.81	+672%
Library Literature	$13.70	$94.29	+688%
Readers' Guide	$10.49	$65.28	+622%

Over the same period the proportion of academic library subscriptions priced above $200.00 increased from one percent to 16 percent. In the past decade, price increases in all categories of serials (except Soviet translations) have averaged 10.1 percent, a *compounding* 10.1 percent!

ACADEMIC LIBRARY RESPONSES

Serial price increases are not new, but library managers have become more aware of both the *extent* and the *permanence* of these increases. Price escalation far in excess of inflation is here to stay. It is no longer possible to treat the gap between available serial funds and the cost of current subscriptions as a temporary imbalance that will right itself when conditions "improve." The funding crisis will continue, and it is no

---

[1] N. Bernard Basch is president of the consulting firm Basch Associates; Judy McQueen is a consultant for Basch Associates.

[2] Editor's Note: Although the data for this article are based on data for 1974–1991, this trend has continued, but with some indication that a leveling-off period is at hand.

longer responsive to management methods that have worked in the past.

In previous years, librarians in colleges and universities have been able to bridge shortfalls in serial funds using a variety of stop-gap measures. At the collection level these included rationalization of subscriptions, the trimming of obvious excesses, the elimination of duplicates, and less frequent updating of annuals and irregular yearbooks and directories. A range of financial techniques also yielded satisfactory short-term results: "one-time" allocations of special funds, temporary cancellation of continuations and irregular serials to move billings from one financial period to the next, reallocation of funds for nonserial materials, and innovative fostering and endowment initiatives to cover serial materials in specific subject areas.

In academic libraries, the impact of current serial price increases has been magnified by the economic and demographic realities common to colleges and universities throughout the English-speaking world. To varying degrees these communities share the challenges of unfavorable currency exchange rates, reduced government support, a shrinking client base for traditional tertiary education, reduced real incomes among the families of potential students, aging and maintenance-intensive physical plants, and increasing retirement and benefits payments to personnel recruited to educate the baby boomers.

Library managers are responding creatively, actively redefining traditional paradigms of serial service. For serials other than core materials, the concept of ownership as the necessary and essential prerequisite for reliable access is eroding. The contours of the new approach are still being defined, and the outlines are anything but clear. Redefinition is made possible by the combination of decades of cooperation, technological developments, and entrepreneurial initiatives. Significant influences include the ready availability of machine-readable catalogs and lists, which allow the rapid identification of holding library locations and collection specializations; the similar availability of access to indexes of journal contents; the spread of speedy, reliable, and inexpensive electronic messaging systems and FAX delivery services; publisher initiatives in exploring alternate formats and licensing and distribution arrangements; and vendor experiments with integrated access systems.

While such redefinition opens up new revenue and service opportunities, it closes out other options. Released from the restrictions of an "access depends on ownership" mind-set, serial managers are free to explore the full range of service options, including some that entail the cancellation of subscriptions.

The evidence for a significant change in serial subscription patterns in academic and research libraries is underground and anecdotal. Although the pace is accelerating, participants and observers are not necessarily interested in publicizing the changes. Library managers can be reluctant to showcase cancellations if their users are not convinced of the feasibility of access outside of ownership. Subscription agencies regard sales data as confidential, and an individual agency cannot discern whether its experience is typical of the industry as a whole or simply a sign of a change in the individual agency's competitive position. Many publishers are also close-mouthed about subscription trends, pricing programs, and plans for nontraditional services.

Be that as it may, there is strong anecdotal evidence that academic and research libraries are cancelling significant numbers of serials, and that such cancellations are permanent, not temporary. Whatever the effect on subscription agencies and publishers, it is clear that library managers do not expect the cancellations to affect the ability of libraries to service the needs of their users.

THE EFFECTS ON SUBSCRIPTION AGENCIES

The majority of library subscriptions are processed through subscription agencies; only a small percentage of orders are placed directly with publishers. A reduction in library subscriptions will affect subscription agencies. As with active orders, the effects extend beyond the initial year of order placement or cancellation. Just as agency revenues accrue over the life of a subscription, so the loss or absence of revenues occasioned by cancellations or decisions not to begin subscriptions has a multiyear impact on revenues.

Revenue vacuums caused by serial cancellations and reductions in the number of subscriptions maintained by libraries are offset by automatic increases in subscription agency revenues attendant upon rising serial prices. Agency revenue sources and the relationships between revenues and profitability are complex. Economic viability depends upon balancing publisher discounts, service charges, and costs. (For more detailed discussion of the economics of subscription agencies refer to N. Bernard Basch and Judy McQueen, *Buying Serials*, New York: Neal-Schuman, 1990.)

Traditionally, many commercial publishers have advanced discounts to subscription agencies. Agencies bill their clients the published subscription rate or a slight discount but forward payments to publisher at the fully discounted rate. Until the mid 1960s, the difference between the amount billed to clients and the amount remitted to publishers paid for agency operations. As agency costs increased, service charges were introduced to fill the gap between costs and revenues from publisher discounts. Different agencies follow different approaches in assessing service charges. An agency may levy a charge on all or any transactions; it might also choose to offer discounts.

Serial prices increased by more than 10 percent a year throughout the 1970s and 1980s. In 1974, the average price of an academic library subscription was $34.55; by 1991, the average price had increased to $153.53. If an agency levied a 5 percent service charge on the list price of each title, its recurring annual revenue on academic library accounts would have grown from $1.73 per title in 1974 to $7.68 in 1991.

Provided that publishers continue to increase serial prices at a rate that significantly outstrips inflation and maintain current levels of discount to agencies, and that agencies maintain current levels of service charges and maintain existing operations without significantly increasing costs, then subscription agencies can be expected to maintain (and even increase) their existing levels of profitability. Serial price increases in excess of inflation are a given for the foreseeable future, and agencies appear to be maintaining services and, in some cases, funding substantial new initiatives within current cost parameters. Publishers, however, are changing their discount policies.

Several major scientific, technical, and medical (STM) publishers announced discount reductions late in 1992. The extent of the reductions varied. Some publishers cut discounts by as much as half and introduced dollar caps on the discounts accruing to any one title: "a discount of 'n' percent, but no more than $300.00 per title," for instance. Publishers make their decisions about discounts behind closed doors, but anecdotal evidence indicates that fears about loss of subscription income, concern that agencies were not passing discounts on to clients and that clients had negative perceptions of publishers, and uncertainty about the future of publishing were contributing factors.

In the late 1980s, many library managers negotiated reductions in service charges with their serial suppliers. Librarians were sensitized to the possibilities for negotiation when their concern over serial expenditures combined with increased awareness of the cumulative size of the discounts agencies received from publishers and thus the value of library accounts. Most agencies responded positively to requests for fee negotiation.

Competition ensured that if one agency was reluctant to negotiate, another would usually be willing to service the account at a lower charge. In fact, during the initial round of fee negotiations, some agencies appeared to be more concerned with gaining market share than with sound business management. The frenzy leveled off as librarians and agents focused on achieving a workable balance between *service* and *fees*. Negotiations became more realistic, resulting in service and cost agreements that both parties could live with comfortably.

As publishers cut their discounts, agencies can be expected to seek to recover their lost revenues through increased service charges. Library managers can be expected to resist such increases, and to apply the techniques they used in negotiating services and fee reductions: considered assessment of institutional needs and available service options and costs.

To reach an accommodation, some agencies may reassess their methods of levying service charges. In North America, it is customary for agencies to provide services in addition to order placement and consolidated invoicing. Whereas some agencies charge for additional capabilities related to automation—provision of MARC serial records, online access to agency files, and electronic messaging, for example—it is unusual for them to levy separate charges for nonautomated services such as submitting claims for missing issues to publishers. These services have traditionally been covered by the general service charge and are provided on an unquantified "all you can eat" basis. Individual library usage of these services and usage variations among libraries are not reflected in variations in service charges. Thus, although three libraries—a library with inadequate records or a poorly tuned automated system that submits hundreds of unnecessary claims a year, a library that lacks the systems or personnel to identify missing issues and thus submits no claims, and a library that submits all claims direct to publishers with no agency intervention—place very different demands on agency resources, this variation is not currently reflected in the service fees paid. The libraries that do not use the agency's claiming services subsidize the claiming services the agency performs for the third library.

In a situation in which the purchasing power of libraries is declining, serials prices are increasing, and subscription agencies seek to increase their service charges, a pricing structure that bases service fees on service use could be attractive to some libraries. Such a structure would allow libraries to choose the level of service they require and pay for only that level of service. Both libraries requiring no-frills basic subscription placement and renewal services and libraries seeking more elaborate claiming and automation support could use an agency's services, but at prices more closely related to their respective consumption of agency resources than is presently the case.

The cumulative pressures of reduced resources, increased prices, and increased service charges can be expected to cause some libraries to abandon subscription agency services in favor of ordering direct from publishers. For others, however, the perceived benefits of contracting out subscription ordering and renewal operations will ensure that there will be a demand for subscription services from agencies that contain costs and provide service less expensively than it would cost libraries to order direct from publishers.

Chapter 2: Communication in Science: The Impact of Information Technology

Julie Hurd[1]

Communication in science is supported by a complex, interrelated system that has evolved gradually since the nineteenth century, when many discipline-specific scientific journals began publication as organs of newly formed scientific societies. The process of producing, organizing, and disseminating scientific information features both formal and informal communication. This communication involves not-for-profit and profit-sector organizations, including universities, academic departments, libraries, professional associations, research institutes, scholarly and trade publishers, database producers, and information industry vendors as well as more loosely structured groups such as "invisible colleges." The study of scientific communication has engaged the interests of historians and sociologists of science as well as science librarians and information scientists; the literature resulting from their research is extensive. References to some key studies are provided at the end of this chapter for those who wish to read beyond this overview.

This chapter will survey the system of scientific communication with attention to formal and informal aspects of the process and with recognition of the diversity of organizations, institutions, and individuals that comprise the system. The role of emerging information technologies will be considered, particularly as these may catalyze changes in the communication system. As we examine scientific communication, it is useful to keep in mind that not all involved share the same personal and organizational goals, sources of financial support, or reward structures. This situation certainly makes the resolution of problems complex and assures varying perspectives on controversial issues.

CHARACTERISTICS OF SCIENTIFIC RESEARCH

Scientific research is directed toward finding answers to questions about the physical universe such as:

- What causes, and cures, Alzheimer's disease?
- What are the properties of this new ceramic material? How can I produce it more efficiently?
- What is the nature of the atmosphere of Venus? How are its observed features explained by known geologic processes?

The answers to some questions may have immediate practical application. For example, the results of research by a pharmaceutical company that hopes to synthesize a profitable new drug are likely to be of immediate use. The answers to other questions may not, at the time the research is done, have an apparent application resulting in a marketable product or process, although useful applications may be developed later. For example, for some years the study of nuclear magnetic resonance seemed of interest only to chemical physicists interested in under-

---

[1] Julie Hurd is Science Librarian at the University of Illinois at Chicago.

standing details of nuclear structure. The techniques developed by those scientists, however, now form the foundation for the medical diagnostic technique of magnetic resonance imaging (MRI), a tool whose applications are rapidly increasing in the health care fields.

The "scientific method" is a phrase used to characterize the process of finding answers to questions or solutions to problems. The first step in the process is to formulate a "hypothesis," a presumed answer or explanation that can be subjected to tests through experiments. An understanding of related research and underlying theory will suggest hypotheses as well as define the nature of appropriate experiments, including data to be collected or observations to be made. That interpretations of theories and previous reported research are not usually controversial is characteristic of science. Thomas Kuhn argues the existence of frameworks of scientific knowledge, which he calls "paradigms" and describes how these influence the course of research (Kuhn, 1970).

Laboratory experiments, field observations, and mathematical or statistical analyses are typical elements of scientific methodology whatever the discipline considered. Organic chemists may work primarily in the laboratory studying reactions and characterizing their products; medical researchers may collect data through case studies that provide input for subsequent laboratory experiments, clinical trials, and statistical analyses; astronomers perform mathematical calculations using data collected by large telescopes and space probes. Analysis of these experimental data or observations leads to a written record of the research project.

Scientific research is often a team-oriented activity. In a research university, a team might consist of a faculty member, graduate students, technicians, and postdoctoral research associates. In a chemical manufacturing firm, a team might include a project leader, organic chemists, chemical engineers, and technicians. Whatever its institutional setting, the team draws together individuals with different backgrounds and skills who collectively can accomplish more than the same individuals working independently. For this reason scientific publications are frequently multi-authored. In the university, team research serves another function: it provides a structured apprenticeship in which graduate students, under faculty guidance, learn how to conduct research and to communicate their findings.

Most scientific research is directed toward publication in the refereed journal, and peer review is perceived as integral to the process of validation of research results. Research reported as dissertations or as patents also undergoes a review process, whether by faculty committee or patent examiners. Although other publication formats exist, it would be difficult to overemphasize the importance of the journal in scientific communication. One measure of the preeminent influence of the scientific journal is provided by citation analyses of references in scientific publications. Citations to the journal literature far outnumber citations to any other form of publication in virtually every field of science.

THE SYSTEM OF SCIENTIFIC COMMUNICATION

Communication in science has been studied extensively by William Garvey, Belver Griffith, and co-workers, who developed a model of the process based on their observations of psychologists (Garvey and Griffith, 1972; Garvey, 1979 and references cited therein). Garvey asserted that "communication is the essence of science" and that scientific communication as a social process would lend itself to the methodology of social psychology. The Garvey-Griffith model was subsequently demonstrated to be generally applicable across both the physical and the social sciences. It outlines the process by which research is communicated and provides details of the various stages with a time frame from initial concept to integration of the research as an accepted component of scientific knowledge. Although the time frame varies from one discipline to another, the essential elements of the model appear to be universal.

The Garvey-Griffith model, as delineated in numerous publications of the 1970s, was based on the communication channels then operational. These were both informal and formal and included personal (oral) communications to individuals and groups as well as publication in paper-based journals and books. Since that time, emerging information technologies have dramatically altered and enhanced options for communicating. The introduction of computers to publishing has resulted in online bibliographic databases and large amounts of machine-readable text created to support the publication of books and journals. Visionaries such as F.W. Lancaster could foresee a "paperless" future (Lancaster, 1978). That future has not become reality yet; the technological foundations are in place, but the economic, social, and political barriers have not been overcome.

The now ubiquitous personal computer, the modem, and the low-cost telecommunications networks also provide new communication channels, but overshadowing these in potential impact are the computer networks of bitnet, the Internet, and the developing National Research and Education Network (NREN). Computer-based communication was not an element in Garvey and Griffith's model, but any observer of contemporary research communities would not need to look far to see how scientists have assimilated information technologies into their daily routines. The discussion that follows draws heavily on the Garvey-Griffith model but also attempts to identify changes caused by technology in the scientific communication structure.

INFORMAL COMMUNICATION

At the earliest stages of a research project, communications of findings are informal and preliminary as befitting their tentative nature. Personal communications within an organization are likely to occur first, with research being discussed casually in serendipitous gatherings and in more structured, but still relatively informal, research group and departmental seminars.

As research progresses the investigators may also consult with colleagues at other institutions. The existence of groups of scientists working on closely related research who are communicating with each other across institutional boundaries was described by sociologist Diana Crane, who used the term "invisible college" to characterize the assemblages (Crane, 1972). These informal contacts may provide information on experimental techniques or data analysis, or may clarify or validate interpretations of findings. At this stage in research, communication elicits feedback that may lead to modifications in experimental design or data interpretation.

The scientific communication that Garvey, Crane, and others described relied on telephone conversations, visits to other laboratories, and encounters at professional meetings, all of which could be limited by time constraints or funds available for travel. As electronic mail and other computer-based forms of communication have evolved, they present much enhanced opportunities for informal communication with known colleagues and with fellow subscribers to a particular "listserve" or discussion group. Reports of use of these new tools and their impact on the communication structure are just beginning to appear.

THE ROLE OF MEETINGS AND CONFERENCES

As research progresses and conclusions can be articulated with some assurance, findings are disseminated in presentations at meetings and conferences. These vary in size and scope from small invitational gatherings on well-defined topics, such as the Gordon conferences, to very large professional association meetings attended by thousands. Invitations to present one's research at a conference may be made on the basis of an abstract submitted to a program committee; thus, a meeting provides an opportunity to present very recent findings without the built-in delays of the publication process. The conference presentation may be published in its entirety in a proceedings, but practice varies greatly. Some presentations may appear only in brief meeting abstracts, while others may be recorded only by a title in a program.

Program presentations, however, are not the only reason scientists attend meetings; conferences serve multiple purposes. First, as observed above, they present the opportunity to describe one's research to an interested audience who might provide additional feedback useful in refining accounts of the research. Second, there are numerous occasions for conversations with invisible college colleagues, editors and publishers of scientific journals, planners of future conferences, and others. The formal structure of the meeting is certainly important to the attendees, but so are all the social events and opportunities for informal conversations (Oseman, 1989 and references therein). If video or computer conferences are to replace the traditional scientific meeting, these less tangible benefits of conferences will need to be recognized in some new means or important aspects of scientific communication will be lost.

FORMAL COMMUNICATION

Publication in a refereed scientific journal marks the completion of a project; that the project's findings have been reviewed and accepted by professional peers signifies acceptance by the scientific community and also certifies a claim on any reported discoveries. The journal serves both a communication function and an archival one in providing the record of authorship on its pages. "Received dates" are common on articles. The received date provides a means of resolving claims should nearly simultaneous discoveries occur. It should be noted that those working in the same specialty probably already know of research that has just been published through all the various informal communication channels described earlier. The journal article will, however, inform those in other specializations.

Despite prior dissemination of the research through informal communication, a sense of urgency is a feature of formal communication, and publication delays are not acceptable to authors. A study of physicists' use of journals by the Institute of Physics identified speed of publication as one of the most important criteria an author would employ in selecting a publisher (King and Roderer, 1982). Although the survey providing that perspective was done some years ago, it is very likely that this sense of urgency has only increased. That is why various forms of electronic publication seem to offer such promise in reducing publication delays and facilitating scientific communication.

Proposals for alternatives to the scientific journal are not new. The library and information science literature as well as the scientific literature contain alternative proposals dating back at least 20 years. Prior to the widespread adoption of computers in publishing, these ideas tended to propose different distribution schemes often involving separate articles as the basic unit. Are and

assesses their minimal impact on scientific communication (Piternick, 1989).

With the advent of computer-assisted publishing and the automatic creation of machine-readable text, new models have emerged that are electronic rather than paper or microform based. Whether these will succeed in supplanting the scientific journal remains to be seen. Perhaps they will provide yet another option in the communication structure. To be successful, electronic journals will need to address all the functions currently served by the more traditional format including the role of print publication in the reward structure for many scientists. A *Chronicle of Higher Education* article identifies determinants of success for the electronic journal and quotes a scholarly scientific publisher, David Rodgers of the American Mathematical Society, who observes that electronic journals "will have to offer compellingly superior capabilities to paper...along with lower production and distribution costs" (Wilson, 1991).

SECONDARY SERVICES IN SCIENCE

Indexing and abstracting services, and now computer-stored bibliographic databases, represent the next communication stage after journal publication. Timely appearance in secondary sources is expected by the scientific community, and it is in this part of the process that information technology has already had significant impact in improving access to published information. The immediacy of a scientist's information need explains why databases first appeared in medicine and the pure sciences and why they were quite readily accepted by many scientists. In addition, technology has provided innovative types of access that have also been assimilated by scientists. The capability of computers to store and manipulate large quantities of text has made possible citation indexes and tables of contents databases. These are especially valued by those with interdisciplinary research interests and those who wish access to very recent materials.

THE ROLE OF THE BOOK

In most scientific disciplines the monograph represents a final stage in the communication process. Its purpose is to synthesize previously published information and provide an overview of a specialized area, perhaps for use as a text or a reference compilation of methodology or theory. Citations in books often reference journal literature where findings first appear. Appearance in a monograph provides evidence that a particular concept, theory, or method has been fully assimilated into a discipline's knowledge. Monographs may be written by faculty to support their course-related activities or by established scientists whose expertise provides a perspective on a phase of scientific development. For university-based scientists the monograph is not necessarily important in the reward structure but rather follows toward the close of a successful career.

FUTURE DIRECTIONS

This chapter has surveyed scientific communication and has identified the most important formal channel, the scientific journal. It has outlined the Garvey-Griffith model of scientific communication and suggested how technologies still under development may lead to future changes. The limitations of space have supported an overview rather than a detailed exploration of each facet of the communication process; complex issues have been identified but not fully explored. The development of the communication process is complex, and changes will likely be evolutionary rather than revolutionary. At the same time, the developments that promise significant change are dynamic. What seems obvious now as a future direction may ultimately prove only a brief perturbation and the real future be something not yet imagined. The question for the future is will technology alter the basic structures that support scientific communication and lead to a model substantially different from one derived before computer use was widespread?

REFERENCES

Diana Crane, *Invisible Colleges: Diffusion of Knowledge in Scientific Communities* (Chicago: University of Chicago Press, 1972).

W.D. Garvey, *Communication: The Essence of Science* (Elmsford, NY: Pergamon Press, 1979).

W.D. Garvey and B.C. Griffith, "Communication and information processing within scientific disciplines: Empirical findings for psychology," *Information Storage and Retrieval*, 8 (1972): 123–26.

Donald W. King and Nancy K. Roderer, "Communication in physics—the use of journals," *Physics Today*, 35 (October 1982): 43–47.

Thomas Kuhn, *The Structure of Scientific Revolutions*, 2nd ed., enlarged (Chicago: University of Chicago Press, 1970).

F.W. Lancaster, *Toward Paperless Information Systems* (London: Academic Press, 1978).

Anne B. Piternick, "Attempts to find alternatives to the scientific journal: A brief review," *Journal of Academic Librarianship*, 15 (1989): 260–66.

David L. Wilson, "Testing time for electronic journals," *Chronicle of Higher Education*, 38 (September 11, 1991): A22–24.

READINGS IN COMMUNICATION IN SCIENCE

These materials are suggested as additional sources that provide more information for those who wish to read further. Although some years old, these books and articles are classic studies of communication in science that continue to influence contemporary scholars of communication. Several of these sources provide historical perspectives. Although these sources were not cited explicitly in this chapter, they have certainly informed the author's perspectives.

T. Allen, "Roles in technical communication networks," in *Communication among Scientists and Engineers*, Carnot E. Nelson and Donald K. Pollock, editors. (Lexington, MA: Health Lexington Books, 1970).

David A. Kronick, *A History of Scientific and Technical Periodicals: The Origins and Development of the Scientific and Technological Press, 1665-1790* (Metuchen, NJ: Scarecrow Press, 1962).

Bruce M. Manzer, *The Abstract Journal, 1790-1920: Origin, Development, and Diffusion* (Metuchen, NJ: Scarecrow Press, 1977).

A.J. Meadows, *Communication in Science* (London: Butterworths, 1974).

A.J. Meadows, editor, *The Scientific Journal* (London: Aslib, 1979).

Herbert Menzel, "Information needs of current scientific research," *Library Quarterly*, 34 (1964): 4–19.

Chapter 3: Sources of Scientific and Technical Information

Research materials are created in a variety of ways by a variety of producers. At one time scientific information was either recorded in a journal or in a book. Today, these same methods are used, but the development of many additional specialized sources has resulted in special acquisition, recording, and archiving problems. All sources may be defined as either primary sources—or secondary sources—material that is repackaging of already published information or sources that provide easier access to the primary sources. For example, articles in the *Journal of the American Chemical Society* are primary sources, while the abstracts of these articles in *Chemical Abstracts* are secondary sources.

The following pages list and describe the different sources of scientific and technical information. The sources are listed alphabetically, not in order of importance.

DATABASES

Databases are key to today's so-called information explosion, providing access more easily, quickly, and through more points of entry. Basically a database is a collection of data loaded into a computer together with special programs that can manipulate information to the user's needs. These data can be furnished in a variety of ways—disks, tapes, online, and CD-ROM. The user accesses data through a computer terminal or personal computer and may have the option to print the data. For bibliographic information, the largest online database is OCLC, with information on books cataloged throughout the world, including the Library of Congress. Most all of the indexing and abstracting services that are listed in chapters 5 through 9 are developed from databases and provide the option of accessing them either electronically or in book form. Large databases, such as those from the National Library of

Medicine, BIOSIS, Engineering Information, Chemical Abstracts Service, Cambridge Abstracts, NTIS, and Inspec, can all be accessed for a fee. Some are available for lease for mounting on a mainframe, thus enabling multiple users to access information simultaneously. Others are furnished as CD-ROM products.

In addition to the indexing and abstracting services available electronically, more and more other reference materials are now produced as electronic databases for the public, including dictionaries, encyclopedias, handbooks, directories, tables, treatises, and cumulative indexes to monographic sets or journals. These all provide another reference option for the user but usually at an added cost.

DISSERTATIONS / THESES

A dissertation is the document that is produced to satisfy the doctoral degree requirements at a university or institute. It is considered a primary source of information for providing new findings in the research. The term *dissertation* is sometimes interchanged with the term *thesis,* but usually *thesis* is reserved for the master's degree level of academic scholarship. Dissertations may develop into books at a later date. Parts of dissertations may appear as technical reports. There are databases as well as print sources that access dissertations. *Dissertations Abstracts International* is one such database.

ELECTRONIC JOURNALS

This format is the newest and fastest growing source of information being developed today. The electronic journal is like any other journal except that the articles are stored and transmitted electronically through the computer. Intended as a fast way for providing information, the electronic journal usually depends on an international network, such as the Internet, may be free, may cost, and may require special equipment to access the information that is provided. Despite its newness, hundreds of titles are already available. *Clinical Trials* is an example of an electronic journal that is available for a fee and requires special equipment, while the *AIDS Book Review Journal* is a free electronic journal. Unfortunately, a whole new field of problems is arising including problems related to cost, archiving, development, and production. Electronic journals are here to stay, however, and will become a major source of research data.

GOVERNMENT DOCUMENTS

Governments are, as a group, the most prolific suppliers of information today. Thousands of documents are produced by governments around the world, with the United States and Great Britain the biggest producers. The level of material ranges from the elementary to the advanced technological. Until recently, access has been extremely difficult, with many libraries keeping government publications separate from the rest of the collection.

U.S. documents have been produced since the 1860s when a depository program was developed so that designated libraries throughout the United States would receive all the published documents. This policy has continued so that today the materials are available to everyone, and, with the MARCIVE and other commercial database catalogs, access is now easier electronically. Buried among government documents are all types of reference sources from encyclopedias, indexes, abstracts, and dictionaries to directories, handbooks, tables, manuals, and bibliographies. Some government documents are selected by commercial publishers, reprinted, and sold as new titles. Most, however, remain as government publications. A few of the classics have been listed in this book, but for the most part the reader is urged to search the government document databases for additional materials. (For helpful search strategies see *Tapping the Government Grapevine,* 2d Edition, Oryx, 1992 and *Using Government Information Sources: Print and Electronic,* 2d Edition, Oryx, 1993).

Government documents can be both primary and secondary sources of information.

MONOGRAPHS

A monograph is a book, usually a scholarly work on a specific topic. Monographs provide an overview of the topic and are normally secondary sources of information, especially in science. Technically, in library cataloging terminology, any book that is not published in parts is considered a monograph, as opposed to a serial which is published in parts. Monographs, however, can be published in several volumes before being complete. What distinguishes monographs, single or multivolume, is the narrow focus on a specific topic. Access to monographs is usually through a card catalog, online catalog, or a bibliography such as *Books in Print.* OCLC provides the world's largest bibliography of books and serial titles. Monographs may be one-time publications, or they may be updated by subsequent editions. They can be purely entertaining, such as the many fiction titles; instructional, such as textbooks and manuals; or informational, such as reference books. They are usually not as up to date as journals because of the longer length of time it takes to publish them, but with computers and desktop publishing, recency has been improved, resulting in very up-to-date information at the time of publication of many monographs.

NONPRINT SOURCES

Nonprint sources are mentioned here to remind users that everything does not always appear in neat printed formats with colorful covers.

Microfilm has been developed for retaining historical materials and for preserving deteriorating print materials. Microfilm requires special handling. Access is usually through the print and electronic indexes since microfilm is cataloged and indexed like any other type of material.

Films, videos, laserdiscs, slides, and other photographic images provide a wide array of information for researchers. Access to them is usually the same as it is for books.

The use of computer disks is increasing, especially as supplemental material to books. The use of disks presents problems for the user who does not have immediate access to the computer and for the provider, who must have backup disks in case the original is damaged or lost. Computer disks require special handling for housing, cataloging, indexing, and insurance against electronic erasing. For example, first the bibliographical description of the book has to identify the disk as an integral part of the book. Then, a decision has to be made as to whether the disk should be kept separate from the book so that it does not become damaged while shelved in the stacks. Finally, disks cannot be subjected to any kind of magnetic field; thus they require extreme caution when part of a collection that has an electronic book detection system.

Some other nonprint research materials are artifacts, museum pieces, and archeological findings. Many of these are converted to print through photographs or, in some cases, to computer images. Written descriptions of these objects usually become printed documents that are accessed as any other printed documents.

SERIALS

Librarians have managed to come up with broad terminology that is sometimes confusing to the nonlibrarian. A *serial* is the accepted professional term for publications intended to be published under the same title in successive parts indefinitely. A serial may change in frequency, format, title, or content, or it may end after several volumes. Serial literature can be both primary and secondary.

Types of Serials

There are many types of serials. First is the *Periodical. Journal* and *periodical* are interchangeable terms, but the scientist opts for the term *journal*. One sees *Journal of . . .* in the names of publications but never sees *Periodical of . . .* On the other hand, librarians make the mistake of calling journal indexes "periodical indexes." *Magazine* is a term reserved for the general public and usually refers to a periodical source of nontechnical information. *Newspapers* are a type dictated by its format, lack of cover, and limited contents. *Series* is a term reserved for those publications where each volume is unique and can be treated as a monograph but where all titles are held together with a common subject series name. Lastly, are all the *Advances in . . . , Progress in . . . , Annual Review of . . . , Trends in . . . , Yearbook of . . . ,* and *Almanac of . . . .* These are usually summary publications bringing together an overview of research over a period of time.

Access to serial literature is very good. Abstracts and indexes permit users to locate materials through a variety of methods. With automation, this process has become faster and more efficient. Because they cover periodicals, abstracts and indexes are also serials, published regularly to keep up with the literature.

The biggest problem with serials is the sheer number of titles that are published. This glut of titles presents monumental problems in housing, preserving, maintaining, selecting, and indexing. Catalogers become frustrated in trying to develop a publishing history for a title that has changed names several times, has had different publishers, and may have split into several sections. Finally, as was seen in Chapter 1, the cost of maintaining a serial collection is monumental, with some budgets spending up to 90 percent or more on just subscriptions. A quick look at the subscription prices for the journals listed in the bibliographical chapters will illustrate why serials pricing is a serious matter.

PREPRINTS

Preprints are usually articles that are issued before they are in their final published format, sometimes without all of the supporting documents, illustrations, and bibliographies. Institutions and societies have preprint series to get research results to others earlier. Preprints are also papers that are going to be presented at meetings. These materials may find their way into the indexing and abstracting literature, but there are many that do not. Preprint articles usually become actual journal articles at later dates and may be identical to the preprint, or the journal articles may not have any resemblance to the originals. Preprints are considered primary sources. Preprints are prime candidates for being published electronically. Several societies are considering this route and may be soon producing an electronic text along with hard copy.

PROCEEDINGS

Proceedings, also called transactions, are the official reports or papers of a society or meeting. They resemble journal articles and may be considered a part of the journal literature. The indexing and abstracting services cover this literature the same as the other serial literature.

REPRINTS

Reprints are materials that have been reprinted from the original and distributed on a limited basis to a select audience. They may be part of a series from an institution or society, but they are rarely indexed and abstracted since they are covered when they appear in their original format. Their main purpose is to facilitate networking among researchers doing the same type of research. Occasionally, a collection of reprints is published as a monograph. Also, some special issues of journals may be reprinted and sold separately as monographs.

SOCIETY PUBLICATIONS

Societies are major publishers of research materials from journals to proceedings, and from books to electronic products. Most materials are from their own members, providing them an avenue for reporting their research progress. The publications are usually reasonable in cost, especially to members. Many provide their own indexing and abstracting access, and some are moving towards publishing material electronically. Many are prolific publishers, such as the American Chemical Society, Institution of Electrical and Electronics Engineers, American Medical Association, American Society for Metals, and American Society for Testing and Materials, each of which publish several hundred titles a year, in addition to thousands of journal articles.

TECHNICAL REPORTS

Technical reports normally result from research grants. They are intended to present the progress of the research from the time it begins until the time it ends. If the project progresses over several years, the technical report for that program may become a serial published in parts until finished. Technical reports may be published in several reference formats, including dictionaries, bibliographies, directories, manuals, or tables.

Institutes, agencies, and societies all produce technical reports. These groups usually have unique numbering systems that help to identify the individual items. They may be indexed and abstracted and may be free for those with a "need to know." Access points to technical reports are many but confusing, because one report may have several agency identification numbers attached to it. For the United States, the largest repository of technical reports is the National Technical Information System (NTIS), managed by the U.S. government. A copy of all technical reports produced from governmental contracts will be found here as well as voluntary deposits of other reports. Some government agencies such as NASA publish thousands of technical reports written within several series.

TEXTBOOKS

Textbooks are those monographs whose main purpose is instruction. A typical textbook begins with background information and then proceeds to basics and continues into ever-more difficult aspects of the topic. Questions or complexed problems may be included as well as bibliographies for further reading. Most textbooks have little reference value, except for the medical fields where a comprehensive textbook is an encyclopedia of the topic covered. Reference departments in medical libraries will have many textbooks as part of their active reference collections. Textbooks are secondary sources of information.

TRADE LITERATURE

Trade publications are all those materials that are published by for-profit organizations such as McGraw-Hill, Elsevier, Lippincott, Scarecrow Press, and Van Nostrand Reinhold. They produce a large portion of the world's literature, sometimes at a high cost to the purchaser. Some of the world's most prestigious reference materials are trade publications, such as the McGraw-Hill handbooks or the Academic Press encyclopedias or the Chapman & Hall dictionaries or the Springer-Verlag treatises. It would be impossible to maintain a reference collection without these publications.

TRANSLATIONS

As more and more countries use English as the main language for publishing in the sciences, *translations* become fewer and fewer. They are still important, however. Their greatest value and use is in journal translation, particularly from Russian, Japanese, and Chinese. Their biggest drawback is lack of recency. Translations may be up to two years behind the original publication, which is far too long for cutting-edge research. For firms doing research that depends on knowledge of foreign results, in-house translators are the only answer. Unfortunately, translation journals are becoming the first category of items to be cancelled when there is a budget crisis. Translations are secondary sources, and access is through the regular indexing and abstracting services for journals.

Chapter 4: Types of Reference Sources

Scientific literature can be classified into types based on format, frequency, and content. Some of these types are easily distinguishable, such as dictionaries, but others may be more difficult to define, such as handbooks, which can include manuals, guides, and tables. Nevertheless, there are some characteristics that can be used to categorize different types of reference sources.

ABSTRACTS

Abstracts are the most important reference sources available for researchers. Without abstracts researchers would have to read through articles to determine their merit. Abstracts also overcome the language barrier because they can be written in any language, allowing the researcher to read a summary of an article in an unfamiliar language. *Chemical Abstracts* is recognized as the world's premier abstracting service. Keep in mind that even though the name of a reference source does not include the word "abstract," the source might still offer an abstract service. For example the *Engineering Index* also provides an abstracting service.

With the continued adoption of new electronic technologies, printed abstracting services are much more up-to-date. Print products still take longer to produce, however, and in some cases are being phased out and replaced completely by online or CD-ROM formats. The majority of the abstracts in this guide are available in some electronic format.

ALMANACS

An *almanac* is often popularly thought of in terms of the *Farmers Almanac*—an annual publication providing a calendar of events of weather, planting, harvesting, astronomy, and folklore. For some scientific disciplines, however, an almanac takes on a different meaning. In these disciplines it is an annual containing charts, tables, and lists of useful information that may or may not change from year to year. Almanacs are common in astronomy; several current astronomical almanacs began in the 1700s. One type of astronomical almanac is the ephemeris, an annual table of past, present, and future coordinates of celestial bodies at a number of specific times during the listed periods. The *Astronomical Almanac for the Year,* previously called *American Ephemeris and Nautical Almanacs,* is an excellent example. In this guide, almanacs are grouped with yearbooks and annuals.

ATLASES

An *atlas* is normally thought of as a collection of maps. Actually, an *atlas* means a collection of tables, charts, or pictures that systematically illustrate a particular subject; an atlas is not limited to cartographical, geographical, or geological subjects, such as the *World Atlas of Geology and Mineral Resources*. There are hundreds of atlases in the medical field that depict the body or body parts in pictures, cross-sections, or radiographs. There are atlases that pictorially depict plants and animals of a region or of the world. There are atlases of mathematical functions, *Atlas of Functions;* chemical compounds, *Atlas of Polymer and Plastics Analysis;* stars, *Cambridge Star Atlas 2000.0;* planets, *Atlas of the Solar System;* and spectra as represented by all the Sadtler Spectra. Atlases are important in science and technology reference, but they are becoming more sophisticated with the new technologies and can be very expensive. The atlases of tables, functions, and chemicals are prime candidates for electronic presentation.

BIBLIOGRAPHIES

A *bibliography* may be a list of works by a single author or publisher, a list of works on a specific subject, or a description of all editions of books or other materials. A true bibliography should list at the least the author, title, publisher, and pagination of a work. Other information may include price, condition, table of contents, locations, and historical notes. Bibliographies come in many forms. There are trade bibliographies in the form of *Books in Print*, national bibliographies in the form of *Cumulative Book Index*, catalogs in the form of Mansell's *The National Union Catalog: Pre-1956 Inprint*, and databases in the form of OCLC. Any library catalog is a bibliography of what that library owns. Bibliographies can be spin-offs of abstracting and indexing services, providing specialized sources on a particular topic. In fact, many indexing services are actually bibliographies. Automation has made compiling custom bibliographies easier because they can be created from electronic databases on demand rather than having to be published for mass distribution. Topics such as AIDS, abortion, drugs, sexual harassment, and individual diseases, however, demand printed bibliographies because they are popular subjects, and many people find printed sources easier to use. Some bibliographices on these topics are even published on a regular basis as serials.

BIOGRAPHICAL SOURCES

The term *biographical source* refers to those sources that provide information about individuals. Biographical information can be found in directories, dictionaries, encyclopedias, handbooks, or catalogs. An entire work may be biographical, or biographical information may be buried within the source. Some biographical sources provide biographical essays on the lives of individuals, while others just list basic directory-type information such as can be found in the *American Men and Women of Science*.

CATALOGS

A *catalog* is a list of items arranged in some order. The most common catalog is the card or online catalog of a library, which arranges books in a variety of ways, including by author, title, subject, and call number. There are catalogs of satellites, chemicals, and astronomical bodies. All of these are important and many become key reference sources in some reference collections.

CURRENT AWARENESS SOURCES

Current awareness services alert researchers about what is to be published or what recently has been published. These services help individuals stay abreast of current research. Some services are computer-produced, while others are photo-offsets of the original publication. Usually, the weekly service issues arrive before the actual journals arrive in the library. These services normally have no lasting value and are rarely kept and bound. *Current Contents,* the current tables of contents of the most recent issues of research journals, is one example of a photo-offset service. *Current Contents* can be accessed online covering the latest six months, and other online are services being developed which bring information faster than printed issues. *Clinical Alerts* is one such example.

DICTIONARIES

Containing alphabetical lists of words, phrases, abbreviations, and other terms, *dictionaries* provide definitions and explanations of the listed terms. They may also include pronunciation, etymology, usage, or grammatical uses. Some dictionaries are encyclopedic in nature, providing some historical background and information about each term. Bilingual or multilingual dictionaries show corresponding terms in another language, but usually contain no definitions. Specialized dictionaries provide definitions for a particular field. Glossaries, another type of dictionary, are lists of specialized words usually found at the back of monographs. Thesauruses list terms pertaining to a specialized field and indicate the various synonyms of words through cross-references. A thesaurus is often used to create a controlled vocabulary for indexing purposes. Some dictionaries become identification sources, such as in chemistry, where a chemical is listed and all its properties are identified along with detailed descriptions such as molecular formulas and diagrams. The *Dictionary of Organic Compounds* is an excellent example of this type of dictionary.

DIRECTORIES

A *directory* is a list of names, organizations, products, of services, providing such identifying information as address, telephone number, personnel, publications, and any other unique information in each entry. Many directories are labeled as biographical or encyclopedic sources, such as the *Encyclopedia of Associations*. Because directories can be extensive and include a wealth of information, many are now available online and in electronic formats to make locating up-to-date information easier, such as the *Encyclopedia of Associations* and *BioScan*. Directories are expensive to produce and maintain, and, as a result, many do not survive because they are too expensive for customers to buy regularly.

ENCYCLOPEDIAS

An important part of any reference collection, *encyclopedias* contain articles on a particular topic or group of topics. Depending on the intended audience, articles can range from dictionary-type definitions to comprehensive essays complete with bibliographies. Articles can also include the etymology of a term and other historical background so that a nonspecialist can better understand what is presented. Although articles are generally arranged alphabetically and include extensive cross-references to other articles, some encyclopedias arrange articles topically within broad subjects. Though indexes are useful, not all encyclopedias have them.

Every discipline has its encyclopedias, ranging from one or two volumes to multivolume sets or serials which may be published in parts over several years with intervening supplements. Encyclopedias can be inexpensive or cost thousands of dollars. The *McGraw-Hill Encyclopedia of Science and Technology* is good example of a encyclopedia.

FIELD GUIDES

A *field guide* explains how to identify items in real life settings. A practical book, small enough to fit into a pocket, a field guide contains detailed descriptions and illustrations of the subjects it identifies. Depending on the discipline, the subjects may be animals, plants, stars, rocks, minerals, fossils, clouds, and so on. Many field guides appear in series, such as the Peterson and Audubon series.

GUIDES

A *guide* explains and illustrates a topic. It is closely related to, though not as specific as, a manual. For the most part, guides are used in laboratories to help researchers perform a particular task the same way each time. Intended to ensure that the task is carried out in the best and safest way possible, guides take researchers through the procedure step-by-step, offering safety warnings and other tips. Some sources described as guides, however, are not how-to books but rather encyclopedias or handbooks, such as guides to hazardous chemicals and field guides.

GUIDES TO THE LITERATURE

Guides to the Literature are bibliographies of recommended materials and sources on a particular topic. This book is an example of a guide to reference literature for science, engineering, medicine, and agriculture. Available for specific topics in many disciplines, guides to the literature help researchers find additional information on a topic. Librarians use them as collections development tools, and students use them to learn about the publications of a particular discipline. Guides may merely list sources or give more detail for each source in an essay or narrative format. Sources may be arranged by subject and listed alphabetically under each type or arranged by type and then listed alphabetically under each subject.

HANDBOOKS

The original purpose of a *handbook* was to provide a one-volume reference source for working professionals, especially in engineering. Today, however, rarely can a professional have just one handbook. The proliferation of information has resulted in hundreds of handbooks of all kinds, sizes, shapes, coverage, and prices.

There are several types of handbooks. One type normally begins with a section covering background or refresher information of a subject, such as the basics of mathematics. Several sections follow, each proceeding in a standard manner beginning with definitions and purposes and then delving into specifics. Generally, the sections become more detailed as the book progresses. Tables, charts, graphs, and illustrations are prolific, and a detailed index is mandatory. The *Handbook of Applied Mathematics for Engineers and Scientists* and *Handbook of Corrosion Data* are examples of this kind of handbook. McGraw-Hill and Van Nostrand Reinhold are two publishers of classic handbooks.

Another type of handbook, such as the *CRC Handbook of Chemistry and Physics,* contains only tables, charts, and similarly formatted information. CRC is the publisher of many such handbooks.

A third type of guidebook/handbook presents how-to information and general information about a subject. Travel handbooks are excellent examples of this type. Many manuals also qualify as handbooks, and the difference between the two can be slight.

HISTORIES

Although not a specific type, *histories,* such as historical encyclopedias, can be important reference works. A chronology is another form of history that is used as a reference source. Chronologies, as the name implies, list events in chronological order to show how something evolved and provide milestones in history so that the user can understand how a process or subject evolved.

INDEXES

The most common type of *index* is an alphabetical listing of names, subjects, or events which indicates where that term can be found in a book or journal by page number or other unique flag. Invaluable for locating nonautomated information, indexes are found in the back of books, volumes of journals, and annual cumulations of abstracting services. Most indexes have controlled vocabularies so that synonyms are cross-referenced, although there are key word (kwic) indexes with uncontrolled vocabularies in which every term has an entry in the index. Though appropriate for science/technology works, kwic indexes do not suit most works in the social sciences and humanities.

The computer provides a variety of ways to produce and search indexes. It is easy to construct an index automatically by setting tags to terms or phrases. In databases, combinations of terms can be identified and found with boolean searching, where terms are searched in conjunction with other terms. The *Science Citation Index* is an example of a computer-generated index.

Other forms of indexes include Union catalogs, in which each entry in the catalog is linked to one or more locations. The card or online catalog in a library is a form of an index because books are linked to call numbers that correspond to shelf locations in the stacks. Some abstracting services are misnamed as indexes, such as the *Engineering Index,* in which the entries are abstracts, and indexes appear at the end of each volume.

MANUALS

A *manual* is a book of instruction, which are more detailed and comprehensive than those in a handbook. The most common manuals in the science/technology fields delineate operating procedures, from operating a piece of equipment, to managing a factory, to providing personnel procedures. There are manuals on how to collect and analyze data, how to conduct a complicated laboratory procedure, how to care for laboratory animals, and how to name plants and animals. Some, but not all, manuals are useful as parts of the reference collection. *Dana's Manual of Minerlogy* and *Bergey's Manual of Systematic Bacteriology* are examples of useful manuals.

MAPS

Maps are common in geology, depicting the earth as it was, is now, and will be. Other maps cover the planets, moons, and the constellations. The term map is sometimes used in place of "atlas," as in "map of the brain." Collections of maps are expensive to maintain, store, and catalog.

PATENTS

A *patent* is an agreement with a government granting an inventor or patentee the sole right to exploit an invention for a period of time within that government's country. Most of the major industrialized countries give patents, but they don't recognize each other's patents; therefore, the inventor must apply for patents in the countries where protecting that invention and its exploitation is necessary. Patents are important in all areas of science and technology, and in some cases, they are the final crown to a research project. Because copies of original patents and any translations are critical in the development of new products, patent searching has become a field in itself, with many indexing and abstracting services covering patents.

REVIEWING SOURCES

Reviews critique the quality and usefulness of books, journals, products, software, or services. A review can appear as an article in a periodical, a collection of articles under a unique title, or an electronic source. Because reviews give guidance on whether an item should be purchased, they are especially useful when expensive items are being considered. Good examples are the *Mathematical Reviews* and the *AIDS Book Review Journal*.

STANDARDS

A *standard* is something that is accepted as an authority or an acknowledged measure of comparison for quantitative or qualitative values. Standards become accepted through the reputation of those who create the standard. They are used on a voluntary basis, but some agencies require certain standards to be followed, such as the federal government, with its "Mil-Specs" (Military Specifications) which all contractors have to follow when constructing military equipment. Standards can also specify the steps for constructing something. Standards become parts of codes and procedures so that products can be compatible. There are several agencies that are prolific in developing standards, including American Society for Testing and Materials (ASTM), American National Standards Institute (ANSI), American Society of Mechanical Engineers (ASME), Institute of Electronic and Electronics Engineers (IEEE), and National Fire Protection Association (NFPA). A well-known index of standards is the *Index and Directory of Industry Standards*.

TABLES

Tables are normally a part of a reference source, but there are works that consist only of tables, particularly in mathematics, physics, and chemistry. There are tables of trigonometric and other mathematical functions, such as *Tables of Integrals, Series, and Products,* as well as tables of chemicals and physical constants, such as *CRC Handbook of Physics and Chemistry*. Some books of tables are published with their own disks and programs that allow users to tailor a particular table to a project.

TREATISES

A *treatise* is a comprehensive work that covers a topic chronologically for a certain period of time, providing extensive bibliographies for additional study. Important for researchers, treatises provide comprehensive overviews of topics incorporating all the pertinent writings for that period of time. By using a treatise a researcher does not have to read the original articles unless more detailed information is needed; therefore, a treatise is the first step in doing research. Treatises can also provide insights on research yet to be done. Chemistry and the biological sciences rely heavily on treatises. Excellent examples are the *Treatise of Invertebrate Paleontology* and *Beilsteins Handbuch der Organischen Chemie*.

YEARBOOKS

Yearbooks, or annuals, are good sources for summaries of what has happened during a year. They are sometimes overlooked, and only a few become part of reference collections. Some yearbooks are supplements to a parent set, such as encyclopedia yearbooks, though others are statistical summaries, such as the yearbooks produced by the United Nations and the Food and Agriculture Organization (FAO). Some yearbooks are published on a timely basis close to the year they cover, such as the *Yearbook of Astronomy,* whereas others can be several years late, such as the *Yearbook of Agriculture. Yearbooks and annuals are actually serials, and some are indexed and covered by abstracting services. The contents of some annuals and yearbooks may never receive detailed indexing, however, and the important information in them may be difficult to find.*

PART 2
Reference Sources

Chapter 5: Multidisciplinary Sources

Categorizing material in guides to the literature can present problems. This guide has four distinct, broadly defined areas: science, engineering/technology, medicine, and agriculture. There are, however, some materials that cut across two or more of these areas. To include those reference works, this first bibliographic chapter lists the titles that cover more than one discipline. Many of the entries are extensive works and go beyond just the four areas covered in this book, and others are more specialized in just two areas. All should be noted, however, and users should be aware that they exist. This chapter does not have a subsection on periodicals as do each of the following chapters. Users should also check the subject and title indexes because some seemingly multidisciplinary sources may be listed in one of the subject chapters.

Abstracts and Indexes

1. Applied Science and Technology Index. New York, NY: Wilson, 1958– , monthly with cumulations. v.1-. service basis. ISSN: 0003-6986.

This is the cumulative subject index to periodical articles from 391 key science, trade, and technology titles with a separate listing for book reviewing and product reviews. It is also available on tape, online, and on CD-ROM.

2. Bibliographic Index. New York, NY: Wilson, 1937– , 3/year. v.1-. service basis. ISSN: 0006-1255.

This subject index to bibliographies lists 50 or more citations published in books, pamphlets, or the some 2,800 periodicals that Wilson indexes. Foreign language publications are included. It is also available online and on tape.

3. Book Review Index. Detroit, MI: Gale Research. 1965– , bimonthly with annual cumulations. $195.00. ISSN: 0524-0581.

This index provides citation to book reviews in some 460 periodicals. All disciplines are covered. It is also available online.

4. Composite Index for CRC Handbooks. 3rd. Boca Raton, FL: CRC, 1990. 3v., index. $1,295.00. ISBN: 0-8493-0284-6.

This index provides author and subject indexes to over 300 handbooks that CRC publishes in the fields of biomedical science, biology, chemistry, engineering, computer science, physics, and mathematics. Annual supplements began in 1991. It is also available on CD-ROM.

5. Comprehensive Dissertation Index. Ann Arbor, MI: University Microfilms, 1861-1972, 1973-1982, 1983-1987, 1988– , annual. 1961-1972 in 37v., 1973-1982 in 38v., 1983-1987 in 22v., 1988– , index. write for prices.

This comprehensive index covers some 450,000 dissertations from U.S. and foreign universities. All disciplines are covered. The dissertations are arranged by discipline.

6. Conference Papers Index. Bethesda, MD: Cambridge Scientific Abstracts, 1973– , bimonthly. v.1– , index. $975.00. ISSN: 0162-704X.

Previously called the *Current Programs* of the World Meetings Information Center, this index is to the authors and titles of papers that have been presented at conferences throughout the world. It is also available online. Another bibliographic guide to conference publications is the *Bibliographic Guide to Conference Publications* (G.K. Hall, 1975-).

7. Current Contents. Philadelphia, PA: Institute for Scientific Information, 1961– , weekly. v.1– , index. price per section varies.

This index reprints the actual tables of contents of key periodicals in all fields. It is divided into the following sections: Agriculture, Biology and Environmental Sciences; Arts and Humanities; Clinical Medicine; Engineering Technology and Applied Sciences; Health Services Administration; Life Sciences; Physical, Chemical, and Earth Sciences; and Social and

Behavioral Sciences. It is also available online, on tape, and on CD-ROM.

8. Directory of Published Proceedings.
Harrison, NY: InterDok, 1965– , frequency varies with each section. v.1– , index. price per section varies. ISSN: 0093-5816 PCE; 0012-3293 SEMT; 0012-3707 SSH.

This index of published conferences and their proceedings is published in 3 sections: Series PCE—Pollution Control and Ecology; Series SEMT—Science, Engineering, Medicine, and Technology; and Series SSH—Social Sciences-Humanities. It compliments the *Index to Scientific and Technical Proceedings* published by the Institute of Scientific Information.

9. Dissertation Abstracts International. Ann Arbor, MI: University Microfilms, 1939– , monthly. v.1– , index. price per section varies.

Previously called *Microfilm Abstracts* (1938-1951) and *Dissertation Abstracts* (1952-1967), this service emphasizes abstracts of dissertations from U.S. institutions. It is published in three sections: A—Humanities and Social Sciences; B—Physical Sciences and Engineering; C—Worldwide. It is also available on CD-ROM.

10. Government Reports Announcement and Index Journal. Springfield, VA: National Technical Information Service, 1975– , semimonthly. v.75, no.7– , index, annual cumulative index called *Government Reports Annual Index.* $495.00. ISSN: 0097-9007.

This is a comprehensive index and current awareness service to some 60,000 research and development reports produced each year. Formed by the union of the *Government Reports Index* and the *Government Reports Announcements*, the *Government Reports Index* was previously called the *U.S. Government Research and Development Reports Index.* Prior to 1975 this service was called *Bibliography of Scientific and Industrial Reports* (1946-1949); *Bibliography of Technical Reports* (1949-1954); *U.S. Government Research and Development Reports* and *U.S. Government Research and Development Reports Index* (1954-1971); and *Government Reports Announcement* and *Government Reports Index* (1971-75). It is also online.

11. Guide to Microforms in Print. New Providence, NJ: K.G. Saur, 1975– , annual. v.1– , index. $516.00. ISSN: 0164-0747.

Incorporating *International Microforms in Print*, this is an alphabetical listing of books, journals, newspapers, government publications, archival materials, and collections that are available in microform. It consists of an author-title and subject sections. Ordering and pricing information is given. A supplement is published that provides only those titles that are new to the previous editions.

12. Index to Scientific and Technical Proceedings. PA: Institute for Scientific Information, Philadelphia. v.1– , index. $1,325.00. ISSN: 0149-8088.

A comprehensive index to published conference proceedings, it is indexed by author, subject, conference sponsor, meeting location, author's organization, and title words. It is also available online. Another smaller index is *Proceedings in Print* (Proceedings in Print Corp., 1964-).

13. Index to U.S. Government Periodicals. Chicago, IL: Infodata International, 1970– , quarterly. v.1– , index. $400.00. ISSN: 0098-4604.

This index covers some 176 U.S. government periodicals, providing author and subject access. It is also available online.

14. Masters Theses in Pure and Applied Sciences. New York, NY: Plenum, 1957– , annual. v.1– , index. price varies per year.

This index to masters theses in the United States and Canada is arranged alphabetically by author within each of the 44 disciplines. Mathematics and the life sciences are excluded.

15. MInd, the Meetings Index: Series SEMT-Science, Engineering, Medicine, Technology. Harrison, NY: InterDok, 1984– , bimonthly. v.1– , index. $425.00. ISSN: 0739-5914.

This work is a listing of future conferences, seminars, workshops, congresses, meetings, institutes, and courses. Another such listing is *World Meetings* (Macmillan, 1963-), which is published in four sections: United States and Canada, outside United States and Canada, medicine, and social and behavioral sciences, human sciences and management. A less comprehensive source is *Scientific Meetings* (Scientific Meetings Publications, 1957-).

16. Monthly Catalog of United States Government Publications. Washington, DC: GPO, 1951– , monthly. no. 672– , index. $199.00. ISSN: 0362-6830.

Previously called *United States Government Publications Monthly Catalog*, this is the official catalog of all U.S. government publications, providing complete bibliographic information, price, and ordering information. SuDoc numbers are included, as well as indications if the item was a depository item. It is also available on CD-ROM. MARCIVE is the online database from which this publication is produced. This database is becoming an integral part of the online catalogs of many libraries.

17. PASCAL Explore; PASCAL Folio; PASCAL Thema. Vand oeure-Les-Nancy Cedex, France: Centre National de la Recherche Scientifique, Institute de l'Information Scientifique et Technique, 1984– , monthly. v.1– , index. price per section varies.

These three titles are the successor to the well-known *Bulletin Signaletique* (1956-1984). They are comprehensive French-language abstracting services with annual author and subject indexes. The various sections, many having changed names several times, include E27—Methodes de Formation et Traitement des Images (1146-5360); T295—Batiment, Travaux Publics (1146-5093); E11—Physique Atomique et Moleculaire, Plasmas (0761-1951); E12—Etat Condense (0761-196X); E13—Structure des Liquides et des Solides Cristallographie (0761-1978); E20—Electronique et Telecommunications (0246-1161); E30—Microscopie Electronique et Diffraction Electronique (0761-2028); E32—Metrologie et Appareillage en Physique et Physicochimie (0761-2044); E33—Informatique (0761-2052); E34—Robotique, Automatique et Automatisation des Processus Industriels (0761-2060); E36—Pollution de l'Eau, de l'Air et du Sol, Dechets, Bruit (0246-117X); E48—Environnement Cosmique Terrestre, Astronomie et Geologie Extraterrestre (0761-2109); E49—Meteorologie (0761-2117); E58—Genetique (0246-1447); E61—Microbiologie: Bacteriologie, Virologie, Mycologie, Protozoaires Pathogenes (0761-2133); E62—Immunologie (0761-2141); E63—Toxicologie (0761-215X); E64—Endocrinologie Humaine et Experimentale, Endocrinopathies (0761-2168); E65—Psychologie, Psychopathologie, Psychiatrie (0761-2176); E71- Ophtalmologie (0761-2184); E72—Otorhinolaryngologie, Stomatologie, Pathologie, Cervicofaciale (0761-2192); E73—Dermatologie, Maladies Sexuellement Transmissliblies (0761-2206); E74—Pneumologie (0761-2214); E75—Cardiologie et Appareil Circulatoire (0761-2222); E76—Gastroenterologie, Foie, Pancreas, Abdomen (0761-2230); E77—Nephrologie, Voies Urinaires (0761-2249); E78- Neurologie (0761-2257); E79—Pathologie et Physiologie Osteoarticulaires (0761-2265); E80—Hematologie (0761-2273); E81—Maladies Metaboliques (0761-2281); E82—Gynecologie, Obstetrique, Andrologie (0761-229X); E83—Aneshesie et Reanimation (0761-2303); E84—Genie Biomedical, Informatique Biomedicale (0761-2311); F10—Mecanique et Acoustique et Transfert de Chaleur (no ISSN); F16—Chimie Analytique Minerale et Organique (0761-1749); F17—Chimie Generale, Minerale et Organique (0761-1757); F21—Electrotechnique (0761-1773); F23—Genie Chimique, Industries Chimique et Parachimique (0761-1781); F24—Polymeres, Peintures, Bois (0761-179X); F25—Transports Terrestres et Maritimes (0761-1803); F40—Mineralogie, Geochimie, Geologie Extraterrestre (0761-1811); F41—Gisements Metalliques et Non-Metalliques, Economie Miniere (0761-182X); F42—Roches Cristallines (0761-1838); F43—Roches Sedimentaires, Geologie Marine (0761-1846);

F44—Stratigraphie, Geologie Regionale, Geologie Generale (0761-1854); F45—Tectonique, Geophysique Interne (0761-1862); F46—Hydrologie, Geologie de l'Ingenieur, Formations Superficielles (0761-1870); F47—Paleontologie (0761-1889); F52—Biochimie, Biophysique Moleculaire, Biologie Moleculaire et Cellulaire (0761-1897); F53—Anatomie et Physiologie des Vertebres (0761-1900); F54—Reproduction des Vertebres, Embryologie des Vertebres et des Invertebres (0761-1919); F55—Biologie Vegetale (0761-1927); F56—Ecologie Anaimale et Vegetale (0246-1153); F70—Pharmacologie, Traitements Medicamenteux (0761-1943); T210—Industries Agroalimentaires (no ISSN); T215—Biotechnologies (0761-165X); T230—Energie (0761-1668); T235—Medecine Tropicale (0761-1676); T240—Metaux, Metallurgie (0761-1684); T260—Zoologie Fondamentale et Appliquee des Invertebres (0761-1714). It is also available online and on CD-ROM.

18. Referativnyi Zhurnal. Moscow, Russia: Vs-esoyuznyi Institut Nauchno-Tekhnicheskoi Informatsii (VINITI), 1953– , frequency varies with each section. v.1– , index. price per section varies.

This Russian journal is the world's most comprehensive abstracting service covering all disciplines, claiming to produce over one million abstracts per year. Both periodical and monographic literature are covered, and it is in Russian. The quality of indexing varies, depending on the section. The sections include: Astronomiya (0486-2236); Aviatsionnye i Raketnye Dvigateli (0373-6407); Avtomatika i Vychislitel'naya Tekhnika (no ISSN); Avtomobil'nye Dorogi (0486-2252); Avtomobil'nyi i Gorodskoi Transport (0034-2297); Biologiya (0034-2300); Biologiya Sel'skokhozyaistvennykh Zhivatnykh (no ISSN); Bionika-Biokibernetika-Bioinzheneriya (0202-912X); Dvigateli Vnutrennego Sgoraniyz (0486-2279); Ekologiya Cheloveka (0202-5140); Ekonomika Promyshlennosti (0203-6223); Elektronika (0206-5452); Elektrotekhnika (0203-5316); Energetika (0203-5308); Environment Management Abstracts (0234-7059); Farmakologiya Effektornykh Sistem, Khimioterapevticheskie Sredstva (0202-5132); Farmakologiya, Obshchaya Farmakologiya Nervnoi Sistemy (0134-580X); Fitopatologiya (0202-9235); Fizika (0034-2343); Fiziologiya i Morfologiya Cheloveka i Zhivotnykh (0207-141X); Fotokinotekhnika (0370-8063); Genetika Cheloveka (0202-9146); Genetika i Selektsiya Vozdelyvaemykh Rastenii (0202-9138); Geodeziya i Aeros'emka (0375-9717); Geofizika (0034-236X); Geografiya (0034-2378); Geologiya (0486-2309); Gornoe Delo (0034-2386); Gornoe i Neftepromyslovoe Mashinostroenie (0373-6415); Immunologiya-Allergologiya (0202-9154); Informatika (0486-235X); Issledovanie Kosmicheskogo Prostranstva (0034-2408); Izdatel'skoe Delo i Poligrafiya (0235-2222); Khimicheskoe, Neftepererabatyvayuschchee i Polimernoe Mashinostroenie (0370-8098); Khimiya (0486-2325); Klinicheskaya Farmakologiya (0202-9162); Kommunal'noe Bytovoe i Torgovoe Oborudovanie (0484-2286); Korroziya i Zashchita ot Korrozii (0131-3533); Kotiostroenie (0034-2424); Legkaya Promyshlennost' (0034-2432); Lesovedenie i Lesovodstvo (0034-2440); Mashinostroitel'nye Materialy, Konstruktsii i Raschet Detali Mashin, Gidroprivod (0034-2459); Matematika (0034-2467); Meditsinskaya Geografiya (0034-2475); Mekhanika (0034-2483); Metallurgiya (0034-2491); Metrologiya i Izmeritel'naya Tekhnika (0034-2505); Nasosostroenie i Kompressorostroenie, Kholodil'noe Mashinostroenie (no ISSN); Oborudovanie Pishchevoi Promyshlennosti (0034-2521); Obshcie Voprosy Pstologicheskoi Anatomii (no ISSN); Okhrana I Uluchshenie Gorodskoi Sredy (0206-6157); Okhrana Prirody i Vosproizvodstvo Pri-rodnykh Resursov (0202-9332); Onkologiya (0202-9197); Organizatsiya i Bezopasnost' Dorozhnogo Dvizheniya (0202-9952); Organizatsiya Upravleniya (0132-5639); Pochvovedenie i Agrokhimiya (0034-2548); Pozharnaya Okhrana (0202-9898); Promy-shlennyi Transport (0034-2556); Radiatsionnaya Bi-ologiya (0131-355X); Radiotekhnika (0034-267X); Raketostroenie i Kosmicheskaya Tekhnika (no ISSN); Rastenievodstvo (0202-9200); Sistemy, Pribory i Me-tody Kontrolya Kachestva Okruzhayushchei Sredy (0206-6149); Stroitel'nye i Dorozhnye Mashiny (0484-2480); Svarka (0131-3525); Tekhnicheskaya Estetika i Ergonomika (no ISSN); Tekhnicheskaya Kibernetika (no ISSN); Tekhnologicheskie Aspekty Okhrany Okruzhayushchei Sredy (0206-6130); Tekhnologiya Mashinostroeniya (0034-2599); Tepio i Massobmen (0203-6436); Toksikologiya (0202-9219); Traktory i Sel'skokhozyaistvennye Mashiny i Orudiya (0034-2602); Truboprovodnyi Transport (0034-2610); Turbostroenie (0034-2629); Vodnyi Transport (0484-2545); Volokonno-opticheskie Sys-temy (0234-9647); Voprosy Tekhnicheskogo Pro-gressa i Organizatsii Proizvodstva v Mashinostroenii (0034-2637); Vozdushnyi Transport (0484-2561); Vzaimodelstvie Raznykh Vidov Transporta i Kontein-ernye Perevozki (0034-2645); Yadernye Reaktory (0034-2653); Zheleznodorozhnyi Transport (0484-2596).

19. World Translation Index. Delft,

Netherlands: International Translations Center, 1978– , 10/year. v.1– , index. $855.00. ISSN: 0259-8264.

Formerly called the *World Transindex*, this service has absorbed numerous other translating reporting services, including the 20-volume *Translations Regis-ter Index*. It provides bibliographic information for existing translations. It is also available online. Also useful is *Index Translationum* (UNESCO, 1948-), which covers over 60,000 translated works from over 60 countries.

Bibliographies

20. American Reference Books Annual.

Littleton, CO: Libraries Unlimited, 1970– , annual. v.1– , index. $85.00. ISSN: 0065-9959.

A source of book reviews of reference works in all disciplines, this work is arranged by subject and type of reference work. There are author, title, and subject indexes.

21. Bibliographies of the History of Science and Technology. New York, NY: Garland,

1982– , irregular. v.1– , index. price per volume varies.

This is a series of bibliographies covering the his-tory of science and technology. The following volumes have been published: v.1 *History of Modern Astron-omy and Astrophysics* by David H. DeVorkin; v.2— *History of Science and Technology in the United States, Volume 1* by Marc Rothenberg; v.3—*History of the Earth Sciences* by Roy Porter; v.4—*History of Modern Physics* by Stephen G. Brush; v.5—*History of Chemical Technology* by Robert P. Multhauf; v.6— *History of Mathematics from Antiquity to the Present* by Joseph W. Dauben; v.7—*History of Geophysics and Meteorology* by Stephen G. Brush; v.8—*History of Classical Physics* by Roderick Weis Home; v.9— *History of Modern Geography* by Gary S. Dunbar; v.10—*History of the Health Care Sciences and Health Care, 1700-1980* by Jonathan Erlen; v.11—*Medieval Science and Technology* by Claudia Kren; v.12—*His-tory of Metal Mining and Metallurgy* by Peter M. Molloy; v.13—*Bronze Age, Greek, and Roman Tech-nology* by John Peter Oleson; v.14—not published; v.15—*History of Biology* by Judith A. Overmier; v.16—*History of Engineering Sciences* by David F. Channell; v.17—*History of Science and Technology in the United States, Volume 2* by Marc Rothenberg; v.18—*History of Electrical Technology* by Bernard S. Finn.

22. Books in Print. New York, NY: Bowker,

1948– , annual. v.1– , index. $397.00. ISSN: 0068-0214.

This is the best source for locating U.S. published and distributed books with brief bibliographic informa-tion and prices. There are 10 volumes per year: v.1-5— Author; v.5-8—Titles; v.9—Out-of-Print; v.10—Pub-lishers and Distributors. Companion volumes are *Sub-ject Guide to Books in Print, Forthcoming Books*, and *Paperbound Books in Print*. There are also spin-offs that are regularly published, including *Scientific and Technical Books and Serials in Print*. All are also available online and on CD-ROM.

23. Core List of Books and Journals in Science and Technology. Russell H. Powell; James R.

Powell, Jr. Phoenix, AZ: Oryx Press, 1987. 134p., bibliog., index. $38.50. ISSN: 0-89774-275-3.

This annotated list of books and journals is appropriate for a general academic library.

24. Encyclopedia of Physical Sciences and Engineering Information Sources: A Bibliographic Guide to Approximately 16,000 Citations for Publications, Organizations, and Other Sources of Information on 450 Subjects Relating to Physical Sciences and Engineering. Steven Wasserman; Martin A. Smith; Susan Mottu. Detroit, MI: Gale Research, 1989. 736p. $140.00. ISSN: 0-8103-2498-9.

Some 16,000 titles are included in this bibliographic guide, some with annotations. It covers abstracting services and indexes, annual reviews and yearbooks, associations and professional societies, bibliographies, directories and biographical sources, encyclopedias and dictionaries, general works, handbooks and manuals, online databases, periodicals, research centers and institutes, specifications and standards, statistical sources, and special sources.

25. Handbooks and Tables in Science and Technology. 3rd. Russell H. Powell. Phoenix, AZ: Oryx Press, 1994. 384p., index. $95.00. ISBN: 0-89774-534-5.

This source is a selective list of over 3,600 handbooks for chemistry, physics, biology, astronomy, geology, agriculture, and other hard sciences.

26. Magazines for Libraries. Bill Katz; Linda Sternberg Katz. New York, NY: Bowker, 1969– , irregular. v.1– , index. $139.95. ISSN: 0000-0914.

A fully annotated list of periodicals listed by subject, this source contains a selective list and provides annotations and suggestions for purchase.

27. New Technical Books. New York Public Library. New York, NY: New York Public Library, 1915– , 6/year. v.1– , index. $30.00. ISSN: 0028-6869.

This selective, annotated list of books received by the New York Public Library is arranged by subject based on the Dewey classification system.

28. Publishers' Trade List Annual. New York, NY: Bowker, 1874– , annual. v.1-. $238.00. ISSN: 0079-7855.

This source consists of book and trade catalogs from publishers, bound together in alphabetical order by name of publisher.

29. Pure and Applied Science Books, 1876-1982. New York, NY: Bowker, 1982. 6v., index. $345.00. ISBN: 0-8352-1437-0.

A bibliography of all books published and distributed in the United States, 1876-1982, this source includes more than 170,000 titles arranged by LC subject headings. A small, useful bibliography is Margaret W.

Batschelet's *Early American Scientific and Technical Literature* (Scarecrow, 1990).

30. Science and Technology Annual Reference Review. H. Robert Malinowsky. Phoenix, AZ: Oryx Press, 1989-91. 3v., index. $55.00v.1; $74.50v.2; $45.00v.3. ISBN: 0-89774-48-Xv.1; 0-89774-527-2v.2; 0-89774-608-2v.3.

This book-reviewing annual covers only reference books in science, engineering, agriculture, and medicine. It is arranged by subject and by type of book.

31. Standard Periodical Directory. Detroit, MI: Gale Research, 1964/65– , biennial. v.1– , index. $395.00. ISSN: 0085-6630.

This listing of worldwide periodicals gives pricing and ordering information to some 70,000 periodicals. It provides such information as full name, address, key personnel, former titles, ISSN, frequency, circulation, advertising rates, and printing method. Also useful is the *Index and Abstract Directory* (Ebsco, 1992), which lists more than 750 indexing and abstracting services and the titles that each covers. It is also available on CD-ROM.

32. Ulrich's International Periodicals Directory. New York, NY: Bowker, 1932– , annual. v.1– , index. $364.00. ISSN: 0000-0175.

This is the most comprehensive listing of periodicals published. Arranged by subject, it provides addresses, prices, frequency, ISSN, title changes, electronic information, and sometimes a brief annotation. Discontinued titles are listed separately but appear in the main index. It has a quarterly supplement: *Ulrich's Update* and is also available online and on CD-ROM. For a historical listing of only abstracts and indexes consult Dolores B. Owen's *Abstracts and Indexes in Science and Technology* (Scarecrow, 1985).

33. World List of Scientific Periodicals Published in the Years 1900-1960. 4th. Peter Brown; George Burden Stratton. Washington, DC: Butterworths/Books on Demand, 1963-1965. 3v., index. $459.30.

Updated by *World List of Scientific Periodicals: New Periodical Titles, 1964-1980*, this is a reprinted bibliography that lists all the known periodicals from 1900-1960. The update extends this list through 1980.

Biographical Sources

34. Asimov's Biographical Encyclopedia of Science and Technology: The Lives and Achievements of 1,510 Great Scientists from Ancient Times to the Present Chronologically Arranged. 2nd revised. Isaac Asimov. Garden City, NY: Doubleday, 1982. 941p., illus., index. $29.95. ISBN: 0-385-17771-2.

This biographical encyclopedia is for the layperson and student, providing 1,510 brief sketches of the lives and achievements of deceased scientists.

35. Biographical Dictionary of Scientists.
David Abbott. New York, NY: P. Bedrick Books, 1984-85. 6v., illus., index. $168.00.

These 6 volumes cover chemists, astronomers, biologists, engineers and inventors, mathematicians, and physicists. Though not a scholarly work, it provides good biographies for a selected number of the more prominent scientists in the various fields.

36. Dictionary of Scientific Biography.
Charles Coulston Gillispie. New York, NY: Scribner, 1980. 16v in 8, bibliog., index. $1,080.00. ISBN: 0-684-16962-2.

This dictionary is the most scholarly and comprehensive source of information available for deceased scientists. Each entry is well-documented and written by an authority. Two supplements have been published as well as an abridged edition: *Concise Dictionary of Scientific Biography* (Scribner, 1981).

37. McGraw-Hill Modern Scientists and Engineers.
New York, NY: McGraw-Hill, 1980. 3v., illus., index. out-of-print. ISBN: 0-07-045266-0.

Although out-of-print, this is still a good source for biographies of scientists and engineers. Some 1,140 biographies are included covering 1920-1978. A portrait is included for each entry. An earlier edition was titled *McGraw-Hill Modern Men of Science.*

38. Who's Who in Science and Engineering, 1992-1993.
premier. Wilmette, IL: Marquis Who's Who, 1992. 1,069p. $199.00. ISBN: 0-8379-5751-6.

This current biographical directory covers some 20,000 leaders worldwide in engineering, life sciences, mathematics, computer science, physical science, and social science. For each entry, in addition to the usual biographical data, selected published works, notable findings, and patents are listed. Also useful is the *Who's Who in Science in Europe* (Gale Research, 1992) and *Who's Who in Technology* (Gale Research, 1989).

Dictionaries, Glossaries, and Thesauri

39. Abbreviations Dictionary.
8th. Ralph De Sola. Boca Raton, FL: CRC, 1992. 1,500p. $69.95. ISBN: 0-8493-4247-3.

This well-accepted reference source provides a listing of abbreviations, acronyms, appellations, contractions, eponyms, geographic equivalents, initials, and slang shortcuts. A myriad of interesting listings include

citizens-band call signs, international vehicle license letters, prisons of the world, and zodiacal signs. For a guide to government acronyms consult William R. Evinger's *Guide to Federal Government Acronyms* (Oryx, 1989).

40. Academic Press Dictionary of Science and Technology.
San Diego, CA: Academic Press, 1992. 2,432p., illus. $115.00. ISBN: 0-12-200400-0.

With close to 124,000 defined entries, this is one of the best sci-tech dictionaries that has been published. It covers 124 fields of science and engineering with each of these fields receiving a special discussion. Some medical terms are included. Pronunciation is given when needed and chronology is included as an appendix.

41. Acronyms, Initialisms, and Abbreviations Dictionary.
17th. Detroit, MI: Gale Research, 1993. 3v. $684.00. ISBN: 0-8103-7538-9v.1; 0-8103-7498-6v.2; 0-8103-7537-0v.3.

Previously called *Acronyms and Initialisms Dictionary*, this is a guide to alphabetic designations, contractions, acronyms, initialisms, abbreviations, and similarly condensed appellations. It is published in 3 volumes: v.1—*Acronyms, Initialisms, and Abbreviations Dictionary*; v.2—*New Acronyms, Initialisms, and Abbreviations*; v.3—*Reverse Acronyms, Initialisms, and Abbreviations Dictionary*. A companion set that expands into the international field is the 3-volume *International Acronyms, Initialisms, and Abbreviations Dictionary* (Gale Research, 1987). For organizational abbreviations consult F.A. Buttress and H.J. Heaney's *World Guide to Abbreviations of Organizations* (Gale Research, 1993).

42. Cambridge Dictionary of Science and Technology.
Peter M.B. Walker. New York, NY: Cambridge University Press, 1990. 1,024p. $39.50. ISBN: 0-521-39441-4.

This is an excellent general science dictionary. Though not as comprehensive as the Academic Press dictionary, it is still a good choice for general science collections. Two other useful dictionaries are the *Barnes & Noble Thesaurus of Science and Technology* (Barnes & Noble, 1985) and the *Chambers Science and Technology Dictionary* (Cambridge University Press, 1988).

43. Dictionary of Science and Technology.
A.F. Dorian. New York, NY: Elsevier, 1980. 2v. $202.75/volume. ISBN: 0-444-41829-6v.1; 0-444-41911-Xv.2.

This is an excellent English-French/French-English language dictionary. It does not include definitions. Another well-known French-English dictionary is Louis DeVries' *French-English Science and Technology Dictionary* (McGraw-Hill, 1976).

44. Dictionary of Science and Technology.
2nd revised. A.F. Dorian. New York, NY:
Elsevier, 1978-1981. 2v. $397.75. ISBN:
0-444-41649-8 English-German;
0-444-41997-7 German-English.

This is a comprehensive English-German/German-English dictionary.

45. McGraw-Hill Dictionary of Scientific and Technical Terms. 5th. Sybil P. Parker. New
York, NY: McGraw-Hill, 1994. 2,194p., illus.
$110.50. ISBN: 0-07-042333-4.

This comprehensive dictionary defines over
100,000 terms from 102 scientific and technical disciplines. Entries indicate disciplines and give pronunciation when needed. Appendixes include measurement systems, fundamental constants, geological time scale, classification of living organisms, and biographical listings. A small but still useful dictionary is the *Thesaurus of Scientific, Technical, and Engineering Terms* (Hemisphere, 1987).

46. Periodical Title Abbreviations. Detroit,
MI: Gale Research, 1969- irregular. v.1-.
$510.00.

This dictionary provides listings for over 130,000
periodical abbreviations and selected monographs covering science, social science, humanities, law, medicine, library science, engineering, education, business, art, and other fields. It is published in 3 volumes: v.1—Abbreviations; v.2—Titles; and v.3—New abbreviations.

47. Report Series Codes Dictionary. 3rd.
Detroit, MI: Gale Research, 1986. 647p.
$180.00. ISBN: 0-8103-2147-5.

This is a guide to more than 20,000 alphanumeric codes used to identify technical reports, arranged both by code and corporate author. It is a revised edition of the *Dictionary of Report Series Codes* edited by Lois E. Godfrey and Helen F. Redman

48. Russian-English Dictionary of Scientific and Technical Usage. B.V. Kuznetsov. New
York, NY: Pergamon Press, 1987. 500p.
$175.00. ISBN: 0-08-032551-3.

This is a good Russian-English language dictionary. Another useful dictionary for translators is Mikhail Zimmerman and Claudia Vedeneera's *Russian-English Translator's Dictionary* (Wiley, 1993).

Directories

49. American Library Directory: A Classified List of Libraries in the United States and Canada, with Personnel and Statistical Data.
New York, NY: Bowker, 1923– , annual. v.1– ,
index. $215.00. ISSN: 0065-910X.

This well-established directory provides detailed information about libraries in the United States and

Canada. Addresses, telephone numbers, personnel, statistics, budgets, branches, and other pertinent information are provided.

50. Annual Register of Grant Support. New
York, NY: Bowker, 1969– , annual. v.1– ,
index. $165.00. ISSN: 0066-4049.

Previously called *Grant Data Quarterly*, this directory is divided into several sections, one of which covers science. It describes those programs for which grants are available from government agencies, foundations, businesses, and professional organizations. A companion source is the *Foundations Dicrectory* (New York University Press, 1960-), which provides detailed information about foundations.

51. Awards, Honors, and Prizes. Paul Wasserman. Detroit, MI: Gale Research, 1969– ,
irregular. v.1– , index. $370.00. ISSN:
0196-6316.

An alphabetically arranged list by administering organization of achievements in all fields, this source is published in two volumes:: v.1—United States and Canada; and v.2—International and foreign.

52. Directory of American Research and Technology. New York, NY: Bowker, 1986– ,
annual. v.20– , index. $297.00. ISSN:
0886-0076.

Previously called *Industrial Research Laboratories in the United States* from 1927-1985, this important directory provides descriptions of industrial research organizations in the United States. Complete descriptions are provided with access through geographic, personnel, and subject indexes. It is also available on CD-ROM. For federal government research organizations consult the *Directory of Federal Laboratory and Technology Resources: A Guide to Services, Facilities, and Expertise* (National Technical Information Services, 1990).

53. Directory of Research Grants. 1994.
Phoenix, AZ: The Oryx Press, 1975-, annual.
v.1-, index. $135.00. ISBN: 0-89774-769-0.

The *Directory of Research Grants* features complete information on over 6,000 government, corporate, organizational, and private funding sources that support geniune research programs in academic, scientific, and technology-related subjects. A related publication is the annual *Directory of Biomedical and Health Care Grants*, which lists over 3,000 funding sources. The entire *GRANTS Database* is available on disc, online, and on tape.

54. Directory of Special Libraries and Information Centers. Detroit, MI: Gale Research,
1963– , irregular. v.1– , index. $300.00.

This very comprehensive directory covers some 20,200 special libraries, providing complete information about each such as data on holdings, personnel, and addresses. It includes over 1,100 listings for foreign libraries from 130 countries. Each edition is in 3 volumes: v.1—Directory of special library and information centers; v.2—Geographic and personnel indexes; and v.3—New special libraries. For subject coverage use the *Subject Directory of Special Libraries and Information Centers* (Gale Research, 1975-) published in 3 volumes each time: v.1—Business, government, and law libraries; v.2—Computers, engineering, and science libraries; and v.3—Health science libraries. Also useful is Helga Lengenfelder's *World Guide to Special Libraries* (K.G. Saur, 1990).

55. Directory of Technical and Scientific Directories: A World Bibliographic Guide to Medical, Agricultural, Industrial, and Natural Science Directories. 5th. Harlow, Great Britain: Longman, 1988. 280p., index. $95.00. ISBN: 0-582-00602-3.

Previously called *Directory of Scientific Directories*, this is a directory of some 1,500 sources in all areas of science, medicine, agriculture, and technology.

56. Encyclopedia of Associations. New York, NY: Gale Research, 1956– , annual. v.1– , index. $320.00. ISSN: 0071-0202.

This is the primary source of information on associations in the United States. Over 22,000 entries provide detailed data on trade, professional, social welfare, public affairs, labor unions, fraternal, patriotic, religious, sports, hobby, and voluntary associations. The main set is called v.1—National Organizations of the U.S. Companion volumes are v.2—Geographic and Executive Indexes and v.3—Supplement. Related directories are *Encyclopedia of Associations: International Organizations* (Gale Research, 1992) and *Regional, State, and Local Organizations* (Gale Research, 1992). It is also available online and on CD-ROM.

57. European Research Centres: A Directory of Scientific, Industrial, Agricultural, and Biomedical Laboratories. 9th. Harlow, Great Britain: Longman, 1993. 2v., index. $630.00. ISBN: 0-582-09625-1.

A directory of some 17,000 scientific, technical, agricultural, and medical laboratories and departments providing titles in original language and English translation and all descriptive information about the organization. Two other related Longman titles are *European Sources of Scientific and Technical Information* (Longman, 1993) and *Pacific Research Centres* (Longman, 1992).

58. Guides to World Science and Technology. Harlow, Great Britain: Longman, 1982-1991. 13v., index. price per volume varies.

These narrative guides review the research and development, science policy, and organizations in all areas of the world. Directories are provided in each volume. The following titles are available: *Science and*

Technology in Africa (1989, 0-582-00086-6, $115.00); *Science and Technology in Australia, Antarctica, and the Pacific Islands* (1989, 0-582-90060-3, $95.00); *Science and Technology in China* (1984, 0-582-90056-5, $88.00); *Science and Technology in Eastern Europe* (1988, 0582-90054-9, $114.00); *Science and Technology in the Federal Republic of Germany* (1990, 0-582-05439-7, $115.00); *Science and Technology in France and Belgium* (1988, 0-582-00084-X, $100.00); *Science and Technology in India* (1990, 0-582-06469-4, $138.00); *Science and Technology in Japan* (1991, 0-582-03684-4, $149.00); *Science and Technology in the Middle East* (1982, 0-582-90052-2, $88.00); *Science and Technology in Scandinavia* (1989, 0-582-01892-7, $115.00); *Science and Technology in the United Kingdom* (1991, 0-582-90051-4, $162.00); *Science and Technology in the United States of America* (1986, 0-582-90061-1, $95.00); *Science and Technology in the USSR* (1988, 0-582-90053-0, $95.00).

59. Libraries, Information Centers and Databases in Science and Technology: A World Guide. 2nd. New York, NY: K.G. Saur, 1988. 697p., index. $225.00. ISBN: 3-598-10757-9.

An international directory of special libraries, information and documentation centers, and databases in science and technology, it provides complete descriptions of the facilities and the holdings of the libraries. A separate publication covers the biomedical sciences. Another database-related source is Tracy Erwin's *Document Retrieval: Sources and Services* (Information Store, 1987).

60. Peterson's Annual Guides to Graduate Study. Princeton, NJ: Peterson's Guides, 1984– , annual. v.1– , indexes with 6v. per year. $181.70.

These are the standard sources for information on graduate programs throughout the United States. The 6 volumes are v.1—*Peterson's Guide to Graduate and Professional Programs*; v.2—*Peterson's Guide to Graduate Programs in the Humanities and Social Sciences*; v.3—*Peterson's Guide to Graduate Programs in Biological and Agricultural Sciences*; v.4—*Peterson's Guide to Graduate Programs in the Physical Sciences and Mathematics*; v.5—*Peterson's Guide to Graduate Programs in Engineering and Applied Sciences*; v.6—*Peterson's Guide to Graduate Programs in Business, Education, Health and Law*. It is also available online and on CD-ROM.

61. Research Centers Directory. Detroit, MI: Gale Research, 1960– , annual. v.1– , index. $420.00. ISSN: 0080-1518.

This directory provides comprehensive coverage of services, facilities, and expertise offered by more than 12,800 nonprofit, university-related research and development companies in the United States and Canada. It covers the usual research centers as well as the new research parks and technology transfer centers. A *New Research Centers Supplement* keeps the main volume up to date between editions. It is also available online. For private sector firms and other for-profit organizations consult *Research Services Directory* (Gale Research, 1992); for government-funded research see *Government Research Directory* (Gale Research, 1992); and for international research consult *International Research Centers Directory* (Gale Research, 1992).

62. Scientific and Technical Organizations and Agencies Directory. 2nd. Margaret Labash Young. Detroit, MI: Gale Research, 1987. 2v., index. $195.00. ISBN: 0-8103-2103-3.

This is a guide to some 15,000 national and international sources of information in the physical and applied sciences and engineering from organizations, agencies, programs, and services. Another very useful source is Michael Sachs' *World Guide to Scientific Associations and Learned Societies* (K.G. Saur, 1990).

63. Subject Collections. 7th. Lee Ash; William G. Miller. New York, NY: Bowker, 1985. 2v., index. $275.00. ISBN: 0-8352-3143-7.

This title is a standard source of information for the special collections found in universities, colleges, public libraries, special libraries, and museums in the United States and Canada. All disciplines are covered.

64. United States Government Manual. Washington, DC: Office of the Federal Register, Archives and Records Service, General Services Administration, 1973/74– , annual. v.1– , index. $21.00.

Previously called *U.S. Government Organizational Manual*, this handbook/directory provides an overview of U.S. government agencies. It includes the main personnel of the agencies, the activities of each, and organizational charts.

65. Yearbook of International Organizations/Annuaire de Organisations Internationales. Brussels, Belgium: Union of International Associations, 1948– , biennial. v.1– , index. $825.00. ISSN: 0084-3814.

This directory provides detailed information on international organizations including embassies and governmental agencies. The three volumes that are published each year cover these topics: v.1—Organization descriptions and index; v.2—International organization participation; v.3—Global action networks.

Encyclopedias

66. Encyclopedia of Physical Science and Technology. 2nd. Rupert A. Meyers. Orlando, FL: Academic Press, 1992. 18v., illus., bibliog., index. $2,500.00. ISBN: 0-12-18138-3.

A comprehensive scholarly encyclopedia, this work covers all areas of physical science, mathematics,

and engineering. The individual entries are covered in-depth, providing the user accurate up-to-date information. Computer science and telecommunications have good coverage as does aeronautics, atmospheric sciences, and space technology.

67. McGraw-Hill Encyclopedia of Science and Technology. 7th. New York, NY: McGraw-Hill, 1992. 20v., illus., bibliog., index. $2,639.00. ISBN: 0-07-909206-3.

This has become the accepted science and technology encyclopedia. It is authoritative, providing clear discussions on the newest theories and latest research. A topical index places all the some 7,500 articles under one or more of the 81 major subject headings. In addition, there is an analytical index for specific terms. Each article begins with an elementary discussion and then proceeds into more advanced coverage. An abridged older edition is also available as *McGraw-Hill Concise Encyclopedia of Science and Technology* (McGraw-Hill, 1989).

68. Van Nostrand's Scientific Encyclopedia. 7th. Douglas M. Considine; Glenn D. Considine. New York, NY: Van Nostrand Reinhold, 1989. 2v., illus., bibliog., index. $195.00. ISBN: 0-442-21750-1.

For those who cannot afford more expensive sets, this work is a good smaller encyclopedia covering all science and technology. The discussions are brief but contain all the needed essential information. An interesting reference source that describes the core concepts in the biological and medical sciences is Radovan Zak's *Basic Facts for Basic Sciences* (Raven, 1990).

Guides to the Literature

69. Best Science and Technology Reference Books for Young People. H. Robert Malinowsky. Phoenix, AZ: Oryx Press, 1991. 216p., index. $24.95. ISBN: 0-89774-580-9.

Although the title specifies young people, this work is a good general guide to reference books for a nontechnical library. All entries are annotated, arranged by subject and by type of publication.

70. Brief Guide to Sources of Scientific and Technical Information. 2nd. Saul Herner; Gene P. Allen; Nancy D. Wright. Arlington, VA: Information Resources Press, 1980. 160p., illus., bibliog., index. $15.00. ISBN: 0-87815-031-5.

A useful, but dated, brief guide that emphasizes directories, research in progress, and U.S. research collections. It provides a comprehensive overview of information pertaining to science and technology.

71. Finding Answers in Science and Technology. Alice Lefler Primack. New York, NY: Van Nostrand Reinhold, 1984. 364p., illus., bibliog., index. out-of-print. ISBN: 0-442-28227-3.

Although the bibliographic examples are dated, the text on how to formulate a search strategy and the general information on how to locate science and engineering information are still useful.

72. Guide to Reference Books. 10th. Eugene P. Sheehy; Rita G. Keckeissen; Richard J. Dionne. Chicago, IL: American Library Association, 1986. 1,560p., index. $80.00. ISBN: 0-8389-0390-8.

This standard guide to reference books has been used for many years. It is arranged by subject and includes both well-known and little-known reference works. Much historical information is provided in the bibliographical citations. A supplement edited by Robert Balay covering 1985-1990 was published in 1992. A new edition is scheduled for 1994.

73. Information Resources for Engineers and Scientists: Workshop Notes. 6th. Washington, DC: INFO/Tek, 1991. 1v., various paging, illus., bibliog. write for price.

This manual for students has become an important guide to engineering and science reference sources. It is arranged by type of reference source, presenting examples and explaining how sources are used.

74. Information Sources in Science and Technology. C.D. Hurt. Englewood, CO: Libraries Unlimited, 1988. 362p., index. $28.50. ISBN: 0-87287-582-2.

This is a good guide to the sci-tech literature. Each annotated entry is arranged by subject and by type. It stresses current U.S. imprints. Although out-of-print, H. Robert Malinowsky and Jeanne M. Richardson's *Science and Engineering Literature* (Libraries Unlimited, 1980) is still useful, as is Denis J. Grogan's *Science and Technology* (C. Bingley, 1982).

75. Scientific and Technical Information Sources. 2nd. Ching-Chih Chen. Cambridge, MA: MIT Press, 1987. 824p., bibliog., index. $55.00. ISBN: 0-262-03120-5.

This comprehensive bibliography lists over 4,000 science and engineering reference sources. Chapters are by type of reference source with entries arranged by subject. Annotations are provided as well as an indication where the book is reviewed.

76. Walford's Guide to Reference Materials, v.1—Science and Technology. 6th. A.J. Walford. Lanham, MD: Unipub, 1993-. 3v., index. $395.00.

An essential guide to reference materials comparable to Sheehy, it is international and includes many little-known titles. The three volumes cover: v.1—Science and Technology; v.2—Social and Historical Sciences; and v.3—Generalia, Language, etc. An abridged edition, *Concise Guide to Reference Material* (Unipub, 1992), is also available.

Handbooks and Manuals

77. Handbook for Scientific and Technical Research. David P. Beach; Torsten K.E. Alvager. Englewood Cliffs, NJ: Prentice-Hall, 1991. 255p., illus., index. $40.00. ISBN: 0-13-431040-3.

A good introduction to research methods, this source is intended for those just embarking on research activities.

78. Handbook of Statistical Methods for Engineers and Scientists. Harrison M. Wadsworth, Jr. New York, NY: McGraw-Hill, 1990. 2v., various paging, illus., bibliog., index. $79.50. ISBN: 0-07-067674-7.

This comprehensive handbook outlining the use of statistics in research and presenting methods in actual use will become a standard reference handbook.

79. McGraw-Hill Style Manual: A Concise Guide for Writers and Editors. Marie Longyear. New York, NY: McGraw-Hill, 1989. 333p., illus., biblio., index. $33.95; $14.95pbk. ISBN: 0-07-038676-5; 0-07-038684-6pbk.

Although this manual is based on McGraw-Hill's in-house editing practices, it is an excellent resource because many of the practices are appropriate for general use. It covers all aspects of writing, editing, and proofreading. Three other useful works are Antoinette M. Wilkinson's *Scientist's Handbook for Writing Papers and Dissertations* (Prentice-Hall, 1991); Harry E. Chandler's *Technical Writer's Handbook* (American Society for Metals, 1983); and Robert A. Day's *How to Write and Publish a Scientific Paper* (Oryx Press, 1994). A good dictionary for writers is the *Oxford Dictionary for Scientific Writers and Editors* (Oxford University Press, 1991). Also useful would be Robert A. Day's *Scientific English: A Guide for Scientists and Other Professionals* (Oryx Press, 1992).

80. Using Government Publications. 2nd. Jean L. Sears; Marilyn K. Moody. Phoenix, AZ: Oryx Press, 1993. 496p., index. $110.00. ISBN: 0-89774-670-8.

This excellent reference source explains the uses of government publications. It provides a checklist of sources and suggests ways of using these sources in the search for information. The electronic sources are also covered. Another useful tool is Judith S. Robinson's *Tapping the Government Grapevine, 2nd Edition* (Oryx, 1993).

Histories

81. Catalogue of Scientific Papers 1800-1900.
Royal Society of London. Cambridge, Great
Britain: Cambridge University Press,
1867-1902. 19v. out-of-print.

This is a classic bibliography for scientific literature
of the 19th century. Arranged alphabetically by author,
it covers periodical articles, proceedings, and transactions. A 3-volume subject index was published 1908-
1914 and continued by the 238-volume *International
Catalogue of Scientific Literature* (1st-14th, Royal Society of London, 1901-1914). Together, these two
works are essential for any history of science collection. Both titles have been reprinted.

**82. Great Events from History: Science and
Technology Series.** Englewood Cliffs, NJ:
Salem Press, 1991. 5v., index. $375.00. ISBN:
0-89356-637-3.

This historical synopsis covers 457 modern scientific and technological breakthroughs that shaped the
20th century. It is arranged chronologically and ends
with 1990.

**83. Historical Catalogue of Scientists and Scientific Books: From the Earliest Times to the
Close of the Nineteenth Century.** *(Garland
Reference Library of the Humanities, v.495).*
Robert Mortimer Gascoigne. New York, NY:
Garland, 1984. 1,177p., index. price not
available. ISBN: 0-8240-8959-6.

This work is a bibliography of early scientific
works and references to the scientists who wrote them.
It is a companion to the *Historical Catalogue of Scientific Periodicals, 1665-1900*.

84. History of Science and Technology: A Narrative Chronology. Edgardo Macorini. New
York, NY: Facts on File, 1988. 2v., illus.,
bibliog., index. $160.00. ISBN:
0-87196-477-5.

This history is a narrative chronology. It is well-illustrated and is excellent for the layperson and student.

**85. History of Scientific and Technical Periodicals: The Origins and Development of the
Scientific and Technical Press, 1665-1790.**
David A. Kronick. New York, NY: Scarecrow
Press, 1962 (c1961). 274p., tables, bibliog.
out-of-print.

This is an excellent history of how the scientific
journal evolved. A large bibliography is included.
Other similar publications are David A. Kronick's
*Scientific and Technical Periodicals of the 17th and
18th Centuries* (Scarecrow Press, 1991) and Jill Lambert's *Scientific and Technical Journals* (Clive Bingley, 1985).

86. Information Sources in the History of Science and Medicine. Pietro Corsi; Paul Weindling. Boston, MA: Butterworths, 1983. 531p.,
illus., bibliog., index. out-of-print. ISBN:
0-408-10764-2.

A good review of how science and medicine developed, including the cultural and social aspects. Major
libraries and archives are also described.

**87. Milestones in Science and Technology: A
Ready Reference Guide to Discoveries, Inventions, and Facts.** Ellis Mount; Barbara A. List.
Phoenix, AZ: Oryx, 1987. 141p., bibliog.,
index. $35.00. ISBN: 0-89774-260-5.

This good general chronology highlights discoveries and inventions.

Tables

**88. International Critical Tables of Numerical
Data, Physics, Chemistry and Technology.**
National Research Council. New York, NY:
McGraw-Hill, 1926-30. 7v., illus. out-of-print.

This is a classic collection of numeric tables that
were termed the best at the time by the specialists who
compiled them. It is now out-of-print but still an important reference source. An index was compiled by
Clarence J. West and Collie Hull in 1933.

**89. Numerical Data and Functional Relationships in Science and Technology, New Series/
Zahlenwerte und Funktionen aus Naturwissenschaften und Technik—Neue Serie.** Hans
Heinrich Landolt; R. Bornstein. New York,
NY: Springer-Verlag, 1961– , irregular. v.1– ,
index. price per volume varies.

This classic, comprehensive collection of critical
tables covers physics, physical chemistry, geophysics,
astronomy, materials engineering, and pure engineering. It is also known just as *Landolt and Bornstein*. The
new series contains 6 groups: 1—Nuclear and particle
physics; 2—Atomic and molecular physics; 3—Crystallography and solid state physics; 4—Macroscopic
and technical properties; 5—Geophysics and space
research; and 6—Astronomy and astrophysics. The
purpose of this collection is to update the 6th edition
completed in 1979 with 4 groups: 1—Atomic and
molecular physics; 2—Properties of matter in its aggregated states; 3—Astronomy and geophysics; and
4—Technology. The new series is in English, and the
6th edition is in German. The 6th edition is called
*Numerical Data and Functional Relationships in
Physics, Chemistry, Astronomy, Geophysics, and
Technology/Zahlenwerte und Funktionen aus Physik,
Chemie, Astronomie, Geophysik und Technik*. The first
edition was published 1883 as *Physakalisch-Chemische Tabellen*.

Chapter 6: Science

Science, from the Latin word *scientia* for knowledge, was referred to as natural philosophy or natural history in the seventeenth and eighteenth centuries. There were no distinct types of science as we know them today. The study of natural philosophy and natural history evolved through the years, so that by the beginning of the twentieth century definite catagories had developed, though now the boundaries between categories are unclear and overlapping, having splintered into biochemistry, geochemistry, agrochemistry, chemical physics, astrochemistry, and marine chemistry to name but a few examples. Some scholars have suggested that a better term for science might be natural science.

Natural science may be divided into exact science and descriptive science. The exact sciences are those based on exact quantitative knowledge, such as physics, chemistry, and mathematics, while descriptive science includes those sciences that describe, such as geology, biology, and astronomy. Even here the boundaries are nebulous because, for example, astronomy can be both an exact science and a descriptive science. Both exact and descriptive science may be called physical sciences, as opposed to the applied sciences of engineering and technology. However, in today's high technology environment, science, engineering, and technology work together so closely that is is difficult to tell one from the other. For the purpose of this book, distinction is made between physical and applied sciences, but users should note possible overlaps and use the indexes for greatest access.

This chapter descibes sources of information for the physical sciences—Astronomy, Biology, Botany, Chemistry, Computer Science (a very fuzzy area), Earth Sciences, Mathematics, Physics, and Zoology.

Astronomy

Astronomy is the study of all the forces and objects outside the earth and its atmosphere. The word "astronomy" comes from Greek terms *astrom* and *nomia* meaning "star arrangement," and as a result, most people think of astronomy as merely the study of stars, their size, features, age, movements, and relative position in the universe. Astronomy, of course, covers much more than that. Any object outside the earth's atmosphere may be studied as part of astronomy, including all of the biological, physical, and chemical aspects of the objects and the space within which they reside. For most researchers, the sun, moon, and planets are the central focus. As a result, a large part of astronomical literature is taken up with atlases, guides, maps, and histories of these bodies. Most of this literature relates to observational astronomy because it focuses on the visual observation of planets, stars, galaxies, nebulae, moons, comets, and meteors. In this area researchers use applied technology to make the observations.

Theoretical astronomy, on the other hand, concerns itself with the theories of how the universe was created (cosmology), the motions of the heavenly bodies, and the predictions of what is to come. This branch of astronomy relies heavily on mathematics and physics and also involves chemistry and biology. Specialized areas or fields of theoretical astronomy have developed. Astrophysics is a quickly evolving field in which the laws of physics are applied to the universe as a whole. Tied to astrophysics is photometry, which covers calculations and measurements of light across the electromagnetic spectrum. This measurement process includes using gamma rays or electromagnetic radiation to "view" objects that were formed in the earliest stages of the universe. Other subbranches of astronomy use different wavelengths of the electromagnetic spectrum to obtain information about the universe.

Reference sources in astronomy are continually updated as more and more sophisticated technologies are developed to observe what is beyond our atmosphere. Field charts, atlases, manuals, guides, and handbooks are numerous. New terminology is being coined every year, resulting in the need for updated dictionaries and encyclopedias. *Astronomy and Astrophysics Abstracts* is the main source to the access of astronomy and related literature.

Biology

Biology is the study of all living organisms whether microscopic bacteria, giant whales, or Sequoia trees. Two subdivisions of biology—botany and zoology—have separate sections in this chapter. As with all science disciplines, biology can be subdivided into many specialized fields which include:

- Cell biology—the study of the individual cells that make up whole organisms.
- Ecology—the study of organisms in relation to their environment.
- Embryology—the study of the early development of organisms.
- Evolution—the study of the historical development of organisms.
- Genetics—the study of the genes and heredity of organisms.
- Morphology—the study of the form and structure of organisms.
- Physiology—the study of all the vital functions of organisms that makes them total and unique.
- Taxonomy—the systematic naming of living organisms.

The prefix "bio" means "life" or "living organism." Science dictionaries list many entries with this prefix, including bioacoustics, bioassay, biocatalyst, biocenology, biochemistry, biocide, biodiversity, bioelectronics, biofeedback, biogenesis, biogeography, biomass, biostatistics, biotic, and biozone. As with other science categories, the boundaries of biology fade as technology and other fields of science become involved in biological research.

The reference sources for biology appear with new editions on a fairly regular basis. Access to the world's research is found through *Biological Abstracts*. Dictionaries and encyclopedias are numerous and handbooks are very important.

Botany

The term "botany" comes from the Greek word for "herb," *botanikas,* which signifies that part of biology concerned with plants. Botany includes the study of plants' physical and chemical makeup, evolution, environmental impact, and interaction with other organisms. Researchers may study the genetic relationships between plants, the growth and development of plants in hostile environments, ways to protect crops from diseases and pests, and new methods for increasing crop yields. Of primary concern to researchers are methods for growing plants without chemicals, producing hardier crops, maintaining rain forests, and protecting endangered species. Botanists generally study either the function and development of plants, or they study plants by types. There is a lot overlap between the distinctions, however, and studying function and development of the total plant community (or type) is not unusual.

The function and development of plants are studied in these fields:

- Plant anatomy—the physical makeup of the plant.
- Plant chemistry—the chemical processes that occur in plants.
- Plant cytology—the study of the plant cells.
- Plant embryology—the study of plant development from seeds.
- Plant genetics—the evolution of plants.
- Plant physiology—the study of how plants function and grow.
- Plant taxonomy—the systematic naming of plants.
- Ethnobotany—the study of the physical differences between plants.
- Paleobotany—the study of fossil plants.

For the study of plants by type of plant, there are

- Agrostology—the study of grasses.
- Algology or phycology—the study of algae.
- Bryology—the study of mosses.
- Mycology—the study of fungi.
- Pteridology—the study of ferns.

For reference purposes, a large number of sources identify plants. Detailed field guides, handbooks, and encyclopedias are important to researchers and laypeople alike, and taxonomic dictionaries are essential. *Biological Abstracts* is the main source for accesses the research literature.

Zoology

Zoology is the branch of biology that deals with all animals from the microscopic to the whales. The study of zoology is based on the structure and function of the animal, usually broken down to a particular class. These structures and functions include

- Physiology—the living processes that make up the whole animal.
- Embryology—the development and new life of animals.
- Genetics—the area of heredity and variation.
- Parasitology—animals living in or on other animals.
- Natural History—behavior of animals in nature.
- Ecology—relation of animals to their environment.
- Evolution—origin and differentiation of animal life.
- Taxonomy—classification and naming of animals.

As experts, zoologists may cover a particular class of animal:

- Entomology—the study of insects.
- Ichthyology—the study of fishes.
- Ornithology—the study of birds.
- Mammalogy—the study of mammals.
- Herpetology—the study of snakes, lizards, crocodiles, turtles, dinosaurs, frogs, toads, and salamanders.

Zoology is intriguing to most individuals because of the wide variety of exotic animals that live on this planet. The literature that has accumulated through the years is voluminous and the access has become more and more sophisticated. *Biological Abstracts* continues, however, to be the primary source for searching this literature. Handbooks are numerous, but field guides and encyclopedias predominate

Earth Sciences

Earth sciences covers all of the disciplines concerned with the earth's origin, composition, physical features, and atmosphere. It encompasses all the forces that have changed and are changing its makeup. It is related to cosmology, the study of how the universe has evolved, because clues about the origins of things in space provide information about how the earth itself was formed. Earth sciences also include the study of physical geography, which is called geomorphology, the study of landforms, their description, classification, origin, history, and ongoing changes. Subfields of geomorphology include glaciology, soil mechanics, remote sensing, fluvial geology, karst landscapes, and to some extent, cartography.

By far the largest branch of earth sciences, geology is the study of the planet from its beginning to its future. The term "geology," however, is now considered too restrictive and has been replaced with geoscience. Other disciplines within earth sciences are:

- Geochemistry—the study of chemical processes within the geological process.
- Geodesy—the science of surveying and mapping the earth's surface.
- Geophysics—the study of the physical forces on and within the earth.
- Mineralogy—the study of minerals found in the earth.
- Petrology—the study of the three types of rocks found in and on the earth: igneous or volcanic, metamorphic or pressure changed, and sedimentary or eroded.
- Meteorology—the study of the atmosphere which includes Climatology or the study of climates.
- Oceanography—study of seas and oceans, including the shores and beaches, subsurface rocks and sediments, waves and related forces, chemistry, and all life that depends on the oceans and seas for survival.
- Paleontology—the study of all fossil life, including Paleobotany, Paleozoology, Invertebrate Paleontology, and Micropaleontology.
- Hydrology—the study of the forces of water on the earth.
- Stratigraphy—the study of the layers of sediments that make up the surface of the earth.
- Economic Geology—the study of all materials that are mined from the earth.

Because earth sciences is a popular discipline for the layperson, guidebooks to landforms and fossils abound. The *Bibliography and Index of Geology* is the major indexing service for this discipline.

Chemistry

Chemistry is a well-structured science based on historical discoveries developed with the help of mathematics and physics. Pertaining to the composition, structure, properties, interactions, and transformations of matter, chemistry is divided into two major subdivisions: organic and inorganic. Organic chemistry concerns itself with only those compounds that contain carbon—basically living matter; while inorganic chemistry is concerned with all of the other elements. These two areas form the basis for all research in the chemical field. Chemists, however, may be physical or analytical chemists or biochemists. Physical chemistry is the marriage of chemistry and physics—the study of the chemical phenomena in solid, liquid, or gaseous states. Analytical chemistry covers the qualitative analysis of chemicals in terms of description of elements, compounds, and structural units, and it is also concerned with the quantitative analysis in terms of measurement of amounts of elements, compounds, or structural units. Biochemistry is the study of the chemical processes of all living organisms.

Research in chemistry is massive. This literature is indexed by the world's largest English language service, *Chemical Abstracts*. There are many handbooks covering all aspects of chemical research, and dictionaries are standard resources, especially those that list the thousands of known compounds with detailed descriptions.

Physics

Physics, from the Greek word *physike* meaning "science of nature," is the study of matter, energy, motion, and force as they all govern nature. Early physics was known as natural philosophy and consisted of two areas—mechanics, which is the relation of motion of objects or particles by the action of given forces, and field theory, which looks at the various fields of energy that produce these forces, such as gravity, electricity, and nuclear power.

Today, physics is a complex field that has applications in all other fields of science. Students going into any field of science must have a thorough understanding of physics. There are many subfields of physics including:

- Acoustics—the science of sound.

- Astrophysics—the application of physics to astronomy and the history of our universe.
- Atomic Physics—the study of the energy properties of atoms.
- Biophysics—the study of the physical properties of living plants and animals.
- Classical Mechanics—the study of early physics that concerned the position of objects in space under the action of forces as a function of time.
- Electricity—the study of electric charges at rest and in motion.
- Electromagnetism—the study of physical laws and principles that connect electricity and magnetism.
- Geophysics—the study of physical laws that affect the earth and its development.
- Heat—the study of energy that is the result of a temperature change.
- Low-Temperature Physics—the study of the properties of materials below minus 452 degrees Fahrenheit.
- Molecular Physics—the study of the interaction of atomic nuclei and their structure.
- Optics—the study of light and vision.
- Solid-State Physics—the study of the physical properties of solids.
- Theoretical Physics—the study of physics in the form of mathematics.

Physics Abstracts is the major indexing tool for locating physics literature. Handbooks are abundant. Compilations of extensive tables are now more accurate than ever with the use of computers.

Mathematics

Mathematics, along with astronomy, is one of the oldest sciences and explains the ordered universe for the other sciences. It is the study using numbers and symbols of all quantities, their relationships with each other, their operation within the total picture, and their measurement. Originally mathematics consisted of simply arithmetic, the art of counting, and geometry or measurement of the properties of space, which include points, lines, curves, planes, and surfaces. The classic divisions of mathematics are algebra, geometry, and analysis. Algebra is the use of symbols in equations to solve problems or an extension of arithmetic, and analysis is calculus. Probability, statistics, and topology are also branches of mathematics.

Handbooks are probably the most important type of reference material for mathematics. Tables are important, and many classic tables developed in earlier centuries are still useful. However, with the computers, published tables are less common because computerized tables can be tailored easily to specific needs and produced automatically at the touch of a key. *Mathematical Reviews* is the major indexing service for research conducted throughout the world.

Computer Science

Although computer science is not a pure science, it is included in this chapter because of its close connection to mathematics. The purely applied aspects or technical aspects of computing are found in the electrical and electronics engineering literature. This discipline is concerned with both theoretical and applied areas of study covering storing and processing, mathematics, and logic. It is a fast-evolving field covering a wide array of interests from sophisticated programming languages to programs, hardware, and artificial intelligence, which is concerned with the understanding of intelligent action, including problem solving, perception, learning, symbolic activity, creativity, and language. Robotics is an applied outgrowth of computer technology.

There is an enormous amount of literature covering computer science. Several specialized indexing and abstracting services are available, but you must search those services in mathematics and engineering fields as well. Handbooks and manuals are prolific in the computer sciences, constantly being updated with each new development in research. Directories and encyclopedias of services and databases are also important in this field, some of which can be very expensive. *Computer and Control Abstracts* is the main indexing and abstracting source in addition to *Mathematical Reviews.*

GENERAL SCIENCE

Abstracts and Indexes

90. General Science Index. New York, NY: Wilson, 1978– , monthly with annual cumulations. v.1– , index. $160.00. ISSN: 0162-1963.

Acknowledged as a distinguished reference work, this subject index covers 106 English-language periodicals. Each cited article has complete bibliographic information, and there is a separate index to science book reviews. All areas of science are covered, including limited food, nutrition, health, and medicine coverage. It is also available online, on tape, and on CD-ROM.

91. Index to Scientific Reviews. Philadelphia, PA: Institute for Scientific Information, 1975– , semiannual. 1975– , index. $830.00. ISSN: 0360-0661.

"An international interdisciplinary index to the review literature of science, medicine, agriculture, technology, and the behavioral sciences." It is also available on tape. Other ISI works that are useful include *Index to Scientific and Technical Proceedings, Index to Scientific Book Contents*, and *Index to Book Reviews in the Sciences*.

92. Science Books and Films. Washington, DC: American Association for the Advancement of Science, 1975– , quarterly. v.11– , index. $35.00. ISSN: 0098-342X.

Previously called *AAAS Science Books*, this reviewing source provides reviews of new science trade/textbooks, science films, and software materials. The reviews are rated and may be critical.

93. Science Citation Index. Philadelphia, PA: Institute for Scientific Information, 1961– , bimonthly with annual cumulations. v.1– , index. $10,175.00. ISSN: 0036-827X.

This comprehensive and indispensable computer-produced index to some 3,500 journals provides access through both cited and citing of an author's works. It covers journals, patents, reports, and conference proceedings. Cumulations are published on a periodic basis. It is also available online and on CD-ROM.

Biographical Sources

94. American Men and Women of Science. New York, NY: Bowker, 1989/90– , irregular. 17th– , index. $750.00. ISBN: 0-8352-3074-0 18th ed.

Previously called *American Men and Women of Science: Physical and Biological Sciences*, this is "A biographical directory of today's leaders in physical, biological and related sciences." It is now in its 18th edition for 1992-93. Biographical information is given for some 121,600 scientists, their areas of expertise, education, experience, current positions, research focus, honors and awards, professional memberships, and mailing addresses. It also available online and on CD-ROM.

95. Biographical Dictionary of American Science: The Seventeenth Through the Nineteenth Centuries. Clark A. Elliott. Westport, CT: Greenwood Press, 1979. 360p., illus., index. out-of-print. ISBN: 0-313-20419-5.

Though out-of-print, this is an essential source of information on some 600 American scientists born between 1609 and 1867.

96. Biographical Encyclopedia of Scientists. John Daintith; Sarah Mitchell; Elizabeth Tootill. New York, NY: Facts on File, 1981. 2v., illus., bibliog., index. $125.00. ISBN: 0-87196-396-5.

This biographical source includes some 2,000 living and deceased scientists. A chronology of scientific achievements is provided. Trevor I. Williams' *Biographical Dictionary of Scientists* (Wiley, 1982) is selective but useful, and David Abbott's *Biographical Dictionary of Scientists* (Facts on File, 1983) covers only biologists and chemists.

97. Biographical Index to American Science: The Seventeenth Century to 1920. *(Bibliographies and Indexes in American History, no.16).* Clark A. Elliott. New York, NY: Greenwood Press, 1990. 300p., index. $65.00. ISBN: 0-313-26566-6.

Biographies of some 2,850 American scientists who died prior to 1921 are included in this work. Referenes are made to other biographic sources and to the *National Union Catalog of Manuscript Collections.*

98. Biographical Memoirs. National Academy of Sciences. Washington, DC: National Academy of Sciences, 1877– , irregular. v.1– , illus., index. price varies per volume. ISSN: 0077-2933.

These volumes provide biographies of deceased members of the Academy. Included for each entry are a list of publications, portrait, and chronology.

99. Biographisch-literarisches Handwörterbuch zur Geschichte der exaten Wissenschaften. Johann Christian Poggendorf. Leipzig, Germany: Barth, 1863-1904; Verlag Chemie, 1925-1940. Dist: Germany. 11v., index (Reprint available from Edwards).

This is the classic biographical source for information about mathematicians, astronomers, chemists, physicists, mineralogists, geologists and other scientists worldwide. With each biographical sketch is a detailed bibliography of the person's writings. This work is supplemented by *Biographisch-literarisches Handwöterbuch der exakten Naturwissenschaften, unter Mitwirkung der Akademien der Wissenschaften* (Akademie-Verlag, 1955-1973).

100. Chambers Concise Dictionary of Scientists. David Millar. New York, NY: Chambers/Cambridge, 1989. 461p., illus. $29.95. ISBN: 1-85296-354-9.

Both deceased and living scientists from all disciplines are included in this work. The biographies are brief but useful. A chronology is included.

101. Prominent Scientists: An Index to Collective Biographies. 2nd. Paul A. Pelletier. New York, NY: Neal-Schuman, 1985. 356p., index. $45.00. ISBN: 0-918212-78-2.

This is an index to some 10,000 scientists in all areas of science. It is indexed by name and field of specialization.

Dictionaries, Glossaries, and Thesauri

102. Companion to the Physical Sciences. David Knight. New York, NY: Routledge, 1989. 192p. $25.00. ISBN: 0-415-00901-4.

The *Companion to the Physical Sciences* is a scholarly dictionary of 225 terms in the physical sciences. Each term is placed in historical context with a bibliography of citations.

103. Concise Science Dictionary. 2nd. New York, NY: Oxford University Press, 1991. 758p., illus. $39.95; $10.95pbk. ISBN: 0-19-866167-3; 0-19-286102-6pbk.

Although not comprehensive, this dictionary is still a good general science work. The definitions are clear and concise. It has standard tables in the appendix covering such topics as conversion tables, geological time scale, and classification of plants and animals.

104. Dictionary of Named Effects and Laws in Chemistry, Physics, and Mathematics. 4th. D.W.G. Ballentyne; D.R. Lovett. New York, NY: Chapman & Hall, 1980. 346p. out-of-print. ISBN: 0-412-22380-5.

This classic dictionary, available since 1958, covers the various laws and named effects that are named for their discoverers. Gives a good historical perspective.

105. Dictionary of Scientific Units: Including Dimensionless Numbers and Scales. 6th. H.G. Jerrard; D.B. McNeill. New York, NY: Chapman & Hall, 1992. 222p., illus., bibliog., index. $29.95. ISBN: 0-412-46720-8.

This standard dictionary provides definitions and historical references of all scientific units. Many of the lesser-known units are included.

106. Dictionary of the Physical Sciences: Terms, Formulas, Data. Cesare Emiliani. New York, NY: Oxford University Press, 1987. 365p., illus., bibliog. $19.95. ISBN: 0-19-503651-4.

This good general science dictionary includes definitions of key terms in physics, chemistry, geology, and astronomy. It also has handbook-type information in the form of some 70 tables.

107. Encyclopedic Dictionary of Science. Candida Hunt; Bernard Dixon. New York, NY: Facts on File, 1988. 256p., color illus., index. $35.00. ISBN: 0-8160-2021-3.

This good, small dictionary for undergraduates covers physics, chemistry, environmental sciences, biology, and medicine. Brief biographies are included. Two earlier works that are still useful are *Facts on File Dictionary of Science* and Robin Kerrod's *Concise Dictionary of Science* (Arco, 1985).

108. German-English Science Dictionary. 4th. Louis DeVries; Leon Jacoler; Phyllis L. Bolton. New York, NY: McGraw-Hill, 1978. 628p. out-of-print. ISBN: 0-07-016602-1.

DeVries is synonymous with science language dictionaries. This is the accepted one for German-English.

109. Houghton Mifflin Dictionary of Science. Robert K. Barnhart. Boston, MA: Houghton Mifflin, 1988. 766p., illus. $21.45. ISBN: 0-395-48367-0.

This general science dictionary is good for schools and public libraries, as well as for undergraduates. Pronunciation is included.

110. Penguin Dictionary of Science. 6th. E.B. Uvarov; Alan Isaacs. New York, NY: Penguin, 1986. 468p., illus. $9.95. ISBN: 0-14-051156-3.

This good student dictionary covers physics, chemistry, mathematics, and astronomy.

Directories

111. Life Sciences Organizations and Agencies Directory. Brigitte T. Darnay; Margaret Labash Young. Detroit, MI: Gale Research, 1988. 864p., index. $175.00. ISBN: 0-8103-1826-1.

"A guide to approximately 8,000 organizations and agencies providing information in the agricultural and biological sciences worldwide." Complete directory-type information is provided.

Encyclopedias

112. Magill's Survey of Science. Frank N. Magill. Englewood Cliffs, NJ: Salem Press, 1990-1992. 17v., index. $425.00 earth sciences; $475.00 life sciences; $475.00 physical sciences. ISBN: 0-89356-606-3 earth sciences; 0-89356-612-8 life sciences; 0-89356-618-7 physical sciences.

This series of several volumes for each subject area contains articles and sources for further study. It is a unique reference source, in which each article includes a listing of key definitions, an essay or discussion, and a bibliography. There are glossaries and comprehensive subject indexes. The three topics covered in the science disciplines are *Earth Science Series* (5v., 1990); *Life Science Series* (6v., 1991); and *Physical Science Series* (6v., 1992).

Handbooks and Manuals

113. Guild Handbook of Scientific Illustration. Elaine R. Hodges. New York, NY: Van Nostrand Reinhold, 1988. 640p., illus., index. $99.95. ISBN: 0-442-23681-6.

This excellent handbook/textbook covers the art of scientific illustrations. All disciplines are included.

114. Handbook of Chemistry and Physics: A Ready Reference Book of Chemical and Physical Data. Boca Raton, FL: CRC, 1913– , annual. 1st– , index. $99.50. ISBN: 0-8493-0472-5 72nd ed.

Also know as the *CRC Handbook of Chemistry and Physics*, this annually published handbook has become a standard classic for librarians. It is comprehensive and easy to use. An abridged student edition is also available for $39.95 (CRC, 1988). The mathematics tables have been pulled and are published separately.

115. Quantities and Units of Measurement: A Dictioanry and Handbook. J.V. Drazil. Bronx, NY: Mansell, 1983. 313p., bibliog., index. $110.00. ISBN: 0-7201-1665-1.

This is a revised and expanded edition of the *Dictionary of Quantities and Units*. The first part is an alphabetical listing of units and the second, of quantities and constants. The work is essential for all rsearchers.

Histories

116. Album of Science. I. Bernard Cohen. New York, NY: Macmillan, 1980-89. 5v., illus., bibliog., index. $375.00. ISBN: 0-684-19074-5.

This is a good, well-illustrated history of science for the undergraduate and layperson. The 5 volumes cover From Leonardo to Lavoisier, 1450-1800; The biological sciences in the 20th century; The nineteenth century; The physical sciences in the 20th century; and Antiquity and the middle ages.

117. Asimov's Chronology of Science and Discovery. Isaac Asimov. New York, NY: HarperCollins, 1989. 707p., color illus., index. $29.95. ISBN: 0-06-015612-0.

This popular, but good, chronology covers science from its beginnings to 1988. A more scholarly chronology is Robert Mortimer Gascoigne's *Chronology of the History of Science, 1450-1900* (Garland, 1987).

118. Dictionary of Concepts in the Philosophy of Science. *(Reference Sources for the Social Sciences and Humanities, no.6).* Paul T. Durbin. New York, NY: Greenwood Press, 1988. 362p., bibliog., index. $59.95. ISBN: 0-313-22979-1.

This is a fairly specialized dictionary that defines and discusses over 100 concepts within the philosophy of science. Also of interest are David Knight's *Companion to the Physical Sciences* (Routledge, 1989) and Robert Olby and Geoffrey Canta's *Companion to the History of Modern Science* (Routledge, 1989).

119. Dictionary of the History of Science. W.F. Bynum; E.J. Browne; Roy Porter. Princeton, NJ: Princeton University Press, 1981. 494p., illus., biblig., index. $75.00; $17.95pbk. ISBN: 0-691-08287-1; 0-691-02384-0pbk.

The some 700 individually authored articles present the major scientific accomplishments and ideas in science.

120. History of Modern Science: A Guide to the Second Scientific Revolution, 1800-1950. *(The Iowa State University Press Series in the History of Technology and Science).* Stephen G. Brush. Ames, IA: Iowa State University Press, 1988. 544p., bibliog., index. $41.95. ISBN: 0-8138-0883-9.

This is a very readable, well-documented history of modern science. Also of interest would be Trevor I. Williams' *Science: A History of Discovery in the Twentieth Century* (Oxford University Press, 1990).

121. Information Sources in the History of Science and Medicine. Pietro Corsi; Paul Weindling. Boston, MA: Butterworth Scientific, 1983. 531p., illus., bibliog., index. out-of-print. ISBN: 0-408-10764-2.

This unique work emphasizes the social aspects in the history of science and medicine. Also included is a description of major scientific and medical libraries and archives.

122. Introduction to the History of Science. *(Carnegie Institution of Washington, Publication no.376).*

George Sarton. Melbourne, FL: Krieger, 1975 (c1927-1948). 5v., illus., index. $425.00. ISBN: 0-88275-172-7.

This reprint of the classic history of science work is comprehensive, very readable, and well documented. George Sarton also has a 2-volume *History of Science* (Norton, 1970). Two other histories that should be mentioned are Charles Joseph Singer's *Short History of Scientific Ideas to 1900* (Oxford University Press, 1959) and David M. Knight's *Sources for the History of Science, 1660-1914* (Cornell University Press, 1975).

123. Isis Cumulative Bibliography. London, Great Britain: Mansell, 1971-, irregular. no.1-, index. price per number varies.

An attempt to compile the most authoritative list of history of science sources in the world, this scholarly work is produced by the History of Science Society with material taken from the *Isis Critical Bibliographies.*

Tables

124. Statistical Tables for the Social, Biological, and Physical Sciences. F.C. Powell. New York, NY: Cambridge University Press, 1982. 96p., illus., bibliog., index. $19.95; $7.95pbk. ISBN: 0-521-24141-3; 0-521-28473-2pbk.

Statistical tables from books, journals, and reports have been brought together in one volume, covering the disciplines of biology, physics, and the social sciences.

125. Tables of Physical and Chemical Constants and Some Mathematical Functions. 15th. G.W.C. Kaye; T.H. Laby. New York, NY: Longman, 1986. 477p., illus., index. $57.95. ISBN: 0-582-46354-8.

This source is a standard, well-known collection of tables of physical and chemical constants. All values are in SI units with bibliographic refernces to the original literature. The *Geigy Scientific Tables* (Ciba-Geigy, 1981-) is another good source produced by an industrial research laboratory.

Periodicals

126. American Midland Naturalist. Notre Dame, IN: University of Notre Dame, 1909–, quarterly. v.1–, index. $60.00. ISSN: 0003-0031.

127. American Scientist. Triangle Park, NC: Sigma Xi, 1913–, bimonthly. v.1–, index. $28.00. ISSN: 0003-0996.

128. Annals of Science. New York, NY: Taylor & Francis, 1936–, bimonthly. v.1–, index. $380.00. ISSN: 0003-3790.

129. Annals of the New York Academy of Sciences. New York, NY: New York Academy of Sciences, 1823– , irregular. v.1– , index. price per volume varies. ISSN: 0077-8923.

130. Discover. Buena Vista, CA: Walt Disney Magazine Publishing, 1980– , monthly. v.1– , index. $27.00. ISSN: 0274-7529.

131. Journal of Research in Science Teaching. New York, NY: Wiley, 1963– , 10/year. v.1– , index. $200.00. ISSN: 0022-4308.

132. Journal of the Franklin Institute. Tarrytown, NY: Pergamon Press, 1826– , 6/year. v.1– , index. $615.00. ISSN: 0016-0032.

133. Nature. London, Great Britain: Macmillan, 1869– , weekly. v.1– , index. $395.00. ISSN: 0028-0836.

134. New Scientist. London, Great Britain: IPC Magazines, 1956– , weekly. v.1– , index. $130.00. ISSN: 0028-6664.

135. Philosophical Transactions of the Royal Society of London: Series A, Physical Sciences and Engineering; Series B, Biological Sciences. London, Great Britain: Royal Society of London, 1665– , monthly. v.1– , index. $753.00 series A; $852.00 series B. ISSN: 0962-8428 series A; 0080-4622 series B.

136. Philosophy of Science. East Lansing, MI: Philosophy of Science Association, 1934– , quarterly. v.1– , index. $55.00. ISSN: 0031-8248.

137. Proceedings of the Academy of Natural Sciences of Philadelphia. Philadelphia, PA: Academy of Natural Sciences of Philadelphia, 1842– , annual. v.1– , index. $30.00. ISSN: 0097-3157.

138. Proceedings of the Royal Society of London; Series A, Mathematical and Physical Sciences; Series B, Biological Sciences. London, Great Britain: Royal Society of London, 1832– , monthly. v.1– , index. $580.00 series A; $320.00series B. ISSN: 0080-4630 series A; 0080-4649 series B.

139. Science. Washington, DC: American Association for the Advancement of Science, 1880– , weekly. v.1– , index. $150.00. ISSN: 0036-8075.

140. Science News. Washington, DC: Science Service, 1921– , weekly. v.1– , index. $39.50. ISSN: 0036-8423.

141. Scientific American. New York, NY: Scientific American, 1845– , monthly. v.1– , index. $36.00. ISSN: 0036-8733.

ASTRONOMY

Abstracts and Indexes

142. Astronomy and Astrophysics Abstracts. New York, NY: Springer-Verlag, 1969– , semiannual. v.1– , index. price varies per year. ISSN: 0067-0022.

Previously called *Astronomischer Jahresbericht* (1899-1968), this is an international abstracting service arranged by subject with added sections for periodicals, proceedings, and books.

Atlases

143. Atlas of the Solar System. Patrick Moore. London, Great Britain: Mitchell Beazley, 1983. 464p., illus. (part in color), bibliog., index. price not available. ISBN: 0-85533-468-1.

This good general atlas of the sun and planets gives general descriptions for the layperson and the researcher. Patrick Moore is a prolific contributor to the literature of astronomy, including another, still useful, work, *Color Star Atlas* (Crown, 1973).

144. Cambridge Atlas of Astronomy. 2nd. Jean Audouze; Guy Israel. New York, NY: Cambridge University Press, 1988. 432p., illus. (part in color), bibliog., index. $90.00. ISBN: 0-521-36360-8.

A translation of the *Grand Atlas de l'Astronomie*, this is a student atlas with beautiful color photographs and illustrations. Still useful is Patrick Moore's *Atlas of the Universe* (Rand McNally, 1970).

145. Cambridge Photographic Atlas of the Planets. Geoffrey Briggs; Frederic Taylor. New York, NY: Cambridge University Press, 1982. 244p., illus. (part in color), index. out-of-print. ISBN: 0-521-23976-1.

This is one of the better atlases covering the planets. Photographs are crisp and clear, accompanied by good text. Another smaller atlas is Paul Doherty's *Atlas of the Planets* (McGraw-Hill, 1980).

146. Cambridge Star Atlas 2000.0. Wil Tirion. New York, NY: Cambridge University Press, 1992 (c1991). 74p., bibliog. $19.95. ISBN: 0-521-26322-0.

This excellent star atlas covers those objects observable with the naked eye or a good pair of binoculars. Contains monthly star maps, star charts, and astronomical information. Also of use is Arthur P. Norton's *Norton's 2000.0: Star Atlas and Reference Handbook* (Wiley, 1989).

147. Color Atlas of the Galaxies. James D. Wray. New York, NY: Cambridge University Press, 1988. 189p., color illus. $79.50. ISBN: 0-521-32236-7.

This is one of the few atlases presenting photographs of celestial objects in their true or natural colors. Technical details are given for each object. Two other interesting atlases are Hans Vehrenberg's *Atlas of Deep-Sky Splendors* (Cambridge University Press, 1984) and Richard C. Henry's *Atlas of the Ultraviolet Sky* (Johns Hopkins University Press, 1988).

148. National Geographic Picture Atlas of Our Universe. Revised. Roy A. Gallant. Washington, DC: National Geographic, 1986. 284p., illus. $18.95. ISBN: 0-685-14522-0.

Excellent illustrations make this a very good atlas, especially for the layperson. Another useful atlas is Patrick Moore's *New Concise Atlas of the Universe* (Mitchell Beazley, 1982).

149. Nearby Galaxies Atlas. R. Brent Tully; J. Richard Fisher. New York, NY: Cambridge University Press, 1987. 7p., 23 leaves, illus., bibliog., index. $65.00. ISBN: 0-521-30136-X.

This atlas covers galaxies other than the Milky Way. Some 22 maps are included.

150. New Photographic Atlas of the Moon. Zdenek Kopal. New York, NY: Taplinger, 1971. 311p., illus., bibliog. out-of-print. ISBN: 0-8008-5515-9.

Although out-of-print, this is still the standard atlas of the moon. Some 200 photographs are included. It is also called the *Photographic Atlas of the Moon.* Another well-known moon atlas is H.A.G. Lewis' *Times Atlas of the Moon* (Times, 1969).

151. Revised New General Catalogue of Nonstellar Astronomical Objects. Jack W. Sulentic; William G. Tifft. Tucson, AZ: University of Arizona Press, 1973. 384p., bibliog. $50.00. ISBN: 0-8165-0421-0.

A revision of J.L.E. Dryer's *New General Catalogue of Nebulae and Clusters of Stars*, this catalog lists some 7,840 objects with data on each.

152. Sky Catalogue 2000.0. Alan Hirshfeld; Roger W. Sinnott; Francois Ochsenbein. New York, NY: Cambridge University Press, 1991– , irregular. v.1– , index. $64.95v.1; $39.95v.1pbk. ISBN: 0-521-41743-0v.1; 0-521-42736-3v.1pbk.

This summary of astronomical data for all stars (5,000) brighter than 8.0. Information for each star includes identification numbers, names, constellation, type, and the inferred distance. A useful, smaller atlas is Wil Tirion's *Sky Atlas 2000.0: 26 Star Charts Covering Both Hemispheres* (Sky Publishing, 1981).

153. Starlist 2000: A Quick Reference Star Catalog for Astronomers. Richard Dibon-Smith. New York, NY: Wiley, 1992. 400p., index. $29.95. ISBN: 0-471-55895-8.

This easy-to-use guide helps in identifying stars. It is intended for students, professionals, and amateur astronomers.

154. True Visual Magnitude Photographic Star Atlas. Christos Papadopoulos. New York, NY: Pergamon, 1979. 3v., illus. $1,065.00. ISBN: 0-08-024458-0.

This comprehensive atlas shows the stars as a person would see them through a telescope. The 3 volumes cover v.1—Southern Stars; v.2—Equatorial Stars; v.3—Northern Stars.

Catalogs

155. Catalogue of the Universe. Paul Muriden; David Allen. New York, NY: Cambridge University Press, 1986. 288p., illus., index. $29.95. ISBN: 0-521-22859-X.

This is an authoritative catalog of the objects in the universe for researchers.

156. General Catalog of HI Observations of Galaxies. W.K. Huchtmeier; O.G. Richter. New York, NY: Springer-Verlag, 1989. 350p., illus., bibliog., index. $66.00. ISBN: 0-387-96997-7.

This is a research catalog of reference data from published neutral hydrogen (HI) spectral observation of external galaxies. It is based on 570 sources, providing some 19,900 entries for over 10,300 galaxies.

157. Master List of Nonstellar Optical Astronomical Objects. Robert S. Dixon; George Sonneborn. Columbus, OH: Ohio State University Press, 1980. 835p., bibliog., index. out-of-print. ISBN: 0-8142-0250-0.

This is a comprehensive compendium of all known catalogs of nonstellar objects. The some 185,000 listings cover every object from every catalog.

158. Messier's Nebulae and Star Clusters. 2nd. Kenneth G. Jones. New York, NY: Cambridge University Press, 1991. 480p., index. $49.50. ISBN: 0-521-37079-5.

This is an historical and biographical description of all objects listed in the 18th century catalog by Messier.

159. NGC 2000.0: The Complete New General Catalogue and Index Catalogues of Nebulae and Star Clusters by J.L.E. Dreyer. Roger W. Sinnott. New York, NY: Cambridge University Press, 1988. 273p., index. $19.95. ISBN: 0-521-37813-3.

This is a corrected catalog of 13,226 deep-sky objects first published by J.L.E. Dreyer in 1888 with indexes in 1895 and 1908. The original work was called *New General Catalogue of Nebulae and Clusters of Stars*, thus NGC. It is intended for individual use and replaces Jack W. Sulentic and William G. Tifft's *Revised New General Catalogue of Nonstellar Astronomical Objects* (University of Arizona Press, 1973).

Dictionaries, Glossaries, and Thesauri

160. Concise Dictionary of Astronomy. Jacqueline Mitton. New York, NY: Oxford University Press, 1991. 423p. $24.95. ISBN: 0-1985-3967-3.

This is a good general dictionary of astronomical terms with brief definitions. A smaller work for the layperson is Jeanne Hopkins' *Glossary of Astronomy and Astrophysics* (University of Chicago Press, 1980).

161. Dictionary of Astronomical Names. Adrian Room. New York, NY: Routledge & K. Paul, 1988. 282p., illus., bibliog. $27.50. ISBN: 0-7102-1115-5.

This useful dictionary provides the origins of the names of stars, asteroids, satellites, and galaxies.

162. Dictionary of Astronomy, Space, and Atmospheric Phenomena. David F. Tver. New York, NY: Van Nostrand Reinhold, 1979. 281p., illus. out-of-print. ISBN: 0-442-24045-7.

This is a good layperson's dictionary of astronomical terms and related terms in physics and mathematics.

163. Dictionary of Minor Planet Names. Lutz D. Schmadel. New York, NY: Springer-Verlag, 1992. 687p. $59.00.

This comprehensive dictionary lists and describes the minor planets of the universe.

164. Facts on File Dictionary of Astronomy. Rev. Valerie Illingworth. New York, NY: Facts on File, 1987 (c1985). 437p., illus. $24.95. ISBN: 0-8160-1357-8.

This dictionary of some 2,300 terms that a layperson would encounter when reading about astronomy. Definitions are clear and succinct. Another smaller dictionary is Malcolm Plant's *Dictionary of Space* (Longman, 1986).

165. HarperCollins Dictionary of Astronomy and Space Science. Dianne F. Moore. New York, NY: HarperPerennial, 1992. 338p., illus. $25.00. ISBN: 0-06-271542-9.

This is a good dictionary for the student. Also of use is the small dictionary by Jacqueline Mitton, *Key Definitions in Astronomy* (Littlefield, 1982).

166. Longman Illustrated Dictionary of Astronomy and Astronautics: The Terminology of Space. Ian Ridpath. Harlow, Great Britain: Longman, 1987. 224p., color illus., index. $12.00. ISBN: 0-582-89381-X.

This dictionary covers not only terminology from astronomy, but also from space sciences.

Encyclopedias

167. Astronomy and Astrophysics Encyclopedia. Stephen P. Maran. New York, NY: Van Nostrand Reinhold, 1992. 1,02p., illus., bibliog., index. $119.95. ISBN: 0-442-26364-3.

This advanced encyclopedia provides some 400 signed articles on all aspects of astronomy. It assumes some previous knowledge of astronomy and astrophysics. An older but still useful work is Simon Mitton's *Cambridge Encyclopedia of Astronomy* (Crown, 1977). There is also the classic *Flammarion Book of Astronomy* (Simon & Schuster, 1964).

168. Cambridge Encyclopedia of Space. Michael Rycroft. New York, NY: Cambridge University Press, 1990. 386p., illus., bibliog., index. $79.50. ISBN: 0-521-36426-4.

A revised edition of *Grand Atlas de l'Espace*, this is an excellent topical encyclopedia covering astronomy and other space related topics. For historical comparison consult the *New Space Encyclopedia* (Dutton, 1973).

169. Encyclopedia of Astronomy and Astrophysics. Robert A. Meyers; Steven N. Shore. San Diego, CA: Academic Press, 1989. 807p., illus., index. $65.00. ISBN: 0-12-226690-0.

This advanced reference source for astronomy and astrophysics is arranged alphabetically. The articles are authored by experts in the field and require some advanced knowledge of astronomy. A smaller and somewhat simpler older work is Alfred Weigert's *Concise Encyclopedia of Astronomy* (A. Hilger, 1976).

170. Extraterrestrial Encyclopedia: Our Search for Life in Outer Space. Revised and updated. Joseph A. Angelo, Jr. New York, NY: Facts on File, 1991. 240p., illus. (part in color), bibliog., index. $40.00. ISBN: 0-8160-2276-3.

The alphabetically arranged encyclopedia presents major space technologies and developments that pertain to the search for extraterrestrial life. Individual entries range from a definition to a page or more of discussion. A good bibliography is included.

171. International Encyclopedia of Astronomy. Patrick Moore. New York, NY: Crown, 1987. 448p., illus., index. $40.00. ISBN: 0-517-56179-4.

This excellent, alphabetically arranged encyclopedia covers all areas of astronomy, as well as related topics in space science. Three older works still useful are Ian Ridpath's *Illustrated Encyclopedia of Astronomy and Space* (Crowell, 1976), David Baker's beautifully illustrated *Larousse Guide to Astronomy* (Larousse, 1978), and Richard S. Lewis' *Illustrated Encyclopedia of the Universe* (Harmony Books, 1983).

172. McGraw-Hill Encyclopedia of Astronomy. Sybil P. Parker. New York, NY: McGraw-Hill, 1983. 450p., illus. (part in color), bibliog., index. $89.95. ISBN: 0-07-045251-2.

Also called the *Encyclopedia of Astronomy*, this work contains all articles pertaining to astronomy from the fifth edition of the *McGraw-Hill Encyclopedia of Science and Technology*.

173. Patrick Moore's A-Z of Astronomy. Patrick Moore. New York, NY: Norton, 1987 (c1986). 240p., illus., bibliog., index. $13.50. ISBN: 0-393-30505-8.

This is a good general encyclopedia of astronomy for the layperson. Entries are concise but accurate.

Guides and Field Guides

174. Audubon Society Field Guide to the Night Sky. Mark R. Chartland. New York, NY: Alfred A. Knopf, 1991. 714p., color illus., index. $18.00.

As with all Audubon Society field guides, this one is well-illustrated, colorful, easy to use, and especially good for the layperson. Also good is William T. Olcott's *Field Book of the Skies* (Putnam, 1954). A good atlas to use with this guide is Erich Karkoschka's *Observer's Sky Atlas* (Springer-Verlag, 1990), a translation of *Atlas fuer Himmelsbeobachter*.

175. Field Guide to the Stars and Planets, Including the Moon, Satellites, Comets and Other Features of the Universe. *(Peterson Field Guide Series, 15).* Donald Howard Menzel; Jay M. Pasachoff. Boston, MA: Houghton Mifflin, 1983. 397p., illus. $19.95; $13.95pbk. ISBN: 0-395-34641-X; 0-395-34835-8pbk.

This is a popular field guide for the amateur, with monthly star charts and a photographic atlas of the sky.

176. Pictorial Guide to the Planets. 2nd. Joseph Hollister Jackson. New York, NY: Crowell, 1973. 248p., illus., bibliog. out-of-print. ISBN: 0-690-62443-3.

Although out-of-print, this guide provides a good introduction to the planets. Two other useful guides from the same publisher are Dinsomore Alter's *Pictorial Guide to the Moon* (Crowell, 1973) and Henry C. King's *Pictorial Guide to the Stars* (Crowell, 1967).

177. Pocket Guide to Astronomy. Patrick Moore. New York, NY: Simon & Schuster, 1985 (c1980). 144p., illus., (part in color), index. $7.95. ISBN: 0-671-25309-3.

This small, useful field guide is produced by a well-known authority in astronomy. Also useful is Peter L. Brown's *Star and Planet Spotting: A Field Guide to the Night Sky* (Sterling, 1990).

178. Universe Guide to Stars and Planets. Ian Ridpath; Wil Tirion. New York, NY: Universe Publishing, 1985. 384p., index. $19.50. ISBN: 0-87663-366-1.

Although not as comprehensive as some other guides, this is still a good general work.

179. Visual Astronomy of the Deep-Sky. Roger N. Clark. New York, NY: Cambridge University Press, 1991. 416p., illus., index. $39.95. ISBN: 0-521-36155-9.

This is an authoritative work for the researcher and student. Illustrations are good, and the text is clear and well written.

180. Whitney's Star Finder: A Field Guide to the Heavens. 5th. Charles Allen Whitney. New York, NY: Knopf, 1989. 111p., illus., index. $16.95. ISBN: 0-679-72582-2.

This well-known field guide covers the observation of sunspots, rainbows, halos, comets, meteors, the moon, and the planets. Two other interesting guides are David H. Levy's *Sky: A User's Guide* (Cambridge University Press, 1991) and Phillip S. Harrington's *Touring the Universe Through Binoculars: A Complete Astronomer's Guidebook* (Wiley, 1990).

Guides to the Literature

181. Astronomy and Astronautics: An Enthusiast's Guide to Books and Periodicals. Andy Lusis. New York, NY: Facts on File, 1986. 302p., illus., index. $35.00. ISBN: 0-8160-1469-8.

This good selective guide to books and periodicals in astronomy and space science emphasizes those for the layperson.

182. Astronomy and Astrophysics: A Bibliographical Guide. *(MacDonald Bibliographical Guides).*

D.A. Kemp. Hamden, CT: MacDonald Technical and Scientific, 1970. 584p., index. out-of-print. ISBN: 0-208-01035-1.

Now out-of-print, this is a selective guide to materials on theory, data, and other astronomical topics. There are over 3,000 entries with special emphasis on star catalogs and ephemerides.

183. Bibliography of Astronomy, 1970-1979. Robert A. Seal; Sarah S. Martin. Littleton, CO: Libraries Unlimited, 1982. 407p., index. out-of-print. ISBN: 0-87287-280-7.

Considered an extension of D.A. Kemp's *Astronomy and Astrophysics: A Bibliographic Guide* (Shoe String Press, 1970) and Robert A. Seal's *Guide to the Literature of Astronomy* (Libraries Unlimited, 1977), this volume covers material published during the 1970s. All entries are annotated.

Handbooks and Manuals

184. Amateur Astronomer's Handbook. 4th. J.B. Sidgwick; James Muriden. Hillside, NJ: Enslow, 1980. 568p., illus., bibliog., index. $9.95. ISBN: 0-89490-049-8.

This handbook, which is more comprehensive than the one by James Muriden, gives the technical aspects of instrumentation, as well as the theory of practical astronomy. For in-depth articles on astronomy, consult Gunter Roth's *Astronomy: A Handbook* (Springer-Verlag, 1975).

185. Amateur Astronomer's Handbook: A Guide to Exploring the Heavens. 3rd. James Muirden. New York, NY: HarperCollins, 1987. 480p., illus., index. $10.95. ISBN: 0-06-091426-2.

This is a more practical handbook for amateur astronomers, especially those wishing to build their own small observatory. A useful companion would be Neale E. Howard's *Telescope Handbook and Star Atlas* (Crowell, 1967). James Muirden also has an older, but smaller, handbook that is still available, *Astronomy Handbook* (Prentice-Hall, 1984).

186. Astronomy Data Book. 2nd. Hedley Robinson; James Muirden. New York, NY: Wiley, 1979. 272p., illus., index. out-of-print. ISBN: 0-470-26594-9.

This good introductory handbook provides information on eclipses, comets, planets, stars, and meteors.

187. Astrophysical Quantities. 3rd. C.W. Allen. London, Great Britain: Athlone Press, 1973. 310p., bibliog., index. $65.00. ISBN: 0-485-11150-0.

The constants and numerical quantities in this very useful handbook are needed by the astronomical and astrophysical researcher.

188. Burnham's Celestial Handbook: An Observer's Guide to the Universe Beyond the Solar System. Robert Burnham, Jr. New York, NY: Dover, 1978-79. 3v., illus., index. $13.95/vol. ISBN: 0-486-23567-Xv.1; 0-486-23568-8v.2; 0-486-23673-0v.3.

This comprehensive handbook gives full descriptions of more than 7,000 celestial objects. The British Meteorological Office also has a useful handbook, *Observer's Handbook* (HMSO, 1982), and Hans Vehrenberg's *Handbook of the Constellations* (Treugesell, 1984) should also be considered.

189. Guide to Amateur Astronomy. Jack Newton; Philip Teece. New York, NY: Cambridge University Press, 1988. 327p., illus., bibliog., index. $24.95. ISBN: 0-521-34028-4.

This excellent handbook for the amateur uses a step-by-step approach, covering such topics as purchasing and using a telescope, time keeping, astrophotography, and building your own equipment. Also useful would be P. Clay Sherrod's *Complete Manual of Amateur Astronomy: Tools and Techniques for Astronomical Observation* (Prentice-Hall, 1981).

190. Handbook of Space Astronomy and Astrophysics. 2nd. Martin V. Zombeck. New York, NY: Cambridge University Press, 1990. 440p., illus., bibliog., index. $75.00; $34.50pbk. ISBN: 0-521-34550-2; 0-421-34787-4pbk.

This compilation of astronomical data covers such areas as radio astronomy, cosmic rays, and x-ray astronomy, as well as handbook data from related physical and mathematical fields.

191. How to Use an Astronomical Telescope: A Beginner's Guide to Observing the Cosmos. James Muriden. New York, NY: Simon & Schuster, 1988. 400p., illus., bibliog., index. $12.95. ISBN: 0-671-66404-2.

This well-written handbook provides guidelines in the selection and use of a telescope by amateur astronomers. Another useful student handbook is Robert J. Traister's *Astronomy and Telescopes: A Beginner's Handbook* (TAB, 1983).

192. Moon Observer's Handbook. Fred W. Price. New York, NY: Cambridge University Press, 1988. 309p., illus., bibliog., index. $37.50. ISBN: 0-521-33500-0.

This excellent handbook for the amateur provides facts about the moon, information on how how to observe it, and detailed maps and charts. Another excellent companion handbook, which is much more comprehensive, is Grant Heiken's *Lunar Sourcebook: A User's Guide to the Moon* (Cambridge University Press, 1991).

193. Observing the Sun. *(Practical Astronomy Handbook Series, 3).* Peter O. Taylor. New York, NY: Cambridge University Press, 1991. 159p., illus., index. $29.95. ISBN: 0-521-40110-0.

This general handbook for observing the sun stresses the need to protect the eyes and describes the best way to make an observatory for looking at the sun.

194. Standard Handbook for Telescope Making. Neale E. Howard. New York, NY: T.Y. Crowell, 1959. 326p., illus., index. out-of-print.

Even though this handbook is out-of-print it is still an excellent introduction to building a telescope. Also useful is Sam Brown's *All About Telescopes* (Edmund Scientific, 1975).

195. Webb Society Deep-Sky Observer's Handbook. Kenneth G. Jones; Webb Society. New York, NY: Enslow, 1979-1990. 8v., illus., bibliog., index. price per volume varies. ISBN: 0-89490-122-2v.1.

This is a very comprehensive treatise/handbook on deep-sky observing. Volume one is now in its second edition with additional volumes being planned. The 8 volumes cover 1—Double Stars; 2—Planetary and Gaseous Nebulae; 3—Open and Globular Clusters; 4—Galaxies; 5—Clusters and Galaxies; 6—Anonymous Galaxies; 7—The Southern Sky; 8—Variable Stars. For the amateur there is Christian B. Luginbuhl's *Observing Handbook and Catalogue of Deep-Sky Objects* (Cambridge University Press, 1990).

Histories

196. Astronomy of the Ancients. Kenneth Brecler; Michael Feirtag. Cambridge, MA: MIT Press, 1979. 206p., illus., bibliog., index. out-of-print. ISBN: 0-262-02137-4.

Now out-of-print this history presents 8 articles covering topics about ancient astronomy and astronomers.

197. History of Ancient Mathematical Astronomy. O. Neugebauer. New York, NY: Springer-Verlag, 1975. 3v., bibliog., index. $335.00. ISBN: 0-387-06995-X.

This is a very comprehensive and scholarly treatise on the history of ancient mathematical astronomy. The 3 volumes cover v.1—The Almagest and Its Direct Predecessors. Babylonian Astronomy; v.2—Egypt. Early Greek Astronomy, Astronomy During the Roman Imperial Period and Late Antiquity; v.3—Appendices and Indices.

198. History of Astronomy. *(Life of Science Library, no. 24).*

Girogio Abetti. New York, NY: Abelart-Schuman, 1952. 338p., illus., index. out-of-print.

This standard, but now out-of-print history of astronomy, is a translation of *Storia dell' Astronomia.*

199. History of Astronomy from Herschel to Hertzsprung. Dieter B. Herrmann. New York, NY: Cambridge University Press, 1984. 220p., illus., bibliog., index. $27.95. ISBN: 0-521-25733-6.

A translation of *Geschichte der Astronomie von Herschel bis Hertzsprung*, this history traces the development of astronomy through its principal directions or main areas of activity, rather than through biographies or chronologies.

200. History of Modern Astronomy and Astrophysics: A Selected Annotated Bibliography. *(Bibliographies of the History of Science and Technology, v.1) (Garland Reference Library of the Humanities, v.304).* David H. DeVorkin. New York, NY: Garland, 1982. 434p., illus., index. $102.00. ISBN: 0-8240-9283-X.

This annotated bibliography covers astronomy from the invention and application of the telescope to astronomy through the middle of the twentieth century. It is arranged by topic and by author.

201. Patrick Moore's History of Astronomy. 6th revised. Patrick Moore. London, Great Britain: Macdonald, 1983. 327p., illus (part in color), index. out-of-print. ISBN: 0-356-08607-0.

Previously called the *Story of Astronomy*, this is an excellent general history through March 1983.

202. Source Book in Astronomy and Astrophysics, 1900-1975. *(Source Books in the History of the Sciences).* Kenneth R. Lang; Owen Gingerich. Cambridge, MA: Harvard University Press, 1979. 922p., illus., bibliog., index. $75.00. ISBN: 0-674-82200-5.

The basis of this book is history presented in the form of excerpts from the original writings about astronomy. It is based partly on an earlier work by Harlow Shapley.

Yearbooks, Annuals, and Almanacs

203. Air Almanac. Washington, DC: U.S. Nautical Office, 1937– , annual. 1938– , index. price varies. ISSN: 0002-2160.

Published jointly with Her Majesty's Nautical Almanac Office, this compendium contains charts, graphs, and other astronomical data needed for air navigation. Also useful is Nathaniel Bowditch's *American Practical Navigator* (Scholarly, 1977).

204. Astronomical Almanac for the Year.
Washington, DC: Nautical Almanac Office,
1981– , annual. v.1– , illus., index. price varies.

Previously issued as *American Ephemeris and Nautical Almanac* (1855-1980), this work provides lists and tables of computed positions of celestial bodies historically and predicted. It contains such topics as eclipses, tables of risings and settings, and planetary movements. Another similar annual is the U.S. Naval Observatory's *Astronomical Phenomena for the Year.*

205. Nautical Almanac. Washington, DC:
U.S. Naval Observatory, 1960– , annual.
1960– , index. price varies. ISSN: 0077-619X.

Also called *American Nautical Almanac*, this is the counterpart to the *Air Almanac*, containing the necessary charts, graphs, and other astronomical data needed for sea navigation.

206. Yearbook of Astronomy. New York,
NY: Norton, 1962– , annual. v.1– , index.
$55.00.

Intended for the amateur, this excellent little annual contains current information of interest to the astronomer, with standard data and charts useful for amateurs. A directory of astronomical societies is included.

Periodicals

207. Astronomical Journal. New York, NY:
American Institute of Physics/American
Astronomical Society, 1849– , monthly. v.1– ,
index. $280.00. ISSN: 0004-6256.

208. Astronomy. Waukesha, WI: Kalmbach,
1973– , monthly. v.1– , index. $30.00. ISSN:
0091-6358.

209. Astronomy and Astrophysics. New
York, NY: Springer-Verlag, 1969– , 28/year.
v.1– , index. $1,174.00. ISSN: 004-6361.

210. Astrophysical Journal. Chicago, IL:
University of Chicago Press/American
Astronomical Society, 1895– , semimonthly.
v.1– , index. $650.00. ISSN: 0004-637X.

**211. Bulletin of the American Astronomical
Society.** New York, NY: American Institute of
Physics/American Astronomical Society,
1969– , quarterly. v.1– , index. $50.00. ISSN:
0002-7537.

212. Earth, Moon, and Planets. Dordrecht,
Netherlands: Kluwer, 1969– , monthly. v.1– ,
index. $724.00. ISSN: 0167-9295.

213. Icarus. San Diego, CA: Academic
Press/American Astronomical Society, 1962– ,
monthly. v.1– , index. $858.00. ISSN:
0019-1035.

214. Meteoritics. Fayetville, AR: University of
Arkansas, 1955– , quarterly. v.1 , index.
$110.00. ISSN: 0026-1114.

215. Observatory. Oxon, Great Britain:
Rutherford Appleton Laboratory, 1877– ,
bimonthly. v.1– , index. $15.00. ISSN:
0029-7704.

**216. Publications of the Astronomical Society
of the Pacific.** San Francisco, CA:
Astronomical Society of the Pacific, 1889– ,
monthly. v.1– , index. $65.00. ISSN:
0004-6280.

217. Sky and Telescope. Belmont, MA: Sky
Publishing, 1941– , monthly. v.1– , index.
$24.00. ISSN: 0037-7704.

218. Vistas in Astronomy. Tarrytown, NY:
Pergamon Press, 1958– , 4/year. v.1– , index.
$352.50. ISSN: 0083-6656.

BIOLOGY

Abstracts and Indexes

219. Biological Abstracts. Philadelphia, PA:
BIOSIS, 1927– , semimonthly. v.1– , index.
$4,900.00. ISSN: 0006-3169.

This source is the most widely known of English abstracting services, covering current research as reported in the biological and biomedical literatures. Each issue is arranged by broad subject categories. Numerous index access points are included as well as cumulative indexes. It is also available online and on CD-ROM.

220. Biological Abstracts/RRM. Philadelphia,
PA: BIOSIS, 1965– , semimonthly. v.1– ,
index. $2,495.00. ISSN: 0192-6985.

This indexed and classified bibliography of research reports, reviews, books on biology and biomedicine, and conference proceedings was previously called *Bioresearch Index* (1965-1980). It is also available online.

221. Biological and Agricultural Index. New
York, NY: H.W. Wilson, 1964– , monthly.
v.19-. service basis. ISSN: 0006-3177.

Previously called *Agricultural Index*, this reference is a cumulative subject index to periodicals in biology, agriculture, and related sciences. It is also available online and on CD-ROM.

222. Cambridge Microbiology Abstracts.
Bethesda, MD: Cambridge Scientific Abstracts, 1965– , monthly. v.1– , index. $755.00 section A; $850.00 section B; $715.00 section C. ISSN: 0300-838X section A; 0300-8398 section B; 0301-2328 section C.

This abstracting service covers some 30,800 abstracts a year in three sections: A—Industrial and applied microbiology; B—Bacteriology; C—Algology, mycology, and protozoology. There are author and subject indexes as well as cumulative indexes. It is also available online.

223. Cambridge Scientific Biochemistry Abstracts. Bethesda, MD: Cambridge Scientific Abstracts, 1971– , monthly. v.1– , index. $665.00 part 1; $675.00 part 2; $760.00 part 3. ISSN: 8756-7504 part 1; 8756-7512 part 2; 8756-7520 part 3.

An interdisciplinary abstracting service covering the literature in biochemistry. It is published in three parts: Part 1—Biological membranes; Part 2—Nucleic acids; Part 3—Amino-acids, peptides, and proteins. Each part is separately indexed and has its own cumulative indexes. It is also available online and CD-ROM.

224. Current Awareness in Biological Sciences. New York, NY: Pergamon Press, 1954-, 144 issues/year. v.1-, index. $4,192.00. ISSN: 0733-4443.

Formerly *International Abstracts of Biological Sciences* (1954-83), this current awareness service is now published in 12 sections: Biochemistry, Cancer Research, Cell and Developmental Biology, Clinical Chemistry, Ecological and Environmental Sciences, Genetics and Molecular Biology, Immunology, Microbiology, Neuroscience, Pharmacology and Technology, Physiology, and Plant Science. It is also available online.

225. Ecology Abstracts. Bethesda, MD: Cambridge Scientific Abstracts, 1975– , monthly. v.1– , index. $745.00. ISSN: 0143-3296.

An abstracting service covering the research literature pertaining to the interactions of living organisms and their environments. Some 11,000 abstracts a year are included. There are author and subject indexes as well as cumulative indexes. It is also available online and on CD-ROM. Another similar British service is *Ecological Abstracts* (Pergamon Press, 1974-).

226. Index to Illustrations of Living Things Outside North America: Where to Find Pictures of Flora and Fauna. Lucile Thompson Munz; Nedra G Slauson. Hamden, CT: Archon Books, 1981. 441p. $55.00. ISSN: 0-208-01857-3.

This unique index gives the source of illustrations of some 9,000 plants and animals appearing in 206

books. The companion work for just North America is *Index to Illustrations of the Natural World* (Archon Books, 1977). A supplement that covers both titles, containing some 6,200 entries, has been produced by Beth Clevis—*Index to Illustrations of Animals and Plants* (Neal-Schuman, 1991).

227. Serial Sources for the BIOSIS Data Base. BioScience Information Services of Biological Abstracts. Philadelphia, PA: BIOSIS, 1938– , annual. 1938– , index. $50.00. ISSN: 0162-2048.

Previously called *BIOSIS List of Serials with Coden, Title Abbreviations, New, Changed and Ceased Titles*; and *Serial Sources for the BIOSIS Database*, this bibliographical listing covers serials that have been accessed by BIOSIS in their indexing and abstracting services.

228. Zentralblatt fur Mikrobiologie. Jena, Germany: G. Fischer, 1895– , 8/year. v.1– , index. $213.00. ISSN: 0232-4393.

Previously called *Zentralblatt fur Bakteriologie, Parasitenkunde, Infektionskrankleiten und Hygiene: Zweite Abteilung-Naturwissenschaft*, this international abstracting service covers microbiology.

Dictionaries, Glossaries, and Thesauri

229. Biological Nomenclature. 3rd. Charles Jeffrey; Systematics Association. New York, NY: Edward Arnold, 1989. 86p. $12.95. ISBN: 0-7131-2983-2.

This small dictionary explains the taxonomic nomenclature that is used in all fields of biology. Another useful thesaurus is Anne C. Gutteridge's *Thesaurus of Biology*, also known as *Barnes and Noble's Thesaurus of Biology* (Barnes & Noble, 1983) or the *Cambridge Illustrated Thesaurus of Biology* (Cambridge University Press, 1983).

230. Cambridge Dictionary of Biology. Peter M.B. Walker. New York, NY: Cambridge University Press, 1990. 336p. $14.95. ISBN: 0-521-39764-2.

This reference is a good general biology dictionary with brief definitions.

231. Chambers Biology Dictionary. Peter M.B. Walker. New York, NY: Chambers, 1989. 324p., illus. $34.50; $14.95pbk. ISBN: 1-85296-152-X; 1-85296-153-8pbk.

This dictionary of terms pertaining to biology is taken from the *Chambers Science and Technology Dictionary*. All areas of biology are covered with the definitions nontechnical.

232. Dictionary of Biochemistry and Molecular Biology. 2nd. J. Stenesh. New York, NY: Wiley, 1989. 125p., bibliog. $74.95. ISBN: 0-471-84089-0.

Previously called *Dictionary of Biochemistry*, this small work covers biochemistry and related areas of chemistry, physics, metabolism, biophysics, genetics, and molecular biology. Also useful would be David M. Glick's *Glossary of Biochemistry and Molecular Biology* (Raven Press, 1990).

233. Dictionary of Ecology, Evolution, and Systematics. Roger J. Lincoln; Geoffrey A. Boxshall; P.F. Clark. New York, NY: Cambridge University Press, 1984. 298p., illus. $24.95. ISBN: 0-521-26902-4.

This advanced dictionary covers the fields of ecology, evolution, and systematics. Peter H. Collin's *Dictionary of Ecology and the Environment* (Collins, 1988) would also be useful.

234. Dictionary of Genetics. 4th. Robert C. King; William D. Stansfield. New York, NY: Oxford University Press, 1990. 406p., bibliog. $39.95; $19.95pbk. ISBN: 0-19-506370-8; 0-19-506371-6 pbk.

This dictionary is a comprehensive work covering the terms used in genetics research. Species and genera useful in genetics research are included. There are other genetics dictionaries including S.G. Oliver and John W. Ward's *Dictionary of Genetic Engineering* (Cambridge University Press, 1985); *Dictionary of Genetics and Cell Biology* (New York University Press, 1987); and Robert C. King's *Encyclopedic Dictionary of Genetics* (VCH, 1989).

235. Dictionary of Life Sciences. 2nd revised. E.A Martin. New York, NY: Pica Press, 1984. 396p., illus. $25.00. ISBN: 0-87663-740-3.

A very practical dictionary, *Dictionary of Life Sciences* emphasizes genetics, molecular biology, microbiology, and immunology. It contains many diagrams and formulas.

236. Dictionary of Microbiology and Molecular Biology. 2nd. Paul Singleton; Diana Sainsbury. New York, NY: Wiley, 1987. 1,019p., illus. (part in color), bibliog. $160.00. ISBN: 0-471-91114-3.

Previously called *Dictionary of Microbiology*, this book is one of the best microbiology dictionaries available. It contains definitions of concepts, terms, and techniques in the fields of microbiology and molecular biology. There are many useful appendixes.

237. Dictionary of the Biological Sciences. Peter Gray. Melbourne, FL: Krieger, 1982 (c1967). 602p., illus., bibliog. $52.50. ISBN: 0-89874-441-5.

This classic biology dictionary originally published by Van Nostrand Reinhold has been reprinted and is still available. It includes some 40,000 terms and is good for the basic biological terms.

238. Dictionary of Theoretical Concepts in Biology. Keith E. Roe; Richard G. Frederick. Metuchen, NJ: Scarecrow Press, 1981. 267p. $32.50. ISBN: 0-8108-1353-X.

Intended for researchers, this dictionary lists and defines biological concepts, plus citations to the initial works and current literature in which they originally were published.

239. Ecology Field Glossary: A Naturalists Vocabulary. Walter Hepworth Lewis. Westport, CT: Greenwood Press, 1977. 152p., bibliog. $38.50. ISBN: 0-8371-9547-0.

This layperson's dictionary to ecological terms is intended as a field book and covers many environmental terms.

240. Enzyme Nomenclature: Recommendations of the Nomenclature Committee of the International Union of Biochemistry on the Nomenclature and Classification of Enzyme-Catalyzed Reactions. Edwin C. Webb; International Union of Biochemistry, Nomenclature Committee. Orlando, FL: Academic Press, 1984. 646p., bibliog., index. $95.00; $55.00pbk. ISBN: 0-12-227164-5; 0-12-227165-3pbk.

This dictionary is the world's authority on enzyme nomenclature.

241. Facts on File Dictionary of Biology. revised and expanded. Elizabeth Tootill. New York, NY: Facts on File, 1988. 326p., illus. $24.95; $12.95 pbk. ISBN: 0-8160-1865-0; 0-8160-2368-9pbk.

Also called *Dictionary of Biology*, this is a very good general biology dictionary. Also good are the *Concise Dictionary of Biology* (Oxford University Press, 1990) and the *New Penguin Dictionary of Biology* (Penguin, 1990).

242. Henderson's Dictionary of Biological Terms. 10th. Eleanor Lawrence; I.F. Henderson. New York, NY: Wiley, 1989. 637p. $49.95. ISBN: 0-470-21446-5.

Previously called *Dictionary of Biological Terms*, this is the Bible of biology dictionaries covering botany, zoology, genetics, and all related areas.

243. Language of Biotechnology: A Dictionary of Terms. (*ACS Professional Reference Book*). Michael Cox; Allan Whitaker. Washington, DC: American Chemical Society, 1988. 255p., illus. $49.95; $29.95 pbk. ISBN: 0-8412-1487-1; 0-8412-1490-5 pbk.

Some 1,500 terms are included in this dictionary covering biotechnology and related areas of genetics, biochemical engineering, and toxicology. It has been published to help standardize the terms in these fields. J. Coombs' *Dictionary of Biotechnology* (Elsevier, 1986) is also useful.

244. Oxford Dictionary of Natural History.
Michael Allaby. New York, NY: Oxford University Press, 1985. 688p., bibliog. $45.00. ISBN: 0-19-217720-6.

Some 12,000 terms are included in this layperson and student's dictionary. The emphasis is on scientific names of plants and animals. It is useful for identification purposes. Roger J. Lincoln and Geoffrey A. Boxshall's *Cambridge Illustrated Dictionary of Natural History* (Cambridge University Press, 1987) would be a good choice for its illustrations.

245. Source Book of Biological Names and Terms.
3rd. Edmund Carroll Jaeger. Springfield, IL: Thomas, 1955. 317p., illus. $48.50. ISBN: 0-398-00916-3.

This is the accepted source for the Greek, Latin, and other elements that are used in scientific biological names. Short biographies are included.

Directories

246. BioScan.
Phoenix, AZ: Oryx Press, 1987– , annual with bimonthly updates. v.1– , index. $750.00. ISSN: 0887-6207.

This directory provides detailed descriptions of almost 1,000 biotechnology companies throughout the world.

247. Naturalists' Directory and Almanac (International).
Gainesville, FL: Sandhill Crane, 1877– , irregular. v.1– , index. $24.95.

Formerly *Naturalists' Directory International*, this irregularly published directory contains a list of amateur and professional naturalists, arranged geographically. It also includes directory information on natural history museums and societies. Another directory is the *Nature Directory* (Walker, 1991).

Encyclopedias

248. Atlas of Endangered Species.
John Burton. New York, NY: Macmillan, 1991. 1v. various paging, bibliog., index. $90.00. ISBN: 0-02-897081-0.

A good general overview of plant and animal species that are on the endangered list. Maps, narrative essays, and illustrations make this atlas an excellent reference work.

249. Cambridge Encyclopedia of Life Sciences.
A.E. Friday; David S. Ingram. New York, NY: Cambridge University Press, 1985. 432p., illus. (part in color), bibliog., index. $60.00. ISBN: 0-521-25696-8.

This work is a topical rather than alphabetically arranged encyclopedia divided into three parts—processes and organization; environments; fossil record. Excellent photographs add to its usefulness.

250. Concise Encyclopedia: Biochemistry.
2nd, expanded, revised, English language. Thomas Scott; Mary Eagleson. New York, NY: De Gruyter, 1988. 649p., illus. $89.90. ISBN: 3-11-011625-1.

Also called *Concise Encyclopedia of Biochemistry*, this encyclopedia is a translation of *Brockhaus ABC Biochemie*. It is a thorough and comprehensive small biochemical encyclopedia.

251. Encyclopedia of Microbiology.
San Diego, CA: Academic Press, 1992. 4v., illus., index. $675.00. ISBN: 0-12-226890-3.

This comprehensive encyclopedia covers all of microbiology including laboratory practices, medical microbiology and immunology, environmental microbiology, genetic and molecular microbiology, and agricultural microbiology.

252. Encyclopedia of the Biological Sciences.
2nd. Peter Gray. New York, NY: Van Nostrand Reinhold, 1970. 1,027p., illus., bibliog. out-of-print.

Although somewhat dated and out-of-print, Gray's encyclopedia is still a good reference source, especially for historical information.

Guides and Field Guides

253. Audubon Society Field Guides.
New York, NY: Knopf, 1977-91. 17v., illus. (part in color), bibliog., index. price per volume varies.

This excellent series of field guides has beautiful illustrations. The volumes that have been published to date cover *Audubon Society Field Guide to North American Mammals* (1980); *...to North American Trees: Western* (1980); *...to North American Trees: Eastern* (1980); *...to North American Butterflies* (1981); *...to North American Fossils* (1982); *...to North American Fishes, Whales, and Dolphins* (1983); *...to North American Insects and Spiders* (1980); *...to North American Mushrooms* (1981); *...to North American Reptiles and Amphibians* (1979); *...to North American Rocks and Minerals* (1979); *...to North American Seashells* (1981); *...to North American Seashore Creatures* (1981); *...to North American Wildflowers* (1979); *...to North American Weather* (1991); *...to North American Birds: Western Region* (1977); *...to North American Birds: Eastern Region* (1977); *...to the Night Sky* (1991). The Audubon Society also publishes field guides for beginners. Macmillan, Brown, and Putnam have all published field guides over the years, many still used.

254. Peterson Field Guide Series. Roger T. Peterson. Boston, MA: Houghton Mifflin, 1947– , irregular. v.1– , illus. (part in color), bibliog., index. price per volume varies.

These field guides have become a classic for those who are nature enthusiasts. They are all excellent reference sources for any library. The titles published so far in the biological sciences are 1—*Field Guide to the Birds* (4th ed., 1980); 2—*Field Guide to Western Birds* (1972); 3—*Field Guide to the Shells of the Atlantic and Gulf Coasts and the West Indies* (3rd ed., 1973); 4—*Field Guide to the Butterflies of North America East of the Great Plains* (1992); 5—*Field Guide to the Mammals* (3rd ed., 1976); 6—*Field Guide to Pacific Coast Shells* (2nd ed., 1974); 8—*Field Guide to the Birds of Britain and Europe* (5th ed., 1993); 9—*Field Guide to Animal Tracks* (2nd. ed., 1975); 10—*Field Guide to the Ferns and Their Related Families of Northeastern and Central North America* (1956); 11—*Field Guide to Eastern Trees* (1988); 12—*Field Guide to Reptiles and Amphibians of Eastern and Central North America* (3rd ed., 1991); 13—*Field Guide to the Birds of Texas and Adjacent States* (1963); 14—*Field Guide to Rocky Mountain Wildflowers from Northern Arizona and New Mexico to British Columbia* (1963); 16—*Field Guide to Western Reptiles and Amphibians* (2nd ed., 1985); 17—*Field Guide to Wildflowers of Northeastern and North Central North America* (1987); 18—*Field Guide to the Mammals of Britain and Europe* (1968); 19—*Field Guide to the Insects of America North of Mexico* (1970); 20—*Field Guide to Mexican Birds* (1973); 21—*Field Guide to Birds Nests of 285 Species Found Breeding in the U.S. East of the Mississippi River* (1975); 22—*Field Guide to Pacific State Wildflowers* (1976); 23—*Field Guide to Edible Wild Plants of Eastern and Central North America* (1978); 24—*Field Guide to the Atlantic Seashore* (1982); 25—*Field Guide to Western Birds' Nests of 250 Species Found Breeding in the U.S. West of the Mississippi River* (1979); 27—*Field Guide to Coral Reefs of the Caribbean and Florida* (1982); 28—*Field Guide to Pacific Coast Fishes of North America from the Gulf of Alaska to Baja, California* (1983); 29—*Field Guide to the Beetles of North America* (1983); 30—*Field Guide to the Moths of Eastern United States* (1984); 31—*Field Guide to Southwestern and Texas Wildflowers* (1984); 32—*Field Guide to Atlantic Coast Fishes of North America* (1986); 33-*Field Guide to Western Butterflies* (1986); 34—*Field Guide to Mushrooms of North America* (1987); 35—*Field Guide to Hawks of North America* (1987); 36—*Field Guide to Southeastern and Caribbean Seashores* (1988); 42—*Field Guide to Freshwater Fishes* (1991); 45—*Field guide to the Ecology of Western Forests* (1993); *Field Guide to the Birds of the West Indies* (5th ed., 1993).

Guides to the Literature

255. Guide to Sources for Agricultural and Biological Research. J. Richard Blanchard; Lois Farrell; U.S. Department of Agriculture, National Agricultural Library. Berkeley, CA: University of California Press, 1981. 735p., index. $60.00. ISBN: 0-520-03226-8.

The emphasis of this guide is on production of food, wildlife management, and pollution. Arranged topically with each chapter providing key guides, abstracts, indexes, and other research sources.

256. Information Sources in the Life Sciences. 4th. H.V. Wyatt. New Providence, NJ: K.G. Saur, 1992. 250p., bibliog., index. $65.00.

Previously called the *Use of Biological Literature*, this authoritative guide covers all forms of literature including government publications, bibliographies, patents, and abstracts. A specialized work covering the fauna and flora of Great Britain and Europe is R.W. Sims' *Key Works to the Fauna and Flora of the British Isles and North-Western Europe* (Oxford University Press, 1988).

257. Using the Biological Literature: A Practical Guide. *(Books in Library and Information Science, v.35).* Elisabeth B. Davis. New York, NY: Dekker, 1981. 286p., bibliog., index. $69.75. ISBN: 0-8247-7209-1.

This book is a good quick guide to biological literature. It is arranged by topic and then by form of publication. Two other useful works, one somewhat dated, are Roger Cletus Smith's *Smith's Guide to the Literature of the Life Sciences* (Burgess, 1980) and David A. Kronick and Wendell D. Winters' *Literature of the Life Sciences* (ISI Press, 1985).

Handbooks and Manuals

258. Biology Data Book. 2nd. Philip L. Altman; Dorothy Dittmer Katz. Bethesda, MD: Federation of American Society for Experimental Biology, 1972-74. 3v., bibliog., index. out-of-print.

Although out-of-print, this classic 3-volume handbook is an excellent source for basic and established data used in biological research. It is intended to be used in the laboratory. Another standard laboratory reference source is *Staining Procedures Used by the Biological Stains Commission* (Williams & Wilkins, 1973).

259. CBE Style Manual: A Guide for Authors, Editors, and Publishers in the Biological Sciences. 5th revised and expanded. CBE Style Manual Committee. Bethesda, MD: Council of Biology Editors, 1983. 324p., illus., bibliog., index. $27.95. ISBN: 0-914340-04-2.

Also called *Council of Biology Editors Style Manual*, this manual is a must for anyone publishing a paper for biological journals or books. It attempts to standardize the style that should be followed.

260. Guidebook to Biochemistry. 4th. Michael Yudkin; Robin Offord; Kenneth Harrison. New York, NY: Cambridge University Press, 1980. 261p., illus., index. $65.00; $24.95 pbk. ISBN: 0-521-23084-5; 0-521-29794-X pbk.

This title is a good basic guide to biochemistry fundamentals and concepts, including macromolecules, metabolic reactions, and molecular genetics. A useful handbook that would supplement this guide is R.M. Dawson's *Data for Biochemical Research* (Oxford University Press, 1986).

261. Handbook of Biological Illustration. 2nd. Frances W. Zweifel. Chicago, IL: University of Chicago Press, 1988. 137p., illus., bibliog., index. $9.95. ISBN: 0-226-99701-4.

A must book for any biology reference collection, the *Handbook of Biological Illustration* shows the proper methods for drawing biological illustrations.

262. Handbook of Ethological Methods. Philip N. Lehner. New York, NY: Garland, 1979. 403p., illus., bibliog., index. out-of-print.

Although out-of-print, this handbook is an excellent guide for those doing research in ethology. It discusses the design of research projects, techniques in collecting and observing, and how to interpret the results.

263. Handbook of Nature Study. Anna B. Comstock. Ithaca, NY: Cornell University Press, 1986. 912p., illus., index. $52.50; $19.95 pbk. ISBN: 0-8013-1913-1; 0-8014-9384-6 pbk.

This reissue of classic text first appeared in 1911. It teaches and illustrates the importance of knowing about the natural world as it was taught at the turn of the century.

264. Handbook of Physiology. New York, NY: Oxford University Press, 1964– , irregular. v.1– , illus., bibliog., index. price per volume varies. ISBN: 0-19-520661-4v.1-4.

This handbook is the most comprehensive source of physiological information available. Each section contains several volumes. The 9 published sections are Section 1—Nervous system; Section 2—Cardiovascular system; Section 3—Respiratory system; Section 4—Adaptation to the environment; Section 5—not published; Section 6—Gastrointestinal system; Section 7—Endocrinology; Section 8—Renal physiology; Section 9—Reactions to environmental agents; Section 10—Skeletal muscle. Also to be noted is the 8-volume *Handbook of Sensory Physiology* (Springer-Verlag, 1971-78).

265. Official World Wildlife Fund Guide to Endangered Species of North America. David W. Lowe; John R. Matthews; Charles J. Moseley. Washington, DC: Beacham Publishing, 1990-92. 3v., illus. (part in color), bibliog., index. $85.00/volume. ISBN: 0-933833-29-6.

Also called the *Official WWF Guide to Endangered Species of North America* or just *Endangered Species of North America*, this subject is a constantly changing area but the 3-volume work documents the various species in North America that are endangered.

266. Practical Handbook of Biochemistry and Molecular Biology. Gerald D. Fasman. Boca Raton, FL: CRC, 1989. 601p., illus., index. $59.95. ISBN: 0-8493-3705-4.

Also called the *Handbook of Biochemistry and Molecular Biology* this handbook is a good general resource for the researcher. Although not as comprehensive as the treatise-type work, it does give most of the primary information that may be needed. A more comprehensive but specialized handbook is Thomas E. Barman's *Enzyme Handbook* (Springer-Verlag, 1985).

267. Synopsis and Classification of Living Organisms. Sybil P. Parker. New York, NY: McGraw-Hill, 1982. 2v., illus. (part in color), bibliog., index. $295.00. ISBN: 0-07-079031-0.

This handbook is a comprehensive source that classifies and describes all living organisms. The index includes some 35,000 scientific and common names.

268. Zinsser Microbiology. 20th. Wolfgang K. Joklik. Norwalk, CT: Appleton & Lange, 1992. 1,053p., illus., bibliog., index. $59.95. ISBN: 0-8385-9983-4.

Zinsser Microbiology is a classic textbook that has become a useful reference source on microbiology. Information is presented in textbook fashion, but every area of microbiology is covered. Other microbiology sources include William M. O'Leary's *Practical Handbook of Microbiology* (CRC, 1989) and Albert Balows' *Manual of Clinical Microbiology* (American Society for Microbiology, 1991).

Histories

269. History of American Ecology: An Original Anthology. 3rd. Frank N. Egerton. Salem, NH: Ayer, 1978. 1v. various paging, illus., bibliog. $36.50. ISBN: 0-405-10399-9.

A good history that discusses the 18th and 19th century developments in limnology, oceanography, plant ecology, and animal ecology.

270. History of Biology: A Selected, Annotated Bibliography. *(Bibliographies of the History of Science and Technology, v.15) (Garland Reference Library of the Humanities, v.419).* Judith A. Overmier. New York, NY: Garland, 1989. 157p., index. $21.00. ISBN: 0-8240-9118-3.

This introductory bibliography of 619 historical works pertaining to biology is arranged by biological topic.

271. History of Biology to about the Year 1900: A General Introduction to the Study of Living Things. Charles Joseph Singer. Ames, IA: Iowa State University Press, 1989 (c1959). 579p., illus., index. $22.95. ISBN: 0-8138-0937-1.

This volume is considered to be one of the better histories of biology. Another useful history is Ben Dawes' *Hundred Years of Biology* (Duckworth, 1952).

272. History of the Life Sciences. Lois N. Magner. New York, NY: Dekker, 1979. 489p., illus., bibliog., index. $49.75. ISBN: 0-8247-8071-X.

This work by Lois Magner is a well-written general history of biology and natural history.

273. History of the Life Sciences: An Annotated Bibliography. Peter Smit. Amsterdam, Netherlands: Asher, 1974. 1,071p., index. $96.00. ISBN: 90-6123-289-9.

This extensive annotated bibliography covers the history of biology to about 1971.

274. Virus: A History of the Concept. Sally Smith Hughes. New York, NY: Science History Publications, 1977. 140p., illus., bibliog., index. $12.00. ISBN: 0-88202-168-0.

Virus is an excellent book for researchers who want background information on virus research.

Periodicals

275. American Biology Teacher. Reston, VA: National Association of Biology Teachers, 1938– , monthly. v.1– , index. $48.00. ISSN: 0002-7685.

276. American Journal of Human Genetics. Chicago, IL: University of Chicago Press/American Society of Human Genetics, 1948– , monthly. v.1– , index. $250.00. ISSN: 0002-9297.

277. American Journal of Physiology. Bethesda, MD: American Physiological Society, 1898– , monthly in 8 separate journals. v.1– , index. $1,075.00. ISSN: 0002-9513.

278. American Midland Naturalist. Notre Dame, IN: University of Notre Dame, 1909– , quarterly. v.1– , index. $60.00. ISSN: 0003-0031.

279. Annals of Applied Biology. Warwickshire, Great Britain: Association of Applied Biologists, 1914– , 6/year. v.1– , index. $330.00. ISSN: 0003-4746.

280. Applied and Environmental Microbiology. Washington, DC: American Society for Microbiology, 1953– , monthly. v.1– , index. $250.00. ISSN: 0099-2240.

281. Archives of Microbiology. Berlin, Germany: Springer-Verlag, 1939– , 12/year. v.1– , index. $1,281.00. ISSN: 0302-8933.

282. Biochemical Journal. Colchester, Great Britain: Portland Press/Biochemical Society, 1906– , semimonthly. v.1– , index. $1,460.00. ISSN: 0264-6021.

283. Biochemistry and Cell Biology/Bichimie et Biologie Cellulaire. Ottawa, Ontario, Canada: National Research Council of Canada, 1929– , monthly. v.1– , index. $220.00. ISSN: 0829-8211.

284. Biological Bulletin. Woods Hole, MA: Marine Biological Laboratory, 1898– , bimonthly. v.1– , index. $155.00. ISSN: 0006-3185.

285. Biological Journal of the Linnean Society. London, Great Britain: Academic Press, 1791– , 12/year. v.1– , index. $564.00. ISSN: 0024-4066.

286. Biological Reviews of the Cambridge Philosophical Society. Cambridge, Great Britain: Cambridge University Press, 1923– , quarterly. v.1– , index. $100.00. ISSN: 0006-3231.

287. Biophysical Journal. New York, NY: Rockefeller University Press/Biophysical Society, 1960– , monthly. v1– , index. $560.00. ISSN: 0006-3495.

288. Bioscience. Washington, DC: American Institute of Biological Sciences, 1951– , monthly. v.1– , index. $105.00. ISSN: 0006-3568.

289. Canadian Journal of Microbiology/Journal Canadienne de Microbiologie. Ottawa, Ontario: National Research Council of Canada, 1954– , monthly. v.1– , index. $223.00. ISSN: 0008-4166.

290. Development. Colchester, Great Britain: Company of Biologists, 1953– , 13/year. v.1– , index. $1,005.00. ISSN: 0950-1991.

291. Developmental Biology. Tempe, AZ: Ecological Society of America, 1931– , quarterly. v.1– , index. $60.00. ISSN: 0012-9615.

292. Ecology. Tempe, AZ: Ecological Society of America, 1920– , bimonthly. v.1– , index. $80.00. ISSN: 0012-9658.

293. Evolution. Lawrence, KS: Allen Press, 1947– , bimonthly. v.1– , index. $100.00. ISSN: 0014-3820.

294. FASEB Journal. Bethesda, MD: Federation of American Society for Experimental Biology, 1942– , monthly. v.1– , index. $225.00. ISSN: 0892-6638.

295. Heredity. Oxford, Great Britain: Blackwell/Genetical Society of Great Britain, 1947– , bimonthly. v.1– , index. $140.00. ISSN: 0018-067X.

296. Human Biology. Detroit, MI: Wayne State University Press, 1929– , 6/year. v.1– , index. $95.00. ISSN: 0018-7143.

297. Journal of Anatomy. Cambridge, Great Britain: Cambridge University Press, 1866– , 6/year. v.1– , index. $525.00. ISSN: 0021-8782.

298. Journal of Animal Ecology. Oxford, Great Britain: Blackwell/British Ecological Society, 1932– , 3/year. v.1– , index. $236.00. ISSN: 0021-8790.

299. Journal of Applied Bacteriology. Oxford, Great Britain: Blackwell/Society for Applied Bacteriology, 1938– , monthly. v.1– , index. $384.00. ISSN: 0021-8847.

300. Journal of Applied Ecology. Oxford, Great Britain: Blackwell/British Ecological Society, 1964– , 3/year. v.1– , index. $237.00. ISSN: 0021-8901.

301. Journal of Applied Physiology. Bethesda, MD: American Physiological Society, 1948– , monthly. v.1– , index. $473.00. ISSN: 8750-7587.

302. Journal of Bacteriology. Washington, DC: American Society for Microbiology, 1916– , semimonthly. v.1– , index. $360.00. ISSN: 0021-9193.

303. Journal of Biological Chemistry. Bethesda, MD: American Society for Biochemistry and Molecular Biology, 1905– , 36/year. v.1– , index. $670.00. ISSN: 0021-9258.

304. Journal of Cell Biology. New York, NY: Rockefeller University Press/American Society for Cell Biology, 1955– , 24/year. v.1– , index. $400.00. ISSN: 0021-9525.

305. Journal of Cellular Physiology. New York, NY: Wiley, 1932– , monthly. v.1– , index. $1,425.00. ISSN: 0021-9541.

306. Journal of Comparative Physiology: A— Sensory, Neural, and Behavioral Physiology; B—Biochemical, Systematic, and Environmental Physiology. Berlin, Germany: Springer-Verlag, 1924– , 12/year A; 6/year B. v.1– , index. $1,207.00A; $599.00B. ISSN: 0340-7594A; 0174-1578B.

307. Journal of Ecology. Oxford, Great Britain: Blackwell/British Ecological Society, 1913– , quarterly. v.1– , index. $237.00. ISSN: 0022-0477.

308. Journal of Experimental Biology. Colchester, Great Britain: Company of Biologists, 1923– , 12/year. v.1– , index. $850.00. ISSN: 0022-0949.

309. Journal of General Microbiology. Spencers Wood, Great Britain: Society for General Microbiology, 1947– , monthly. v.1– , index. $780.00. ISSN: 0022-1287.

310. Journal of General Physiology. New York, NY: Rockefeller University Press/Society of General Physiologists, 1918– , monthly. v.1– , index. $190.00. ISSN: 0022-1295.

311. Journal of General Virology. Spencers Wood, Great Britain: Society for General Microbiology, 1967– , monthly. v.1– , index. $780.00. ISSN: 0022-1317.

312. Journal of Heredity. New York, NY: Oxford University Press/American Genetic Association, 1910– , bimonthly. v.1– , index. $105.00. ISSN: 0022-1503.

313. Journal of Molecular Biology. London, Great Britain: Academic Press, 1959– , 24/year. v.1– , index. $1,692.00. ISSN: 0022-2836.

314. Journal of Morphology. New York, NY: Wiley, 1887– , monthly. v.1– , index. $820.00. ISSN: 0362-2525.

315. Journal of Neurochemistry. New York, NY: Raven Press, 1956– , monthly. v.1– , index. $1,057.00. ISSN: 0022-3042.

316. Physiological Reviews. Bethesda, MD: American Physiological Society, 1921– , quarterly. v.1– , index. $200.00. ISSN: 0031-9333.

317. Proceedings of the National Academy of Sciences of the United States of America. Washington, DC: National Academy of Sciences, 1915– , semimonthly. v.1– , index. $250.00. ISSN: 0027-8424.

318. Quarterly Review of Biology. Chicago, IL: University of Chicago Press, 1926– , quarterly. v.1– , index. $70.00. ISSN: 0033-5770.

319. Social Biology. Port Angeles, WA: Society for the Study of Social Biology, 1954– , quarterly. v.1– , index. $65.00. ISSN: 0037-766X.

320. Soil Biology and Biochemistry. Tarrytown, NY: Pergamon Press, 1969– , 12/year. v.1– , index. $696.00. ISSN: 0038-0717.

BOTANY

Abstracts and Indexes

321. Abstracts of Mycology. Philadelphia, PA: BIOSIS, 1967– , monthly. v.1– , index. $200.00. ISSN: 0001-3617.
Contains English abstracts of research involving fungi, lichens, and fungicides. Abstracts are taken from the *Biological Abstracts and Research Index.*

322. Botanical Abstracts. Baltimore, MD: Williams & Wilkins, 1918-1926. 15v., index. out-of-print.
Botanical Abstracts is a good retrospective source of botanical information. Since 1926 all botanical abstracts now appear in the *Biological Abstracts.*

323. Excerpta Botanica. International Association for Plant Taxonomy. Stuttgart, Germany: G. Fischer, 1959– , irregular. v.1– , index. $132.00section A; $445.00section B. ISSN: 0014-4037section A; 0014-4045section B.
Published in two sections:—*Section A—Taxonomica et Chorologica*; *Section B—Sociologica*—this abstracting service covers the world's botanical literature.

324. Flowering Plant Index of Illustration and Information. Richard T. Isaacson. Boston, MA: G.K. Hall, 1979. 2v. $230.00; supplement 1979-1981 $260.00. ISBN: 0-8161-0301-1.
This G.K. Hall index is still useful. It lists by common and botanical name the flowering plants of the world, indicating where an illustration of each plant can be found.

325. Index Hepaticarum: Index to the Liverworts of the World. Stuttgart, Germany: J. Cramer in der Gebrueder Borntraeger Verlag buchhandlung, 1962– , irregular. v.1– , index. price varies per volume. ISSN: 0073-5787.
This highly specialized work covers the literature pertaining to the world's liverworts.

326. Index Kewensis: Plantarum Phanerogamarum Nomina et Synonyma Omnium Generum et Specierum a Linnaeo Usque ad Annum MDCCCLXXXV Complectens. Champaign, IL: Koeltz Science Books (reprint), 1895. 2v. $180.00; $104.00/supplement. ISBN: 3-87429-190-1.
This printed index is for a repository of names for flowering plants giving generic nomenclature and common names together with the sources of their original publication. Supplements have been issued every five years since 1895. A more comprehensive computer-generated registry is the *International Plant Index* (The Index, 1962-).

327. Index of Fungi. Tucson, AZ: C.A.B. International, 1940– , semiannual. v.1– , index. $73.00. ISSN: 0019-3895.
Originally a supplement to the *Review of Applied Mycology*, this work is a registry of new genera and species of the world's fungi. It is also available online.

328. Kew Record of Taxonomic Literature Relating to Vascular Plants. London, Great Britain: HMSO, 1971– , annual. v.1– , index. $20.00/number.
Previously called *Index to European Taxonomic Literature*, this publication of the Royal Botanic Gardens lists references to all publications on the taxonomy of flowering plants, gymnosperms, and ferns.

Atlases

329. Atlas and Manual of Plant Pathology.
Ervin H. Barnes. New York, NY: Plenum
Press, 1979. 325p., illus., bibliog., index.
$45.00.

This very well organized work includes graphs,
data charts, experiments, equipment lists, and discussion questions pertaining to the pathology of plants.

**330. Atlas Florae Europaeae: Distribution of
Vascular Plants in Europe.** Jaakko Jalas; Juha
Suominen. New York, NY: Cambridge
University Press, 1989. 3v., illus., index.
$175.00. ISBN: 0-521-34272-4v.3.

Orginally published in 7 volumes, the new 3-volume work is as follows: v.1—1-Pteridophyta (Psilotaceae to Azollaceae); 2-Gymmospermae (Pinaceae to
Ephedraceae); v.2—3-Salicaceae to Balanophoraceae;
4-Polygonaceae; 5-Chenopodiaceae to Basellaceae;
v.3—6-Caryophyllaceae (Alsinoideae and Paronychicideae); 7-Caryophyllaceae (Silenoaideae). This
valuable atlas shows the distribution of European flora.

Bibliographies

**331. Bibliography of Plant Viruses and Index
to Research.** Helen Purdy Beale. New York,
NY: Columbia University Press, 1976. 1,495p.
$172.00. ISBN: 0-231-03763-5.

This classic bibliography of over 29,000 articles
covers some 6,500 periodicals with emphasis on Japanese and Russian works covering 1892-1970. It is
arranged alphabetically by author.

332. Bibliography of Seeds. Lela V. Barton.
New York, NY: Columbia University Press,
1967. 858p. $127.50. ISBN: 0-231-02937-3.

Some 20,000 citations to the literature of seeds are
included in this bibliography derived from the files of
the Boyce Thompson Institute for Plant Research.

**333. Botanical Bibliographies: A Guide to
Bibliographic Materials Applicable to Botany.**
Lloyd H. Swift. Minneapolis, MN: Burgess,
1970. 804p. $160.00 reprint. ISBN:
0-8087-1960-2.

This good historical bibliography is divided into 4
sections covering general, background, botanical, and
applied subjects.

**334. Geographical Guide to Floras of the
World.** S.F. Blake; Alice C. Atwood.
Champaign, IL: Koeltz Science Books, 1944.
2v., index. $140.00. ISBN: 3-87429-068-9v.1;
3-87429-060-3v.2.

Originally *Miscellaneous Publications 401 and
797* of the U.S. Department of Agriculture, this guide
is an annotated bibliography of flora literature. It is
arranged by continent and then alphabetically by
author.

**335. Guide to Standard Floras of the World:
An Annotated, Geographically Arranged Systematic Bibliography of the Principal Floras,
Enumerations, Checklists, and Chronological
Atlases of Different Areas.** D.G. Frodin. New
York, NY: Cambridge University Press, 1984.
619p., bibliog., index. out-of-print. ISBN:
0-521-23688-6.

Now out-of-print, this guide is still an excellent
bibliography of the standard floras of the world.

**336. Herbs: An Indexed Bibliography, 1971-
1980: The Scientific Literature on Selected
Herbs and Aromatic and Medicinal Plants of
the Temperate Zone.** James E. Simon; Alena
F. Chadwick; Lyle E. Craker. New York, NY:
Elsevier, 1984. 770p., index. out-of-print.
ISBN: 0-444-99626-5.

This comprehensive, specialized bibliography contains some 8,000 entries. Sixty-three major economical
herbs are listed with short descriptions and detailed
bibliographies. It is now out-of-print.

**337. Taxonomic Literature: A Selective Guide
to Botanical Publications and Collections with
Dates, Commentaries, and Types.** 2nd. *(Regnum Vegetabile v. 94, 98, 105, 110, 112, 115,
116).* Frans A. Stafleu; Richard S. Cown.
Forestburgh, NY: Lubrecht & Cramer,
1979-1988. 7v., bibliog., index. $1,650.00.
ISBN: 90-313-0224-4set.

An extensive but expensive guide to the botanical
publications of the world, this work includes dates,
commentaries, types, and other pertinent information.

Biographical Sources

338. Biographical Notes Upon Botanists.
John Hendley Barnhart. Boston, MA: G.K.
Hall, 1965. 3v., bibliog. $370.00. ISBN:
0-8161-0695-9.

This historical biographical source contains information on some 44,000 botanists, including those who
were living at the time of publication. It is taken from
the resources of the New York Botanical Garden Library.

Dictionaries, Glossaries, and
Thesauri

**339. Ainsworth and Bisby's Dictionary of the
Fungi.** 7th. G.C. Ainsworth; Guy Richard
Bisby; D.L. Hawsworth; B.C. Sutton. Kew,
Great Britain: Commonwealth Mycological
Institute, 1983. 445p., illus. $31.50. ISBN:
0-85198-515-7.

Also called *Dictionary of the Fungi*, this authoritative dictionary covers all terms associated with fungi and related areas. A smaller but useful work is Walter Henry Snell and Esther A. Dick's *Glossary of Mycology* (Harvard University Press, 1971).

340. B-P-H: Botanico-Periodicum-Huntianum. G.M. Lawrence. Pittsburgh, PA: Hunt Institute for Botanical Documentation, 1968. 1,063p. $20.00. ISBN: 0-913196-10-X.

This title is a very comprehensive list of abbreviations for more than 12,000 periodical titles that pertain to botany and plant sciences. It is intended to standardize abbreviations in the field of botany.

341. Botanical Latin: History, Grammar, Syntax, Terminology, and Vocabulary. 4th. William Thomas Stearn. North Pomfret, VT: Trafalgar, 1992. 546p., illus., bibliog., index. $39.25. ISBN: 0-7153-0052-0.

This textbook instructs students on how to assign the various Latin prefixes and suffixes used in describing plants. A dictionary of botanical terms is included.

342. Cacti: The Illustrated Dictionary. Rod Preston-Mafham; Ken Preston-Mafham. New York, NY: Sterling, 1991. 224p., illus. $50.00. ISBN: 0-7137-2092-1.

This small specialized dictionary lists cacti plants and the terminology associated with them.

343. Dictionary of Botany. R. John Little; C. Eugene Jones. New York, NY: Van Nostrand Reinhold, 1980. 400p., illus., bibliog. out-of-print.

Although out-of-print, this title is still an excellent botanical dictionary covering some 5,500 terms. Two other useful, but older works, are George Usher's *Dictionary of Botany* (Constable, 1966) and Delbert Swartz's *Collegiate Dictionary of Botany* (Roland Press, 1971).

344. Dictionary of Plant Pathology. Paul Holliday. New York, NY: Cambridge University Press, 1989. 369p., illus. $64.95. ISBN: 0-521-33117-X.

This excellent dictionary covers plant diseases. It includes crop names and pathology, disease names, disorders, fungicide names, taxonomic groups, toxins, and pathogens. Some 100 plant pathologists are included with brief biographical information.

345. Elsevier's Dictionary of Botany. Paul Macura. New York, NY: Elsevier, 1979-1982. 2v., index. $208.00/volume. ISBN: 0-444-41787-7v.1; 0-444-41977-2v.2.

This multilingual dictionary is useful to those working with literature in English, French, German, and Russian. Volume one also has a Latin section. The 2 volumes cover: v.1—Plant names; v.2—General terms. A good Russian-English botanical dictionary is

Paul Macura's *Russian-English Botanical Dictionary* (Slavica, 1981).

346. Facts on File Dictionary of Botany. Elizabeth Tootill; Stephen Blackmore. New York, NY: Facts on File, 1984. 400p., illus. $24.95. ISBN: 0-87196-861-4.

This work is a very good botanical dictionary. Two other useful works for the layperson and student are the *Longman Illustrated Dictionary of Botany* (Longman, 1984) and *Concise Oxford Dictionary of Botany* (Oxford University Press, 1992).

347. Glossary of Botanic Terms with Their Derivation and Accent. Benjamin D. Jackson. Forestburgh, NY: Lubrecht & Cramer, 1986. 481p. $35.00. ISBN: 81-211-0005-4.

The best aspect of this dictionary is the inclusion of pronunciation guides. It is fairly comprehensive.

348. International Code of Botanical Nomenclature. *(Regnum Vegetabile, v.118)*. W. Greuter. Champaign, Il: Koeltz Science Books, 1988. 328p., index. $36.00. ISBN: 3-87429-278-9.

Based on the 14th International Botanical Congress held in Berlin, 1987, this is a handbook of the code that is used to officially name the world's plants.

349. Names of Plants. 2nd. D. Gledhill. New York, NY: Cambridge University Press, 1989. 202p., illus., bibliog. $17.95. ISBN: 0-521-36675-5.

This book is a concise dictionary of plant names. Another useful source is Allen J. Coombe's *Timber Press Dictionary of Plant Names* (Timber Press, 1985).

350. Synonymized Checklist of the Vascular Flowers of the United States, Canada, and Greenland. 2nd revised. John T. Kartesz. Portland, OR: Timber Press, 1992. 550p., illus. $59.95. ISBN: 0-88192-204-8.

Alphabetically organized by hierarchy, this list contains over 57,000 names and 20,000 synonyms of North American flora. It contains subspecies, varieties, and hybrids.

Directories

351. International Directory of Botanic Gardens. 5th revised and enlarged. Christine A. Heywood. Champaign, IL: Koeltz Science Books, 1990. 1,000p., index. $150.00. ISBN: 1-878762-01-X.

This frequently published directory is arranged geographically and provides information on some 500 gardens giving location, staff, and publication information.

Encyclopedias

352. Encyclopedia of Ferns. David Jones. Portland, OR: Timber Press, 1987. 433p., illus. (part in color), bibliog., index. $55.95. ISBN: 0-88192-054-1.

This encyclopedia covers only cultivated ferns, including some 700 of the more common species. Information is given on cultural and nutritional requirements, pests and diseases, propagation, and hybridization.

353. Encyclopedia of Plant Physiology: New Series. W. Ruhland; A. Pirson; Martin Huldrych Zimmermann. New York, NY: Springer-Verlag, 1975– , irregular. v.1– , illus., bibliog., index. price per volume varies.

The previous edition of this comprehensive treatise-type work was called *Handbuch der Pflanzenphysiologie*. It is a topical encyclopedia intended for research. The volumes published so far are v.1-3—Transport in plants; v.4—Physiological plant pathology; v.5-6—Photosynthesis; v.7—Physiology of movements.

354. Ferns and Allied Plants: With Special Reference to Tropical America. Rolla Milton Tryon; Alice F. Tryon; W.H. Hodge. New York, NY: Springer-Verlag, 1982. 857p., illus., maps, bibliog., index. $259.00. ISBN: 0-387-90672-X.

This title is the authority for ferns in the United States. It includes plants normally associated with ferns as well as those found in tropical America.

355. Flowering Plants of the World. V.H. Heywood. Englewood Cliffs, NJ: Prentice-Hall, 1985. 335p., illus. (part in color), index. $39.95. ISBN: 0-13-322405-8.

This title is a reissue of a 1978 Oxford University Press edition by the same name. It provides information on 250,000 species of Angiospermae, including classification, structure, contributions, and terminology.

356. Mushrooms of North America: The Most Comprehensive Mushroom Guide Ever. Roger Phillips. New York, NY: Little, Brown & Co, 1991. 319p.,color illus., index. $39.95. ISBN: 0-316-70612-4.

An excellent guide to mushrooms with over 1,000 full color illustrations. Information for each entry includes Latin name, mycologist who first described it, and detailed description.

357. New Flora of the British Isles. Clive A. Stace. New York, NY: Cambridge University Press, 1991. 1,226p., illus., bibliog., index. $75.00. ISBN: 0-521-42793-2.

New Flora of the British Isles is an alphabetically arranged encyclopedia of British flora. Each entry is fully described and includes a black-and-white illustration.

358. Rodale's Illustrated Encyclopedia of Herbs. William Hylton; Rodale Press Staff. Emmaus, PA: Rodale, 1987. 522p., illus., index. $24.95. ISBN: 0-87857-699-1.

This well-written encyclopedia covers 140 herbs, giving scientific name, family, botanical description, flowering behavior, range of cultivation, and habitat. Another more recent book on herbs is Elisabeth Lambert-Ortiz's *Encyclopedia of Herbs, Spices, and Flavorings* (Dorling Kindersley, 1992).

359. Trees of North America. Alan Mitchell. New York, NY: Facts on File, 1987. 208p., illus., index. $35.00. ISBN: 0-8160-1806-5.

This well-illustrated work contains information about over 500 species and 250 varieties of North American trees. Three other useful works are Thomas S. Elias' *Complete Trees of North America* (Van Nostrand Reinhold, 1980); F. Bayard Hora's *Oxford Encyclopedia of Trees of the World* (Oxford University Press, 1980), and for the British Isles W.J. Bean's *Trees and Shrubs Hardy in the British Isles* (St Martins Press, 1981).

360. Tropica: Color Cyclopedia of Exotic Plants and Trees. 4th. Alfred Byrd Graf. New York, NY: Macmillan, 1992. 1,157p., color illus., index. $165.00. ISBN: 0-025-4990-7.

This beautifully illustrated encyclopedia has become an important reference work to the exotic flora of the world. The descriptions are complete along with some 7,000 color photographs.

Guides and Field Guides

361. Field Guide to North American Edible Wild Plants. Thomas S. Elias. New York, NY: Van Nostrand Reinhold, 1983. 286p., illus., index. $19.95. ISBN: 0-442-22254-8.

This general guide is for locating, identifying, harvesting, and preparing wild plants. It is arranged by season and then by plant type. Two other guides on edible plants are Madeline Angell's *Field Guide to Berries and Berrylike Fruits* (Bobbs-Merrill, 1981) and *Field Guide to Edible Wild Plants of Eastern and Central North America, Peterson Field Guide Series, v. 23* (Houghton-Mifflin, 1978).

362. Guide to the Vegetation of Britain and Europe. Oleg Polunin; Martin Walters. New York, NY: Oxford University Press, 1985. 238p., illus. (part in color), maps, bibliog., index. $39.95. ISBN: 0-19-217713-3.

This guide provides good descriptions of Europe's vegetation excluding Russia. The descriptions are for the layperson.

363. Mushroom Hunter's Field Guide: All Color and Enlarged. Alexander Hanchett Smith; Nancy Weber. Ann Arbor, MI: University of Michigan Press, 1980. 336p., illus., bibliog., index. $18.95. ISBN: 0-472-85610-3.

One of many field guides for identifying mushrooms, this one is well-illustrated and fairly easy to use. Other mushroom guides include Orson K. Miller's *Mushrooms of North America* (Dutton, 1977); U. Nonis' *Mushrooms and Toadstools: A Color Field Guide* (Hippocrene Books, 1982); and Phyllis G. Glick's *Mushroom Trail Guide* (Holt, Rinehart & Winston, 1979).

364. Mushrooms Demystified. revised. David Arora. Berkeley, CA: Ten Speed Press, 1990. 1,020p., illus., index. $39.95; $24.95pbk. ISBN: 0-89815-170-8; 0-89815-169-4pbk.

From the basis of the number of pages, this book is the most comprehensive field guide to mushrooms that is available. Over 2,000 species are included and fully described with some 800 photographs. Another useful field guide is David W. Fischer's *Edible Wild Mushrooms of North America* (University of Texas Press, 1992).

365. Mycology Guidebook. Russell B. Steven; Mycological Society of America. Seattle, WA: Washington University Press, 1981. 712p., illus., bibliog., index. $50.00. ISBN: 0-295-95841-3.

This title is a well-accepted guide to mycology, providing information on identification, ecological aspects, fungus physiology, and genetics.

366. North American Trees: Exclusive of Mexico and Tropical Florida. 4th. Richard Joseph Preston. Ames, IA: Iowa State University Press, 1989. 407p., illus., index. $41.95; $20.95pbk. ISBN: 0-8138-1171-6; 0-8138-1172-4pbk.

This field handbook provides extensive descriptions of trees. Logical identification keys are provided. Another useful guide is Herbert L. Edlin's *Tree Key* (Scribner, 1978).

Guides to the Literature

367. Guide to Information Sources in the Botanical Sciences. Elisabeth B. Davis. Englewood, CO: Libraries Unlimited, 1987. 300p., index. $35.00. ISBN: 0-87287-439-7.

This excellent guide to the literature of botany is comprehensive and well-indexed.

Handbooks and Manuals

368. AMA Handbook of Poisonous and Injurious Plants. Kenneth F. Lampe; Mary Ann McCann. Chicago, IL: American Medical Association, 1985. 432p., color illus., bibliog., index. $28.00. ISBN: 0-89970-183-3.

This title is both a handbook that provides medical information about poisonous plants and a field guide that can be used for identifying the plants. It is arranged basically by the name of the plant. Two other sources of information about poisonous plants are Adam Sczawinski and Nancy J. Turner's *Common Poisonous Plants and Mushrooms of North America* (Timber Press, 1991) and *Poisonous Plants: A Source Guide* (Gordon Press, 1991). For an atlas, consult Dietrich Frohne and Hans Jurgen Pfander's *Colour Atlas of Poisonous Plants* (Wolf, 1984).

369. Complete Guide to the Trees of Britain and Northern Europe. Alan Mitchell. Limpsfield, Great Britain: Dragon's World, 1985. Dist: Manchester, NH: Salem House. 208p., illus. (part in color), index. $27.95. ISBN: 1-85208-000-2.

Some 500 species and 250 varieties of trees are described and illustrated giving scientific name, history, characteristics, distribution, and varieties. A useful companion would be Alan Mitchell's *Field Guide to the Trees of Britain and Northern Europe* (Houghton Miffilin, 1974).

370. CRC Handbook of Flowering. A.H. Halevy. Boca Raton, FL: CRC, 1985. 5v., bibliog., index. $1,275.00. ISBN: 0-8493-3910-3.

This treatise-type handbook provides authoritative articles on flowering. Each plant entry provides information on what is required for flowering including environment, development, and chemical regulation.

371. Diseases of Trees and Shrubs. Wayne A. Sinclair; Howard H. Lyon; Warren T. Johnson. Ithaca, NY: Comstock Publishing Assoc, 1987. 574p., color illus., bibliog., index. $52.50. ISBN: 0-8014-1517-9.

This pictorial survey of diseases and environmental damage of trees and shrubs in the United States and Canada is arranged by disease, then by plant part, and finally by taxonomic relationship.

372. Endangered and Threatened Plants of the United States. Edward S. Ayensu; Robert A. DeFilipps. Washington, DC: Smithsonian Institution, 1978. 403p., bibliog., index. $42.00. ISBN: 0-87474-222-6.

This handbook contains useful information about the plants that are endangered in the United States. A complete list of extinct plants is also given. For worldwide lists of endangered plants contact the International Union for the Conservation of Nature and Natural Resources (IUCN) which frequently publishes lists including the *IUCN Plant Red Data Book* (IUCN, 1978).

373. Handbook of Applied Mycology. D.K. Aurora; Bharat Rai. New York, NY: Dekker, 1991. 5v., illus., bibliog., index. $150.00/volume. ISBN: 0-8247-8380-8v.1.

This comprehensive treatise-like handbook covers topics pertaining to the applied aspects of research in mycology. The 5 chapters cover v.1—Soils and plants; v.2—Humans, animals and insects; v.3—Foods and feeds; v.4—Fungal biotechnology; v.5—untitled.

374. Handbook of Hawaiian Weeds. 2nd. E.L. Haselwood; G.G. Motten. Honolulu, HI: University of Hawaii Press, 1983. 501p., illus., bibliog., index. $18.50. ISBN: 0-8248-0885-1.

This unique book describes the 226 species of weeds of Hawaii. It provides information on how the plant propagates, habitats of growth history, origin, and other ecological topics.

375. Handbook of Phycological Methods. Phycological Society of America. New York, NY: Cambridge University Press, 1973-85. 4v., illus., bibliog., index. out-of-print. ISBN: 0-521-20049-0v.1.

This comprehensive, technical handbook provides information on the research methods used in phycology. The 4 volumes cover v.1—Culture methods and growth measurements; v.2—Physiological and biochemical methods; v.3—Developmental and cytological methods; v.4—Ecological field methods.

376. Handbook of Plant Cell Culture. New York, NY: McGraw-Hill, 1983– , irregular. v.1– , illus., bibliog., index. price per volume varies. ISBN: 0-07-010848-Xv.6.

This treatise-type handbook provides detailed information on cell culture, especially as it pertains to crops. There are extensive bibliographies throughout the volumes. The 6 volumes published so far cover v.1—Techniques for propagation and culture; v.2-3—Crop species; v.4—Techniques and applications; v.5—Ornamental species; v.6—Perennial crops.

377. Integrated System of Classification of Flowering Plants. Arthur Cronquist. New York, NY: Columbia University Press, 1981. 1,262p., illus., bibliog., index. out-of-print. ISBN: 0-231-03880-1.

Three hundred eighty families in 83 orders are described in detail with the major families illustrated. For a good regional manual consult Henry A. Gleason and Arthur Cronquist's *Manual of Vascular Plants of the Northeast United States and Adjacent Canada* (New York Botanical Garden, 1991). Also of use is P.H. Davis and J. Cullen's *Identification of Flowering Plant Families* (Cambridge University Press, 1989).

378. Ornamental Grasses and Grasslike Plants. A.J. Oakes. New York, NY: Van Nostrand Reinhold, 1990. 614p., illus., maps, index. $64.95. ISBN: 0-442-23931-9.

This highly specialized handbook describes the various ornamental grasses used in landscape gardening. Each grass includes common name, synonym, cultivars, origin, habitat, hardiness, description, use, and cultivation.

379. Weeds of the United States and Their Control. Harri Lorenzi; Larry S. Jeffrey. New York, NY: Van Nostrand Reinhold, 1987. 355p., illus. (part in color), bibliog., index. $69.50. ISBN: 0-442-25884-4.

Some 305 weed species are described with habitat and distribution provided along with control suggestions.

380. Westcott's Plant Disease Handbook. 5th. R. Kenneth Horst. New York, NY: Van Nostrand Reinhold, 1990. 953p., illus., index. $69.95. ISBN: 0-442-31853-7.

This handbook is the best authority on plant diseases available. It is arranged by common name of plant disease providing information on identification and control of organisms that invade plants.

Treatises

381. Biochemistry of Plants: A Comprehensive Treatise. P.K. Stumpf; Eric E. Conn. Orlando, FL: Academic Press, 1980– , irregular. v.1– , illus., bibliog., index. $102.00/volume. ISBN: 0-12-675412-8v.12.

This ongoing treatise provides up-to-date research information on all aspects of plant biochemistry. Volumes published so far are v.1—The plant cell; v.2—Metabolism and respiration; v.3—Carbohydrates; v.4—Lipids; v.5—Amino acids and derivatives; v6—Proteins and nucleic acids; v.7—Secondary plant products; v.8—Photosynthesis; v.9—Lipids: structure and function; v.10—Photosynthesis; v.11—Biochemistry of metabolism; v.12—Physiology of metabolism; v.13—Methodology; v.14—Carbohydrates; v.15—Molecular Biology. Another useful work is David W. Newman and Kenneth G. Wilson's *Models in Plant Physiology and Biochemistry* (CRC, 1987).

382. Plant Disease: An Advanced Treatise. James Gordon Horsfall; Ellis Brevier Cowling. Orlando, FL: Academic Press, 1977-1980. 5v., illus., bibliog., index. out-of-print.

Although out-of-print this title is an excellent treatise covering plant diseases. The 5 volumes cover v.1—How disease is managed; v.2—How disease develops in populations; v.3—How plants suffer from disease; v.4—How pathogens induce disease; v.5—How plants defend themselves. Another much older treatise that is also of value is James Gordon Horsfall's

Plant Pathology: An Advanced Treatise (3v., Academic Press, 1959-60).

383. Plant Physiology: A Treatise. F.C. Steward. San Diego, CA: Academic Press, 1959-1972. 6v. in 11, illus., bibliog., index. $131.00/volume. ISBN: 0-12-668609-2v.9.

This authoritative treatise covers the physiology of plants. The 6 volumes cover v.1—Cellular organization and respiration; Photosynthesis and chemosynthesis; v.2—Plants in relation to water and solutes; v.3—Inorganic nutrition of plants; v.4—Metabolism; v.5—Analysis of growth; v.6—Physiology of development.

Periodicals

384. Botanical Review. Bronx, NY: New York Botanical Garden, 1935– , quarterly. v.1– , index. $55.00. ISSN: 0006-8101.

385. Bryologist. Omaha, NE: American Bryological and Lichenological Society, 1898– , quarterly. v.1– , index. $40.00. ISSN: 0007-2745.

386. Bulletin of the Torrey Botanical Club. Bronx, NY: New York Botanical Garden, 1870– , quarterly. v.1– , index. $45.00. ISSN: 0040-9618.

387. Canadian Journal of Botany/Journal Canadienne de Botanique. Ottawa, Ontario, Canada: National Research Council of Canada, 1929– , monthly. v.1– , index. $316.00. ISSN: 0008-4026.

388. Economic Botany. Bronx, NY: New York Botanical Garden, 1947– , quarterly. v.1– , index. $55.00. ISSN: 0013-0001.

389. Environmental and Experimental Botany. Tarrytown, NY: Pergamon Press, 1961– , quarterly. v.1– , index. $368.00. ISSN: 0098-8472.

390. International Journal of Plant Sciences. Chicago, IL: University of Chicago Press, 1875– , quarterly. v.1– , index. $42.00.

391. Journal of Experimental Botany. Oxford, Great Britain: Oxford University Press, 1950– , monthly. v.1– , index. $420.00. ISSN: 0022-0957.

392. Journal of Phycology. Lawrence, KS: Allen Press/Phycological Society of America, 1965– , 6/year. v.1– , index. $210.00. ISSN: 0022-3646.

393. Journal of Phytopathology/Phytopathologische Zeitschrift. Berlin, Germany: Paul Parey, 1930– , 12/year. v.1– , index. $645.00. ISSN: 0931-1785.

394. Journal of Plant Physiology. Stuttgart, Germany: Gustav Fischer, 1909– , irregular. v.1– , index. $850.00. ISSN: 0176-1617.

395. Mycologia. Bronx, NY: New York Botanical Garden, 1909– , bimonthly. v.1– , index. $80.00. ISSN: 0027-5514.

396. Mycological Research. Cambridge, Great Britain: Cambridge University Press, 1896– , 12/year. v.1– , index. $550.00. ISSN: 0953-7562.

397. New Phytologist. Cambridge, Great Britain: Cambridge University Press, 1902– , monthly. v.1– , index. $525.00. ISSN: 0028-646X.

398. Phytochemistry. Tarrytown, NY: Pergamon Press/Phytochemical Society of Europe, 1962– , 12/year. v.1– , index. $1,216.00. ISSN: 0031-9422.

399. Phytomorphology. Jodpur, India: Scientific Publishers/International Society of Plant Mycologists, 1951– , quarterly. v.1– , index. $55.00. ISSN: 0031-9449.

400. Phytopathology. St Paul, MN: APS Press/American Phytopathological Society, 1911– , monthly. v.1– , index. $225.00. ISSN: 0031-949X.

401. Plant and Cell Physiology. Kyoto, Japan: Nihon Shokubutsu Sein Gahkai/Japanese Society of Plant Physiologists, 1960– , 8/year. v.1– , index. $180.00. ISSN: 0032-0781.

402. Plant and Soil. Dordrecht, Netherlands: Kluwer/Royal Netherlands Society of Agricultural Science, 1949– , 18/year. v.1– , index. $1,345.00. ISSN: 0032-079X.

403. Plant Physiology. Rockville, MD: American Society of Plant Physiologists, 1926– , monthly. v.1– , index. $450.00. ISSN: 0032-0889.

404. Plant Science. New York, NY: Elsevier, 1973– , 18/year. v.1– , index. $1,683.00. ISSN: 0168-9452.

405. Planta. Berlin, Germany: Springer-Verlag, 1925– , 12/year. v.1– , index. $1,546.00. ISSN: 0032-0935.

406. Taxon. Berlin, Germany: International Bureau for Plant Taxonomy, 1951– , quarterly. v.1– , index. $108.00. ISSN: 0040-0262.

407. Tropical Ecology. Varanasi, India: International Society for Tropical Ecology, 1960– , semiannual. v.1– , index. $60.00. ISSN: 0564-3295.

CHEMISTRY

Abstracts and Indexes

408. Analytical Abstracts. London, Great Britain: Royal Society of Chemistry, 1954– , monthly. v.1– , index. $636.00. ISSN: 0003-2689.

This abstracting service covers both journals and books pertaining to analytical chemistry. It is also available online and on CD-ROM.

409. Chemical Abstracts. Columbus, OH: Chemical Abstracts Service, 1907– , weekly. v.1– , index. $14,094.00.

This is the world's most comprehensive English abstracting service that covers chemistry in all languages. It is well-indexed on a weekly, volume (6-month), and collective (5 or 10 years) basis. The indexes include author, subject, chemical substance, ring system, molecular formula, numerical patent, patent concordance, and hetero-atom-in-context. The abstracts are issued in sections: *Applied Chemistry and Chemical Engineering Section* (0090-8363); *Biochemistry Section (0009-2304); Macromolecular Section* (0009-2274); *Organic Chemistry Section* (0009-2282); *Physical, Inorganic, and Analytical Chemistry Section* (0278-1832); and *Section Groupings* (0009-2258). Also available is *CA Selects* which are 240 separate areas of chemistry that present the abstracts from the parent abstracting service. This abstracting service is also available online.

410. Chemical Abstracts Service Source Index. Columbus, OH: Chemical Abstracts Service, 1907/69– , quinquennial. 1907/69– , index. $990.00/base volume; $210.00/yearly supplements. ISSN: 0001-0634.

Also called *CASSI* and kept up-to-date with quarterly supplements beginning in 1975, each quinquennial or base volume supersedes the previous volume (most current is 1907/89). This is an alphabetical list of all periodicals that have ever had an article abstracted for *Chemical Abstracts*. In addition to giving complete bibliographical information and history of the title, library holdings are indicated. It is also available online.

411. Chemical Titles. Columbus, OH: Chemical Abstracts Service, 1961– , biweekly. v.1– , index. $425.00. ISSN: 0009-2711.

Also available online, this source is a computer-produced KWIC current awareness index to some 900 international chemical periodicals based on the tables of contents of the issue of each title. The Institute for Scientific Information provides a citation index called *Chemistry Citation Index* on CD-ROM.

412. Cheminform. Weinheim, Germany: VCH, 1907– , weekly. v.1– , index. $2,105.00. ISSN: 0009-2975.

Previously called *Chemisches Zentralblatt*, this weekly is published by the German Chemical Society. It duplicates much of what *Chemical Abstracts* abstracts but is especially strong on European and Russian materials. Abstracts can appear from two to three months after publication of an article.

413. Chromatography Abstracts. New York, NY: Elsevier, 1958– , 11/year. v.1– , index. $727.00. ISSN: 0268-6287.

Previously called *Gas and Liquid Chromatography Abstracts* and *Gas Chromatography Abstracts*, this service covers advances in chromatographic techniques and their applications to specific problems in chemistry.

414. Current Chemical Reactions. Philadelphia, PA: Institute for Scientific Information, 1979– , monthly. v.1– , index. $815.00. ISSN: 0163-6278.

Also called *CCR*, this service indexes new or modified reactions or syntheses as reported in the periodical literature. It is also available as an in-house database.

415. Index Chemicus. Philadelphia, PA: Institute of Scientific Information, 1960– , weekly with quarterly and annual cumulations. v.1– , index. $4,725.00. ISSN: 0891-6055.

Previously called *Current Abstracts of Chemistry and Index Chemicus*, this specialized service reports on the synthesis, isolation, and identification of new organic compounds as reported in the periodical literature.

Biographical Sources

416. American Chemists and Chemical Engineers. Wyndham D. Miles. Washington, DC: American Chemical Society, 1976. 544p., index. $32.95. ISBN: 0-8412-0278-8.

This biographical dictionary contains 517 men and women who have figured prominently in the fields of chemistry and chemical engineering over the past 300 years.

417. Great Chemists. Eduard Farber. New York, NY: Wiley, 1961. 1,642p., illus., bibliog. out-of-print.

Although out-of-print this is an excellent source for biographical sketches with portraits of 100 historically important chemists. Another useful and similar book is Henry M. Smith's *Torchbearers of Chemistry, Portraits and Brief Biographies of Scientists Who Have Contributed to the Making of Modern Chemistry* (Academic Press, 1949).

Dictionaries, Glossaries, and Thesauri

418. Acronyms and Abbreviations in Molecular Spectroscopy: An Encyclopedic Dictionary. Detlaf A.W. Wendisch. New York, NY: Springer-Verlag, 1990. 315p., illus., bibliog. $59.50. ISBN: 0-387-51348-5.

This work is a guide and dictionary to the multitude of acronyms and abbreviations associated with spectroscopy.

419. Compendium of Chemical Technology: IUPAC Recommendations. Victor Gold. Boston, MA: Blackwell Scientific, 1987. 456p., illus., bibliog. price not available. ISBN: 0-632-01765-1.

Recommendations by the International Union of Pure and Applied Chemistry make this title a very authoritative chemical dictionary. The 3,100 terms are from analytical, inorganic, macromolecular, organic, and physical chemistry.

420. Compendium of Macromolecular Nomenclature. W.V. Metanomski; International Union of Pure and Applied Chemistry. Boston, MA: Blackwell Scientific, 1991. 171p., illus., bibliog. price not available. ISBN: 0-632-02846-7.

Standard definitions as prescribed by the IUPAC are included in this dictionary covering polymer molecules, assemblies of polymer molecules, polymer solutions, and polymer crystals.

421. Concise Chemical and Technical Dictionary. 4th enlarged. H. Bennett. New York, NY: Chemical Publishing Co, 1986. 1,271p. $125.00. ISBN: 0-8206-0204-3.

Some 100,000 terms are included in this dictionary covering chemicals, drugs, trade names, and chemistry in general. Another newer physical chemistry dictionary is the *Comprehensive Dictionary of Physical Chemistry* (E. Horwood, 1992).

422. Concise Dictionary of Chemistry. new. New York, NY: Oxford University Press, 1990. 320p., illus. $8.95. ISBN: 0-19-286110-7.

Derived from the *Concise Science Dictionary*, this small dictionary covers some 3,000 terms in chemistry and biochemistry. It is intended for undergraduate use.

423. Dictionary of Alkaloids. Ian Southan; John Buckingham. New York, NY: Chapman & Hall, 1989. 2v., illus., index. $1,295.00. ISBN: 0-412-24910-3.

This dictionary covers over 9,900 alkaloids giving descriptions, physical and spectral properties, and other distinguishing information. There are name, molecular formula, CAS registry number, types of compound, and species indexes.

424. Dictionary of Chromatography. 2nd. Ronald C. Denney. New York, NY: Wiley, 1982. 229p., illus., bibliog. out-of-print. ISBN: 0-471-87477-9.

A specialized dictionary covering the terms and concepts that are encountered in chromatographic literature and its related fields. It is still useful even though it is out-of-print.

425. Dictionary of Colloid and Surface Science. Paul Becher. New York, NY: Marcel Dekker, 1990. 202p., bibliog. $79.75. ISBN: 0-8247-8326-3.

Colloid and surface science are covered in this dictionary that includes mini-encyclopedia coverage of some concepts, biographical notes, and biographical sketches.

426. Dictionary of Electrochemistry. 2nd. London, Great Britain: Macmillan, 1984. 308p., illus., bibliog. $35.00. ISBN: 0-333-34983-0.

A well-written dictionary covering electrochemical terms and concepts that might be encountered by biochemists, biologists, chemists, geologists, pharmacists, physicists, and applied scientists.

427. Dictionary of Inorganic Compounds. Jane Macintyre. New York, NY: Chapman & Hall, 1992. 5v., illus., index. $4,600.00. ISBN: 0-412-30120-2.

This dictionary contains physical, structural, and bibliographical information for some 50,000 inorganic compounds. There are master formula, name, CAS registry number, and structural type indexes. The first supplement was published in 1993.

428. Dictionary of Natural Products CD-ROM: The Chapman & Hall Chemical Database. New York, NY: Chapman & Hall, 1992– , annual. 1992– , index. $4,999.00 for first year with updates; $2,975.00/annual renewal. ISSN: 0966-2146.

This database covers over 80,000 organic substances including all the natural products contained in the *Dictionary of Organic Compounds*, *Dictionary of Antibiotics*, *Dictionary of Alkaloids*, *Dictionary of*

Drugs, and *Dictionary of Terpenoids*. Complete descriptions and physical data are included as well as the extensive bibliographies.

429. Dictionary of Organic Compounds. 5th. New York, NY: Chapman & Hall, 1982. 7v., illus., index. $2,550.00/base volume; $5,485.00 for 10 supplements. ISBN: 0-412-17000-0set.

This title is the most comprehensive dictionary of organic compounds available giving physical, structural, and bibliographic information for over 151,800 compounds. Ten supplements have been issued since 1983.

430. Dictionary of Organometallic Compounds. New York, NY: Chapman & Hall, 1984. 3v., bibliog., index. $1,100.00/base volume; $350.00/each supplement 1 and 2; $571.50/supplement 3; $594.00/supplement 4; $895.00/supplement 5. ISBN: 0-412-24710-0set.

This comprehensive dictionary covers just organometallic compounds giving physical, structural, and bibliographic information. Annual supplements have been issued since 1985 with a structure index issued to the first 5 supplements.

431. Elsevier's Dictionary of Chemistry: Including Terms from Biochemistry: English, French, Spanish, Italian, and German. A.F. Dorian. New York, NY: Elsevier, 1989 (c1983). 686p., index. $208.50. ISBN: 0-444-42230-7.

A standard bilingual dictionary of chemistry containing some 9,000 terms. Other chemistry dictionaries from Elsevier include *Dictionary of Chemistry and Chemical Technology: Japanese, English, and Chinese* (1989, 85,000 terms); *Dictionary of Chemical Terminology: English, German, French, Polish, and Russian* (1980, 3,805 terms); and *Dictionary of Analytical Chemistry: English, German, French, Polish, and Russian* (1991, 2,400 terms).

432. Facts on File Dictionary of Chemistry. revised and expanded. John Daintith. New York, NY: Facts on File, 1988. 249p., illus. $24.95. ISBN: 0-8160-1866-9.

This work is a good general dictionary of chemistry covering terms, chemicals, names, and processes. Another good layperson's chemical dictionary is the *Penguin Dictionary of Chemistry* (Viking-Penguin, 1991).

433. French-English Dictionary for Chemistry. 2nd. Austin M. Patterson. New York, NY: Wiley, 1966 (c1954). 476p. out-of-print.

Although out-of-print this is still the standard French-English chemistry dictionary.

434. Gardner's Chemical Synonyms and Trade Names. 9th. Jill Pearce; John Buckingham. Brookfield, VT: Gower, 1987. 2,081p., index. $185.00. ISBN: 0-291-39703-4.

This book is one of the most comprehensive sources of information on chemical synonyms and trade names found in the fields of pharmaceuticals, agricultural chemicals, petrochemicals, plastics, polymers, and synthetics.

435. Grant and Hackh's Chemical Dictionary. 5th. Roger L. Grant; Claire Grant. New York, NY: McGraw-Hill, 1987. 641p., illus. $84.50. ISBN: 0-07-024067-1.

Some 55,000 chemical terms are included in this well-known chemistry dictionary, including synonyms, formulas, melting points, and primary use for terms listed. Also of use would be Raj Kumar's *Dictionary of Analytical Chemistry* (South Asia Books, 1990).

436. Hawley's Condensed Chemical Dictionary. 12th. Richard J. Lewis, Sr. New York, NY: Van Nostrand Reinhold, 1993. 1,275p., illus., index. $69.95. ISBN: 0-442-01131-8.

Previously called the *Condensed Chemical Dictionary*, this work is one of the best accepted chemistry dictionaries to date (first edition published in 1919), giving descriptions of chemicals, raw materials, processes, and equipment; definitions; and descriptions and identification of trademarked products. A smaller dictionary that still is useful is Clifford A. Hamel's *Glossary of Chemical Terms* (Van Nostrand Reinhold, 1982).

437. Miall's Dictionary of Chemistry. 5th. Essex, Great Britain: Longman, 1981. 501p., illus. $45.00. ISBN: 0-582-35152-9.

Previously called *New Dictionary of Chemistry*, Miall's is a good standard dictionary of chemical terms. Also still of value but out-of-print are the *McGraw-Hill Dictionary of Chemical Terms* (McGraw-Hill, 1985) and *McGraw-Hill Dictionary of Chemistry* (McGraw-Hill, 1984).

438. Patterson's German-English Dictionary for Chemists. 4th. Austin M. Patterson; James Cox; George E. Condoyannis. New York, NY: Wiley, 1992. 944p. $75.00. ISBN: 0-471-66991-1.

This excellent, well-respected German-English chemistry dictionary, first published in 1917, covers some 65,000 terms. See also Louis DeVries' *Dictionary of Chemistry and Chemical Engineering*.

439. Russian-English Chemical and Polytechnical Dictionary. 4th. Ludmilla Ignatiev Callaham. New York, NY: Wiley, 1992. 852p. $100.00. ISBN: 0-471-61139-5.

Previously called *Russian-English Technical and Chemical Dictionary*, this is a standard Russian-English dictionary.

440. Vocabular of Organic Chemistry. Milton Orchin. New York, NY: Wiley, 1980. 609p., illus., index. $64.95. ISBN: 0-471-04491-1.

Prepared at the Organic Division, Department of Chemistry, University of Cincinnati, this dictionary covers those terms more commonly associated with organic chemistry.

Directories

441. American Chemical Society Directory of Graduate Research. Washington, DC: American Chemical Society, 1991. 1,561p.; index. $69.00.

Also called *ACS Directory of Graduate Research* and *Directory of Graduate Research*, this is an excellent source of information about chemical graduate programs and related areas of chemical engineering, biochemistry, pharmaceutical chemistry, medicinal chemistry, clinical chemistry, and polymer science. Also from the American Chemical Society is the *College Chemistry Faculties*.

442. Chemcyclopedia. Joseph H. Kuney; Joanne M. Mullican. Washington, DC: American Chemical Society, 1982– , irregular. v.1– , illus., index. $60.00. SuDoc: 0736-6019

This directory of commercially available chemicals lists various substances and their suppliers.

443. Chemical Research Faculties: An International Directory, 1988. Washington, DC: American Chemical Society, 1988. 558p., index. $159.95. ISBN: 0-8412-1017-9.

This directory lists chemical research faculties outside United States in 107 countries. It contains the same kind of directory information as the *American Chemical Society Directory of Graduate Research*.

Encyclopedias

444. Concise Encyclopedia of Biochemistry. 2nd revised and expanded. Thomas Scott; Mary Eagleson. New York, NY: DeGruyter, 1988. 649p., illus. $89.90. ISBN: 0-89925-457-8.

Being a translation of *Brockhaus ABC Biochemie*, this biochemical encyclopedia emphasizes metabolism, metabolic regulation, molecular biology, enzymology, and natural products. Although out-of-print, the *Encyclopedia of Biochemistry* (Van Nostrand Reinhold, 1967) is useful for historical and standard terminology.

445. Encyclopedia of Electrochemistry of the Elements. Allen J. Bard. New York, NY: Marcel Dekker, 1973– , irregular. v.1– , illus., bibliog., index. price per volume varies. ISBN: 0-8247-6093-Xv.1.

This comprehensive encyclopedia covers electrochemistry of the elements. The first 10 volumes cover inorganic chemistry with volume 11 and following covering organic.

446. Encyclopedia of the Alkaloids. John Stephen Glasby. New York, NY: Plenum Press, 1975-1983. 4v., illus., bibliog., index. $110.00/volume. ISBN: 0-306-30845-2v.1.

This alphabetically arranged encyclopedia of chemical compounds provides physical and chemical information including formulas, melting points, occurrence, special properties, and reactions with relation to their alkaloids.

447. McGraw-Hill Encyclopedia of Chemistry. 2nd. Sybil P. Parker. New York, NY: McGraw-Hill, 1993. 1,236p., illus., index. $95.00. ISBN: 0-07-045455-8.

All the articles in this excellent encyclopedia were taken from the seventh edition of the *McGraw-Hill Encyclopedia of Science and Technology*. The articles are written for the student as well as the researcher.

448. Merck Index: An Encyclopedia of Chemicals and Drugs. Rahway, NJ: Merck, 1889– , annual. 1st– , index. $35.00. ISBN: 0-911910-28-X 11th ed.

This "Bible" of chemicals and drugs gives full descriptions that include variant names, trademarks, properties, formulas, and uses.

449. Physical Chemistry Source Book. Sybil P. Parker. New York, NY: McGraw-Hill, 1988. 406p., illus., index. $48.00. ISBN: 0-07-045504-X.

The material for this source book has been taken from the sixth edition of the *McGraw-Hill Encyclopedia of Science and Technology*. Some 130 articles on physical chemistry have been conveniently brought together in a small encyclopedia for easy consultation.

450. Spectroscopy Source Book. Sybil P. Parker. New York, NY: McGraw-Hill, 1988. 288p., illus., index. $48.00. ISBN: 0-07-045505-8.

Material for this source book has been taken from the sixth edition of the *McGraw-Hill Encyclopedia of Science and Technology*. All of the 70 articles that pertain to spectroscopy are brought together in a convenient small encyclopedia.

451. Van Nostrand Reinhold Encyclopedia of Chemistry. 4th. Douglas M. Considine; Glenn D. Considine. New York, NY: Van Nostrand Reinhold, 1984. 1,082p., illus., bibliog., index. out-of-print. ISBN: 0-442-22572-5.

Previously called *Encyclopedia of Chemistry*, this is still a good general encyclopedia of chemistry containing some 1,300 entries.

Guides to the Literature

452. Chemical Information: A Practical Guide to Utilization. 2nd revised and enlarged. Yecheskel Wolman. New York, NY: Wiley, 1988. 291p., illus., index. $39.95. ISBN: 0-471-91704-4.

This guide to the areas of information including the scientific journal, library organization, handbooks, numerical data, patents, and bibliographic databases is a narrative rather than bibliographic guide.

453. Chemical Information Sources. Gary D. Wiggins. New York, NY: McGraw-Hill, 1990. 256p., bibliog., index. $42.35. ISBN: 0-07-909939-4.

This excellent guide to the use of chemical sources of information discusses sources, problem-solving, and computer-readable databases. A disk is included containing over 2,000 records of chemistry reference sources.

454. Chemical Publications, Their Nature and Use. 5th. M.G. Mellon. New York, NY: McGraw-Hill, 1982. 419p., illus., bibliog., index. $34.65. ISBN: 0-02-041514-5.

A standard guide to the literature discussing those reference materials needed in the chemical field. An older but still useful guide is George Antony's *Guide to Basic Information Sources in Chemistry* (J. Norton, 1979).

455. How to Find Chemical Information: A Guide for Practicing Chemists, Educators and Students. 2nd. Robert E. Maizell. New York, NY: Wiley, 1987. 402p., illus., bibliog., index. $55.00. ISBN: 0-471-86767-5.

Arranged by type of information, this authoritative guide covers all the reference materials needed by a chemical researcher. For a good discussion on the makeup of chemical literature consult Herman Skolnik's *Literature Matrix of Chemistry* (Wiley, 1982).

456. Information Sources in Chemistry. 4th. R.T. Bottle. London, Great Britain: Bowker-Saur, 1993. 341p., index. $70.00. ISBN: 1-857-39016-4.

Previously called *Use of Chemical Literature*, this well-known guide covers all types of chemical literature including the periodical literature.

Handbooks and Manuals

457. Beilstein Guide: A Manual for the Use of Beilstein's Handbuch der Organische Chemie. Oskar Weissbach. New York, NY: Springer-Verlag, 1976. 95p., index. price not available. ISBN: 0-387-07457-0.

Being a translation of *Beilstein-Leitfaden*, this is a good guide for those who need to understand how to use and get the most out of *Beilstein*.

458. Chemical Demonstrations: A Handbook for Teachers of Chemistry. Bassam Z. Shakhashiri. Washington, DC: American Chemical Society, 1983-1992. 4v., illus., index. $25.00/volume. ISBN: 0-299-12860-1v.4.

This very useful handbook illustrates chemical phenomena. Each demonstration includes description, materials list, preparation procedures, instructions for presentation, hazard information, and discussion of the phenomena.

459. Chemical Technician's Ready Reference Handbook. 3rd. Gershom J. Shugar; Jack T. Ballinger. New York, NY: McGraw-Hill, 1990. 889p., illus., index. $62.50. ISBN: 0-07-057183-X.

Intended for the laboratory technician, this handbook outlines "every single step" to be followed when performing normal laboratory procedures. It is in textbook format.

460. Chemist's Companion: A Handbook of Practical Data, Techniques and References. Arnold J. Gordon; Richard A. Ford. New York, NY: Wiley, 1972. 537p., illus., bibliog., index. $64.75. ISBN: 0-471-31590-7.

Although somewhat dated, the *Chemist's Companion* is still a useful little handbook giving such information as the properties of atoms and molecules, spectroscopic data, and discussions on photochemistry, chromatography, kinetics, thermodynamics, experimental techniques, and mathematical data. Also of use is Tim Clark's *Handbook of Computational Chemistry* (Wiley, 1985).

461. Chemist's Ready Reference Handbook. Gershom J. Shugar; John A. Dean. New York, NY: McGraw-Hill, 1990. 1v. various paging, illus., bibliog., index. $79.50. ISBN: 0-07-057178-3.

This general overview of analytical laboratory techniques is not intended to be comprehensive and should be used in conjunction with other handbooks.

462. CRC Handbook of Basic Tables for Chemical Analysis. Thomas J. Bruno; Paris D.N. Svoronos. Boca Raton, FL: CRC, 1989. 417p., illus., bibliog., index. $119.95. ISBN: 0-8493-3935-9.

Although the tables found in this handbook can be found in other books, this one is useful because they are all brought together under one cover. All tables pertain to analytical chemistry with the emphasis on organic. Another older book of chemical tables is Roy A. Keller's *Basic Tables in Chemistry* (McGraw-Hill, 1967).

463. CRC Handbook of Chromatography.
Boca Raton, FL: CRC, 1982-1990. 21v., tables, bibliog., index. price per volume varies.

This multivolume treatise/handbook of data pertaining to chromatography is divided into several sections: Amino Acids and Amines (1983-89, 2v., $229.95); Peptides (1986, $179.95); Carbohydrates (1982-90, 2v., $319.45); Drugs (1981-88, 6v., $979.50); Phenols (1982, $119.95); Nucleic Acids and Related Compounds (1987, 2v., $354.95); Lipids (1984, 2v., $340.00); Inorganics (1987, $110.00); Polymers (1982, $129.95); Steroids (1986, $139.95); and Hydrocarbons (1987, $235.00).

464. CRC Handbook of Data on Organic Compounds. 2nd. Robert C. Weast; Jeanette G. Grasselli. Boca Raton, FL: CRC, 1988. 9v., illus., bibliog., index. $2,655.00; $295.00/supplement. ISBN: 0-8493-0420-2.

Over 25,000 compounds are covered in this organic chemistry handbook. It includes physical and chemical data as well as spectral. Supplements begin at volume 10 and following in 1990.

465. CRC Handbook of Laboratory Safety.
3rd. Keith Furr. Boca Raton, FL: CRC, 1990. 704p., illus., bibliog., index. $110.00. ISBN: 0-8493-0353-2.

This handbook attempts to help persons interpret and place into operation the many regulatory standards that are needed in the chemical laboratory as well as other types of research labs.

466. CRC Handbook of Organic Analytical Reagents. K.L. Cheng; Keihei Meno; Toshiaki Imamura. Boca Raton, FL: CRC, 1982. 534p., illus., bibliog., index. $117.00. ISBN: 0-8493-0771-6.

This handbook can be considered as an update for the 4-volume *Organic Analytical Reagents* (Van Nostrand Reinhold, 1947). It includes classical reagents from the original work as well as newer ones.

467. Feiser and Feiser's Reagents for Organic Synthesis. Mary Feiser. New York, NY: Wiley, 1980– , irregular. v.8– , illus., index. price per volume varies.

Previously called *Reagents for Organic Synthesis*, this well-known encyclopedic handbook gives structural and physical properties of reagents, including preferred methods of preparation or purification.

468. First Aid Manual for Chemical Accidents. 2nd English-language. M.J. Lefaevre; Shirley A. Conibear. New York, NY: Van Nostrand Reinhold, 1989. 261p., index. $32.95. ISBN: 0-492-70490-6.

Being a translation of *Manuel de Premiers Soins d'Urgence*, this manual focuses on the immediate care for a chemical accident victim. It does, however, have a complex arrangement that needs studying before using. Also of use would be E.R. Plunkett's *Handbook of Industrial Toxicology* (Chemical Publishing Co., 1987).

469. Handbook of Chemical Property Estimation Methods: Environmental Behavior of Organic Compounds. Warren J. Lyman; William F. Reehl; David H. Rosenblatt. Washington, DC: American Chemical Society, 1990 (c1982). 2v. various paging, illus., bibliog., index. $49.95. ISBN: 0-8412-1761-0.

Some 26 properties of organic chemicals in regard to their transport and fate in the environment are covered in this handbook. Methods for determining their properties are given, taking into consideration range of applicabilities, ease of use, minimum input data requirements, and accuracy.

470. Handbook on the Physics and Chemistry of Rare Earths. Karl A. Gschneidner, Jr.; LeRoy Eyring. New York, NY: North-Holland, 1978– , irregular. v.1– , illus., bibliog., index. price per volume varies. ISBN: 0-444-85022-8.

With 15 volumes published as of 1993, this ongoing treatise-type handbook documents information and synthesizes other information on the rare earths.

471. International Thermodynamic Tables of the Fluid State. S. Angus. New York, NY: Pergamon, 1976-1988. 10v., illus., bibliog., index. price per volume varies. ISBN: 0-08-021981-0v.5.

This series of very authoritative handbooks contains tables on the thermodynamic properties of gases and liquids.

472. Lange's Handbook of Chemistry. 14th. John A. Dean. New York, NY: McGraw-Hill, 1992. 1v. various paging, index. $79.50. ISBN: 0-07-016194-1.

Previously called *Handbook of Chemistry*, this chemical handbook is well-known. It is less comprehensive than the *Handbook of Chemistry and Physics* but very helpful for laboratory use. It is revised every 6 years.

473. Methoden der Organische Chemie (Houben-Weyl): Erweiterungs-und Folge-bande zur Vierten Aufl. K.H. Buchel. New York, NY: G. Thieme, 1982– , irregular. v.1– , illus., bibliog., index. price not available. ISBN: 3-13-217104-2.

Also called *Houben-Weyl's*, this German handbook is considered an authority on all organic chemistry laboratory methods of preparation of compounds. It is a classic set.

474. Organic Reactions. W. Dauben. New York, NY: Wiley, 1942– , irregular. v.1– , bibliog., index. price per volume varies. ISSN: 0078-6179.

An irregularly published set that is "collections of chapters, each devoted to a single reaction, or a definite phase of a reaction, or wide applicability." Detailed procedures are given along with examples and extensive bibliographies. The annual *Organic Synthesis* (Wiley, 1941-) provides checked laboratory methods for preparing organic compounds.

475. Practical Handbook of Spectroscopy. Boca Raton, FL: CRC, 1991. 880p., illus., index. $65.00. ISBN: 0-8493-3708-9.

This handbook is condensed information taken from the out-of-print 3-volume *CRC Handbook of Spectroscopy* and updated for ease of use. All areas of the use of spectroscopy are covered.

476. Ring Systems Handbook. Columbus, OH: American Chemical Society, 1984– , 2/year. 1v., 2 cumulative supplements/year, index. $475.00/base volume; $215.00/year for 2 supplements. ISSN: 0742-5996.

This unique handbook leads the user from the chemical structure to the name and CAS registry number of ring systems. Over 75,000 ring systems are covered in ring analysis order. For each entry the following are given: sequential ring file number, CAS registry number, latest CA index name, molecular formula, Wiswesser line notation (WLN), CA reference, and structural diagram. It is issued in 4 parts: Ring Systems File I, Ring Systems File II, Ring Formula Index, and Ring WLN Index.

477. Standard Methods of Chemical Analysis. 6th. New York, NY: Van Nostrand Reinhold, 1962-66. 3v. in 5, illus., bibliog., index. $548.50 (reprint by Krieger). ISBN: 0-88275-940-X (reprint by Krieger).

The standard handbook for chemical analysis. The 3 volumes cover: v.1—The elements; v.2—Industrial and natural products and noninstrumental methods; and v.3—Instrumental Methods.

478. Thermochemical Data of Organic Compounds. 2nd. J.B. Pedley; R.D. Naylor; S.P. Kirby. New York, NY: Chapman & Hall, 1986. 792p., bibliog., index. $120.00. ISBN: 0-412-27100-1.

Being a revision of *Sussex-N.P.L. Computer Analysed Thermochemical Data*, this handbook provides information on the standard enthalpy of formation for over 3,000 organic compounds. Also included are the standard enthalpies of 42 common inorganic compounds.

Histories

479. Chemical Literature, 1700-1860: A Bibliography with Annotations, Detailed Descriptions, Companies, and Locations. William A. Cole. New York, NY: Mansell, 1988. 582p. $165.00. ISBN: 0-7201-1967-7.

This comprehensive bibliography lists books pertaining to the history of chemistry.

480. Documentary History of Biochemistry, 1770-1940. M. Kulas Teich; Dorothy M. Needham. Leicester, Great Britain: Leicester University Press, 1992. 579p., illus., bibliog., index. $155.00. ISBN: 0-718-51341-X.

This title is a comprehensive history of biochemistry. Another useful work is Marcel Florkin's *History of Biochemistry* (Elsevier, 1972-79).

481. History of Chemistry. John Hudson. New York, NY: Chapman & Hall, 1992. 275p., illus., index. $59.95; $24.950pbk. ISBN: 0-412-03641-X; 0-412-03651-7pbk.

A good basic overview of the history of chemistry from the Neolithic Age to the present. It covers both themes and personalities. Two other useful history of chemistry works are David M. Knight's *Classical Scientific Papers: Chemistry* (Elsevier, 1968) and Kenneth M. Reese's *Century of Chemistry: The Role of Chemists and the American Chemical Society* (American Chemical Society, 1976). Also, David Knight's *Ideas in Chemistry: A History of the Science* (Rutgers University Press, 1992) is a collection of history of chemistry essays.

482. History of Chemistry. James Riddick Partington. New York, NY: Macmillan, 1961-1970. 4v., bibliog., index. out-of-print.

Now out-of-print, this well-documented work is the most widely accepted history of chemistry. Another more popular work is E.S.C. Von Meyer's *History of Chemistry from Earliest Times to the Present Day* (Arno Press, 1975). Also, for just analytical chemistry consult Fenenc Szabadvary's *History of Analytical Chemistry* (Pergamon, 1966) and for organic chemistry consult Tetsuo Nozoe's *Seventy Years in Organic Chemistry* (American Chemical Society, 1991).

483. Select Bibliography of Chemistry, 1492-1902. *(Smithsonian Miscellaneous Collection, v.36, 40:7, 41:3, 44:5)*. Henry Carrington Batton. Washington, DC: Smithsonian Institution, 1893-1904; Krause reprint 1973. 4v., index. $128.00v.1; $35.00/volume 2-3. ISBN: 0-527-09400-5v.1; 0-527-09420-Xv.2; 0-527-09426-9v.3; 0-527-09432-3v.4.

A bibliography of some 18,000 chemical books published in Europe and the United States. For excerpts from some of these books consult Henry M. Leicester's *Source Book in Chemistry, 1400-1900* (McGraw-Hill, 1952) and *Source Book in Chemistry, 1900-1950* (Harvard University Press, 1968).

Treatises

484. Advanced Treatise on Physical Chemistry. James Riddick Partington. New York, NY: Wiley, 1949-1962. 5v., illus., bibliog., index. out-of-print.

Although out-of-print, this title is a classical treatise on physical chemistry. The 5 volumes cover v.1—Fundamental principles: the properties of gases; v.2—The properties of liquids; v.3—The properties of solids; v.4—Physico-chemical optics; v.5—Molecular spectra and structures: dielectrics and dipole moments. Also of importance is H. Eyring's *Physical Chemistry: An Advanced Treatise* (Academic Press, 1967-1975, 11v.).

485. Beilsteins Handbuch der Organischen Chemie. 4th. Friedrich Konrad Beilstein. New York, NY: Springer-Verlag, 1918-1940; supplement 1928– , irregular. 27v.; supplement 1-5 in ongoing volumes, index. price per volume varies.

This German work is the world's most comprehensive treatise on organic chemistry giving for each compound constitutes and configuration; natural occurrence and isolation from natural products; preparation, formation, and purification; structural and energy parameters; physical properties; chemical properties; characterization and analysis; and salt and additional compounds. Until supplement 5, it is in German. The main set covers the literature up to 1909; first supplement, 1910-1919; second supplement, 1920-1929; third supplement, 1930-1949 and 1930-1959 for heterocyclic compounds; fourth supplement, 1950-1959; and sixth supplement (currently being published), 1960-1979. It is also available online.

486. Compendium of Organic Synthetic Methods. Ian T. Harrison; Shuyen Harrison. New York, NY: Wiley, 1971-1988. 6v., illus., index. $216.00. ISBN: 0-471-50135-2.

This systematic listing of functional group transformations is designed for the bench chemists and persons planning syntheses. It is arranged by reacting functional group of the starting material and the functional group formed.

487. Comprehensive Biochemistry. Marcel Florkin; Elmer H. Stotz. New York, NY: Pergamon Press, 1962-1979. 6 sections in 34v., illus., bibliog. $1,900.00. ISBN: 0-08-030732-9.

This well-known treatise covers all areas of biochemistry. The 6 sections cover 1—Physico-chemical and organic aspects of biochemistry; 2—Chemistry and biological compounds; 3—Biochemical reaction mechanisms; 4—Metabolism; 5—Chemical biology; 6—History of biochemistry.

488. Comprehensive Chemical Kinetics. New York, NY: Elsevier, 1969– , irregular. v.1– , illus., index. price per volume varies.

Comprehensive Chemical Kinetics is an ongoing treatise with each volume covering a different topic including practice and theory of the kinetics of organic, inorganic, and polymerization reactions.

489. Comprehensive Coordination Chemistry: The Synthesis, Reactions, Properties, and Applications of Coordination Compounds. Geoffrey Wilkinson; Robert D. Gillard; Jon A. McCleverty. New York, NY: Pergamon Press, 1987. 7v., illus., bibliog., index. $3,200.00. ISBN: 0-08-026232-5set.

This comprehensive treatise is a companion to *Comprehensive Organometallic Compounds*. It provides a convenient source of information on coordination compounds with the 7 volumes covering v.1—Theory and background; v.2—Ligands; v.3—Main group and early transition elements; v.4—Middle transition Elements; v.5—Late transition elements; v.6—Industrial, medical, and synthetic applications; v.7—Indexes.

490. Comprehensive Heterocyclic Chemistry: The Structure, Reactions, Synthesis, and Uses of Heterocyclic Compounds. Alan R. Katritzky; Charles W. Rees. New York, NY: Pergamon, 1984. 8v., illus., bibliog., index. $2,200.00. ISBN: 0-08-026200-7set.

This treatise covers organic heterocyclic compounds, which are the compounds that play a vital role in the metabolism of all living cells. It stresses basic principles and the chemistry and synthesis of different heterocyclic systems. The 8 volumes cover v.1—Introduction, nomenclature, review literature, biological aspects, industrial uses, less-common heteroatoms; v.2—Six-membered rings with one nitrogen atom; v.3—Six-membered rings with oxygen, sulfur or 2 or more nitrogen atoms; v.4—Five-membered rings with one oxygen, sulfur or nitrogen atoms; v.5—Five-membered rings with 2 or more nitrogen atoms; v.6—Five-membered rings with 2 or more oxygen, sulfur or nitrogen atoms; v.7—Small and large rings; v.8—Indexes.

491. Comprehensive Inorganic Chemistry.
M. Cannon Sneed; J. Lewis Maynard; Robert C. Brasted. New York, NY: Pergamon Press, 1953. 5v., illus., bibliog., index. out-of-print.

This title is a good treatise covering inorganic chemistry including physical, chemical, and biological properties.

492. Comprehensive Organic Chemistry.
Derek Baron. New York, NY: Pergamon Press, 1978. 6v., illus., bibliog., index. $1,900.00. ISBN: 0-08-030732-9.

This well-known treatise of organic chemistry covers properties and reactions. It includes some synthetic compounds and natural products.

493. Comprehensive Organic Synthesis.
Barry M. Trost. New York, NY: Pergamon Press, 1991. 9v., illus., index. $2,950.00. ISBN: 0-08-035929-9.

Comprehensive Organic Synthesis is a detailed, critical account of organic synthesis covering the formation of carbon-carbon bonds, introduction to heteroatoms, and heteroatom interconversions, all of which are important in the preparation of organic compounds.

494. Comprehensive Organometallic Chemistry: The Synthesis, Reactions, and Structures of Organometallic Compounds. Geoffrey Wilkinson; F. Gordon A. Stone; Edward W. Abel. New York, NY: Pergamon Press, 1982. 9v., illus., index. $3,000.00. ISBN: 0-08-025269-9.

This companion to *Comprehensive Coordination Chemistry* covers organometallic and carbon monoxide chemistry. This treatise provides coverage for the past 25 years of research.

495. Comprehensive Treatise of Electrochemistry. New York, NY: Plenum, 1980– , irregular. v.1– , index. price per volume varies. ISBN: 0-306-40275-0v.1.

This ongoing treatise of electrochemistry is well documented and comprehensive.

496. Comprehensive Treatise on Inorganic and Theoretical Chemistry. J.W. Mellor. New York, NY: Longman, 1922-37. 16v., illus., bibliog., index. $160.00/volume (reprint from Books on Demand).

Also known as *Mellor's Comprehensive Treatise on Inorganic and Theoretical Chemistry*, this classical treatise covers inorganic and theoretical chemistry. Three supplements have been published for volume 2 and 3 for volume 8.

497. Gmelin's Handbuch der Anorganischen Chemie. 8th. Leopold Gmelin. New York, NY: Springer-Verlag, 1924– , irregular. v.1– , bibliog., index. price per volume varies.

Gmelin's is the world's most comprehensive treatise on inorganic chemistry. For each entry the history, occurrence, properties, scientific methods of preparation, and commercial process of manufacture are given. Supplements are being issued for each volume. It is also available online.

498. Rodd's Chemistry of Carbon Compounds: A Comprehensive Treatise. 2nd. E.H. Rodd; S Coffey. New York, NY: Elsevier, 1964– , irregular. v.1– , illus., bibliog., index. price per volume varies. ISSN: 0080-3758.

Rodd's is one of the world's most comprehensive carbon compound treatises. It is divided into four parts and has been kept current with supplements since 1974.

499. Techniques of Chemistry. A. Weissberger. New York, NY: Wiley, 1971– , irregular. v.1– , index. price per volume varies. ISSN: 0082-2531.

Formed by the merger of *Technique of Organic Chemistry* and *Technique of Inorganic Chemistry*, this comprehensive classical treatise covers techniques in all areas of chemistry, including allied fields such as photochemistry.

500. Treatise on Analytical Chemistry. 2nd. I.M. Kolthoff; Philip J. Elving. New York, NY: Wiley, 1978– , irregular. v.1– , illus., bibliog., index. price per volume varies. ISSN: 0082-6243part 1; 0082-6251part 2; 0082-626Xpart 3.

This multivolume organic treatise in three parts is the authoritative work on analytical chemistry. It is also known as just *Kolthoff's*. The 3 parts cover part 1—Theory and practice of analytical chemistry; part 2—Analytical chemistry of the elements; analytical chemistry of inorganic and organic compounds; part 3—Analytical chemistry in industry.

Periodicals

501. Accounts of Chemical Research.
Washington, DC: American Chemical Society, 1968– , monthly. v.1– , illus., index. $170.00. ISSN: 0001-4842.

502. Analytical Chemistry. Washington, DC: American Chemical Society, 1929– , semimonthly. v.1– , illus., index. $373.00. ISSN: 0003-2700.

503. Angewandte Chemie: International Edition. Weinheim, Germany: VCH, 1961– , monthly. v.1– , illus., index. $440.00. ISSN: 0570-0833.

504. Biochemistry. Washington, DC: American Chemical Society, 1964– , weekly. v.1– , index. $1,040.00. ISSN: 0006-2960.

505. Canadian Journal of Chemistry/Journal Canadienne de Chimie. Ottawa, Ontario, Canada: National Research Council of Canada, 1929– , monthly. v.1– , illus., index. $141.00. ISSN: 0008-4042.

506. Chemical Reviews. Washington, DC: American Chemical Society, 1924– , 8/year. v.1– , illus., index. $320.00. ISSN: 0009-2665.

507. Faraday Discussions. Cambridge, Great Britain: Royal Society of Chemistry, 1946– , semiannual. v.1– , illus., index. $186.00. ISSN: 0301-7249.

508. Inorganic Chemistry. Washington, DC: American Chemical Society, 1962– , semimonthly. v.1– , illus., index. $864.00. ISSN: 0020-1669.

509. Journal of Chemical and Engineering Data. Washington, DC: American Chemical Society, 1959– , quarterly. v.1– , illus., index. $289.00. ISSN: 0021-9568.

510. Journal of Chemical Education. Washington, DC: American Chemical Society, 1924– , monthly. v.1– , illus., index. $60.00. ISSN: 0021-9584.

511. Journal of Chemical Research. Cambridge, Great Britain: Royal Society of Chemistry, 1977– , monthly. v.1– , illus., index. $534.00. ISSN: 0308-2342.

512. Journal of Chromatography. New York, NY: Elsevier, 1958– , 54/year. v.1– , illus., index. $4,015.00. ISSN: 0021-9673.

513. Journal of Organic Chemistry. Washington, DC: American Chemical Society, 1936– , biweekly. v.1– , illus., index. $670.00. ISSN: 0022-3263.

514. Journal of Physical Chemistry. Washington, DC: American Chemical Society, 1896– , biweekly. v.1– , illus., index. $998.00. ISSN: 0022-3654.

515. Journal of Polymer Science: Part A, Polymer Chemistry; Part B, Polymer Physics. New York, NY: Wiley, 1962– , 27/year. v.1– , illus., index. $1,595.00A; !$1,565.00B. ISSN: 0887-624XA; 0887-6266B.

516. Journal of the American Chemical Society. Washington, DC: American Chemical Society, 1879– , biweekly. v.1– , illus., index. $925.00. ISSN: 0002-7863.

517. Journal of the Electrochemical Society. Pennington, NJ: Electrochemical Society, 1902– , monthly. v.1– , illus., index. $325.00. ISSN: 0013-4651.

518. Journal of the Royal Society of Chemistry. Cambridge, Great Britain: Royal Society of Chemistry, 1972– , 12/year and fortnightly. v.1– , illus., index. see below. ISSN: see below.

The journal consists of 4 sections: *Dalton Transactions*, 12/year, $1,115.00, 0300-9246; *Faraday Transactions*, fortnightly, $1,076.00, 0956-5000; *Perkin Transactions 1*, fortnightly, $903.00, 0300-922X; *Perkin Transactions 2*, 12/year, $766.00, 0300-9580.

519. Liebig's Annalen der Chemie. Weinheim, Germany: VCH, 1832– , monthly. v.1– , illus., index. $460.00. ISSN: 0170-2041.

520. Talanta. Tarrytown, NY: Pergamon Press, 1958– , monthly. v.1– , illus., index. $720.00. ISSN: 0039-9140.

521. Tetrahedron. Tarrytown, NY: Pergamon Press, 1957– , 60/year. v.1– , illus., index. $4,275.00. ISSN: 0040-4020.

522. Tetrahedron Letters. Tarrytown, NY: Pergamon Press, 1959– , weekly. v.1– , illus., index. $3832.00. ISSN: 0040-4039.

COMPUTER SCIENCE

Abstracts and Indexes

523. ACM Guide to Computing Literature. New York, NY: Association for Computing Machinery, 1964– , annual. v.1– , index. $175.00. ISSN: 0149-1199.

Previously called *Bibliography and Subject Index of Current Computing Literature*, this bibliographic listing of computer literature has author, keyword, category, subject, reviewer, and source indexes. Some 18,000 entries per year are included. A new CD-ROM product from ACM called *Computing Archive* provides a database of computing literature plus the full-text reviews that appear in *Computing Reviews*.

524. Collected Algorithms for ACM. Association for Computing Machinery. New York, NY: Association for Computing Machinery, 1980-83. 5v., supplements 1983– , index. $400.00v.1-5; $60.00/supplement.

This publication offers code listings for all algorithms printed in ACM journals, including both machine readable and microfiche forms.

525. Computer and Control Abstracts. Stevenge, Great Britain: Inspec, 1966– , monthly. v.1– , index. $1,200.00. ISSN: 0036-8113.

This title is Section C of *Science Abstracts* providing a subject arrangement of abstracts pertaining to all areas of computers and control engineering. It is also available online and on CD-ROM. It is supplemented with *Current Papers in Computers and Control*. Also useful but containing fewer abstracts is *Computer Abstracts* (Anbar Abstracts, 1957-).

526. Computer and Information Systems Abstracts Journal. Riverdale, MD: Cambridge Scientific Abstracts, 1962– , monthly. v.1– , index. $1,125.00. ISSN: 0191-9776.

Previously called *Computer and Information Systems* and *Information Processing Journal*, this international abstracting journal emphasizes software, applications, and electronics. Acronyms, author, and subject indexes are included. It is also available online.

527. Computer Literature Index. Phoenix, AZ: Applied Computer Research, 1971– , quarterly. v.1– , index. $195.00. ISSN: 0270-4846.

Previously called *Quarterly Bibliography of Computers and Data Processing*, CLI is an annotated bibliography of books, articles, and various published reports that are concerned with computers and data processing. It is cumulated annually.

528. Computing Reviews. New York, NY: Association for Computing Machinery, 1960– , monthly. v.1– , index. $115.00. ISSN: 0010-4884.

This monthly is a good reviewing source of computer publications. It covers hardware, software, computer systems, organizations, theory of computation, information systems, and computer applications. It is also available online.

529. Micro Computer Index. Medford, NJ: Learned Information, Inc., 1980– , bimonthly. v.1– , index. $159.00. ISSN: 8756-7040.

This abstracting journal covers over 2,400 periodical articles and news items per year, including reviews of software, hardware, and books. All popular computer magazines are covered. It is also available online.

Bibliographies

530. Computer Literature Bibliography, 1946-67. W.W. Youden. Salem, NH: Ayer, 1970 (c1967). 2v., index. $55.00. ISBN: 0-405-00068-5.

This good historical bibliography was originally published by the National Bureau of Standards with citations from periodicals, books, workshops, and proceedings. It is considered the most exhaustive work for the period.

Dictionaries, Glossaries, and Thesauri

531. Artificial Intelligence Dictionary. Ellen Thro; Lance A. Leventhal. San Marcos, CA: Microtrend Books, 1991. 407p., illus. $24.95. ISBN: 0-915391-36-8.

This dictionary of terms used in the field of artificial intelligence is intended for users and specialists. Two other useful but smaller dictionaries are Jenny Raggett's *Artificial Intelligence from A to Z* (Chapman & Hall, 1992) and the *Facts on File Dictionary of Artificial Intelligence* (Facts on File, 1989).

532. Butterworths Security Dictionary: Terms and Concepts. John J. Fay. Stoneham, MA: Butterworth-Heinemann, 1987. 277p., bibliog. $29.95. ISBN: 0-409-90033-8.

This specialized dictionary covers the terminology associated with security as it pertains to computers. It covers procedural, organizational, and legal terminology. Dennis Longley and Mike Shoin's much larger *Data and Computer Security* (Stockton Press, 1987) would also be useful, but it is about four times as expensive.

533. Computer Animation Dictionary: Including Related Terms Used in Computer Graphics, Film and Video, Production, and Desktop Publishing. Rabi Roncarelli. New York, NY: Springer-Verlag, 1989. 124p. $28.00. ISBN: 0-387-97022-3.

More than 1,500 terms are included in this specialized dictionary covering computer art, animation, video, film production, electronic and desktop publishing, and general computer operations.

534. Computer Dictionary. 3rd. Donald D. Spencer. Marietta, GA: Camelot, 1992. 468p. $24.95. ISBN: 0-89218-209-1.

Computer Dictionary is one of many computer dictionaries that has proven itself acceptable to the public. The definitions are clear and relatively nontechnical. Two other small dictionaries are the *Microsoft Press Computer Dictionary* (Microsoft, 1991) and *HarperCollins Dictionary of Computer Terms* (HarperPerrenial, 1991).

535. Computer Glossary: The Complete Illustrated Desk Reference. 6th. Alan Freedman. New York, NY: AMACOM, 1993. 574p., illus. price not available. ISBN: 0-8144-7809-3.

This frequently revised dictionary is compiled by the well-known Alan Freedman. It is intended for the technical users as well as the practioneer. Two other useful glossaries are the British Computer Society's *Glossary of Computing Terms* (Pitman, 1991) and Jerry Martin Rosenberg's *Business Dictionary of Computers* (Wiley, 1993). Freedman also has a *Computer Glossary Sourcebook* (AMACOM, 1990).

536. Computer Science Abbreviations and Acronyms: A Professional Reference Guide. Mark W. Greenia. Sacramento, CA: Lexikon Services, 1990. 100p. $25.00. ISBN: 0-944601-22-7.

This fairly comprehensive dictionary lists definitions for some 5,500 abbreviations and acronyms associated with the computer industry and its associated fields. Other abbreviations and acronyms guides include Julie E. Towell's *Computer and Telecommunication Acronyms* (Gale, 1986); for historical acronyms, see Claude P. Wrathall's *Computer Acronyms, Abbreviations, etc.* (Petrocelli, 1981); and Jerry Martin Rosenberg's *McGraw-Hill Dictionary of Information Technology and Computer Acronyms, Initials, and Abbreviations* (McGraw-Hill, 1992).

537. Data and Computer Communications: Terms, Definitions and Abbreviations. Gilbert Held. New York, NY: Wiley, 1989. 254p., illus. $44.95. ISBN: 0-471-92066-5.

The emphasis on this dictionary is telecommunications. It includes both terms and abbreviations or acronyms.

538. Dictionary of Computer Graphics Technology and Applications. Roy Latham. New York, NY: Springer-Verlag, 1991. 160p., illus., bibliog. $24.95. ISBN: 0-387-97540-3.

The field of computer graphics is an everchanging field with new terms coined on a regular basis. This dictionary covers the most encountered terms. Other good graphics dictionaries include Donald D. Spencer's *Illustrated Computer Graphics Dictionary* (Camelot, 1992) and John Vince's *Language of Computer Graphics* (Architecture Design and Technology, 1990).

539. Dictionary of Computing. 3rd. Valerie Illingworth. New York, NY: Oxford University Press, 1990. 510p., illus. $39.95. ISBN: 0-19-853825-1.

This dictionary of computer terminology is very authoritative and frequently updated. Another good British-oriented dictionary is Don B. Lynch's *Concise Dictionary of Computing and Information Technology* (Chartwell-Bratt, 1991).

Directories

540. CD-ROM Directory with Multimedia CD's. London, Great Britain: TFPL, 1986– , semiannual. v.1– , index. $72.00.

This semiannual worldwide listing of CD-ROM database companies gives information about the company and its products. It also includes some 3,500 titles of electronic books and multimedia titles plus hardware and software information. A listing of some 1,400 commercially available CD-ROMs can be found in *CD-ROMs in Print, 1991: An International Guide* (Meckler, 1991). Also of use is Chris Sherman's *CD-ROM Handbook* (McGraw-Hill, 1994).

541. Computer Directory and Buyer's Guide. Newtonville, MA: Berkely Enterprises, 1974– , annual. v.1– , index. $35.00.

This alphabetical list by name of some 3,600 firms in the computing field gives a brief description of firms' services, products, facilities, and hardware leasing. Also useful is the *Microcomputer Market Place* (Random House, 1992).

542. Computer Publishers and Publications. Detroit, MI: Gale, 1984– , irregular. v.1– , index. $205.00. ISSN: 0740-4085.

CPP describes some 240 book publishers covering the computer field and lists some 1,200 computer journals. It has periodic supplements between editions.

543. Computer-Readable Data Bases. Kathleen Y. Marcaccio. Detroit, MI: Gale,v.1– , index. $170.00. ISSN: 0271-4477.

Also called *Computer-Readable Databases* and previously called *Computer-Readable Bibliographic Data Bases*, this directory covers over 6,000 databases. Each database is profiled and described in detail. It covers online and transactional databases produced worldwide, CD-ROM databases, electronic bulletin boards, off-line files available for batch processing, and databases on magnetic tape or diskette. For just portable databases consult *Directory of Portable Databases* (Gale, 1970-) which describes more than 1,900 databases.

544. Computers and Computing Information Resources Directory. Detroit, MI: Gale, 1986– , biennial. v.1– , index. $195.00; $100.00/supplement. ISSN: 0894-8941.

A source of information about computer applications, including publications, associations, research organizations, consultants, trade shows, libraries, publishers, online services, and teleprocessing networks.

545. Database Directory. White Plains, NY: Knowledge Industry, 1984– , annual with mid-year supplement. v.1– , index. $395.00. ISSN: 0749-6680.

This directory lists databases and their distributors, including pricing information. It is also available online.

546. Datapro Directory of Microcomputer Software. Delran, NJ: Datapro, 1981– , 3 annual base volumes with monthly issues. v.1– , index. $820.00. ISSN: 0730-8795.

This comprehensive directory lists proprietary microcomputer software. Datapro publishes several directories of this type, all with a main volume and then monthly updates. Another well-established one is the *Datapro Directory of Software* (Datapro, 1975-). The periodically published *Software Catalog* (Elsevier, 1984-1990) also is a source that is published in several volumes: *Microcomputers* (1989), *Science and Engineering* (1987), *Systems* (1985), *Health Professions* (1984), and *Business* (1985).

547. Directory of Online Databases. Detroit, MI: Gale, 1979– , quarterly. v.1– , index. ISSN: 0193-6840.

This directory describes some 4,900 databases that are publicly available to online users. It gives information on database producers and the names of online services or vendors. For a directory that stresses British sources consult J.L. Hall and Marjorie J. Brown's *Online Bibliographic Databases* (Aslib, 1986).

548. PC-SIG Encyclopedia of Shareware. 4th. Blue Ridge Summit, PA: TAB, 1982. 704p., illus., index. $19.95. ISBN: 0-8306-2669-7.

PC-SIG shareware is described in this directory, covering spreadsheets, word processors, databases, educational programs, graphics, programming tools, and games.

549. Software Encyclopedia: A Guide for Personal, Professional and Business Users. New York, NY: Bowker, 1992. 2v., index. $209.95. ISBN: 0-8352-3182-8.

This extensive listing of some 16,000 available software packages is indexed by title and by compatible system and application. It is revised frequently.

Encyclopedias

550. Concise Encyclopedia of Information Processing in Systems and Organizations. *(Advances in Systems, Control and Information Engineering).* Andrew P. Sage. New York, NY: Pergamon Press, 1990. 548p., illus., bibliog., index. $290.00. ISBN: 0-08-035954-X.

Based on the *Systems and Control Encyclopedia* (Pergamon Press, 1987) this is a concise source of information on information processing, both human and machine.

551. Encyclopedia Macintosh. Craig Danuloff; Deke McClelland. San Francisco, CA: Sybex, 1990. 782p., illus., index. $27.95. ISBN: 0-89588-628-6.

This very practical encyclopedia is for those who use the popular Macintosh pcs. It provides information on the selection of hardware and software, subscriptions, books, bulletin boards, user groups, and vendors.

552. Encyclopedia of Computer Science. 3rd. Anthony Ralston; Edwin D. Reilly, Jr. New York, NY: Van Nostrand Reinhold, 1992. 1,736p., illus. (part in color), glossary. $125.00. ISBN: 0-442-27679-6.

Previously called *Encyclopedia of Computer Science and Engineering*, this has become the authoritative encyclopedia for computer science. It is arranged by 9 topical headings with each article separately authored. For information on artificial intelligence, consult Stuart C. Shapiro's *Encyclopedia of Artificial Intelligence* (Wiley, 1992).

553. Encyclopedia of Computer Science and Technology. New York, NY: Dekker, 1975– , irregular. v.1– , index. $170.00/volume. ISBN: 0-8247-2273-6v.23.

This very well-accepted encyclopedic series covers all aspects of computer science. Each volume contains a review of research and technology for that period.

554. Encyclopedia of Microcomputers. Allen Kent; James G. Williams; Rosalind Kent. New York, NY: Dekker, 1988– , irregular. v.1– , bibliog., index. $175.00/volume. ISBN: 0-8247-2279-5v. 10.

This encyclopedic series provides current articles pertaining to microcomputers. Each volume stands alone with no overall index to all volumes.

555. Macmillan Encyclopedia of Computers. Gary G. Bitter. New York, NY: Macmillan, 1992. 2v., illus., index. $175.00. ISBN: 0-02-897045-4.

This British counterpart to the Van Nostrand work *Encyclopedia of Computer Science* is a comprehensive source of information.

556. McGraw-Hill Encyclopedia of Electronics and Computers. 2nd. Sybil P. Parker. New York, NY: McGraw-Hill, 1988. 992p., illus., index. $79.95. ISBN: 0-07-045499-X.

Material from the *McGraw-Hill Encyclopedia of Science and Technology* has been used to compile this authoritative work on computers and electronics. The language is technical but understandable for the layperson and student.

557. McGraw-Hill Personal Computer Programming Encyclopedia: Languages and Operating Systems. 2nd. William J. Birnes. New York, NY: McGraw-Hill, 1989. 752p., illus., bibliog., index. $95.00. ISBN: 0-07-005393-6.

Also called *Personal Computer Programming Encyclopedia*, this encyclopedia is a very good reference source on pc programming. All languages and operating systems are discussed and examples of features are included.

Guides to the Literature

558. Computing Information Directory. Pullman, WA: Hildebrandt, 1985– , irregular. v.1– , index. $229.95. ISBN: 0-933113-13-7 1992 ed.

Also called *CID*, this directory is the most comprehensive guide to computer literature available. It contains lists with descriptions of journals, newsletters, books, dictionaries, indexes, abstracts, software resources, review resources, directories, computer languages, ACM publications, standards, and publishers. An older work is Darlene Meyers' *Computer Science Resources: A Guide to Professional Literature* (Greenwood, 1981).

559. Keyguide to Information Sources in Artificial Intelligence/Expert Systems. Peter J. Hancox; William J. Mills; Bruce J. Reid. Lawrence, KS: Ergosyst Associates, 1990. 288p., index. $75.00. ISBN: 0-916313-18-2.

A good bibliographic guide to artificial intelligence information. Another specialized guide is John Cox's *Keyguide to Information Sources in CAD/CAM* (Mansell, 1988).

Handbooks and Manuals

560. Computer Security Handbook. 2nd. Richard H. Baker. Blue Ridge Summit, PA: TAB, 1991. 310p., illus., bibliog., index. $34.95; $24.95pbk. ISBN: 0-8306-7592-2; 0-8306-3592-0pbk.

This practical handbook contains information pertaining to the ever-changing security of computers. It is understandable for the layperson. Another useful handbook is Richard Levin's *Computer Virus Handbook* (Osborne-McGraw-Hill, 1990).

561. Handbook of Artificial Intelligence. Avron Barr; Edward A. Feigenbaum. Redding, MA: Addison-Wesley, 1981-1989. 4v., illus., bibliog., index. price per volume varies. ISBN: 0-201-51819-8v.4.

This comprehensive handbook covers artificial intelligence, including searching, knowledge representation, and natural language. The material is detailed and well-documented.

562. Handbook of Computer-Communication Standards. William Stallings. New York, NY: Macmillan, 1987-1990. 3v., illus., index. price per volume varies. ISBN: 0-672-22696-0.

This collection of informative chapters brings together a wealth of communications information that is usually in technical reports. It has excellent illustrations. The 3 volumes cover v.1—The open system interconnection (OSI) model and OSI-related standards; v.2—Local network standards; v.3—TCP-IP protocol suite (Department of Defense).

563. Handbook of Software Maintenance: A Treasury of Technical and Managerial Tips, Techniques, Guidelines, Ideas, Sources, and Case Studies for Efficient, Effective, and Economical Software Maintenance. Girish Parikh. New York, NY: Wiley, 1986. 421p., illus., bibliog., index. $62.95. ISBN: 0-471-82813-0.

This title is a very good practical handbook for those who manage software products.

564. McGraw-Hill Computer Handbook. Harry L. Helms. New York, NY: McGraw-Hill, 1983. 1v. various paging, illus., bibliog., index. $89.95. ISBN: 0-07-027972-1.

Although becoming somewhat dated, this work is still a good handbook of computer basics. It duplicates some information found in other McGraw-Hill handbooks and encyclopedias.

565. Microcomputer Applications Handbook. William J. Birnes. New York, NY: McGraw-Hill, 1990. 645p., illus., index. $79.95. ISBN: 0-07-005397-9.

This practical handbook for the nonprofessional covers operating systems, various applications, and languages that are found in the use of microcomputer systems.

Histories

566. Bibliographic Guide to the History of Computing, Computers, and the Information Processing Industry. James W. Cortada. New York, NY: Greenwood Press, 1990. 644p. $79.50. ISBN: 0-313-26810-X.

This expanded version of the *Annotated Bibliography on the History of Data Processing* is a comprehensive guide to the history of computing.

567. Historical Dictionary of Data Processing. James W. Cortada. New York, NY: Greenwood Press, 1987. 3v., index. $65.00v.1; $65.00v.2; $75.00v.3. ISBN: 0-313-25651-9v.1; 0-313-23303-9v.2; 0-313-25652-7v.3.

This good historical overview of data processing covers in 3 volumes: Biographies, Organizations, and Technology.

568. History of Programming Languages. Richard L. Wexelblat. New York, NY: Academic Press, 1981. 758p., illus., index. $57.00. ISBN: 0-12-745040-8.

Based on the proceedings of a 1978 conference in Los Angeles, this interesting work covers just programming languages, showing how they have evolved. For an interesting general history of computing consult N. Metropolis' *History of Computing in the Twentieth Century* (Academic Press, 1980).

Periodicals

569. Byte. Peterborough, NH: McGraw-Hill, 1975– , monthly. v.1– , index. $29.95. ISSN: 0360-5280.

570. Compute. Greensboro, NC: Computer Publications, 1979– , monthly. v.1– , index. $19.95. ISSN: 0194-357X.

571. Computer Journal. New York, NY: Cambridge University Press, 1958– , 6/year. v.1 , index. $355.00. ISSN: 0010-4620.

572. Computers and Education. Tarrytown, NY: Pergamon Press, 1977– , 8/year. v.1– , index. $552.00. ISSN: 0360-1315.

573. Computers in Education Journal. Port Royal, VA: American Society for Engineering Education, 1965– , quarterly. v.1– , index. $45.00.

574. Data Processing Digest. Los Angeles, CA: Data Processing Digest, 1955– , monthly. v.1– , index. $175.00. ISSN: 0011-6858.

575. Datamation. Newton, MA: Cahners, 1957– , 24/year. v.1– , index. $69.00. ISSN: 0011-6963.

576. IBM Journal of Research and Development. Thornwood, NY: IBM, 1957– , bimonthly. v.1– , index. $30.00. ISSN: 0018-8646.

577. Information Sciences. New York, NY: Elsevier, 1969– , 24/year. v.1– , index. $1,088.00. ISSN: 0020-0255.

578. Infoworld. San Mateo, CA: Infoworld Publishing, 1979– , weekly. v.1– , index. $110.00. ISSN: 0199-6649.

579. Journal of the Association for Computing Machinery. New York, NY: Association for Computing Machinery, 1954– , quarterly. v.1– , index. $85.00. ISSN: 0004-5411.

580. MacWorld. San Francisco, CA: MacWorld Communications, 1984– , monthly. v.1– , index. $30.00. ISSN: 0741-8647.

581. PC Magazine: The Independent Guide to IBM Standard Personal Computing. New York, NY: Ziff-Davis, 1982– , fortnightly. v.1– , index. $29.97. ISSN: 0888-8507.

582. PC World. San Francisco, CA: PC World Communications, 1982– , monthly. v.1– , index. $29.90. ISSN: 0737-8939.

583. SIAM Journal on Computing. Philadelphia, PA: Society for Industrial and Applied Mathematics, 1972– , bimonthly. v.1– , index. $198.00. ISSN: 0001-4842.

EARTH SCIENCES

Abstracts and Indexes

584. Bibliography and Index of Micropaleontology. New York, NY: American Museum of Natural History, 1971– , monthly. v.1– , index. $660.00. ISSN: 0300-7227.

This work is an index of the world's literature pertaining to micropaleontology

585. Geotechnical Abstracts. Essen, Germany: German National Society/Soil Mechanics and Foundation Engineering. Dist: no.1– , index. 1970– , monthly. ISSN: 0016-8491.

This international abstracting service covers soil mechanics, foundation engineering, and engineering geology.

586. IMM Abstracts and Index. London, Great Britain: Institution of Mining and Metallurgy, 1950– , bimonthly. v.1– , index. $200.00.

Previously called *IMM Abstracts*, this publication surveys the world's literature on the economic geology and mining of all minerals except coal, mineral processing, and nonferrous extraction metallurgy. It is also available online.

587. Meteorological and Geoastrophysical Abstracts. Littleton, MA: American Meteorological Society, 1950– , monthly. v.1– , index. $750.00. ISSN: 0026-1130.

Called *Meteorological Abstracts and Bibliography 1950-59*, this abstracting service covers books, reports, research papers, and other literature pertaining to environmental sciences, meteorology, astrophysics, hydrology, glaciology, and physical oceanography. It is also available online and on CD-ROM.

588. Mineral Index. 3rd. A. Clark. New York, NY: Chapman & Hall, 1992. 700p. $95.00.

Popularly known as *Hey's Index*, this reference work indexes recognized mineral species on the basis of their chemical composition giving source of name, varieties, chemical composition, and type locality.

589. Mineralogical Abstracts. London, Great Britain: Oxford University Press, 1920– , quarterly. v.1– , index. $235.00. ISSN: 0026-4601.

Published for Mineralogical Society of Great Britain and Mineralogical Society of America, this service covers all the literature pertaining to mineralogy. It is also available online.

590. Oceanic Abstracts. Bethesda, MD: Cambridge Scientific Abstracts, 1964– , bimonthly. v.1– , index. $1,075.00. ISSN: 0748-1489.

Previously called *Oceanic Index* and *Oceanic Citation Index*, this source covers the literature in the fields of marine biology, oceanography, ships and shipping, marine pollution, and offshore engineering.

591. Zentralblatt fur Geologie und Paleontologie. Stuttgart, Germany: E. Schweizerbartsche, 1807– , monthly. v.1– , index. price varies. ISSN: 0340-5109 teil 1; 0044-4189 teil 2.

Previously called *Zentralblatt fur Mineralogie, Geologie und Palaeontologie*, this international index to geology and paleontology is arranged by broad subject topics. It is in 2 parts: Teil 1—Allgemeine, Angewandte, Regionale und Historische Geologie; Teil 2—Palaeontologie. A comparable service for mineralogy from the same publisher is *Zentralblatt fur Mineralogie* in two parts: teil 1—Kristallographie, Mineralogie; teil 2—Petrographie, Technische Mineralogie, Geochemie und Logerstaettenkunde.

Atlases

592. Atlas Geologique du monde/Geological World Atlas: 1:10,000,000. G. Chaubert; A. Faure-Muret. Paris, France: UNESCO, 1976– , irregular. 1v. looseleaf, maps, bibliog. price per piece varies. ISBN: 92-3-099916-4.

This work contains sheets issued on an irregular basis by the Commission for the Geological Map of the World providing a clear, concise geological map of the world. The geologic features are described and sources of data and references are provided. Peter A. Ziegler's *Geologic Atlas of Western and Central Europe* (Elsevier, 1982) is also useful.

593. Atlas of Continental Displacement: 200 Million Years to the Present. *Cambridge Earth Science Series.* H.G. Owen. New York, NY: Cambridge University Press, 1983. 159p., illus., maps, bibliog. price not available. ISBN: 0-521-25817-0.

This interesting atlas shows how the earth's crust has moved over the last 200 million years.

594. Atlas of Economic Mineral Deposits. Colin J. Dixon. Ithaca, NY: Cornell University Press, 1979. 143p., illus., bibliog., index. $130.00. ISBN: 0-8014-1231-5.

This valuable reference source provides maps and information on the distribution of 48 solid, noncombustible mineral deposits. Another newer atlas is R.A. Ixer's *Atlas of Opaque and Ore Minerals and Their Associations* (Van Nostrand Reinhold, 1990).

595. Atlas of Landforms. 3rd. H. Allen Curran. New York, NY: Wiley, 1984. 165p., illus. (part in color), maps, bibliog., index. $56.95. ISBN: 0-471-87434-5.

This excellent source of information for the physical geographer and geomorphologist provides information on land forms through the use of full-color images, topographic maps, and remote sensing images.

596. Atlas of Metamorphic Rocks and Their Textures. B.W.D. Yardley; W.S. MacKenzie; C. Guilford. New York, NY: Wiley, 1990. 120p., illus. $39.95. ISBN: 0-582-30166-1.

This specialized photographic atlas of metamorphic rocks shows the detailed make-up and textures of these rocks.

597. Climatic Atlas of Europe/Atlas Climatique de l'Europe. F. Steinhauser. Geneva, Switzerland: World Meteorological Organization, 1970. 1v., various paging, maps. out-of-print.

This atlas and the edition *Climatic Atlas of North and Central America* (World Meteorological Organization, 1979) comprise 2 excellent sources of climate information for Europe and North America.

598. National Atlas of the United States of America. Arch C. Gerlach; U.S. Geological Survey. Washington, DC: U.S. Geological Survey, 1970. 417p., maps, index. out-of-print.

This first national atlas covering the United States contains 756 maps divided by the following topics: general reference, physical, historical, economic, sociocultural, administrative, mapping and charting, and the world.

599. Our Magnificent Earth: A Rand McNally Atlas of Earth Resources. New York, NY: Rand McNally, 1979. 208p., illus., maps, bibliog., index. out-of-print.

Previously called *Atlas of Earth Resources*, this atlas shows the location of such resources as minerals, energy sources, food, and forests. It includes text, bibliography, and index.

600. Random House Atlas of the Oceans. Danny Elder; John Pernetta. New York, NY: Random House, 1991. 200p., illus., index. $40.00. ISBN: 0-679-40830-4.

This atlas shows the environmental status of the world's oceans, examining factors such as human impact, threatened species, topographical features, and other important regional issues. Another older source is the *Rand McNally Atlas of the Oceans* (Rand McNally, 1977).

601. Stratigraphic Atlas of North and Central America. T.D. Cook; A.W. Bally; Shell Oil Company Exploration Department. Princeton, NJ: Princeton University Press, 1977. 272p., maps, bibliog. $37.50. ISBN: 0-691-08189-1.

This extensive set of maps and reports covers the sedimentary basins of all geological periods and epochs. Emphasis is on hydrocarbon occurrence.

602. Times Atlas and Encyclopedia of the Sea. 2nd. Alastair Couper. London, Great Britain: Times Books, 1989. 272p., illus. (part in color), maps, index. $65.00. ISBN: 0-7230-0318-1.

Previously called *Times Atlas of the Oceans* this encyclopedic atlas covers the ocean environment, resources of the ocean, ocean trade, and the world ocean. Its purpose is to present the "activities of people in the context of the physical and biological features of the ocean."

603. World Atlas of Geology and Mineral Deposits. Duncan R. Derry; Lawrence Curtis. New York, NY: Halsted Press, 1980. 110p., color illus., maps, bibliog. out-of-print. ISBN: 0-470-26996-0.

Also called a *Concise World Atlas of Geology and Mineral Deposits*, this title is a general atlas of the major mineral resources of the world plus geological information.

604. World Atlas of Geomorphic Features. Rodman E. Snead. Huntington, NY: R.E. Krieger, 1980. 301p., color illus., maps, bibliog. $39.50. ISBN: 0-88275-272-3.

This excellent atlas of 63 major worldwide geomorphic features includes several man-made lakes.

605. World Ocean Atlas. Sergei G. Goishkov. New York, NY: Pergamon Press, 1976– , irregular. v.1– , illus., maps, index. price per volume varies. ISBN: 0-08-021953-5v.2.

This is the largest and most authoritative atlas of the world's oceans covering meteorology, physical oceanography, marine chemistry, biology, and geology. The 3 volumes published so far are v.1—Pacific Ocean; v.2—Atlantic and Indian Oceans; v.3—Arctic Ocean.

Bibliographies

606. Annotated Bibliographies of Mineral Deposits in Europe. John Drew Ridge. New York, NY: Pergamon Press, 1990. 2v., index. $280.00. ISBN: 0-08-024022-4.

This comprehensive bibliography provides locations of deposits, probable age of formation, metals or minerals for which it is being mined, and the Lindgren classification category. The 2 volumes cover v.1—Northern Europe including examples from the USSR in both Europe and Asia; v.2—Western and southern central Europe. Two similar bibliographies are John Drew Ridge's *Annotated Bibliographies of Mineral Deposits in Africa, Asia (Exclusive of USSR), and Australia* (Pergamon Press, 1976) and John Drew Ridge's *Annotated Bibliographies of Mineral Deposits in the Western Hemisphere* (Geological Society of America, 1972).

607. Antarctic Bibliography. Washington, DC: GPO, 1965– , every 18 months. v.1– , index. price per volume varies. ISSN: 0066-4626.

This index to the literature of Antarctica covers expeditions, biology, geology, logistics, and other related areas. A 26-volume work on the Arctic was prepared by the Arctic Institute of North America called *Arctic Bibliography* (McGill-Queen's University Press, 1947-1975). It is also available online and on CD-ROM.

608. Bibliography and Index of Geology. Falls Church, VA: American Geological Institute, 1969– , monthly with annual cumulations. v.33– , index. $1,295.00. ISSN: 0098-2784.

Continuing *Bibliography and Index of Geology Exclusive of North America* (1923-1971); *Bibliography of North American Geology* (1923-1971); and *Abstracts of North American Geology* (1966-1971), this publication is the major indexing source for the geosciences. In addition to periodicals it covers books, papers, and maps. It is also available online and on CD-ROM. Other retrospective sources include the *Geological Abstracts* (Geological Society of America, 1953-1958) and *Geoscience Abstracts* (American Geological Institute, 1959-1966). For retrospective coverage of economic geology consult the *Annotated*

Bibliography of Economic Geology (Economic Geology, 1929-1966).

609. Bibliography of American Published Geology, 1669-1850. Robert M. Hazen. Boulder, CO: Geological Society of America, 1976. 1v., index. out-of-print.

Some 13,700 entries are included covering the geological literature published in the United States during 1669-1850.

610. Bibliography of Fossil Vertebrates. Society of Vertebrate Paleontology. Lincoln, NE: Society of Vertebrate Paleontology, 1902– , annual. v.1– , index. $135.00. ISSN: 0272-8869.

These specialized bibliographies periodically published as an issue of the *Memoirs of the Geological Society of America* are now an annual providing the latest citations to fossil vertebrate literature.

611. Catalogue of Published Bibliographies in Geology, 1896-1920. *NAS-NRC Bulletin 36.* Edward Bennett Mathews. Washington, DC: National Research Council, 1923. 228p., index. out-of-print.

Now out-of-print, this government document is a good source of published bibliographies pertaining to the geosciences.

612. Earth Sciences: An Annotated Bibliography. *(Bibliographies of the History of Science and Technology, v.3) (Garland Reference Library of the Humanities, v.315).* Roy Porter. New York, NY: Garland, 1983. 192p., index. out-of-print. ISBN: 0-8240-9267-8.

This small annotated bibliography is to key materials in the geosciences.

613. Gemology: An Annotated Bibliography. John Sinkankas. Metuchen, NJ: Scarecrow Press, 1993. 2v., illus., index. $179.50. ISBN: 0-8108-2652-6.

Based on John and Marjorie Sinkankas' personal library of over 14,000 materials, this comprehensive bibliography contains some 7,500 entries describing in detail rare books from the 16th and 17th centuries as well as currently published materials. It covers all types of materials in all languages and includes biographical details of noted gemologists.

614. Geotitles. Didcat, Great Britain: Geosystem, 1969– , monthly. v.1– , index. $800.00.

Previously called *Geotitles Weekly*, this publication is a current awareness source to the published geological literature. It is also available online.

615. Index of State Geological Survey Publications Issued in Series. John Boyd Corbin. Metuchen, NY: Scarecrow Press, 1965. 667p., index. out-of-print.

This history of all monographic publications that have been issued in series through 1962 by the state geological surveys is arranged by state, then series. A supplement was published for 1963-1980.

616. Index to Maps in Earth Science Publications, 1963-1983. John Van Balen. Westport, CT: Greenwood Press, 1985. 400p. price not available. ISBN: 0-813-24963-6.

Maps in earth science publications are indexed for 1963-1983. Each is identified by type and topic with full bibliographic citation.

617. New Publications of the Geological Survey. Washington, DC: GPO, 1971– , monthly. no.1– , index. price varies.

This title contains lists of publications of the U.S. Geological Survey and supplements the permanent catalogs: *Publications of the Geological Survey 1879-1961* and *Publications of the Geological Survey 1962-1970.* For information on how to obtain USGS publications consult Kurt Dodd's *Guide to Obtaining USGS Information* (GPO, 1989).

618. Union List of Geologic Field Trip Guidebooks of North America. 5th. Charlotte Derksen; Geoscience Information Society. Alexandria, VA: American Geological Institute, 1989. 223p., index. $60.00. ISBN: 0-913312-97-5.

Kept up to date by the Geoscience Information Society, this excellent union list identifies the illusive fieldtrip guidebooks, giving complete citations and indicating libraries that have the particular titles.

Dictionaries, Glossaries, and Thesauri

619. Challinor's Dictionary of Geology. 6th. John Challinor; Antony Wyatt. New York, NY: Oxford University Press, 1986. 374p., index. $16.95. ISBN: 0-19-520506-5.

Previously called a *Dictionary of Geology*, this small dictionary covers geological terms and places them in relation to those terms and concepts in other fields. Other small dictionaries are P.M.B. Walker's *Chambers Earth Sciences Dictionary* (Chambers, 1992) and D.G.A. Whitten's *Penguin Dictionary of Geology* (Penguin, 1978).

620. Chambers World Gazetteer: An A-Z of Geographical Information. 5th. David Munro. New York, NY: Cambridge University Press, 1988. 733p., maps, index. price not available. ISBN: 1-85296-200-3.

This is one of the best regularly updated geographical dictionaries available. It includes an atlas.

621. Concise Oxford Dictionary of Earth Sciences. Ailsa Allaby; Michael Allaby. New York, NY: Oxford University Press, 1990. 410p., bibliog. $35.00. ISBN: 0-19-866146-0.

Though not as comprehensive as other geological dictionaries this work is an excellent, up-to-date source for most terms associated with earth sciences.

622. Dictionary of Earth Science, English-French, French-English/Dictionnaire des Sciences de la Terre, Anglais-Francais, Francais-Anglais. 2nd. Jean Pierre Michel; Rhodes Whitmore Fairbridge. New York, NY: Wiley/Masson Science Reference, 1992. 301p. $70.00. ISBN: 0-47193-535-2.

This publication is one of the better French language dictionaries for the earth sciences.

623. Dictionary of Earth Sciences. Stella E. Stiegeler. Lanham, MD: Rowman, 1983 (c1976). 301p., illus. $9.95. ISBN: 0-8226-0377-2.

Being a companion to a *Dictionary of Life Sciences* and a *Dictionary of Physical Sciences*, this popular dictionary is still useful in spite of its 1976 copyright.

624. Dictionary of Gemology. 2nd. Peter G. Read. Boston, MA: Butterworths, 1988. 256p., illus. $54.95. ISBN: 0-408-00571-8.

This dictionary covers all terms associated with the field of gemology and related areas including some mineralogical terms. Other useful related books are Richard S. Mitchell's *Dictionary of Rocks* (Van Nostrand Reinhold, 1985); Michael Fleischer's *Glossary of Mineral Species* (Glossary Mineralogical Record, 1980); Richard S. Mitchell's *Mineral Names: What Do They Mean?* (Van Nostrand Reinhold, 1979); and Robert Latimer Bates' *Mineral Resources A-Z* (Enslow, 1991).

625. Dictionary of Geosciences: Containing Approximately 38,000 Terms. Adolf Watznauer. New York, NY: Elsevier, 1982. 2v., index. $154.00. ISBN: 0-444-99701-6v.1; 0-444-99702-4v.2.

This dictionary is a translation of a well-established German language dictionary, *Worterbuch Geowissenschaften*.

626. Dictionary of Geotechnics. S.H. Somerville; M.A. Paul. Boston, MA: Butterworths, 1983. 283p., illus., index. $70.00. ISBN: 0-408-00437-1.

This dictionary covers the terms associated with soil and rock mechanics and other fields of engineering geology.

627. Dictionary of Landscape: A Dictionary of Terms Used in the Description of the World's Land Surface. George A. Goulty. Brookfield, VT: Gower, 1991. 309p. $59.95. ISBN: 1-85628-214-7.

This useful dictionary defines terms in the field of geomorphology and physical geography.

628. Dictionary of Petrology. S.I. Tomkeieff; E.K. Walton. New York, NY: Wiley, 1983. 680p., bibliog., index. $180.00. ISBN: 0-471-10159-1.

This work is the most authoritative dictionary covering terms associated with sedimentary, metamorphic, and igneous petrology.

629. Dictionary of Soil Science. 2nd. Jean Lozet; Clement Mathieu. Rotterdam, Netherlands: A.A. Balkema, 1991. 348p., illus., bibliog. $80.00. ISBN: 90-5410201-2.

This translation of *Dictionaire de Science du Sol* contains some 2,800 terms pertaining to soil science and related areas of mineralogy, petrology, geomorphology, and hydrology.

630. Elsevier's Dictionary of Geosciences: Russian-English. K.P. Bhatnagar. New York, NY: Elsevier, 1991. 1,023p. $225.75. ISBN: 0-444-88425-4.

This bilingual dictionary contains some 56,000 terms used in geochemistry, physical chemistry, geology, tectonics, meteorology, climatology, mineralogy, oceanography, paleontology, petroleum exploration, petrology, petrography, rock mechanics, and sedimentology. Another related work is V.M. Kotlyakov and N.A. Smolyarova's *Elsevier's Dictionary of Glaciology in English, Russian, French and German* (Elsevier, 1991).

631. Elsevier's Dictionary of Hydrological and Hydrogeological Environment: Russian-English/English-Russian. R.G. Dzhamalov; I.S. Zektser; R.A. Kanivetsky. New York, NY: Elsevier, 1992. 510p., index. $171.50. ISBN: 0-444-88419-X.

Close to 10,000 specialized terms from hydrology, hydrogeology, environmental sciences, and related fields are included with the emphasis on concepts. Also of interest would be J.D. Van der Turin's *Elsevier's Dictionary of Hydrogeology and Water Quality Management: English, French, Spanish, Dutch, and German* (Elsevier, 1991).

632. Facts on File Dictionary of Geology and Geophysics. Dorothy Lapidus; Donald R. Coates. New York, NY: Facts on File, 1987. 347p., illus. $24.95. ISBN: 0-87196-703-0.

This publication is a popular but authoritative dictionary of geology and geophysics.

633. Facts on File Dictionary of Marine Sciences. Barbara Charton. New York, NY: Facts on File, 1988. 325p., illus. $12.95. ISBN: 0-8160-2369-7.

This good general dictionary covers terminology associated with marine science, oceanography, and other related fields. An older but still useful work is David F. Tver's *Ocean and Marine Dictionary* (Cornell Maritime, 1979).

634. GeoRef Thesaurus and Guide to Indexing. 5th. Ruth H. Shimomura. Alexandria, VA: American Geological Institute, 1989. 731p., illus., bibliog. $75.00. ISBN: 0-913312-98-3.

Also called *GeoRef Thesaurus*, this is the Bible for a GeoRef database search.

635. Glossary of Geology. 3rd. Robert Latimer Bates; Julia A. Jackson. Alexandria, VA: American Geological Institute, 1987. 788p. $75.00. ISBN: 0-913312-89-4.

This well-accepted dictionary of geological terms is published by the American Geological Institute. An abridged edition was published as *Dictionary of Geological Terms* (Anchor Press, 1976).

636. McGraw-Hill Dictionary of Earth Sciences. 3rd. Sybil P. Parker. New York, NY: McGraw-Hill, 1984. 837p., illus. $46.95. ISBN: 0-07-045252-0.

This comprehensive dictionary covers some 15,000 terms in the fields of climatology, geology, mineralogy, and petrology. It includes synonyms, acronyms, and abbreviations.

637. New Illustrated Dinosaur Dictionary. Helen Roney Sattler. New York, NY: Lothrop, Lee & Shepard Books, 1990. 363p., illus. (part in color). $27.95.

This revision of the *Illustrated Dinosaur Dictionary* describes all known dinosaurs and other animals of the Mesozoic era and includes general topics relating to dinosaurs. Another useful dictionary is Donald F. Glut's *Complete Dinosaur Dictionary* (Citadel, 1992), which is a reprint of the 1982 *New Dinosaur Dictionary*, also called in 1972 the *Dinosaur Dictionary*.

638. Penguin Dictionary of Physical Geography. J.B. Whittow. London, Great Britain: A. Lane, 1984. 591p., illus. $17.00. ISBN: 0-7139-1256-1.

This excellent small dictionary defines terms encountered in physical geography, geomorphology, and related areas of geology. Two other useful books in physical geography are F.J. Monkhouse and John Small's *Dictionary of the Natural Environment* (Wiley, 1978) and Dudley Stamp and Audrey N. Clark's *Glossary of Geographical Terms* (Longman, 1979).

Directories

639. Directory of Geoscience Departments, North America. Alexandria, VA: American Geological Institute, 1989– , annual. v.28– , index. $22.00.

Previously called *Directory of Geoscience Departments, United States and Canada*, this annual provides names, addresses, and other information on the geoscience departments on the North American continent.

640. E & MJ International Directory of Mining. New York, NY: Engineering and Mining Journal, 1968– , annual. v.1– , illus., index. $126.00.

Previously called *E & MJ International Directory of Mining and Mineral Processing Operations* this annual issue of the *Engineering and Mining Journal* provides up-to-date information about the world's mining industry.

641. Earth and Astronomical Sciences Research Centers. Jennifer M. Fitch. Detroit, MI: Gale/Longman, 1991. 630p., index. $475.00. ISBN: 0-582-08274-9.

This directory provides a country-by-country survey of some 3,000 national and international government and university research centers, industrial and academic laboratories, consultants, and societies in over 100 countries. Covers geology, cartography, surveying, oceanography, meteorology, climatology, planetary and galactic observatories, geochemistry, mineralogy, petrology, mining, and seismology.

642. Geophysical Directory. Houston, TX: Geophysical Directory, Inc, 1946– , annual. v.1– , index. $45.00.

This directory lists oil companies and key personnel who use geophysical techniques plus supply and service companies in petroleum and mineral exploration. Also useful is W. O'Reilly's *International Directory of Geophysical Research* (Elsevier, 1986).

643. Map Collections in the United States and Canada: A Directory. 4th. David K. Carrington; Richard W. Stephenson. Washington, DC: Special Libraries Association, 1985. 178p., index. $35.00. ISBN: 0-87111-306-6.

Alphabetically arranged by city within state or province sections, this directory describes over 700 map libraries in the United States and Canada.

644. World Directory of Map Collections. 2nd. *(IFLA Publications, 31)*. John A. Wolter; Ronald E. Grim; David K. Carrington. New York, NY: K.G. Saur, 1986. 405p., bibliog., index. $36.50. ISBN: 0-86291-296-2.

This directory describes some 285 worldwide map collections giving addresses, personnel, size, range of collections, services provided, and classification schemes used.

Encyclopedias

645. Cambridge Encyclopedia of Earth Sciences. David G. Smith. New York, NY: Cambridge University Press, 1982. 496p., illus. (part in color), bibliog., index. $47.50. ISBN: 0-521-23900-1.

This general earth science encyclopedia is for the layperson and undergraduate but still useful at the research level. Another useful but out-of-date work is Cornelius S. Hurlburt Jr.'s the *Planet We Live On* (Abrams, 1976).

646. Clouds of the World: Complete Color Encyclopedia. Richard S. Scorer. Harrisburg, PA: Stackpole Books, 1972. 176p., color illus., bibliog. out-of-print. ISBN: 0-8117-1961-8.

Although out-of-print, this is an excellent encyclopedia of cloud formations with some 330 color photographs.

647. Encyclopedia of Earth Sciences Series. Rhodes Whitmore Fairbridge. Stroudsburg, PA: Dowden, Hutchison & Ross, 1966– , irregular. v.1– , illus., bibliog., index. price per volume varies.

This comprehensive treatise-like encyclopedia covers all areas of the earth sciences. Volumes published so far are v.1- *Encyclopedia of Oceanography*, 1966; v.2—*Encyclopedia of Atmospheric Sciences and Astrogeology*, 1967; v.3—*Encyclopedia of Geomorphology*, 1968; v.4a—*Encyclopedia of Geochemistry and Environmental Sciences*, 1972; v.4b—*Encyclopedia of Sedimentology*, 1978; v.7—*Encyclopedia of Paleontology*, 1979; v.8—*Encyclopedia of World Regional Geology*, 1975; v.9—*Encyclopedia of Solid Earth Geopohysics*, 1989; v.10—*Encyclopedia of Structural Geology and Plate Tectonics*, 1987; v.11—*Encyclopedia of Climatology*, 1987; v.12—*Encyclopedia of Soil Science*, 1979; v.13—*Encyclopedia of Applied Geology*, 1984; v.14—*Encyclopedia of Field and General Geology*, 1988; v.15—*Encyclopedia of Beaches and Coastal Environments*, 1982; v.16—*Encyclopedia of Igneous and Metamorphic Petrology*, 1989.

648. Encyclopedia of Earth System Sciences. William A. Niernberg. San Diego, CA: Academic Press, 1992. 4v., illus., bibliog., index. $950.00. ISBN: 0-12-226720-6.

This encyclopedia of articles stresses human interactions with the earth's environment. A detailed index refers one to the specific topics.

649. Encyclopedia of Gemstones and Minerals. Martin Holden. New York, NY: Facts on File, 1991. 303p., illus., bibliog., index. $45.00. ISBN: 0-8160-2177-5.

This alphabetically arranged encyclopedia of some 225 minerals and gemstones gives descriptions, physical properties, where found, how formed, and uses. Also as useful and colorful is Joel E. Arem's *Color Encyclopedia of Gemstones* (Van Nostrand Reinhold, 1987). See also, the more comprehensive *Encyclopedia of Minerals*.

650. Encyclopedia of Marine Sciences. J.G. Baretta-Bekker; E.K. Duursma. New York, NY: Springer-Verlag, 1992. 311p., bibliog. $39.00. ISBN: 0-387-54501-8.

This small encyclopedia of some 1,850 entries covers marine biology, marine geology, physical oceanography, and marine chemistry in concise entries.

651. Encyclopedia of Minerals. 2nd. Willard Lincoln Roberts; George Robert Rapp, Jr.; Thomas J. Campbell. New York, NY: Van Nostrand Reinhold, 1990. 979p., illus. $109.95. ISBN: 0-442-27681-8.

This comprehensive and colorful encyclopedia of minerals is alphabetically arranged, giving complete descriptions and illustrations of minerals. For a smaller, but still useful work, see *Encyclopedia of Gemstones and Minerals*. A spin-off of the first edition was called *VNR Color Dictionary of Minerals and Gemstones* (1982). Other older, well-known encyclopedias covering minerals include *Larousse Guide to Minerals, Rocks, and Fossils* (Larousse, 1974) and *Encyclopedia of Minerals and Gemstones* (Orbis, 1976).

652. Encyclopedia of the Solid Earth Sciences. Philip Kearey. Cambridge, MA: Blackwell, 1993. 713p., illus., bibliog., index. $180.00. ISBN: 0-632-02577-8.

Some 2,700 entries are included in this comprehensive encyclopedia covering geochemistry, geomorphology, geophysics, petrology, mineralogy, paleontology, stratigraphy, sedimentology, structural geology, economic geology, and volcanology. Entries are brief, up to 1,500 words in length.

653. Geologic Names of the U.S. Through 1975. *(U.S. Geological Survey Bulletin 1535).* Roger W. Swanson. Washington, DC: GPO, 1981. 643p., bibliog., index. $9.00.

This publication is a summary index of U.S. geologic names. For detailed information about geologic formations and stratigraphic classifications and nomenclatures with descriptions, citations where first described and type locality consult the following: *North American Geologic Formation Names* by Fred B. Weeks (USGS Bulletin 191); *Names and Definitions of the Geologic Units of California* by M. Grace Wilmarth (USGS Bulletin 826); *Lexicon of Geologic*

Names of the U.S. (Including Alaska) by M. Grace Wilmarth (USGS Bulletin 896); *Geologic Names of North America Introduced in 1936-1966* by Druid Wilson (USGS Bulletin 1056A); *Index to the Geologic Names of North America* by Druid Wilson (USGS Bulletin 1956B); *Lexicon of Geologic Names of the United States for 1936-1960* by Grace C. Keroher (USGS Bulletin 1200); *Lexicon of Geologic Names of the United States for 1961-1967* by Grace C. Keroher (USGS Bulletin 1350); *Lexicon of Geologic Names of the United States for 1968-1975* by Gwendolyn W. Luttrell (USGS Bulletin 1520).

654. Illustrated Encyclopedia of Dinosaurs. David Norman. London, Great Britain: Salamander, 1985. 208p. (illus., (part in color), index. $12.98. ISBN: 0-8610-1225-9.

This encyclopedia provides descriptions of the more common dinosaurs for the lay reader. George S. Paul's *Predatory Dinosaurs of the World* (Simon & Schuster, 1988) is also an important source.

655. Illustrated Encyclopedia of Fossils. Giovanni Pinna. New York, NY: Facts on File, 1990. 256p., illus. $35.00. ISBN: 0-8160-2149-X.

Good illustrations and concise text make this an excellent encyclopedia of fossils, including the dinosaurs. Rodney Steel and Anthony P. Harvey's *Encyclopedia of Pre-Historic Life* (McGraw-Hill, 1979) is also useful.

656. Index Fossils of North America: A New Work Based on the Complete Revision and Reillustration of Grabau and Shimer's "North American Index Fossils". H.W. Shimer. New York, NY: Wiley, 1944. 837p., illus., bibliog., index. out-of-print.

Though out-of-print, this work is the authority on index fossils and their localities for the North American Continent. Each one is identified with bibliographic notations.

657. Index of Generic Names of Fossil Plants, 1820-1965. *(U.S. Geological Survey Bulletin 1300).* Henry Nathaniel Andrews. Washington, DC: GPO, 1970. 354p., index. out-of-print.

This index revises and updates the *U.S. Geological Survey Bulletin 1013* and is based on the *Compendium Index of Paleobotany*. Each entry gives age, geographic origin, and taxonomic status. It has two supplements, one for 1966-73 by Anna M. Blazer (*U.S. Geological Survey Bulletin 1396*) and 1974-78 by Arthur Dwight Watt (*U.S. Geological Survey Bulletin 1517*).

658. Magill's Survey of Science: Earth Science Series. Frank N. Magill; James A. Woodhead. Pasadena, CA: Salem Press, 1990. 5v., illus., bibliog., index. $400.00. ISBN: 0-89356-606-3.

Arranged by topic, this encyclopedia covers all the major topics in earth sciences. The articles are all in the same format with summary of phenomena, methods of study, summary of methodology, and applications. A detailed index provides access to specific topics.

659. McGraw-Hill Encyclopedia of the Geological Sciences. Daniel Lapedes. New York, NY: McGraw-Hill, 1988. 915p., illus., index. $89.95. ISBN: 0-07-045265-2.

This title and Sybil P. Parker's *McGraw-Hill Encyclopedia of Ocean and Atmospheric Sciences* (McGraw-Hill, 1980) cover all of the earth sciences with most articles having appeared in the *McGraw-Hill Encyclopedia of Science and Technology*.

660. Meteorology Source Book. McGraw-Hill Editors. New York, NY: McGraw-Hill, 1989. 304p., index. $45.00. ISBN: 0-07-045511-2.

This small textbook/encyclopedia covers meteorology.

661. Mineral Deposits of Europe. London: Institution of Mining and Metallurgy, 1978-89. 5v., illus. (part in color), bibliog., index. price per volume varies. ISBN: 0-900488-44-1v.1.

This comprehensive survey describes the mineral resources of Europe. The 5 volumes cover v.1—Northwest Europe; v.2—Southeast Europe; v.3—Central Europe; v.4/5—Southwest and Eastern Europe with Iceland. Also useful is Donald D. Can's *Concise Encyclopedia of Mineral Resources* (Pergamon Press, 1989).

662. Ocean World Encyclopedia. Donald G. Groves; Lee M. Hunt. New York, NY: McGraw-Hill, 1980. 443p., illus., index. out-of-print. ISBN: 0-07-025010-3.

Using non-technical terminology, this encyclopedia has some 425 articles covering oceanography. There are also some biographical entries.

663. Rand McNally Encyclopedia of World Rivers. Rand McNally and Co. Chicago, IL: Rand McNally, 1980. 350p., illus., index. price not available.

This authoritative work covers 1,750 of the world's rivers giving such information as source, length, physical features, history, and other pertinent data.

664. Standard Encyclopedia of the World's Mountains. Anthony Julian Huxley. New York, NY: Putnam, 1962. 383p., illus., maps. out-of-print.

This encyclopedia gives information about the world's mountain ranges, including geology, fauna, and flora as well as history.

665. Standard Encyclopedia of the World's Oceans and Islands. Anthony Julian Huxley. New York, NY: Putnam, 1962. 383p., illus. (part in color), maps, index. out-of-print.

Gives detailed information about the world's oceans and islands, including fauna, flora, and history.

666. Standard Encyclopedia of the World's Rivers and Lakes. R. Kay Gresswell; Anthony Julian Huxley. New York, NY: Putnam, 1965. 384p., illus. (part in color), maps, index. out-of-print.

This encyclopedia provides detailed information about the world's rivers and lakes, including location, source, outlet, length, and area.

667. Volcanoes of the World: A Regional Directory, Gazetteer, and Chronology of Volcanism During the Last 10,000 Years. Tom Simkin. Stroudsburg, PA: Hutchinson Ross Publishing Co, 1981. 232p., illus., bibliog., index. out-of-print. ISBN: 0-87933-408-8.

This detailed source of the location of the world's volcanoes gives data and history about each volcano. A newly published work is David Ritchie's *Encyclopedia of Earthquakes and Volcanoes* (Facts on File, 1994).

Guides and Field Guides

668. Classic Mineral Localities of the World: Asia and Australia. Philip Scalisis; David Cook. New York, NY: Van Nostrand Reinhold, 1982. 226p., illus., bibliog., index. $44.95. ISBN: 0-442-28685-6.

This publication contains detailed descriptions of classic mines, dates of discovery, activity, and types of minerals mined in Asia and Australia.

669. Fossil Collecting in the Mid-Atlantic States. Jasper Burns. Baltimore, MD: Johns Hopkins University, 1991. 208p., illus., index. $39.95; $18.95pbk. ISBN: 0-8018-4121-6; 0-8018-4145-3pbk.

This work is an excellent guide to collecting fossils on the east coast of the United States. Also useful is Russell P. MacFall and Jay Wollin's *Fossils for Amateurs* (Van Nostrand Reinhold, 1983).

670. Pictorial Guide to Fossils. Gerald Ramon Case. New York, NY: Van Nostrand Reinhold, 1982. 515p., illus., bibliog., index. out-of-print. ISBN: 0-442-22651-9.

Intended for the hobbyist this guide provides information for identifying fossils worldwide. It covers invertebrates as well as vertebrates.

671. Simon and Schuster's Guide to Fossils. Paolo Arduini; Giorgio Teruzzi. New York, NY: Simon & Schuster, 1987. 320p., illus., index. $22.95; $12.95pbk. ISBN: 0-671-63219-1; 0-671-63132-2pbk.

In keeping with other Simon & Schuster guides this one provides excellent illustrations for identifying fossils with emphasis on invertebrates. Another smaller guide is Chris Pellant's *Rocks, Minerals, and Fossils of the World* (Little, Brown, 1990).

672. Simon and Schuster's Guide to Gems and Precious Stones. Curzio Cipprian; Alessando Borelli. New York, NY: Simon & Schuster, 1986. 384p., illus., index. $11.95. ISBN: 0-671-60430-9.

This beautifully illustrated guide for the gemologist provides good descriptions for identification.

673. Simon and Schuster's Guide to Rocks and Minerals. Martin Prinz; George Harlow; Joseph Peters. New York, NY: Simon & Schuster, 1978. 607p., illus., index. $13.95. ISBN: 0-671-24417-5.

Being a translation of *Mineralie Rocce*, this guide provides extensive information on identifying over 370 rocks and mineral groups. Another useful guide is James R. Tindall's *Collector's Guide to Rocks and Minerals* (Van Nostrand Reinhold, 1975).

Guides to the Literature

674. Dinosaurs: A Guide to Research. *(Garland Reference Library of the Humanities, 1196).* New York, NY: Garland, 1992. 468p., bibliog., index. $73.00. ISBN: 0-8240-5344-3.

This guide provides a general overview to the literature pertaining to dinosaurs. It is arranged by topic with each chapter containing annotated bibliographies.

675. Geologic Reference Sources: A Subject and Regional Bibliography of Publications and Maps in the Geological Sciences. 2nd. Dederick C. Ward; Marjorie W. Wheeler; Robert A. Bier, Jr. Metuchen, NJ: Scarecrow Press, 1981. 560p., index. $49.50. ISBN: 0-8108-1428-5.

This guide to the literature of geology and related areas includes books, indexes, articles, and maps.

676. Information Sources in the Earth Sciences. 2nd. Joan E. Hardy; David Wood; Anthony P. Harvey. New York, NY: Bowker-Saur, 1990. 518p., bibliog., index. $85.00. ISBN: 0-408-01406-7.

Previously called *Use of Earth Sciences Literature*, this resource is a well-accepted guide to the earth science literature.

677. Keyguide to Information Sources in Cartography. A.G. Hodgkiss. New York, NY: McGraw-Hill, 1986. 253p., bibliog., index. $50.00. ISBN: 0-7201-1768-2.

This work is a good general guide to sources of information on maps and map making.

678. Map Librarianship: An Introduction. 2nd. Mary Lynette Larsgaard. Littleton, CO: Libraries Unlimited, 1987. 382p., illus., bibliog., index. $43.50. ISBN: 0-87287-537-7.

Map Librarianship is an authoritative guide to the literature of map librarianship, including the computer aspects.

679. Research Guide to the Arid Lands of the World. Stephen T. Hopkins; Douglas E. Jones. Phoenix, AZ: Oryx Press, 1983. 391p., bibliog., index. out-of-print. ISBN: 0-89774-066-1.

This title is a good guide for physical geographers working on the environment of arid lands.

Handbooks and Manuals

680. Alkaline Rocks and Carbonatites of the World. Alan Robert Woolley. London, Great Britain: British Museum (Natural History), 1987– , irregular. v.1– , illus., bibliog., index. $65.00/v.1. ISBN: 0-565-00971-0v.1.

This projected multi-volume work, with volume one covering North and South America, is a cataloged inventory of localities for alkaline rocks and carbonites.

681. Atmosphere: An Introduction to Meteorology. 4th. Frederick K. Lutgens; Edward J. Tarback. Englewood Cliffs, NJ: Prentice-Hall, 1989. 492p., illus., bibliog., index. price not available. ISBN: 0-13-050196-4.

This standard textbook on meteorology includes much tabular and graphical information. An older out-of-date handbook that also includes useful information on the atmosphere is Hans Volland's *CRC Handbook of Atmospherics* (CRC, 1982). For a good field guide/handbook consult David M. Ludlum's *Audubon Society Field Guide to North American Weather* (Knopf, 1991).

682. Climate Data and Resources: A Reference and Guide. Edward Linarce. New York, NY: Chapman & Hall, 1992. 384p., illus., index. $74.50; $29.95pbk. ISBN: 0-415-05702-7; 0-415-05703-5pbk.

This handbook provides a review of climate theory and practice and describes solar radiation, wind, and precipitation. It describes how climate can be measured and estimated, and data analyzed.

683. Foraminiferal Genera and Their Classification. Alfred Richard Loeblich, Jr.; Helen Tappan. New York, NY: Van Nostrand Reinhold, 1988. 2v., illus., bibliog., index. $249.95. ISBN: 0-442-25937-9.

This highly specialized catalog of foraminifera is useful in identifying this microfossil.

684. Gems, Their Sources, Descriptions, and Identification. 4th. Robert Webster; B.W. Anderson. Boston, MA: Butterworths, 1983. 1,006p., illus. (part in color), bibliog., index. $90.00. ISBN: 0-408-01148-3.

This comprehensive handbook and guide covers all known gems and is especially useful for its descriptions and as an identification guide.

685. Gemstone and Mineral Data Book: A Compilation of Data, Recipes, Formulas, and Instructions for the Mineralogist, Gemologist, Lapidary, Jeweler, Craftsman, and Collector. John Sinkankas. Phoenix, AZ: Geoscience Press, 1988. 368p., index. $17.95. ISBN: 0-945005-07-6.

This small compact handbook of data about gems and minerals is not as comprehensive as *Gems, Their Sources, Description and Identification* but is still useful for the layperson. For detailed mineralogical statistics consult the *Minerals Handbook, 1992-1993* (Stockton Press, 1992).

686. Guide to Fossils. Helmut Mayr. Ithaca, NY: Princeton University Press, 1992. 256p., illus., bibliog., index. $24.95. ISBN: 0-691-08789-X.

This good, compact, general handbook/guide to fossils providing excellent photographs emphasizes European species.

687. Handbook of Applied Meteorology. David D. Houghton. New York, NY: Wiley, 1985. 1,461p., illus., bibliog., index. price not available. ISBN: 0-471-08404-2.

This very useful handbook contains numerous tables, charts, and graphs pertaining to meteorology.

688. Handbook of Paleozoology. Emil Kuhn-Schnyder. Baltimore, MD: Johns Hopkins University Press, 1986. 394p., illus., bibliog., index. $38.00. ISBN: 0-8018-2837-6.

Being a translation of *Palaezoologie*, this small introductory handbook covers only paleozoology.

689. Handbook of Physical Properties of Rocks. Robert S. Carmichael. Boca Raton, FL: CRC, 1982-1984. 3v., illus., bibliog., index. price per volume varies. ISBN: 0-8493-022-9v.1; 0-8493-0227-7v.2; 0-8493-0228-5v.3.

Also called *CRC Handbook of Physical Properties of Rocks*, this comprehensive treatise/handbook covers all rocks giving detailed physical data about each.

690. Handbook of World Salt Resources.
Stanley J. Lefond. New York, NY: Plenum Press, 1969. 384p., illus., bibliog. out-of-print.

Although out-of-print this handbook is still a useful source of information on salt deposits, solar salt operations, and salt springs. Histories of the salt localities are included.

691. International Stratigraphic Guide: A Guide to Stratigraphic Classification, Terminology, and Procedure.
Hollis D. Hedberg; International Subcommission on Stratigraphic Classification of the International Union of Geological Sciences. New York, NY: Wiley, 1976. 200p., illus., bibliog., index. out-of-print. ISBN: 0-471-36743-5.

Intended for stratigraphers, this guide provides individuals with information on how to classify and name strata using the internationally accepted terminology.

692. Manual of Mineralogy.
21th. James Dwight Dana; Cornelis Klein; Cornelius S. Hurlburt, Jr. New York, NY: Wiley, 1993. 681p., illus. (part in color), bibliog., index. $68.57. ISBN: 0-471-57452-X.

Also known as *Dana's Manual of Mineralogy*, this manual is the mineralogist's Bible. It is both a field and laboratory guide based on James Dwight Dana's *System of Mineralogy* (7th ed., Wiley, 1944-62). The *Practical Handbook of Physical Properties of Rocks and Minerals* (CRC, 1985) is also a useful work as is Phillip Crowson's *Mineral Handbook* (Groves, 1988).

693. Map Catalog.
revised. Joel Makower; Laura Bergheim. New York, NY: Random House, 1990. 368p., illus. (part in color), index. $16.95. ISBN: 0-679-71767-1.

This useful handbook covers maps and charts of the earth and some moons and planets.

694. Maps for America: Cartographic Products of the U.S. Geologic Survey and Others.
revised. Morris Mordecai Thompson. Washington, DC: GPO, 1988 (c1981). 265p., illus., bibliog., index. $25.00. ISBN: 0-16-003363-2.

This detailed handbook covers all the map products produced by the USGS and other related agencies. It provides information on how to acquire such materials.

695. Practical Handbook of Marine Science.
Michael Kennish. Boca Raton, FL: CRC, 1989. 710p., illus., bibliog., index. $59.95. ISBN: 0-8493-3700-3.

Also called *CRC Practical Handbook of Marine Sciences*, this source includes a wide array of information about the oceans, their make-up, life, and history.

696. Soil Technicians' Handbook.
K.H. Head. New York, NY: Wiley, 1989. 158p., illus., bibliog., index. $47.95. ISBN: 0-470-21443-0.

This manual is for those needing to make soil tests. It is brief and intended for use in the field. K.H. Head also wrote a manual for the laboratory.

697. Times Books World Weather Guide.
E.A. Pearce; Gordon Smith. New York, NY: Times Books/Random House, 1990. 480p., illus., index. $17.95. ISBN: 0-8129-1881-9.

In addition to the standard weather statistics for selected cities worldwide, a brief paragraph is provided describing the country in terms of its landscape features and climatic variants.

698. Weather Handbook: A Survey of Climatic Conditions and Weather Phenomena for Selected Cities in the United States and around the World.
3rd revised. McKinley Conway; Linda L. Liston. Norcross, GA: Conway Data, 1990. 548p., maps, tables, index. $39.95. ISBN: 0-910436-29-0.

This handbook provides statistics on temperatures, degree days, sky cover, humidity, precipitation, and wind on a month-to-month basis.

Histories

699. American Geological Literature, 1669 to 1850.
Robert M. Hazen; Margaret Hindle Hazen. Stroudsburg, PA: Dowden, Hutchison & Ross, 1980. 431p., index. out-of-print. ISBN: 0-87933-371-5.

This comprehensive bibliography of over 11,000 entries covers American geology from 1669-1850.

700. Birth and Development of the Geological Sciences.
Frank Dawson Adams. New York, NY: Dover, 1990 (c1938). 506p., illus., bibliog. $10.95. ISBN: 0-486-26372-X.

Birth and Development of the Geological Sciences is one of the best general histories of geology from ancient Greece to the 1930s. For historical biographies consult Archibald Geikie's *Founders of Geology* (Macmillan, 1905).

701. Century of Weather Service: A History of the Birth and Growth of the National Weather Service, 1870-1970.
Patrick Hughes. New York, NY: Gordon & Breach, 1970. 212p., illus., maps. $57.00. ISBN: 0-677-02640-4.

This authoritative history of meteorology in the United States also includes a chronology from 1644 to 1970.

702. Contributions to the History of Geological Mapping. E. Dudich. New York, NY: State Mutual Books, 1984. 442p., index. $140.00. ISBN: 0-569-08805-4.

The history of geological mapping is covered in this comprehensive text, including early mapping in Europe through the beginning of modern technologies in 1980.

703. Edge of an Unfamiliar World: A History of Oceanography. Susan Schlee. New York, NY: Dutton, 1973. 398p., illus., bibliog., index. out-of-print. ISBN: 0-525-09673-6.

This small, very readable, historical account of oceanography has good illustrations. Two other interesting histories are Margaret Deacon's *Scientists and the Sea, 1650-1900: A Study of Marine Science* (Academic, 1971) and C. P. Idyll's *Exploring the Ocean World* (Crowell, 1969).

704. Geologists and the History of Geology: An International Bibliography from the Origins to 1978. William Antony S. Sarjeant. New York, NY: Arno Press, 1980. 5v., index. $450.00. ISBN: 0-405-10469-3.

This comprehensive work presents over 10,000 biographical sketches of geologists and mineralogists, providing a unique history of geology.

705. History of Geology. revised. Gabriel Gohau. New Brunswick, NJ: Rutgers University Press, 1991. 249p., illus., index. $35.00; $12.95pbk. ISBN: 0-8135-1665-X; 0-8135-1666-8pbk.

This good, scholarly history of geology is a translation of *Histoire de la Geologie*.

706. Meteorology in America 1800-1870. James R. Fleming. Baltimore, MD: Johns Hopkins University, 1990. 336p., index. $45.00. ISBN: 0-8018-3958-0.

This work is an excellent general history of meteorology in America. For a bibliography covering geophysics and meteorology consult Stephen G. Brush's *History of Geophysics and Meteorology* (Garland, 1985).

707. Source Book in Geology, 1400-1900. *(Source Books in the History of the Sciences).* Kirtley Fletcher Mather; Shirley L. Mason. Cambridge, MA: Harvard University Press, 1970 (c1939). 502p., illus., index. $43.00. ISBN: 0-674-82277-3.

This title and *Source Book in Geology, 1900-1950* (Harvard University Press, 1967) provide historical excerpts from the early geological writings.

Tables

708. Climates of the States. 4th. Detroit, MI: Gale Research, 1992. 2v., index. $255.00. ISBN: 0-8103-0449-X.

This reference provides climatological data from the National Oceanic and Atmospheric Administration in the form of tables, graphs, maps, and figures for the United States and Puerto Rico. A useful companion is *Climate Normals for the U.S.: (Base: 1951-80)* (Gale, 1983). Summaries of U.S. weather station reports can be found in the *Climatological Data* reports also published by the National Oceanic and Atmospheric Administration.

709. International Tables for X-Ray Crystallography. 2nd. *(Mathematical Tables Series, v.2).* John S. Kasper; Kathaleen Lonsdale; International Union of Crystallography. Norwell, MA: Kluwer, 1985. 1v. various paging, index. $85.00. ISBN: 90-277-1956-X.

This title contains highly specialized tables used by crystallographers and mineralogists for describing and defining crystals. Another similar work is Theo Hahn's *International Tables for Crystallography* (Reidel, 1987).

710. Smithsonian Meteorological Tables. *(Smithsonian Miscellaneous Collection, v.114).* Robert J. List. Washington, DC: Smithsonian Institution, 1984 (c1966). 527p., index. $30.00.

In spite of its copyright, this is still the standard handbook of tables that are used in meteorological work.

711. Weather of U.S. Cities: A Guide to the Weather History of 296 Key Cities and Weather Observation Stations in the United States and Its Island Territories. 4th. James A. Ruffner; Frank E. Bair. Detroit, MI: Gale Research/Longman, 1993. 1,131p., index. $185.00. ISBN: 0-8103-4827-6.

This very useful compilation lists weather information for 296 key cities in the United States and its island territories giving temperature highs and lows, precipitation, heat degree days, etc. For world weather information consult Willy Rudloff's *World Climates* (Wissanschaftliche Verlagsgesellschaft, 1981).

Treatises

712. Treatise on Invertebrate Paleontology. Joint Committee on Invertebrate Paleontology. New York, NY: Geological Society of America, 1953– , irregular. v.1– , bibliog., index. price per volume varies.

The second edition of this authoritative treatise began in 1970. There is no other work such as this providing descriptions, photographs, and references of every known invertebrate fossil. Also useful are the many catalogs that are published including Brooks F. Ellis and Angelina R. Messina's *Catalogue of Ostracoda* (American Museum of Natural History, 1952-); *Catalogue of Foraminifera* (American Museum of Natural History, 1940-); and *the Fossilium Catalogus* in 2 parts, *Animalia* and *Plantae* (W. Junk, 1913-).

713. Water: A Comprehensive Treatise. New
York, NY: Plenum Press, 1972-1982. 7v., illus., bibliog., index. price per volume varies. ISBN: 0-306-37181-2v.1.

This specialized treatise provides methods of testing the chemistry physics of water, solutions, and hydrates.

714. World Survey of Climatology. New
York, NY: Elsevier, 1969- , irregular. v.1- , illus., index. price per volume varies.

This title is an ongoing treatise/survey of climatological topics. each volume covers a different topic but all are comprehensive.

Yearbooks, Annuals, and Almanacs

715. Minerals Yearbook. Washington, DC:
U.S. Bureau of Mines, 1932/33- , annual. v.1- , bibliog., index. price per volume varies.

This yearbook is the most used source of information on minerals worldwide. Although published in 4 volumes each year, information can be several years late in being reported. A British counterpart is the *Financial Times International Year Books: Mining*, previously called the *Mining Yearbook,* which goes back to 1887.

716. Ocean Almanac. Robert Hendrickson.
New York, NY: Doubleday, 1989. 456p., index. $17.50. ISBN: 0-385-14077-0.

This compilation of interesting facts and lore about the oceans and the life there-in includes sea creatures, master mariners, and naval disasters.

717. Ocean Yearbook. Chicago, IL:
University of Chicago Press, 1978- , irregular. v.1- , index. ISSN: 0191-8575.

A useful periodically published work (not yearly) this yearbook provides information about the oceans, including facts on transportation, commerce, and technology.

718. Weather Almanac. 6th. Detroit, MI: Gale
Research, 1991. 1v. various paging, index. $120.00. ISBN: 0-8103-2843-7.

This almanac is a comprehensive compilation of weather data and related environmental phenomena in the United States and its key cities. It provides useful information for the layperson as well as scientific data for researchers.

Periodicals

719. American Journal of Science. New
Haven, CT: Yale University Press, 1818- , monthly. v.1- , index. $90.00. ISSN: 0002-9599.

720. American Mineralogist. Washington,
DC: Mineralogical Society of America, 1916- , monthly. v.1- , index. $200.00. ISSN: 0003-004X.

721. Bulletin of the American Meteorological
Society. Boston, MA: American Meteorological Society, 1920- , monthly. v.1- , index. $60.00. ISSN: 0003-0007.

722. Bulletin of the Association of Engineering
Geologists. Sudbury, MA: Association of Engineering Geologists, 1963- , quarterly. v.1- , index. $70.00. ISSN: 0004-5691.

723. Bulletin of the Geological Society of
America. Boulder, CO: Geological Society of America, 1888- , monthly. v.1- , index. $170.00. ISSN: 0016-7606.

724. Bulletin of the Seismological Society of
America. El Cerrito, CA: Seismological Society of America, 1911- , bimonthly. v.1- , index. $125.00. ISSN: 0037-1106.

725. Canadian Journal of Earth Sciences/Journal Canadienne des Sciences de la
Terre. Ottawa, Ontario: National Research Council of Canada, 1964- , monthly. v.1- , index. $105.00. ISSN: 0008-4077.

726. Cartographic Journal. Newcastle, Great
Britain: British Cartographic Society, 1964- , semiannual. v.1- , index. $22.00. ISSN: 0008-7041.

727. Clay Minerals. London, Great Britain:
Mineralogical Society, 1947- , quarterly. v.1- , index. $150.00. ISSN: 0009-8558.

728. Climatological Data. Asheville, NC: U.S.
National Climatic Data Center, 1897- , monthly. v.1- , index. $25.00.

729. Contributions to Mineralogy and Petrology. Berlin, Germany: Springer-Verlag,
1947- , 12/year. v.1- , index. $1,345.00. ISSN: 0010-7999.

730. Economic Geology and The Bulletin of the Society of Economic Geologists. El Paso, TX: Economic Geology Publishing/Society of Economic Geologists, 1906– , 8/year. v.1– , index. $65.00. ISSN: 0361-0128.

731. Geological Journal. Chichester, Great Britain: Wiley, 1955– , quarterly. v.1– , index. $235.00. ISSN: 0072-1050.

732. Geological Magazine. Cambridge, Great Britain: Cambridge University Press, 1864– , bimonthly. v.1– , index. $205.00. ISSN: 0016-7568.

733. Geology. Boulder, CO: Geological Society of America, 1973– , monthly. v.1– , index. $140.00. ISSN: 0091-7613.

734. Geophysical Research Letters. Washington, DC: American Geophysical Union, 1974– , monthly. v.1– , index. $480.00. ISSN: 0094-8276.

735. Geotimes. Alexandria, VA: American Geologic Institute, 1956– , monthly. v.1– , index. $24.95. ISSN: 0016-8556.

736. JGR: Journal of Geophysical Research. Washington, DC: American Geophysical Union, 1896– , monthly. v.1– , index. $2,555.00 all sections. ISSN: 0148-0227.
   Contains the following sections: Solid Earth, $1,385.00, 0196-6936; Oceans, $1,542.00, 0196-2256; Space Physics, $2,285.00, 0196-6928; Atmosphere, $90.00; Planets, $335.00, 0196-6936.

737. Journal of Applied Meteorology. Boston, MA: American Meteorological Society, 1962– , monthly. v.1– , index. $165.00. ISSN: 0733-3021.

738. Journal of Atmospheric and Oceanic Technology. Boston, MA: American Meteorological Society, 1984– , bimonthly. v.1– , index. $135.00. ISSN: 0739-0572.

739. Journal of Climate. Boston, MA: American Meteorological Society, 1986– , monthly. v.1– , index. $175.00. ISSN: 0894-8755.

740. Journal of Geology. Chicago, IL: University of Chicago Press, 1893– , bimonthly. v.1– , index. $63.00. ISSN: 0022-1376.

741. Journal of Glaciology. Cambridge, Great Britain: International Geological Society, 1947– , 3/year. v.1– , index. $220.00. ISSN: 0022-1430.

742. Journal of Paleontology. Ithaca, NY: Paleontological Society, 1927– , bimonthly. v.1– , index. $99.00. ISSN: 0022-3360.

743. Journal of Petrology. Oxford, Great Britain: Oxford University Press, 1960– , 6/year. v.1– , index. $240.00. ISSN: 0022-3530.

744. Journal of Physical Oceanography. Boston, MA: American Meteorological Society, 1971– , monthly. v.1– , index. $185.00. ISSN: 0022-3670.

745. Journal of Sedimentary Petrology. Tulsa, OK: SEPM, 1931– , bimonthly. v.1– , index. $120.00. ISSN: 0022-4472.

746. Journal of the Atmospheric Sciences. Boston, MA: American Meteorological Society, 1944– , semimonthly. v.1– , index. $320.00. ISSN: 0022-4928.

747. Journal of the Geological Society. Bath, Great Britain: Geological Society of London, 1845– , 6/year. v.1– , index. $467.00. ISSN: 0016-7649.

748. Local Climatological Data. Asheville, NC: U.S. National Climatic Data Center, 1897– , monthly. v.1– , index. $17.00.

749. Meteorological Magazine. London, Great Britain: HMSO, 1866– , monthly. v.1– , index. $32.00. ISSN: 0026-1149.

750. Micropaleontology. New York, NY: American Museum of Natural History, 1954– , quarterly. v.1– , index. $120.00. ISSN: 0026-2803.

751. Monthly Weather Review. Boston, MA: American Meteorological Society, 1872– , monthly. v.1– , index. $205.00. ISSN: 0027-0644.

752. Physics and Chemistry of the Earth. Tarrytown, NY: Pergamon Press, 1956– , 6/year. v.1– , index. $472.00. ISSN: 0079-1946.

753. Quarterly Journal of the Royal Meteorological Society. Reading, Great Britain: Royal Meteorological Society, 1871– , 6/year. v.1– , index. $250.00. ISSN: 0035-9009.

754. Rocks and Minerals. Washington, DC: Heldref Publications, 1926– , bimonthly. v.1– , index. $53.00. ISSN: 0035-7529.

755. Transactions of the Institution of Mining and Metallurgy: Section A: Mining Industry; Section B: Applied Earth Sciences; Section C: Mineral Processing and Extractive Metallurgy. London, Great Britain: Institution of Mining and Metallurgy, 1892– , 9/year. v.1– , index. $205.00. ISSN: 0371-7844 Section A; 0371-7453 Section B; 0371-9553 Section C.

MATHEMATICS

Abstracts and Indexes

756. CompuMath Citation Index. Philadelphia, PA: Institute for Scientific Information, 1982- . 3/year. v.1– , indexes. $1,495.00/year. ISSN: 0730-6199.

Also called *CMCI*, this citation index covers computer science, mathematics, statistics, operations research, and other related areas. It includes source, research, citation, permuterm, and corporate indexes. There is a cumulative index for 1976-1980 with the current issues available online.

757. Current Index to Statistics: Applications, Methods and Theory. Washington, DC: American Statistical Association, 1976- . annual. v.1– , indexes. $60.00/year. ISSN: 0364-1228.

This annual index to the statistical literature is also available online.

758. Current Mathematical Publications. Providence, RI: American Mathematical Society, 1969- . 17/year. v.1– , indexes. $314.00/year. ISSN: 0361-4794.

Formed by *American Mathematical Society New Publications* and *Contents of Contemporary Mathematical Journals*, this is a list of those materials that will be reviewed in *Mathematical Reviews*. It is also available online and on CD-ROM.

759. Jahrbuch uber de Fortschritte der Mathematik. Berlin, Germany: DeGruyter, 1968-1942. 60v., indexes. out-of-print.

This German abstracting/indexing service preceded the *Mathematical Reviews* and is the only one covering the years 1868-1942.

760. Mathematical Reviews. Providence, RI: American Mathematical Society, 1940- . monthly. v.1– , indexes. $4,010.00/year. ISSN: 0025-5629.

This foremost international abstracting service covers periodical articles, books, and technical reports. It is arranged by subject and is also available online and on CD-ROM.

761. Mathematics of Computation. Washington, DC: National Academy of Sciences/National Research Council, 1943- . quarterly. v.1– , indexes. $205.00/year. ISSN: 0025-5718.

Previously called *Mathematical Tables and Other Aids to Computation*, 1943-1959, this journal provides articles and research pertaining to numerical mathematics, tables, and other related topics.

762. Zentralblatt fur Mathematik und ihre Grenzgebiete/Mathematics Abstracts. New York, NY: Springer-Verlag, 1931- . 30/year. v.1– , indexes. $2,689.00/year. ISSN: 0044-4235.

Also called *Mathematics Abstracts*, this journal covers mathematics and related materials in physics, astrophysics, and geophysics. The abstracts may be in English, French, or German. It is also available online.

Bibliographies

763. Omega Bibliography of Mathematical Logic. *(Perspectives in Mathematical Logic).* Gert H. Muller; Wolfgang Lenski. New York, NY: Springer Verlag, 1987. 6v., index. $1,178.00. ISBN: 0-387-17457-5.

This very comprehensive bibliography covers the mathematics literature from 1879 to 1985 which pertains to classical and nonclassical logic, and model, recursion, set, and proof theory.

Biographical Sources

764. Biographical Dictionary of Mathematicians. New York, NY: Macmillan, 1991. 4v., index. $175.00. ISBN: 0-684-19282-9.

This comprehensive biographical dictionary of mathematicians gives brief information on each mathematician.

765. Makers of Mathematics. Alfred Hooper. New York, NY: Random House, 1948. 402p., illus., bibliog., index. out-of-print.

Now out-of-print, this classic book discusses great mathematicians and their concepts. Also of use and similar is Eric Temple Bell's *Men of Mathematics* (Simon & Schuster, 1937).

766. Women of Mathematics: A Biobibliographical Sourcebook. Louise S. Grinstein; Paul J. Campbell. New York, NY: Greenwood Press, 1987. 292p., bibliog., index. $65.00. ISBN: 0-313-24849-4.

Only notable women mathematicians are covered in this biobibliographical reference source.

767. World Directory of Mathematicians, 1990. 9th. Walter Feit. Providence, RI: American Mathematical Society, 1990. 1,239p. $40.00. ISBN: 0-685-38654-6.

This address directory lists some 35,000 mathematicians throughout the world from 81 countries.

Dictionaries, Glossaries, and Thesauri

768. Concise Dictionary of Mathematics. Christopher Clapham. New York, NY: Oxford University Press, 1990. 203p., illus. $29.95; $7.95pbk. ISBN: 0-19-866156-8; 0-19-286103-4pbk.

Also called *Concise Oxford Dictionary of Mathematics*, this is a good general mathematics dictionary. Another general mathematics dictionary is Jeanne Bendick's *Mathematics Illustrated Dictionary* (McGraw-Hill, 1965).

769. Dictionary of Mathematics. J.A. Glen; G.H. Littler. Totowa, NJ: Barnes & Noble, 1984. 230p. price not available. ISSN: 0-389-20451-X.

Although this work has a British slant, it is still a good general mathematics dictionary for students and laypersons.

770. Dictionary of Mathematics: In English, German, French, Russian. Gunther Eisenreich; Ralph Sube. New York, NY: Elsevier, 1982. 2v., index. $254.50. ISBN: 0-444-99706-7.

This book is a comprehensive multi-lingual mathematics dictionary. For just English-German consult Sheila Macintyre's *German-English Mathematical Vocabulary* (Wiley, 1966) and for Russian-English consult A.J. Lohwater's *Russian-English Dictionary of the Mathematical Sciences* (American Mathematical Society, 1990).

771. Dictionary of Mathematics Terms. Douglas Downing. Hauppauge, NY: Barron's Educational Series, 1987. 247p. $8.95. ISBN: 0-8120-2641-1.

This good general dictionary covers algebra, geometry, trigonometry, probability, statistics, logic, computer mathematics, and calculus.

772. Dictionary of Real Numbers. Jonathan M. Borwein; Peter Borwein. Pacific Grove, CA: Brooks/Cole Publishing Co, 1990. 424p. $79.95. ISBN: 0-534-12840-8.

Intended for the applied mathematician, this unique dictionary/handbook is arranged by the first 8 digits

after the decimal of the specified functions and then gives the value to which the function is evaluated.

773. HarperCollins Dictionary of Mathematics. E.J. Brawski; Jonathan M. Borwein. New York, NY: HarperPerennial, 1991. 659p., illus. $25.00; $14.95pbk. ISBN: 0-06-271525-9; 0-06-461019-5pbk.

This general dictionary is good for the student and layperson. Also published in Great Britain by Collins as *Dictionary of Mathematics*.

774. HarperCollins Dictionary of Statistics. Roger Porkess. New York, NY: HarperPerennial, 1991. 267p., illus. $25.00; $12.95pbk. ISBN: 0-06-271527-5; 0-06-461020-9pbk.

This general dictionary of statistical terminology is for the student and educated layperson. Also useful would be F.H.C. Marriott's *Dictionary of Statistical Terms* (Wiley, 1990).

775. Mathematics Dictionary. 5th. Robert C. James. New York, NY: Van Nostrand Reinhold, 1992. 548p., illus., index. $42.95. ISBN: 0-442-00741-8.

More than 8,000 topics are defined in this well-known dictionary covering all areas of mathematics as well as brief biographies of key mathematical scientists. There is a French, German, Russian, and Spanish index.

776. Quantities and Units of Measurement: A Dictionary and Handbook. J.V. Drazil. New York, NY: H.W. Wilson, 1983. 313p., bibliog., index. $25.00. ISBN: 0-7201-1665-1.

Previously called *Dictionary of Quantities and Units*, the first part of this dictionary covers units of measurement, their symbols, and abbreviations and the second part covers the quantities and selected constants. Two older books on the metric system are John Louis Feirer's *SI Metrics Handbook* (Scribner, 1977) and William J. Semioli's *Conversion Tables for SI Metrication* (Industrial Press, 1974).

777. Webster's New World Dictionary of Mathematics. William Karush. New York, NY: Webster's New World, 1989. 317p., illus., bibliog. $11.95. ISBN: 0-13-192667-5.

Previously called the *Crescent Dictionary of Mathematics*, this title is a good general dictionary of mathematics for the student and layperson. Also of use would be Carol Gibson's *Facts on File Dictionary of Mathematics* (Facts on File, 1988).

Directories

778. Mathematical Sciences Professional Directory, 1989. Providence, RI: American Mathematical Society, 1989. 190p., index. $27.00. ISBN: 0-8218-0132-5.

This directory lists institutions and organizations with mathematics as their main interest. Complete directory information is given including name, address, telephone numbers, and personnel.

Encyclopedias

779. Encyclopaedia of Mathematics. Norwell, MA: Kluwer Academic, 1988. 10v., illus., index. $490.00. ISBN: 1-55608-010-7.

A translation of the *Soviet Mathematical Encyclopaedia* (1977-1985), this comprehensive work defines mathematical terms as well as surveys major mathematical topics, concepts, and theories.

780. Encyclopedia of Statistical Sciences. Samuel Kotz; Norman L. Johnson. New York, NY: Wiley, 1982-89. 10v., illus., bibliog., index. $1,003.00. ISBN: 0-471-05544-1.

This very comprehensive encyclopedia covers statistical theory and the applications of statistical methods in various scientific disciplines.

781. Encyclopedic Dictionary of Mathematics. 2nd. Mathematical Society of Japan. Cambridge, MA: MIT Press, 1987. 4v., illus., bibliog., index. $350.00. ISBN: 0-262-09026-0.

This alphabetically arranged encyclopedia covers all of mathematics in some 450 entries. It includes biographical information on a few noted mathematicians. For special sub-areas of mathematics consult A.G. Howson's *Handbook of Terms Used in Algebra and Analysis* (Cambridge University Press, 1972) and the *International Dictionary of Applied Mathematics* (Van Nostrand Reinhold, 1960).

782. VNR Concise Encyclopedia of Mathematics. 2nd. S. Gottwald; W. Gellert. New York, NY: Van Nostrand Reinhold, 1989. 776p., illus., index. price not available. ISBN: 0-442-20590-2.

Previously called *Mathematics at a Glance*, this excellent mathematical encyclopedia covers elementary mathematics, higher mathematics, and special areas. Another much older but still useful source of historical information on pure mathematics is the *Universal Encyclopedia of Mathematics* (Simon & Schuster, 1969).

Guides to the Literature

783. Guide to the Literature of Mathematics and Physics Including Related Works on Engineering Sciences. 2nd. Nathan Grier Parke. New York, NY: Dover, 1958. 436p., index. out-of-print.

This title, together with Elie M. Dick's *Current Information Sources in Mathematics* (Libraries Unlimited, 1973), brings together some 6,600 mathematics titles that would be essential to any comprehensive mathematics collection. Some brief annotations are included.

784. Mathematics Journals: An Annotated Guide. Diana F. Liang. Metuchen, NJ: Scarecrow Press, 1992. 235p., index. $29.50. ISBN: 0-8108-2585-6.

This annotated list describes some 350 mathematics and statistics journals with a few in computer science. Full bibliographical information is given plus a brief annotation and publication history. This is an excellent selection guide to mathematics periodicals.

785. Statistics and Econometrics: A Guide to Information Sources. Joseph Zaremba. Detroit, MI: Gale, 1980. 701p., index. out-of-print. ISBN: 0-8103-1466-5.

This annotated guide lists some 1,700 books that pertain to probability or statistical concepts.

786. Using the Mathematics Literature: A Practical Guide. *(Books in Library and Information Science, v.25).* Barbara Kirsch Schaefer. New York, NY: Marcel Dekker, 1979. 141p., bibliog., index. $38.80. ISBN: 0-8247-6675-X.

Although somewhat dated this work is still a useful guide to the sources of mathematical literature. Its intent is to give background information on doing research in the field of mathematics. Two other older guides are John E. Pemberton's *How to Find Out in Mathematics* (Pergamon, 1969) and A.R. Dorling's *Use of Mathematical Literature* (Butterworth, 1977).

Handbooks and Manuals

787. CRC Handbook of Mathematical Curves and Surfaces. 2nd. David H. Von Seggern. Boca Raton, FL: CRC, 1992. 400p., illus., bibliog., index. $39.95. ISBN: 0-8493-0196-3.

A useful handbook for those working in the computer graphics field, this book illustrates curves and surface features in two-dimensions.

788. CRC Handbook of Mathematical Sciences. 6th. William H. Beyer. Boca Raton, FL: CRC, 1987. 860p., illus., bibliog., index. $84.95. ISBN: 0-8493-0656-6.

Previously called the *Handbook of Tables for Mathematics*, this standard handbook has all of the major mathematical tables that are used by students and researchers.

789. CRC Handbook of Tables for Probability and Statistics. 2nd. William H. Beyer. Boca Raton, FL: CRC, 1988 (c1968). 642p., index. $54.95. ISBN: 0-8493-0692-2.

This classic handbook reprints tables, charts, and graphs pertaining to probability and statistics.

790. CRC Standard Mathematical Tables and Formulae. 29th. Boca Raton, FL: CRC, 1991. 609p., index. $37.50.

Tables taken from the *CRC Handbook of Physics and Chemistry* are included in this handbook covering all of the mathematical functions used by mathematicians and other researchers. Two other useful compilations are Milton Abramowitz's *Handbook of Mathematical Functions, with Formulas, Graphs, and Mathematical Tables* (Dover, 1965) and Richard Steven Burington's *Handbook of Mathematical Tables and Formulas* (McGraw-Hill, 1973).

791. Fundamentals of Mathematics. H. Behnke. Cambridge, MA: MIT Press, 1984. 3v., illus., bibliog., index. $75.00. ISBN: 0-685-07931-7.

This treatise-type handbook covers all of the fundamentals that pertain to mathematics. The 3 volumes cover v.1—Foundations of Mathematics: The Real Number System and Algebra; v.2—Geometry; v.3—Analysis. Another comprehensive 7-volume work is Walter Lederman's *Handbook of Applicable Mathematics* (Wiley, 1980-91).

792. Handbook of Mathematics. 3rd. I.N. Bronshtein; K.A. Semendyayev. New York, NY: Van Nostrand Reinhold, 1985. 973p., illus., bibliog., index. $52.95. ISBN: 0-442-21171-6.

A translation of *Spravochnik po Matematike*, this book presents an excellent overview of mathematics. For the special area of numerical analysis consult P.G. Ciarlet's ongoing publication *Handbook of Numerical Analysis* (Elsevier, 1990-).

793. Handbook of Statistical Methods for Engineers and Scientists. Harrison M. Wadsworth, Jr. New York, NY: McGraw-Hill, 1990. 1v. various paging, illus., bibliog., index. $79.50. ISBN: 0-07-067674-7.

The use of statistics in all areas of engineering is covered in this comprehensive handbook. Two other statistics books of use are Vic Barnett's *Outlines in Statistical Data* (Wiley, 1985) and Francis J. Wall's *Statistical Data Analysis Handbook* (McGraw-Hill, 1986).

Histories

794. Bibliography and Research Manual of the History of Mathematics. Kenneth O. May. Buffalo, NY: University of Toronto Press, 1973. 818p., index. out-of-print. ISBN: 0-8020-1764-9.

Although now out-of-print, some 30,000 titles are included in this bibliography on the history of mathematics. Also included is a discussion on how to do research and retrieve information.

795. History of Mathematics: From Antiquity to the Beginning of the Nineteenth Century. 2nd. J.F. Scott. London, Great Britain: Taylor & Francis, 1969. 266p., illus., bibliog., index. out-of-print.

This chronology lists events that have shaped the history of mathematics over the past 2,000 years. Also of interest are Florian Cajori's *History of Mathematics* (Macmillan, 1924), Howard Eves' *Introduction to the History of Mathematics* (Holt, Rinehart & Winston, 1969), and *History of Mathematics* (W.C. Brown, 1991).

796. History of Mathematics from Antiquity to the Present: A Selective Bibliography. *(Bibliographies of the History of Science and Technology, v.6; Garland Reference Library of the Humanities, v.313).* Joseph W. Dauben. New York, NY: Garland, 1985. 467p., illus., index. out-of-print. ISBN: 0-8240-9284-8.

This comprehensive bibliography covers all areas of the history of mathematics. Another useful bibliography is Robin E. Rider's *Bibliography of Early Modern Algebra, 1500-1800* (University of California Press, 1982).

797. Mathematics and Its History. John Stillwell. New York, NY: Springer-Verlag, 1989. 371p., illus., bibliog., index. $49.80. ISBN: 0-387-96981-0.

This well-written book presents an overview of mathematics from the Greeks to the present. For an early history of statistics consult Anders Hald's *History of Probability and Statistics and Their Applications Before 1750* (Wiley, 1990).

798. Source Book in Mathematics, 1200-1800. *(Source Books in the History of the Sciences).* D.J. Struik. Princeton, NJ: Princeton University Press, 1969. 427p., illus., bibliog., index. $45.00. ISBN: 0-69108-404-1.

This excellent history of mathematics is based on the actual writings of 75 mathematicians from the 13th century to the end of the 18th.

Tables

799. Atlas of Functions. Jerome Spanier;
Keith B. Oldham. Washington, DC:
Hemisphere Publishing Co, 1987. 700p., illus.
(part in color), bibliog., index. $165.00. ISBN:
0-89116-573-8.

This comprehensive book of functions is arranged
in an atlas-format.

800. Basic Statistics Tables: Tables of Distribution. Chris Spatz; James O. Johnston.
Monterey, CA: Brooks/Cole Publishing Co,
1976. 380p., illus., bibliog., index. out-of-print.
ISBN: 0-8185-0183-9.

Even though this title is now out-of-print, it is still
a good source of tables for statical use. Two other
useful statistics books are E.S. Pearson's *Biometrika
Tables for Statisticians* (Lubrecht & Cramp, 1976) and
William H. Beyer's *CRC Handbook of Tables for
Probability and Statistics* (CRC, 1968).

801. Index of Mathematical Tables. 2nd. *(Addison-Wesley International Series).* A. Fletcher.
Reading, MA: Addison-Wesley, 1962. 2v.,
bibliog., index. out-of-print.

Although out-of-print, this comprehensive index to
mathematical tables is for the 16th century to 1961.
Another similar work is A.V. Lebedev's *Guide to
Mathematical Tables* (Pergamon, 1960).

802. Selected Tables in Mathematical Statistics. Providence, RI: American Mathematical
Society, 1973-1981. 7v., index. price per
volume varies. ISBN: 0-8218-1901-1v.1.

All tables in this set have been checked for accuracy. They cover many areas of statistics that researchers use on a regular basis. Both the former
National Bureau of Standards and the Royal Society
have long series of tables that would be also of interest
to statistics users.

**803. Tables of Fourier Transforms and
Fourier Transforms of Distribution.** Fritz
Oberhettinger. New York, NY:
Springer-Verlag, 1990. 259p., index. $35.00.
ISBN: 0-387-50630-6.

This highly specialized handbook of tables is a
translation of *Tabellen zur Fourier Transformation.*
Other specialized handbooks include Alexander Apelblat's *Table of Definite and Infinite Integrals* (Elsevier,
1983) and Eugene Jahnke's *Tables of Higher Functions* (McGraw-Hill, 1960).

804. Tables of Integrals, Series, and Products.
I.S. Gradshteyn. San Diego, CA: Academic
Press, 1980. 1,160p., bibliog., index. $49.95.
ISBN: 0-12-294760-6.

This translation of *Tablitsy Integralov, Summ,
Riadov i Proizvedenii* is one of the most comprehen-
sive compilations of tables containing integrals, series,
and products. Two other less comprehensive works are
Eldon R. Hansen's *Tables of Series and Products*
(Prentice-Hall, 1975) and H.B. Dwight's *Tables of
Integrals and Other Mathematical Data* (Macmillan,
1961).

Periodicals

805. Advances in Mathematics. San Diego,
CA: Academic Press, 1967– , monthly. v.1– ,
index. $687.00. ISSN: 0001-8708.

806. American Journal of Mathematics.
Baltimore, MD: Johns Hopkins University,
1878– , 6/year. v.1– , index. $150.00. ISSN:
0002-9327.

807. American Mathematical Monthly.
Washington, DC: Mathematical Association of
America, 1894– , 10/year. v.1– , index.
$128.00. ISSN: 0002-9890.

808. Annals of Mathematics. Baltimore, MD:
Johns Hopkins University Press, 1884– ,
bimonthly. v.1– , index. $180.00. ISSN:
0003-486X.

809. Arithmetic Teacher. Reston, VA:
National Council of Teachers of Mathematics,
1954– , monthly. v.1– , index. $45.00. ISSN:
0004-136X.

**810. Bulletin of the American Mathematical
Society.** Providence, RI: American
Mathematical Society, 1894-1978; new series,
1979– , 4/year. v.1– , index. $202.00. ISSN:
0273-0979.

811. Bulletin of the London Mathematical Society. London, Great Britain: London
Mathematical Society, 1969– , 6/year. v.1– ,
index. $236.00. ISSN: 0024-6093.

812. College Mathematics Journal.
Washington, DC: Mathematical Association of
America, 1970– , 5/year. v.1– , index. $85.00.
ISSN: 0746-8342.

813. Duke Mathematical Journal. Durham,
NC: Duke University Press, 1935– , 9/year.
v.1– , index. $264.00. ISSN: 0012-7094.

814. Journal of Algebra. San Diego, CA:
Academic Press, 1964– , 18/year. v.1– , index.
$1,085.00. ISSN: 0021-8693.

815. Journal of Differential Equations. San
Diego, CA: Academic Press, 1965– , monthly.
v.1– , index. $759.00. ISSN: 0022-0396.

816. Journal of Differential Geometry. Bethlehem, PA: Lehigh University Press, 1967– , 6/year. v.1– , index. $190.00. ISSN: 0022-040X.

817. Journal of the American Mathematical Society. Providence, RI: American Mathematical Society, 1988– , 4/year. v.1– , index. $136.00. ISSN: 0894-0347.

818. Journal of the London Mathematical Society. London, Great Britain: London Mathematical Society, 1926– , 6/year. v.1– , index. $440.00. ISSN: 0024-6107.

819. Mathematical Gazette. Leicester, Great Britain: Mathematical Association, 1894– , 4/year. v.1– , index. $45.00. ISSN: 0025-5572.

820. Mathematical Proceedings of the Cambridge Philosophical Society. Cambridge, Great Britain: Cambridge University Press, 1843– , 6/year. v.1– , index. $299.00. ISSN: 0305-0041.

821. Mathematics Magazine. Washington, DC: Mathematical Association of America, 1926– , bimonthly. v.1– , index. $68.00. ISSN: 0025-570X.

822. Mathematics Teacher. Reston, VA: National Council of Teachers of Mathematics, 1908– , monthly. v.1– , index. $45.00. ISSN: 0025-5769.

823. Notices of the American Mathematical Society. Providence, RI: American Mathematical Society, 1953– , 10/year. v.1– , index. $131.00. ISSN: 0002-9920.

824. Proceedings of the American Mathematical Society. Providence, RI: American Mathematical Society, 1950– , monthly. v.1– , index. $508.00. ISSN: 0002-9939.

825. Proceedings of the London Mathematical Society. London, Great Britain: London Mathematical Society, 1865– , 6/year. v.1– , index. $480.00. ISSN: 0024-6115.

826. Quarterly Journal of Mathematics. Oxford, Great Britain: Oxford Journals, 1930– , quarterly. v.1– , index. $125.00. ISSN: 0033-5606.

827. Quarterly of Applied Mathematics. Providence, RI: Brown University, 1943– , quarterly. v.1– , index. $50.00. ISSN: 0033-569X.

828. SIAM Journal on Applied Mathematics. Philadelphia, PA: Society for Industrial and Applied Mathematics, 1953– , bimonthly. v.1– , index. $210.00. ISSN: 0036-1399.

829. SIAM Journal on Control and Optimization. Philadelphia, PA: Society for Industrial and Applied Mathematics, 1963– , bimonthly. v.1– , index. $242.00. ISSN: 0363-0129.

830. SIAM Journal on Discrete Mathematics. Philadelphia, PA: Society for Industrial and Applied Mathematics, 1980– , quarterly. v.1– , index. $188.00. ISSN: 0895-4801.

831. SIAM Journal on Mathematical Analysis. Philadelphia, PA: Society for Industrial and Applied Mathematics, 1970– , bimonthly. v.1– , index. $305.00. ISSN: 0036-1410.

832. SIAM Journal on Matrix Analysis and Applications. Philadelphia, PA: Society for Industrial and Applied Mathematics, 1980– , quarterly. v.1– , index. $150.00. ISSN: 0895-4798.

833. SIAM Journal on Numerical Analysis. Philadelphia, PA: Society for Industrial and Applied Mathematics, 1964– , bimonthly. v.1– , index. $220.00. ISSN: 0036-1429.

834. SIAM Journal on Optimization. Philadelphia, PA: Society for Industrial and Applied Mathematics, 1991– , quarterly. v.1– , index. $160.00. ISSN: 1052-6234.

835. SIAM Journal on Scientific and Statistical Computing. Philadelphia, PA: Society for Industrial and Applied Mathematics, 1980– , bimonthly. v.1– , index. $210.00. ISSN: 0196-5204.

836. SIAM Review. Philadelphia, PA: Society for Industrial and Applied Mathematics, 1959– , quarterly. v.1– , index. $129.00. ISSN: 0036-1445.

837. Topology: An International Journal of Mathematics. New York, NY: Pergamon, 1962– , 4/year. v.1– , index. $455.00. ISSN: 0040-9383.

838. Transactions of the American Mathematical Society. Providence, RI: American Mathematical Society, 1900– , monthly. v.1– , index. $842.00. ISSN: 0002-9947.

PHYSICS

Abstracts and Indexes

839. Acoustics Abstracts. Brentwood, Great Britain: Multi-Science Publishing Co, 1967– , monthly. v.1– , index. $362.00. ISSN: 0001-4974.

Previously called *Acountics and Ultrasonics Abstract*, this 2-part abstracts journal (A—non-core journals, B—core journals) covers solid, liquid, and gaseous state acoustics; acoustic diagnostic techniques; acoustics measurements; ultrasonic applications; vibration; and shock and noise.

840. Colour Index. 3rd. Society of Dyers and Colourists; American Association of Textile Chemists and Colourists. Bradford, Great Britain: Society of Dyers and Colourists, 1971-1982. 7v., index. price not available. ISBN: 0-901056-06-6.

This guide to colorants gives comprehensive descriptions and properties of every recognized colorant in the world. Volumes 6 and 7 are supplements to the first 5 volumes.

841. Current Physics Index. New York, NY: American Institute of Physics, 1975– , quarterly. v.1– , index. $490.00. ISSN: 0098-9819.

This index covers research in physics as reported in the core physics journals that are published worldwide. It is also available online.

842. Eight Peak Index of Mass Spectra: The Eight Most Abundant Ions in 66,720 Mass Spectra, Indexed by Molecular Weight, Elemental Composition, and Most Abundant Ions. 3rd. Mass Spectrometry Data Centre. Nottingham, Great Britain: Mass Spectrometry Data Centre: The Royal Society of Chemistry, 1983. 3v. in 7, tables, index. price not available.

This title is a comprehensive index to mass spectra.

843. Physics Abstracts. Stevenage, Great Britain: Inspec/Institution of Electrical Engineers, 1898– , bimonthly. v.1– , index. $2,350.00. ISSN: 0036-8091.

This abstracting service, Section A of Science Abstracts, is the major source of physics information covering all areas of physics. Another useful service is *Physical Review Abstracts* from the American Physical Society. It is also available online and on CD-ROM.

844. Physics Briefs/Physikalische Berichte. Information Center for Energy, Physics, Mathematics, GW. Weinheim, Germany: VCH Verlagsgesellschaft, 1845– , bimonthly. v.1– , index. $2,390.00. ISSN: 0170-7434.

Superseding *Physikalische Berichte*, this abstracting service covers physics, astronomy, and related fields. It abstracts journals, reports, conference proceedings, books, patents, and dissertations. It is also available online.

845. Solid State and Superconductivity Abstracts. Bethesda, MD: Cambridge Scientific Abstracts, 1957– , quarterly. v.1– , index. $995.00. ISSN: 0896-5900.

Previously called *Solid State Abstracts* (1960-1965) and *Solid State Abstracts Journal* (1966-1987) and incorporating several specialized journals, this service covers theory, production, and application of solid state materials, emphasizing superconductivity. It contains over 8,000 abstracts per year and is also available online.

846. Thermophysical Properties Research Literature Retrieval Guide, 1900-1980. J.F. Chaney. New York, NY: IFI/Plenum, 1982– , irregular. v.1– , index. price per volume varies. ISBN: 0-306-67225-1v.5.

This guide is a comprehensive compilation of scientific and technical literature pertaining to thermophysical properties and prepared by the Center for Information and Numerical Data Analysis and Synthesis (CINDAS). The 7 volumes published so far cover v.1—Element; v.2—Inorganic compounds; v.3—Organic compounds and polymeric materials; v.4—Alloys, intermetallic compounds, and cermets; v.5—Oxide mixtures and minerals; v.6—Mixtures and solution; v.7—Coatings, systems, composites, foods, and animal and vegetable products.

Dictionaries, Glossaries, and Thesauri

847. Cambridge Illustrated Thesaurus of Physics. Teresa Rickards; Ronald C. Denney; Stephen Foster. New York, NY: Cambridge University Press, 1984. 256p., color illus., index. $29.95. ISBN: 0-521-26363-8.

Also published as *Barnes and Noble Thesaurus of Physics*, this dictionary is popular with the layperson.

848. Concise Dictionary of Physics: New Edition. 2nd. New York, NY: Oxford University Press, 1990. 308p., illus. $8.95. ISBN: 0-19-286111-5.

Some 2,000 definitions are included in this small dictionary covering physics. Some astronomy terms are included as they pertain to astrophysics. Also of use, but somewhat dated, is James Thewlis' *Concise*

Dictionary of Physics and Related Subjects (Pergamon, 1979).

849. Dictionary of Effects and Phenomena in Physics: Descriptions, Applications, Tables. Joachim Schubert. New York, NY: VCH, 1987. 140p., bibliog. $30.00. ISBN: 0-89573-487-7.

This translation of *Physikalische Effekte* contains discussions of some 400 effects and phenomena giving a definition, effects and relationships to other effects, full name of scientist responsible for naming, and citations to the literature.

850. Dictionary of Physics. 3rd. H.J. Gray; Alan Isaacs. Harlow, Great Britain: Longman, 1991. 640p. $52.50. ISBN: 0-582-03797-2.

Previously called a *New Dictionary of Physics*, this comprehensive dictionary covers physics and allied fields.

851. Dictionary of Physics: Russian, English, German, and French. V.J. Rydnik; E.A. Sviridenkov; N.D. Voropaev. New York, NY: Elsevier, 1989. 392p. $143.00. ISBN: 0-444-70490-6.

This multilingual dictionary lists some 6,000 terms in all fields of physics. Other Elsevier bilingual dictionaries in physics related areas include *Dictionary of High-Engery Physics: English, German, French, and Russian* (1987, 4,500 terms); *Dictionary of Nuclear Engineering: English, German, French, and Russian* (1985, 30,000 terms); and *Elsevier's Dictionary of High Vacuum Science and Technology: German, English, French, (Italian, Spanish, and Russian* (1968, 3,692 terms). For just Russian to English consult Irving Emin's *Russian-English Physics Dictionary* (Wiley, 1963).

852. Dictionary of Pure and Applied Physics. Louis DeVries. New York, NY: Elsevier, 1963-64. 2v. out-of-print.

Although this title is out-of-print, it is still the standard English-German/German-English dictionary for physics. It is comprehensive with v.1 covering German-English and v.2 English-German. Another useful German language dictionary is Charles J. Hyman's *Dictionary of Physics and Allied Sciences* (F. Unger, 1958-62).

853. Dictionary of Scientific Units: Including Dimensionless Numbers and Scales. 6th. *(Science Paperbacks, 210).* H.G. Jerrard; D.B. McNeill. New York, NY: Chapman & Hall, 1992. 244p., illus., bibliog., index. $29.95. ISBN: 0-412-46720-8.

Some 900 entries are included in this dictionary covering fundamental physics constants, standards, weights and measures, and conversion factors.

854. Encyclopaedic Dictionary of Physics. James Thewlis. New York, NY: Pergamon, 1961-64, 1966-75. 9v., 5suppl., index. $1,200.00. ISBN: 0-08-018296-8.

Although dated, this work is still considered the major dictionary in the physics field. It covers general, nuclear, solid state, molecular, chemical, metal, and vacuum physics; astronomy, geophysics, biophysics, and related subjects.

855. Facts on File Dictionary of Physics. revised. John Daintith. New York, NY: Facts on File, 1988. 235p., illus. $24.95. ISBN: 0-8160-1868-5.

Over 2,000 definitions are included in this small dictionary that stresses classical physics but also covers atomic, nuclear, and particle physics. Two other good concise dictionaries for the layperson are M.P. Lord's *Macmillan Dictionary of Physics* (Macmillan, 1986) and Valerie Illingworth's *Penguin Dictionary of Physics* (Penguin Books, 1991).

856. McGraw-Hill Dictionary of Physics. Sybil P. Parker. New York, NY: McGraw-Hill, 1985. 646p., illus. ISBN: 0-07-045418-3.

Material for this dictionary was previously published in the third edition of the *McGraw-Hill Dictionary of Scientific and Technical Terms*. It includes terms from all fields of physics. For specialized coverage there are many dictionaries such as Ronald C. Denney's *Dictionary of Spectroscopy* (Wiley, 1982) and A.M. James' *Dictionary of Thermodynamics* (Wiley, 1976).

Directories

857. Directory of Physics and Astronomy Staff Members. New York, NY: American Institute of Physics, 1975/76– , annual. 1975/76– , index. $30.00.

Previously called *Directory of Physics and Astronomy Faculties in North American Colleges and Universities*, this directory is the accepted source of information on college and university physics and astronomy departments, providing description, staff, and other related data. Another companion annual is *Graduate Programs in Physics, Astronomy, and Related Fields* (American Institute of Physics).

Encyclopedias

858. Encyclopedia of Applied Physics. George L. Trigg. New York, NY: American Institute of Physics, 1991– , irregular. 20v. projected. $295.00/vol., $5,950.00/set.

This alphabetically arranged encyclopedia is to be published over several years (v.7 begins in 1993) covering every area of physics and its related fields. When finished it will be the authoritative reference source for researchers in the field of physics.

859. Encyclopedia of Physics. 3rd. Robert M. Besancon. New York, NY: Van Nostrand Reinhold, 1985. 1,378p., illus., bibliog., index. $149.50. ISBN: 0-442-25778-3.

This good concise encyclopedia covers physics and related areas. Also of use would be Sybil P. Parker's *McGraw-Hill Encyclopedia of Physics* (McGraw-Hill, 1983).

860. Encyclopedia of Physics. 2nd. Rita G. Lerner; George L. Trigg. New York, NY: VCH, 1991. 1,408p., illus., bibliog., index. $150.00. ISBN: 0-89573-752-3.

This is one of the best one-volume encyclopedias covering physics. Articles are separately authored with entries for all areas of physics as well as related fields. A concise dictionary from the first edition was published as *Concise Encyclopedia of Solid State Physics* (Addison-Wesley, 1983).

861. Nuclear and Particle Physics Source Book. *(The McGraw-Hill Science Reference Series).* Sybil P. Parker. New York, NY: McGraw-Hill, 1988. $48.00. ISBN: 0-07-045509-0.

Material for this sourcebook has been taken from the sixth edition of the *McGraw-Hill Encyclopedia of Science and Technology*. It is arranged by topic and covers the structure of atomic nuclei and their interactions with each other.

862. Optics Source Book. Sybil P. Parker. New York, NY: McGraw-Hill, 1988. 399p., illus., index. $48.00. ISBN: 0-07-045506-6.

Material for this sourcebook has been taken from the sixth edition of the *McGraw-Hill Encyclopedia of Science and Technology*. All materials on optics and optical engineering have been brought together in a convenient volume.

863. Solid-State Physics Source Book. Sybil P. Parker. New York, NY: McGraw-Hill, 1988. 381p., illus., bibliog., index. $48.00. ISBN: 0-07-045503-1.

Material for this sourcebook was taken from the sixth edition of the *McGraw-Hill Encyclopedia of Science and Technology*. It is arranged by topic, covering all the material on solid state physics that was contained in the parent encyclopedia.

Guides to the Literature

864. Information Sources in Physics. 2nd. *(Butterworths Guide to Information Sources).* Dennis F. Shaw. Boston, MA: Butterworths, 1985. 456p., index. $80.00. ISBN: 0-408-01474-1.

Previously called *Use of Physics Literature*, this is the best guide to physics literature available. It covers the nature of the literature, the subfields of physics, and how to locate physics information. There are three other older out-of-date guides, which if updated, would be useful, including L.R.A. Melton's *Introductory Guide to Information Sources in Physics* (American Institute of Physics, 1978); Robert H. Whitford's *Physics Literature* (Scarecrow Press, 1968); and B. Yates' *How to Find Out About Physics* (Pergamon, 1965).

Handbooks and Manuals

865. American Institute of Physics Handbook. 3rd. Bruce H. Billings; Dwight E. Gray. New York, NY: McGraw-Hill, 1972. 1v. various paging, illus., bibliog., index. $159.50. ISBN: 0-07-001485-X.

Also called *AIP Handbook*, this title is a standard handbook for physicists. It is somewhat dated, but most of the tables and data included do not need updating. Another useful translation is N. Koshkin's *Handbook of Elementary Physics* (Gordon and Breach, 1982) as well as Edward Condon's *Handbook of Physics* (McGraw-Hill, 1967) for historical information.

866. Color Science: Concepts and Methods, Quantitative Data and Formulae. 2nd. *(Wiley Series in Pure and Applied Optics).* Gunter Wyszecki; W.S. Stiles. New York, NY: Wiley, 1982. 950p., illus., bibliog., index. $123.00. ISBN: 0-471-02106-7.

This handbook covers concepts and methods, quantitative data, and formulae pertaining to color science including details of light sources, color filters, monochromators, and photon detectors.

867. CRC Handbook of Laser Science and Technology. Boca Raton, FL: CRC, 1982-1987. 5v., 2suppl. illus., bibliog., index. $177.00/vol. ISBN: 0-8493-3501-9v.1, 0-8493-3502-7v.2, 0-8493-3503-5v.3, 0-8493-3504-5v.4, 0-8493-3505-1v.5, 0-8493-3506-X suppl.1.

This comprehensive handbook covers lasers and masers, gas lasers, and optical materials. The volumes and supplements cover v.1—Lasers and masers (1982); v.2—Gas lasers (1982); v.3—Optical materials, part 1: Nonlinear optical properties/radiation damage (1986); v.4—Optical materials, part 2: Properties (1986); v.5—Optical materials, part 3: Applications, coatings, and fabrication (1987); supplement 1—Lasers (1990); supplement 2—Optical materials (1992). Also useful is F.T. Arrechi's six-volume set *Laser Handbook* (Elsevier, 1972-1991).

868. Handbook of Optics. Walter G. Driscoll; William Vaughn; Optical Society of America. New York, NY: McGraw-Hill, 1978. 1,600p., illus., bibliog., index. $124.50. ISBN: 0-07-047710-8.

This comprehensive handbook covers all aspects of optics. It is well documented and contains numerous charts and graphs.

869. Handbook of Physical Calculations: Definitions, Formulas, Technical Applications, Physical Tables, Conversion Tables, Graphs, Dictionary of Physical Terms. 2nd enlarged & revised. Jan J. Tuma. New York, NY: McGraw-Hill, 1983. 478p., illus., bibliog., index. $39.95. ISBN: 0-07-065439-5.

This is an authoritative and well-established handbook of physics information.

870. Handbuch der Physik. New York, NY: Springer-Verlag, 1956-1988. 55v., illus., diagrams, bibliog., index. price per volume varies.

Also called the *Encyclopedia of Physics*, this treatise-type handbook covers the entire field of physics in a systematic method. It is in German, English, and French with volumes 5:2 and 43 never published.

871. Physicist's Desk Reference. 2nd. Herbert L. Anderson. New York, NY: American Institute of Physics, 1989. 356p., illus., bibliog., index. $60.00, $35.00pbk. ISBN: 0-88318-629-2, 0-88318-610-1pbk.

Previously called *Physics Vade Mecum*, this handy desk reference provides facts, formulas, graphs, and tables that the practicing physicist would need on a day-to-day basis.

872. Sadtler Standard Spectra. Philadelphia, PA: Sadtler Research Labs, 1980– , irregular. Multivolume with supplements in several series, all in loose-leaf volumes, index. price per volume varies.

The Sadtler Research Labs is the world's foremost producer of spectra data. The data are constantly updated and added to. The major spectra series include infrared grating; infrared prism; proton nuclear magnetic resonance; 13c nuclear magnetic resonance; ultraviolet; infrared vapor phase; Raman; infrared high resolution evaluated quantitative; ultraviolet in nonpolar solvents; 100 MHz nuclear magnetic resonance; and fluorescence. These are very expensive sets to purchase in their entirety with one series costing more than $50,000 to purchase all at once.

873. Superconductivity Sourcebook. V. Daniel Hunt. New York, NY: Wiley, 1989. 308p., illus., bibliog., index. $39.95. ISBN: 0-471-61706-7.

This comprehensive handbook covers all areas of superconductivity from magnetic applications to supercollider. The market potential for superconductivity is also discussed.

874. Wiley/NBS Registry of Mass Spectral Data. 5th. Fred W. McLafferty; Douglas B. Stauffer. New York, NY: Wiley, 1989. 7v., illus., bibliog., index. $6,000.00. ISBN: 0-471-62886-7.

This comprehensive compilation of mass spectral data is formed from the combination of the two previously published works: *Registry of Mass Spectra Data* and *EPA/NIH Mass Spectral Data Base* and its supplements.

Histories

875. History of Classical Physics: A Selected Annotated Bibliography. *(Bibliographies of the History of Science and Technology, v.8) (Garland Reference Library of the Humanities, v.444).* Roderick Weis Home. New York, NY: Garland Publishing, 1984. 324p., index. out-of-print. ISBN: 0-8240-9067-5.

Some 1,300 entries are included in this historical bibliography. It covers the years 1700-1900 and excludes entries for materials that appear in other bibliographies of this series such as astronomy and geophysics. Another very brief bibliography that is useful is Stephen G. Brush's *Resources for the History of Physics* (University Press of New England, 1972).

876. History of Modern Physics, 1800-1950. Los Angeles, CA: Tomash Publishing, 1947– , irregular. v.1– , index. price per volume varies. ISBN: 0-88318-523-7v.7.

Each volume in this ongoing history of physics covers a particular topic in detail. To date, the following have been published: v.1—*Alsos*; v.2—*Project Y—The Los Alamos Story*; v.3—*American Physics in Transition: A History of Conceptual Change in the Late 19th Century*; v.4—*The Question of the Atom: From the Karlsruhe Congress to the First Solvay Conference, 1860-1911*; v.5—*Physics for a New Century*; v.6—*Basic Bethe: Seminal Articles on Nuclear Physics, 1936-1937*; v.7—*A History of the Theories of Aether and Electricity*. Some one-volume histories that are also useful include *History of Twentieth Century Physics* (Academic Press, 1977) and Laurie M. Brown's *Birth of Particle Physics* (Cambridge University Press, 1983).

877. History of Modern Physics: An International Bibliography. *(Bibliographies of the History of Science and Technology, v.4); (Garland Reference Library of the Humanities, v.420).* Stephen G. Brush; Lanfranco Belloni. New York, NY: Garland Publishing, 1983. 334p., index. $55.00. ISBN: 0-8240-9117-5.

Over 2,000 entries are included in this bibliography covering modern physics from the discovery of X-rays in 1895 to the mid-1900s. Companion titles are the *Isis Cumulative Bibliography* (Mansell, 1913-1965) and

Literature on the History of Physics in the 20th Century (University of California Press, 1981).

878. History of Physics. *(Readings from Physics Today, no. 2).* Spencer R. Weart; Melba Phillips. New York, NY: American Institute of Physics, 1985. 375p., illus. (part in color), bibliog. $25.00. ISBN: 0-88318-468-0.

This good general history of physics is based on published articles in *Physics Today*. Another more comprehensive history is Isaac Asimov's *History of Physics* (Walker, 1984). Other good general histories are Joseph Norwood's *Twentieth Century Physics* (Prentice-Hall, 1976), Claude Garrod's *Twentieth Century Physics* (Blackwell, 1984), and Olaf Pedersen's *Early Physics and Astronomy* (Cambridge University Press, 1992).

Tables

879. Astrophysical Formulae: A Compendium for the Physicist and Astrophysicist. Kenneth R. Lang. New York, NY: Springer-Verlag, 1978. 735p., illus., bibliog., index. $49.00. ISBN: 0-387-09064-9.

This easy-to-use source lists hundreds of formula used by physicists and astrophysicists.

880. Atomic Data and Nuclear Data Tables. San Diego, CA: Academic Press, 1969– , irregular. v.12– , illus., index. $297.00. ISSN: 0092-640X.

This "journal devoted to compilations of experimental and theoretical results" in atomic physics, nuclear physics, and related areas was formed by the union of *Atomic Data* and *Nuclear Data Tables.*

881. Fundamental Formulas of Physics. Donald Howard Menzel. New York, NY: Dover, 1960. 2v., illus., index. $18.00. ISBN: 0-486-60595-7v.1, 0-486-60596-5v.2.

This unabridged and revised version of a work published in 1955 is a good standard source of physics formulas. Also of use but long out-of-date is the *Smithsonian Physical Tables* (Smithsonian Institution, 1954).

882. Steam Tables in SI-Units: Concise Steam Tables in SI-Units (Student's Tables). 3rd enlarged. Ulrich Grigull; Johannes Straub; Peter Schiebener. New York, NY: Springer-Verlag, 1990. 133p. $19.95. ISBN: 0-387-51888-6.

Properties of ordinary water substance up to 1,000C and 100 megapascal are included in these tables. There are numerous specialized compendiums of tables including Joseph Henry Keenan's *Gas Tables* (Wiley, 1983) and C. Michael Lederer's *Table of Isotopes* (Wiley, 1978).

883. Thermophysical Properties of Matter. Y.S. Touloukian; Purdue University Thermophysical Properties Research Institute. New York, NY: IFI/Plenum (reprinted by Books on Demand), 1970-79. 13v., illus., index. $160.00/vol.

Also called *TPRC Data Series*, this is a revision and expansion of a work published in 1960-66 as *TPRC Data Book*. The thermophysical properties cover thermal conductivity, specific heat, thermal radiative properties, thermal diffusivity, viscosity, and thermal expansion.

Periodicals

884. Advances in Physics. Basingstoke, Great Britain: Taylor & Francis, 1952– , bimonthly. v.1– , index. $420.00. ISSN: 0001-8732.

885. American Journal of Physics. College Park, MD: American Association of Physics, 1933– , monthly. v.1– , index. $205.00. ISSN: 0002-9505.

886. Annals of Physics. San Diego, CA: Academic Press, 1957– , 16/year. v.1– , index. $1,152.00. ISSN: 0003-4916.

887. Applied Physics, A: Solids and Surfaces; B: Photophysics and Laser Chemistry. Berlin, Germany: Springer-Verlag/Deutsche Physikalische Gesellschaft, 1973– , 24/year. v.1– , index. $683.00pt A; $715.00pt B. ISSN: 0721-7250pt A; 0721-7269pt B.

888. Applied Physics Letters. New York, NY: American Institute of Physics, 1962– , weekly. v.1– , index. $820.00. ISSN: 0003-6951.

889. Bulletin of the American Physical Society. New York, NY: American Institute of Physics, 1956– , 9/year. v.1– , index. $400.00. ISSN: 0003-0503.

890. Canadian Journal of Physics/Journal Canadien de Physique. Ottawa, Ontario, Canada: National Research Council of Canada, 1929– , monthly. v.1– , index. $92.00. ISSN: 0008-4204.

891. Chemical Physics. New York, NY: Elsevier, 1973– , 27/year. v.1– , index. $2,050.00. SuDoc: 0301-0104

892. Chemical Physics Letters. New York, NY: Elsevier, 1967– , 72/year. v.1– , index. $6,084.00. ISSN: 0009-2614.

893. Contemporary Physics. Basingstoke, Great Britain: Taylor & Francis, 1959– , bimonthly. v.1– , index. $272.00. ISSN: 0010-7514.

894. Journal of Applied Physics. New York, NY: American Institute of Physics, 1931– , semi-monthly ,semi-monthly. v.1– , index. $1,240.00. ISSN: 0021-8979.

895. Journal of Chemical Physics. New York, NY: American Institute of Physics, 1931– , semi-monthly. v.1– , index. $1,830.00. ISSN: 0021-9606.

896. Journal of Mathematical Physics. New York, NY: American Institute of Physics, 1960– , monthly. v.1– , index. $875.00. ISSN: 0022-2488.

897. Journal of Physics, A: Mathematical and General; B: Atomic; Molecular, and Optical Physics; Condensed Matter; D: Applied Physics; E: Measurement Science and Technology; G: Nuclear and Particle Physics. Bristol, Great Britain: Institute of Physics, 1968– , 134/year. v.1– , index. $1,677.00pt A; $1,422.00ptB; $2,894.00Condensed Matter; $694.00pt D; $409.00pt E; $978.00pt G. ISSN: 0305-4470pt A; 0953-4075pt B; 0953-8984Condensed Matter; 0022-3727pt D; 0957-0233pt E; 0954-3899pt G.

898. Journal of Physics and Chemistry of Solids. Tarrytown, NY: Pergamon Press, 1956– , 12/year. v.1– , index. $1,095.00. ISSN: 0022-3697.

899. Journal of the Acoustical Society of America. New York, NY: American Institute of Physics, 1929– , monthly. v.1– , index. $600.00. ISSN: 0001-4966.

900. Journal of the Optical Society of America, Pt A; Pt B. Washington, DC: Optical Society of America, 1917– , 24/year. v.1– , index. $350.00pt A; $490.00pt B. ISSN: 0740-3232pt A; 0740-3224pt B.

901. Nuovo Ciemento della Societa Italiana di Fisica, A: Nuclei, Particles and Fields; B: General Physics, Relativity, Astronomy, and Mathematical Physics and Methods; C: Geophysics and Space Physics; D: Condensed Matter, Atomic, Molecular, and Chemical Physics, Fluids, Plasmas, Biophysics. Bologna, Italy: Editrice Compositori SRL, 1971– , A: bimonthly; B: monthly; C: bimonthly, D: monthly. v.1– , index. $835.00pt A; $583.00pt B; $295.00pt C; $505.00pt D. ISSN: 0369-4097pt A; 0369-4100pt B; 0390-5551pt C; 0392-6737pt D.

902. Philosophical Magazine, Pt A: Defects and Mechanical Properties; Pt B: Electronic, Optical and Magnetic Properties. Basingstoke, Great Britain: Taylor & Francis, 1798– , monthly. v.1– , index. $1,190.00. ISSN: 0031-8086.

903. Physica, A: Statistical and Theoretical Physics; B: Physics of Condensed Matter; C: Superconductivity; D: Nonlinear Phenomena. New York, NY: North-Holland/European Physical Society, 1934– , A: 40/year; B: 32/year; C: 68/year; D: 32/year. v.1– , index. $7,133.00. ISSN: 0378-4371pt A; 0921-4526pt B; 0921-4534pt C; 0167-2789pt D.

904. Physical Review, A: General Physics; B: Condensed Matter. New York, NY: American Institute of Physics/American Physical Society, 1970– , A: 24/year; B: 48/year. v.1– , index. $1,535.00pt A; $2380.00pt B. ISSN: 0556-2791pt A; 0163-1829pt B.

905. Physical Review Letters. New York, NY: American Institute of Physics/American Physical Society, 1958– , weekly. v.1– , index. $1,000.00. ISSN: 0031-9007.

906. Physics Education. Bristol, Great Britain: Institute of Physics, 1966– , 6/year. v.1– , index. $138.00. ISSN: 0031-9120.

907. Physics Teacher. College Park, MD: American Association of Physics Teachers, 1963– , 9/year. v.1– , index. $133.00. ISSN: 0031-921X.

908. Physics Today. New York, NY: American Institute of Physics, 1948– , monthly. v.1– , index. $115.00. ISSN: 0031-9228.

909. Physics World. Bristol, Great Britain: Institute of Physics, 1950– , monthly. v.1– , index. $120.00. ISSN: 0953-8585.

910. Reports on Progress in Physics. Bristol, Great Britain: Institute of Physics, 1934– , monthly. v.1– , index. $770.00. ISSN: 0034-4885.

911. Review of Scientific Instruments. New York, NY: American Institute of Physics, 1930– , monthly. v.1– , index. $650.00. ISSN: 0034-6748.

912. Reviews of Modern Physics. New York, NY: American Institute of Physics/American Physical Society, 1929– , quarterly. v.1– , index. $230.00. ISSN: 0034-6861.

ZOOLOGY

Abstracts and Indexes

913. Animal Behavior Abstracts. Bethesda, MD: Cambridge Scientific Abstracts, 1972– , quarterly. v.1– , index. $485.00. ISSN: 0301-8695.

Previously called *Behavioural Biology Abstracts: Section A—Animal Behavior*, this abstracting service covers field and laboratory studies of all aspects of animal behavior. Some 5,000 abstracts a year are published. It is also available online and on CD-ROM.

914. Aquatic Sciences and Fisheries Abstracts. Bethesda, MD: Cambridge Scientific Abstracts, 1969– , monthly. v.1– , index. $855.00 part 1; $615.00 part 2; $225.00 part 3. ISSN: 0140-5373 part 1; 0140-5381 part 2; 1045-6031 part 3.

Previously called *Aquatic Biology Abstracts* and *Current Bibliography for Aquatic Sciences and Fisheries*, this service is now published in 3 parts: Part 1—Biological sciences and living resources; Part 2—Ocean technology, policy and non-living resources; Part 3—Aquatic pollution and environmental quality. This abstracting services publishes some 40,000 abstracts a year and is also available online and on CD-ROM.

915. Entomology Abstracts. Bethesda, MD: Cambridge Scientific Abstracts, 1969– , monthly. v.1– , index. $765.00. ISSN: 0013-8924.

This abstracting service covers insects, arachnids, myriapods, onychophorans, and terrestrial isopods with some 8,800 abstracts each year. It is also available online and on CD-ROM.

916. Index Bergeyana: An Annotated Alphabetic Listing of Names of the Taxa of the Bacteria. Robert E. Buchanan. Baltimore, MD: Williams & Wilkins, 1966. 1,472p., bibliog. out-of-print.

This alphabetical list of names of the taxa of bacteria is the most comprehensive index available. The main volume evaluates some 20,000 taxa with a 1981 supplement adding several more thousand. It is a companion to *Bergey's Manual of Determinative Bacteriology*.

917. Nomenclator Zoologicus. London, Great Britain: Zoological Society of London, 1939– , irregular. v.1– , index. $45.00. ISSN: 0078-0952.

This source records the bibliographic origins of published generic and subgeneric names in zoology.

918. Wildlife Review. Ft Collins, CO: U.S. Fish and Wildlife Service, 1935– , bimonthly. v.1– , index. free. ISSN: 0043-5511.

This indexing service for wildlife management covers fish and wildlife magazines in the United States. It is also available on CD-ROM.

919. Zoological Record. London, Great Britain: Zoological Society of London, 1864– , annual. v.1– , index. $2,200.00. ISSN: 0144-3607.

This comprehensive retrospective bibliography of the world's zoological literature was previously called *Record of Zoological Literature* (1906-1914) and published as the 6th to 14th issues of the *International Catalogue of Scientific Literature, Class N, Zoology*. It includes 27 separate sections, each covering a special genera, each published separately, and each with its own indexes. It is also available online and on CD-ROM.

Bibliographies

920. Animal Identification: A Reference Guide. R.W. Sime; D. Hollis. New York, NY: Wiley, 1980. 3v., bibliog., index. out-of-print. ISBN: 0-471-27765-7v.1.

Although out-of-print, this title is an excellent bibliography of the various scientific books and papers that are used to identify aquatic and terrestrial animals. It is arranged systematically and then geographically in 3 volumes: v.1—Marine and brackish water animals; v.2—Land and freshwater animals (not insects); v.3—Insects.

921. Bibliography of Reproduction: A Classified Monthly List of References Compiled from the Research Literature. Cambridge, Great Britain: Reproduction Research Information Service, 1963– , monthly. v.1– , index. $365.00. ISSN: 0006-1565.

A current bibliography of books, papers, and articles pertaining to reproduction in the fields of biology, medicine, agriculture, and veterinary science.

922. Endangered Vertebrates: A Selected, Annotated Bibliography, 1981-1988. *(Garland Reference Library of Social Sciences, v.480).* Sylva Baker. New York, NY: Garland, 1990. 197p., index. $32.00. ISBN: 0-8240-4796-6.

This small specialized bibliography contains materials pertaining to endangered vertebrates. All entries contain full bibliographic information and are annotated.

923. Entomological Nomenclature and Literature. 3rd revised and enlarged. W.J. Chamberlin. Westport, CT: Greenwood Press, 1970 (c1952). 141p., index. $49.75. ISBN: 0-8371-3810-8.

This classic bibliography is arranged chronologically, covering nomenclature associated with insects. There is a separate annotated bibliography of serials.

Dictionaries, Glossaries, and Thesauri

924. Amphibian Species of the World: A Taxonomic and Geographical Reference. Darrel R. Frost. Lawrence, KS: Allen Press/Association of Systematics Collections, 1985. 732p., bibliog., index. $85.00. ISBN: 0-942924-11-8.

This dictionary lists species names of amphibians of the world. Arranged alphabetically within the taxonomic hierarchy, each entry contains scientific name, authority, year of citation, type of species, type specimens, type locality, distribution, and comments.

925. Birds of the World: A Checklist. 3rd. Michael Walters. Neptune City, NJ: TFH, 1980. 704p., index. $69.95. ISBN: 0-87666-894-5.

This important reference source on birds of the world contains a common-name index. Another checklist of over 9,700 living species is Burt L. Monroe's *World Checklist of Birds* (Yale University Press, 1993).

926. Birdwatcher's Dictionary. Peter Weaver. San Diego, CA: Academic Press, 1990. 156p. $16.00. ISBN: 0-85661-028-3.

This handy little dictionary explains the terminology encountered by birdwatchers.

927. Collegiate Dictionary of Zoology. Robert W. Pennak. Melbourne, FL: Krieger, 1987. 594p. $28.50. ISBN: 0-89874-921-2.

This is a very good general zoological dictionary for the student.

928. Common Names of North American Butterflies. Jacqueline Y. Miller. Washington, DC: Smithsonian Institution Press, 1992. 177p., bibliog., index. $14.95. ISBN: 1-56098-122-9.

This dictionary lists all the recorded species and subspecies of butterflies found north of Mexico. The geographical distribution of each is noted.

929. Complete Checklist of the Birds of the World. 2nd. Richard Howard; Alick Moore. San Diego, CA: Academic Press, 1991. 622p., index. $49.50. ISBN: 0-12-356910-9.

This work is an excellent checklist down to the subspecies level of the world's birds. It includes geographical distribution and common name.

930. Concise Oxford Dictionary of Zoology. Michael Allaby. New York, NY: Oxford University Press, 1991. 508p., illus. $39.95. ISBN: 0-19-866162-2.

Some 6,000 entries are included in this dictionary of zoology covering ecology, evolution, animal behavior, earth history, cell structure, physiology, zoogeography, taxonomic principles, and genetics. It replaces A.W. Leftwich's *Dictionary of Zoology* (Constable, 1973).

931. Dictionary of Birds. Bruce Campbell; Elizabeth Lack. Friday Harbor, WA: Harrell Books, 1985. 700p. $75.00. ISBN: 0-931130-12-3.

This dictionary is a revision and update of A. Landsborough Thomas' *New Dictionary of Birds.* Entries for birds are at the family level by common name and provide characteristics, habitat, taxonomy, distribution, population, movement, food, behavior, breeding, and voice. Another older and smaller but still useful work is Bruce Campbell and Richard J. Holmes' *Dictionary of Birds in Color* (Viking Press, 1974). For anatomical information on birds consult J.J. Baumel's *Nomina Anatomica Avium: An Annotated Dictionary of Birds* (Academic Press, 1979).

932. Dictionary of Entomology. A.W. Leftwich. New York, NY: Crane Russak, 1976. 360p., bibliog. out-of-print. ISBN: 0-8448-0983-7.

This well-known but now out-of-print dictionary contains over 3,000 definitions of species plus some biological terms. For just butterflies and moths consult Allan Watson and Paul E.S. Whalley's *Dictionary of Butterflies and Moths in Color* (McGraw-Hill, 1975).

933. Dictionary of Ethology. Klaus Immelmann; Colin Beer. Cambridge, MA: Harvard University Press, 1989. 336p., illus., bibliog. $35.00. ISBN: 0-674-20506-5.

This translation of *Worterbuch der Verhaltensforschung* covers those terms pertaining to animal behavior. The definitions are nearly encyclopedic in length.

934. Dictionary of Scientific Bird Names.
James A. Jobling. New York, NY: Oxford
University Press, 1991. 272p., illus. $29.95.
ISBN: 0-19-854634-3.

This up-to-date dictionary of the scientific names
of birds is alphabetically arranged. Other useful titles
are Ernest A. Choate's *Dictionary of American Bird
Names* (Harvard Common Press, 1985) and A.F.
Gotch's *Birds, Their Latin Names Explained* (Blandford Press, 1981).

935. Invertebrates: An Illustrated Glossary.
Michael Stachowitsch. New York, NY:
Wiley-Liss, 1992. 690p., illus., index. $175.00;
$79.95pbk. ISBN: 0-471-83294-4;
0-471-56192-4pbk.

This unique dictionary covers 77 living invertebrate taxa, giving detailed definitions of all anatomical
characteristics. Each phylum's entry has all definitions
that refer to that phylum.

**936. Reptiles, Their Latin Names Explained:
A Guide to Animal Classification.** A.F.
Gotch. New York, NY: Blandford Press, 1986.
176p., illus., bibliog., index. price not
available. ISBN: 0-7137-1704-1.

This guide explains the Latin names that are assigned to reptiles showing how they are used and how
to develop a name.

**937. Venomous Snakes of the World: A
Checklist.** Keith A. Harding; Kenneth R.G.
Welch. New York, NY: Pergamon Press, 1980.
188p., bibliog., index. $100.00. ISBN:
0-08-025495-0.

Published as supplement number one, 1980, to the
journal *Toxicon* this is a checklist of poisonous snakes
of the world.

938. World List of Mammalian Species. 3rd.
G.B. Corbet; J.E. Hill. New York, NY: Oxford
University Press, 1991. 243p., illus., bibliog.
$72.00. ISBN: 0-19-854017-5.

This publication is an authoritative complete list of
the mammalian species in the world. Should be used
with such works as *Walker's Mammals of the World*,
listed elsewhere in this chapter. Also useful would be
James H. Honacki's *Mammal Species of the World*
(Allen Press, 1982) and A.F. Gotch's *Mammals, Their
Latin Names Explained* (Blandford Press, 1979).

939. Zoological Catalogue of Australia. D.W.
Walton. Canberra, Australia: Australian
Government Publishing, 1984– , irregular.
v.1– , index. $29.95/volume. ISBN:
0-644-02839-4v.1.

When finished, this will be an authoritative catalog
of all the known species of animals found in Australia.
It is a list providing accepted genus and species names
plus synonyms.

Directories

940. Aquariums: Windows to Nature.
Leighton Taylor. New York, NY:
Prentice-Hall, 1993. 192p., illus. (part in color),
bibliog., index. $35.00. ISBN: 0-671-85019-9.

This excellent directory/encyclopedia of North
American aquariums provides descriptions, collections, and research. Also included is a traveler's guide
to North American aquariums and a directory of great
aquariums from around the world.

**941. Zoological Parks and Aquariums in the
Americas.** Wheeling, WV: American
Association of Zoological Parks and
Aquariums, 1992-93. 1v., various paging,
index. $60.00. ISBN: 0-686-16897-6.

Formerly *Zoos and Aquariums in the Americas*, this
regularly published book provides a wealth of information on zoos and aquariums in the United States.
Another useful annual is the *International Zoo Yearbook* (Zoological Society of London, 1960-). Although dated, Jefferson G. Ulmer and Susan Gower's
Lions and Tigers (Garland, 1985), is a guide to zoological parks, visitor farms, nature centers, and marine
life displays in the United States and Canada.

Encyclopedias

**942. Audubon Society Encyclopedia of Ani-
mal Life.** Ralph Buchsbaum. New York, NY:
Clarkson N. Potter, 1982. 606p., illus., index.
out-of-print. ISBN: 0-517-54657-4.

This interesting, well-illustrated encyclopedia
traces the evolution of the 33 phyla and 7 classes of the
phylum Chordata. Four other animal life encyclopedias that could be considered are Philip Whitfield's
Macmillan Illustrated Animal Encyclopedia (Macmillan, 1984); Maurice and Robert Burton's *Encyclopedia
of the Animal Kingdom* (Crescent Books, 1984); Elena
Marcon and Manuel Mongini's *World Encyclopedia
of Animals* (Orbis, 1984); and the colorful, coffee-table
work *New Larousse Encyclopedia of Animal Life* (Bo-
nanza Books, 1980).

**943. Audubon Society Encyclopedia of North
American Birds.** John K. Terres. New York,
NY: Knopf, 1980. 1,109p., illus, bibliog.,
index. out-of-print. ISBN: 0-394-46651-9.

This very comprehensive work contains some
6,000 cross-referenced entries to the birds of North
America. It also includes definitions of terms, a bibliography, and 126 biographies of famous naturalists.
Also useful is Christopher M. Perrins and Alex L.A.
Middleton's *Encyclopedia of Birds* (Facts on File,
1986).

944. Cambridge Encyclopedia of Ornithology.
Michael Brooke; Tim Birkhead. New York,
NY: Cambridge University Press, 1991. 362p.,
illus., index. $49.50. ISBN: 0-521-36205-9.

This well-written and beautifully illustrated topical
encyclopedia of birds has a list of ornithological organizations as well as a glossary of the more common
terms.

945. Coral Reefs of the World. International
Union for the Conservation of Nature and Natural Resources. Gland, Switzerland: IUCN,
1988. 3v., illus., bibliog., index. $100/set.
ISBN: 0-318-35599-X.

This 3-volume set is the definitive encyclopedia of
coral reefs. Detailed descriptions are given. The 3
volumes cover v.1—Atlantic and Eastern Pacific;
v.2—Indian Ocean, Red Sea, and Gulf; v.3—Central
and Western Pacific.

946. Encyclopedia of Aquatic Life. Keith Banister; Andrew Campbell. New York, NY: Facts
on File, 1985. 349p., illus. (part in color),
bibliog., index. $45.00. ISBN: 0-8160-1257-1.

Fishes, marine invertebrates, and marine mammals
are included in this well-illustrated encyclopedia.

947. Encyclopedia of Insects. Christopher
O'Toole. New York, NY: Facts on File, 1986.
160p., illus., index. $24.95. ISBN:
0-8160-1358-6.

Each of the 28 different orders of insects is treated
separately in this beautifully illustrated encyclopedia.
The major aspects of each order are described using
numerous charts, lists, and boxed illustrations.

948. Encyclopedia of Mammals. David W.
MacDonald. New York, NY: Facts on File,
1984. 960p., illus., index. $65.00. ISBN:
0-87196-871-1.

Every living species of mammals is covered in this
encyclopedia with arrangement by order—carnivores,
sea mammals, primates, large herbivores, small herbivores, insect eaters, and marsupials.

949. Encyclopedia of Marine Animals.
Neville Coleman. New York, NY:
HarperCollins, 1991. 324p., color illus. $50.00.
ISBN: 0-20-716429-0.

This well-illustrated encyclopedia shows a selected
number of marine animals with general descriptions.
Also of use would be Steven K. Katona's *Field Guide
to Whales, Porpoises, and Seals from Cape Cod to
Newfoundland* (Smithsonian, 1993).

950. Encyclopedia of Marine Invertebrates.
Jerry G. Walls. Neptune City, NJ: TFH, 1982.
736p., illus. (part in color), bibliog., index.
$49.95. ISBN: 0-87666-495-8.

This encyclopedia provides detailed descriptions of
marine invertebrates that are suitable for aquariums.
Entries are arranged phylogenetically from Protozoa
to Cephalochoradata.

**951. Encyclopedia of Reptiles and Amphibi-
ans.** Tim Halliday; Kraig Alder. New York,
NY: Facts on File, 1986. 160p., illus., index.
$27.95. ISBN: 0-8160-1359-4.

Reptiles and amphibians are described in detail
with some striking photographs. The articles include
such things as characteristics of an order, physiological
form, and descriptions of each group's families. An
older, out-of-print, but still useful work is Alan E.
Leviton's *Reptiles and Amphibians of North America*
(Doubleday, 1971).

952. Encyclopedia of Shells. Kenneth R. Wye.
New York, NY: Facts on File, 1991. 288p.,
bibliog., index. $45.00. ISBN: 0-8160-2702-1.

This general guide to shells includes some 1,200
species in this encyclopedia. Common and scientific
names as well as complete descriptions are given.

**953. Field Guide to the Birds of South-East
Asia, Covering Burma, Malaya, Thailand,
Cambodia, Vietnam, Laos, and Hong Kong.**
Ben F. King; Edward C. Dickinson. Boston,
MA: Houghton Mifflin, 1975. 480p., illus.
(part in color), bibliog., index. out-of-print.
ISBN: 0-395-19113-0.

Arranged in the format of the *Peterson Field
Guides*, this guide covers some 1,200 species of birds.

954. Grzimek's Animal Life Encyclopedia.
Bernhard Grzimek. New York, NY: Van
Nostrand Reinhold, 1972-75. 13v., illus., index.
out-of-print.

This authoritative encyclopedia is arranged by animal group with each volume arranged by animal orders
and families. The mammals section has been revised
as *Grzimek's Encyclopedia of Mammals*, listed elsewhere in this chapter.

955. Grzimek's Encyclopedia of Evolution.
Bernhard Grzimek. New York, NY: Van
Nostrand Reinhold, 1976. 560p., illus. (part in
color), bibliog., index. out-of-print.

As a companion to *Grzimek's Animal Life Encyclopedia*, this volume covers information on animal evolution.

956. Grzimek's Encyclopedia of Mammals.
2nd. Bernhard Grzimek. New York, NY:
McGraw-Hill, 1990. 5v., illus. (part in color),
bibliog., index. $500.00. ISBN:
0-07-909508-9.

This translation of *Grzimeks Enzyklopadie
Sangetiere* is a revision of those volumes covering
mammals in the 13-volume *Grzimek's Animal Life*

Encyclopedia. It is comprehensive, including such domestic species as cats and dogs. The illustrations are outstanding.

957. Illustrated Encyclopedia of Birds: The Definitive Reference to Birds of the World. Christopher M. Perrins. New York, NY: Prentice-Hall, 1991. 420p., illus. $50.00. ISBN: 0-13-083635-4.

Some 9,300 species from every family of living birds are included in this encyclopedia with each entry providing common and scientific name, range, habitat, and size.

958. Illustrated Encyclopedia of Wildlife. Lakeville, CT: Grey Castle Press, 1990. 15v., illus., bibliog., index. $495.00. ISBN: 1-55905-052-7.

This 15-volume set is an excellent illustrated encyclopedia of the animal kingdom. Volumes 1-5 cover mammals; 6-8 birds; 9 reptiles and amphibians; 10 fish; and 11 invertebrates. This source is good for the layperson. A good popular one-volume work is Stanley Klein's *Encyclopedia of North American Wildlife* (Facts on File, 1983).

959. Mammals of North America. 2nd. E. Raymond Hall. New York, NY: Wiley, 1981. 2v., illus., bibliog., index. out-of-print. ISBN: 0-471-05443-7v.1.

Mammals of North America is the most comprehensive work covering the North American mammals from Greenland to Panama. Over 3,600 mammals are covered in great detail.

960. Marshall Cavendish International Wildlife Encyclopedia. Maurice Burton; Robert Burton. North Bellmore, NY: Marshall Cavendish, 1991. 25v., color illus., bibliog., index. $499.95. ISBN: 0-86307-734-X.

This is a good general encyclopedia for the student and layperson.

961. Naturalized Birds of the World. Christopher Lever. New York, NY: Wiley, 1987. 615p., illus., bibliog., index. price not available. ISBN: 0-470-20789-2.

This book provides detailed descriptions and discussions of birds that have been naturalized or domesticated throughout the world.

962. Walker's Mammals of the World. 5th. Ronald M. Nowak. Baltimore, MD: Johns Hopkins University Press, 1991. 2v., illus., bibliog., index. $89.95. ISBN: 0-8018-2525-7.

Previously called *Mammals of the World*, this authoritative encyclopedic work was first published by Ernest P. Walker. Some 1,100 genera and 4,000 species are described in detail.

963. World Encyclopedia of Fishes. Alwyne C. Wheeler. London, Great Britain: Macdonald, 1985. 368p., illus. (part in color), index. price not available. ISBN: 0-356-10715-9.

This general encyclopedia covers the fishes of the world and is intended for the layperson. It has excellent color illustrations.

Guides and Field Guides

964. Butterflies of North America: A Natural History and Field Guide. James A. Scott. Stanford, CA: Stanford University Press, 1986. 583p., illus. (part in color), bibliog., index. $65.00; $24.95pbk. ISBN: 0-8047-1205—; 0-8047-2013-4pbk.

This excellent field guide identifies North American butterflies. The descriptions are well-written and the illustrations are outstanding.

965. Collector's Guide to Seashells of the World. Jerome M. Eisenberg. Avenal, NJ: Outlet Book Co, 1989. 224p., illus., index. $15.99. ISBN: 0-517-69096-9.

This small field guide for the amateur covers the more common seashells.

966. Field Guide to Seabirds of the World. Peter Harrison. New York, NY: Viking Penguin, 1987. 288p., illus., index. $24.95. ISBN: 0-8289-0610-6.

Although small in size, this work is an excellent field guide to seabirds. The photographs include some of the more rare birds. Complete information needed for identification is given for each described species.

967. Field Guide to the Birds of North America. Thomas B. Allen; Teresa S. Purvis. Washington, DC: National Geographic Society, 1983. 464p., color illus., index. $16.95. ISBN: 0-87044-472-7.

This publication is one of the most beautiful field guides for birds available. The 200 color paintings are truly works of art.

968. Guide to Animal Tracking and Behavior. Donald W. Stokes; Lillian O. Stokes. Boston, MA: Little, Brown, and Co, 1986. 418p., illus., bibliog., index. $10.95. ISBN: 0-36-81730-9.

Also called *Animal Tracking*, this unique guide covers all types of evidence that can help identify an animal including footprints, tree scratches, and droppings.

969. Henry Holt Guide to Shells of the World. A.P.H. Oliver. New York, NY: Henry Holt, 1989 (c1975). 320p., color illus., bibliog., index. $12.95. ISBN: 0-8050-1119-6.

Originally published as the *Hamlyn Guide to Shells of the World*, this guide describes over 1,200 species. Beautiful paintings of the shells are by James Nicholls. For a small beginner's guide consult Sandra D. Romashko's *Shell Book* (Windward, 1984) Also *Simon & Schuster's Pocket Guide to Shells of the World* (Simon & Schuster, 1989) is useful.

970. Living Snakes of the World in Color. John M Mehrtens. New York, NY: Sterling, 1987. 480p., color illus., index. $55.00. ISBN: 0-8069-6560-X.

A good, fairly comprehensive guide covering the snakes of the world. Another colorful guide but smaller is *Simon and Schuster's Guide to Reptiles and Amphibians of the World* (Simon & Schuster, 1989).

Guides to the Literature

971. Birds: A Guide to the Literature. *(Garland Reference Library of the Humanities, v.680).* Melanie Miller. New York, NY: Garland, 1986. 912p., index. $86.00. ISBN: 0-8240-8710-0.

This comprehensive bibliographical guide covers the literature pertaining to birds. Complete citations are given with some brief annotations. The classic bibliography of birds now out-of-print is Reuben M. Strong's *Bibliography of Birds* (Chicago, Natural History Museum, 1939-1949). Its counterpart for fishes is Bashford Dean's *Bibliography of Fishes* (American Museum of Natural History, 1916-1923).

972. Entomology: A Guide to Information Sources. Pamela Gilbert; Chris J. Hamilton. London, Great Britain: Mansell, 1990. 259p., index. $60.00. ISBN: 0-7201-2052-7.

A well-organized guide to entomological literature covering taxonomy, collections, searching, current events, and organizations. It is arranged by topical chapters.

973. Keyguide to Information Sources in Animal Rights. Charles R. Magel. Jefferson, NC: McFarland, 1989. 267p., bibliog., index. $39.95. ISBN: 0-89950-405-1.

This small guide provides an overview of animal rights literature, an annotated bibliography, and a list of selected animal rights organizations.

Handbooks and Manuals

974. American Insects: A Handbook of the Insects of America North of Mexico. Ross H. Arnett, Jr. New York, NY: Van Nostrand Reinhold, 1985. 850p., illus., bibliog., index. $114.95. ISBN: 0-442-20866-9.

This comprehensive guide to the insects of the United States includes chapters on insect classification and systematics. Could be used as a field guide. A good

brief guide to insects for the layperson is the *Audubon Society Book of Insects* (Abrams, 1983).

975. Bergey's Manual of Systematic Bacteriology. Noel R. Krieg; John G. Holt; Peter H.A. Sneath; James T. Staley; Stanley T. Williams. Baltimore, MD: Williams & Wilkins, 1984-89. 4v., illus., bibliog., index. $98.95.v.1; $81.95v.2; $93.95v.3; $73.95v.4. ISBN: 0-683-04108-8v.1; 0-683-07893-3v.2; 0-683-07908-5v.3; 0-683-09001-5v.4.

Based on *Bergey's Manual of Determinative Bacteriology*, this comprehensive work provides a descriptive classification of all known bacteria. Another useful book would be V.B. Skorman's *Approved Lists of Bacterial Names* (American Society for Microbiology, 1989).

976. Birder's Handbook: A Field Guide to the Natural History of North American Birds, Including All Species That Regularly Breed North of Mexico. Paul R. Ehrlich; David S. Dobkin; Darryl Wheye. New York, NY: Simon & Schuster, 1988. 785p., illus., bibliog., index. $16.95. ISBN: 0-671-62133-5.

This handbook is not a field guide to identification (although it could be used as such) but rather a comprehensive handbook about the birds that have already been identified. Each species is fully described with numerous illustrations of the birds, their nests, eggs, etc. For information on birdwatching consult the *Audubon Society Handbook for Birders* (Scribners, 1981).

977. Birds of Africa. Leslie H. Brown; Emil K. Urban; Kenneth Newman. San Diego, CA: Academic Press, 1982– , irregular. v.1– , illus. (part in color), bibliog., index. price per volume varies. ISBN: 0-12-137301-0v.1.

Projected to 7 volumes, this comprehensive work covers all of the birds of Africa. Each species is fully described giving range and status, physical characteristics, voice, general habits, food, breeding habits, field characteristics, and references.

978. Complete Guide to Monkeys, Apes, and Other Primates. Michael Kavanagh. London, Great Britain: Cape, 1983. 224p., color illus., bibliog., index. out-of-print. ISBN: 0-224-02168-0.

Although out-of-print this book for the layperson contains good general descriptions, color illustrations, and a short bibliography. A much older, but still useful, work is J.R. Napier and P.H. Napier's *Handbook of Living Primates: Morphology, Ecology and Behavior of Nonhuman Primates* (Academic Press, 1967). Since primates are on the endangered list consult the *Threatened Primates of Africa: The IUCN Red Data Book* (IUCN, 1988).

979. Fishes of the World. 2nd. Joseph S. Nelson. New York, NY: Wiley, 1984. 523p., bibliog., index. $64.95. ISBN: 0-471-86475-7.

Fishes of the World is a detailed classified guide to the fishes of the world.

980. Handbook for Butterfly Watchers. Robert Michael Pyle. Boston, MA: Houghton Mifflin, 1992 (c1984). 280p., illus., index. $11.70. ISBN: 0-395-61629-8.

This small book is useful to those who study butterflies in the wild. It would be a good book to use with field guides.

981. Handbook of Fish Diseases. Dieter Untergasser. Neptune City, NJ: TFH Publications, 1989. 160p., color illus., index. $29.95. ISBN: 0-86622-703-2.

This excellent handbook for the aquarist has outstanding color illustrations. It covers such topics as recognition and prevention of diseases, anatomy, diseases and heredity, treatment and diagnosis, as well as environmental factors.

982. Handbook of Marine Mammals. Sam H. Ridgway; Richard J. Harrison. San Diego, CA: Academic Press, 1981-1989. $105.00/volume. ISBN: 0-12-588501-6v.1; 0-12-588502-4v.2; 0-12-588503-2v.3; 0-12-588504-0v.4.

This well-researched handbook covers all marine mammals. Each species is described giving anatomy, physiology, behavior, distribution, reproduction, effects of man, and history of the scientific name. The 4 volumes are v.1—The walrus, sea lions, fur seals, and sea otters; v.2—Seals; v.3—The Sirenians and baleen whales; v.4—River dolphins and the larger toothed whales. For a good one-volume work on whales and dolphins consult Stephen Leatherwood and Randall R. Reeves' *Sierra Club Handbook of Whales and Dolphins* (Sierra Club, 1983).

983. Handbook of North American Birds. Ralph S. Palmer. New Haven, CT: Yale University Press, 1961– , irregular. v.1– , illus., bibliog., index. $45.00/volume. ISBN: 0-300-04059-8v.4.pt.1.

This ongoing handbook is intended to cover all species of birds in North America. Each species is described in detail including physical description, field identification, voice, habitat, distribution, migration, banding status, reproduction, habits, and food. The 5 volumes published so far cover loons, flamingos, waterfowl, osprey, kites, bald eagles, buteos, and golden eagles.

984. Handbook of the Birds of Europe, the Middle East, and North America. Stanley Cramp. New York, NY: Oxford University Press, 1980-1993. 7v., illus. (part in color), bibliog., index. $135.00v.1; $145.00v.2; $150.00v.3; $165.00v.4; $175.00v.5; $175.00v.6; $130.00v.7. ISBN: 0-19-857358-8v.1; 0-19-857505-Xv.2; 0-19-857506-8v.3; 0-19-857507-6v.4; 0-19-857508-4v.5; 0-19-85709-3v.6; 0-19-857510-6v.7.

This highly recommended book covers the birds of Europe. Each species is described in detail. The 7 published volumes (some volumes in several parts) are v.1—Ostrich to Ducks; v.2—Hawks to Buzzards; v.3—Waders to Gulls; v.4—Terns to Woodpeckers; v.5—Tyrant Flycatchers to Thrushes; v.6—Warblers; v.7—Old World Flycatchers to Shrikes.

985. Handbook of the Birds of India and Pakistan, Together with Those of Nepal, Sikkim, Bhutan, and Ceylon. 2nd. Salim Ali; S. Dillon Ripley. New York, NY: Oxford University Press, 1979– , irregular. v.1– , illus. (part in color), maps, bibliog., index. $42.50/volume. ISBN: 0-19-561115-2v.1.

This comprehensive ongoing handbook covers all the birds of the India/Pakistan area. The 10 volumes will cover v.1—Divers to Hawks; v.2—Megapodes to Crab Plover; v.3—Stone Curlews to Owls; v.4—Frog Mouths to Pittas; v.5—Larks to the Grey Hypocolius; v.6—Cuckoo-Shrikes to Babaxes; v.7—Laughing Thrushes to the Mangrove Whistler; v.8—Warblers to Red Starts; v.9—Robins to Wagtails; v.10—Flowerpeckers to Butings. A compact edition, *Compact Handbook of the Birds of India and Pakistan* was issued in 1983.

986. Handbook of Tropical Aquarium Fishes. Herbert R. Axelrod; Leonard P. Schultz. Neptune City, NJ: TFH, 1989. 718p., color illus., index. $9.95. ISBN: 0-87666-491-5.

This work is an excellent handbook for anyone working with aquariums. It contains information about all the species of fishes that can be kept in aquariums.

987. Illustrated Guide to Shrimp of the World. Ian Dove; Claus Frimodt. Huntington, NY: Osprey Books, 1987. 229p., illus. (part in color), bibliog., index. $85.00. ISBN: 0-943738-20-2.

The first 3 chapters of this handbook provide information on how to identify shrimp and information for shrimp producers and users. The largest chapter is the one that gives complete descriptions of the shrimp.

988. International Code of Zoological Nomenclature/Code International de Nomenclature Zoologique. 3rd. International Commission on Zoological Nomenclature. Berkeley, CA: University of California Press, 1985. 338p., bibliog., index. $45.00. ISBN: 0-520-05546-2.

Adopted by the 20th General Assembly of the International Union of Biological Sciences, this code sets forth the rules and regulations for assigning scientific names to animals and groups of animals.

989. IUCN Mammal Red Data Book. Jane Thornback; Martin Jenkins; International Union for the Conservation of Nature and Natural Resources. Gland, Switzerland: IUCN, 1982– , irregular. v.1– , bibliog., index. price per volume varies. ISBN: 2-88032-600-1v.1.

This title is one of several *Red Data Books* published by the International Union for the Conservation of Nature and Natural Resources (IUCN) that outlines conservation measures for protecting the animals of the world. It indicates specific endangered species. Volume one covers threatened mammalian taxa of the Americas and Australasian zoogeographic region (excluding Cetacea). Other handbooks by IUCN include *IUCN Red List of Threatened Animals* (1986); the *IUCN Amphibia-Reptilia Red Data Book* (1982–); and the *IUCN Invertebrate Red Data Book* (1983). Also, there are other books covering endangered species such as Paul R. Ehrlich's *Birds in Jeopardy* (Stanford University Press, 1992); Guy Mountfort's *Rare Birds of the World* (S. Greene Press, 1988); and the 3-volume *Official World Wildlife Fund Guide to Endangered Species of North America* (Beecham, 1990-92).

990. Lizards of the World. Chris Mattison. New York, NY: Facts on File, 1989. 192p., illus. (part in color), bibliog., index. $24.95. ISBN: 0-8160-1900-2.

This good overview handbook has excellent illustrations. Chapters cover history, feeding, habitats, etc. The chapters for individual families cover distribution, habitats, and foodstuffs.

991. Poisonous and Venomous Marine Animals of the World. 2nd revised. Bruce W. Halstead. Princeton, NJ: Darwin Press, 1988. 1,168p., illus. (part in color), bibliog., index. $250.00. ISBN: 0-87850-050-2.

This excellent handbook covers those marine animals that are venomous. Each is fully described including the symptoms when bitten or scratched, reactions, and medical care. A small book that just identifies venomous animals in general is Marcos A. Frieberg's *World of Venomous Animals* (TFH, 1984).

992. Sierra Club Handbook of Seals and Sirenians. Randall R. Reeves; Brent S. Stewart; Stephen Leatherwood. San Francisco, CA: Sierra Club Books, 1992. 359p., bibliog., index. $18.00. ISBN: 0-87156-656-7.

This outstanding handbook provides complete descriptions of seals and sirenians. Illustrations show all stages of life and discussions of conservation are included.

993. Snakes of the World. Kenneth L. Williams. Malabar, FL: Krieger, 1993. 2v., bibliog., index. $59.50. ISBN: 0-89464-302-9.

This is the most complete book available covering the technical names of the snakes of the world. The first volume includes all known generic and subgeneric names while the second volume covers living and extinct snake species.

994. South American Birds: A Photographic Aid to Identification. John S. Dunning. Newton Square, PA: Harrowood Books, 1988 (c1987). 351p., color illus., maps, index. $47.50; $35.00pbk. ISBN: 0-915180-25-1; 0-915180-26-Xpbk.

Some 2,700 species are described with over 1,400 color photographs. This work should be used with more detailed field guides.

995. Spiders of the World. Rod Preston-Mafham; Ken Preston-Mafham. New York, NY: Facts on File, 1984. 191p., illus. (part in color), bibliog., index. $24.95. ISBN: 0-87196-996-3.

A selected list of spiders is included in this colorful handbook. Information is given about the anatomy, habitats, and distribution of spiders with selected species fully described. For more comprehensive coverage of spiders consult R.F. Foelix's *Biology of Spiders* (Harvard University Press, 1982) and W.J. Gertsch's *American Spiders* (Van Nostrand Reinhold, 1979).

996. Turtles of the World. Carl H. Ernst; Roger Barbour. Washington, DC: Smithsonian Institution Press, 1989. 313p., illus., bibliog., index. $45.00. ISBN: 0-87474-414-8.

This well-designed guide identifies the 257 turtle species in the world. Full descriptions are given. The authors' *Turtles of the United States* (University Press of Kentucky, 1972) is still a classic. Also of interest would be *Encyclopedia of Turtles* (TFH, 1979) and *Turtles and Tortoises of the World* (Facts on File, 1988).

997. UFAW Handbook on the Care and Management of Laboratory Animals. 6th. Trevor B. Poole; Ruth Robinson. New York, NY: Churchill Livingstone, 1987. 933p., illus., bibliog., index. $115.00. ISBN: 0-582-40911-X.

The UFAW Handbook is the Bible for the care and management of laboratory animals. The latest techniques are considered as well as the humane treatment of each animal. No animal laboratory should be without this handbook.

Histories

998. History of Entomology. Ray F. Smith; Thomas E. Mittler; Carroll N. Smith. Palo Alto, CA: Annual Reviews, 1973. 517p., illus., bibliog., index. out-of-print.

Now out-of-print, this excellent work outlines the history of entomology and the research that has been carried out in this discipline.

999. History of Fishes. 34d. J.R. Norman. New York, NY: Wiley, 1975. 467p., illus., bibliog., index. out-of-print. ISBN: 0-470-32641-7.

This book is a very readable history of research in the field of fish.

Treatises

1000. Comprehensive Insect Physiology, Biochemistry, and Pharmacology. G.A. Kerkut; L.I. Gilbert. New York, NY: Pergamon Press, 1985. 15v., illus., bibliog., index. $4,000.00. ISBN: 0-08-926850-1.

This work is an authoritative treatise on insects. The 13 volumes cover v.1- Embryogenesis and reproduction; v.2—Postembryonic development; v.3—Integument, respiration, and circulation; v.4—Regulation: digestion, nutrition, excretion; v.5—Nervous system: structure and motor functions; v.6—Nervous system: sensory; v.7—Endocrinology I; v.8—Endocrinology II; v.9—Behavior; v.10—Biochemistry; v.11—Pharmacology; v.12—Insect control; v.13—Cumulative Indexes.

1001. Fish Physiology. W.S. Hoar; D.J. Randall. San Diego, CA: Academic Press, 1969– , irregular. v.1– , illus., bibliog., index. price per volume varies. ISBN: 0-12-350435-Xv.12.

This authoritative treatise covers fish physiology. The 12 volumes published so far are v.1—Excretion, ionic regulation, and metabolism; v.2—Endocrine system; v.3—Reproduction and growth, bioluminescence, pigments, and poisons; v.4—Nervous system, circulation, and respiration; v.5—Sensory systems and electric organs; v.6—Environmental relations and behavior; v.7—Locomotion; v.8—Bioenergetics and growth; v.9—Reproduction, Part A: Endocrine tissues and hormones; Part B: Ion and water transfer; v.11—Physiology of developing fish, Part B: Viviparity and posthatching juveniles; v.12—Cardiovascular systems. For a treatise covering reptiles consult Carl Gans' 10-volume *Biology of the Reptilia* (Liss, 1969-79).

1002. Microscopic Anatomy of Invertebrates. Frederick W. Harrison. New York, NY: Wiley, 1991. 4v., illus., bibliog., index. $150.00/volume. ISBN: 0-471-5684-2v.1.

This 4-volume set is one of the newer treatises covering invertebrates. It essentially replaces Libbie Henrietta Hyman's *The Invertebrates* (McGraw-Hill, 1940).

1003. Reproduction of Marine Invertebrates. Arthur C. Gipse; John S. Pearse. San Diego, CA: Academic Press, 1974-1979. 5v., illus., bibliog., index. price per volume varies. ISBN: 0-12-282501-2v.1.

Although not as comprehensive as some other treatises, this is still an authoritative work. The 5 volumes cover v.1—Acoelomate and pseudocoplomate metazoans; v.2—Entopracts and lesser Ooelomates; v.3—Annelids and echiurans; v.4—Molluscs: gastropods and cephalopods; v.5—Molluscs: pelecypods and lesser classes.

1004. Traite de Zoologie: Anatomie, Systematique, Biologie. Pierre Paul Grasse. Paris, France: Masson, 1948– , irregular. v.1– , illus., bibliog., index. price per volume varies.

Published in parts, this is the world's authoritative treatise on zoology. There is no other work that is as comprehensive. A comparable German work is *Handbuch der Zoologie* (W. de Gruyter, 1968-) and a similar British work is the *Cambridge Natural History* (10v., Macmillan, 1895-1909).

Periodicals

1005. American Entomologist. Lanham, MD: Entomological Society of America, 1955– , quarterly. v.1– , index. $30.00. ISSN: 1046-2821.

1006. American Zoologist. New Orleans, LA: American Society of Zoologists, 1961– , bimonthly. v.1- index. $127.00. ISSN: 0003-1569.

1007. Anatomical Record. New York, NY: Wiley-Liss, 1906– , monthly. v.1– , index. $813.00. ISSN: 0003-276X.

1008. Animal Behaviour. London, Great Britain: Academic Press, 1952– , monthly. v.1– , index. $374.00. ISSN: 0003-3472.

1009. Annals of the Entomological Society of America. Lanham, MD: Entomological Society of America, 1908– , bimonthly. v.1– , index. $150.00. ISSN: 0013-8746.

1010. Applied Animal Behavior Science.
New York, NY: Elsevier, 1975– , 12/year.
v.1– , index. $630.00. ISSN: 0168-1591.

1011. Applied Entomology and Zoology.
Tokyo: Japanese Society of Applied
Entomology and Zoology, 1966– , quarterly.
v.1– , index. $50.00. ISSN: 0003-6862.

1012. Audubon Magazine. New York, NY:
National Audubon Society, 1899– , bimonthly.
v.1– , index. $30.00. ISSN: 0004-7694.

1013. Auk: A Journal of Ornithology.
Lawrence, KS: University of Kansas, 1884– ,
quarterly. v.1– , index. $60.00. ISSN:
0004-8038.

**1014. Behavior: An International Journal of
Comparative Ethology.** Leiden, Netherlands:
E.J. Brill, 1947– , 8/year. v.1– , index. $265.25.
ISSN: 0005-7959.

1015. Canadian Entomologist. Ottawa,
Ontario, Canada: Entomological Society of
Canada, 1868– , bimonthly. v.1– , index.
$180.00. ISSN: 0008-347X.

**1016. Canadian Journal of Zoology/Journal
Canadienne de Zoologie.** Ottawa, Ontario:
National Research Council of Canada, 1929– ,
monthly. v.1– , index. $140.00. ISSN:
0008-4301.

1017. Condor. Tempe, AZ: Arizona State
University/Cooper Ornithological Society,
1899– , quarterly. v.1– , index. $30.00. ISSN:
0010-5422.

1018. Copeia. Carbondale, IL: Southern
Illinois University/American Society of
Ichthyologists and Herpetologists, 1913– ,
quarterly. v.1– , index. $50.00. ISSN:
0045-8511.

1019. Environmental Entomology. Lanai,
MD: Entomological Society of America,
1972– , bimonthly. v.1– , index. $150.00.
ISSN: 0046-225X.

1020. Ethology. Berlin, Germany: Verlag Paul
Parey, 1937– , 8/year. v.1– , index. $375.00.
ISSN: 0179-1613.

1021. Herpetological Journal. London, Great
Britain: British Herpetological Society, 1948– ,
semiannual. v.1– , index. $60.00. ISSN:
0268-0130.

1022. Insect Biochemistry and Molecular Biology. Tarrytown, NY: Pergamon Press,
1971– , 8/year. v.1– , index. $616.00. ISSN:
0965-1748.

1023. Journal of Applied Entomology/Zeitschrift fur Angewandte Entomologie.
Hamburg, Germany: Verlag Paul Parey,
1914– , 10/year. v.1– , index. $629.00. ISSN:
0044-2240.

1024. Journal of Economic Entomology.
Lanham, MD: Entomological Society of
America, 1908– , bimonthly. v.1– , index.
$190.00. ISSN: 0022-0493.

1025. Journal of Experimental Zoology. New
York, NY: Wiley, 1904– , 16/year. v.1– ,
index. $1,440.00. ISSN: 0022-104X.

1026. Journal of Field Ornithology. Ohio
Wesleyan University, OH: Department of
Zoology, 1930– , quarterly. v.1– , index.
$45.00. ISSN: 0273-8570.

1027. Journal of Fish Biology. London, Great
Britain: Academic Press, 1969– , monthly.
v.1– , index. $623.00. ISSN: 0022-1112.

1028. Journal of Herpetology. Oxford, OH:
Miami University, 1967– , quarterly. v.1– ,
index. $60.00. ISSN: 0022-1511.

1029. Journal of Insect Physiology.
Tarrytown, NY: Pergamon Press, 1957– ,
monthly. v.1– , index. $864.00.

1030. Journal of Invertebrate Pathology. San
Diego, CA: Academic Press, 1959– ,
bimonthly. v.1– , index. $316.00. ISSN:
0022-2011.

1031. Journal of Mammalogy. Provo, UT:
Brigham Young University, 1919– , quarterly.
v.1– , index. $33.00. ISSN: 0022-2372.

1032. Journal of Nematology. Lake Alfred,
FL: University of Florida, 1969– , quarterly.
v.1– , index. $70.00. ISSN: 0022-300X.

1033. Journal of Protozoology. Lawrence,
KS: Allen Press, 1954– , 6/year. v.1– , index.
$122.00. ISSN: 0022-3921.

1034. Journal of Zoology. Oxford, Great
Britain: Oxford University Press, 1833– ,
monthly. v.1– , index. $685.00. ISSN:
0952-8369.

1035. Physiological Zoology. Chicago, IL: University of Chicago Press/American Society of Zoologists, 1928– , bimonthly. v1– , index. $178.00. ISSN: 0031-935X.

1036. Transactions of the American Entomological Society. Philadelphia, PA: American Entomological Society, 1867– , quarterly. v.1– , index. $18.00. ISSN: 0002-8320.

1037. Wilson Bulletin. Richmond, VA: Virginia Commonwealth University/Wilson Ornithological Society, 1889– , quarterly. v.1– , index. $30.00. ISSN: 0043-5643.

Chapter 7: Engineering/Technology

Engineering is the application of scientific or physical knowledge to the development of a product. Technology refers to the tools that are used to develop these products. Engineering is an old profession dating to the times before Christ, but it has become a highly technical field relying on "cutting edge technology." The results of engineering surround our existence, but to achieve these results engineers consume an enormous amount of research and development time. Today's engineering researchers have to have a strong background in the sciences.

Specialization is the basis of all engineering. These specialized subfields include:

- Agricultural Engineering—an expanding field that is concerned with developing better ways to produce food and fibers. It includes machinery, plant engineering, genetic engineering, and soil engineering and works closely with areas of science such as chemistry, medicine, nutrition, botany, zoology, and environmental science.
- Chemical Engineering—a discipline that studies how basic raw materials, such as ores, salts, sulfur, limestone, coal, natural gas, petroleum, air, and water are converted into a variety of products through various chemical processes. These products include aluminum, magnesium, and titanium metals; fuels; solvents; synthetic fertilizers; resins; plastics; antibiotics; paper; and petrochemicals.
- Civil Engineering—a field that is basically concerned with the planning, design, construction, and management of any work project or facility, including buildings, structures, transportation facilities, water resource projects, dams, bridges, power generation plants, roads, harbors, river management, canals, wastewater facilities, sanitation facilities, soil mechanics, and foundations. Specialized

areas within civil engineering include building engineering, structural engineering, highway engineering, traffic engineering, transportation engineering, bridge engineering, tunnel engineering, coastal engineering, harbor and river engineering, dam engineering, hydraulics engineering, sanitary engineering, engineering geology, and soils engineering.

- Electrical Engineering—an area that is concerned with the development of electric power through any number of processes, including generators, wind, solar, water, and nuclear means. It is closely related to electronics, which is the control and use of electricity.
- Engineering Design—an area that covers the initial creation of systems, devices, and processes. It is actually a part of all areas of engineering, with each engineer practicing engineering design.
- Environmental Engineering—a fast-expanding field concerned with all aspects of the environment and how to protect it. It includes such concerns as pollution, pesticide control, cleaner air, waste, ecology, and nuclear safety. These engineers work closely with engineers in all areas to ensure the best environmental conditions possible.
- Industrial Engineering—the branch of engineering that uses mathematics, physics, and chemistry to design, improve, and install integrated systems that involve people, materials, equipment, and energy. In other words, it is the branch of engineering that seeks to improve efficiency. It is concerned with machines, robotics, materials, energy, and management.
- Mechanical Engineering—this field of engineering is the application of physics in the development of any useful product. There is a little bit of mechanical engi-

neering in all fields of engineering, including engineering graphics, robotics, engineering instruments, mechanics, strains and stresses, strength of materials, and testing.

- Mining Engineering—the area that is concerned with all aspects of mining for minerals and hard fuels, such as coal. Liquid fuels are part of Petroleum Engineering.
- Nuclear Engineering—the broad area of engineering that is concerned with all aspects of producing energy through the use of nuclear power.
- Petroleum Engineering—the study of producing oil and gas from the well to the consumer.

This chapter has taken all of these disciplines and grouped them into the following subcategories:

- General Engineering/Technology.
- Chemical and Petroleum Engineering.
- Civil Engineering, Building, and Construction.
- Electrical and Electronics Engineering.
- Environmental Engineering.
- Industry and Manufacturing.
- Mechanical Engineering.
- Transportation.

The major indexing service for engineering research is the *Engineering Index*. The engineering field is the major developer of handbooks. The first handbooks were intended to be a one-volume reference work that could be carried around in an engineer's pocket. Today, however, many of these handbooks are larger and more comprehensive.

GENERAL ENGINEERING/TECHNOLOGY

Abstracts and Indexes

1038. Applied Science and Technology Index. New York, NY: Wilson, 1958– , monthly with quarterly cumulations. v.1– , index. service basis. ISSN: 0003-6986.

This subject index lists the articles in the more popular periodicals in science and technology. Citations to book reviews are listed separately. It covers aeronautics, space science, chemistry, computer technology, construction, engineering, petroleum and gas, robotics, telecommunications, and transportation. It is also available online and on CD-ROM.

1039. Bibliographical Guide to Technology. Boston, MA: G.K. Hall, 1974– , annual. v.1– , index. $250.00. ISSN: 0360-2761.

Previously called *Technology Book Guide*, this guide gives full bibliographic information of books cataloged by the New York Public Library and the Library of Congress in the fields of industrial, structural, civil, transportation, hydraulic, sanitary, highway, mechanical, electrical, nuclear, and mining engineering.

1040. Current Technology Index. London, Great Britain: Bowker-Sauer, 1962– , bimonthly. v.1– , index. $920.00. ISSN: 0260-6593.

Previously called the *British Technology Index*, this index covers periodicals in engineering, chemical technology, instrumentation, building, transport, and computerization. It is also available online and on CD-ROM.

1041. Engineering Index Monthly. New York, NY: Engineering Index, Inc, 1906– , monthly with annual cumulations. v.1– , index. $1,625.00 monthly; $1,145.00 annual index; $1,500.00 cumulation. ISSN: 0742-1974.

This monthly indexing/abstracting service covers all areas of engineering technology. Access to information can be made by numerous special indexes. It is also available online and on CD-ROM. *Bioengineering and Biotechnology Abstracts* is a spin-off from this database.

1042. Official Gazette of the United States Patent and Trademark Office: Patents. Washington, DC: U.S. Patent and Trademark Office, 1872– , weekly. v.1– , index. $375.00. ISSN: 0098-1133.

This weekly publication gives abstracts to patents that were issued for that week. The British counterpart is the *Official Journal* (British Patent Office, 1986-). There are various indexes to the *Official Gazette* including the *Index of Patents* (1920-) and its *Index to Classification and Manual of Classification*, which is revised on a regular basis and guides one through the classification scheme. Patents can be searched from 1969 to the present through CASSIS/CD-ROM (Classification and Search Support Information System).

Biographical Sources

1043. American Engineers of the Nineteenth Century: A Biographical Index. *(Garland Reference Library of Social Sciences, v.53).* Christine Roysdon; Linda A. Khatri. New York, NY: Garland, 1978. 247p., index. out-of-print. ISBN: 0-8240-9827-7.

Arranged by name of engineer, each entry gives the profession, followed by citations to several articles or works about the engineer. A related work of historical interest is Roland Turner's *Great Engineers and Pioneers in Technology* (St Martins Press, 1981).

1044. Marquis Who's Who in Science and Engineering. 1992-93. Wilmette, IL: Marquis Who's Who, 1992. 1,096p. $199.00. ISBN: 0-8379-5751-6.

This biographical directory contains over 21,000 entries for engineers throughout the world. In addition to biographical information, it includes published works, awards, notable findings, patents, and works in progress.

1045. Who's Who in Engineering. 7th. New York, NY: Hemisphere, 1988. 846p. $200.00. ISBN: 0-89116-648-3.

Previously called *Engineers of Distinction*, this directory lists engineers living in the U.S. Brief biographical information is given for each entry. Also included are sections listing various awards and information about the major engineering societies. For British engineers consult *Who's Who of British Engineers* (St Martins Press, 1981).

1046. Who's Who in Technology, Biography and Index. 6th. Detroit, MI: Gale Research, 1989. 2v., index. $380.00. ISBN: 0-8103-4950-7.

Over 38,000 entries are included in this biographical directory which includes Canada. Typical who's-who type of information is given plus access by geographic region, by employer, and by discipline.

Dictionaries, Glossaries, and Thesauri

1047. Comprehensive Dictionary of Engineering and Technology, with Extensive Treatment of the Most Modern Techniques and Processes. Richard Ernst. New York, NY: Cambridge University Press, 1985. 2v., illus., index. $270.00. ISBN: 0-521-30377-Xv.1; 0-521-30378-8v.2.

This very comprehensive bilingual dictionary covers engineering terminology in French and English. Richard Ernst also has the same dictionary in German and English called *Dictionary of Engineering Technology* (Oxford University Press, 1985-89).

1048. Dictionary of Biotechnology. J. Coombs. New York, NY: Elsevier, 1986. 330p., illus. $39.50; $24.95pbk. ISBN: 0-444-01087-4; 0-444-01070-Xpbk.

Also published as the *Macmillan Dictionary of Biotechnology*, this dictionary contains approximately 4,000 terms with brief definitions. It stresses the biological aspect of biotechnology.

1049. Dictionary of Engineering Acronyms and Abbreviations. Harald Keller; Uwe Erb. New York, NY: Neal-Schuman, 1989. 312p. $75.00. ISBN: 1-55570-028-4.

Over 30,000 engineering-related terms are included in this acronyms dictionary. The source of the acronym is given. Two other useful similar dictionaries are M. Gordon's *Dictionary of New Information Technology Acronyms* (Gale Research, 1986) and *Pugh's Dictionary of Acronyms and Abbreviations* (Oryx Press, 1981).

1050. Dictionary of Patent, Copyright and Trademark Terms. Elias Stephen. Berkeley, CA: Nola Press, 1991. 225p. $15.95. ISBN: 0-87337-154-2.

Previously called *Nalo's Intellectual Property Law Dictionary*, this specialized dictionary is for patent searchers, attorneys, and inventors. Terms are defined for the specialist.

1051. Ei Thesaurus. Jessica L. Milstead. New York, NY: Engineering Information, 1992. 790p. $130.00.

This thesaurus provides some 9,000 terms used in compiling the Engineering Information's publications and databases. It replaces the "Subject Heading for Engineering" that was part of *Ei Vocabulary*.

1052. Language of Biotechnology: A Dictionary of Terms. John M. Walker; Michael Cox; Allan Whitaker. Washington, DC: American Chemical Society, 1988. 255p. $49.95; $29.95pbk. ISBN: 0-8412-1489-1; 0-8412-1490-5pbk.

This small dictionary lists some 1,500 terms in the fields of biotechnology and its allied areas of biology and chemical engineering.

1053. McGraw-Hill Dictionary of Engineering. Sybil P. Parker. New York, NY: McGraw-Hill, 1984. 659p., illus. price not available. ISBN: 0-07-045412-4.

This spin-off from the 1983 edition of the *McGraw-Hill Dictionary of Scientific and Technical Terms*, contains some 16,000 engineering terms. Each term has an indication of which field of engineering it is associated with. Another good general engineering dictionary is *Gerrish's Technical Dictionary* (Goodheart-Willcox, 1982).

1054. Quantification in Science: The VNR Dictionary of Engineering Units and Measures. Michele G. Melaragno. New York, NY: Van Nostrand Reinhold, 1991. 333p., index. $42.95. ISBN: 0-442-00641-1.

This new dictionary covers all international weights, measures, and units, giving definitions, descriptions, uses, and conversions.

Directories

1055. Biotechnology Directory. New York, NY: Stockton Press, 1984– , annual. v.1– , index. $195.00.

Previously called the *International Biotechnology Directory*, this work provides information on companies, research centers, and academic institutions involved in new and established biotechnology research.

1056. Directory of Engineering Societies and Related Organizations. New York, NY: Engineers Joint Council, 1956– , biennial. v.1– , index. $150.00. ISSN: 0070-5470.

Previously called the *Engineering Societies Directory*, this directory lists U.S. and foreign technical and engineering societies.

1057. Engineering College Research and Graduate Study. Washington, DC: American Society for Engineering Education, 1967– , annual. v.1– , index. $45.00.

Previously called the *Annual Directory of Engineering College Research and Graduate Study*, this annual gives information about programs and research in various universities and colleges throughout the United States.

1058. Engineering Research Centres: A World Directory of Organizations and Programmes. 2nd. Harlow, Great Britain: Longman Group, 1988. 599p., index. $400.00. ISBN: 0-582-01778-5.

This international directory gives information on over 5,000 facilities, including official laboratories, industrial research centers, and educational institutions with R&D activities in all engineering fields.

1059. GEN Guide to Biotechnology Companies. New York, NY: Genetic Engineering News/Mary Ann Liebert, 1992. 204p., index. $95.00. ISBN: 0-913-113-56-5.

This guide covers bioprocess engineering firms, biotechnology consultants, peptide companies, state biotech centers, and other related areas.

1060. Genetic Engineering and Biotechnology Related Firms Worldwide Directory, 1992/93. 11th. Marshall Sittig. Bristol, PA: International Publications Service, 1993. 606p., illus., index. $299.00. ISBN: 1-880866-00-5.

Over 2,000 firms from 57 countries are listed in this biotechnology directory. The listings are by country and by state within the U.S., giving pertinent data on the kind of research conducted. Each entry is assigned one or more of 26 activity codes that further identify its major interest.

1061. High Technology Market Place Directory. 9th. Princeton Junction, NJ: Princeton Hightech Group, 1992. 1,100p., index. $175.00. ISBN: 0-934603-53-7.

This directory provides profiles of over 2,500 high technology companies. Information is given on names, executives, sales, major customers, products, markets served, and foreign operations.

1062. MacRae's Blue Book. New York, NY: Business Research Publications, 1893– , annual. v.1– , index. $145.00.

Previously called *MacRae's Industrial Directory*, this work provides names, addresses, and services of over 45,000 leading manufacturers. It also gives product information.

1063. Thomas Register of American Manufacturers and Thomas Register Catalog File. New York, NY: Thomas Publishing, 1905– , annual. 1st– , index (25 volumes each year). $240.00. ISSN: 0362-7721.

This classic and indispensable source provides information on American and Canadian manufacturers. Sixteen of the volumes contain over 1,750,000 listings per year under 50,000 product and service headings. Two volumes list company profiles of over 125,000 companies. There are also 7 catalog file volumes of some 1,600 company catalogs.

Encyclopedias

1064. G.K. Hall Encyclopedia of Modern Technology. David Blackburn; Geoffrey Holister. Boston, MA: G.K. Hall, 1987. 248p., color illus., bibliog., index. $40.00. ISBN: 0-8161-9056-9.

This topically arranged encyclopedia is for the student and layperson. Its main use is for its many color illustrations rather than an in-depth discussion of the topics. Also of interest would be the *Oxford Illustrated Encyclopedia of Information and Technology* (Oxford University Press, 1992).

1065. McGraw-Hill Encyclopedia of Engineering. Sybil P. Parker. New York, NY: McGraw-Hill, 1983. 1,264p., illus., bibliog., index. $89.95. ISBN: 0-07-045486-8.

Material on engineering has been taken from the 5th edition of the *McGraw-Hill Encyclopedia of Science and Technology* to make a one-volume encyclopedia. The discussions are for the student as well as the researcher.

Guides to the Literature

1066. Information Resources for Engineers and Scientists: Workshop Notes. 6th. Washington, DC: INFO/Tek, 1991. 1v., various paging, bibliog. $49.95.

Arranged as notes for a workshop, this excellent guide to engineering literature covers the major resources that are available. A complete description of each entry is given with an indication of how it should be used. There is a strong emphasis on government sources.

1067. Information Sources in Engineering. 2nd. L.J. Anthony. Boston, MA: Butterworth, 1985. 579p., illus., bibliog., index. $95.00. ISBN: 0-408-11475-4.

Previously called *Use of Engineering Literature*, this work is the most comprehensive guide to engineering literature available. It covers all areas and types of publications. Three older sources that also could be used are Ellis Mount's *Guide to Basic Information Sources in Engineering* (Wiley, 1976); S. Parsons' *How to Find Out about Engineering* (Pergamon, 1972); and Margaret T. Schenk's *What Every Engineer Should Know about Engineering Information Sources* (Dekker, 1984).

1068. Information Sources in Patents. C.P. Auger. New Providence, NJ: Bowker-Saur, 1992. 187p., index. $86.25. ISBN: 0-86291-906-1.

This guide helps locate information about patents including European patents.

1069. Lesko's New Tech Sourcebook: A Directory to Finding Answers in Today's Technology-Oriented World. Matthew Lesko; Sharon Zarozny. New York, NY: Harper & Row, 1986. 726p., index. price not available. ISBN: 0-06-181509-8.

This general guide to information sources pertaining to engineering is oriented more to the student and layperson.

Handbooks and Manuals

1070. Engineering Mathematics Handbook: Definitions, Theorems, Formulas, Tables. 3rd. Jan J. Tuma. New York, NY: McGraw-Hill, 1987. 498p., illus., bibliog., index. $44.50. ISBN: 0-07-065443-3.

This useful handbook contains all of the various formulas, definitions, and theorems that are used in solving complex engineering problems. A newer companion to this handbook is Jan J. Tuma's *Handbook of Numerical Calculations in Engineering* (McGraw-Hill, 1989). Also useful would be the *ASM Handbook of Engineering Mathematics* (ASM International, 1983).

1071. Eshbach's Handbook of Engineering Fundamentals. 4th. Ovid W. Eshbach. New York, NY: Wiley, 1990. 1v., various paging, illus., bibliog., index. $85.00. ISBN: 0-471-89084-7.

Previously called *Handbook of Engineering Fundamentals*, *Eshbach's* is a standard handbook of engineering fundamentals.

1072. Handbook of Applied Mathematics for Engineers and Scientists. Max Kurtz. New York, NY: McGraw-Hill, 1991. 1v., various paging, illus., bibliog., index. $69.95. ISBN: 0-07-035685-8.

This problem solving handbook gives the definitions, basic equations, principles, and techniques of mathematics, using fully solved problems. Also of use would be Edward E. Grazda's *Handbook of Applied Mathematics* (Krieger, 1977).

1073. Handbook of Bioengineering. Richard Skalak; Shu Chien. New York, NY: McGraw-Hill, 1987. 1v., various paging, illus., index. $107.50. ISBN: 0-07-057783-8.

This handbook is more for biomedical engineering than the more broadly defined bioengineering. It stresses such areas as orthopedics, blood transmission, pulmonary mechanics, and the senses such as hearing. It includes information for the nonspecialist as well as the specialist.

1074. Handbook of Dimensional Measurement. 2nd. Francis T. Farago. New York, NY: Industrial Press, 1982. 524p., illus., index. $49.95. ISBN: 0-8311-1136-4.

All methods of measurement from traditional to computer are covered in this handbook.

1075. Handbook of Engineering Management. Dennis Lock. Boston, MA: Butterworths-Heinemann, 1989. 832p., illus., bibliog., index. $65.00. ISBN: 0-434-91170-4.

This excellent handbook covers engineering management or the management of technology. It is intended for the practicing engineer, covering the concepts needed to direct engineering technical resources, huge engineering projects, and the day-to-day administration of an engineering firm.

1076. Handbook of Measurement Science. P.H. Sydenham. New York, NY: Wiley, 1982-83. 2v., illus., bibliog., index. $322.00. ISBN: 0-471-10037-4v.1; 0-471-10493-0v.2.

The many methods of measurement in all areas of engineering are discussed in this 2-volume work. The 2 volumes cover v.1—Theoretical fundamentals; v.2—Practice fundamentals.

1077. Inventing and Patenting Sourcebook: How to Sell and Protect Your Idea. Richard C. Levy; Robert J. Huffman. Detroit, MI: Gale Research, 1990. 922p., illus., index. $75.00. ISBN: 0-8103-4871-3.

This well-written guide and sourcebook explains patenting for inventors, innovators, marketers, and researchers. An older work, but still useful, is Orville Greene's *Practical Inventor's Handbook* (McGraw-Hill, 1979) and a newer book with general information is *General Information Concerning Patents* (Gordon Press, 1991). For a layperson's guide to patents consult Frank H. Foster's *Patents, Copyrights and Trademarks* (Wiley, 1989). Information on chemical patents can be found in John T. Maynard's *Understanding Chemical Patents* (American Chemical Society, 1991).

1078. McGraw-Hill Handbook of Essential Engineering Information and Data. Ejup N. Ganic; Tyler G. Hicks. New York, NY: McGraw-Hill, 1991. 1v., various paging, illus., index. $89.50. ISBN: 0-07-022764-0.

This handbook presents the essential information that practicing engineers need in their daily activities of design, operation, analysis, and economic evaluation.

1079. Standard Handbook of Engineering Calculations. 2nd. Tyler G. Hicks; S. David Hicks. New York, NY: McGraw-Hill, 1985. 1v., various paging, illus., index. $84.50. ISBN: 0-07-028735-X.

The emphasis of this handbook is on calculations pertaining to mechanical, civil, and architectural engineering. A procedure is described followed with detailed calculations and examples.

1080. Wiley Engineer's Desk Reference: A Concise Guide for the Professional Engineer. Sanford I. Heisler. New York, NY: Wiley, 1984. 567p., illus., bibliog., index. $59.95. ISBN: 0-471-86632-6.

This handbook is a replacement to 2 older classic handbooks: *Engineer's Manual* and *Engineer's Companion*. It presents engineering information of facts, formulas, and techniques that are used on a regular basis by practicing engineers.

Histories

1081. Dictionary of Inventions and Discoveries. 2nd. E.F. Carter. New York, NY: Crane, Russak, 1976. 208p. out-of-print. ISBN: 0-8448-0867-9.

This alphabetically arranged account of inventions and discoveries indicates to whom each discovery is attributable and the year in which they were introduced.

1082. Early Scientific Instruments. Anthony Turner. New York, NY: Sotherby, 1987. 320p., illus., bibliog. $115.00. ISBN: 0-85667-319-6.

This title is a good history of the scientific instruments that have been developed through time. It is interesting to read and has good illustrations.

1083. Encyclopaedia of the History of Technology. Ian McNeil. New York, NY: Routledge, 1990. 1,062p., illus., bibliog., index. price not available. ISBN: 0-415-01306-2.

This topical encyclopedia is arranged in 5 parts—materials, power and engineering, transport, communications and calculations, and technology and society. It is a very good introduction to the history of technology.

1084. History of Technology. New York, NY: Oxford University Press, 1954-84. 8v., index. price per volume varies. ISBN: 0-19-872905-4v.8.

This classic history covers technology from earliest times to about 1950. The 8 volumes cover v.1—From early times to fall of ancient empires; v.2—The Mediterranean civilizations and the middles ages; v.3—From the Renaissance to the industrial revolution 1500-1750; v.4—The industrial revolution 1750-1850; v.5—The late 19th century 1850-1900; v.6-7—The 20th Century 1900-1950; v.8—Index.

1085. Technical Americana: A Checklist of Technical Publications Printed Before 1831. Evald Rink. Millwood, NY: Kraus International, 1981. 776p., index. $90.00. ISBN: 0-527-75447-1.

This bibliography is arranged by the topics of general, technology, agriculture, crafts and trades, medical technology, military technology, civil engineering, mechanical engineering, manufacturing, mining and mineral production, sea transportation, and inland transportation. It also contains an indication of which libraries own copies.

Standards

1086. Annual Book of ASTM Standards. Philadelphia, PA: American Society for Testing and Materials, 1939– , annual. v.1– , illus., bibliog., index. (59v. per year). price per volume varies.

This book is the world's most comprehensive compilation of standards, tests, and specifications of one society, the American Society for Testing and Materials. Each of the 59 annual volumes is published at a different time during the year and covers a specific topic such as coated steel or electrical conductors. The standards are accepted industry-wide and written into specifications.

1087. Compilation of ASTM Standard Definitions. 6th. Philadelphia, PA: American Society for Testing and Materials, 1986. 907p., illus. $74.00. ISBN: 0-8031-0928-8.

This dictionary lists the terms used in the *Annual Book of ASTM Standards.*

1088. Index and Directory of Industry Standards. Englewood, CO: Information Handling Services, 1983– , annual. v.1– , index (several volumes per year). price per year varies.

Previously called *Index and Directory of U.S. Industry Standards*, this standard source helps locate over 113,000 international and domestic standards of some 373 professional societies by subject and numerical designation. For just those standards from the American National Standards Institute, consult the *Catalog of American National Standards, 1990-91* (ANSI, 1990).

1089. Index of Federal Specifications Standards and Commercial Item Descriptions. Washington, DC: U.S. Federal Supply Service, 1952– , annual. v.1– , index. $27.00.

This source provides alphabetical, numerical, and Federal Supply classification indexing to government specifications in general use.

1090. Standards: A Resource and Guide for Identification, Selection and Acquisition. Patricia L. Ricci; Linda Perry. St Paul, MN: Stinz, Bernards, and Co, 1990. 239p., index. $60.00.

This introduction to the source of standards lists worldwide organizations that produce standards, giving detailed information about each. Also included are lists of libraries and information centers having collections of standards, vendors of standards, and consultants.

Tables

1091. CRC Handbook of Tables for Applied Engineering Science. 2nd. Ray E. Bolz; George L. Ture. Boca Raton, FL: CRC, 1973. 1,166p., illus., index. $84.95. ISBN: 0-8493-0252-8.

This handbook of readily available tables for the practicing engineer is used by the engineering profession as the *Handbook of Chemistry and Physics* is used by the chemistry and physics professions.

1092. Engineering Formulas. 6th. Kurt Gieck. New York, NY: McGraw-Hill, 1990. 1v., various paging, illus., index. $29.95. ISBN: 0-07-023455-8.

This translation of *Technische Formelsammlung* is a well-established listing of the various formulas used in all fields of engineering. Another similar work is A.M. Howatson's *Engineering Tables and Data* (Chapman & Hall, 1991).

Periodicals

1093. Consulting-Specifying Engineer. Des Plaines, IL: Cahners, 1987– , 15/year. v.1– , index. $74.95. ISSN: 0892-5046.

1094. Engineer. London, Great Britain: Morgan-Grampian, 1856– , weekly. v.1– , index. $160.00. ISSN: 0013-7758.

1095. Engineering. London, Great Britain: Design Council, 1866– , monthly. v.1– , index. $100.00. ISSN: 0013-7782.

1096. Engineering Times. Alexandria, VA: National Society of Professional Engineers, 1979– , monthly. v.1– , index. $30.00. ISSN: 0195-6876.

1097. International Journal of Engineering Science. Tarrytown, NY: Pergamon Press, 1963– , monthly. v.1– , index. $1,064.00. ISSN: 0020-7225.

1098. Popular Mechanics. New York, NY: Hearst Magazines, 1902– , monthly. v.1– , index. $15.94. ISSN: 0032-4558.

1099. Popular Science. New York, NY: Times Mirror Magazines, 1872– , monthly. v.1– , index. $13.94. ISSN: 0161-7370.

1100. Research and Technology. Des Plaines, IL: Cahners, 1959– , monthly. v.1– , index. $69.95. ISSN: 0746-9179.

1101. Technology and Culture. Chicago, IL: University of Chicago Press, 1960– , quarterly. v.1– , index. $60.00. ISSN: 0040-165X.

CHEMICAL AND PETROLEUM ENGINEERING

Abstracts and Indexes

1102. Aluminum Industry Abstracts. Washington, DC: Aluminum Association, 1968– , monthly. v.1– , index. $525.00. ISSN: 1066-0623.

Produced by the Aluminum Association and formerly called *World Aluminum Abstracts*, this highly specialized abstracting service covers worldwide information on aluminum as published in the business and technical literature. It is also available online.

1103. Ceramic Abstracts. Columbus, OH: American Ceramic Society, 1922– , bimonthly. v.1– , index. $120.00. ISSN: 0095-9960.

Contains close to 10,000 abstracts and patents per year on ceramic and related fields. It covers such areas as art, glass, electronics, kilns, engineering materials, and chemistry. It is also available online and on CD-ROM.

1104. Corrosion Abstracts. Houston, TX: National Association of Corrosion Engineers, 1962– , bimonthly. v.1– , index. $200.00. ISSN: 0010-9339.

This specialized abstracting service covers materials pertaining to all aspects of corrosion. It is also available on CD-ROM.

1105. Metals Abstracts and Metals Abstracts Index. Materials Park, OH: ASM International, 1968– , monthly. v.1– , index. $1,620.00 abstracts; $700.00 indexes. ISSN: 0026-0924 abstracts; 0026-0932 indexes.

Formed by the merger of *Review of Metal Literature* and *Metallurgical Abstracts*, this service monitors the international literature on all aspects of metallurgical sciences and technology. It is also available online and on CD-ROM.

1106. Metals and Alloys in the Unified Numbering System: With a Description of the System and a Cross-Index of Chemically Similar Specifications. 5th. *(ASTM DS-56D; SAE HS1086Jun89).* Warrendale, PA: Society of Automotive Engineers, 1989. 384p., index. $105.00. ISBN: 0-89883-428-7.

This standard index lists all metals and alloys with a unified number developed by the Society of Automotive Engineers and the American Society for Testing and Materials. For each entry the unified number is given, a description, the chemical composition, and a list of cross-reference specifications is also included.

1107. Parat Index of Polymer Trade Names. 2nd. New York, NY: VCH, 1992. 456p. $190.00. ISBN: 1-56081-194-3.

Previously called *Index of Polymer Trade Names*, this index covers close to 24,000 polymers, monomers, and other substances used in producing polymers; the entries are alphabetically arranged. The CA registry numbers are given as well as molecular formulas so that additional information can be located through *Chemical Abstracts.*

1108. Theoretical Chemical Engineering. Cambridge, Great Britain: Royal Society of Chemistry, 1964– , bimonthly. v.1– , index. $236.00. ISSN: 0960-5053.

Formerly called *Theoretical Chemical Engineering Abstracts* , this source provides worldwide coverage of theoretical chemical engineering including theory and laboratory experimentation. It is also available online and on CD-ROM.

1109. World Textile Abstracts. Oxford, Great Britain: Elsevier Advanced Technology, 1969– , monthly. v.1– , index. $467.00. ISSN: 0043-9118.

Previously called *Shirley Institute of Current Literature* and *Textile Abstracts*, this service provides abstracts of technical and technico-economic literature relevant to fiber-forming polymers, textile and related industries and the applications of fibrous and textile materials in other products. Over 500 worldwide publications are covered. It is also available online.

Bibliographies

1110. Chemical Engineering: Bibliography (1967-1988). Martyn S. Ray. Park Ridge, NJ: Noyes, 1990. 887p., bibliog., index. $98.00. ISBN: 0-8155-1241-4.

This bibliography lists some 20,000 references from 40 journals published between 1967 and 1988. It is arranged by subject, then chronologically with complete citations. For an older bibliography covering vapor deposition consult Donald T. Hawkins' *Chemical Vapor Deposition, 1960-1980: A Bibliography* (Plenum, 1981).

Dictionaries, Glossaries, and Thesauri

1111. Chemical Engineering Drawing Symbols. D.G. Austin. New York, NY: Wiley, 1979. 96p., illus., bibliog., index. $31.95. ISBN: 0-470-26601-5.

This useful and easy-to-use source shows symbols used in making chemical engineering drawings.

1112. Consumer's Dictionary of Cosmetic Ingredients. 3rd revised. Ruth Winter. New York, NY: Crown, 1989. 330p., bibliog. $12.00. ISBN: 0-517-57263-X.

This consumer's dictionary contains information about the harmful and desirable ingredients found in men's and women's cosmetics.

1113. Dictionary of Chemical Technology. 2nd revised. Dorit L. Noether. New York, NY: VCH, 1992. 320p., illus. $59.50. ISBN: 0-89573-329-3.

This good general dictionary of terms relating to chemical engineering includes short descriptions of industrial processes and products. It is also issued as the *Encyclopedic Dictionary of Chemical Technology* (VCH, 1993).

1114. Dictionary of Composite Materials Technology. Lancaster, PA: Technomic, 1989. 160p. $65.00. ISBN: 0-87762-600-6.

This concise dictionary covers composite materials including fibers and particulates. Also included are the terms associated with the manufacture of these materials.

1115. Dictionary of Named Processes in Chemical Technology. Alan E. Comyns. New York, NY: Oxford University Press, 1993. 352p. $75.00. ISBN: 0-19-855385-4.

This dictionary lists some 3,000 chemical processes that are used in industry and have special names that are personal names or corporate names. Each entry is fully described.

1116. Dictionary of Organophosphorus Compounds. F.S. Edmundson. New York, NY: Chapman & Hall, 1987. 1,347p., illus., index. $725.00. ISBN: 0-412-25790-4.

Organophosphorous compounds are covered in this typical Chapman & Hall dictionary giving physical, structural, and bibliographical information. It is of particular interest to those in the fields of synthetic organic chemistry, agro-chemicals, pesticides, pharmaceuticals, anticancer drugs, detergents, solvents, surfactants, and other special chemical fields.

1117. Dictionary of Plastics Technology. R.J. Heath; A.W. Birley. New York, NY: Chapman & Hall, 1992. 256p., index. $59.95. ISBN: 0-216-93179-7.

This comprehensive dictionary of plastics terminology includes tables and diagrams. An appendix of conversion tables is included.

1118. Fairchild's Dictionary of Textiles. 6th. Isabel B. Wingate. New York, NY: Fairchild Publications, 1979. 691p., illus. $40.00. ISBN: 0-87005-198-9.

This dictionary of textile terms includes all fiber-based products, technologies for producing fibers, all yarn and yarn technologies, weaving, knitting, felting, lacemaking, dyeing, printing, finished products, inventors, and standards. A smaller, less comprehensive textile dictionary but much more up-to-date is George M.C. Tubbs' *Textile Terms and Definitions* (Textile Institute, 1991).

1119. Illustrated Glossary of Process Equipment/Glossaire Illustre des Equipements de Procede/Glosario Illustrado de Equipos. Bernard H. Paruit. Houston, TX: Gulf Publishing, 1982. 318p., illus. $23.00. ISBN: 0-87201-691-9.

This multilingual glossary lists processing equipment terms used in the chemical industries. There is an English-French-Spanish edition as well as an English-French-Chinese edition. Another multilingual dictionary is Aksel L. Lydersen's *Dictionary of Chemical Engineering: English, French, German, Spanish* (Wiley, 1992).

1120. Industrial Chemical Thesaurus. Michael Ash; Irene Ash. New York, NY: VCH, 1992. 2v. $295.00. ISBN: 1-56081-615-5.

This thesaurus identifies some 40,000 international tradenames found in the chemical industry. It provides the tradename equivalents of generic products. Another smaller work is Michael and Irene Ash's *Chemical Tradename Dictionary* (VCH, 1992).

1121. Macmillan Dictionary of Biotechnology. J. Coombs. London, Great Britain: Macmillan, 1986. 330p., illus. out-of-print. ISBN: 0-333-39464-X.

This small dictionary of biotechnology is especially good for historical terms. For a multilingual dictionary consult the *Biotechnology Glossary* (Elsevier, 1991).

1122. Polymer Science Dictionary. Mark S.M. Alger. New York, NY: Elsevier, 1989. 532p. ISBN: 1-85166-220-0.

This comprehensive dictionary defines over 6,000 terms pertaining to polymer science but not technology, including polymerization, polymer structure, properties, and individual polymer materials. Definitions are longer, encyclopedic style.

1123. Whittington's Dictionary of Plastics. 2nd. Lloyd R. Whittington. Westport, CT: Technomic, 1978. 344p. $35.00.

Sponsored by the Society of Plastics Engineers this dictionary is a good source of definitions for historical terms relating to the plastics industry.

Directories

1124. Biotechnology Directory 1992. J. Coombs; Y.R. Alston. New York, NY: Stockton Press, 1991. 682p., index. $215.00. ISBN: 1-56154-023-1.

This directory of quick information lists more than 10,000 companies, research centers, and academic institutions involved in biotechnology in 22 countries. A buyer's guide of products and services is included.

1125. Biotechnology Guide U.S.A.: Companies, Data, and Analysis. 2nd. M. Dibner. New York, NY: Stockton Press, 1991. 652p., index. $199.00. ISBN: 1-56159-015-0.

This directory contains information on 742 U.S. biotechnology companies and 142 corporations with biotechnology programs.

1126. Chem Sources International. Ormond Beach, FL: Chemical Sources International, 1986– , semiannual. v.1– , index. $250.00.

This directory covers 80,000 chemical compounds from 80 countries. Access is by trade name, supplier, and application. It is also available online.

1127. Chem Sources USA. Ormond Beach, FL: Chemical Sources International, 1958– , annual. v.1– , index. $250.00.

Chem Sources USA is a comprehensive directory of chemicals and suppliers for the United States. Access is by trade name, supplier, and application. It is also available online.

1128. Chemical Engineering Faculties. New York, NY: American Institute of Chemical Engineers, 1960– , annual. v.1– , index. $50.00. ISSN: 0589-5465.

Previously called *Chemical Engineering Faculties of the United States, Canada, and Great Britain*, this directory now lists chemical engineering departments worldwide, giving status, personnel, and other departmental information.

1129. Chemical Guide to the United States. Pearl River, NJ: Noyes, 1962– , irregular. 1st– , index. $96.00. ISSN: 0069-2972.

This guide describes some 220 of the largest U.S. chemical companies. It gives information about all manufacturing divisions, subdivisions, and affiliates.

1130. Davison's Textile Blue Book. Ridgewood, NJ: Davison, 1866– , annual. v.1– , index. $100.00.

This long standing annual directory gives information about mills, dyers, and finishers in the U.S. and Canada.

1131. Dictionary of Ceramic Science and Engineering. Loran S. O'Bannon. New York, NY: Plenum Press, 1984. 303p., bibliog., index. $55.00. ISBN: 0-306-41324-8.

This alphabetically arranged dictionary defines terms related to all aspects of ceramics.

1132. Directory of Chemical Engineering Consultants. 7th. M.P. Healy-Stagen. New York, NY: American Institute of Chemical Engineers, 1988. 16p. free to members. ISBN: 0-8169-0344-1.

Listed by firm name, this small directory gives addresses, personnel, scope of service, type of organization, licenses, and specialties.

1133. Directory of World Chemical Producers. Dallas, TX: Chemical Information Services, 1980/81– , annual. v.1– , index. $350.00. ISSN: 0196-0555.

This directory contains approximately 50,000 alphabetically listed product titles manufactured worldwide by some 5,000 chemical producers.

1134. Guide to Directories for the Rubber and Plastics Industry. new. Rien van den Honel. Shawbury, Great Britain: Rapra Technology, 1992. 100p., index. $115.00.

This guide is an index to over 400 published directories that pertain to rubber, plastics, and composites, giving full bibliographic descriptions and annotation.

1135. Industrial Minerals Directory: A World Guide to Producers and Processors. 2nd. New York, NY: Metals Bulletin, 1991. 704p., index. $210.00. ISBN: 0-900542-99-3.

This source of information on industrial minerals contains the latest information on mineral processing companies as well as mine owners and operators. It is arranged by company, with each entry giving the standard directory information. Another related directory from the same publisher is the *Mining Directory* (6th, 1991).

1136. Iron and Steel Works of the World. 10th. Richard Serjeantson. New York, NY: Metals Bulletin, 1991. 725p., illus., index. $322.00. ISBN: 0-947671-43-9.

This directory arranged by country covers the world's leading iron and steel producers, re-rollers, tube makers, iron powder producers, strip coaters, and cold rolled section makers. This same publisher produces other specialized directories including *Non-Ferrous Metal Works of the World* (5th, 1990); *Steel Traders of the World* (5th, 1990); *Metal Traders of the World* (4th, 1990); and *Foundry Directory and Register of Forges Europe* (16th, 1991).

1137. Materials Research Centres: A World Directory of Organizations and Programmes in Materials Science. 4th. Eric Mitchell; Elizabeth Lines. Harlow, Great Britain: Longman Group, 1991. 726p., index. $475.00. ISBN: 0-582-08124-6.

Arranged by country, this directory gives information about industrial centers and laboratories worldwide, including names, addresses, personnel, expenditures, scope of services, and publications.

1138. OPD Chemical Buyer's Guide. Oil, Paint, and Drug Reporter. New York, NY: Schnell Publishing, 1913– , annual. v.1– , index. price not available. ISSN: 0276-539X.

Previously called *Chemical Buyer's Guide*, this resources is one of the oldest chemical buyer's guides. It gives sources for 1,000s of chemicals in the U.S. Also of use is the annual issue of *Chemical Week* called *Chemical Week Buyer's Guide* (Chemical Week Assoc.).

Encyclopedias

1139. Encyclopedia of Chemical Processing and Design. John J. McKetta; William A. Cunningham. New York, NY: Dekker, 1976-1991. 38v., illus., bibliog., index. $175.00/volume. ISBN: 0-8247-2487-9v.37.

This ongoing publication has 38 volumes published. It is one of many authoritative sources of information on all aspects of chemical processing and design. See also *Ullmann's Encyclopedia of Industrial Chemistry* and the *Kirk Othmer Encyclopedia of Chemical Technology* which are equally as comprehensive. Each of the titles has unique materials.

1140. Encyclopedia of Emulsion Technology. Paul Becher. New York, NY: Dekker, 1983-87. 3v., illus., bibliog., index. $165.00/volume. ISBN: 0-8247-1876-3v.1; 0-8247-1877-1v.2; 0-8247-1878-Xv.3.

The specialized topic of emulsion technology is covered in this 3-volume set. The 3 volumes cover v.1—Basic theory; v.2—Application; v.3—Basic theory measurement application.

1141. Encyclopedia of Industrial Chemical Additives. Michael Ash; Irene Ash. New York, NY: Chemical Publishing, 1984-87. 4v., index. $93.50/volume. ISBN: 0-8206-0299-Xv.1; 0-8206-0308-2v.3; 0-8206-0309-0v.3; 0-8206-0320-1v.4.

The main work is the first 3 volumes with the fourth being an update volume. It gives national and international coverage of additives used in industry listed alphabetically according to use and then alphabetically by trade name. Each entry gives trade name, manufacturer, chemical name, application, composition, properties, and description.

1142. Encyclopedia of Materials Science and Engineering. Michael B. Bever. Oxford, Great Britain: Pergamon Press, 1986. 8v., illus., bibliog., index. $2,050.00; $295.00/supplement. ISBN: 0-262-02233-8.

Materials science and engineering is concerned with the fundamental nature of materials and their practical application. It covers basic theory as well-as engineering practice. Articles are brief to extensive, signed, and include bibliographies. Supplements began in 1988.

1143. Encyclopedia of Plastics, Polymers, and Resins. Michael Ash; Irene Ash. New York, NY: Chemical Publishing, 1982-88. 4v., index. $85.00/volume. ISBN: 0-8206-0290-6v.1.

This encyclopedia contains practical information on plastics, polymers, and resins that are trademarked. Information is from manufacturers' printed materials.

1144. Encyclopedia of Polymer Science and Engineering. 2nd. Herman F. Mark; Jacqueline I. Kroschwitz. New York, NY: Wiley, 1985-90. 23v., illus., bibliog., index. $3,610.00. ISBN: 0-471-86519-2.

Previously called *Encyclopedia of Polymer Science and Technology*, this is the definitive work on polymers. It gives information on chemical substances, polymer properties, methods and processes, uses, and general background. A concise version was published in 1991 as *Concise Encyclopedia of Polymer Science and Engineering*.

1145. Encyclopedia of PVC. 2nd. Leonard I. Nass. New York, NY: Dekker, 1986. 2v., illus., bibliog., index. $165.00/volume. ISBN: 0-8247-7427-2v.1; 0-8247-7695-Xv.2.

With the environmental concerns of PVC, this specialized encyclopedia covers in 2 volumes information any researcher or field engineer needs. The 2 volumes cover v.1—Resin manufacture and properties; v.2—Compound design and additives.

1146. Encyclopedia of Surfactants. Judith Jecde; Michael Ash; Irene Ash. New York, NY: Facts on File, 1992. 260p., illus., bibliog., index. $45.00. ISBN: 0-8160-2105-8.

Written for the layperson with excellent illustrations, this encyclopedia covers the fascinating area of textiles. Another equally as useful work on the same topic is Martin Grayson's *Encyclopedia of Textiles, Fibers, and Non-Woven Fabrics* (Wiley, 1984).

1147. International Encyclopedia of Composites. Stuart M. Lee. New York, NY: VCH, 1990– , irregular. v.1– , illus., bibliog., index. $275.00/volume. ISBN: 0-89573-290-4set.

This projected multivolume work covers materials science, processing, and manufacturing technology plus fluid and solid mechanics, and engineering construction and design. It covers the behavior of composite materials, special properties, and design aspects. For a one-volume work on composites consult Anthony Kelly's *Concise Encyclopedia of Composite Materials* (Pergamon Press, 1989).

1148. Kirk-Othmer Concise Encyclopedia of Chemical Technology. New York, NY: Wiley, 1985. 1,318p., illus., bibliog., index. $139.00. ISBN: 0-471-86977-5.

This work is the abridged version of the third edition 24-volume set. It covers chemical technology in its broadest sense from coatings, inks, dyes, pigments, fats, waxes, and fibers to glass, ceramics, industrial chemicals, wood, paper, and product and processes. For more current information consult the 4th edition of the *Kirk-Othmer Encyclopedia of Chemical Technology* (1991- , Wiley).

1149. Kirk-Othmer Encyclopedia of Chemical Technology. 4th. New York, NY: Wiley, 1991– , irregular. 27 volume projected, illus., bibliog., index. $5,400.00. ISBN: 0-471-52704-1.

This and the *Ullmann's Encyclopedia of Industrial Chemistry* are the two most authoritative works covering chemical engineering. Each covers the field with authored articles, presenting the latest information. This 4th edition is also available on CD-ROM. A spin-off of the third edition was the *Encyclopedia of Composite Materials and Components* (Wiley, 1983). See also the *Encyclopedia of Chemical Processing and Design*.

1150. Modern Plastics Encyclopedia. New York, NY: McGraw-Hill, 1966– , annual. v.1– , illus., index. $39.75. ISSN: 0026-8275.

A product of the journal, *Modern Plastics*, this is an encyclopedia and directory of information about plastics. The encyclopedia section covers resins and compounds, chemicals and additives, reinforced plastics and compounds, primary processing, auxiliary equipment and components, and fabricating and finishing. There are also sections of engineering data, buyer's guide, and directory of trade names.

1151. Ullmann's Encyclopedia of Industrial Chemistry. 5th completely revised. Fritz Ullmann; Wolfgang Gerhartz. Deerfield Beach, FL: VCH, 1985– , irregular. 36v. projected, illus., bibliog., index. $8,460.00.00.

Previously in German and called *Ullmann's Encyklopadie der Technischen Chemie*, this encyclopedia is a comprehensive and authoritative source of information on industrial chemistry. It is divided into an A and B series of volumes. The 28 A volumes will contain alphabetically arranged articles on chemicals, product groups, areas of application, processes, and technological concepts. The 8 B volumes will contain comprehensive coverage of specific topics such as environmental protection and plant safety.

Guides to the Literature

1152. Biotechnology and the Research Enterprise: A Guide to the Literature. William F. Woodman; Mark C. Shelley; Brian J. Reichel. Ames, IA: Iowa State University Press, 1989. 358p., bibliog., index. $49.95. ISBN: 0-8138-0164-8.

This general guide provides good coverage of the literature in all areas of biotechnology. It covers all types of materials. Another good guide is Y. Alston's *Biosciences: Information Sources and Services* (Stockton Press, 1992).

1153. Chemical Industries: An Information Sourcebook. Phae H. Dorman. Phoenix, AZ: Oryx Press, 1988. 95p., index. $32.50. ISBN: 0-89774-257-5.

This guide covers books and periodicals pertaining to the chemical industries including drugs, paints, plastics, and textiles. A directory of associations and consultants is also included. An older and larger work is Theodore P. Peck's *Chemical Industries: Information Sources* (Gale Research, 1979).

1154. Information Sources in Biotechnology. 2nd. A. Crafts-Lighty. New York, NY: Stockton Press, 1986. 403p., illus., bibliog., index. $130.00. ISBN: 0-943818-18-4.

Although somewhat dated, this work is a usable source of materials pertaining to biotechnology including printed materials, abstracting services, databases, patents, companies, organizations, and library services.

1155. Information Sources in Metallic Materials. M.N. Patten. New York, NY: Bowker-Saur, 1989. 415p., bibliog., index. $75.00. ISBN: 0-408-01491-1.

Written in narrative form rather than bibliographic, this guide covers both materials and applications. Each chapter is separately authored. The index does not cover the specific titles mentioned in the text.

1156. Information Sources in Polymers and Plastics. R.T. Adkins. New York, NY: Bowker-Saur, 1989. 352p., bibliog., index. $75.00. ISBN: 0-408-02027-X.

This narrative bibliographic guide to the literature covers polymers and plastics.

Handbooks and Manuals

1157. Adhesives Handbook. 3rd. J. Shields. Boston, MA: Butterworths, 1984. 360p., illus., bibliog., index. out-of-print. ISBN: 0-408-01356-7.

Although out-of-print, this publication is still a good handbook covering adhesives. It covers such areas as selection, materials and properties, surface preparation, bonding process, and testing, plus having a directory of products.

1158. ASM Engineered Materials Reference Book. Metals Park, OH: ASM International, 1989. 517p., illus., index. $87.00. ISBN: 0-87170-350-5.

This handbook contains data and information on new materials including composites, ceramics, plastics, and electronic materials. Information is presented in tabular form with molecular structure, phase diagrams, and references. It is designed to be a companion volume to the *ASM Metals Reference Book* (ASM International, 1983). Also of use is Cyril A. Dostal's

Engineered Materials Handbook (ASM International, 1988) and the *Structural Alloys Handbook* (CINDAS, 1990).

1159. Biochemical Engineering and Biotechnology Handbook. 2nd. B. Atkinson. New York, NY: Stockton Press, 1991. 1,285p., illus., index. $265.00. ISBN: 1-56159-012-6.

This source is the authoritative handbook for persons working in the pharmaceutical industries, brewing and distilling, food technology, dairy and beverage industries, and the treatment of water.

1160. Chemical Formulary. H. Bennett. New York, NY: Chemical Publishing Co, 1933– , irregular. v.1– , index. $52.50/volume.

This handbook gives formulas for a variety of commercial products including adhesives, foods and beverages, cosmetics, coatings, detergents, elastomers, polymers, and resins.

1161. Chemical Products Desk Reference. Michael Ash; Irene Ash. New York, NY: Chemical Publishing Co, 1990. 1,312p., index. $330.00. ISBN: 0-8206-0324-4.

This desk reference provides definitions of over 32,000 trademark products followed by a classification of each product by function and identified by the ingredients contained within each. Two companion volumes by Michael and Irene Ash are *Industrial Chemical Thesaurus* (VCH, 1992) and *Chemical Tradename Dictionary* (VCH, 1993).

1162. Composite Materials Handbook. 2nd. Mel M. Schwartz. New York, NY: McGraw-Hill, 1992. 1v., various paging, illus., bibliog., index. $79.50. ISBN: 0-07-055819-1.

Materials, processes, and applications of composite materials are covered in this new edition of this specialized handbook. Each chapter is authored separately and includes general introduction, detailed discussions, and bibliographies.

1163. Corrosion Resistant Materials Handbook. 4th. D.J. DeRenzo. Park Ridge, NJ: Noyes, 1985. 965p., index. $125.00. ISBN: 0-8155-1023-3.

This handbook provides detailed coverage of all materials that have resistance to any type of corrosion. Each entry is described giving all the information needed to determine if a particular material would be useful based on its corrosion resistance.

1164. CRC Handbook of Applied Thermodynamics. David A. Palmer. Boca Raton, FL: CRC, 1987. 275p., illus., bibliog., index. $237.00. ISBN: 0-8493-3271-0.

This specialized handbook covers the fundamentals of thermodynamics. Numerous tables, charts, and other information are included.

1165. CRC Handbook of Solubility Parameters and Other Cohesion Parameters. 2nd. Allan F.M. Barton. Boca Raton, FL: CRC, 1992. 680p., illus., bibliog., index. $195.00. ISBN: 0-8493-0176-9.

This specialized handbook covers solubility parameters and their application to liquid, gas, solid, and polymer systems. Information has been taken from over 2,900 reports.

1166. Dechma Corrosion Handbook: Corrosive Agents and Their Interactions with Materials. New York, NY: VCH, 1987– , irregular. v.1– , index. $115.00/volume v.1-6; $480.00/volume v.7-12; $5,895.00 full set of 12 volumes. ISBN: 0-89573-623-3v.1.

This ongoing set is the most comprehensive collection of corrosion information available. The volumes published so far cover v.1—Acetates, aluminum chloride, chlorine and chlorinated water, fluorides, potassium hydroxide, steam, sulfuric acids; v.2—Aliphatic aldehydes, ammonia and ammonium hydroxide, sodium hydroxide, soil (underground corrosion); v.3—Acid halides, amine salts, bromine and bromides, carbonic acid, lithium hydroxide; v.4—Alkanecarboxylic acids, formic acid, hot oxidizing gases, polyols; v.5—Alphatic amines, alkaline earth chlorides, alkaline earth hydroxides, flourine hydrogen fluoride, hydrochloric acid; v.6—Acetic acid, alkanols, benzene and benzene homologues, hydrogen chloride; v.7—Alphatic ketones, ammonium salts, atmosphere; v.8—Sulfuric acid; v.9 Methanol, sulfur dioxide, key to materials composites; v.10—Corrosive agents and their interaction with materials.

1167. Handbook of Applied Chemistry: Facts for Engineers, Scientists, Technicians, and Technical Managers. Vollrath Hopp; Ingo Henning. New York, NY: McGraw-Hill, 1983. 1v., various paging, bibliog., index. $54.95. ISBN: 0-07-030320-7.

This translation of *Chemie Kopendium fur das Selbstudieum* is a good general chemical engineering handbook for those who are working in laboratories. The information is concise but accurate and well-documented.

1168. Handbook of Chemical Engineering Calculations. Nicholas P. Chopey; Tyler G. Hicks. New York, NY: McGraw-Hill, 1984. 1v., various paging, illus., bibliog., index. $69.50. ISBN: 0-07-010805-6.

In addition to calculations unique to chemical engineering, the basic mathematical and engineering calculations are covered.

1169. Handbook of Chemicals Production Processes. Robert A. Meyers. New York, NY: McGraw-Hill, 1986. 1v., various paging, illus., bibliog., index. $89.50. ISBN: 0-07-041765-2.

This title is one of a 3-volume set covering the production processes of materials used in synthesizing fuels, chemicals, and polymers. The other 2 books in this area are *Handbook of Synfuels and Technology* (McGraw-Hill, 1984) and *Handbook of Petroleum Refining Processes* (McGraw-Hill, 1986). Information includes chemistry and thermodynamics of the process, by-products, wastes, emissions, specifications, and operating costs.

1170. Handbook of Chemistry Specialties: Textile Fiber Processing, Preparation, and Bleaching. John E. Nettles. Malabar, FL: Krieger, 1991(c1983). 488p., index. price not available. ISBN: 0-89464-539-0.

This small concise handbook for textile engineers covers processing, preparation, and bleaching.

1171. Handbook of Composites. George Lubin. New York, NY: Van Nostrand Reinhold, 1982. 786p., illus., bibliog., index. $104.95. ISBN: 0-442-24897-0.

Previously called *Handbook of Fiberglass and Advanced Plastics Composites*, this work presents useful data on composites. Chapters cover such areas as materials, processes, design, analysis, and applications.

1172. Handbook of Corrosion Data. Bruce D. Craig. Metals Park, OH: ASM International, 1989. 683p., index. $128.00. ISBN: 0-87170-361-0.

Arranged by chemical compound, each entry gives a description of corrosion information followed by tables that pertain to the type, concentration, duration, and rate of corrosion. More detailed information on each compound can be found in the *Metals Handbook*. Two other similar and useful books are Philip A. Schweitzer's *Corrosion and Corrosion Protection Handbook* (Dekker, 1989) and Philip A. Schweitzer's *Corrosion Resistance Tables* (Dekker, 1986).

1173. Handbook of Glass Data. (Physical Sciences Data Series). New York, NY: Elsevier, 1983. 4v., illus., bibliog., index. $200.00v.1; $251.50v.2; $338.50v.3; $360.00v.4. ISBN: 0-444-41689-7set.

This detailed treatise-like handbook lists data on all glass-forming melts and glasses. All information is the form of tables, charts, and diagrams. The 4 volumes cover v.1—Silica glass and binary silicate glasses; v.2—Single-component and binary nonsilicate oxide glasses; v.3—Ternary silicate glasses; v.4—Ternary nonsilicate glasses. For a one-volume work on glass properties consult N.P. Bansal's *Handbook of Glass Properties* (Academic Press, 1986).

1174. Handbook of Heat and Mass Transfer. Nicholas P. Cheremisinoff. Houston, TX: Gulf Publishing, 1986– , irregular. 7v. projected, illus., bibliog., index. $195.00/volume. ISBN: 0-87201-411-8v.1.

This very comprehensive handbook covers the transmission and mass transfer of heat. The projected 7 volumes cover v.1—Heat transfer operations; v.2—Mass transfer and reactor design; v.3—Catalysis, kinetics and reactor engineering; v.4—Combustion science and technology; v.5—Multiphase reactor operations; v.6—Multiphase reactor design; v.7—Radiation technology. Also of interest would be James J. Christensen's *Handbook of Heats of Mixing* (Wiley, 1982).

1175. Handbook of Plastic Materials and Technology. Irvin I. Rubin. New York, NY: Wiley, 1990. 1,745p., illus., index. $115.00. ISBN: 0-471-09634-2.

The purpose of this handbook is to present a review of polymers and how they are processed and utilized. It gives history, descriptions, and advantages/disadvantages of each polymer listed. Since this book was published under the sponsorship of the Society of Plastics Engineers, see also the *Plastics Engineering Handbook* of the Society of the Plastics Industry. Another handbook on technology is Vishu Shah's *Handbook of Plastics Testing Technology* (Wiley, 1984). For additives to plastics consult R. Gachter's *Plastics Additives Handbook* (Oxford University Press, 1991); Jesse Edenbaum's *Plastics Additives and Modifiers Handbook* (Van Nostrand Reinhold, 1991); or Michael Ash's *Handbook of Industrial Chemical Additives* (VCH, 1991).

1176. Handbook of Polymer Science and Technology. Nicholas P. Cheremisinoff. New York, NY: Dekker, 1988-91. 4v., illus., index. $185.00/volume. ISBN: 0-8247-8173-2v.1; 0-8247-8174-0v.2; 0-8247-8004-3v.3; 0-8247-8021-3v.4.

Originally part A of the *Encyclopedia of Engineering Materials*, and now a separate handbook, this 4-volume comprehensive work covers the science and technology of polymers. The 4 volumes cover v.1-Synthesis and properties; v.2—Performance properties of plastics and elastomers; v.3—Applications and processing operations; v.4—Composites and specialty applications. Also, a one-volume work that is useful is J. Brandrup's *Polymer Handbook* (Wiley, 1989).

1177. Handbook of Powder Science and Technology. M.E. Fayed; L. Otten. New York, NY: Van Nostrand Reinhold, 1984. 850p., illus., bibliog., index. $109.95. ISBN: 0-442-22610-1.

This specialized handbook covers the physical and chemical aspects of all powders including character, storage, mixing, transport, and collection.

1178. Handbook of U.S. Colorants: Foods, Drugs, Cosmetics, and Medical Devices. 3rd. Daniel M. Marmion. New York, NY: Wiley, 1991. 473p., illus., bibliog., index. $89.95. ISBN: 0-471-50074-7.

This handbook is a major source of information on color additives used in foods, drugs, cosmetics, and medical devices. It gives the history, regulation, description, and use of colorants; colorant analysis; and resolution of mixtures and analysis of commercial products. Charts and tables are used throughout. Also useful would be J. Knowlton and S. Pearce's *Handbook of Cosmetic Science and Technology* (Elsevier, 1993).

1179. Industrial Solvent Handbook. 3rd. Ernest W. Flick. Park Ridge, NJ: Noyes, 1985. 648p., illus., bibliog., index. $86.00. ISBN: 0-8155-1010-1.

This useful handbook gives data on the physical properties of industrial solvents plus information on selecting the solvents. Information is presented in tables, charts, and figures.

1180. Materials Handbook. 13th. George Stuart Brady. New York, NY: McGraw-Hill, 1991. 1v., various paging, illus., bibliog., index. $74.50. ISBN: 0-07-007074-1.

Also known as *Brady's Materials Handbook*, this handbook is the classic work on materials of all types. It is alphabetically arranged with each material entry giving composition, method of production, major properties, and uses. Another 4-volume more technical set, but now out-of-date, is the *CRC Handbook of Materials Science* (CRC, 1974-80). Also of interest would be James F. Shackelford's *CRC Materials Science and Engineering Handbook* (CRC, 1992).

1181. Metallic Materials Specification Handbook. 4th. Robert B. Ross. New York, NY: Chapman & Hall, 1992. 830p., illus., bibliog., index. $192.50. ISBN: 0-4123-6940-0.

Over 50,000 trade names are included in this handbook classified according to chemical analysis. Complete descriptions are given including corrosion protection, machinability, and uses.

1182. Metals Handbook. 10th. Cleveland, OH: American Society for Metals, 1990– , irregular. 17v. projected, illus., bibliog., index. price per volume varies.

This very comprehensive multivolume handbook covers information on metals. Each volume covers a specific topic including the physical metallurgy of each of these topics. The volumes published in the 9th edition and not yet superseded by the 10th edition are v.8—Mechanical testing; v.9—Metallography and microstructure; v.10—Materials characterization; v.11—Failure analysis and prevention; v.12—Fractography; v.13—Corrosion; v.14—Forming and forging; v.15—Casting; v.16—Machinery; v.17—Nondestructive evaluation and quality control. The 7 volumes of the 10th edition published to date are v.1—Properties and selection: irons, steels, and high performance alloys; v.2—Properties and selection: nonferrous alloys and special purpose materials; v.3—Heat treating; v.4—

Friction, lubrication, and wear technology; v.5—Surface cleaning, finishing and coating; v.6—Welding, brazing, and soldering; v.7—Microstructural analysis. There is a one-volume edition available, published in 1985. See also *Smithsell's Metals Reference Book*. Another good one-volume source of metals information is the *ASM Metals Reference Book* (American Society for Metals, 1983).

1183. Paint Handbook. Guy E. Weismantel. New York, NY: McGraw-Hill, 1981. 1v., various paging, illus., bibliog., index. $69.95. ISBN: 0-07-069061-8.

This handbook covers paint and coating, including surface preparation, testing, and troubleshooting. Emphasis is on architectural and industrial coatings with paint specifications more important than paint formulation. For information on formulation consult Michael Ash's 2-volume *Formulary of Paint and Other Coatings* (Chemical Publishing, 1978-82).

1184. Perry's Chemical Engineers' Handbook. 6th. Robert H. Perry; Don W. Green; James O. Maloney. New York, NY: McGraw-Hill, 1984. 1v., various paging, illus., bibliog., index. $112.50. ISBN: 0-07-049479-7.

This classic handbook, also used as a textbook, is the standard source of information on all aspects of chemical engineering. It includes information on economics as well as production. Environmental topics are also included. See also *Riegel's Handbook of Industrial Chemistry*. Two specialized works are Frank L. Evans' *Equipment Design Handbook for Refineries and Chemical Plants* (Guld Publishing, 1979-80) and Philip A. Schweitzer's *Handbook of Separation Techniques for Chemical Engineers* (McGraw-Hill, 1988).

1185. Plastics Engineering Handbook of the Society of the Plastics Industry. 5th. Michael L. Berins. New York, NY: Van Nostrand Reinhold, 1991. 845p., illus., index. $89.95. ISBN: 0-442-31799-9.

The Society of the Plastics Industry (SPI) is an internationally recognized facility that sets standards for the plastics industry. This handbook is the widely accepted handbook for all engineers working with plastics. It is sometimes referred to as the *SPI Plastics Engineering Handbook*. Another older but still useful work is H. Saechtling's *International Plastics Handbook* (Oxford University Press, 1987) as well as the *Handbook of Plastic Compounds, Elastomers, and Resins* (VCH, 1991) and Manas Chanda's *Plastics Technology Handbook* (Dekker, 1993). For additional information about plastics standards, consult the *Specifications and Standards for Plastics and Composites* (ASM International, 1990).

1186. Riegel's Handbook of Industrial Chemistry. 9th. Emil Raymond Riegel; James A. Kent. New York, NY: Van Nostrand Reinhold, 1992. 1,288p., illus., bibliog., index. $99.95. ISBN: 0-442-00175-4.

This well-established handbook for the chemical process industry covers all areas—from synthetic organic chemicals to agro-chemicals to materials. The book can also be used as a textbook.

1187. Smithsell's Metals Reference Book. 7th. Colin J. Smithell; Eric A. Brandes. Boston, MA: Butterworths, 1991. 1v., various paging, illus., bibliog., index. $300.00. ISBN: 0-750-61020-4.

Previously called *Metals Reference Book*, this handbook gives a summary of metallurgical data, mainly in the form of tables. Such topics as hard metals, friction and wear, corrosion, and solders are covered as well as various coatings.

1188. Standard Methods for Analysis and Testing of Petroleum and Related Products, 1991. Institute of Petroleum. New York, NY: Wiley, 1991. 2v., illus., bibliog., index. $440.00. ISBN: 0-471-92949-2.

This important work continues the *IP Standard for Petroleum and Its Products* and is also called *Methods for Analysis and Testing of Petroleum and Related Products*. It contains over 250 methods for analyzing and testing all petroleum products, including chemical and physical methods and some small-scale rig tests. The tests are listed in numerical order and give such information as scope, definition, summary of method, significance and use, apparatus, procedure, calculations, reporting, and precision.

1189. Woldman's Engineering Alloys. 7th revised. Norman Emme Woldman; John P. Frick. Metals Park, OH: American Society for Metals, 1990. 1,459p., index. $128.00. ISBN: 0-87170-408-0.

Previously called *Engineering Alloys*, *Woldman's* is the source of information on alloys. Alphabetically arranged, each alloy is identified and its general use indicated. A list of manufacturers is included as well as a table of obsolete alloys.

Histories

1190. American Chemical Industry. William Haynes. New York, NY: Garland, 1983(c1954). 6v., illus., bibliog., index. out-of-print. ISBN: 0-8240-5362-1.

American Chemical Industry is a very comprehensive, but out-of-print, history of chemical engineering in the United States. The 6 volumes cover v.1—Background and beginning; v.2-3—The World War I period, 1912-1922; v.4—The merger era; v.5—Decade of new products; v.6—The chemical companies.

1191. History of Chemical Engineering. *(Advances in Chemistry Series, 190).* William F. Furter. Washington, DC: American Chemical Society, 1980. 435p., illus., bibliog., index. $46.95. ISBN: 0-8412-0512-4.

This publication is an authoritative history of chemical engineering. For a history of metallurgy consult R.F. Tylecote's *History of Metallurgy* (Institution of Materials, 1992).

1192. History of Chemical Technology: An Annotated Bibliography. *(Bibliographies of the History of Science and Technology v.5) (Garland Reference Library of the Humanities, v.348).* Robert P. Multhauf. New York, NY: Garland, 1984. 299p., index. price not available. ISBN: 0-8240-9255-4.

Arranged both by country and topic, this comprehensive annotated bibliography covers all areas of chemical technology.

1193. Textiles in America, 1650-1870: A Dictionary Based on Original Documents; Prints and Paintings, Commercial Records, American Merchant Papers, Shopkeepers' Advertisements, and Pattern Books with Original Swatches of Cloth. Florence M. Montgomery. New York, NY: Norton, 1984. 412p., illus., bibliog. $45.00. ISBN: 0-393-01703-6.

This historical account explains how textiles were used in the United States, plus it has a dictionary of historical terminology in the textile industry. There are excellent photographs.

Tables

1194. Gas Tables: International Version, Thermodynamic Properties of Air Products of Combustion and Component Gases Compressible Flow Functions. 2nd. Joseph Henry Keenan; Jing Chao; Joseph Kaye. New York, NY: Wiley, 1983. 211p., illus., bibliog. $61.95. ISBN: 0-471-08874-9.

This book contains conveniently arranged gas tables of various types for the practicing engineer.

Treatises

1195. Comprehensive Polymer Science. Geoffrey Allen; J.C. Bevington. New York, NY: Pergamon Press, 1988. 7v., illus., bibliog., index. $2,190.00. ISBN: 0-08-032515-7.

This multivolume treatise with supplements presents an excellent overview of polymer science. It covers all areas from research to uses.

1196. Treatise on Materials Science and Technology. San Diego, CA: Academic Press, 1972-1989. 31v., illus., bibliog., index. $107.00/volume. ISBN: 0-12-341831-3v.31.

This very extensive treatise covers the fundamental properties and characterization of materials, ranging from simple solids to complex heterophase systems. Each volume is separately indexed and individual chapters are separately authored. The following volumes have unique subtitles: v.3—Ultrasonic investigation of mechanical properties; v.6—Plastic deformation of materials; v.7—Microstructure of irradiated materials; v.9—Ceramic fabrication processes; v.10—Properties of solid polymeric materials; v.11—Properties of microstructure; v.12—Glass I; v.13—Wear; v.14—Metallurgy of superconductivity materials; v.15—Neutoron scattering; v.16—Erosion; v.17—Glass II; v.18—Ion implantation; v.19—Experimental methods; v.20—Ultrarapid quenching of liquid alloys; v.21—Electronic structures and properties; v.22—Glass III; v.23—Corrosion; v.24—Preparation and techniques for thin films; v.25—Embrittlement of engineering alloys; v.26—Glass IV; v.27—Analytical techniques for thin films; v.28—Materials for marine systems and structures; v.29—Structural ceramics; v.30—Auger electron spectroscopy; v.31—Aluminum alloys.

Periodicals

1197. AIChE Journal. New York, NY: American Institute of Chemical Engineers, 1955– , monthly. v.1– , index. $349.00. ISSN: 0001-1541.

1198. Canadian Journal of Chemical Engineering. Ottawa, Ontario, Canada: Canadian Society for Chemical Engineering, 1922– , 6/year. v.1– , index. $120.00. ISSN: 0008-4034.

1199. Chemical and Engineering News. Washington, DC: American Chemical Society, 1923– , weekly. v.1– , index. $105.00. ISSN: 0009-2347.

1200. Chemical Engineer. Basinstoke, Great Britain: Taylor & Francis, 1923– , 23/year. v.1– , index. $153.00. ISSN: 0302-0797.

1201. Chemical Engineering. New York, NY: McGraw-Hill, 1902– , monthly. v.1– , index. $46.00. ISSN: 0009-2460.

1202. Chemical Engineering Education. Gainsville, FL: American Society for Engineering Education, 1965– , quarterly. v.1– , index. $20.00. ISSN: 0009-2479.

1203. Chemical Engineering Progress. New York, NY: American Institute of Chemical Engineers, 1947– , monthly. v.1– , index. $60.00. ISSN: 0360-7275.

1204. Chemical Engineering Research and Design. Basinstoke, Great Britain: Taylor & Francis, 1923– , bimonthly. v.1– , index. $240.00. ISSN: 0263-8762.

1205. Chemical Engineering Science. Tarrytown, NY: Pergamon Press, 1951– , 18/year. v.1– , index. $1,448.00. ISSN: 0009-2509.

1206. Chemical Week. New York, NY: Chemical Week Associates, 1914– , weekly. v.1– , index. $99.00. ISSN: 0009-272X.

1207. Chemtech. Washington, DC: American Chemical Society, 1970– , monthly. v.1– , index. $365.00. ISSN: 0009-2703.

1208. Composites. Oxford, Great Britain: Butterworth-Heinemann, 1969– , bimonthly. v.1– , index. $376.00. ISSN: 0010-4361.

1209. Industrial and Engineering Chemistry Research. Washington, DC: American Chemical Society, 1962– , monthly. v.1– , index. $512.00. ISSN: 0888-5885.

1210. Journal of Applied Polymer Science. New York, NY: Wiley, 1956– , 36/year. v.1– , index. $2,355.00. ISSN: 0021-8995.

1211. Journal of Composite Materials. Lancaster, PA: Technomic, 1967– , 18/year. v.1– , index. $760.00.

1212. Journal of Materials Science. London, Great Britain: Chapman & Hall, 1966– , 24/year. v.1– , index. $2,650.00. ISSN: 0022-2461.

1213. Materials and Design. Oxford, Great Britain: Butterworth-Heinemann, 1978– , 6/year. v.1– , index. $208.00. ISSN: 0264-1275.

1214. Materials Evaluation. Columbus, OH: American Society for Nondestructive Testing, 1942– , monthly. v.1– , index. $85.00. ISSN: 0025-5327.

1215. Materials Science and Engineering: A—Structural Materials; B—Solid-State Materials for Advanced Technology. Lausanne, Switzerland: Elsevier, 1967– , 46/year. v.1– , index. $3045.00 A; $812.00 B. ISSN: 0921-5093 A; 0921-5107 B.

1216. Process Engineering. London, Great Britain: Morgan-Grampian, 1972– , monthly. v.1– , index. $130.00. ISSN: 0370-1859.

CIVIL ENGINEERING, BUILDING, AND CONSTRUCTION

Abstracts and Indexes

1217. Civil Engineering DataBase (CEDB). New York, NY: American Society of Civil Engineering, 1975– , bimonthly. v.1– , index. price varies.

This database provides access to all ASCE publications. It contains over 48,000 searchable records back to 1975 and adds about 4,000 new records each year.

1218. Concrete Abstracts. Detroit, MI: American Concrete Institute, 1972– , bimonthly. v.1– , index. $155.00. ISSN: 0045-8007.

This abstracting journal covers publications that report on developments in concrete and concrete technology. It is of interest to civil engineers, structural engineers, architects, and others involved in designing and working with concrete.

1219. Fluid Abstracts. Barking, Great Britain: Elsevier, 1969– , monthly. v.1– , index. $1,184.00. ISSN: 0962-7170; 0962-7162.

This work, published in 2 sections—Civil Engineering and Process Engineering—covers civil and process engineering applications of fluid mechanics, hydraulics, flow metering and measuring, offshore engineering, environmental hydraulics, and other related topics. It was formed by the merger of *Civil Engineering Hydraulics Abstracts, Industrial Aerodynamics Abstracts, Offshore Engineering Abstracts, World Ports and Harbours Abstracts, Fluid Power Abstracts, Fluid Sealing Abstracts, Solid-Liquid Flow Abstracts, Pumps and Other Fluids Machinery Abstracts, Fluid Flow Measurement Abstracts, Pipelines Abstracts, Computer-Aided Process Control Abstracts, Mixing and Separation Technology Abstracts,* and *International Dredging Abstracts.* It is also available online.

1220. International Civil Engineering Abstracts. Dublin, Ireland: CITIS, 1974– , monthly. v.1– , index. $595.00. ISSN: 0332-4095.

Previously called *ICE Abstracts* and *European Civil Engineering Abstracts,* this abstracting service covers the international journal literature in civil engineering. It is also available online and on CD-ROM.

Biographical Sources

1221. Macmillan Encyclopedia of Architects. Adolf K. Placzek. New York, NY: Free Press, 1982. 4v., illus., bibliog., index. $400.00. ISBN: 0-02-925000-5.

Entries in this biographical encyclopedia had to be born before December 31, 1930, or be deceased. The biographies are complete and include a list of works and extensive bibliographies. A smaller biographical dictionary with briefer entries is J.M. Richards' *Who's Who in Architecture: From 1400 to the Present Day* (Holt, Rinehart & Winston, 1971).

Dictionaries, Glossaries, and Thesauri

1222. Architectural and Building Trades Dictionary. 3rd. Robert E. Putnam; G.E. Carlson. New York, NY: Van Nostrand Reinhold, 1982 (c1974). 510p., illus. $19.95. ISBN: 0-442-27461-0.

This excellent dictionary covers terms related to all aspects of building, including tools, materials, methods, and acronyms.

1223. Building Trades Dictionary. L.P. Toenjes. Homewood, IL: American Technical Publishers, 1989. 314p., illus. $34.95. ISBN: 0-8269-0403-3.

This dictionary includes terms from the building trades, basic engineering, and architecture. Definitions are concise and descriptive.

1224. Complete Dictionary of Wood. Thomas Corkill. New York, NY: Dorset Press, 1989 (c1979). 655p., illus. $24.95, $14.95 pbk. ISBN: 0-88029-346-2, 0-88029-329-2 pbk.

Originally published as *Glossary of Wood* in Great Britain, this dictionary covers all terms that relate to wood as a product, material for building, or related areas in the engineering field.

1225. Construction Glossary: An Encyclopedic Reference and Manual. 2nd. J. Stewart Stein. New York, NY: Wiley, 1993. 1,137p., index. $95.00. ISBN: 0-471-56933-X.

Some 30,000 terms, phraseology, and expressions pertaining to construction are included in this work which is based on the CSI Masterformat. It includes specification language, building and zoning code interpretations, and reference standards.

1226. Construction Regulations Glossary: A Reference Manual. J. Stewart Stein. New York, NY: Wiley, 1983. 930p., index. price not available. ISBN: 0-471-89776-0.

This companion to *Construction Glossary* is a dictionary covering the terms related to regulations in the construction industry. Over 500 ordinances, codes, and other works were consulted.

1227. Dictionary of Architecture and Construction. 2nd. Cyril M. Harris. New York, NY: McGraw-Hill, 1993. 924p. $59.50. ISBN: 0-07-026888-6.

This title is a well-written authority for terminology related to architecture and building construction. It includes definitions in all areas of building, materials, styles, and history of architecture.

1228. Dictionary of Building. Randall McMullan. New York, NY: Nichols, 1988. 262p., illus. $59.50. ISBN: 0-89397-319-X.

Words used in the English-speaking world are included in this small dictionary of building terms. It has a British slant but is still a good dictionary. Another out-of-print work that is equally useful is John S. Scott's *Dictionary of Building* (Halsted, 1984).

1229. Dictionary of Building and Civil Engineering: English, German, French, Dutch, Russian. S.N. Korchomkin. Boston, MA: Nijhoff, 1985. 935p. $195.00. ISBN: 0-8288-0222-X.

This dictionary lists over 14,000 English terms with their German, French, Dutch, and Russian equivalents. It covers civil engineering, materials, soil mechanics, buildings, construction, and site terminology.

1230. Dictionary of Civil Engineering. 3rd. John S. Scott. New York, NY: Wiley, 1981. 308p., illus. $19.95. ISBN: 0-470-27087-X.

This general dictionary covers the broad civil engineering terms including soil mechanics, construction, and some mining terminology.

1231. Dictionary of Geotechnics. S.H. Somerville; M.A. Paul. Woburn, MA: Butterworths, 1983. 283p., illus. $70.00. ISBN: 0-408-00437-1.

Some 1,600 terms pertaining to geotechnical engineering are defined along with related terms in geology and geomorphology.

1232. Dictionary of Soil Mechanics and Foundation Engineering. John Arthur Barker. New York, NY: Construction Press, 1981. 210p. price not available. ISBN: 0-86095-885-X.

Over 2,500 terms are included in this dictionary covering the terms and equipment that are associated with all aspects of soil mechanics and foundation engineering.

1233. Dictionary of Woodworking Tools, c1700-1970. revised. Raphael Salaman; Philip Walker. Newton, CT: Taunton Press, 1990. 546p., illus. $27.95. ISBN: 0-942391-51-9.

This excellent encyclopedic dictionary covers all woodworking tools that have been developed in Eng-

land. Good illustrations aid in the book's usefulness. Two multilingual dictionaries covering tools are L.Y. Chaballe and J.P. Vandenberghe's *Elsevier's Dictionary of Building Tools and Materials: In English/American, French, Spanish, German, and Dutch* (Elsevier, 1982, 5,833 terms) and W.E. Clason's *Elsevier's Dictionary of Tools and Ironware: In English/American, French, Spanish, Italian, Dutch and German* (Elsevier, 1982, 2,576 terms).

1234. Elsevier's Dictionary of Building Construction: English/French; French/English. James Maclean. New York, NY: Elsevier, 1988-89. 1v., illus. $226.00. ISBN: 0-444-42966-2 English/French; 0-444-42931-X French/English.

All terms associated with the building industry are included in this bilingual dictionary. In addition to building terms, there is emphasis on terms related to the mechanical and electrical services as they pertain to building. Other Elsevier multilingual dictionaries include: U. Gelbrich's *Dictionary of Architecture and Building* (1989, 30,000 terms); J.P. Vandenberghe's *Elsevier's Dictionary of Architecture: In English, French, Spanish, German, and Dutch* (1988, 4,543 terms); C.J. Van Manscum's *Elsevier's Dictionary of Building Construction: In English/American, French, Dutch, and German* (1959, 5,328 terms); and R. Zimmermann's *Dictionary of Lighting Engineering: In English, German, French, and Russian* (1989, 11,000 terms).

1235. Elsevier's Dictionary of Civil Engineering: In English, German, Spanish and French. Marcos F. Gutierrez. Amsterdam, Netherlands: Elsevier, 1991. 392p. $157.00. ISBN: 0-444-88987-6.

Some 5,560 terms are included in this multilingual dictionary of all areas of civil engineering. Other related Elsevier dictionaries include K.P. Ghatnagar's *Elsevier's Dictionary of Civil Engineering: Russian-English* (1988, 40,000 terms).

1236. Illustrated Dictionary for Building Construction. John E. Traister. Albany, NY: Delmar, 1992. 525p., illus. $21.95. ISBN: 0-8273-4960-2.

This small, concise dictionary lists some 1,000 terms unique to the building industry and construction trades. Also useful are Paul Marsh's *Illustrated Dictionary of Building* (Construction Press, 1982) and Cyril M. Harris's *Dictionary of Architecture and Construction* (McGraw-Hill, 1975).

1237. Illustrated Dictionary of Building Materials and Techniques: An Invaluable Sourcebook to the Tools, Terms, Materials and Techniques Used by Building Professionals. Paul Bianchina. New York, NY: Wiley, 1993. 238p., illus., bibliog., index. $39.95. ISBN: 0-471-57656-5.

This dictionary contains some 4,000 terms and abbreviations pertaining to the tools, materials, techniques, and terminology used by building contractors, architects, electricians, plumbers, masons, roofers, and other building professionals.

1238. Means Illustrated Construction Dictionary. new unabridged. Kornelis Smit; Haward M. Chandler. Kingston, MA: R.S. Means, 1991. 691p., illus. $99.95. ISBN: 0-876-29218-X.

More than 13,000 construction terms are defined in this comprehensive dictionary. It includes materials products, methods, equipment, uses, and other related construction terminology.

Directories

1239. Directory of Construction Industry Consultants. New York, NY: Wiley, 1992. 441p., index. $95.00. ISBN: 0-471-56947-X.

This frequently published directory lists some 300 consultants specializing in engineering, project management, claims consulting, litigation support, and alternative dispute resolution. Each entry gives officers and key personnel, contact person, background and history, special expertise, projects, and representative clients.

1240. Directory of International Periodicals and Newsletters on the Built Environment. 2nd. Frances C. Gretes. New York, NY: Van Nostrand Reinhold, 1992. 442p., index. $79.95. ISBN: 0-442-00792-2.

This directory provides full bibliographic details on international periodicals and newsletters covering architecture, building, interior design, and historic preservation as well as landscape and urban design. It includes descriptive annotations that describe audience, quality, and reputation.

1241. Sweet's Catalog File: Architecture Products for General Buildings. New York, NY: Sweet's, 1977– , annual. v.1– , index.

Sweet's Catalog File is an annually produced multivolume set of product catalogs pertaining to construction and building. It covers everything that an architect or builder may be interested in using in a project.

1242. World Cement Directory. Brussels, Belgium: World Cement Directory, 1956– , irregular. v.1– , index. $400.00.

This directory presents information about the international cement industry, including company management, location of plants, type of kilns and fuels used, and production and capacity figures.

Encyclopedias

1243. Concise Encyclopedia of Building and Construction Materials. *(Advances in Materials Science and Engineering, v.4).* Fred Moavenzadeh; Robert W. Cahn. New York, NY: Pergamon Press, 1990. 682p., illus., bibliog., index. $175.00. ISBN: 0-08-034728-2.

Much of this material is based on information from the multivolume work, *Encyclopedia of Materials Science and Engineering.* It is one of 10 such concise encyclopedias. It covers all topics pertaining to building and construction materials such as adhesives, cement, wood, metals, and polymers.

1244. Concise Encyclopedia of Interior Design. 2nd. A. Allen Dizik. New York, NY: Van Nostrand Reinhold, 1988. 220p., bibliog. $39.95. ISBN: 0-442-22109-6.

This alphabetically arranged encyclopedia lists interior design terms, stressing furnishings but including all decorating terminology. There are no illustrations.

1245. Encyclopedia of Architecture: Design, Engineering, and Construction. Joseph A. Wilkes; Robert T. Packard. New York, NY: Wiley, 1990. 5v., illus., bibliog., index. $850.00. ISBN: 0-471-63351-8.

Prepared by the American Institute of Architects, this encyclopedia covers all aspects of architectural design, including design, engineering, and construction. A smaller one-volume work that is also useful is Pedro Guedes' *Encyclopedia of Architectural Technology* (McGraw-Hill, 1979).

1246. Encyclopedia of Building Technology. Henry J. Cowan. Englewood Cliffs, NJ: Prentice-Hall, 1988. 344p., illus., bibliog., index. $75.00. ISBN: 0-13-275520-3.

This encyclopedia covers the building and construction technologies, written for the student. It includes references to other sources.

1247. Encyclopedia of How It's Built. Donald Clarke. New York, NY: A&W, 1979. 184p., illus. (part in color). out-of-print. ISBN: 0-89479-047-1.

Also called *How It's Built* this layperson's encyclopedia covers such topics as the arch, bridges, cathedrals, frame construction, lighthouses, sewage and water supplies, ships and docks, tunnels, and wells.

1248. Encyclopedia of Wood: Wood as an Engineering Material. revised. Forest Products Laboratory. 1989. 376p., illus., bibliog., index. $19.95. ISBN: 0-8069-6994-6.

Originally published as the *Wood Handbook*, this is a general encyclopedia about wood and its uses as an engineering material.

1249. Plumber's and Pipe Fitter's Library.
4th. Charles N. McConnell. New York, NY:
Macmillan, 1989. 3v., illus., index. $64.95.
ISBN: 0-02-582914-9.

This publication is a comprehensive source of technical information on all aspects of plumbing and pipe fitting as they pertain to the building trades, including basic tools, fixtures, environmental concerns, water supply, materials, sewage disposal, and safety. It has been established as a classic.

Guides and Field Guides

1250. ACI Manual of Concrete Practice.
Detroit, MI: American Concrete Institute,
1967– , annual. v.1– , illus., bibliog., index (5
volumes published per year to make a set).
$320.00. ISSN: 0065-7875.

This annual produced by the American Concrete Institute is the Bible for the concrete industry giving all the procedures, specifications, and standards that are needed for proper construction with concrete.

1251. Concrete Manual: A Manual for the Control of Concrete Construction. 8th revised. Washington, DC: GPO, 1981. 627p.,
illus., bibliog., index. $18.00. ISBN:
0-16-003371-3.

Published by the Water and Power Resource Services, this manual provides engineering data and outlines of methods and procedures that are to be followed in administering construction specifications and contracts by the federal government and used by the Bureau of Reclamation.

1252. Field Engineers Manual. Robert O.
Parmley. New York, NY: McGraw-Hill, 1981.
608p., illus., index. $44.95. ISBN:
0-07-048513-5.

This practical manual for the construction engineer provides useful information on problems and planning related to materials, surveying, mechanic and electrical systems, drainage, and other related areas.

1253. Geotechnical Engineering Investigation Manual. Roy E. Hunt. New York, NY:
McGraw-Hill, 1984. 983p., illus., bibliog.,
index. $89.00. ISBN: 0-07-031309-1.

This detailed manual covers those areas of geology that have an impact on engineering projects including rock types and masses, soils, groundwater, flooding, erosion, landslides, ground heave, subsidence and collapse, and earthquakes.

1254. Manual of Geology for Civil Engineers.
John Pitts. River Edge, NJ: World Scientific,
1985. 228p., illus., index. $38.00. ISBN:
9971-97-805-9.

A brief overview of geology is provided for civil engineers covering geotechnics and soil mechanics.

1255. Manual of Soil Laboratory Testing.
2nd. K.H. Head. New York, NY: Halsted,
1982-92. 3v., illus., bibliog., index. $258.85.
ISBN: 0-470-21842-8v.1; 0-470-27289-9v.2;
0-470-20236-Xv.3.

This practical field manual covers soil testing. It discusses equipment, description of soils, testing and techniques, and safety. Only volume one is in the second edition. The 3 volumes cover v.1—Soil classification and compaction tests; v.2—Permeability, quick shear strength and compressibility tests; v.3—Effective stress testing principles, theory and applications.

1256. Manual of Steel Construction. 9th.
American Institute of Steel Construction.
Chicago, IL: American Institute of Steel
Construction, 1990. 1v., various paging, illus.,
index. $60.00. ISBN: 0-685-41193-1.

Also called *Steel Construction Manual*, this is the Bible for steel construction engineers. Through formulas, charts, and diagrams it presents all of the specifications and data needed to safely design steel into any structure. For the properties of steel consult Philip D. Harvey's *Engineering Properties of Steel* (American Society for Metals, 1982).

1257. Timber Construction Manual. 3rd.
American Institute of Timber Construction.
New York, NY: Wiley, 1985. 836p., illus.,
index. $64.95. ISBN: 0-471-82758-4.

This manual covers all the techniques, methods, and uses of timber. There are numerous illustrations, charts, and graphs. Also of interest is Karl Heinz Gotz's *Timber Design and Construction Sourcebook* (McGraw-Hill, 1989), a translation of *Holzbau Atlas*.

Guides to the Literature

1258. Information Sources in Architecture.
Valerie J. Bradfield. Boston, MA:
Butterworths, 1983. 419p., illus., bibliog.,
index. $85.00. ISBN: 0-408-10763-4.

This useful guide covers the sources of information pertaining to the building industry including information retrieval, organizations, periodicals, reference materials, abstracting services, trade literature, and government publications.

Handbooks and Manuals

1259. American Metric Construction Handbook. R.J. Lytle; Dorothy T. Burrows. New
York, NY: McGraw-Hill, 1983 (c1976). 304p.,
illus., bibliog., index. $14.95. ISBN:
0-07-039277-3.

This useful handbook helps architects and engineers understand and use the American metric system. Numerous conversion charts and diagrams are included. A similar publication is Susan Braybrooke's

AIA Metric Building and Construction Guide (Wiley, 1980).

1260. Architect's Data. 2nd. Ernest Neufert. New York, NY: Halsted Press, 1988. 433p., illus., bibliog., index. $45.00. ISBN: 0-470-26947-2.

This useful handbook gives basic building forms with layouts, sizes, and properties. Covers all types of buildings. Also useful is *Architectural Graphic Standards* (Wiley, 1991) and Joseph DeChiara's *Time-Saver Standards for Building Types* (McGraw-Hill, 1990).

1261. Architect's Handbook of Construction Detailing. David K. Ballast. New York, NY: Prentice-Hall, 1990. 484p., illus., bibliog., index. $69.95. ISBN: 0-13-044694-7.

This well-written handbook outlines all aspects of drawing and drafting as used by the architect or builder. Another useful book on the same topic is John A. Nelson's *Handbook of Architectural and Civil Drafting* (Van Nostrand Reinhold, 1983).

1262. Architect's Remodeling, Renovation, and Restoration Handbook. H. Leslie Simmons. New York, NY: Van Nostrand Reinhold, 1989. 348p., illus., bibliog., index. $75.95. ISBN: 0-442-20574-0.

This handbook is intended to help architects in the production of effective drawings and specifications for remodeling, renovation, and restoration projects. A related book covering architectural details is Joseph DeChiara's *Handbook of Architectural Details for Commercial Buildings* (McGraw-Hill, 1980).

1263. Architectural Handbook: Environmental Analysis, Architectural Programming, Design and Technology, and Construction. Alfred M. Kemper. New York, NY: Wiley, 1979. 591p., illus., bibliog., index. out-of-print. ISBN: 0-471-02697-2.

This handbook covers a wide variety of topics of interest to architects and building engineers. Areas covered include environmental analysis, architectural programming, design and technology, and construction techniques.

1264. Building Design and Construction Handbook. 4th. Frederick S. Merritt. New York, NY: McGraw-Hill, 1982. 1v., various paging, illus., bibliog., index. $106.50. ISBN: 0-07-041521-8.

Previously called *Building Construction Handbook*, this very comprehensive handbook provides the best of building design and construction practices, including anything pertaining to the selection of building materials and construction methods. Another handbook covering building construction is Edward Allen's *Professional Handbook of Building Construction* (Wiley, 1985).

1265. Building Systems Integration Handbook. Richard D. Rush. Stoneham, MA: Butterworths-Heinemann, 1991. 445p., illus., bibliog., index. $29.95. ISBN: 0-7506-9198-0.

The purpose of this handbook is to help architects and designers integrate the systems of structure, envelope, mechanical, and interior so that the final result is a building that is efficient and pleasing.

1266. Chemical Materials for Construction: Handbook of Chemicals for Concrete, Flooring, Caulks and Sealants, Epoxies, Latex Emulsions, Adhesives, Roofing, Waterproofing, Technical Coatings and Heavy Construction Specialties. Philip Maslow. New York, NY: McGraw-Hill, 1982. 570p., illus., bibliog., index. price not available. ISBN: 0-07-040664-2.

This useful handbook for engineers describes the properties of various chemical materials used in construction. It explains in detail the effect of the chemicals on the materials involved.

1267. Civil Engineering Handbook. 4th. Leonard C. Urquhart. New York, NY: McGraw-Hill, 1959. 1,184p., illus., index. $94.00. ISBN: 0-07-066148-0.

Although dated, this well-known handbook is still being published as an authoritative source of information for civil engineers. It covers all areas from surveying to sewage disposal and water supply.

1268. Civil Engineering: Reference Guide. Frederick S. Merritt. New York, NY: McGraw-Hill, 1986. 1v., various paging, illus., index. $49.50. ISBN: 0-07-041522-6.

This abridged edition of the *Standard Handbook for Civil Engineers* (McGraw-Hill, 1983) provides the key material that civil engineers need in their day-to-day work.

1269. Civil Engineer's Reference Book. 4th. Leslie S. Blake. Stoneham, MA: Butterworths-Heinemann, 1989. 960p., illus., bibliog., index. $150.00. ISBN: 0-408-01208-0.

This authoritative handbook of civil engineering fundamentals is useful for other engineers as well as architects and geological engineers. Also of interest is Michael Lindeburg's *Civil Engineering Reference Manual* (Professional Publications, 1992).

1270. Concrete Construction Handbook. 3rd. Joseph J. Waddell; Joseph A. Dobrowolski. New York, NY: McGraw-Hill, 1993. 1v., various paging, illus., bibliog., index. $92.50. ISBN: 0-07-067666-6.

This comprehensive handbook covers all aspects of concrete from properties, mixing, using, and finishing to special uses, precast, prestressed and repair. Also of use is J.T. Adams' *Complete Concrete, Masonry, and Brick Handbook* (Van Nostrand Reinhold, 1983).

1271. Construction Inspection Handbook: Quality Assurance/Quality Control. 3rd. James Jerome O'Brien. New York, NY: Van Nostrand Reinhold, 1989. 773p., illus., bibliog., index. $64.95. ISBN: 0-442-20559-7.

This handbook outlines the controls of quality, time, and cost in detail giving facts, figures, and guidelines for such areas as sitework, concrete, metal, thermal moisture protection, equipment, and special construction.

1272. Construction Materials for Architects and Designers. Terry L. Patterson. Englewood Cliffs, NJ: Prentice-Hall, 1990. 301p., illus., index. $46.00. ISBN: 0-13-168345-4.

This handbook outlines the properties of various construction materials used in building, including wood, masonry, steel, and concrete. Another similar handbook that is also useful is Harold J. Rosen's *Construction Materials for Architects* (Wiley, 1985).

1273. Data Book for Civil Engineers. 3rd. Elwyn E. Seelye. New York, NY: Wiley, 1954-59. 3v., illus., index. $420.00. ISBN: 0-471-77286-0v.1.

This classic set of handbooks, still in-print, provides the day-to-day data used by the practicing civil engineer. The 3 volumes cover v.1—Design; v.2—Specifications and costs; v.3—Field practices.

1274. Excavation Planning Reference Guide. Horace K. Church; Jeremy Robinson. New York, NY: McGraw-Hill, 1988. 2v., various paging, illus., bibliog., index. $89.00. ISBN: 0-07-010840-4.

Previously called *Excavation Handbook*, this small handbook covers all open-air excavation from the initial location in situ to their final deposition in construction or mining.

1275. Foundation Engineering Handbook. 2nd. Hsai-Yang Fang. New York, NY: Van Nostrand Reinhold, 1991. 923p., illus., bibliog., index. $134.95. ISBN: 0-442-22487-7.

This very good handbook provides information about foundation engineering including soil mechanics.

1276. Ground Engineer's Reference Book. F.G. Bell. Boston, MA: Butterworth, 1987. 1v., various paging, illus., bibliog., index. $225.00. ISBN: 0-408-01173-4.

This comprehensive handbook covers those topics that deal with the ground and civil engineering projects. The 5 parts cover properties and behavior of the ground, investigation in ground engineering, treatment of the ground, construction in ground engineering, and numerical methods and modelling.

1277. Handbook of Architectural Technology. Henry J. Cowan. New York, NY: Van Nostrand Reinhold, 1991. 490p., illus., bibliog., index. $79.95. ISBN: 0-442-20525-2.

This handbook covers the technical aspects of architectural technology and the various management and research methods.

1278. Handbook of Concrete Engineering. 2nd. Mark Fintel. New York, NY: Van Nostrand Reinhold, 1985. 892p., illus., bibliog., index. $109.95. ISBN: 0-442-22623-3.

Reinforced concrete is stressed in this important handbook. It covers materials, design, specialized structures, and structural analysis.

1279. Handbook of Dam Engineering. Alfred R. Golze. New York, NY: Van Nostrand Reinhold, 1977. 793p., illus., bibliog., index. price not available. ISBN: 0-442-22752-3.

Although somewhat dated this still useful handbook covers the planning, location, selection of types, design, and construction of dams. Related areas of hydroelectric plants and ship-locks are also included.

1280. Handbook of Geology in Civil Engineering. 3rd. Robert F. Legget; Paul F. Karrow. New York, NY: McGraw-Hill, 1983. 1v., various paging, illus., bibliog., index. price not available. ISBN: 0-07-037061-3.

Portions of this book were taken from *Geology and Engineering* and *Cities and Geology*. It is both a handbook and history of geology as it pertains to civil engineering. It stresses the importance of geology to civil engineers and provides numerous worldwide case histories.

1281. Handbook of HVAC Design. Nils R. Grimm; Robert C. Rosaler. New York, NY: McGraw-Hill, 1990. 1v., various paging, illus., bibliog., index. $99.50. ISBN: 0-07-024841-9.

A handbook that gives information on how to design, install, and operate heating, ventilating, and air conditioning systems. Topics covered include project planning, duct work, safety, conservation, and noise control.

1282. Handbook of Soil Mechanics. Arpad Kezdi. New York, NY: Elsevier, 1974-88. 4v., illus., bibliog., index. price not available. ISBN: 0-444-99890-Xv.1.

This standard handbook on soil mechanics is a translation of *Handbuch der Bodenmechanik*. These four volumes cover in detail all the laws and theories that are needed to understand how soils react. The 4 volumes cover v.1—Soil physics; v.2—Soil testing; v.3—Soil mechanics of earthwork, foundations, and highway engineering; v.4—Application of soil mechanics in practice; examples and case histories.

1283. Handbook of Structural Concrete.
F.K. Kong. New York, NY: McGraw-Hill, 1983. 1v., various paging, illus., bibliog., index. price not available. ISBN: 0-07-011573-7.

This international reference handbook covers the science of structural concrete providing its behavior, design, analysis, construction, maintenance, demolition, and design uses.

1284. Means Estimating Handbook. Kinston, MA: R.S. Means, 1990. 905p., illus., index. $89.95. ISBN: 0-87629-177-9.

This very useful handbook helps in estimating quantities of materials as well as labor required for construction projects. It is to be used with all R.S. Means cost data directories. Also of interest is the *National Construction Estimator* (Craftsman, 1991).

1285. Practical Construction Equipment Maintenance Reference Guide. Lindley R. Higgins. New York, NY: McGraw-Hill, 1987. 1v., various paging, illus., bibliog., index. price not available.

Previously called *Handbook of Construction Equipment Maintenance*, this book is most useful to maintenance workers and equipment operators. The 3 sections cover maintenance technology, power systems, and ground contact.

1286. Reinforced Concrete Designer's Handbook. 9th. Charles E. Reynolds; James C. Steedman. New York, NY: Chapman & Hall, 1988. 505p., illus., bibliog., index. $95.00. ISBN: 0-7210-1198-5.

This excellent handbook is intended to help any designer who uses reinforced concrete. It covers such areas as safety factors, structural analysis, materials and stress, and structures and foundations.

1287. Standard Handbook for Civil Engineers. 3rd. Frederick S. Merritt. New York, NY: McGraw-Hill, 1983. 1v., various paging, illus., bibliog., index. $120.00. ISBN: 0-07-041515-3.

This handbook is considered the Bible for civil engineers. It is comprehensive, covering all areas of civil engineering and related topics. It presents the best of engineering practices that affect the selection of engineering materials and construction methods. A condensed version is also available as *Civil Engineering Reference Guide* (McGraw-Hill, 1986).

1288. Structural Engineering Handbook.
3rd. Edwin H. Gaylord, Jr.; Charles N. Gaylor. New York, NY: McGraw-Hill, 1990. 1v., various paging, illus., bibliog., index. $84.50. ISBN: 0-07-023188-5.

All types of structures are covered in this handbook including buildings, tall buildings, bridges, roofs, tanks for liquid storage, transmission towers, chimneys, and conduits. It covers such materials as reinforced concrete, prestressed concrete, steel, composites, wood, aluminum, and masonry.

1289. Surveying Handbook. Russell C. Brinker; Ray Minnick. New York, NY: Van Nostrand Reinhold, 1987. 1,270p., illus., index. $99.95. ISBN: 0-442-21423-5.

This excellent handbook covers all areas of surveying. It should become a classic.

1290. Thermal Insulation Handbook. William C. Turner; John F. Malloy. New York, NY: McGraw-Hill, 1981. 629p., illus., bibliog., index. $0-07-039805-4.

Previously called *Thermal Insulation*, this handbook covers the theory and fundamentals of all areas of heat transfer and the application to thermal insulation.

1291. Wood Engineering and Construction Handbook. Keith F. Faherty; Thomas G. Williamson. New York, NY: McGraw-Hill, 1989. 1v., various paging, illus., bibliog., index. $67.50. ISBN: 0-07-019895-0.

This handbook is intended to provide the necessary techniques for designing wood structures and structural components. Also included is a chapter on wood properties. Two other useful handbooks are Morton Newman's *Structured Details for Wood Construction* (McGraw-Hill, 1988) and the U.S. Forest Products Laboratory's *Wood Engineering Handbook* (Prentice-Hall, 1990).

Histories

1292. Early Years of Modern Civil Engineering. Richard Shelton Kirby; Philip Gustave Laurson. New Haven, CT: Yale University Press, 1932. 324p., illus., bibliog., index. out-of-print.

Although out-of-print, this book gives a good summary of the history of civil engineering to the 1930s. A brief historical account of civil engineering is covered in Mike Chrimes' *Civil Engineering 1839-1889: A Photographic History* (Gloucester, 1991).

1293. History of Building. 3rd. Jack Bowyer. Panscastle, Great Britain: Attic Books, 1993. 275p., illus, index. $20.00. ISBN: 0-948-08318-2.

This book is a good general history of building.

1294. History of Civil Engineering Since 1600: An Annotated Bibliography. *(Bibliographies on the History of Science and Technology, no.14) (Garland Reference Library of the Humanities, v.519).* Darwin H. Stapleton; Roger L. Shumaker. New York, NY: Garland, 1986. 232p., index. $40.00. ISBN: 0-8240-8948-0.

Each chapter covers an historical period: Renaissance 1600-1750; Industrial Revolution 1750-1830; Victorian Era 1830-1900; Modern Era 1900-1950; and Recent Times, since 1950. There are over 1,200 entries.

Standards

1295. Architectural Graphic Standards. 9th. Charles G. Ramsey; Harold R. Sleeper; John R. Hahe, Jr. New York, NY: Wiley, 1988. 928p., illus., index. $190.00. ISBN: 0-471-57369-6.

This reference source on graphic standards is used by architects and other individuals doing drafting. It illustrates every aspect of drawing architectural details so that the final blueprints are in a standard format. Over 10,000 architectural drawings are included.

1296. ASTM Standards in Building Codes: Specifications, Test Methods, Practices, Classifications, Definitions. Philadelphia, PA: American Society for Testing and Materials, 1955– , annual. v.1– , illus., bibliog., index. $245.00. ISSN: 0192-2998.

Published in 3 volumes annually, this set pulls together all of the ASTM standards from the *Annual Book of ASTM Standards* that cover the building industry. It includes all pertinent specifications, tests, definitions, and practices that are recommended by the ASTM.

1297. Time-Saver Standards for Interior Design and Space Planning. Joseph De Chiara; Julius Panero; Martin Zelnik. New York, NY: McGraw-Hill, 1991. 1,200p., illus., index. $95.00.

This well-written handbook describes design data, detail types, guidelines, and techniques for interior design and space planning. It covers architectural woodwork, construction details and finishes, and special materials and it gives actual drawings to help in planning and design.

Tables

1298. Berger Building and Design Cost File: Unit Prices. Wantagh, NY: Building Cost File, Inc, 1981– , annual. v.1– , tables, index (2 volumes each year).

This 2-volume per year set was formed by the merger of the *Berger Design Cost File* and the *Berger Building Cost File*. It gives data useful for estimating the cost of building any facility. It is an invaluable set for any architectural engineering collection and for those in the building trades. The 2 volumes cover v.1—General construction trades; v.2—Mechanical and electrical trades. Three other smaller, less comprehensive manuals are Martin D. Kiley's *Building Cost Manual* (Craftsman, 1990); Edward J. Tyler's *Electrical Construction Estimator* (Craftsman, 1990); and Martin D. Kiley's *National Construction Estimator* (Craftsman, 1990).

1299. Means Cost Data Books. Kingston, MA: R.S. Means. many titles per year.

R.S. Means publishes many cost data books that give up-to-date figures for estimating what costs are involved in building and construction. They are presented in easy-to-follow tabular format and are revised on a regular basis, many annually. Currently, the following are published: *Landscape Cost Data* ($74.95); *Construction Cost Indexes* ($169.00); *Labor Rates for the Construction Industry* ($145.00); *Electrical Change Order Cost Data* ($72.95); *Facilities Cost Data* ($179.95); *Interior Cost Data* ($71.95); *Mechanical Cost Data* ($55.95); *Plumbing Cost Data* ($71.95); *Repair and Remodeling Cost Data* ($72.95); *Residential Cost Data* ($68.95); *Site Work Cost Data* ($71.95); *Square Foot Costs: Residential* ($68.95); *Assemblies Cost Data* ($115.95); *Heavy Construction Cost Data* ($76.95); *Electrical Cost Data* ($72.95); *Open Shop Building—Construction Cost Data* ($76.95); *Concrete Cost Data* ($67.95); *Building Construction Cost Data* ($79.95); *Light Commercial Cost Data* ($68.95).

Treatises

1300. Civil Engineering Practice. Paul N. Cheremisinoff; Nicholas P. Cheremisinoff; Su Ling Cheng. Lancaster, PA: Technomic, 1987-88. 5v., illus, bibliog., index. $750.00. ISBN: 0-685-19617-8.

This comprehensive treatise covers the following in 5 volumes: v.1—Structures; v.2—Hydraulics-mechanics; v.3—Geotechnical ocean engineering; v.4—Surveying/construction/transportation/energy/economics and government/computers; v.5—Water resources/environmental. It is intended to provide the practicing civil engineer with authoritative information about all aspects of civil engineering.

Periodicals

1301. ACI Structural Journal. Detroit, MI: American Concrete Institute, 1905– , bimonthly. v.1– , index. $88.00. ISSN: 0889-3241.

1302. Builder. Washington, DC: Hanley-Wood/National Association of Home Builders of the U.S, 1942– , monthly. v.1– , index. $29.95. ISSN: 0744-1193.

1303. Building and Environment. Tarrytown, NY: Pergamon Press, 1965– , quarterly. v.1– , index. $344.00. ISSN: 0360-1323.

1304. Building Design and Construction. Des Plaines, IL: Cahners, 1950– , monthly. v.1– , index. $89.95. ISSN: 0007-3407.

1305. Building Research and Development. London, Great Britain: Chapman & Hall/International Council for Building Research, Studies and Documentation, 1968– , bimonthly. v.1– , index. $185.00. ISSN: 0961-3218.

1306. Building Today. London, Great Britain: International Thomson Business, 1877– , weekly. v.1– , index. $126.00. ISSN: 0954-0652.

1307. Canadian Journal of Civil Engineering/Revue Canadienne de Genie Civil. Ottawa, Ontario, Canada: National Research Council of Canada, 1974– , bimonthly. v.1– , index. $73.00. ISSN: 0315-1468.

1308. Cement and Concrete Research. Tarrytown, NY: Pergamon Press, 1971– , 6/year. v.1– , index. $400.00. ISSN: 0008-8846.

1309. Civil Engineering ASCE. New York, NY: American Society of Civil Engineers, 1930– , monthly. v.1– , index. $72.00. ISSN: 0360-0556.

1310. Coastal Engineering. Amsterdam, Netherlands: Elsevier, 1977– , 8/year. v.1– , index. $388.00. ISSN: 0378-3839.

1311. Construction Equipment. Des Plaines, IL: Cahners, 1949– , 16/year. v.1– , index. $79.95. ISSN: 0192-3978.

1312. Construction Record. Don Mills, Ontario: Southam Business Communications, 1889– , monthly. v.1– , index. $48.00. ISSN: 0013-7804.

1313. Constructor. Washington, DC: Associated General Contractors of America, 1919– , monthly. v.1– , index. $100.00. ISSN: 0162-6191.

1314. Doors and Hardware. Chantilly, VA: Door and Hardware Institute, 1936– , monthly. v.1– , index. $40.00. ISSN: 0361-5294.

1315. Engineering Geology. Amsterdam, Netherlands: Elsevier, 1965– , 12/year. v.1– , index. $583.00. ISSN: 0013-7952.

1316. Engineering Journal. Chicago, IL: American Institute of Steel Construction, 1964– , quarterly. v.1– , index. $15.00. ISSN: 0013-8029.

1317. ENR (Engineering News Record). New York, NY: McGraw-Hill, 1874– , weekly. v.1– , index. $55.00. ISSN: 0891-9526.

1318. Highway and Heavy Construction Products. Des Plaines, IL: Cahners, 1892– , 6/year. v.1– , index. $74.95. ISSN: 0035-7340.

1319. International Construction. Barnet, Great Britain: Maclean Hunter, 1962– , monthly. v.1– , index. $100.00. ISSN: 0020-6415.

1320. Materials and Structures/Materiaux et Constructions. London, Great Britain: Chapman & Hall/RILEM, 1968– , bimonthly. v.1– , index. $285.00. ISSN: 0025-5432.

1321. Municipal Engineer. London: Thomas Telford/Institution of Civil Engineers, 1873– , bimonthly. v.1– , index. $120.00. ISSN: 0263-788X.

1322. Proceedings of the American Society of Civil Engineers. New York, NY: American Society of Civil Engineers, 1873-. v.1– , index. $1,770.00 all sections. ISSN: 0003-1119 all sections as a set.

Now published as Division journals: *Journal of Aerospace Engineering* (1988- , quarterly, $76.00, 0893-1321); *Journal of Performance of Constructed Facilities* (1987- , quarterly, $68.00, 0887-3828); *Journal of Construction Engineering and Management* (1956- , quarterly, $76.00, 0733-9364); *Journal of Computing in Civil Engineering* (1987- , quarterly, $68.00, 0887-3801); *Journal of Cold Regions Engineering* (1987- , quarterly, $64.00, 0887-381X); *Journal of Environmental Engineering* (1956- , bimonthly, $108.00, 0733-9372); *Journal of Professional Issues in Engineering Education and Practice* (1956- , quarterly, $72.00, 1052-3928); *Journal of Engineering Mechanics* (1956- , monthly, $224.00, 0733-9399); *Journal of Energy Engineering* (1956- , 2-3/year, $64.00, 0733-9402); *Journal of Geotechnical Engineering* (1956- , monthly, $156.00, 0733-9410); *Journal of Hydraulic Engineering* (1956- , monthly, $152.00, 0733-9429); *Journal of Irrigation and Drainage En-*

gineering (1956- , bimonthly, $92.00, 0733-9437); *Journal of Management in Engineering* (1985- , quarterly, $76.00, 0742-597X); *Journal of Materials in Civil Engineering* (1989- , quarterly, $68.00, 0899-1561); *Journal of Structural Engineering* (1956- , monthly, $240.00, 0733-9445); *Journal of Surveying Engineering* (1956- , quarterly, $88.00, 0733-9453); *Journal of Transportation Engineering* (1969- , bimonthly, $88.00, 0733-947X); *Journal of Urban Planning and Development* (1956- , 2-3/year, $64.00, 0733-9488); *Journal of Water Resources Planning and Management* (1956- , bimonthly, $92.00, 0733-9496); *Journal of Waterway, Port, Coastal and Ocean Engineering* (1956- , bimonthly, $92.00, 0733-950X).

1323. Professional Builder and Remodeler. Des Plaines, IL: Cahners, 1936– , 16/year. v.1– , index. $139.95. ISSN: 0033-0043.

1324. Public Roads. Washington, DC: U.S. Federal Highway Administration, 1918– , quarterly. v.1– , index. $12.00. ISSN: 0033-3735.

1325. Structural Engineer. London: Institution of Structural Engineering, 1922– , 24/year. v.1– , index. $192.00. ISSN: 0039-2553.

1326. Tunnels and Tunneling. London: Construction Press, 1969– , monthly. v.1– , index. $80.00. ISSN: 0041-414X.

ELECTRICAL AND ELECTRONICS ENGINEERING

Abstracts and Indexes

1327. Electrical and Electronics Abstracts. Piscataway, NJ: Institution of Electrical Engineers/INSPEC, 1903– , monthly. v.1– , index. $1,955.00. ISSN: 0036-8105.

This comprehensive abstracting journal, Section B of Science Abstracts, covers journals, reports, books, dissertations, and conference papers published worldwide pertaining to all aspects of electronics and electrical engineering. Indexes include subject, author, bibliography, book, corporate author, and conference. Also available online. Also available are tailored abstracts called *Key Abstracts* covering specific topics.

1328. Electronics and Communications Abstracts Journal. Bethesda, MD: Cambridge Scientific Abstracts, 1967– , bimonthly. v.1– , index. $800.00. ISSN: 0361-3313.

Previously called *Electronics Abstracts Journal*, this specialized abstracting journal covers theoretical and applied research in electronic systems, physics, circuits, and devices plus communications. It is

also available online. Also of use but duplicating much of the information is the British publication *Electronics and Communications Abstracts* (Multi-Science, 1961– .).

1329. Index to IEEE Publications. New York, NY: Institute of Electrical and Electronics Engineers, 1973– , annual. v.1– , index. free with publications of IEEE.

This is an annual author and subject index to the *Proceedings of the IEEE, IEEE Transactions*, IEEE journals, *IEEE Spectrum*, IEEE sponsored conferences, IEEE standards, and books from the IEEE Press.

Biographical Sources

1330. IEEE Membership Directory. New York, NY: Institute of Electrical and Electronics Engineers, 1991. 2v. $189.95. ISBN: 0-7803-9951-X.

This simple directory lists the members of the Institute of Electrical and Electronics Engineers, the world's largest organization in this field. It is also available online.

Catalogs

1331. Electronic Engineers Master Catalog: EEM. 34th. Garden City, NY: United Technical Publications, 1991/92. 4v., illus., index. price not available. ISSN: 0732-9016.

Previously called *Electronics Engineers Master*, this annual is a comprehensive catalog of all equipment and components that are used in the electronics industries. The 4 volumes cover v.1—Electronics; v.2—Electromechanical and electro-optical; v.3—Packaging hardware; v.4—Computers, instruments, and power sources. For each product a complete description is given with features, specifications, dimensions, illustrations, and other useful data. Also useful is the annual *Electronic Market Data Book* (Electronic Industries Association).

Dictionaries, Glossaries, and Thesauri

1332. Audio Dictionary. 2nd revised and expanded. Glenn D. White. Seattle, WA: University of Washington Press, 1991. 413p., illus., bibliog. $19.95. ISBN: 0-295-97088-X.

This basic dictionary covers the terms in the fields of sound recording, sound reinforcement, and musical acoustics, as well as basic terms in acoustics, elementary electroacoustics, digital audio, and electronics.

1333. Dictionary of Electrical Engineering and Electronics. 4th. Peter-Klaus Budig. New York, NY: French and European Publications, 1987. 2v. $185.00v.1; $195.00v.2. ISBN: 0-8288-0288-2v.1; 0-8288-0287-4v.2.

This bilingual dictionary has 2 volumes covering v.1—English-German; V.2—German-English.

1334. Dictionary of Electronics. 2nd. S.W. Amos. Boston, MA: Butterworths, 1987. 324p., illus. $42.95. ISBN: 0-408-02750-9.

This good general dictionary gives electronics terms with concise definitions. A somewhat older but still useful dictionary is John Markus's *Electronics Dictionary* (McGraw-Hill, 1978).

1335. Dictionary of Electronics: English-German/German-English. Alfred Opperman. New York, NY: French and European Publications, 1987. 2v. $195.00v.1; $225.00v.2. ISBN: 0-8288-024-7v.1; 0-8288-0293-9v.2.

This 2-volume bilingual dictionary covers the terms in electronics.

1336. Electronics Sourcebook for Engineering. 2nd. George Loveday. New York, NY: State Mutual Book and Periodical Services, 1986. 293p., illus., index. $120.00. ISBN: 0-273-02667-4.

This sourcebook is a concise guide to the theorems, parameters, circuits, and concepts that pertain to electronics. It is arranged in alphabetical order ranging from acceptor impurity to potentiometer and ending with zero crossing detector.

1337. Elsevier's Dictionary of Electronics. G.G King. New York, NY: Elsevier, 1987-88. 2v. $359.00. ISBN: 0-444-42642-6v.1; 0-444-42643-4v.2.

This typical bilingual dictionary lists terms in electronics in its broadest definition including some physics terms as well as telecommunications terminology. The 2 volumes cover v.1—English-French; v.2—French-English

1338. Encyclopedic Dictionary of Electronic Terms. John E. Traister; Robert J. Traister. Englewood Cliffs, NJ: Prentice-Hall, 1984. 604p., illus. $18.95. ISBN: 0-13-276998-0.

This concise dictionary lists terms related to electronics.

1339. Facts on File Dictionary of Telecommunications. revised and updated. John Graham; Sue J. Lowe. New York, NY: Facts on File, 1991. 240p., illus. $24.95. ISBN: 0-8160-2029-9.

This good dictionary covers the field of telecommunications with excellent definitions for the student

and layperson as well as the researcher. Another useful work is S.J. Aries's *Dictionary of Telecommunications* (Butterworths, 1981).

1340. Fiber Optics Standard Dictionary. 2nd. Martin H. Weik. New York, NY: Van Nostrand Reinhold, 1989. 366p., illus., bibliog. $40.95. ISBN: 0-442-23387-6.

Previously called *Fiber Optics and Lightwave Communications Standard Dictionary*, this edition has tried to comply with draft international, national, federal, industrial, and technical society standards. Older terms have been eliminated and newer terms in associated fields are included. Another useful dictionary in the electro-optical field is Dennis Bodson's *Electro-Optical Communications Dictionary* (Heyden Book, 1983).

1341. HarperCollins Dictionary of Electronics. Ian R. Sinclair. New York, NY: HarperPerennial, 1991. 363p., illus. $25.00; $12.95pbk. ISBN: 0-06-271528-3; 0-06-461022-5pbk.

This basic dictionary lists electronics terms with concise definitions. Also useful is Rudolf F. Graf's *Modern Dictionary of Electronics*.

1342. IEEE Standard Dictionary of Electrical and Electronics Terms. 5th. *(ANSI/IEEE Standard 100-1988)*. Frank Jay. New York, NY: Institute of Electrical and Electronics Engineers, 1993. 1,270p., illus. $90.00. ISBN: 1-55937-000-9.

This dictionary covers the terms used by the American Standards Association that pertain to electrical and electronics engineering. For each term the source or standard is given for the definition. It covers some 30,000 terms and 15,000 acronyms. Another good dictionary of electrical and electronics terms is the *McGraw-Hill Dictionary of Electrical and Electronic Engineering* (McGraw-Hill, 1984). A useful small dictionary for electrical technicians is John E. Traister's *Illustrated Dictionary for Electrical Workers* (Delmar, 1991).

1343. Illustrated Dictionary of Electronics. 6th. Rufus P. Turner; Stan Gibilisco. Blue Ridge Summit, PA: TAB, 1994. 760p., illus. $39.95. ISBN: 0-8306-4397-4.

Although not really illustrated, this is an excellent dictionary of electronics. It includes abbreviations and acronyms as well as words and phrases.

1344. Illustrated Encyclopedic Dictionary of Electronic Circuits. 2nd. John Douglas-Young. Englewood Cliffs, NJ: Prentice-Hall, 1987. 768p., illus., index. $39.95. ISBN: 0-13-450701-0.

This is one of the standard dictionaries of electronic circuits. The circuits are clearly illustrated and described.

1345. Multilingual Dictionary of Electricity, Electronics, and Telecommunications. International Electrotechnical Commission. New York, NY: Elsevier, 1992. 5v., index. $984.00. ISBN: 0-444-89510-8v.1.

Previously called *IEC Multilingual Dictionary of Electricity*, this dictionary contains terms and definitions from the fields of electrical and electronics engineering and telecommunications in French and English with equivalents in Russian, German, Spanish, Italian, Dutch, Polish, and Swedish. A one-volume edition is available covering 15,000 terms: *IEC Multilingual Dictionary of Electricity, Electronics and Telecommunications* (IEEE, 1993). Also of use would be the *Dictionary of Electrical Engineering: English, German, French, Dutch, Russian* (Kluwer, 1985).

1346. Parat Index of Acronyms and Abbreviations in Electrical and Electronic Engineering. Buro Scientia. New York, NY: VCH, 1989. 538p. $175.00. ISBN: 0-89573-812-0.

Also known as the *Index of Acronyms and Abbreviations in Electrical and Electronic Engineering*, this dictionary contains some 45,000 entries of acronyms and abbreviations. Also useful and including some additional terms is Phil Brown's *Electronics and Computers Acronyms* (Butterworths, 1988).

1347. Telecommunications Fact Book and Illustrated Dictionary. Ahmed S. Khan. Albany, NY: Delmar, 1992. 200p., illus. $21.95. ISBN: 0-8273-4615-8.

This dictionary contains some 1,500 of the latest telecommunications terms. Some encyclopedic appendices are included covering such topics as radio emissions, agencies, journals, and codes.

Directories

1348. Electronics Research Centres: A World Directory of Organizations and Programmes. 2nd. Harlow, Great Britain: Longman Group, 1989. 523p., index. $475.00. ISBN: 0-582-03604-6.

This directory contains information about electronics research centers throughout the world. Great Britain and the United States are covered well with many other countries only mentioning educational institutions.

1349. European Electronics Directory 1983: Components and Sub-Assemblies. New York, NY: Elsevier, 1993. 574p., index. $405.00. ISBN: 1-85617-175-2.

This directory is a guide to manufacturers, distributors and agents for some 550 components and sub-assembly products giving names, addresses, size of firm, products covered, and manufacturers represented. It is arranged by country.

1350. Sources: A Directory of Electronics Information Agencies Outside the U.S. Washington, DC: Electronic Industries Association, 1987. 147p. $50.00.

Somewhat dated and ready for a new edition, this directory covers basically foreign industries from some 78 countries. Addresses, contact persons, and publications are given. Also given is information about chambers of commerce, industrial and business groups, and embassies.

1351. World Satellite Directory. 11th. Potomac, MD: Phillips Publishing, 1989. 1,187p., maps, index. $227.00. ISBN: 0-934960-56-9.

One of the most comprehensive directories, *World Satellite Directory* covers satellite communications services. All satellites are described, giving a wealth of statistical and technical data. It includes manufacturing information as well as a buyer's guide. Also useful is the *International Satellite Directory* (Design Publications, 1990).

Encyclopedias

1352. Encyclopedia of Electronic Circuits. Rudolf F. Graf. Blue Ridge Summit, PA: TAB, 1985-92. 4v., illus., index. $60.00/volume; $29.95/volume pbk. ISBN: 0-8306-0938-5v.1; 0-8306-1938-0b.1 pbk.

This 4-volume encyclopedia contains several thousand circuits arranged by subject. Each circuit's purpose is indicated and described, including the source. Another useful one-volume encyclopedia is John Douglas-Young's *Illustrated Encyclopedic Dictionary of Electronic Circuits* (Prentice-Hall, 1983).

1353. Encyclopedia of Electronics. 2nd. Stan Gibilisco; Neil Sclater. Blue Ridge Summit, PA: TAB, 1990. 960p., illus. $69.50. ISBN: 0-8306-3389-8.

This general encyclopedia covers electronic terms with some related terms from other disciplines. It is well-illustrated and has a good index.

1354. Encyclopedia of Semiconductor Technology. New York, NY: Wiley, 1984. 941p., illus., bibliog., index. $127.00. ISBN: 0-471-88102-3.

All material in this specialized encyclopedia consists of reprinted articles from the *Kirk-Othmer Encyclopedia of Chemical Technology*. It provides information on methods of manufacturing, properties and uses of semiconductors, common elements used in their manufacture, and other related substances.

1355. Encyclopedia of Telecommunications. Robert A. Meyers. San Diego, CA: Academic Press, 1989. 575p., illus., bibliog., index. $65.00. ISBN: 0-12-226691-9.

All material for this encyclopedia was taken from the Academic Press's *Encyclopedia of Physical Science and Technology*. This is a topical encyclopedia, necessitating the use of the index to locate specific information. A glossary is included at the beginning of each topic.

1356. Illustrated Encyclopedia of Solid-State Circuits and Applications. Donald R. Mackenroth; Leo G. Sands. Englewood Cliffs, NJ: Prentice-Hall, 1984. 353p., illus., index. $32.95. ISBN: 0-13-450537-9.

This workbench or hobbyist's encyclopedia covers semiconductor devices. Each chapter discusses a specific type such as diodes and progresses from the simple to the more complex.

1357. International Encyclopedia of Integrated Circuits. 2nd. Stan Gibilisco. Blue Ridge Summit, PA: TAB, 1992. 1,142p., illus., index. $84.95. ISBN: 0-8306-3026-0.

This good encyclopedia covers currently available integrated circuits. It is arranged by application and then by manufacturer. Such topics as clocks, timers, logic circuits, and power supplies are covered. Also useful is Walter H. Buchsbaum's *Encyclopedia of Integrated Circuits* (Prentice-Hall, 1987).

1358. McGraw-Hill Encyclopedia of Electronics and Computers. 2nd. Sybil P. Parker. New York, NY: McGraw-Hill, 1988. 992p., illus., bibliog., index. $79.95. ISBN: 0-07-045487-6.

Information for this encyclopedia was taken from the 6th edition of the *McGraw-Hill Encyclopedia of Science and Technology*. It contains all the articles on electricity, semiconductors, integrated circuitry, computer hardware and software, robotics, data management, communications, and microprocessors.

Guides to the Literature

1359. Guide to the Literature of Electrical and Electronics Engineering. Susan B. Ardis. Littleton, CO: Libraries Unlimited, 1987. 170p., bibliog., index. $37.50. ISBN: 0-87287-474-5.

This guide covers bibliographic sources, ready reference materials, handbooks, reference texts, journals and newsletters, product literature, patents, and standards that pertain to electrical energy, power engineering, communications, circuits, control systems, solid state devices, signal processing, and computer engineering.

Handbooks and Manuals

1360. American Electricians' Handbook. 12th. Terrell Groft; Wilford I. Summers. New York, NY: McGraw-Hill, 1991. 1v, various paging, illus., index. $69.50. ISBN: 0-07-013933-4.

This standard handbook for the practicing engineer gives information on the selection, installation, operation, and maintenance of all types of electrical equipment and electrical wiring. It reflects the current standards established by NEC, ANSI, NEMA, and NESC.

1361. ARRL Handbook for Radio Amateurs. 68th. Newington, CT: American Radio Relay League, 1992. 1v., various paging, illus., index. price not available. ISBN: 0-87259-168-9.

Previously called the *Radio Amateur's Handbook* and published since 1926, this title is the Bible for the amateur radio operator. Every aspect of being an operator is covered including radio principles, modulation methods, transmission, construction, and maintenance. Another well-respected handbook is William T. Orr's *Radio Handbook* (Sams, 1987) and a newer title is Joe Pritchard's *Newnes Amateur Radio Computing Handbook* (Butterworths, 1990).

1362. Audio Engineering Handbook. K. Blair Benson. New York, NY: McGraw-Hill, 1988. 1v., various paging, illus., bibliog., index. $89.95. ISBN: 0-07-004777-4.

This very comprehensive handbook covers every aspect of audio engineering, including principles, design, transmission, equipment, production, tests, and standards. See also John D. Lenk's *Lenk's Audio Handbook* and K. Blair Benson's *Television and Audio Handbook for Technicians and Engineers* for additional information on audio engineering.

1363. Complete Handbook of Magnetic Recording. 3rd. Finn Jorgensen. Blue Ridge Summit, PA: TAB, 1988. 740p., illus. (part in color), bibliog., index. $49.95. ISBN: 0-8306-1979-8.

This handbook is the Bible for magnetic recording. It begins with a history of magnetic recording and ends with tutorials that model magnetic recording processes.

1364. Electric Motor Handbook. B.J. Chalmers. Boston, MA: Butterworths, 1988. 546p., illus. (part in color), bibliog., index. $130.00. ISBN: 0-408-00707-9.

This basic handbook covers the design, construction, operation, and maintenance of rotating electric motors of 10KW or higher output.

1365. Electrical Engineer's Reference Book.
15th. M.A. Laughton; M.G. Say. Boston, MA:
Butterworth-Heineman, 1993. 1v., 1,000p.,
illus., bibliog., index. $160.00. ISBN:
0-7506-1202-9.

This well-established handbook brings together a
wide range of information for the electrical engineer.
It covers the fundamentals of electrical engineering,
energy supply, the power plant, applications, and a
guide to standards that are relevant to electrical engineering. Earlier editions were known as *Newnes Electrical Engineer's Reference Book.*

1366. Electronic Communications Handbook.
Andrew F. Inglis. New York, NY:
McGraw-Hill, 1988. 624p., illus., bibliog.,
index. $59.50. ISBN: 0-07-031711-9.

Information on telecommunications for the electronics communications industry is covered in this
comprehensive handbook. The first half covers transmission and switching technologies while the second
discusses electronic communications systems. For
older historical information consult Gary M. Miller's
Handbook of Electronic Communication (Prentice-
Hall, 1979). Also of interest would be Stephen R.
Cheshier's *Electronic Communication Applications
Handbook* (Wiley, 1987).

**1367. Electronic Conversions, Symbols and
Formulas.** 2nd. Rufus P. Turner. Blue Ridge
Summit, PA: TAB, 1987. 271p., illus.,
glossary, index. $21.95; $14.95pbk. ISBN:
0-8306-0865-6; 0-8306-2865-7pbk.

All conversions, symbols, and formulas that are
given in this book pertain only to the field of electronics. It is organized by subject and also contains some
special sections on schematic symbols, Greek letter
symbols, English letter symbols, and circuit and conversion formulas. Another similar handbook is Raymond H. Ludwig's *Illustrated Handbook of Electronic
Tables, Symbols, Measurements, and Values* (Prentice-Hall, 1984).

**1368. Electronic Filter Design Handbook: LC
Active, and Digital Filters.** 2nd revised. Arthur Bernard Williams; Fred J. Taylor. New
York, NY: McGraw-Hill, 1988. 1v., various
paging, illus., bibliog., index. $64.95. ISBN:
0-07-070434-1.

The design of electronic filters is covered in this
comprehensive handbook with the emphasis on LC
active and digital filters. For RC active filters consult
F.N. Stephenson's *RC Active Filter Design Handbook*
(Wiley, 1985).

1369. Electronics Engineers' Handbook. 3rd.
Donald G. Fink; Donald Christiansen. New
York, NY: McGraw-Hill, 1989. 1v., various
paging, illus., bibliog., index. $89.95. ISBN:
0-07-020982-0.

This publication is the classic handbook for elec-
tronics. The typical handbook format is utilized. See
also the *Electronics Engineer's Reference Book.* Three
older technical handbooks are Milton Kaufman's
Handbook for Electronics Engineering Technicians
(McGraw-Hill, 1984); George H. Olsen's *Beginner's
Handbook of Electronics* (Prentice-Hall, 1980); and
Walter H. Buchsbaum's *Buchsbaum's Complete
Handbook of Practical Electronic Reference Data*
(Prentice-Hall, 1987).

1370. Electronics Engineer's Reference Book.
6th. F.F. Mazda. Boston, MA:
Butterworths-Heinemann, 1989. 1v, various
paging, illus., bibliog., index. $135.00. ISBN:
0-408-00590-4.

This, along with the *Electronics Engineers' Handbook*, make up the two best handbooks covering electronics. It covers techniques, physical phenomena, materials and components, electronic design, and applications.

**1371. Fiber Optics Handbook: For Engineers
and Scientists.** Frederick C. Allard. New York,
NY: McGraw-Hill, 1990. 1v., various paging,
illus., bibliog., index. $69.95. ISBN:
0-07-001013-7.

Fiber optics are used in a variety of industries. This
handbook covers some history, fundamentals, and
uses. Applications for scientists doing laboratory research are also covered.

**1372. Fundamentals Handbook of Electrical
and Computer Engineering.** Sheldon S.L.
Chang. New York, NY: Wiley, 1982-83. 3v.,
illus., bibliog., index. $189.95. ISBN:
0-471-89690-X.

The 3 volumes of this handbook cover v.1—Circuits, fields, and electronics; v.2—Communication,
control, devices, and systems; v.3—Computer hardware, software, and applications. The emphasis is on
electrical computer engineering.

1373. Handbook of Batteries and Fuel Cells.
David Linden. New York, NY: McGraw-Hill,
1984. 1v., various paging, illus., bibliog.,
index. $112.50. ISBN: 0-07-037874-6.

This handbook is devoted solely to batteries and
battery technology with the emphasis on providing
information on advantages and disadvantages, characteristics, properties, and performance.

**1374. Handbook of Electrical and Electronic
Insulating Materials.** W. Tiller Shugg; Ken-
neth N. Mathes. New York, NY: Van Nostrand
Reinhold, 1986. 598p., illus., bibliog., index.
$89.50. ISBN: 0-442-28122-6.

Dielectric materials are covered in this handbook
giving information on manufacturing techniques, test
methods, development programs, and market trends.
For a work specific to polymer coatings consult James

J. Licari's *Handbook of Polymer Coatings for Electronics* (Noyes, 1990).

1375. Handbook of Electronics Calculations for Engineers and Technicians. 2nd. Milton Kaufman; Arthur T. Seidman. New York, NY: McGraw-Hill, 1989. 1v., various paging, illus., bibliog., index. $49.95. ISBN: 0-07-033528-1.

Electronics calculations are outlined and discussed in detail in this handbook with examples. Another useful work would be John R. Brand's *Handbook of Electronic Formulas, Symbols, and Definitions* (Van Nostrand Reinhold, 1992).

1376. Handbook of Microwave and Optical Components. Kai Chang. New York, NY: Wiley, 1988-91. 4v., illus., bibliog., index. $255.00. ISBN: 0-471-61366-5v.1.

This handbook provides a compendium of principles and design data for engineers. The 4 volumes cover v.1- Microwave passive and antenna components; v.2—Microwave solid-state components; v.3—Optical components; v.4—Fiber optical components. Also of use would be the 3-volume set *Microwave Engineering Handbook* (Van Nostrand Reinhold, 1992-94) and Ronald W. Waynant's *Electro-Optics Handbook* (McGraw-Hill, 1993).

1377. Handbook of Modern Electronics and Electrical Engineering. Charles Belove; Phillip Hopkins. New York, NY: Wiley, 1986. 2,401p., illus., bibliog., index. $115.00. ISBN: 0-471-09754-3.

Although becoming dated, this still useful handbook covers such topics as components, transducers, active filters, and radar.

1378. Handbook of Practical Electrical Design. Joseph F. McPartland; Brian J. McPartland. New York, NY: McGraw-Hill, 1984. 1v., various paging, illus., index. $59.50. ISBN: 0-07-045695-X.

This practical handbook covers the design of electrical systems for buildings. It follows the *National Electric Code*. Another newer and useful handbook is Joseph F. McPartland's *McGraw-Hilll's Handbook of Electrical Construction Calculations* (McGraw-Hill, 1993).

1379. Handbook of Practical Electronics Circuits. John D. Lenk. Englewood Cliffs, NJ: Prentice-Hall, 1982. 334p., illus., index. $39.00. ISBN: 0-13-380741-X.

This handbook is a collection of over 270 electronic circuits used in digital and analog equipment. Each circuit is fully described.

1380. Handbook of Transformer Applications. William M. Flanagan. New York, NY: McGraw-Hill, 1986. 1v., various paging, illus., bibliog, index. $75.00. ISBN: 0-07-021290-2.

Transformers and other related magnetic components are covered in this handbook with the emphasis on performance of power, wideband, rectifiers, pulse, and inverter transformers. Another related book of interest is John E. Traister's *Handbook of Power Generation* (Prentice-Hall, 1983).

1381. Handbook on Semiconductors. T.S. Moss. New York, NY: North-Holland, 1980-82. 4v., illus., bibliog., index. $228.25v.1; $184.75v.2; $246.25v.3; $259.00v.4. ISBN: 0-444-85346-4v.1; 0-444-85273-5v.2; 0-444-85275-3v.3; 0-444-85347-2v.4.

This comprehensive handbook/treatise covers semiconductors in 4 volumes: v.1—Band theory and transport properties; v.2—Optical properties of solids; v.3—Materials, properties and preparation; v.4—Device physics.

1382. IES Lighting Handbook. revised. John E. Kaufman; Illuminating Engineering Society of North America. New York, NY: Illuminating Engineering Society of North America, 1987. 2v., illus., bibliog., index. $200.00. ISBN: 0-87995-024-2.

The 2 volumes of this well-established handbook cover v.1—Reference volume and v.2—Applications volume. All aspects of lighting are covered, including physics of light, color, light sources, lighting calculations, lighting design, and lighting for various types of facilities.

1383. Lenk's Audio Handbook. John D. Lenk. New York, NY: McGraw-Hill, 1991. 1v., various paging, illus., index. $39.95. ISBN: 0-07-037503-8.

John D. Lenk has produced an excellent handbook on the operation of audio equipment. He also includes troubleshooting techniques that will benefit technicians responsible for maintenance of audio equipment.

1384. Lenk's Video Handbook: Operation and Troubleshooting. John D. Lenk. New York, NY: McGraw-Hill, 1990. 1v., various paging, illus., index. $39.95. ISBN: 0-07-037291-8.

John D. Lenk is a prolific writer on electrical and electronic subjects. His video handbook is a respected handbook covering operation and troubleshooting of all video equipment.

1385. Lineman's and Cableman's Handbook. 8th. Edwin B. Kurtz; Thomas M. Shoemaker. New York, NY: McGraw-Hill, 1992. 1v., various paging, illus., index. $69.50. ISBN: 0-07-035685-5.

This practical handbook is for anyone involved in the design, construction, maintenance, and control of both overhead and underground cables. For information on just electric cables consult D. McAllister's *Electric Cables Handbook* (CRC, 1990) and on transmission lines consult Brian C. Wadell's *Transmission Line Design Handbook* (Artech House, 1991).

1386. Master Handbook of Electronic Tables and Formulas. 5th. Martin Clifford. Blue Ridge Summit, PA: TAB, 1992. 544p., illus., index. $39.95; $22.95pbk. ISBN: 0-8306-2192-X; 0-8306-2191-1pbk.

This handbook covers the latest data used in everyday electronics practice including such areas as resistance formulas, meters and meter multipliers, sine waves, capacitors, impedance vectors, and other formulas used in the electronics field.

1387. Master Handbook of IC Circuits. 2nd. Delton J. Horn. Blue Ridge Summit, PA: TAB, 1989. 533p., illus., index. $34.95; $24.95pbk. ISBN: 0-8306-9185-5; 0-8306-3185-2.

There are a multitude of books covering electrical and electronic circuits. All are useful and each has material that is unique. This handbook has become a recommended one for IC circuits. Three other good handbooks are Arthur H. Seidman's *Integrated Circuits Applications Handbook* (Wiley, 1983); David L. Hiserman's *Handbook of Digital IC Applications* (Prentice-Hall, 1980); and Arthur Bernard Williams's *Designer's Handbook of Integrated Circuits* (McGraw-Hill, 1984).

1388. Modern Electronic Circuits Reference Manual. John Markus. New York, NY: McGraw-Hill, 1980. 1,238., illus., index. $96.95. ISBN: 0-07-040446-1.

Some 3,600 different transistors and integrated circuits are covered in this handbook. Each circuit is presented with references to the original source. Also of interest is Raymond A. Collins' *Giant Handbook of Electronic Circuits* (TAB, 1980).

1389. Power Electronics Handbook: Components, Circuits and Applications. F.F. Mazda. Boston, MA: Butterworths, 1990. 417p., illus., bibliog., index. $79.95. ISBN: 0-408-03004-6.

This practical handbook for the working engineer contains information on power components, circuit design, and applications. It is a concise, well-written, and well-illustrated handbook.

1390. Printed Circuits Handbook. 3rd. Clyde F. Coombs, Jr. New York, NY: McGraw-Hill, 1988. 1v., various paging, illus., bibliog., index. $59.50. ISBN: 0-07-012609-7.

First published in 1967, this handbook has become a standard work on wiring technology, covering the design, manufacture, testing, and repair of wiring boards and assemblies.

1391. Reference Data for Engineers: Radio, Electronics, Computers, and Communications. 7th. Edward Jordan. Carmel, IN: Sams, 1985. 1v., various paging, illus., bibliog., index. $99.95. ISBN: 0-672-21563-2.

This frequently revised standard handbook for engineers covers the fundamentals, theory, and applications of radio, electronics, computers, and communications equipment.

1392. Reference Manual for Telecommunications Engineering. Roger L. Freeman. New York, NY: Wiley, 1985. 1,504p., illus., bibliog., index. $115.00. ISBN: 0-471-86753-5.

This comprehensive handbook contains all the relevant material from many sources that would be of interest to the telecommunications engineer. There is a heavy use of charts, graphs, and tables giving facts and data on such topics as signaling, networks, fiber optics, radio propagation, and television transmission. There is much newer research in this field which can be found in Daniel Minoli's *Telecommunications Technology Handbook* (Artech House, 1991).

1393. Standard Handbook for Electrical Engineers. 13th. Donald G. Fink; H. Wayne Beaty. New York, NY: McGraw-Hill, 1993. 1v., various paging, illus., bibliog., index. $110.50. ISBN: 0-07-020984-7.

This is the standard source of handbook information for electrical engineers, having been first published in 1907. It presents the practical data needed by the engineer and covers generation, transmission, distribution, control, conservation, and applications of electrical power. Another book that contains excerpts from this handbook is H. Wayne Beaty's *Electrical Engineering Materials Reference Guide* (McGraw-Hill, 1990).

1394. Switchgear and Control Handbook. 2nd. Robert W. Smeaton. New York, NY: McGraw-Hill, 1987. 1v., various paging, illus., bibliog., index. price not available. ISBN: 0-07-058449-4.

Switchgear and controls are essential to any power system. This handbook covers these components in detail with information used by plant and maintenance engineers, technicians, and electricians. Information includes classification, selection, installation, servicing, load and motor characteristics, and planning.

1395. Television and Audio Handbook for Technicians and Engineers. K. Blair Benson. New York, NY: McGraw-Hill, 1990. 1v., various paging, illus., bibliog., index. $39.95. ISBN: 0-07-004787-1.

Intended for service technicians but also of interest to other engineers, this handbook covers practical information about television and audio engineering, including fundamentals, maintenance, and testing.

1396. Tube Substitution Handbook. 21st. Indianapolis, IN: Sams, 1980. 128p. out-of-print. ISBN: 0-672-21746-5.

Although out-of-print, this Handbook is a good cross-reference book for information on now outdated tubes giving substitutions that can work in place of the original. This information would be useful for the hobbyist or museum workers who are reconstructing early appliances that used tubes. For transistors consult the *Transistor Substitution Handbook* (Sams, 1978) and for semiconductors consult the 2-volume work *Master Semiconductor Replacement Handbook* (TAB, 1982).

1397. World Radio TV Handbook. New York, NY: Watson Guptill, 1970– , annual. v.1– , illus., index. $19.95.

Previously called *World Radio-Television Handbook*, this annual gives a summary of events and information about radio and TV.

Histories

1398. Bibliographical History of Electricity and Magnetism. Paul Fleury Mottelay. Salem, NH: Arno Press, 1975 (c1922). 673p., bibliog., index. $48.00. ISBN: 0-405-06605-8.

This comprehensive bibliography covers all areas of electricity and magnetism from the earliest discovery and reporting to the 1920s. Another bibliography covering electronics is George Shiers' *Bibliography of the History of Electronics* (Scarecrow Press, 1972).

1399. Electrical and Electronic Technologies: A Chronology of Events and Invention to 1900. Henry B.O. Davis. Metuchen, NJ: Scarecrow Press, 1981. 213p., bibliog., index. $32.50. ISBN: 0-8108-1464-1.

This chronology documents events, worldwide, that had an impact on electrical and electronic technologies. Included are major discoveries and inventions, laws, individuals, and corporations. Two additional chronologies have been published by Davis: *Electrical and Electronics Technologies: A Chronology of Events and Inventions from 1900 to 1940* (Scarecrow Press, 1983) and *Electrical and Electronics Technologies: A Chronology of Events and Inventions from 1900 to 1980* (Scarecrow Press, 1985).

1400. Electronic Inventions and Discoveries: Electronics from the Earliest Beginnings to the Present Day. 3rd revised and expanded. G.W.A. Dummer. New York, NY: Pergamon Press, 1983. 233p., illus., bibliog., index. $68.00; $28.00pbk. ISBN: 0-08-029354-9; 0-08-029353-0pbk.

Previously called *Electronic Inventions from 1745 to 1976*, this very readable history covers material to about 1980.

1401. History of Electrical Technology: An Annotated Bibliography. *(Garland Reference Library of Science and Technology, v.18).* Bernard S. Finn. New York, NY: Garland, 1991. 342p., index. $48.00. ISBN: 0-8240-9120-5.

Some 1,500 entries are included in this annotated bibliography covering the secondary sources through 1986. It is published in 4 sections: general historical, communications, power, and miscellaneous.

Standards

1402. McGraw-Hill's National Electrical Code Handbook. New York, NY: McGraw-Hill, 1979– , every 3 years with annual supplements. v.16– , illus., bibliog., index. $54.50.

Previously called *NFPA Handbook of the National Electrical Code*, this handbook aids in the interpretation of the *National Electrical Code (NEC)* which is the official set of rules and regulations guiding the safe installation of electrical wiring and equipment. It is revised every 3 years with supplements published in the intervening years. It has become the most widely used handbook covering the code. For legal purposes consult Thomas L. Harman's *Guide to the National Electrical Code* (Prentice-Hall, 1990).

1403. National Electrical Code—1990. Quincy, MA: National Fire Protection Association, 1897– , every 3 years with annual supplements. v.1– , various paging, index. price not available. ISBN: 0-87765-361-5.

Revised every 3 years, this code was first developed in 1897 and has been the recommended code for electrical, architectural, and allied interests. Its purpose is to safeguard persons and properties from hazards arising from the use of electricity in all installations. It appears in many formats including the *National Electrical Safety Code* (IEEE, ANSI C2-1990).

1404. National Electrical Code—1990 Handbook: With Complete Text of the 1990 Code. Mark W. Earley; Richard H. Murray; John M. Caloggero. Quincy, MA: National Fire Protection Association, 1989. 1,186p., index. price not available. ISBN: 0-87765-365-8.

This handbook describes the code in detail so that all sections are understandable. Example calculations are included. For a section-by-section explanation of the code consult Paul Rosenberg's *Guide to the 1993 National Electrical Code* (Macmillan, 1993).

Periodicals

1405. EDN Magazine. Newton, MA: Cahners, 1956– , 26/year. v.1– , index. $119.95. ISSN: 0012-7515.

1406. Electric Light and Power. Tulsa, OK: PennWell, 1922– , monthly. v.1– , index. $42.00.

1407. Electrical Review. Sutton, Great Britain: Reed Business, 1872– , 6/year. v.1– , index. $124.00. ISSN: 0013-4384.

1408. Electrical World. New York, NY: McGraw-Hill, 1874– , monthly. v.1– , index. $55.00. ISSN: 0013-4457.

1409. Electronic Engineering. London, Great Britain: Morgan-Grampian, 1928– , monthly. v.1– , index. $48.00. ISSN: 0013-4902.

1410. Electronics. San Jose, CA: Penton, 1930– , monthly. v.1– , index. $60.00. ISSN: 0883-4989.

1411. Electronics and Communication Engineering Journal. Stevenage, Great Britain: Institution of Electrical Engineers, 1939– , bimonthly. v.1– , index. $100.00. ISSN: 0954-0695.

1412. Electronics World and Wireless World. Sutton, Great Britain: Reed Business, 1911– , monthly. v.1– , index. $56.00. ISSN: 0266-3244.

1413. IEE Proceedings. Stevenage, Great Britain: Institution of Electrical Engineers, 1980– , each section is bimonthly. v.1– , index. price not available.

Part A: Science, Measurement and Technology; Part B: Electric Power Applications (0143-7038); Part C: Generation, Transmission and Distribution (0143-7046); Part D: Control Theory and Applications (0143-7054); Part E: Computers and Digital Techniques (0143-7062); Part F: Radar and Signal Processing (0956-375X); Part G: Circuits, Devices and Systems (0956-3768); Part H: Microwaves, Antennas & Propagation (0950-107X); Part I: Communications, Speech and Vision (0956-3776); Part J: Optoelectronics (0267-3932).

1414. IEEE Journal of Microelectromechanical Systems. New York, NY: Institute of Electrical and Electronics Engineers, 1992– , quarterly. v.1– , index. $100.00. ISSN: 1057-7157.

1415. IEEE Journal of Oceanic Engineering. New York, NY: Institute of Electrical and Electronics Engineers, 1976– , quarterly. v.1– , index. $115.00. ISSN: 0364-9059.

1416. IEEE Journal of Quantum Electronics. New York, NY: Institute of Electrical and Electronics Engineers, 1965– , monthly. v.1– , index. $390.00. ISSN: 0018-9197.

1417. IEEE Journal of Selected Areas in Communications. New York, NY: Institute of Electrical and Electronics Engineers, 1983 , 9/year. v.1– , index. $185.00. ISSN: 0733-8716.

1418. IEEE Journal of Solid State Circuits. New York, NY: Institute of Electrical and Electronics Engineers, 1966– , bimonthly. v.1– , index. $215.00. ISSN: 0018-9200.

1419. IEEE Spectrum. New York, NY: Institute of Electrical and Electronics Engineers, 1964– , monthly. v.1– , index. $139.00. ISSN: 0018-9235.

1420. IEEE Transactions. New York, NY: Institute of Electrical and Electronics Engineers, 1945– , frequency varies per section. v.1– , index.

These transactions are made up of the following 45 sections: Aerospace and Electronic Systems (1965- , quarterly, 0018-9251, $140.00); Antennas and Propagation (1952- , monthly, 0018-926X, $212.00); Applied Superconductivity (1991- , quarterly, 1051-8223, $80.00); Automatic Control (1951- , monthly, 0018-9286, $225.00); Biomedical Engineering (1953- , monthly, 0018-9294, $215.00); Broadcasting (1955- , quarterly, 0018-9316, $50.00); Circuits and Systems for Video Technology (1981- , quarterly, 1051-8215, $100.00); Circuits and Systems Part 1 (1952- , monthly, 1057-7122, $177.00); Circuits and Systems Part 1 (1952- , monthly, 1057-7130, $163.00); Communications (1953- , monthly, 0090-6778, $195.00); Component Hybrids and Manufacturing Technology (1978- , quarterly, 0148-6411, $185.00); Computer-Aided Design of Integrated Circuits and Systems (1982- , monthly, 0278-0070, $260.00); Computers (1952- , monthly, 0018-9340, $295.00); Consumer Electronics (1952- , quarterly, 0098-3063, $135.00); Education (1958- , quarterly, 0018-9359, $98.00); Electrical Insulation (1965- , bimonthly, 0018-9367, $150.00); Electromagnetic Compatibility (1959- , quarterly, 0018-9375, $93.00); Electron Devices (1952- , monthly, 0018-9383, $315.00); Energy Conversion (1986- , quarterly, 0885-8969, $125.00); Engineering Management (1954- , quarterly, 0018-9391, $105.00); Geoscience and Remote Sensing (1963- , bimonthly, 0196-2892, $147.00); Industrial Electronics (1953- , bimonthly, 0278-0046, $120.00); Industry Applications (1965, bimonthly, 0093-9994, $183.00); Information Theory (1953- , bimonthly, 0018-9448, $215.00); Instrumentation and Measurement (1952- , bimonthly, 0018-9456, $135.00); Knowledge and Data Engineering (1989- , quarterly, 1041-4347, $170.00); Magnetics (1965- , bimonthly, 0018-9464, $263.00); Medical Imaging (1982- , quarterly, 0278-0062, $110.00); Microwave Theory and Techniques (1953- , monthly, 0018-9480, $225.00); Neural Networks (1990- , bimonthly, 1045-9227, $95.00); Nuclear Science (1954- , bimonthly, 0018-9499, $170.00); Parallel and Distributed Systems (1990- , quarterly, 1045-9219, $185.00); Pattern Analysis and Machine Intelligence (1979- , monthly, 0162-8828, $255.00); Plasma Science (1973- , bimonthly, 0093-3813, $180.00); Power Delivery (1986- , quarterly, 0885-8977, $155.00); Power Electronics (1986- , quarterly, 0885-8993, $120.00); Power Systems (1986- , quarterly, 0885-8950, $145.00); Professional Communication (1958- , quarterly, 0361-1434, $80.00); Reliability (1952- , 5/year, 0018-9529, $100.00); Robotics and Automation (1985- , bimonthly, 1042-296X, $124.00); Signal Processing (1951- , monthly, 1053-587X, $310.00); Software Engineering (1975- , monthly, 0098-5589, $275.00); Systems, Man and Cybernetics (1945- , bimonthly, 0018-9472, $146.00); Ultrasonics, Ferroelectrics and Frequency (1954- , bimonthly, 0885-3010, $220.00); Vehicular Technology (1952- , quarterly, 0018-9545, $90.00).

1421. International Journal of Electronics. Basingstoke, Great Britain: Taylor & Francis, 1965– , monthly. v.1– , index. $850.00. ISSN: 0020-7217.

1422. Power Engineering. Tulsa, OK: PennWell, 1896– , monthly. v.1– , index. $38.00. ISSN: 0032-5961.

1423. Proceedings of the Institute of Electrical and Electronics Engineers. New York, NY: Institute of Electrical and Electronics Engineers, 1930– , monthly. v.1– , index. $235.00. ISSN: 0018-9219.

1424. Semiconductor Science and Technology. Bristol, Great Britain: IOP Publishing, 1986– , monthly. v.1– , index. $748.00. ISSN: 0268-1242.

1425. Solid State Technology. Port Washington, WA: PennWell, 1958– , monthly. v.1– , index. $60.00. ISSN: 0038-111X.

ENERGY, MINING, AND NATURAL RESOURCES

Abstracts and Indexes

1426. EIA Publications Directory, 1977-1989. U.S. Energy Information Administration. Washington, DC: GPO, 1990. 389p., index. price unavailable.

A regularly updated index to the Energy Information Administration publications.

1427. Energy Bibliography and Index. Susan Lytle; Texas A&M Libraries. Houston, TX: Gulf Publishing, 1978-82. 5v., index. $90.00/volume. ISBN: 0-87201-975-6v.3.

This set of 5 volumes contains abstracts and indexes to all the energy-related materials held at the Texas A&M University Libraries up to 1982. It does not include periodical articles.

1428. Energy Information Abstracts. New York, NY: Bowker, 1976– , monthly with annual cumulations. v.1– , index. $625.00 monthly; $475.00 annual; $990.00 both. ISSN: 0147-6521 monthly; 0739-3679 annual.

Previously called *Energy Index*, an abstracting service covering research and development, resources, consumption, conservation, economics, and applications. Sources include periodicals, conference proceedings, and reports. The annual cumulation is titled *Energy Information Abstracts Annual*. It is also available online and on CD-ROM.

1429. Energy Research Abstracts. U.S. Department of Energy. Washington, DC: GPO, 1976– , irregular. v.1– , index. $146.00. ISSN: 0160-3604.

Previously called *ERDA Energy Research Abstracts*, this service of the U.S. Department of Energy covers only those publications produced by that agency. All areas of energy concerns are covered from storage, planning, and chemistry to conservation, consumption, and utilization. Several indexes help in accessing the information. It is also available online.

1430. INIS Atomindex/INIS Atomindeks. Vienna, Austria: International Atomic Energy Agency, 1970– , semimonthly. v.1– , index. price unavailable. ISSN: 0004-7139.

Previously called *Atomindex* and incorporating *Nuclear Science Abstracts* in June, 1976, this comprehensive index directs readers to the world's literature covering nuclear energy. It is available online and on CD-ROM.

1431. International Petroleum Abstracts. Institute of Petroleum. New York, NY: Wiley, 1973– , quarterly. v.1– , index. $550.00. ISSN: 0309-4944.

Incorporating the *Offshore Abstracts* and sponsored by the Institute of Petroleum, this abstracting service abstracts articles, worldwide, covering all aspects of petroleum engineering from exploration to production. It is also available online. See also *Petroleum Abstracts* which is published more frequently.

1432. Petroleum Abstracts. Tulsa, OK: University of Tulsa, 1961– , weekly. v.1– , index. service basis. ISSN: 0031-6423.

This service abstracts articles from around the world dealing with the exploration and production of petroleum. It is produced by the University of Tulsa on a weekly basis and is available online. See also the *International Petroleum Abstracts* which is published quarterly.

1433. Solar Energy Index. Arizona State University. New York, NY: Pergamon, 1980. 942p., index. out-of-print. ISBN: 0-08-023888-2.

This is an index to the Arizona State University solar energy collection, one of the largest in the country. It contains some 10,500 citations from the 1800s. Journal articles are included. Supplements have been published since 1982.

Atlases

1434. Atlas of Renewable Energy Resources in the United Kingdom and North America. Julian E.H. Mustoe. New York, NY: Wiley, 1984. 202p., illus. (part in color), maps, bibliog., index. $129.00. ISBN: 0-471-10293-8.

Renewable energy in this atlas pertains to solar, wind, wave, tidal, river, ocean thermal, and geothermal energies and biofuels. For each of these types, statistics are given together with a narrative, maps, charts, and graphs. This source is a good overview of renewable energy.

1435. Atlas of Selected Oil and Gas Reservoir Rocks From North America: A Color Guidebook to the Petrology of Selected Oil and Gas Reservoir Rocks from the United States and Canada. Edwin N. Biederman, Jr. New York, NY: Wiley, 1986. 399p., illus. (part in color), bibliog., index. price not available. ISBN: 0-471-81666-3.

A unique atlas of the rocks that contain or have the potential to contain oil and gas. Since the world's oil reserves are decreasing, this atlas has become an important reference source for exploration geologists and petroleum engineers working on first-time oil drillings.

1436. United States Energy Atlas. 2nd. David J. Cuff; William J. Young. New York, NY: Macmillan, 1986. 385p., illus. (part in color), bibliog., index. $85.00. ISBN: 0-01-691240-6.

Although not literally an atlas (the information is not presented via maps in this particular "atlas"), this is still an excellent summary and historical account of the status of energy production and reserves in the U.S. Encyclopedic information is given as well as statistical data on nonrenewable and renewable resources. A very good glossary is included.

Bibliographies

1437. Sun Power: A Bibliography of United States Government Documents on Solar Energy. Sandra McAninch. Westport, CT: Greenwood Press, 1981. 944p., index. $125.00. ISBN: 0-313-20992-8.

A comprehensive bibliography of all government documents through 1980 that pertain or make reference to sun power or energy. It is arranged in broad topical chapters such as biomass, ocean thermal, solar, and wind.

1438. Wind Energy 1975-1985: A Bibliography. Penny Farmer. New York, NY: Springer-Verlag, 1986. 167p., index. $95.00. ISBN: 0-387-16103-1.

This is a historical bibliography of government publications, symposia, conference papers, periodical articles, and monographs that pertain to wind energy. It does not include annotations but does indicate the language of the publications cited. Another, older book on wind power that may be useful is the *Wind Power Book* (Cheshire Books, 1981).

Biographical Sources

1439. Energy and Nuclear Science International Who's Who. Harlow, Great Britain: Longman Group, 1992. 388p., index. $310.00. ISBN: 0-8103-9956-3.

Previously called *International Who's Who in Energy and Nuclear Science* and *Who's Who in Atoms*, this book gives brief biographical information on persons working in the fields of energy and nuclear science. It is revised on an irregular basis.

Dictionaries, Glossaries, and Thesauri

1440. A-Z of Offshore Oil and Gas: An Illustrated International Glossary and Reference Guide to the Offshore Oil and Gas Industries and Their Technology. 2nd. Harry Whitehead. Houston, TX: Gulf Publishing, 1983. 438p., illus., bibliog. $118.30. ISBN: 0-87201-052-X.

This glossary and reference guide is a very useful dictionary for terms that are associated with offshore oil and gas exploration, drilling, and production. It includes information about the world's oil and gas fields.

1441. Desk and Derrick Standard Oil Abbreviations. 3rd. Desk and Derrick Club. Tulsa, OK: PennWell, 1986. 320p. $27.75. ISBN: 0-87814-299-1.

This is a dictionary of some 10,500 oilfield terms and abbreviations.

1442. Dictionary of Coal Science and Technology. Roy D. Merritt. Park Ridge, NJ: Noyes, 1987. 389p., illus., bibliog. $48.00. ISBN: 0-8155-1124-8.

Close to 2,500 terms pertaining to coal geology, mining, reclamation, exploration, and resource classification are included in this specialized dictionary.

1443. Dictionary of Energy. *(Energy, Power and Environment, 18).* Carl W. Hall; George W. Hinman. New York, NY: Dekker, 1983. 286p., illus., bibliog. $75.00. ISBN: 0-8247-1793-7.

A good small dictionary covering the energy field. Definitions are intended for the researcher. Martin Counihan's *Dictionary of Energy* (Routledge, 1981) is also a good energy dictionary.

1444. Dictionary of Energy Technology. Alan Gilpin; Alan Williams. Boston, MA: Butterworths, 1982. 392p., illus., bibliog. out-of-print. ISBN: 0-408-01108-4.

This was previously published as *Dictionary of Fuel Technology.* This dictionary covers terms in the energy field, including those associated with nuclear energy.

1445. Dictionary of Nuclear Engineering in Four Languages: English, German, French, Russian. Ralph Sube. New York, NY: Elsevier, 1985. 1,199p., index. $200.00. ISBN: 0-444-99593-5.

Being a translation of *Worterbuch Kerntechnik,* this is a typical Elsevier bilingual dictionary with terms listed in English followed by their equivalents in German, French, and Russian. Indexes are included for each of the three languages.

1446. Dictionary of Nuclear Power and Waste Management with Abbreviations. Foo-Sun Lau. New York, NY: Wiley, 1987. 396p., bibliog. $200.00. ISBN: 0-471-91517-3.

Although somewhat expensive this is a good specialized dictionary on nuclear power and waste management. Commonly used abbreviations are also identified. Appendixes include half-lives of nuclides, atomic masses of elements, and tables of scientific units and equivalencies.

1447. Dictionary of Petroleum Exploration, Drilling and Production. Norm J. Hyne. Tulsa, OK: PennWell, 1991. 625p., illus. $79.95. ISBN: 0-87814-352-1.

This is an up-to-date dictionary of terms covering exploration, drilling, and production of petroleum. Also useful is Jodie Leecraft's *Dictionary of Petroleum Terms* (PETEX, 1983).

1448. Elsevier's Oil and Gas Field Dictionary in Six Languages: English/American, French, Spanish, Italian, Dutch, and German. L.Y. Chaballe; L. Masuy; J.P. Vandenberghe. New York, NY: Elsevier, 1980. 672p., index. $200.00. ISBN: 0-444-41833-4.

A typical Elsevier multilingual dictionary, this work is alphabetically arranged by the English term followed with the equivalents in French, Spanish, Italian, Dutch, and German. Each language has an index that refers back to the English term.

1449. Energy and Environmental Terms: A Glossary. *(Energy Paper No.24).* Peter Brackley. Brookfield, VT: Gower, 1988. 199p. $42.95. ISBN: 0-566-05759-X.

This small dictionary contains brief definitions to the more common terms in the energy and environmental science fields. Two other useful, but dated, dictionaries are the World Energy Conference's *Standard Terms of the Energy Economy* (Pergamon, 1978) and David Kut's *Dictionary of Applied Energy Conservation* (Nichols, 1982).

1450. Energy Terminology: A Multi-Lingual Glossary. 2nd. World Energy Conference. New York, NY: Pergamon, 1986. 539p. $200.00; $78.00pbk. ISBN: 0-08-034071-7; 0-08-034072-5pbk.

This multilingual glossary contains close to 1,500 terms arranged by English term with corresponding French, German, and Spanish equivalents. Unlike most multilingual dictionaries, this one contains definitions.

1451. Handbook of Oil Industry Terms and Phrases. 4th. Robert D. Langenkamp. Tulsa, OK: PennWell, 1984. 347p., bibliog. $32.95. ISBN: 0-87814-258-4.

Close to 3,200 terms pertaining to the oil industry are included in this dictionary. See also the *Illustrated Petroleum Reference Dictionary.*

1452. Illustrated Petroleum Reference Dictionary. 3rd. Robert D. Langenkamp. Tulsa, OK: PennWell, 1985. 695p., illus. $64.95. ISBN: 0-87814-272-X.

This is an excellent dictionary of petroleum industry terms. It includes illustrations plus the Desk and Derrick Clubs of North America's *D&D Standard Oil Abbreviations* and a section of "Universal Conversion Factors." See also the *Handbook of Oil Industry Terms and Phrases*. David F. Tver's *Petroleum Dictionary* (Van Nostrand Reinhold, 1980) is another useful dictionary.

1453. Macmillan Dictionary of Energy. 2nd. Malcolm Slesser. London, Great Britain: Macmillan, 1988. 300p., illus. $59.95. ISBN: 0-333-45461-8.

Previously called *Dictionary of Energy*, this is a good up-to-date dictionary of energy terminology. It includes terms in the related fields of environmental engineering, fuels and fuel technology, and bioenergies. An older but useful dictionary for historical terms is V. Daniel Hunt's *Energy Dictionary* (Van Nostrand Reinhold, 1979).

1454. Oil and Gas Dictionary. Paul Stevens. New York, NY: Nichols, 1988. 270p., illus. $78.50. ISBN: 0-89397-325-4.

This dictionary, aimed at the entrepeneur rather than the engineer, covers the technical jargon of the oil and gas industries. The definitions vary from brief to extensive entries.

1455. Solar Energy Dictionary. V. Daniel Hunt. New York, NY: Industrial Press, 1982. 411p., illus., bibliog. out-of-print. ISBN: 0-8311-1139-9.

Although out-of-print, this is a good dictionary dealing with the historical terminology associated with solar energy. It covers processes, products, and renewable solar energies in addition to covering terms in wind energy, ocean energy, and waste energy conversion. A dictionary covering just renewable energy is Margaret Crouch's *Renewable Energy Dictionary* (Volunteers in Technical Assistance, 1982).

Directories

1456. Asia-Pacific-Africa-Middle East Petroleum Directory. Tulsa, OK: PennWell, 1979– , annual. v.1– , illus., index. $115.00. ISSN: 0748-4089.

Formerly *Asia-Pacific Petroleum Directory* and incorporating *Africa-Middle East Petroleum Directory*, this directory lists companies involved in drilling, refining, exploration, pipelines, engineering, field services, construction, and other petroleum-related operations.

1457. Energy, Sources of Print and Nonprint Materials. Maureen Crowley. New York, NY: Neal-Schuman, 1980. 341p., index. $35.00. ISBN: 0-918212-16-2.

Although one will need to use this in conjunction with the *Encyclopedia of Associations* for the latest names and addresses, it is still useful. This reference identifies some 800 organizations, which are sources of information, and publications on all aspects of energy. Full descriptions of each organization are given with representative listings of publications.

1458. European Petroleum Directory. Tulsa, OK: PennWell, 1979– , annual. v.1– , illus., index. $115.00. ISSN: 0275-3871.

This directory supersedes *Eastern Hemisphere Petroleum Directory* listing companies involved in drilling, refining, exploration, pipelines, engineering, field services, construction and other petroleum-related operations.

1459. Offshore Contractors and Equipment Worldwide Directory. Tulsa, OK: PennWell, 1969– , annual. v.1– , illus., index. $125.00.

Previously called *Offshore Contractors and Equipment Directory* and *Worldwide Offshore Contractors Directory*, this work lists over 3,500 companies and personnel in drilling, construction, geophysical drilling, services, supply manufacturing, and transportation.

1460. Petroleum Software Directory. Tulsa, OK: PennWell, 1984– , annual. v.1– , index. $165.00. ISSN: 0743-6750.

This annual provides an access to the many software packages that are used in the petroleum industry. Each program is fully described and followed by the applications. Information can be located by application, by software producer, and by software name.

1461. Solar Energy Directory. Sandra Oddo; Martin McPhillips; Richard Gottlieb. New York, NY: Wilson, 1983. 312p., index. out-of-print. ISBN: 0-939300-06-0.

It is hoped that this directory will be updated. This source currently lists U.S. organizations, institutions, agencies, and industries working in the solar energy field. Its emphasis is on heating and cooling, solar thermal, and photovoltaics. Full directory information is given. Because of the date of publication, keep in mind that some information may be out of date.

1462. SYNERJY: A Directory of Renewable Energy. New York, NY: Synerjy, 1974– , semiannual. v.1– , index. $50.00. ISSN: 0163-2183.

Intended to present information on alternative energy sources, this directory is basically an index of informational sources that lists books, patents, government publications, periodical articles, manufacturers, and research facilities. It also includes an annual manufacturer's directory. This directory includes information on solar, wind, biomass, and hydropower energies.

1463. USA Oil Industry Directory. Tulsa, OK: PennWell, 1962– , annual. v.1– , illus., index. $125.00. ISSN: 0082-8599.

This annual covers the principal oil companies whose headquarters are in the United States. It provides profiles for each company including address, telephone numbers, personnel, subsidiary, and refining information. The financial status and production figures for each company are also given.

1464. USA Oilfield Service, Supply, and Manufacturers Directory. Tulsa, OK: PennWell, 1983– , annual. v.1– , illus., index. $115.00.

Previously called *Oilfield Service, Supply and Manufacturers Worldwide Directory* and *Oilfield Service, Supply, and Manufacturers Directory*, this annual provides information on oil field services, the wholesale and retail sale of oil field products as well as information on companies engaged in the design, manufacture, and construction of equipment used in the oil fields.

1465. World Directory of Energy Information. Christopher Swain; Andrew Buckley. New York, NY: Facts on File, 1981-1984. 3v., illus., index. price not available. ISBN: 0-87196-563-1v.1.

This excellent overview of energy for each country is arranged within each volume by country. Each volume contains sections on energy framework, country review, energy organizations, and energy publications. The lists of publications are especially useful in providing various statistical annuals.

1466. World Energy and Nuclear Directory. 4th. Harlow, Great Britain: Longman Group, 1991. 573p., index. $450.00. ISBN: 0-582-07933-0.

Previously called *World Energy Directory* and *World Nuclear Directory*, this rather expensive directory provides detailed profiles of research laboratories and institutions that carry out all types of research in energy, including nuclear. It provides the usual names, addresses, and telephone numbers plus information about the facilities research. Topics covered include electricity, direct energy conversion, biological energy sources, natural gas, coal technology, and other renewable forms of power.

1467. Worldwide Refining and Gas Processing Directory. Tulsa, OK: PennWell, 1942– , annual. v.1– , illus., index. $140.00. ISSN: 0277-0962.

Incorporating *Refining and Petrochemical Yearbook* this directory lists over 3,000 plant sites in the U.S. and Canada, Europe, Latin America, Asia-Pacific, Africa, and the Middle East involved in crude oil and natural gas processing, including refining, construction, and equipment. Statistical surveys are also included from the *Oil and Gas Journal.* Two other related publications are the *Worldwide Petrochemical Directory* (PennWell, annual) and the *Whole World Oil Directory* (Whole World, irregular).

Encyclopedias

1468. International Petroleum Encyclopedia. Tulsa, OK: PennWell Books, 1968– , annual. v.1– , index. $110.00.

This is one of the best annual encyclopedias available covering petroleum. The main section is an atlas divided by region, and each region is alphabetically divided by country. The encyclopedia displays various petroleum-related information such as oil fields, gas fields, pipelines, refineries, tanker terminals, and major cities. The narrative for each country summarizes petroleum activity.

1469. Kaiman's Encyclopedia of Energy Topics. Kaiman Lee; Jacqueline Masloff. Newtonville, MA: Environmental Design & Research Center, 1979. 2v., illus., index. $150.00. ISBN: 0-915250-31-4.

This is a good source for historical information on energy topics. It is alphabetically arranged with discussions ranging from a few sentences to several pages.

1470. Landman's Encyclopedia. 3rd. Robert L. Hankinson. Houston, TX: Gulf Publishing, 1988. 496p., illus., index. $89.00. ISBN: 0-87201-424-X.

An excellent encyclopedia containing sample documents pertaining to such topics as securing oil and gas leases, lease agreements, and utilization agreements. A database is included.

1471. McGraw-Hill Encyclopedia of Energy. 2nd. Sybil P. Parker. New York, NY: McGraw-Hill, 1981. 838p., illus., bibliog., index. $79.95. ISBN: 0-07-045268-7.

Materials for this encyclopedia were taken from the 4th edition of the *McGraw-Hill Encyclopedia of Science and Technology.* It is somewhat dated but provides good background information on such topics as conservation, choices of energy, production, consumption, fuel reserves, protecting the environment, and technologies.

1472. Oilfields of the World. 3rd revised. E.N. Tiratsoo. Houston, TX: Gulf Publishing, 1986. 392p., illus., maps, bibliog., index. $79.00. ISBN: 0-87201-668-4.

An excellent overview of the worldwide oil fields, this work gives historical insights, statistics, and other information about oil reserves. It is arranged in chapters that cover groups of countries.

Guides to the Literature

1473. Energy Information Guide. R. David Weber. San Carlos, CA: Energy Information Press, 1982. 3v., index. $100.00. ISBN: 0-87436-388-8.

Although somewhat dated, this information guide is still useful for identifying reference works on energy and energy-related topics. The guide includes organizations, government agencies, books, and articles. Each of the 3 volumes covers a particular topic: v.1—General and alternative energy sources; v.2—Nuclear and electric power; v.3—Fossil fuels.

1474. Guide to the Petroleum Reference Literature. Barbara C. Pearson; Katherine B. Ellwood. Littleton, CO: Libraries Unlimited, 1987. 193p., index. $45.00. ISBN: 0-87287-473-7.

Arranged by type of reference work, this guide lists and describes those materials that are key in the Petroleum Engineering Library. In addition, 118 periodical titles have been included as well-as 80 databases. As a reference work, it is a good initial source to use before doing in-depth research on petroleum topics. Another useful, specialized bibliographic guide is Marjorie Chryssostomidis' *Offshore Petroleum Engineering: A Bibliographic Guide to Publications and Information Sources* (Noyes, 1978).

1475. Information Sources in Energy Technology. L.J. Anthony. Boston, MA: Butterworths, 1988. 324p., bibliog., index. $105.00. ISBN: 0-408-03050-X.

This is a very good guide to the various sources of information on energy. Arranged by subject, each chapter is separately authored and begins with an overview of the subject and then is followed by a list of sources including books, monographs, reviews, journals, patents, conference proceedings, reports, encyclopedias, handbooks, dictionaries, standards, statistics and databooks, abstracts, indexes, bibliographies, and directories.

Handbooks and Manuals

1476. Energy Handbook. 2nd. Robert L. Loftness. New York, NY: Van Nostrand Reinhold, 1984. 763p., illus., bibliog., index. $81.95. ISBN: 0-442-25992-1.

An excellent general handbook giving background information pertaining to energy, this handbook covers such topics as energy and humans, fossil energy, energy consumption trends, nuclear power, geothermal energy, solar energy, energy transport, and energy futures. Other useful but somewhat dated energy handbooks include Wayne C. Turner's *Energy Management Handbook* (Wiley, 1982) and Peter G. Norback's *Consumer's Energy Handbook* (Van Nostrand Reinhold, 1981).

1477. Energy Reference Handbook. 3rd. Thomas F.P. Sullivan; Martin L. Heavner. Rockville, MD: Government Institutes, 1981. 417p., illus., index. $45.00. ISBN: 0-86587-082-9.

This handbook presents a good overview of energy in all forms. Another good handbook covering trends and perspectives as related to energy is V. Daniel Hunt's *Handbook of Energy Technology* (Van Nostrand Reinhold, 1982).

1478. Energy Statistics Sourcebook, 1987. Tulsa, OK: PennWell Books, 1987. 444p., index. $115.00. ISBN: 0-889-5260-1.

This sourcebook provides the key statistical information needed to analyze oil and gas data. It is produced from a database on energy maintained by the *Oil and Gas Journal* and covers such topics as exploration, production, reserves, imports and exports, pricing, and transportation. The book includes monthly as well as annual data. For up-to-date energy statistics consult the Institute of Gas Technology's *Energy Statistics*, a quarterly published since 1978.

1479. Handbook of Energy Audits. 2nd. Albert Thumann. Atlanta, GA: Fairmont Press, 1983. 443p., illus., bibliog., index. $43.00; $25.00pbk. ISBN: 0-925586-76-2; 0-915586-75-4pbk.

"An energy audit serves the purpose of identifying where a building or plant facility uses energy and identifies energy conservation opportunities." This is a comprehensive handbook showing all aspects of how to conduct this audit, including various governmental guidelines.

1480. Handbook of Energy Engineering. 2nd. Albert Thumann; D. Paul Mehta. Lilburn, GA: Fairmont Press, 1991. 429p., illus., bibliog., index. $58.00. ISBN: 0-88173-124-2.

This up-to-date handbook for energy engineers covers all areas from safety to conservation.

1481. Handbook of Energy for World Agriculture. B.A. Stout. New York, NY: Elsevier, 1990. 504p., illus., bibliog., index. $135.00. ISBN: 1-85166-349-5.

A comprehensive source of information on energy for agriculture, this handbook covers summaries and discussions on such topics as fuel woods, biomass, and nonrenewable petroleum sources. It provides a basis for understanding energy production and consumption in agriculture.

1482. Handbook of Petroleum Refining Processes. Robert A. Meyers. New York, NY: McGraw-Hill, 1986. 1v., various paging, illus., bibliog., index. $59.50. ISBN: 0-07-041763-6.

This is a companion volume to Robert A. Meyers' *Handbook of Synfuels Technology* (McGraw-Hill, 1984). The 2 volumes cover all aspects of the production and synthesis of petrochemicals including ethlylene, propylene, benzene, toluene, and styrene. It does not discuss the refined chemicals such as gasoline, diesel, lubricants, and waxes.

1483. Hydropower Engineering Handbook.
John S. Gulliver; Roger E.A. Arndt. New York,
NY: McGraw-Hill, 1991. 1v., various paging,
illus., bibliog., index. $69.50. ISBN:
0-07-025193-2.

This is one of the first new hydropower engineering handbooks since the 1970s. Through the use of case studies the handbook provides cost-estimating techniques and hydrologic and hydraulic guidelines for conducting hydropower site studies. It is an essential book for hydropower project planning, design, and development.

1484. Petroleum Engineering Handbook.
Howard B. Bradley; Fred W. Gipson.
Richardson, TX: Society of Petroleum
Engineers, 1987. 1v., various paging, illus.,
bibliog., index. price not available.

Previously called *Petroleum Production Handbook* this very comprehensive handbook presents information and data on production equipment and reservoir engineering. Representative topics covered include gas lift, sucker-rods, pumping units, oil storage, measuring and sampling, gas properties, well performance, chemical flooding, and oil and gas leases. It is a highly recommended handbook.

1485. Solar Energy Handbook. Jan F.
Kreider; Frank Kreith. New York, NY:
McGraw-Hill, 1981. 1v., various paging, illus.,
bibliog., index. out-of-print. ISBN:
0-07-035474-X.

Although somewhat dated and now out-of-print, this handbook gives a solid historical perspective to solar energy. It has good discussions on the uses of solar energy and systems and on the social impact of solar energy use. Another similar handbook is William C. Dickinson's *Solar Energy Technology Handbook* (Dekker, 1980) and a handbook for architects and designers, *Passive Solar Design Handbook* (Van Nostrand Reinhold, 1984).

**1486. World Energy Book: An A-Z, Atlas, and
Statistical Source Book.** David Crabbe; Richard McBride. New York, NY: Nichols, 1978.
259p., illus. out-of-print. ISBN:
0-89397-032-8.

Although out-of-print, this is still a good source for the definitions and discussions of the standard terms that relate to the energy field. The atlas portions have very general maps showing such things as oil and gas reserves, coal reserves, distribution of solar radiation, tidal energy sets, and geothermal energy sites.

1487. World Nuclear Handbook. New York,
NY: Facts on File, 1988. 228p., illus., glossary,
index. $65.00. ISBN: 0-8160-1924-X.

Although flawed by some problems and errors, this handbook does have information on nuclear matters, including fuel extraction, fuel processing, waste disposal, power generation, medical uses, agricultural uses, and weapons.

Yearbooks, Annuals, and Almanacs

1488. Energy Statistics Yearbook. New York,
NY: United Nations, 1952– , annual. v.1– ,
index. price varies per volume. ISSN:
0256-6400.

Previously called *Yearbook of World Energy Statistics and World Energy Supplies*, this is a comprehensive collection of international energy statistics. It is intended to present comparable data on long-term trends in the commercial primary and secondary forms of energy. All information is in tabular format.

**1489. Financial Times International Year
Books: Oil and Gas.** Harlow, Great Britain:
Longman Group, 1910– , annual. v.1– , index.
$110.00. ISSN: 0141-3228.

Previously called *Oil and Petroleum Yearbook*, this long-time published handbook from the *Financial Times* gives an annual summary of information on oil and gas exploration and production.

Periodicals

1490. Applied Energy. Barking, Great Britain:
Elsevier, 1975– , 12/year. v.1– , index.
$680.00. ISSN: 0306-2619.

1491. Energy. Tarrytown, NY: Pergamon
Press, 1976– , monthly. v.1– , index. $632.00.
ISSN: 0360-5442.

1492. Energy Engineering. Lilburn, GA:
Fairmont Press, 1904– , bimonthly. v.1– ,
index. $99.00. ISSN: 0199-8595.

1493. Energy Journal. Weston, MA:
International Association of Energy
Economists, 1980– , quarterly. v.1– , index.
$150.00. ISSN: 0195-6574.

1494. Energy Policy. Oxford, Great Britain:
Butterworth-Heinemann, 1973– , 10/year.
v.1– , index. $340.00. ISSN: 0301-4215.

1495. Energy Report. Arlington, VA: Pasha
Publications, 1973– , weekly. v.1– , index.
$635.00. ISSN: 0888-8183.

1496. Energy Sources. Bristol, PA: Taylor &
Francis, 1973– , quarterly. v.1– , index.
$209.00. ISSN: 0090-8312.

1497. Fuel. Oxford, Great Britain:
Butterworth-Heinemann, 1922– , monthly.
v.1– , index. $912.00. ISSN: 0016-2361.

1498. Hydrocarbon Processing. Houston, TX: Gulf Publishing, 1922– , monthly. v.1– , index. $20.00. ISSN: 0018-8190.

1499. Independent Power Report. New York, NY: McGraw-Hill, 1985– , fortnightly. v.1– , index. $715.00.

1500. International Journal of Energy Research. Chichester, Great Britain: Wiley, 1976– , 9/year. v.1– , index. $875.00. ISSN: 0363-907X.

1501. International Journal of Hydrogen Energy. Tarrytown, NY: Pergamon Press, 1976– , monthly. v.1– , index. $712.00. ISSN: 0360-3199.

1502. Journal of the Institute of Energy. London, Great Britain: Institute of Energy, 1927– , quarterly. v.1– , index. $241.00. ISSN: 0144-2600.

1503. JPT: Journal of Petroleum Technology. Richardson, TX: Society of Petroleum Engineering, 1949– , monthly. v.1– , index. $30.00. ISSN: 0149-2136.

1504. Nuclear Science and Engineering. LaGrange Park, IL: American Nuclear Society, 1956– , monthly. v.1– , index. $390.00. ISSN: 0029-5639.

1505. Nucleonics Week. New York, NY: McGraw-Hill, 1960– , weekly. v.1– , index. $1,295.00. ISSN: 0048-105X.

1506. Oil and Gas Journal. Tulsa, OK: PennWell, 1902– , weekly. v.1– , index. $48.50. ISSN: 0030-1388.

1507. Resources and Energy. Amsterdam, Netherlands: North-Holland, 1979– , 4/year. v.1– , index. $254.00. ISSN: 0165-0572.

1508. Solar Energy. Tarrytown, NY: Pergamon Press, 1957– , 12/year. v.1– , index. $550.00. ISSN: 0038-092X.

1509. Wind Engineering. Brentwood, Great Britain: Multi-Science, 1977– , 6/year. v.1– , index. $203.00. ISSN: 0309-524X.

1510. World Oil. Houston, TX: Gulf Publishing, 1916– , monthly. v.1– , index. $24.00. ISSN: 0043-8790.

ENVIRONMENTAL ENGINEERING

Abstracts and Indexes

1511. EIS: Digests of Environmental Impact Statements. Bethesda, MD: Cambridge Scientific Abstracts, 1970– , bimonthly. v.1– , index. $435.00.

Previously called *EIS: Key to Environmental Impact Statements*, this publication summarizes and indexes all environmental impact statements filed with the U.S. federal government. It covers air transportation, defense programs, energy, hazardous substances, land use, manufacturing, parks, refuges, forests, R&D, roads, railroads, urban planning, waste, and water. It is also available on CD-ROM.

1512. Environment Abstracts. New York, NY: Bowker A and I Publishing, 1970– , monthly. v.1– , index. $695.00 abstracts; $495.00 annual ; $1,070.00 combined. ISSN: 0093-3287 abstracts; 0000-1198 annual.

Previously called *Environment Information Access* with the annual cumulation called *Environment Abstracts Annual* and the index called *Environment Index* and incorporating *Acid Rain Abstracts*, this service abstracts materials pertaining to all areas of the environment and pollution. It is also available online and on CD-ROM.

1513. EPA Publications Bibliography: Quarterly Abstract Bulletin. Washington, DC: U.S. Environmental Protection Agency, 1970– , quarterly. v.1– , index. $80.00.

This quarterly contains abstracts for reports generated by the EPA and its predecessor agencies. It has indexes arranged by report title, keyword subject, corporate and personal author, contract number, and accession/report number. The 4th issue annually contains cumulative indexes for that year. There is an *EPA Cumulative Bibliography* covering 1970-1976 and another for 1977-1983.

1514. Pollution Abstracts. Bethesda, MD: Cambridge Scientific Abstracts, 1970– , bimonthly. v.1– , index. $635.00. ISSN: 0032-3624.

This abstracting journal covers radiation, air pollution, land pollution, noise pollution, marine and freshwater pollution, sewage and wastewater treatment, waste management, toxicology and health, and environmental policies. Some 2,500 primary sources are screened each year. It is also available online and on CD-ROM.

1515. Selected Water Resources Abstracts.
Washington, DC: Water Resources Scientific
Information Center, 1968– , monthly. v.1– ,
index. $115.00. ISSN: 0037-136X.

This service abstracts materials from the U.S. Geological Survey collection that pertain to water resources, conservation, and pollution. It is also available
online and on CD-ROM.

Atlases

1516. Atlas of Environmental Issues. Nick
Middleton. New York, NY: Facts on File,
1989. 63p., color illus., index. $16.95. ISBN:
0-8160-2023-X.

This is a resource for young readers—grades six
and up. It describes and explains major environmental
issues of the world: the effects of soil erosion, defor-
estation, mechanical agriculture, oil pollution of the
oceans, acid rain, overfishing, and nuclear power. Another useful source is Joni Seager's *State of the Earth
Atlas* (Unwin Hyman, 1990).

1517. Atlas of U.S. Environmental Issues.
Robert J. Mason. New York, NY: Macmillan,
1990. 252p., color illus., maps, bibliog., index.
$95.00. ISBN: 0-0289-7261-9.

This is an atlas of 150 maps that show environmental issues in agriculture, coastal zone management,
air quality, noise and light pollution, and the economics
and politics of environment.

Bibliographies

**1518. Acid Rain and the Environment, 1984-
1988.** Leslie Grayson. Corning, NY: Air
Science Co, 1988. 240p., index. $69.50. ISBN:
0-946655-25-1.

This bibliography, together with an earlier one
covering the literature from 1980-1984, gives good
historical coverage on the effects of acid rain. It is
arranged into 5 sections: the issue, the scientific con-
troversy, the research, the effects, and the litigation
strategies. Another bibliography that could be consulted is G. Harry Stopp's *Acid Rain* (Scarecrow Press,
1985).

**1519. Environmental Periodicals Bibliog-
raphy: A Current Awareness Bibliography
Featuring Serial Publications in the Area of
Environmental Studies.** Santa Barbara, CA:
International Academy at Santa Barbara,
1972– , bimonthly. v.1– , index. price per
volume varies.

Previously called *Environmental Periodicals: Indexed Article Titles* and *Environmental Periodicals
Bibliography: Indexed Article Titles*, this publication
gives the tables of contents of over 380 international
periodicals on the environment, including the areas of
human ecology, air, energy, land resources, water re-

sources, and nutrition and health. It is also available
online and on CD-ROM. For historical coverage of
environmental impact assessment consult Brian D.
Clark's *Environmental Impact Assessment: A Bibliography with Abstracts* (Bowker, 1980).

Dictionaries, Glossaries, and Thesauri

**1520. Dictionary of Dangerous Pollutants,
Ecology and Environment.** David F. Tver. NY
347p., illus. out-of-print. ISBN:
0-8311-1060-0.

This small dictionary identifies the major pollutants
that are a threat to the ecology and environment.

**1521. Dictionary of Environmental Science
and Technology.** revised. Andrew Porteous.
Chichester, Great Britain: Wiley, 1991. 439p.,
illus. $20.00. ISBN: 0-47193-544-1.

This good up-to-date dictionary of terms and
phrases pertains to all aspects of environmental concern. Also useful for further reference would be Andy
Crump's *Dictionary of Environment and Development: People, Places, Ideas, and Organizations* (MIT,
1993).

1522. Dictionary of the Environment. 3rd.
Michael Allaby. New York, NY: New York
University Press, 1989. 423p. $17.50. ISBN:
0-8147-0591-X.

Environmental concerns in their broadest sense are
covered in this well-written dictionary. It includes
information on relevant government agencies, voluntary organizations, and significant environmental
regulations.

**1523. Environment in Key Words: A Multilin-
gual Handbook of the Environment, English,
French, German, Russian.** Isaac Paenson.
New York, NY: Pergamon Press, 1990. 2v.,
illus., index. $300.00. ISBN: 0-0802-4524-2.

This handbook deals with terms pertaining to the
environment and is alphabetized by the English term
with indexes to French, German, and Russian terms.
For an English-French/French-English handbook consult Peter H. Collin's *Dictionary of Ecology and Environment* (Peter Collin, 1992) and for an English-Ger-
man/German-English handbook see Dieter Lukhaup's
Parat Dictionary of Environmental Protection (VCH,
1992).

1524. Environmental Engineering Dictionary.
C.C. Lee. Rockville, MD: Government
Institutes, 1990. 630p. $68.00. ISBN:
0-86587-786-6.

Published by Government Institutes, which has
numerous materials pertaining to the environment, this
dictionary covers those terms and phrases be encountered in other publications of Government Institutes,

specifically that terminology germane to the fields of engineering.

1525. Environmental Glossary. 4th. G. William Frick; Thomas F.P. Sullivan. Rockville, MD: Government Institutes, 1986. 360p. $42.00. ISBN: 0-86587-134-5.

This glossary lists and defines the terms used in various statutes and regulations controlling pollution. Each definition is taken from an official source such as an EPA document.

1526. Environmental Planning: A Condensed Encyclopedia. Alan Gilpin. Park Ridge, NJ: Noyes, 1986. 348p., illus. $48.00. ISBN: 0-8155-1103-5.

This is an encyclopedia of terms and phrases concerned with environmental impact assessment, including laws, statutes, organizations, and the like. It is international in scope.

1527. Environmental Regulatory Glossary. 5th. G. William Frick; Thomas F.P. Sullivan. Rockville, MD: Government Institutes, 1990. 449p. $59.00. ISBN: 0-8658-7798-X.

Previously called *Environmental Glossary*, this dictionary covers terms that may be encountered in publications pertaining to regulatory concerns. Another dated but still useful dictionary is Marc Landy's *Environmental Impact Statement Glossary* (IFI/Plenum, 1979).

1528. Facts on File Dictionary of Environmental Science. L. Harold Stevenson; Bruce C. Wyman. New York, NY: Facts on File, 1991. 294p., illus. $24.95. ISBN: 0-8160-2317-4.

This is another general dictionary from a publisher that has many dictionaries for the student and layperson. Environment is covered in the broadest sense in this work.

1529. Glossary: Water and Wastewater Control Engineering. 2nd. American Water Works Association. Denver, CO: American Water Works Association, 1981. 456p. $30.00. ISBN: 0-89867-263-5.

This work is published by the American Water Works Association which is the major association concerned with all aspects of water engineering. This dictionary covers terminology associated with water and wastewater control. Another dictionary covering the same terminology is John S. Scott's *Dictionary of Waste and Water Treatment* (Butterworths, 1981).

1530. HarperCollins Dictionary of Environmental Science. Gareth Jones; Alan Robertson; Jean Forbes; Graham Hollier. New York, NY: HarperPerennial, 1992. 453p., illus. $25.00; $13.00pbk. ISBN: 0-06-271533-X; 0-06-461040-3pbk.

Also called *Dictionary of Environmental Science*, this work is for the student and laypublic and covers the physical world, the biological world, the built environment, and the agro-economic infrastructure. The emphasis is on the interaction of people and their environment. Another recent work is the U.S. Department of Energy's *Dictionary and Thesaurus of Environment, Health and Safety* (C.K. Smoley, 1992).

1531. Land Use A-Z. David E. Newton. Hillside, NJ: Enslow, 1991. 128p., bibliog. $17.95. ISBN: 0-8949-0260-1.

This dictionary covers the terms related to the scientific, technological, and social problems affecting the use of land.

Directories

1532. Acid Rain Resource Directory. Raleigh, NC: Acid Rain Foundation, Inc, 1982– , irregular. v.1– , index. $10.00.

This small directory lists organizations and gives other information pertaining to acid rain.

1533. Conservation Directory. Washington, DC: National Wildlife Federation, 1956– , annual. v.1– , index. $18.00. ISSN: 0069-911X.

Previously called *Directory of Organizations and Officials Concerned with the Protection of Wildlife and Other Natural Resources*, this directory lists organizations, agencies, and officials concerned with natural resource use and management. It covers the U.S.A. and Canada as well as selected international groups. Local, state, regional, and federal agencies are included.

1534. Directory of Toxicological and Related Testing Laboratories. Washington, DC: Hemisphere, 1991. 1v., various paging, index. $50.00. ISBN: 0-89116-904-0.

This is a specialized directory with information about testing laboratories that conduct toxicological and related testing. Names, addresses, and types of laboratories are provided.

1535. Gale Environmental Sourcebook: A Guide to Organizations, Agencies, and Publications. Karen Hill. Detroit, MI: Gale Research, 1992. 688p., index. $86.25. ISBN: 0-8103-8403-5.

An excellent source of information about organizations and agencies concerned with the environment, this book gives full descriptions, addresses, and the like. A bibliographical list of notable environmental publications is also included.

1536. Indoor Air Quality Directory, 1992-1993. Bethesda, MD: IAQ Publications, 1992. 362p., index. $75.00. ISBN: 0-963303-1-8.

This directory provides a comprehensive source of information for all areas of indoor air quality. It covers a variety of factors that affect the quality of indoor air: the pollutants of asbestos, combustible products, electro-magnetic fields, environmental tobacco smoke, lead, microbials, radon, and volatile organic compounds. Access to information is by manufacturer, government agency, and associations.

1537. Radon Directory. Chevy Chase, MD: Radon Press, 1990/91– , annual. v.1– , index. $75.00.

Previously called *Radon Industry Directory*, this directory includes lists of radon detection companies, radon mitigation companies, and radon consultants. This directory also lists the manufacturers and distributors of radon detection products, state and federal radon agencies, and other radon related materials.

1538. Regulated Chemicals Directory 1992. ChemADVISOR. New York, NY: Chapman & Hall, 1992. 1,472p. (looseleaf), index. $375.00. ISBN: 0-412-03481-6.

This annually revised directory, with intervening quarterly updates regarding the regulations and recommendations that pertain to chemical substances, is intended to help in compliance efforts. Complete regulatory data is given as it pertains to health and safety, environmental state, and international impact.

1539. World Directory of Environmental Organizations: A Handbook of National and International Organizations and Programs, Governmental and Non-Governmental, Concerned with Protecting the Earth's Resources. Claremont, CA: Public Affairs Clearinghouse for the Sierra Club, 1973– , irregular. v.1– , index. $35.00. ISSN: 0092-0908.

Also called *Sierra Club's World Directory of Environmental Organizations*, this comprehensive global guide to organizations is concerned with the environment and natural resources. It lists more than 2,100 governmental and nongovernmental organizations in over 200 countries.

Encyclopedias

1540. Concise Encyclopedia of Environmental Systems. P.C. Young. Tarrytown, NY: Pergamon Press, 1993. 750p., illus., index. price not available. ISBN: 0-08-036198-6.

This encyclopedia provides good general summaries of agricultural systems and atmospheric processes plus information on air quality, ecosystems, environ-

mental chemistry, geology, soil processes and geophysics, hydrology, fluid dynamics and water quality, marine processes, meteorology, and climatology.

1541. Encyclopedia of Environmental Science and Engineering. James R. Pfafflin; Edward N. Ziegler. New York, NY: Gordon and Breach, 1983. 3v., illus., index. $798.00. ISBN: 0-677-06430-6.

This comprehensive treatise-like coverage of environmental science and engineering is filled with well-document and comprehensive articles.

1542. Encyclopedia of Environmental Studies. William Ashworth. New York, NY: Facts on File, 1991. 470p., illus., index. $60.00. ISBN: 0-8160-1531-7.

This good up-to-date general encyclopedia covers the environment and related areas. Excellent illustrations are provided.

1543. Information Please Environmental Almanac. World Resources Institute. Boston, MA: Houghton Mifflin, 1991. 606p., index. $21.95. ISBN: 0-395-59625-4.

This is a good source on environmental topics because it includes statistical data, lists, and other tabular information.

1544. McGraw-Hill Encyclopedia of Environmental Science. 3rd. Sybil P. Parker. New York, NY: McGraw-Hill, 1993. 749p., illus., bibliog., index. $85.00. ISBN: 0-07-051396-1.

Material for this excellent encyclopedia has been taken from the fifth edition of the *McGraw-Hill Encyclopedia of Science and Technology*. This is a good source of well-established information about all areas of environmental science. Entries are signed and well-documented.

1545. State of the Environment. Paris, France: Organization for Economic Co-Operation and Development, 1991. 297p., illus., bibliog. price not available.

Although not a true encyclopedia, this work presents the progress achieved as of 1990 concerning the relationships between the state of the environment and the economic growth and structural changes in OECD countries. It covers a wide spectrum of topics: global atmospheric issues, air, inland water, marine environment, land, forest, wildlife, solid waste, noise, agriculture, industry, transport, energy, and economics.

1546. Water Encyclopedia. 2nd. Frits van der Leeden; Fred L. Troise; David Keith Todd. Chelsea, MI: Lewis, 1990. 808p., illus., bibliog. $135.00. ISBN: 0-87371-120-3.

This is really a handbook of tables, charts, graphs, and maps. The tables and illustrations provide information on such topics as weather, hydrology, surface and ground water, acid rain, sea level rise, solid waste, and urban runoff.

Guides to the Literature

1547. Acid Rain Information Book. 2nd. David V. Bubenick. Park Ridge, NJ: Noyes, 1984. 397p., illus., bibliog., index. $39.00. ISBN: 0-8155-0967-7.

Originally published as a U.S. Office of Environment Assessment document in 1981, this guide discusses major aspects of the acid rain phenomenon, points out areas of uncertainty, and summarizes research.

1548. Directory of Environmental Information Resources. 4th. Thomas F.P. Sullivan. Washington, DC: Government Institutes, 1992. 262p., index. $74.00. ISBN: 0-86587-326-7.

This excellent guide covers some 1,400 sources of environmental information including federal and state government; professional, scientific, and trade organizations; and databases, reference materials, and journals.

1549. Energy and Environment Information Resource Guide. M. Lynn Neufeld. Philadelphia, PA: National Federation of Abstracting and Indexing Services, 1982. 53p. $12.50. ISBN: 0-942308-15-8.

This small but useful guide to materials associated with energy and the environment. The user must realize, however, that many sources need to be checked in newer editions.

1550. Environmental Bibliography Search Guide. 4th. Environmental Studies Institute. Santa Barbara, CA: International Academy at Santa Barbara, 1990. 44p. 3-ring binder. $60.00. ISBN: 0-9610590-4-4.

This publication is a brief but useful guide on how to search for information about the environment.

1551. Guide to State Environmental Programs. 2nd. Deborah Hitchcock Jessup. Washington, DC: Bureau of National Affairs, 1990. 700p., bibliog., index. $54.00. ISBN: 0-87179-655-4.

Arranged by state, this guide outlines each state's environmental agencies and programs giving titles of programs, names of persons to contact, fees, and other information. Directory information is given for federal agencies and programs.

1552. Toxic and Hazardous Materials: A Sourcebook and Guide to Information Sources. *(Bibliographies and Indexes in Science and Technology, no.2).* James K. Webster. New York, NY: Greenwood Press, 1987. 431p., index. $55.00. ISBN: 0-313-24575-4.

This sourcebook covers some 1,600 entries on toxic and hazardous materials including books, periodicals, databases, audiovisual materials, organizations, etc. Another older but useful historical work is the *Toxic Substances Sourcebook* (Environmental Information Center, 1980).

Handbooks and Manuals

1553. Bretherick's Handbook of Reactive Chemical Hazards. 4th. L. Bretherick. Boston, MA: Butterworths, 1990. 2,005p., illus., bibliog., index. $195.00. ISBN: 0-408-04983-9.

Previously called *Handbook of Reactive Chemical Hazards*, this is a well-established handbook covering reactive chemical hazards. Each entry is described in detail emphasizing the hazards involved. Another similar book, which is aimed at schools and colleges, is the *Compendium of Hazardous Chemicals in Schools and Colleges* (Lippincott, 1990).

1554. CRC Handbook of Incineration of Hazardous Wastes. William S. Rickman. Boca Raton, FL: CRC, 1991. 608p., illus., index. $259.00. ISBN: 0-8493-0557-8.

This comprehensive handbook covers the emerging incinerator technologies. It reviews regulatory and technical requirements, choosing an incinerator, engineering calculations, and the bid process. Of equal importance, but covering other aspects of incineration is Calvin R. Brunner's *Handbook of Incineration Systems* (McGraw-Hill, 1991). Another useful book on hazardous waste is the *Hazardous Waste Management Compliance Handbook* (Van Nostrand Reinhold, 1991).

1555. CRC Handbook of Radiation Measurement and Protection. Allen B. Brodsky. Boca Raton, FL: CRC, 1978-82. 2v., illus., bibliog., index. $240.00. ISBN: 0-8493-3756-9v.1; 0-8493-3757-7v.2.

A specialized handbook outlining all aspects of radiation measurement and protection, this work presents numerous examples that include much graphic and tabular information. Another similar publication is Alfred W. Klement's *CRC Handbook of Environmental Radiation* (CRC, 1982).

1556. Environmental Health Reference Book. M.H. Jackson. Boston, MA: Butterworths, 1989. 521p., illus., bibliog., index. $210.00. ISBN: 0-408-02600-6.

All things concerned with the health and well-being of the general public are found in this handbook. It touches such areas as water pollution, pest control, radioactive waste disposal, and other types of waste management. Another handbook that deals more with the chemical aspect of environmental engineering is William H. Lederer's *Regulatory Chemicals of Health*

Environmental Concern (Van Nostrand Reinhold, 1985).

1557. Environmental Law Handbook. 11th.
Washington, DC: Government Institutes, 1991. 670p., index. $65.00.

This frequently revised handbook serves as a source of information on environmental law. It is written for the layperson and covers the various laws and regulations concerning the envrionment, including laws and/or regulations regarding the control of water pollution, toxic substances, noise, and pesticides. Two other similar handbooks are Nicholas A. Robinson's *Environmental Law Handbook* (New York State Bar Assoc., 1987) and Sidney M. Wolf's *Pollution Law Handbook* (Quorum, 1988).

1558. Environmental Statutes. Rockville,
MD: Government Institutes, 1992. 1,171p., index. $55.00; $39.50pbk. ISBN: 0-86587-252-X; 0-86587-251-1pbk.

There are hundreds of environmental statutes throughout the U.S.A. This handbook, published by a very reputable publisher, has compiled those statutes in one easy-to-use volume. For comprehensive weekly information on laws and statutes see the *Environment Reporter*.

1559. Firefighter's Hazardous Material Reference Book. Daniel J. Davis; Grant T. Christianson. New York, NY: Van Nostrand Reinhold, 1991. 1,100p., index. $119.95. ISBN: 0-442-00377-3.

This handbook presents the numerous hazardous materials firefighters may have to confront during a fire. By presenting the hazardous substances and discussing what can happen to them under extreme environmental conditions, such as fire, this references explains how to fight the fire safely. Another smaller and simpler handbook that can be consulted is Charles J. Baker's *Firefighter's Handbook of Hazardous Materials* (Matese Enterprises, 1990).

1560. Groundwater Chemicals Desk Reference. John H. Montgomery; Linda M. Welkom. Chelsea, MI: Lexis, 1990-91. 1v., illus., bibliog., index. $90.00. ISBN: 0-87371-286-2v.1; 0-87371-430-Xv.2.

This comprehensive work deals with the many hazardous chemicals that may find their way into groundwater. Each entry gives a complete description of the chemical, including all the physical and chemical properties and its potential as a fire hazard. Two other useful handbooks are John H. Montgomery's *Groundwater Chemicals Field Guide* (Lewis, 1991) and David M. Nielson's *Practical Handbook of Groundwater Monitoring* (Lewis, 1991).

1561. Handbook of Acoustical Measurements and Noise Control. 3rd. Cyril M. Harris. New York, NY: McGraw-Hill, 1991. 1v, various paging, illus., index. $89.50. ISBN: 0-07-026868-1.

Industrial expansion and construction has created noise pollution, an increasing medical concern. This handbook, previously called *Handbook of Noise Control*, covers all methods of measuring noise and presents ways of instituting noise-control systems.

1562. Handbook of Air Pollution Analysis.
2nd. Roy M. Harrison; Roger Perry. New York, NY: Chapman & Hall, 1986. 634p., illus., bibliog., index. $85.00. ISBN: 0-412-24410-1.

The increased public concern regarding air pollution makes this a timely publication. This handbook covers the various methods of analysis of air polution: meteorology, chemistry, rain water analysis, and air quality control. Another similar book is E. Willard Miller's *Environmental Hazards: Air Pollution—A Reference Book* (ABC-Clio, 1989). Seymour Calvert's *Handbook of Air Pollution Technology* (Wiley, 1984) gives a good treatment of technologies associated with air pollution control, and *Air Pollution Engineering Manual* (Van Nostrand Reinhold, 1992) is a newer manual on air pollution.

1563. Handbook of Environmental Degradation Rates. Philip H. Haward. Chelsea, MI: Lewis, 1991. 725p., bibliog., index. price not available. ISBN: 0-87371-358-3.

This handbook lists the rate constants of individual abiotic and biotic degradation processes for chemicals of anthropogenic origin as they pertain to the soil, water, and air. For each chemical the following information is given: structure, half-lives, aqueous biodegradation, photolysis, photooxidation half-life, reduction half-life, hydrolysis, and the CAS registry number.

1564. Handbook of Environmental Fate and Exposure Data for Organic Chemicals.
Philip H. Haward. Chelsea, MI: Lewis, 1989-92. 4v., illus., bibliog., index. $311.85. ISBN: 0-87371-151-3v.1; 0-87371-204-8v.2; 0-87371-328-1v.3; 0-87371-413-Xv.4.

This reference source is a treatise-like handbook listing the physical properties of organic compounds and their origins, their interactions in the environment, and their various by-products. The author has fully described each substance and has included a selected bibliography. The 4 volumes cover: v.1—Large production and priority pollutants; v.2—Solvents; v.3—Pesticides; v.4—Organic chemicals. Another older but still useful handbook on organic chemicals is Karel Verschueren's *Handbook of Environmental Data on Organic Chemicals* (Van Nostrand Reinhold, 1983).

1565. Handbook of Industrial Toxicology.
3rd. E.R. Plunkett. New York, NY: Chemical Publishing, 1987. 605p., bibliog., index. $82.50. ISBN: 0-8206-0321-X.

An alphabetical listing of hazardous materials frequently encountered in the industrial workplace, this handbook provides synonyms of the chemical, drug, or pesticide; discusses the types of occupational exposures; explains the threshold limit values; gives brief toxicity profiles; and suggests preventive measures. Also useful in conjunction with this handbook is the *Toxic and Hazardous Industrial Chemicals Safety Manual* (International Technical Information Institute, 1982).

1566. Handbook of Mass Spectra of Environmental Contaminants. 2nd. R.A. Hites. Chelsea, MI: Lewis, 1992. 450p., illus., bibliog., index. $69.95. ISBN: 0-87371-534-9.

Previously called *CRC Handbook of Mass Spectra of Environmental Contaminants*, this is a collection of electron mass spectra of 394 commonly encountered environmental pollutants. They are indexed by common chemical name, CAS registry number, exact molecular weight, and intense peaks.

1567. Handbook of Pollution Control Processes. Robert Noyes. Park Ridge, NJ: Noyes, 1991. 750p., illus., index. $127.00. ISBN: 0-8155-1290-2.

This handbook covers pollution-control processes that are used today to treat inorganic air emissions, solid waste, dust, radioactive waste, hazardous chemicals, drinking water, and landfills.

1568. Handbook of Toxic and Hazardous Chemicals and Carcinogens. 3rd. Marshall Sittig. Park Ridge, NJ: Noyes, 1992. 2v., bibliog., index. $197.00. ISBN: 0-8155-1286-4.

Now in its third edition, this handbook is an excellent source of information about hazardous wastes and industrial chemicals. Approximately 800 alphabetically arranged compounds are covered, and first-aid procedures and personal protection measures are given for each of the compounds.

1569. Hazardous Chemicals Desk Reference.
3rd. Richard J. Lewis, Sr. New York, NY: Van Nostrand Reinhold, 1993. 1,742p., index. $69.95. ISBN: 0-442-01408-2.

This handbook of some 6,000 common industrial and laboratory materials is taken from the more comprehensive *Sax's Dangerous Properties of Industrial Materials* by Irving Sax. The information is less technical than in the parent volume and is intended to be a source of quick reference. There are many other books of this type including Richard J. Lewis' *Rapid Guide to Hazardous Chemicals in the Workplace* (Van Nostrand Reinhold, 1990); *Hazardous Chemicals Data Book* (Noyes, 1986); and Craig J. Norback's *Hazardous Chemicals On File* (3v., Facts on File, 1988).

1570. Hazardous Materials Training Handbook. P. David Shafer. Madison, CT: Business & Legal Reports, 1987. 1v., looseleaf, index. $89.95. ISBN: 1-55645-320-5.

This is a good manual to use in training individuals to handle and cope with hazardous materials.

1571. Hazardous Substances: A Reference.
Melvin Berger. Hillside, NJ: Enslow, 1986. 128p., bibliog., index. $17.95. ISBN: 0-89490-116-8.

Although it is difficult to find a reference source for the younger readers, this book (for grades 6-12) is one such reference source. It covers such commonly used materials as benzene, formaldehyde, sulfuric acid, and xylene. Each is described as well as the procedures for handling the substances.

1572. International Handbook of Pollution Control. Eward J. Kormondy. New York, NY: Greenwood Press, 1989. 466p., bibliog., index. $95.00. ISBN: 0-313-24017-5.

This informational handbook presents discussions on how 24 countries are responding to the global problems of pollution and pollution control. Each country has its own chapter. This handbook also includes a useful list of 150 source books on pollution and pollution control.

1573. Land Planner's Environmental Handbook. William B. Honachefsky. Park Ridge, NJ: Noyes, 1991. 722p., illus., bibliog., index. $96.00. ISBN: 0-8155-1267-8.

This handbook provides technical information on the environment and covers such topics as landfilling, incineration, composting, leaking underground tanks, radon, medical waste, ocean pollution, and wildlife protection. Included are some important reprints of statistics that pertain to farmlands.

1574. Pesticide Users' Health and Safety Handbook: An International Guide. Andrew Watterson. New York, NY: Van Nostrand Reinhold, 1988. 504p., illus., bibliog., index. $78.95. ISBN: 0-442-23487-2.

This is a very useful handbook covering the many pesticides in use today. After a discussion of general characteristics of pesticides, toxicity, and methods of use, the work describes some 200 commonly used pesticides and gives name variations, regulatory controls, and recommended precautions.

1575. Red Book on Transportation of Hazardous Materials. 2nd. Lawrence W. Bierlein. New York, NY: Van Nostrand Reinhold, 1988. 1,203p., illus., index. $125.95. ISBN: 0-442-21044-2.

This is the essential guide to the regulations that govern the transport of hazardous materials. The many regulations are outlined and summarized for easy understanding. Another work that might be of interest is Gary F. Bennett's *Hazardous Materials Spills Handbook* (McGraw-Hill, 1982).

1576. Reference Guide to Clean Air. Cass R. Sandak. Hillside, NJ: Enslow, 1990. 128p., bibliog., index. $17.95. ISBN: 0-894-90261-X.

Arranged in alphabetical order by topic, this guide discusses the many environmental problems that are presently plaguing our air and atmosphere.

1577. Sax's Dangerous Properties of Industrial Materials. 8th. N. Irving Sax; Richard J. Lewis, Sr. New York, NY: Van Nostrand Reinhold, 1994(c1992). 3v. $399.95. ISBN: 0-442-01675-1.

Also known as *Sax's*, this is the Bible for information about the dangerous properties of all industrial materials. The information, given in tabular and narrative form, provides all the necessary toxicity data to determine how dangerous a particular material may be.

1578. Standard Handbook of Environmental Engineering. Robert A. Corbitt. New York, NY: McGraw-Hill, 1990. 1v., various paging, illus., bibliog., index. $89.50. ISBN: 0-07-013158-9.

This manual covers such topics as air quality control, water supply, wastewater disposal, and environmental legislation. The information is given in easy-to-read text and in numerous tables, graphs, and formulas. Although out-of-date, the 5-volume treatise-like handbook, *CRC Handbook of Environmental Control* (CRC, 1972-80) is also worth considering as a resource.

1579. Standard Handbook of Hazardous Waste Treatment and Disposal. Harry M. Freeman. New York, NY: McGraw-Hill, 1989. 1v., various paging, illus., bibliog., index. $97.50. ISBN: 0-07-022042-5.

This handbook is for those who handle waste that may contain hazardous materials. The work covers methods of handling waste, provides lists of waste disposal system vendors, and discusses the new technologies for handling waste. This is an extremely important reference work that demonstrates concern over the amount of waste currently generated in our world.

1580. Standard Methods for the Examination of Water and Wastewater: Including Bottom Sediments and Sludges. American Public Health Association; American Water Works Association; Water Pollution Control Federation. New York, NY: American Public Health Association, 1960– , irregular. 11th– , illus., index. price not available.

Previously called *Standard Methods for the Examination of Water, Sewage, and Industrial Wastes*, this is the Bible for examining all water and sludges to determine their level of contamination or cleanliness. It is kept up to date with supplements. Another useful handbook is H.H. Rump and H. Krist's *Laboratory Manual for the Examination of Water, Waste Water and Soil* (VCH, 1992).

1581. Suspect Chemicals Sourcebook: A Guide to Industrial Chemicals Covered under Major Regulatory and Advisory Programs. Kenneth Clansky. Burlingame, CA: Raytech, 1989. 1v., various paging, index. $155.00. ISSN: 0893-7036.

In this guide, some 5,000, primarily industrial, hazards are listed. The information presented is reprinted forms of federal statutes, regulations, and advisory programs. All documentation is listed. The guide is updated on a quarterly basis and is also available electronically.

1582. Toxics A to Z: A Guide to Everyday Pollution Hazards. John Harte. Berkeley, CA: University of California Press, 1991. 576p., index. $75.00; $29.95pbk. ISBN: 0-520-07223-5; 0-420-07224-3pbk.

The first part of this general reference handbook covers such topics as petrochemicals, pesticides, and toxins in the air, water, food, and in consumer products. The second part is a guide to commonly encountered toxics, including chemical elements, compounds, food colors, and laser light. Another useful book on toxicology is Philip Wexler's *Information Resources in Toxicology* (Elsevier, 1988).

1583. Water Quality and Treatment: A Handbook of Community Water Supplies. 4th. Frederick W. Pontius; American Water Works Association. New York, NY: McGraw-Hill, 1990. 1,194p., illus., bibliog., index. $89.50. ISBN: 0-07-001540-6.

Intended for any water supply manager, this handbook outlines the prodedures of maintaining water quality through the many methods of treatment. Since water quality is an increasing concern the investigator should also consult John DeZuane's *Handbook of Drinking Water Quality* (Van Nostrand Reinhold, 1990).

Histories

1584. American Environmental History: The Exploitation and Conservation of Natural Resources. 2nd. Joseph M. Petulla. New York, NY: Macmillan, 1988. 464p., illus., bibliog., index. $28.50. ISBN: 0-675-20885-8.

This is a well-written, easy-to-understand history of the environmental movement in the United States. It includes suggestions for additional reading.

Periodicals

1585. Air Pollution Control. Washington, DC: Bureau of National Affairs, 1980– , biweekly. v.1– , index. $630.00. ISSN: 0196-7150.

1586. Ambio. Lawrence, KS: Allen Press, 1972– , 8/year. v.1– , index. $170.00. ISSN: 0044-7447.

1587. Archives of Environmental Contamination and Toxicology. New York, NY: Springer-Verlag, 1972– , 8/year. v.1– , index. $469.00. ISSN: 0090-4341.

1588. Atmospheric Environment: Part A—General; Part B—Urban Atmosphere. Tarrytown, NY: Pergamon Press, 1967– , 22/year. v.1– , index. $1,776.00. ISSN: 0960-1686 A; 0957-1272 B.

1589. BNA's National Environment Watch. Washington, DC: Bureau of National Affairs, 1990– , weekly. v.1– , index. $420.00. ISSN: 1049-8893.

1590. Bulletin of Environmental Contamination and Toxicology. New York, NY: Springer-Verlag, 1966– , 12/year. v.1– , index. $338.00. ISSN: 0007-4861.

1591. Bulletin of the Ecological Society of America. Tempe, AZ: Arizona State University/Ecological Society of America, 1917– , quarterly. v.1– , index. $15.00. ISSN: 0012-9623.

1592. Chemical Regulation Reporter. Washington, DC: Bureau of National Affairs, 1977– , weekly. v.1– , index. $1,395.00. ISSN: 0148-7973.

1593. Critical Reviews in Environmental Control. Boca Raton, FL: CRC, 1970– , quarterly. v.1– , index. $225.00. ISSN: 1040-838X.

1594. Daily Environment Report. Washington, DC: Bureau of National Affairs, 1992– , daily. v.1– , index. $3,400.00. ISSN: 1060-2976.

1595. Ecological Applications. Tempe, AZ: Arizona State University/Ecological Society of America, 1991– , quarterly. v.1– , index. $60.00. ISSN: 1051-0761.

1596. Ecological Monographs. Tempe, AZ: Arizona State University/Ecological Society of America, 1931– , quarterly. v.1– , index. $60.00. ISSN: 0012-9615.

1597. Ecology. Tempe, AZ: Arizona State University/Ecological Society of America, 1920– , bimonthly. v.1– , index. $150.00. ISSN: 0012-9658.

1598. Environment International. Tarrytown, NY: Pergamon Press, 1978– , bimonthly. v.1– , index. $356.00. ISSN: 0160-4120.

1599. Environment Reporter. Washington, DC: Bureau of National Affairs, 1970– , weekly. v.1– , index. $2,180.00. ISSN: 0013-9211.

1600. Environmental Pollution. Barking, Great Britain: Elsevier, 1970– , 12/year. v.1– , index. $1,032.00. ISSN: 0269-7491.

1601. Environmental Research. San Diego, CA: Academic Press, 1967– , bimonthly. v.1– , index. $519.00. ISSN: 0013-9351.

1602. Environmental Science and Technology. Washington, DC: American Chemical Society, 1967– , monthly. v.1– , index. $395.00. ISSN: 0013-936X.

1603. Environmental Toxicology and Chemistry. Tarrytown, NY: Pergamon Press, 1982– , 12/year. v.1– , index. $415.00. ISSN: 0730-7268.

1604. Global Climate Change Digest. New York, NY: Elsevier, 1988– , monthly. v.1– , index. $325.00. ISSN: 0897-4268.

1605. Hazardous Waste and Hazardous Materials. New York, NY: Mary Ann Liebert, 1984– , quarterly. v.1– , index. $136.00. ISSN: 0882-5696.

1606. International Environmental Reporter. Washington, DC: Bureau of National Affairs, 1978– , monthly. v.1– , index. $1,405.00. ISSN: 0149-8738.

1607. Journal of Applied Toxicology. New York, NY: Wiley, 1970– , bimonthly. v.1– , index. $395.00. ISSN: 0260-437X.

1608. Journal of Chemical Ecology. New York, NY: Plenum, 1975– , monthly. v.1– , index. $575.00. ISSN: 0098-0331.

1609. Journal of Environmental Science and Health: Part A—Environmental Science and Engineering; Part B—Pesticides, Food Contaminants, and Agricultural Wastes; Part C—Environmental Carcinogenesis and Ecotoxicology Reviews. New York, NY: Dekker, 1968– , 16/year. v.1– , index. $975.00. ISSN: 0360-1226 A; 0360-1234 B; 0882-8164 C.

1610. Journal of the Air and Waste Management Association. Pittsburgh, PA: Air and Waste Management Association, 1951– , monthly. v.1– , index. $200.00. ISSN: 1047-3289.

1611. Journal of the Institute of Environmental Sciences. Mt Prospect, IL: Institute of Environmental Sciences, 1959– , bimonthly. v.1– , index. $30.00. ISSN: 1052-2883.

1612. Journal of Toxicology and Environmental Health. Bristol, PA: Hemisphere, 1975– , monthly. v.1– , index. $649.00. ISSN: 0098-4108.

1613. Radioactive Waste Management and the Nuclear Fuel Cycle. New York, NY: Harwood, 1980– , 8/year. v.1– , index. $146.00. ISSN: 0739-5876.

1614. Resources, Conservation, and Recycling. Amsterdam, Netherlands: Elsevier, 1975– , 8/year. v.1– , index. $462.00. ISSN: 0921-3449.

1615. Science of the Total Environment. Amsterdam, Netherlands: Elsevier, 1972– , 42/year. v.1– , index. $2,002.00. ISSN: 0048-9697.

1616. Toxicology. Limerick, Ireland: Elsevier, 1973– , 24/year. v.1– , index. $1,514.00. ISSN: 0300-483X.

1617. Toxicology and Applied Pharmacology. San Diego, CA: Academic Press, 1959– , monthly. v.1– , index. $690.00. ISSN: 0041-008X.

1618. Toxicology Letters. Amsterdam, Netherlands: Elsevier, 1977– , 15/year. v.1– , index. $1,071.00. ISSN: 0378-4274.

1619. Toxics Law Reporter. Washington, DC: Bureau of National Affairs, 1986– , weekly. v.1– , index. $1,150.00. ISSN: 0887-7394.

1620. Waste Management and Research. London, Great Britain: Academic Press, 1983– , bimonthly. v.1– , index. $228.00. ISSN: 0734-242X.

1621. Water, Air, and Soil Pollution. Dordrecht, Netherlands: Kluwer, 1971– , 24/year. v.1– , index. $1,173.00. ISSN: 0049-6979.

INDUSTRY AND MANUFACTURING

Dictionaries, Glossaries, and Thesauri

1622. Boiler Operator's Dictionary: A Quick Reference of Boiler Operation Terminology. L.E. LaRocque; Phil Roman. Troy, MI: Business News, 1988. 151p. $12.95. ISBN: 0-912524-41-3.

Although not an in-depth dictionary, this small pocket-size volume gives brief and clear definitions of terms associated with boilers and related areas.

1623. CAD/CAM Dictionary. Edward J. Preston; George W. Crawford; Mark E. Coticchia. New York, NY: Dekker, 1985. 210p. $79.95. ISBN: 0-8247-7524-4.

Computer Aided Design/Computer Aided Manufacturing (CAD/CAM) is the process by which computers are used to assist in creating, modifying, and displaying a design. This practical dictionary covers the terms encountered in this field.

1624. Comprehensive Dictionary of Instrumentation and Control: Reference Guides for Instrumentation and Control. W.H. Cuberly. Research Triangle Park, NC: Instrument Society of America, 1988. 352p. $59.95. ISBN: 1-55617-125-0.

This dictionary of over 9,000 terms covers instrumentation, control, and related fields, especially the use of computers in instrumentation, automatic control devices, and monitoring data collection and processing.

1625. Dictionary of Drying. New York, NY: Dekker, 1979. 350p., illus., bibliog. $110.00. ISBN: 0-8247-6652-0.

More than 4,000 terms related to all aspects of drying are included in this dictionary.

1626. Dictionary of Industrial Security. Stewart Kidd. New York, NY: Routledge & Kegan, 1987. 141p., bibliog. $45.00. ISBN: 0-7102-0794-8.

This small dictionary lists terms relating to all aspects of security including locks and locking devices.

1627. Dictionary of Robot Technology in Four Languages: English, German, French, and Russian. E. Burger; G. Korzak. New York, NY: Elsevier, 1988. 275p., index. $150.00. ISBN: 0-8288-0681-0.

Robotics is a worldwide research and development venture. This multilingual dictionary gives the English term followed by the German, French, and Russian equivalents.

1628. Dictionary of Robotics. Harry Waldman. New York, NY: Macmillan, 1985. 303p., illus. out-of-print. ISBN: 0-02-948530-4.

Although out-of-print, this dictionary covers the basic terminology of robotics. It also includes brief biographies, companies, robot names, initialisms, and spacecraft. Another still useful dictionary is David F. Tver's *Robotics Sourcebook and Dictionary* (Industrial Press, 1983).

1629. Dictionary of Terms Used in the Safety Profession. 3rd. Stanley Abercrombie. Des Plaines, IL: American Society of Safety Engineers, 1988. 72p. $25.00. ISBN: 0-939874-79-2.

This small dictionary is intended to help those involved in interpreting the codes, laws, and guidelines that pertain to safety in the workplace. An appendix of associations, institutes, societies, and governmental agencies is included.

1630. Elsevier's Dictionary of Machine Tools and Elements. Marcos F. Gutierrez. New York, NY: Elsevier, 1990. 298p., bibliog., index. $157.25. ISBN: 0-444-88697-4.

One of the typical multilingual dictionaries from Elsevier covering machine tools and their elements giving English terms with German and Spanish equivalents.

1631. Encyclopedic Dictionary of Industrial Technology: Materials Processes, and Equipment. David F. Tver; Roger W. Bolz. New York, NY: Chapman & Hall, 1984. 353p., illus., bibliog. $37.50. ISBN: 0-412-00501-8.

This small dictionary is for engineers and industrial and technical managers, covering such topics as materials, minerals, metals, machine tools, robots, and other production equipment and manufacturing processes.

1632. Industrial Engineering Terminology. revised. New York, NY: McGraw-Hill, 1991. 1v., various paging, index. $80.95. ISBN: 0-07-031730-5.

The American National Standards Institute (ANSI) is one of the highly respected standard agencies in the world. This dictionary covers ANSI Standard Z94.0 which is the terminology used in industrial engineering.

Directories

1633. Directory of Foreign Manufacturers in the United States. 4th. Atlanta, GA: Georgia State University Business Press, 1990. 437p., bibliog. $150.00. ISBN: 0-88406-219-8.

This directory gives full information about foreign manufacturers that operate in the United States.

1634. U.S. Industrial Directory. Stamford, CT: Cahners, 1975– , annual. v.1– , illus., index. $125.00. ISSN: 0095-7046.

This directory is an index to availability of industrial products in the U.S. Four volumes make up each year. The first 2 are an alphabetical listing of industrial products; the third is a literature directory and catalog file arranged by product, listing over 6,000 catalogs that are available; and the fourth volume is a telephone/address directory arranged alphabetically by manufacturer.

Encyclopedias

1635. Automation Encyclopedia: A to Z in Advanced Manufacturing. Glenn A. Graham; Robert E. King. Dearborn, MI: Society of Manufacturing Engineers, 1988. 497p., illus., bibliog. $99.00. ISBN: 0-87263-304-7.

This encyclopedia is an alphabetical listing of manufacturing terms. The definitions are brief to multi-page. Most of the terms were taken from the *Tool and Manufacturing Engineers Handbook*.

1636. Encyclopedia/Handbook of Materials, Paints, and Finishes. new revised. Henry R. Clauser. Westport, CT: Technomic, 1987 (c1976). 569p., illus., index. $29.00. ISBN: 0-87762-189-6.

Much of the material in this handbook is taken from the *Encyclopedia of Engineering Materials and Processes*. It is a good but somewhat dated work that would be useful for historical terminology.

1637. Encyclopedia of How It's Made. Donald Clarke. New York, NY: A&W Publishers, 1978. 198p., illus., index. out-of-print. ISBN: 0-89479-035-8.

This out-of-print but popular encyclopedia covers some common manufacturing processes, including glass, linoleum, paper, wire, and wine. Although the discussions are brief they give an excellent explanation for the student and general reader.

1638. Encyclopedia of Lasers and Optical Technology. Robert A. Meyers. San Diego, CA: Academic Press, 1991. 764p., illus., bibliog., index. $69.95. ISBN: 0-12-226693-5.

This general encyclopedia covers lasers including history, key information, and applications. Each article begins with a glossary followed by an introduction, discussion, review, and bibliography.

1639. International Encyclopedia of Robotics: Applications and Automation. Richard C. Dorf; Shimon Y. Nof. New York, NY: Wiley, 1988. 3v., illus., bibliog., index. $410.00. ISBN: 0-471-87868-5.

This title is one of the better encyclopedias covering robotics and its various applications. It is written for the professional but the entries are understandable for the educated layperson and student. A smaller concise edition has also been published as the *Concise International Encyclopedia of Robotics: Applications and Automation* (Wiley, 1990).

1640. Systems and Control Encyclopedia: Theory, Technology, Applications. M.G. Singh. New York, NY: Pergamon Press, 1987. 8v., illus., bibliog., index. $3,200.00. ISBN: 0-08-028709-3.

This extensive encyclopedia covers the basic theory, technology, and applications of systems and control. It is intended to present the latest information at the time of writing and covers extensively such subjects as artificial intelligence and robotics. Supplements began in 1990.

1641. Wiley Encyclopedia of Packaging Technology. Marilyn Bakker. New York, NY: Wiley, 1986. 746p., illus., bibliog., index. $135.00. ISBN: 0-471-80940-3.

This handbook covers the basics involved with packaging including related areas of recycling and labeling. The illustrations are very good.

Handbooks and Manuals

1642. AGA Gas Handbook: Properties and Uses of Industrial Gases. Kersti Ahlberg. Philadelphia, PA: Coronet Books, 1985. 582p., illus., bibliog., index. $97.50. ISBN: 91-970061-1-4.

This useful handbook covers the various uses of gases in industry. It is well-documented with good illustrations.

1643. Basic Machining Reference Handbook. Arthur R. Meyers; Thomas J. Slattery. New York, NY: Industrial Press, 1988. 281p., illus., index. $26.95. ISBN: 0-8311-1174-7.

This book covers machining operations, including cut-off processes, turning on the lathe, milling, drill presses, and grinding. Definitions and some historical notes are included. For a more detailed and comprehensive handbook on machining, consult the *Tool and Manufacturing Engineers Handbook.* Another one-volume work covering only metal cutting tools is the *Metal Cutting Tool Handbook* (Industrial Press, 1989).

1644. Computer-Integrated Manufacturing Handbook. V. Daniel Hunt. New York, NY: Chapman & Hall, 1989. 322p., bibliog., glossary, index. $57.50. ISBN: 0-412-01651-6.

This handbook provides an introduction to computer-integrated manufacturing (CIM). It is divided into four sections: System fundamentals; Application of CIM; Technology assessment; and Competiveness. Although not a true handbook, it is an excellent introductory source for managers in CIM. Another similar, newer, and useful handbook on the manufacture of integrated circuits is Robert Zorich's *Handbook of Quality Integrated Circuit Manufacturing* (Academic Press, 1991).

1645. Handbook of Expert Systems in Manufacturing. Rex Maus; Jessica Keyes. New York, NY: McGraw-Hill, 1991. 561p., illus., bibliog., index. $54.95. ISBN: 0-07-040984-6.

An expert system is supposed to clone the knowledge of a human expert but done electronically. This handbook guides the user through the development of expert systems using theory and examples as case histories.

1646. Handbook of Industrial Engineering. 2nd. Gavriel Salvendy. New York, NY: Wiley, 1992. 1v., various paging, illus., bibliog., index. $150.00. ISBN: 0-471-50276-6.

Industrial engineering is the process of how humans use resources—machines, humans, materials—to make a product or perform a service. This handbook covers all of these areas by applying the knowledge of solving real-world problems.

1647. Handbook of Industrial Robotics. Shimon Y. Nof. New York, NY: Wiley, 1985. 1,358p., illus., bibliog., index. $110.00. ISBN: 0-471-89684-5.

This comprehensive handbook covers the basics of industrial robotics, including design, social and economic aspects, and applications. Two other older handbooks that are still useful are V. Daniel Hunt's *Industrial Robotics Handbook* (Industrial Press, 1983) and Edward L. Safford's *Handbook of Advanced Robotics* (TAB Books, 1982).

1648. Handbook of Metal Forming. Kurt Lange; Klaus Pohlandt. New York, NY: McGraw-Hill, 1985. 1v., various paging, illus., bibliog., index. $112.50. ISBN: 0-07-036285-8.

If metals are not formed properly there can be failure of the equipment or structures. This handbook covers the technical aspects of metal forming that engineers need to know.

1649. Handbook of Microcomputer-Based Instrumentation and Controls. John D. Lenk. Englewood Cliffs, NJ: Prentice-Hall, 1984. 307p., illus., index. $44.00. ISBN: 0-13-380519-0.

This small handbook is intended to be a quick guide to digital or microcomputer-based instrumentation and control systems. For coverage of sensors, consult Nello Zuech's *Handbook of Intelligent Sensors for Industrial Automation* (Addison-Wesley, 1992).

1650. Handbook of Package Engineering. 2nd. Joseph F. Hanlon. New York, NY: McGraw-Hill, 1984. 1v., various paging, illus., index. $87.50. ISBN: 0-07-025994-1.

This handbook covers the materials used in packaging, giving history, properties, manufacture, and utilization of each material. Also included is information on tests, quality control, laws, and regulations.

1651. Handbook of Statistical Methods in Manufacturing. Richard B. Clements. New York, NY: Prentice-Hall, 1991. 392p., illus., bibliog., index. $49.95. ISBN: 0-13-372947-8.

This handbook lists statistical methods as they are applied to the manufacturing processes.

1652. Human Factors Design Handbook: Information and Guidelines for the Design of Systems, Facilities, Equipment and Products for Human Use. 2nd. Wesley E. Woodson; Peggy Tillman. New York, NY: McGraw-Hill, 1991. 1,056p., illus., bibliog., index. $96.50. ISBN: 0-07-071768-0.

This handbook covers all the aspects of designing systems, facilities, equipment, and products so that the human factor is considered in each case.

1653. Industrial Control Handbook. E.A. Parr. New York, NY: Industrial Press, 1987-89. 3v., illus., index. $34.95/volume. ISBN: 0-00-383097-1v.1; 0-632-01835-6v.2; 0-8311-1179-8v.3.

This useful handbook covers the uses of transducers in industry; the techniques that have been developed to make the best use of transducers; and the theory and applications of process control in general. The 3 volumes cover v.1—Transducers; v.2—Techniques; v.3—Theory and applications.

1654. Instrument Engineers' Handbook: Process Control. revised. Bela G. Liptak; Kriszta Venczel. Radnor, PA: Chilton, 1985. 1,110p., illus., bibliog., index. $75.00. ISBN: 0-8019-7290-6.

This handbook covers all areas of process instrumentation in typical handbook fashion giving an introduction to the topic, discussion, and conclusions. Another useful recently revised handbook is Douglas M. Considine's *Process/Industrial Instruments and Controls Handbook* (McGraw-Hill, 1993).

1655. Juran's Quality Control Handbook. 4th. J.M. Juran; Frank M. Gryna. New York, NY: McGraw-Hill, 1988. 1v., various paging, illus., bibliog, index. $89.50. ISBN: 0-07-033176-6.

Previously called *Quality Control Handbook*, this well-established handbook covers the important manufacturing topics of quality control, including manufacturing support activities, business processes, and the need of internal customizing.

1656. Laser Handbook. F.T. Arecchi; E.O. Schulz-Dubois. New York, NY: Elsevier, 1972– , irregular. v.1– , illus., bibliog, index. price per volume varies. ISBN: 0-444-86953-0v.6.

This comprehensive treatise-like handbook covers the latest technology in the laser industry as it is applied to all disciplines.

1657. Maintenance Engineering Handbook. 4th. Lindley R. Higgins. New York, NY: McGraw-Hill, 1988. 1v., various paging, illus., index. $92.50. ISBN: 0-07-028766-X.

This handbook covers the overall maintenance concerns of a plant engineer. It covers such areas as organization, personnel, scheduling, and budgeting.

1658. Materials Handling Handbook. 2nd. Raymond A. Kulwiec. New York, NY: Wiley, 1985. 1,458p., illus., bibliog., index. $109.95. ISBN: 0-471-09782-9.

Sponsored by the American Society of Mechanical Engineers and the International Material Management Society, this handbook covers all aspects of unit and bulk materials handling including transportation and safety. Also of interest are two management handbooks: T.H. Allegri's *Materials Management Handbook* (TAB, 1991) and Peter Bailey's *Materials Management Handbook* (State Mutual Books, 1989).

1659. Maynard's Industrial Engineering Handbook. 4th. Harold Bright Maynard; William K. Hodson. New York, NY: McGraw-Hill, 1992. 1v., various paging, illus., bibliog., index. $99.50. ISBN: 0-07-041086-0.

This well-known handbook provides basic as well as specific information for industrial engineers. It includes not only the traditional methods and systems but also the new computerized technologies.

1660. Microelectronic Packaging Handbook.
Rao R. Tummala; Eugene J. Rymaszewski.
New York, NY: Van Nostrand Reinhold, 1989.
1,194p., illus., bibliog., index. $104.95. ISBN:
0-442-20578-3.

This handbook covers the science of microelectronics as it pertains to packaging. The *Handbook of Electronics Packaging Design and Engineering* (Van Nostrand Reinhold, 1990) is also a useful companion to this handbook.

1661. Piping Design Handbook. John J.
McKetta. New York, NY: Dekker, 1992.
1,216p., illus., index. $195.00. ISBN:
0-8247-8570-3.

Material for this book was taken from the *Encyclopedia of Chemical Processing and Design* (Dekker, 1976-91). It brings together information on the principles of piping design, pipeline construction, rules of thumb for piping engineers, operation and maintenance, and economics and costs. Two other useful handbook are R.H. Warring's *Handbook of Valves, Piping, and Pipelines* (Gulf Publishing, 1982) and Mohinder L. Nayyar's *Piping Handbook* (McGraw-Hill, 1992).

1662. Plastic Blow Molding Handbook. C.
Lee Norman. New York, NY: Van Nostrand
Reinhold, 1990. 560p., illus., bibliog., index.
$85.95. ISBN: 0-442-20752-2.

Sponsored by the Society of Plastics Engineers, this specialized handbook covers the processes needed in plastic blow moldings, which are used in packaging.

1663. Production Handbook. 4th. John A.
White. New York, NY: Wiley, 1987. 1,008p.,
illus., bibliog., index. $95.00. ISBN:
0-471-86347-5.

The production side of manufacturing is emphasized in this handbook. It covers manpower, methods, machines, materials, moving, space, and systems.

1664. Standard Handbook of Plant Engineering. Robert C. Rosaler; James O. Rice. New
York, NY: McGraw-Hill, 1983. 1v., various
paging, illus., bibliog., index. $114.50. ISBN:
0-07-052160-3.

This handbook covers the complex management of any plant and how to make it operate smoothly and efficiently. It covers the traditional rather than the new automation technologies. Another related book covering quality control is Allan I. Young's *Complete Plant Operations Handbook: A Guide to Cost Reduction, Quality Control, and On-Time Delivery* (Prentice-Hall, 1990).

1665. Stationary Engineering Handbook.
K.L. Petrocelly. Lilburn, GA: Fairmont Press.
259p., illus., index, glossary. $58.00. ISBN:
0-88173-078-5.

Stationary engineering is that field interested in the operation of power plants. This handbook is intended to be an instructional guide for persons who operate power plants, covering the maintenance aspects and repairs of the engines, as well as the use of public emergency services.

**1666. TAB Handbook of Hand and Power
Tools.** Rudolf F. Graf; George J. Whalen. Blue
Ridge Summit, PA: TAB, 1984. 501p., illus.,
index. $26.95; $16.95pbk. ISBN:
0-8306-0638-6; 0-8306-1638-1pbk.

This practical guide covers hand tools and power tools. It lists each kind and gives a description with numerous illustrations. Hand tools covered include tools used for masonry, carpentry, and automobile maintenance. Some 40 power tools are described including drills, saws, vacuum cleaners, and lawn mowers.

**1667. Tool and Manufacturing Engineers
Handbook: A Reference Book for Manufacturing Engineers, Managers and Technicians.**
4th. Thomas J. Drozda; Charles Wick.
Dearborn, MI: Society of Manufacturing
Engineers, 1983-88. 5v., illus., bibliog., index.
$115.00/volume. ISBN: 0-87263-085-4v.1.

This well-established handbook is a unique compilation of practical data covering the specifications and uses of modern manufacturing equipment and processes. The 5 volumes cover v.1—Machining; v.2—Forming; v.3—Materials, finishing and coating; v.4—Quality control and assembly; v.5—Manufacturing management.

1668. Welding Handbook. 8th. R.L. O'Brien.
Miami, FL: American Welding Society, 1991.
3v., illus., bibliog., index. price not available.

This 3-volume handbook is the welding Bible. It covers standards, specifications, processes, and equipment. Welding safety is stressed. New editions are published on a regular basis. The 8th edition has condensed the material from 5 volumes into 3. Another useful, less comprehensive handbook covering the same material is the *Science and Practice of Welding* (Cambridge University Press, 1989).

Tables

**1669. Nomograms for Steam Generation and
Utilization.** V. Ganapathy. New York, NY:
Van Nostrand Reinhold, 1985. 176p., illus.,
bibliog., index. $54.95. ISBN: 0-442-23731-6.

This title is a collection of charts, nomograms, and short articles related to fuels, combustion, heat transfer, boilers, heat recovery, energy conservation, life cycle costing, and equipment sizing.

1670. Plant Engineer's Handbook of Formulas, Charts, Tables. 3rd. Donald W. Moffat. New York, NY: Prentice Hall, 1991. 561p., illus., bibliog., index. $57.95. ISBN: 0-13-680298-2.

This comprehensive handbook contains charts, formulas, tables, and other tabular data that can be used on a day-to-day basis by any plant engineer. It has became a standard handbook of tables.

Yearbooks, Annuals, and Almanacs

1671. World Yearbook of Robotics and CIM Research and Development. London, Great Britain: Kogan Page, 1985– , annual. v.1– , index. $80.00.

This yearbook is based in part on the *International Robotics Yearbook* and was previously called the *World Yearbook of Robotic Research and Development*. It is intended to present a review of advancement in robotics technology throughout the world. The key part is the section on robotics research and development activities which lists for each country the areas of interest in robotics.

Periodicals

1672. Design News. Newton, MA: Cahners, 1946– , 24/year. v.1– , index. $94.95. ISSN: 0011-9407.

1673. IIE Transactions. Norcross, GA: Industrial Engineering and Management Press/Institute of Industrial Engineers, 1969– , quarterly. v.1– , index. $75.00. ISSN: 0569-5554.

1674. Industrial Engineering. Norcross, GA: Institute of Industrial Engineers, 1969– , monthly. v.1– , index. $47.50. ISSN: 0019-8234.

1675. Integrated Manufacturing Systems. Bradford, Great Britain: MCB University Press, 1985– , quarterly. v.1– , index. $329.95. ISSN: 0957-6061.

1676. International Journal of Machine Tools and Manufactures. Tarrytown, NY: Pergamon Press, 1961– , 6/year. v.1– , index. $456.00. ISSN: 0890-6955.

1677. Machinery and Production Engineering. Horton Kirby, Great Britain: Findlay Publications, 1912– , semimonthly. v.1– , index. free. ISSN: 0024-919X.

1678. Manufacturing Review. Fairfield, NJ: American Society of Mechanical Engineers, 1988– , quarterly. v.1– , index. $100.00. ISSN: 0896-1611.

1679. Material Handling Engineering. Cleveland, OH: Penton, 1945– , monthly. v.1– , index. $45.00. ISSN: 0025-5262.

1680. Modern Materials Handling. Newton, MA: Cahners, 1946– , 14/year. v.1– , index. $74.95. ISSN: 0026-8038.

1681. Tooling and Production. Solon, OH: Huebcore Communications, 1934– , monthly. v.1– , index. $90.00. ISSN: 0040-9243.

MECHANICAL ENGINEERING

Abstracts and Indexes

1682. Applied Mechanics Reviews. New York, NY: American Society of Mechanical Engineers, 1948– , monthly. v.1– , index. $360.00. ISSN: 0003-6900.

This comprehensive journal reviews literature pertaining to mechanical engineering. Each issue contains 2 or 3 feature articles, book reviews and notes, and a review of the journal literature. All reviews are fully annotated. Occasionally part of an issue reprints the proceedings of a conference.

1683. Fluid Flow Measurement Abstracts. Oxford, Great Britain: STI, 1974– , quarterly. v.1– , index. $250.00. ISSN: 0305-9235.

This specialized abstracting service covers information on the measurement of flow and other parameters and the physical properties of gas.

Bibliographies

1684. Bibliography on the Fatigue of Materials, Components, and Structures. J.Y. Mann. New York, NY: Pergamon Press, 1970-1990. 4v., index. price per volume varies. ISBN: 0-08-040507-X v.4.

This chronologically arranged bibliography lists sources on the fatigue of materials, components, and structures. The 4 volumes cover the years: v.1—1838-1950; v.2—1951-1960; v.3—1961-1965; v.4—1966-1969.

Biographical Sources

1685. Mechanical Engineers in America Born Prior to 1861: A Biographical Dictionary. American Society of Mechanical Engineers. New York, NY: American Society of Mechanical Engineers, 1980. 330p., portraits, bibliog., index. price not available.

Some 500 biographies are included in this historical reference work. Fifty of the entries have portraits. Information has been noted from other comprehensive sources. Biographies include personal as well as professional activities.

Dictionaries, Glossaries, and Thesauri

1686. Dictionary of Mechanical Engineering. 3rd. G.H.F. Nayler. Boston, MA: Butterworth-Heinemann, 1985. 394p. $80.00. ISBN: 0-408-01505-5.

Although not a comprehensive dictionary this one covers terms associated with moving parts and machines plus some power-related terminology. Also useful would be the *Dictionary of Mechanical and Design Engineering* (McGraw-Hill, 1985).

1687. Illustrated Dictionary of Mechanical Engineering: English, German, French, Dutch, Russian. Vladimir V. Schwartz. Boston, MA: Nijhoff, 1984. 416p., illus., index. $99.50. ISBN: 90-201-1668-1.

This unique multilingual dictionary is arranged by broad topics with subterms following in alphabetical order by English term and then German, French, Dutch, and Russian equivalents. Most all terms are illustrated with a line drawing or equation. There are indexes for each of the languages referring to the English equivalent. Another recently published dictionary is Hans-Dieter Junge's *Dictionary of Machine Tools and Mechanical Engineering: English/German* (VCH, 1992).

1688. McGraw-Hill Dictionary of Mechanical and Design Engineering. Sybil P. Parker. New York, NY: McGraw-Hill, 1984. 387p., illus. $15.95. ISBN: 0-07-045414-0.

This spin-off from the *McGraw-Hill Dictionary of Scientific and Technical Terms* covers aerospace engineering, control systems, mechanisms, thermodynamics, and fluid mechanics.

Encyclopedias

1689. Encyclopedia of Fluid Mechanics. Nicholas P. Cheremisinoff. Houston, TX: Gulf Publishing, 1986-1990. 10v., bibliog., index. $195.00/volume. ISBN: 0-87201-513-0v.1.

This comprehensive treatise-type encyclopedia covers all areas of fluid mechanics. The 10 volumes cover v.1—Flow phenomena and measurement; v.2—Dynamics of single-fluid flows and mixing; v.3—Gas-liquid flows; v.4—Solids and gas-solids flows; v.5—Slurry flow technology; v.6—Complex flow phenomena and modeling; v.7—Rheology and non-Newtonian flows; v.8—Aerodynamics and compressible flow; v.9—Polymer flow engineering; v.10—Surface and groundwater flow phenomena.

Handbooks and Manuals

1690. ASHRAE Handbook. Atlanta, GA: American Society of Heating, Refrigeration, and Air-Conditioning Engineers, 1922– , annual. v.1– , illus, bibliog., index. $109.00/volume. ISSN: 1041-2344.

This comprehensive compilation lists data pertaining to the air conditioning, heating, ventilating, and refrigeration fields. There are four volumes to a set with each volume published in a different year, and updates to a particular volume are occasionally published in another volume. It is the standard reference source for these industries. The 4 volumes cover Equipment; Fundamentals; Heating, Ventilating, and Air-Conditioning Systems and Applications; Refrigeration Systems and Applications. It had various previous titles: *ASHRAE Handbook and Product Specification File*; *ASHRAE Handbook and Product Directory*; *ASHRAE Handbook of Fundamentals*; and *ASHRAE Guide and Data Book*.

1691. Diesel Engine Reference Book. Boston, MA: Butterworths, 1984. 1v., various paging, illus., bibliog., index. price not available. ISBN: 0-408-00443-6.

This handbook covers diesel engines manufactured in Europe, U.S., and Japan. The major areas covered include theory, design practice, lubrication, environmental pollution, crankcase explosions, engine types, testing, and maintenance. Numerous photographs, charts, and diagrams are included.

1692. Fatigue Design Handbook. 2nd. Richard C. Rice; Brian N. Leis; Drew W. Nelson. New York, NY: McGraw-Hill, 1990. 369p., illus., bibliog., index. $89.00. ISBN: 0-89883-011-7.

The purpose of this handbook is to describe "the major elements of the fatigue-design process and how those elements must be tied together in a comprehensive product evaluation." It emphasizes current technologies and procedures.

1693. Flow Measurement Engineering Handbook. 2nd. R.W. Miller. New York, NY: McGraw-Hill, 1989. 1v., various paging, illus., bibliog., index. $87.50. ISBN: 0-07-042046-7.

This handbook is a single source of information on selective criteria, installation practices, and computational equations for flow meters. Emphasis is on the most widely used flowmeter: the square-edged-orifice flowmeter. For a small pocket book consult Nicholas P. Cheremisinoff's *Fluid Flow Pocket Handbook* (Gulf, 1984).

1694. Fluid Mechanics Source Book. New York, NY: McGraw-Hill, 1988. 274p., illus., index. $48.00. ISBN: 0-07-045502-3.

This sourcebook of information covers such topics as fluid statics, fluid flow, and fluid dynamics. All information is reprinted from the 6th edition of the *McGraw-Hill Encyclopedia of Science and Technology*.

1695. Fluid Power Design Handbook. 2nd revised and expanded. *(Fluid Power and Control, 10).* Franklin D. Yeaple. New York, NY: Dekker, 1990. 769p., illus., index. price not available. ISBN: 0-8247-7949-5.

This comprehensive handbook covers the field of hydraulics. It covers hydraulic cylinders and motors with information on electronic analog and digital control, microprocessors, and computer-aided design. Another older but useful work is Robert D. Blevins' *Applied Fluid Dynamics Handbook* (Van Nostrand Reinhold, 1984). Also, John S. Gulliver's *Hydropower Engineering Handbook* (McGraw-Hill, 1991) should be considered.

1696. Gear Handbook. Alec Stokes. Boston, MA: Butterworth-Heinemann, 1992. 256p., illus., index. $95.00. ISBN: 0-7506-1149-9.

This comprehensive handbook covers all types of gears, including spur, helical, straight bevel, spiral bevel, zero bevel, hypoid, and worm. Also of use is the *Dudley's Gear Handbook* (McGraw-Hill, 1991).

1697. Handbook of Measurement Science. P.H. Sydenham. New York, NY: Wiley, 1982-83. 2v., illus., bibliog., index. $146.00v.1; $176.00v.2. ISBN: 0-471-10037-4v.1; 0-471-10493-0v.2.

This handbook provides the basic fundamentals of design of measurement that have endured over the years. It is an essential handbook for anyone working in instrumentation. The 2 volumes cover theory in volume 1 and actual practice in volume 2.

1698. Handbook of Mechanics, Materials, and Structures. Alexander Blake. New York, NY: Wiley, 1985. 710p., illus., bibliog., index. $87.95. ISBN: 0-471-86239-8.

This general handbook gives basic mechanical engineering information along with data on materials and structures.

1699. Handbook of Practical Gear Design. Darle W. Dudley. New York, NY: McGraw-Hill, 1984. 1v., various paging, illus., bibliog., index. $82.50. ISBN: 0-07-017951-4.

Previously called *Practical Gear Design*, this highly specialized handbook covers the design and manufacture of all types of gears and the tools needed to make the gears. It is the most authoritative work available on the topic.

1700. Handbook of Tribology. Bharat Bhushan; Balkishan K. Gupta. New York, NY: McGraw-Hill, 1991. 1v., various paging, illus., bibliog., index. $92.50. ISBN: 0-07-005249-2.

What is destined to be a standard handbook on lubrication, this typical McGraw-Hill work is comprehensive, covering all aspects of friction, wear, and lubrication. Another older but useful work is Richard Booser's *CRC Handbook of Lubrication* (CRC, 1984).

1701. Machinery's Handbook: A Reference Book for the Mechanical Engineer, Designer, Manufacturing Engineer, Draftsman, Toolmaker, and Machinist. 23rd. New York, NY: Industrial Press, 1988. 2,511p., illus., index. $55.00. ISBN: 0-8311-1200-X.

Previously called *Handbook for Machine Shop and Drafting-Room*, this work covers such topics as tooling and toolmaking, machinery operation, manufacturing processes, fasteners, threads, gearing, bearings, and measuring units. It stresses metal-working industries and tool design. There is a companion guide that helps one understand the handbook: *Machinery's Handbook Practical Companion: Machinery's Handbook Guide* (Industrial Press, 1988).

1702. Marks' Standard Handbook for Mechanical Engineers. 9th. Lionel S. Marks. New York, NY: McGraw-Hill, 1987. 1v., various paging, illus., bibliog., index. $104.50. ISBN: 0-07-004127-X.

Previously called *Standard Handbook for Mechanical Engineers*, this work is a classic in mechanical engineering handbooks. It covers the traditional areas such as shop processes, fuels, furnaces, and welding as well as the modern technologies of environmental control and automation. See also *Mechanical Engineer's Handbook*. This could be considered the replacement of the *ASME Handbook* last published in 1965 by McGraw-Hill.

1703. Mechanical Design and Systems Handbook. 2nd. Harold A. Rothbart. New York, NY: McGraw-Hill, 1985. 1v., various paging, illus., bibliog., index. $124.50. ISBN: 0-07-054020-9.

Partially republished as *Mechanical Engineering Essentials Reference Guide* (1988), this handbook covers the fundamentals of mechanical engineering, system analysis, design, fastener components, and power-controlled components. Special emphasis is given to computer-aided design. Also useful is Joseph E. Shigley's *Standard Handbook of Machine Design* (McGraw-Hill, 1986).

1704. Mechanical Engineer's Handbook.
Myer Kutz. New York, NY: Wiley, 1986.
2,316p., illus., bibliog., index. $95.00. ISBN:
0-471-08817-X.

In 2 parts: Design and Production and Power, this
and *Mark's Standard Handbook for Mechanical Engineers* are the two most important handbooks available
in this discipline. The handbook covers digital computers, materials, design, manufacturing, systems, controls, instrumentation, management, research, energy,
and power. Another handbook for technicians is M.J.
Webb's *Mechanical Technician's Handbook*
(McGraw-Hill, 1983).

**1705. Mechanisms and Mechanical Devices
Sourcebook.** Nicholas P. Chironis. New York,
NY: McGraw-Hill, 1991. 447p., illus., index.
$57.95. ISBN: 0-07-010918-4.

This handbook covers modern mechanisms, classical linkages, and machinery devices that provide a
wide variety of motions and functions. It gives information on how mechanical components can be combined with electrical, hydraulic, pneumatic, optical,
thermal, and photoelectric devices to perform complex
tasks. Two other similar and useful works are Ichiro
Kato's *Mechanical Hands Illustrated* (Hemisphere,
1987) and Robert O. Parmley's *Mechanical Components Handbook* (McGraw-Hill, 1985).

1706. Pressure Vessel Design Handbook.
2nd. Henry H. Bednar. Melbourne, FL:
Krieger, 1991. 431p., illus., bibliog., index.
$56.50. ISBN: 0-89464-503-X.

All pressure vessels are designed according to specific codes for safety. This handbook aids those who
are designing pressure vessels. Numerous examples of
worked solutions are presented. A working knowledge
is assumed of the *ASME Boiler and Pressure Code*,
which is the accepted code that is used in design
applications.

1707. Pump Handbook. 2nd. Igor J. Karassik;
William C. Krutzch. New York, NY:
McGraw-Hill, 1986. 1v., various paging, illus.,
bibliog., index. $102.50. ISBN:
0-07-033302-5.

All types of pumps are described in this handbook
including centrifuge, power, steam, screw, rotary, and
jet. It also covers such things as couplings, controls and
valves plus all the instrumentation that makes a pump
work properly. A smaller, older, but still useful work
is Raymond P. Lambeck's *Hydraulic Pumps and Motors: Selection and Application for Hydraulic Power
Control Systems* (Dekker, 1983).

1708. Shock and Vibration Handbook. 3rd.
Cyril M. Harris. New York, NY: McGraw-Hill,
1988. 1v., various paging, illus., bibliog.,
index. $92.50. ISBN: 0-07-026801-0.

This comprehensive handbook covers the mechanics of shock and vibration as it is applied to machines.

Detailed charts, diagrams, and illustrations along with
extensive bibliographies make this a useful handbook.

1709. Spring Designer's Handbook. Harold
Carlson. New York, NY: Dekker, 1978. 350p.,
illus., index. $99.75. ISBN: 0-8247-6623-7.

Although a 1978 work, this is the standard handbook for the design of springs. With current robotic
technology, springs are essential in all mechanical
devices.

**1710. Standard Application of Mechanical
Details.** Jerome F. Mueller. New York, NY:
McGraw-Hill, 1985. 331p., illus., index.
$49.95. ISBN: 0-07-043962-1.

This handbook presents accepted methods for installing equipment that an engineer specifies. It presents theory that can be used with common sense to
solve engineering installation problems. It covers heating, air conditioning, refrigeration, water source,
wastewater, energy conservation, control systems, and
emergency power.

**1711. Standard Handbook of Fastening and
Joining.** 2nd. Robert O. Parmley. New York,
NY: McGraw-Hill, 1989. 1v., various paging,
illus., bibliog., index. $69.50. ISBN:
0-07-048522-4.

Fastening and joining are vital in any mechanical
engineer's work. This authoritative work covers such
areas as threaded fasteners, standard pins, retaining
rings, concrete fastening, wire, rope, and cable as well
as areas of timber, welding, and adhesive bonding.

**1712. Structural Engineering and Applied
Mechanics Data Handbook.** Teng H. Hsu.
Houston, TX: Gulf Publishing, 1988-90. 3v.,
illus., bibliog., index. $75.00/volume. ISBN:
0-87201-335-9v.3.

This comprehensive and technical handbook covers all aspects of structural engineering, giving useful
data on how to determine the mechanical behavior of
beams and frames. It is presented in the form of cases
that have been fully described with all calculations
worked out. The 3 volumes cover: v.1—Beams; v.2—
Frames; v.3—Plates. For a one-volume concise coverage of structural engineering, consult Edwin H. Gaylord Jr.'s *Structural Engineering Handbook* (McGraw-Hill, 1990).

Histories

1713. History of Mechanics. Rene Dugas.
New York, NY: Central Book, 1988 (c1955).
671p., illus., index. $14.95. ISBN:
0-486-65632-2.

This classic book on the history of mechanics covers the topic from earliest times to the turn of the 20th
century. For just a history of mechanics in the middle
ages consult Marshall Clagett's *Science of Mechanics*

in the Middle Ages (University of Wisconsin Press, 1959).

1714. History of Tribology. D. Dowson. Ann Arbor, MI: Books on Demand, 1979. 677p., illus., bibliog., index. 180.00. ISBN: 0-8357-2992-3.

This excellent history covers lubrication from prehistoric times to the present.

Periodicals

1715. Acta Mechanica. Berlin, Germany: Springer-Verlag, 1965– , 20/year. v.1– , index. $1,035.00. ISSN: 0001-5970.

1716. European Journal of Mechanical Engineering. Amsterdam, Netherlands: Elsevier/Belgian Society of Mechanical Engineers, 1954– , quarterly. v.1– , index. $165.00. ISSN: 0777-2734.

1717. International Journal of Heat and Mass Transfer. Tarrytown, NY: Pergamon Press, 1960– , 12/year. v.1– , index. $1,448.00. ISSN: 0017-9310.

1718. Machine Design. Cleveland, OH: Penton, 1929– , 28/year. v.1– , index. $100.00. ISSN: 0024-9114.

1719. Mechanical Engineering. New York, NY: American Society of Mechanical Engineers, 1906– , monthly. v.1– ,index. $45.00. ISSN: 0025-6501.

1720. Numerical Heat Transfer: Part A—Applications; Part B—Fundamentals. Bristol, PA: Hemisphere, 1978– , 12/year. v.1– , index. $530.00 part A; $220.00 part B. ISSN: 1040-7782 part A; 1040-7790 part B.

1721. Power. New York, NY: McGraw-Hill, 1882– , monthly. v.1– , index. $50.00. ISSN: 0032-5929.

1722. Proceedings of the Institution of Mechanical Engineers. Bury St Edmund, Great Britain: Mechanical Engineering Publications, 1983-. v.1– , index. $1,420.00 A-H.

Consists of the following 8 parts: A—*Journal of Power and Energy* (quarterly, $220.00, 0263-7138); B—*Journal of Engineering Manufacture* (quarterly, $220.00, 0954-4054); C—*Journal of Mechanical Engineering Science* (6/year, $288.00, 0263-7154); D—*Journal of Automobile Engineering* (quarterly, $220.00, 0954-4070); E—*Journal of Process Mechanical Engineering* (2/year, $114.00, 0954-4089); F—*Journal of Rail and Rapid Transit* (2/year, $129.00, 0954-4097); G—*Journal of Aerospace Engi-*

neering (2/year, $129.00, 0954-4100); H—*Journal of Engineering in Medicine* (quarterly, $220.00, 0954-4119).

1723. Transactions of the American Society of Mechanical Engineers. New York, NY: American Society of Mechanical Engineers, 1935– , quarterly per section. v.1– , index.

Consists of 16 sections: *Journal of Applied Mechanics* ($120.00, 0021-8936); *Journal of Biomechanical Engineering* ($100.00, 0148-0731); *Journal of Dynamic Systems, Measurement and Control* ($100.00, 0022-0434); *Journal of Energy Resources Technology* ($100.00, 0195-0738); *Journal of Engineering for Gas Turbines and Power* ($100.00, 0742-4795); *Journal of Engineering for Industry* ($100.00, 0022-0817); *Journal of Engineering Materials and Technology* ($100.00, 0094-4289); *Journal of Fluids Engineering* ($100.00, 0098-2202); *Journal of Heat Transfer* ($100.00, 0022-1481); *Journal of Mechanical Design* ($100.00, 1050-0472); *Journal of Offshore Mechanics and Arctic Engineering* ($100.00, 0892-7219); *Journal of Pressure Vessel Technology* ($100.00, 0094-9930); *Journal of Solar Energy Engineering* ($100.00, 0199-6231); *Journal of Tribology* ($120.00, 0742-4787); *Journal of Turbomachinery* ($100.00, 0889-504X); *Journal of Vibration and Acoustics* ($100.00, 1048-9002).

1724. Wear. Lausanne, Switzerland: Elsevier, 1958– , 20/year. v.1– , index. $2,210.00. ISSN: 0043-1648.

TRANSPORTATION

Abstracts and Indexes

1725. Highway Research Abstracts. Washington, DC: Highway Research Information Council, 1968– , quarterly. v.1– , index. $85.00.

Previously called *HRIS Abstracts* and *Transportation Research Abstracts*, this service abstracts reports and journal articles that are related to highway research. It is also available online.

1726. International Aerospace Abstracts. New York, NY: American Institute of Aeronautics and Astronautics, 1961– , semimonthly. v.1– , index. $1,050.00. ISSN: 0020-5842.

This title provides abstracts of papers and articles on aerospace and astronautics. It should be used in conjunction with the *Scientific and Technical Aerospace Abstracts (STAR)* which covers technical reports. It is available online and on CD-ROM.

1727. Scientific and Technical Aerospace Abstracts (STAR). Baltimore, MD: NASA, 1963– , semimonthly. v.1– , index. $185.00. ISSN: 0036-8741.

This is the main source for areas of aerospace research conducted by NASA. The material is fully identified and abstracted with availability indicated. Indexes cover all areas from subject and author to report number. There is also an online service available.

1728. Urban Transportation Abstracts. Washington, DC: National Research Council, 1982– , annual. v.1– , index. $65.00. ISSN: 0734-0648.

This work abstracts research reports, technical papers, periodical articles, and other materials that pertain to urban transportation and public transit. The Urban Mass Transportation Institute also publishes another work called *Urban Mass Transportation Abstracts*.

Atlases

1729. Railways Atlas of the World. Short Hill, NJ: Railway Atlas, 1982. 1v., various paging, maps. $23.00.

This general atlas shows the major railways of the world. For those just in the United States consult the *Railroad Atlas of the U.S.* (Rand McNally, 1988).

Bibliographies

1730. Airline Bibliography: The Salem College Guide to Sources on Commercial Aviation. Myron J. Smith, Jr. West Cornwall, CT: Locust Hill Press, 1986-88. 2v., illus., index. price not available. ISBN: 0-933951-13-2.

This excellent bibliography of historical aviation materials covers in volume 1—United States and in volume 2—Foreign. Each volume is arranged by broad topics and then by author. Historical notes and narrative are included.

1731. Information Sources in Transportation, Material Management, and Physical Distribution: An Annotated Bibliography and Guide. Bob J. Davis. Westport, CT: Greenwood Press, 1976. 715p., index. out-of-print. ISBN: 0-8371-8379-0.

Now out-of-print, this excellent bibliography contains background information on transportation, materials management, and physical distribution. It covers books, government materials, organizations, educational materials, statistical publications, and atlases and maps. All entries are annotated.

1732. Motorcycle Books: A Critical Survey and Checklist. Kirby Congdon. Metuchen, NJ: Scarecrow, 1987. 135p. $16.00. ISBN: 0-8108-1985-6.

This publication is a good source for books on motorcycles and motorcycling with 117 titles fully annotated plus an addition listing of 522 catalogs and handbooks that cover over 48 brands of motorcycles.

1733. Rural Transport and Planning: A Bibliography with Abstracts. David Banister. New York, NY: Mansell, 1985. 448p., bibliog., index. price not available. ISBN: 0-7201-1692-9.

This international bibliography focuses on the rural environmaient of transportation. It is arranged into 6 broad categories—context, policy and planning, accessibility and mobility, modes, methods and evaluations, and area-based studies.

Biographical Sources

1734. Men of Space: Profiles of the Leaders in Space Research, Development and Exploration. Shirley Thomas. Philadelphia, PA: Chilton Books, 1960-65. 7v., illus., bibliog., index. out-of-print.

This biographical set covers prominent individuals who have been instrumental in space technology, including the legal, institutional, and economic aspects. Sixty-six biographies are included in the 7 volumes.

1735. Who's Who in Space: The First 25 Years. Michael Cassutt. Boston, MA: G.K. Hall, 1987. 311p., portraits, index. price not available. ISBN: 0-8161-8801-7.

Detailed biographies of astronauts with portraits are included in this biographical source. Arranged in three sections—American, Soviet, and International. It includes the crew of the *Challenger*.

Dictionaries, Glossaries, and Thesauri

1736. Automotive Reference: A New Approach to the World of Auto/Related Information. G.J. Davis. Boise, ID: Whitehorse, 1987. 460p. ISBN: 0-937591-01-7; 0-937591-00-9pbk.

Automotive Reference is a good dictionary of terms and phrases associated with the automotive industry. It is unique in that common words are listed for easy access. Another source is John Dinkel's *Road and Track Illustrated Dictionary* (Norton, 1981, c1977).

1737. Aviation/Space Dictionary. 7th. Larry Reithmaier. Blue Ridge Summit, PA: TAB, 1990. 461p., illus. price not available. ISBN: 0-8306-8092-6.

Previously called *Aviation and Space Dictionary*, this is a good dictionary of terms associated with all areas of aviation and flying plus the new age terms in space flight.

1738. Chambers Air and Space Dictionary.
P.M.B. Walker; J.E. Allen; D.J. Shapland. Edinburgh, Great Britain: Chambers, 1990. 215p., illus. $25.00. ISBN: 0-550-13243-0.

This dictionary lists some 6,000 terms in aeronautics, astronomy, meteorology, space, and radar plus associated terms for acoustics, physics, telecommunications, and engineering. It was also published by Cambridge University Press as the *Cambridge Air and Space Dictionary*.

1739. Complete Multilingual Dictionary of Aviation and Aeronautical Terminology: English, French, Spanish. Henri Demaison.
Lincolnwood, IL: Passport Books, 1984. 671p. $75.00. ISBN: 0-844291-06-4.

This standard multilingual dictionary is arranged by English term with corresponding terms in French and Spanish.

1740. Dictionary of Automotive Engineering.
Hans-Dieter Junge. New York, NY: VCH, 1991. 388p. $84.00. ISBN: 0-89573-988-7.

This bilingual dictionary defines automotive terminology in English and German.

1741. Dictionary of Marine Technology.
D.A. Taylor. Boston, MA: Butterworths, 1989. 244p., illus., tables, charts. $105.00. ISBN: 0-408-02195-0.

This dictionary lists terms pertaining to marine and offshore engineering, naval architecture, shipbuilding, shipping, and ship operation. It basically updates G.O. Watson's *Dictionary of Marine Engineering and Nautical Terms* (Newnes, 1965). Also of use would be John V. Noel Jr.'s *VNR Dictionary of Ships and the Sea* (Van Nostrand Reinhold, 1981).

1742. Dictionary of Space Technology. Mark
Williamson. New York, NY: A. Hilger, 1990. 401p., illus. $50.00. ISBN: 0-85274-339-4.

This dictionary contains terms pertaining to space engineering and related scientific and engineering disciplines.

1743. Elsevier's Dictionary of Ports and Shipping: In English, French, Spanish, Italian, Portuguese, Dutch and German. J.D. Van der
Turin; D.L. Newman. New York, NY: Elsevier, 1993. 368p., index. $203.00. ISBN: 0-444-89542-6.

This multilingual dictionary has some 2,655 terms covering both the economic and engineering aspects of ports, waterways, and shipping. Where appropriate short explanations have been added.

1744. Glossary of Automotive Terms.
Warrendale, PA: Society of Automotive Engineers, 1988. 609p. $54.00. ISBN: 0-89883-677-8.

This glossary lists some 10,500 terms that are contained in the *SAE Handbook*. Reference is made to the handbook for each term. A smaller SAE dictionary that does not refer the reader to the handbook is Don Goodsell's *Dictionary of Automotive Engineering* (SAE, 1989). For an English-French-German dictionary consult Jean de Coster's *Dictionary for Automotive Engineering* (Saur, 1982).

1745. Jane's Aerospace Dictionary. 3rd. Bill
Gunston. Alexandria, VA: Jane's, 1988. 605p. $39.95. ISBN: 0-706-0580-3.

This comprehensive dictionary covers aerospace-related terms including acronyms and abbreviations with brief definitions. Some biographical information is included.

1746. Naval Terms Dictionary. 5th. John V.
Noel, Jr.; Edward L. Beach. Annapolis, MD: Naval Institute Press, 1988. 316p. $21.95. ISBN: 0-87021-571-X.

This dictionary lists naval and naval-related terms in current usage. Acronyms are not included except those that are common. For acronyms consult Bill Wedertz's *Dictionary of Naval Abbreviations* (Naval Institute Press, 1984). For an in-depth historical dictionary of maritime terms consult Rene de Kerchove's *International Maritime Dictionary* (Van Nostrand Reinhold, 1983 c1961). Also of use but somewhat dated is Joseph Palmer's *Jane's Dictionary of Naval Terms* (Jane's, 1975).

1747. Norton Encyclopedic Dictionary of Navigation. David F. Tver. New York, NY:
Norton, 1987. 283p., illus. $19.95. ISBN: 0-393-02406-7.

This dictionary contains currently used navigational terms with definitions in navigation jargon. It covers navigation, weather, navigational stars, and navigational alphabet.

1748. Railway Age's Comprehensive Railroad Dictionary. Robert G. Lewis. Omaha, NE:
Simmons-Boardman Books, 1984. 160p. $17.95. ISBN: 0-911382-00-3.

This title is a good dictionary of terms pertaining to railroading including communications, signaling, tracks, administration, and specific cars and locomotives.

1749. Space Sciences Dictionary: In English, French, German, Spanish, Portuguese and Russian. J. Kleczek; H. Kleczkova. New York,
NY: Elsevier, 1990-92. 4v., index. $686.00. ISBN: 0-444-98872-6v.1.

This 4-volume multilingual dictionary covers terms used in space science, space technology, space research, and related disciplines. Each of the volumes can be purchased separately covering: v.1—Radiation and matter; v.2—Motion, space flight and data; v.3—Space technology and space research; v.4—Earth sciences, solar system and deep space.

1750. Transportation-Logistics Dictionary.
2nd. Joseph L. Cavinato. Washington, DC: Traffic Service Corp, 1982. 323p. price not available. ISBN: 0-87408-022-3.

This business-oriented dictionary lists terms in the field of transportation including logistics, environmental hazards, distribution, equipment, and administration.

1751. Urban Public Transportation Glossary.
Benita H. Gray. Washington, DC: National Research Council, 1989. 74p. $14.00. ISBN: 0-309-04718-8.

This small dictionary covers 1,500 terms, including acronyms and abbreviations in urban transportation. It updates the *Transportation Research Boards Special Report 179* published in 1978.

Directories

1752. Aerospace Facts and Figures. New
York, NY: Aviation Week and Space Technology/McGraw-Hill, 1945– , annual. v.1– , illus., index. $16.95.

Also called *Aviation Facts and Figures*, this is an annual collection of facts and figures pertaining to aviation. It covers space programs, aviation, finance, employment, R&D, missiles, and production. It is all summarized with only the highlights presented.

1753. Aerospace Technology Centres. Brenda
Wren. Harlow, Great Britain: Longman Group, 1988. 194p., index. $245.00. ISBN: 0-582-01773-4.

This directory, arranged by country, gives information about centers and laboratories working in the aerospace science field. Standard directory-type data is provided such as addresses, telephone numbers, status, product ranges, personnel, expenditures, scope of activities, and publications.

1754. Directory of Transportation Libraries/Information Centers in North America.
5th. Daniel Krummes; Michael Kleiber. Cincinnati, OH: ATE Information Service, 1987. 175p., index. price not available.

Formerly a publication of the Special Libraries Association but still produced by the Transportation Division of SLA, this small directory lists all transportation libraries and information centers in North America, giving such information as location, size, coverage, etc.

1755. International ABC Aerospace Directory. New York, NY: Jane's, 1951– , annual.
v.1– , illus., index. $340.00.

Previously called *Interavia ABC Aerospace Directory*, this is a good general source of information about the aerospace industry. Standard directory information is given on companies that are involved in any aspect of aerospace commerce. Another useful directory of this type is the *World Aviation Directory* (Ziff-Davis, 1940–).

1756. Jane's Space Directory. New York,
NY: Jane's, 1985– , annual. v.1– , index. $245.00.

Previously called *Interavia Space Directory* and *Jane's Space Flight Directory*, this excellent annual encyclopedic source covers information on all areas of spaceflight including history, worldwide space programs, military space, launches, solar system, world space enters, spacemen, and space contractors. For information on just U.S. spacecraft consult Bill Yenne's *Encyclopedia of U.S. Spacecraft* (Exeter Books, 1985).

1757. Lloyd's Ports of the World. Colchester,
Great Britain: Lloyd's of London Press, 1990. 815p., illus., index. $152.00.

Also called *Ports of the World*, this listing of the major world shipping ports gives information about each as to size, location, etc.

1758. Maritime Services Directory. San
Diego, CA: Aegis, 1989/90– , annual. v.1– , index. $85.00.

This comprehensive directory contains maritime-related information including shipbuilding and repair, products, cargo management, organizations, schools, shipyards, vessel operation, and statistics. A list of U.S. Flag oceangoing fleets is included as well as all ships in service in the U.S. Navy, Coast Guard, and Army Corps of Engineers.

Encyclopedias

1759. Concise Encyclopedia of Traffic and
Transportation Systems. Markos Papageorgiou. New York, NY: Pergamon Press, 1991. 658p., illus., bibliog., index. $350.00. ISBN: 0-08-036203-6.

Most articles in the encyclopedia are revised from the *Systems and Control Encyclopedia*. It covers topics related to traffic control and transportation systems including highway, railroad, air transport, and maritime transport plus an emphasis on the infrastructure of all transport systems.

1760. Guiness Book of Aircraft: Records, Facts, Feats. 5th. David Mondey; Michael J.H. Taylor. New York, NY: Sterling, 1988. 256p., illus. (part in color), index. 0-85112-355-4.

This book of aviation records and firsts is similar to Joe Christy's *1001 Flying Facts and Firsts* (TAB, 1988). It is arranged by topic, then chronologically.

1761. Illustrated Encyclopedia of Aircraft. London, Great Britain: Orbis, 1981-83. 156p., illus. (part in color). $5.00/volume.

This encyclopedia is an interesting collection of individual volumes, each covering a particular aircraft. Descriptions are general and include good illustrations.

1762. Illustrated Encyclopedia of General Aviation. 2nd. Paul Garrison. Blue Ridge Summit, PA: TAB, 1990. 462p., illus. $34.95; $24.95pbk. ISBN: 0-8306-8316-X; 0-8306-3316-2pbk.

This work is an alphabetically arranged encyclopedia of acronyms, initialisms, aircraft names, companies, and subjects. Included are detailed specifications of individual aircraft and engines.

1763. Illustrated Encyclopedia of Space Technology. 2nd. Kenneth Gatland. New York, NY: Orion, 1989. 303p., color illus., bibliog. price not available. ISBN: 0-517-57427-6.

This topically arranged encyclopedia of spaceflight is written for the student and layperson. The index must be used to access specific bits of information. A chronology of spaceflight is excellent.

1764. Jane's Airport and ATC Equipment. David F. Rider. New York, NY: Jane's, 1982– , annual. v.1– , illus., bibliog., index. $225.00.

A typical Jane's publication, this encyclopedic work describes all types of airport equipment including environmental controls, terminal equipment, computers, emergency equipment, radar, and especially the security equipment. It is arranged by type of equipment, then by manufacturer.

1765. Jane's Airports and Handling Agents. New York, NY: Jane's, 1987– , irregular. v.1– , illus., bibliog., index. $1,240.00.

This reference source provides information on some 1,700 airports (with runways over 1,000 meters) giving location, runway specifications, operating hours, parking, and communications. It also provides information on some 2,540 handling agents, customs and immigration requirements, fuellers and caterers, banks, and hotels. It is published in 5 sections: Europe (6th, 1993-94, 0-7106-1085-8, $310.00); U.S./Canada (6th, 1993-94, 0-7106-1087-4, $310.00); Middle East/Africa (6th, 1993-94, 0-7106-1086-6, $310.00); Far East/Asia (6th, 1993-94, 0-7106-1088-2, $310.00); and South America (6th, 1993-94, 0-7106-1089-0, $310.00).

1766. Jane's All the World's Aircraft. New York, NY: Jane's, 1909– , annual. v.1– , illus., bibliog., index. $245.00.

Also called *All the World's Aircraft*, this is the world's most comprehensive source of information on aircraft. It gives detailed descriptions with specifications and illustrations on all types of aircraft including sport, microlight, sailplane, hang gliders, lighter-than-air, balloons, and aero engines. Another Jane's publication is *Jane's Civil and Military Aircraft Upgrades* (1st ed, 1993/94, $245.00). Four other interesting, but not as up-to-date sources are Gordon Swanborough's *Civil Aircraft of the World* (I. Allen, 1980); David Mondey's *Complete Illustrated Encyclopedia of the World's Aircraft* (A&W, 1978); Alain-Yves Berger's *Berger-Burr's Ultralight and Microlight Aircraft of the World* (Haynes, 1985); and David Mondey's *International Encyclopedia of Aviation* (Crescent, 1988).

1767. Jane's Avionics. New York, NY: Jane's, 1982– , annual. v.1– , illus., index. $245.00.

This encyclopedia defines devices used in flying an airplane, including sensors; data processing, management, and displays; radio communications; and various training systems. It describes each as fully as possible but is somewhat limited because of information not being available from the manufacturer.

1768. Jane's Containerisation Directory. New York, NY: Jane's, 1968/69– , annual. v.1– , illus., index. $245.00.

Previously called *Jane's Freight Containers*, this is a unique reference source covering containers used in transportation including roll on/roll off. The terminals section is arranged geographically and includes descriptions of ports, railway handling centers, and inland container terminals. Another section is a directory of operators arranged by firm name plus a section of airports, information on the International Air Transport Association, cargo-carrying airlines, and container manufacturers and services.

1769. Jane's Fighting Ships. New York, NY: Jane's, 1888– , annual. v.1– , illus., bibliog., index. $245.00.

This title is the world's standard source of information on warships. Data for each ship includes main machinery, speed, missiles, countermeasures, combat data systems, radars, programs, and modernization/sales.

1770. Jane's High-Speed Marine Craft. New York, NY: Jane's, 1967– , annual. v.1– , illus., index. $245.00.

Previously called *Jane's Surface Skimmers* and *Jane's High-Speed Marine Craft and Air Cushion Vehicles*, this work gives descriptions of builders and designers, operating components, and services that pertain to exclusively marine craft.

1771. Jane's Urban Transport Systems. New York, NY: Jane's, 1982– , annual. v.1– , illus., index. $245.00.

This title is a comprehensive source of information on urban transit systems. The main portion is a directory of urban transit operators alphabetically arranged by city covering heavy rail, light rail, trolly bus, motor bus, ferryboats, and other forms. Descriptions include miles of coverage, routes, equipment, fare system, finance, and research.

1772. Jane's World Airlines. New York, NY: Jane's, 1993– , annual. v.1– , looseleaf with 4 updates per year, illus., index. $950.00.

This encyclopedia covers some 500 airlines worldwide providing key personnel, fleet structures, corporate structures, financial data, routes operated, traffic statistics, and cargo capacity.

1773. Jane's World Railways. New York, NY: Jane's, 1950/51– , annual. v.1– , illus., index. $245.00.

Also known as *World Railways*, this is the major source of information on statistical data pertaining to railways. It provides data about manufacturers, casualty services, rapid transit systems, freight car leasing companies, operators of international rail services in Europe, associates, and agencies.

1774. Magill's Survey of Science: Space Exploration Series. Frank N. Magill. Pasadena, CA: Salem Press, 1989. 5v., bibliog., index. $425.00. ISBN: 0-89-356600-4.

Although not a true encyclopedia, this topically arranged work gives an excellent general overview of space and other exploration sciences. It includes space technology, astronomy, astrophysics, and other related topics written at the undergraduate level.

1775. Oxford Companion to Ships and the Sea. Peter Kemp. New York, NY: Oxford University Press, 1976. 972p., illus. (part in color). out-of-print. ISBN: 0-19-211553-7.

Although out-of-print, this is still a standard historical encyclopedia covering ships, seafaring, and related topics. For current information on military ships see *Jane's Fighting Ships* and for a general encyclopedia on ships consult Peter Kemp's *Encyclopedia of Ships and Seafaring* (Crown, 1980).

1776. Space Almanac: Facts, Figures, Names, Dates, Places, Lists, Charts, Tables, Maps covering Space from Earth to the Edge of the Universe. Anthony R. Curtis. Woodsboro, MD: Arcsoft, 1989. 955p., illus. $19.95. ISBN: 0-86668-065-9.

This encyclopedic work gives information on such topics as space stations, astronauts, cosmonauts, shuttles, rockets, planetary explorers, solar system, and other astronautically related topics.

1777. Standard Catalog of American Cars, 1976-1986. 2nd. James M. Flammang. Iola, WI: Krause, 1989. 484p., illus. $19.95. ISBN: 0-87341-133-1.

Complete descriptions of each car are given for the years 1976-1986 providing basic specifications, factory prices, and estimates of current value. Two other books make this a 3-volume set: Beverley Rae Kines' *Standard Catalog of American Cars, 1805-1942* (Krause, 1989) and John A. Gunnell's *Standard Catalog of American Cars, 1946-1975* (Krause, 1982).

1778. Standard Catalog of American Light Duty Trucks: Pickups, Panels, Vans, All Models 1896-1986. John A. Gunnell. Iola, WI: Krause, 1987. 776p., illus., bibliog. $24.95. ISBN: 0-87341-091-2.

This comprehensive historical work provides information on models, specifications, prices, sales, and production totals of all American light duty trucks. Each entry is illustrated. It includes historical background information on the major manufacturers.

1779. United States Military Aircraft Since 1909. 3rd. Gordon Swanborough; Peter M. Bowers. Washington, DC: Smithsonian Institution Press, 1989. 766p., illus., index. $49.95. ISBN: 0-87474-880-1.

This work is a good history of the development of all aircraft used by the U.S. Army and U.S. Air Force. Each aircraft is fully described giving history and military use. The technical data about each model is given in detail with photographs.

1780. World Guide to Automobile Manufacturers. Nick Baldwin; G.N. Georgano. New York, NY: Facts on File, 1987. 544p., illus. (part in color), index. $50.00. ISBN: 0-8160-1844-8.

The emphasis in this historical encyclopedia is corporate histories and then key people. It is stated to have "every make of car with a life history of ten years or more listed, and many with less." There are excellent color illustrations.

Guides and Field Guides

1781. Chilton Manuals. Radnor, PA: Chilton. multivolume.

The Chilton Book Company is the foremost publisher of automotive repair manuals. There are manuals for most all makes of cars and trucks and individual manuals for repair of specific parts of the automobile. A large majority of the manuals are revised, if not annually, on a regular basis. They are durable and made to be used in the repair bays of the mechanic. There are close to 200 currently available manuals. Examples of the many types are *Professional Automotive Service Manual, Chilton's Labor Guide, Truck and Van Service Manual, Emission Diagnosis and Tune-Up Man-*

ual, *Auto Heating and Air Conditioning Manual, Automatic Transmission Manual, Import Car Wiring Diagram Manual, Electronic Engine Controls Manual, Chassis Electronic Manual, Chilton's Buick Century and Regal, Chilton's Chevrolet Mid-Size, Chilton's Chevrolet, Chilton's Dodge, Chilton's Import Car Repair Manual, Chilton's Mercedes-Benz, Chilton's Porsche, Chilton's Spanish Auto Repair Manual, Chilton's Toyota Corolla-Tercel, Chilton's Ford Pickups,* and *Chilton's GM Sub-Compacts.* For complete catalogs of all publications, contact Chilton Book Company, 201 King of Prussia Road, Radnor, PA 19089-0230.

1782. Intertec Manuals. Overland Park, KS: Intertec Publishing Corp.

The Intertec Publishing Corporation is an authoritative publisher of manuals other than automotive, including farm equipment, tractors, outdoor power equipment, small engines, marine equipment, recreational water and snow vehicles, and most motorcycles. For a complete catalog contact the Intertec Publishing Corp., PO Box 12901, Overland Park, KS 66282-2901.

Handbooks and Manuals

1783. Automotive Handbook. 3rd. Society of Automotive Engineers. Warrendale, PA: Society of Automotive Engineers, 1993. 840p., illus., bibliog., index. $29.00. ISBN: 1-67091-372-X.

This important handbook covers automotive engineering, including actuators, cellular communications, driver information systems, navigation systems, quality reliability, sensors, and tribology/wear and tear.

1784. Concise Encyclopedia of Aeronautics and Space Systems. M. Plegrin. Tarrytown, NY: Pergamon, 1993. 496p., illus., bibliog. $280.00. ISBN: 0-08-037049-7.

This technical encyclopedia covers all aspects of automatic control of aeronautical and space systems. Safety controls are stressed.

1785. Gale's Auto Sourcebook 1991: A Guide to 1987-1991 Cars and Light Trucks. Karen Hill. Detroit, MI: Gale Research, 1991. 750p., index. $89.50. ISBN: 0-8103-8312-8.

This sourcebook is arranged by car or truck model giving citations, summaries, and excerpts of car evaluations, tests, recalls, repairs, lawsuits, and awards.

1786. Goodheart-Wilcox Automotive Encyclopedia: Fundamental Principles, Operation, Construction, Service, Repair. William K. Tobolt; Larry Johnson; Steven W. Olive. South Holland, IL: Goodheart-Willcox, 1989. 815p., illus., index. $28.00. ISBN: 0-87006-691-9.

This encyclopedia is really a handbook. It is topically arranged with chapters on such things as fasten-

ers, gaskets, and seals; emission controls; and speedometers. Each topic is fully discussed giving numerous examples and definitions.

1787. Highway Design Reference Guide. Kenneth B. Woods; Steven S. Ross. New York, NY: McGraw-Hill, 1988. 1v., various paging, illus., bibliog., index. price not available. ISBN: 0-07-053924-3.

Previously called *Highway Engineering Handbook*, this is an updated book on highway design, covering such areas as administration and finance, drainage, earthwork, weather, maintenance and landscaping. For information on the construction of roads and bridges consult Michael Lapinski's *Road and Bridge Construction Handbook* (Van Nostrand Reinhold, 1978), as well as Petros P. Xanthakos' *Theory and Design of Bridges* (Wiley, 1994).

1788. Motorcycle Identification: A Guide to the Identification of All Makes and Models of Motorcycles, Including Off Road Machines and Mopeds. Lee S. Cole. Novato, CA: Lee Books, 1986. 159p., illus. $15.00. ISBN: 0-939818-11-6.

The basic use of this small handbook is to trace stolen motorcycles. After a brief history of motorcycles, records, thefts, and tracing, the book lists various motorcycle brands with special emphasis on the placement of the vehicle identification number (VIN) used in identifying stolen vehicles. The publisher has similar books on other vehicles.

1789. New Observer's Book of Aircraft. 35th. William Green. London, Great Britain: Warne, 1986. 255p., illus. $10.00.

This small handbook/field guide was previously called the *Observer's Book of Aircraft*; it is intended for identification of most aircraft. Brief descriptions are given. Another useful recognition type handbook is *Jane's World Aircraft Recognition Handbook* (Jane's, 1982).

1790. SAE Aerospace Standards Handbook. Warrendale, PA: Society of Automotive Engineers, 1992. 14v., illus., index. price per volume varies.

This set of 14 separate handbooks contains AS, AIR, and ARP documents that represent a comprehensive collection of standards pertaining to the aerospace industries. The individual titles are *Aerospace Fluid Power, Actuation, and Control Technologies Handbook* ($190.00, $70.00 for annual updates); *Aircraft Instruments Handbook* ($190.00, $40.00 for annual updates); *Aerospace Composite Materials Handbook* ($210.00, $125 for annual updates); *Aerospace Flight Deck and Handling Qualities Standards for Transport Aircraft* ($140.00, $40.00 for annual updates); *Aircraft Noise Handbook* ($140.00, $50.00 for annual update); *Air Transport Cabin and Flight Deck Safety Provi-*

sions Handbook ($140.00, $50.00 for annual update); *Electromagnetic Compatibility Handbook* ($130.00, $35.00 for annual update); *Air Cargo and Ground Equipment Handbook* ($160.00, $40.00 for annual update); *Aerospace Landing Gear Systems Handbook* ($150.00, $50.00 for annual update); *Aerospace Couplings, Fittings, Hose and Tubing Assemblies Handbook* ($295.00, $150.00 for annual update); *Aircraft Lighting Handbook* ($140.00, $50.00 for annual update); *Aerospace Fuel, Oil, and Oxidizer Systems Handbook* ($140.00, $35.00 for annual update); *Aircraft Fasteners and Engine Utility Parts Handbook* ($350.00, $150.00 for annual update); *Aircraft Oxygen Equipment Handbook* ($130.00, $50.00 for annual update).

1791. SAE Handbook. New York, NY: Society of Automotive Engineers, 1918– , annual. 1st– , (4v. per year), illus. (part in color), bibliog., index. $200.00.

This is the major source of information on automotive engineering, stressing ground vehicle design, manufacturing, testing, performance standards, recommended practices, and specifications. Information is presented with numerous tables, charts, and drawings. The 4 volumes cover v.1—Material; v.2—Parts and components; v.3—Engines, fuels, lubricants, emissions, and noise; v.4—On-highway vehicles and off-highway machinery.

1792. Traffic Engineering Handbook. 4th. James L. Pline. Englewood Cliffs, NJ: Prentice-Hall, 1992. 481p., illus., bibliog., index. $60.00. ISBN: 0-13-926791-3.

This book and its companion, John D. Edwards' *Transportation Planning Handbook* (Prentice-Hall, 1992), make an excellent set of handbooks covering traffic and transportation engineering. The 2 books replace the earlier handbook, *Transportation and Traffic Engineering Handbook* (Prentice-Hall, 1982).

1793. World Truck Handbook. new. G.N. Georgano. New York, NY: Jane's, 1986. 328p., illus., index. $16.95. ISBN: 0-7106-0366-5.

This handbook covers only truck manufacturers that are currently making trucks. It is arranged by axle layout and contain brief descriptions along with a photograph.

Histories

1794. Airplanes of the World from Pusher to Jet, 1490-1954. Douglas Rolfe. New York, NY: Simon & Schuster, 1954. 319p., illus. out-of-print.

Although out-of-print, this book presents a good overview of the history of airplanes to 1954.

1795. 50 Years of American Automobiles, 1939-1989. Consumer Guide. New York, NY: Crown, 1989. 720p., illus. (part in color), index. $49.95. ISBN: 0-517-68640-6.

This excellent work gives the history of each car listed, including information about manufacturers, prices, models, and interesting facts. Photographs of all models are included. Also useful for historical coverage is Richard M. Langworth's *Great American Automobiles of the 50s* (Crown, 1989).

1796. Heroes in Space: From Gagarin to Challenger. Peter Bond. New York, NY: Blackwell, 1987. 467p., illus., bibliog., index. $24.95. ISBN: 0-631-15349-7.

This well-written history covers U.S. and Russian space flight up through the *Challenger* disaster. It gives a detailed account of each mission and an appendix lists each mission, crew, and launch date.

1797. History of Man-Powered Flight. D.A. Reay. New York, NY: Pergamon Press, 1977. 355p., illus., bibliog., index. out-of-print. ISBN: 0-08-021738-9.

Now out-of-print, this small work gives a good readable history of man and the quest to fly.

1798. Rocket: The History and Development of Rocket and Missile Technology. David Baker. London, Great Britain: New Cavendish Books, 1978. 276p., illus., bibliog., index. out-of-print. ISBN: 0-904568-10-5.

Rockets are a standard technology today that are being ever improved. This out-of-print history discusses the history of how rocket technology has developed.

Tables

1799. RAE Table of Earth Satellites, 1957-1986. 3rd. Royal Aircraft Establishment. New York, NY: Macmillan, 1987. 936p., index. price not available. ISBN: 0-333-39275-2.

Each new edition of this work is a cumulative edition. It is a chronological list of 2,869 launches of satellites and space vehicles between 1957 and 1986 giving name and international designation with date of launch, lifetime, mass, shape, dimensions, and at least one set of orbital parameters. Satellite fragments are also listed making more than 17,000 entries. Also of use would be Anthony R. Curtis's *Space Satellite Handbook* (Arcsoft, 1989) which lists all satellites ever in orbit and all satellites now in orbit with facts, figures, names, dates, places, lists, tables, and maps. For an annual update on satellites consult the *Satellite Directory* (Instructional Telecommunications Unit).

Periodicals

1800. AIAA Journal. Washington, DC: American Institute of Aeronautics and Astronautics, 1963– , monthly. v.1– , index. $340.00. ISSN: 0001-1452.

1801. Air Cargo World. Atlanta, GA: Communication Channels, 1910– , monthly. v.1– , index. $45.00. ISSN: 0745-5100.

1802. American Shipper. Jacksonville, FL: Howard Publications, 1949– , monthly. v.1– , index. $30.00. ISSN: 0160-225X.

1803. Automobile Quarterly. Kutztown, PA: Automobile Quarterly, 1962– , quarterly. v.1– , index. $69.95. ISSN: 0005-1438.

1804. Automotive Engineer. Bury St Edmunds: Mechanical Engineering Publications, 1962– , 6/year. v.1– , index. $99.00. ISSN: 0307-6490.

1805. Automotive Engineering Magazine. Warrendale, PA: Society of Automotive Engineers, 1972– , monthly. v.1– , index. $72.00. ISSN: 0098-2571.

1806. Automotive Week. Wayne, NJ: Automotive Week, 1975– , weekly. v.1– , index. $110.00. ISSN: 0889-3918.

1807. Aviation Week and Space Technology. New York, NY: McGraw-Hill, 1916– , weekly. v.1– , index. $82.00. ISSN: 0005-2175.

1808. Car and Driver. New York, NY: Hachette Magazines, 1955– , monthly. v.1– , index. $19.94. ISSN: 0008-6002.

1809. Chilton's Distribution Magazine. Radnor, PA: Chilton, 1901– , monthly. v.1– , index. $55.00. ISSN: 0273-6721.

1810. Flying. New York, NY: Hachette Magazines, 1927– , monthly. v.1– , index. $24.00. ISSN: 0015-4806.

1811. International Railway Journal and Rapid Transit Review. New York, NY: Simmons-Boardman, 1960– , monthly. v.1– , index. $33.00. ISSN: 0744-5326.

1812. Journal of Aircraft. Washington, DC: American Institute of Aeronautics and Astronautics, 1963– , bimonthly. v.1– , index. $185.00. ISSN: 0021-8669.

1813. Journal of Navigation. Cambridge, Great Britain: Cambridge University Press, 1947– , 3/year. v.1– , index. $129.00. ISSN: 0373-4633.

1814. Journal of Ship Research. Jersey City, NJ: Society of Naval Architects and Marine Engineers, 1957– , quarterly. v.1– , index. $70.00. ISSN: 0022-4502.

1815. Journal of Spacecraft and Rockets. Washington, DC: American Institute of Aeronautics and Astronautics, 1964– , bimonthly. v.1– , index. $185.00. ISSN: 0022-4650.

1816. Marine Engineer's Review. London, Great Britain: Institute of Marine Engineers, 1970– , monthly. v.1– , index. $96.00. ISSN: 0047-5955.

1817. Mass Transit. Melville, NY: PTN Publishing, 1974– , monthly. v.1– , index. $30.00. ISSN: 0364-3484.

1818. Modern Railways. Shepperton, Great Britain: Ian Allan, 1946– , monthly. v.1– , index. $46.00. ISSN: 0026-8356.

1819. Motor Trend. Los Angeles, CA: Peterson, 1949– , monthly. v.1– , index. $19.94. ISSN: 0027-2094.

1820. Parking. Washington, DC: National Parking Association, 1952– , 10/year. v.1– , index. $95.00. ISSN: 0031-2193.

1821. Railroad History. Akron, OH: Railway and Locomotive History Society, 1921– , semiannual. v.1– , index. $25.00. ISSN: 0090-7847.

1822. Railway Age. New York, NY: Simmons-Boradman, 1856– , monthly. v.1– , index. $35.00. ISSN: 0033-8826.

1823. Railway Gazette International. Sutton, Great Britain: Reed Business Publishing Group, 1835– , monthly. v.1– , index. $61.20. ISSN: 0373-5346.

1824. Railway Magazine. Cleam, Great Britain: IPC Magazine, 1897– , monthly. v.1– , index. $32.00. ISSN: 0033-8923.

1825. Road and Track. Newport Beach, CA: Hachette Magazines, 1947– , monthly. v.1– , index. $19.94. ISSN: 0035-7189.

1826. Shipping World and Shipbuilder.
Basingstoke, Great Britain: Marine
Publications International, 1883– , monthly.
v.1– , index. $64.00. ISSN: 0037-3931.

1827. TR News. Washington, DC:
Transportation Research Board, 1963– ,
bimonthly. v.1– , index. $38.00. ISSN:
0738-6826.

1828. Traffic Engineering and Control.
London, Great Britain: Printerhall, 1960– ,
monthly. v.1– , index. $98.00. ISSN:
0041-0683.

1829. Traffic Management. Newton, MA:
Cahners, 1962– , monthly. v.1– , index. $69.95.
ISSN: 0041-0691.

1830. Transportation. Dordrecht,
Netherlands: Kluwer, 1972– , quarterly. v.1– ,
index. $159.00. ISSN: 0049-4488.

1831. Transportation Journal. Louisville,
KY: American Society of Transportation and
Logistics, 1961– , quarterly. v.1– , index.
$50.00. ISSN: 0041-1612.

**1832. Transportation Research: A—General;
B—Methodological.** Tarrytown, NY:
Pergamon Press, 1967– , 12/year. v.1– , index.
$624.00. ISSN: 0191-2607A; 0191-2615B.

1833. Transportation Research Record.
Washington, DC: Transportation Research
Board, 1963– , irregular. v.1– , index. $865.00.
ISSN: 0361-1981.

1834. Truck and Off-Highway Industries.
Radnor, PA: Chilton, 1979– , bimonthly. v.1– ,
index. $55.00. ISSN: 0194-1410.

1835. Trucks. Southampton, PA: Truck
Magazine, 1986– , 6/year. v.1– , index. $17.50.
ISSN: 0884-8947.

Chapter 8: Medicine

Medicine, from the Latin word *medicina* meaning "to heal," is concerned with preventing and treating disease, as well as maintaining good health. It is an applied science using all of the physical sciences and some engineering disciplines in its research. It is usually divided into clinical and basic fields: clinical includes all the specialties and basic covers the areas more closely related to the biological sciences. The basic medical sciences attempt to discover and describe how the human body functions. They include:

- Anatomy—the study of all parts of the human body.
- Biochemistry—the study of all chemical processes that take place in the human body.
- Biophysics—the application of physics to biology in the study of the human body.
- Embryology—the study of the early development of life.
- Endocrinology—the study of the body's endocrine system.
- Genetics—the study of genes and heredity.
- Microbiology—the study of microorganisms that may affect the human body.
- Pathology—the study of how diseases alter the human body.
- Pharmacology—the study of how drugs or other chemicals affect the human body.
- Physiology—the study of the vital functions of the human body and how they all work together to maintain life.
- Psychology—the study of human behavior as it functions biologically and with the social environment.

Clinical medicine has resulted in many specialties in the medical profession. There are two broad specialties, preventive medicine and public health, and many finely defined specialities:

- Preventive Medicine—the study of how to prevent diseases.
- Public Health—the study of how to maintain and promote good health.

- Anesthesiology—the study of anesthesia and anesthetics.
- Cardiology—the study of the heart and how it functions.
- Dentistry—the study of teeth and the oral cavity.
- Dermatology—the study of diagnosis and treatment of skin diseases.
- Gastroenterology—the study of the stomach and intestines.
- Geriatrics—treating the aged.
- Gerontology—the study of the chemical, biological, historical, and sociological aspects of aging.
- Gynecology—study and treatment of the diseases that affect the genital tract in women.
- Immunology—the study of how human organisms react to antigens.
- Internal Medicine—a general study of all internal parts of the human body.
- Neurology—the study of the nervous system, including neurosurgery.
- Nursing—the professions of helping individuals in their promotion, maintenance, and restoration to good health.
- Obstetrics—the treatment of all aspects of child bearing.
- Ophthalmology—the study of all aspects of the eye.
- Orthopedics—the part of surgery that is concerned with the restoration of the functions of bones.
- Otorhinolarygology—the study of medical and surgical treatment of the head and neck including ears, nose, and throat.
- Pediatrics—the study and treatment of health and diseases in children.
- Plastic Surgery—the restoration or changing of physical features.
- Psychiatry—the treating of problems of the mind.
- Radiology—the study of the use of radioactive substances in the diagnosis and treatment of disease.

- Rehabilitation—the study of restoring individuals to normal functions or as close to normal as possible.
- Serology—the study of serums and their reactions on the body.
- Surgery—the treating of diseases and injuries through operations.
- Urology—the study of the male and female urinary tract.
- Venereology—the study of sexually transmitted diseases.

The most important indexing source for medical research is the *Index Medicus,* which provides print and electronic access. Other reference materials are many and include numerous well-established dictionaries and encyclopedias. There are also handbooks, some multivolume. Medicine is one where textbooks become reference books. Every special sub-discipline of medicine has older well-established textbooks as well as newly written ones. These become mini-treatises/handbooks/encyclopedias for that discipline. A few have been included in this chapter but for the most part they are not listed because of the sheer numbers.

GENERAL MEDICINE

Abstracts and Indexes

1836. Excerpta Medica Abstract Journals. Amsterdam, Netherlands: Excerpta Medica, 1947– , 794/year. v.1– , index. $22,638.00. ISSN: 0921-822X.

This comprehensive medical abstracting collection consists of 46 sections covering some 3,500 journals in all fields of medicine and allied sciences. The journals are produced from EMBASE, an Excerpta Medica database. Each section can be purchased separately and all are available online and via CD-ROM. Section 37, *Drug Literature Index*, ceased publication in 1990. The sections currently being published are 1—Anatomy, Anthropology, Embryology and Histology; 2—Physiology; 3—Endocrinology; 4—Microbiology; 5—General Pathology and Pathological Anatomy; 6—Internal Medicine; 7—Pediatrics and Pediatric Surgery; 8—Neurology and Neurosurgery; 9—Surgery; 10—Obstetrics and Gynecology; 11—Otorhinolaryngology; 12—Ophthalmology; 13—Dermatology and Venereology; 14—Radiology; 15—Chest Diseases, Thoracic Surgery and Tuberculosis; 16—Cancer; 17—Public Health, Social Medicine and Epidemiology; 18—Cardiovascular Diseases and Cardiovascular Surgery; 19—Rehabilitation and Physical Medicine; 20—Gerontology and Geriatrics; 21—Developmental Biology and Teratology; 22—Human Genetics; 23—Nuclear Medicine; 24—Anesthesiology; 25—Hematology; 26—Immunology, Serology and Transplantation; 27—Biophysics, Bioengineering and Medical Instrumentation; 28—Urology and Nephrology; 29—Clinical Biochemistry; 30—Pharmacology; 31—Arthritis and Rheumatism; 32—Psychiatry; 33—Orthopedic Surgery; 34—Plastic Surgery; 35—Occupational Health and Industrial Medicine; 36—Health Policy, Economics and Management; 38—Adverse Reactions Titles; 40—Drug Dependence, Alcohol Abuse and Alcoholism; 46—Environmental Health and Pollution Control; 47—Virology; 48—Gastroenterology; 49—Forensic Science Abstracts; 50—Epilepsy Abstracts; 52—Toxicology; 53—AIDS; 130—Clinical Pharmacology. All are also available online and on CD-ROM.

1837. Index Medicus. Bethesda, MD: National Library of Medicine, 1960– , monthly. v.1– , index. $319.00. ISSN: 0019-3879.

Previously called *Current List of Medical Literature* and absorbing *Bibliography of Medical Reviews*, this indexing service is produced from MEDLARS (Medical Literature Analysis and Retrieval System). It covers several thousand journals, proceedings, reports, and monographs each year providing subject, author, and title indexes. It is available online, as CD-ROM, and on tape. A much smaller version covering some 118 journals is also published as the *Abridged Index Medicus*.

Atlases

1838. Atlas of Human Cross-Sectional Anatomy. 2nd. Donald R. Cahill; Matthew J. Orland; Carl C. Reading. New York, NY: Wiley, 1990. 251p., illus., bibliog., index. $149.95. ISBN: 0-471-50988-4.

This highly specialized atlas provides detailed cross-sections of the human body.

1839. Atlas of the Human Brain Stem and Spinal Cord. James Fix. Frederick, MD: Aspen, 1987. 163p., illus., bibliog., index. $32.00. ISBN: 0-87189-858-6.

This work is an excellent atlas with both gross and cross-sectional views of the brain, spinal cord, and brain stem.

1840. Grant's Atlas of Anatomy. 9th. Anne M. R. Agor; Ming T. Lee. Baltimore, MD: Williams & Wilkins, 1991. 650p., illus. (part in color), index. $49.00. ISBN: 0-683-03701-3.

This is the classic atlas of anatomy used by medical students. It provides the most detailed views of any atlas. Three other of the many useful atlases are J.A. Gosling's *Human Anatomy: A Text and Colour Atlas* (Gower, 1991), Chihiro Yokochi's *Photographic Atlas of the Human Body* (Igaku-Shoin, 1989) and M.H. McMinn's *Color Atlas of Human Anatomy* (Mosby, 1993).

Bibliographies

1841. Bibliography of Bioethics. Washington, DC: Kennedy Institute of Ethics, Georgetown University, 1975– , annual. v.1– , index. $45.00. ISSN: 0363-0161.

This bibliography covers English-language articles from periodicals, newspapers, books, and legal documents that deal with medical ethics. It is available online.

1842. Encyclopedia of Health Information Sources: A Bibliographic Guide to Approximately 13,000 Titles for Publications and Organizations, and Other Sources of Information on More than 450 Health-Related Subjects. Paul Wasserman; Suzanne Grefsheim. Detroit, MI: Gale Research, 1987. 483p. $155.00. ISBN: 0-8103-2135-1.

This subject guide to some 13,000 sources provides full bibliographical information.

1843. Federal Information Sources in Health and Medicine: A Selected Annotated Bibliography. *(Bibliographies and Indexes in Medical Studies, no.1).* Mary Glen Chitty; Natalie Schatz. New York, NY: Greenwood Press, 1988. 306p., index. $55.00. ISBN: 0-313-25530-X.

This guide to finding, using, and obtaining government medical information is arranged by subject with full bibliographical citations.

1844. Health Sciences Books, 1876-1982. New York, NY: Bowker, 1982. 4v. $225.00. ISBN: 0-8352-1447-8.

This work is a compilation of health-related books that have appeared in *BIP* through 1982.

1845. Medical and Health Care Books and Serials in Print. New York, NY: Bowker, 1972– , annual. v.1– , index. $175.00. ISSN: 0000-085X.

Previously called *Medical Books and Serials in Print* and *Medical Books in Print*, this annual produced from *BIP* and *Ulrich's International Periodical Directory*, provides bibliographical and ordering information. It is arranged in sections by subject and author/title with an index to publishers. It is also available online and on CD-ROM.

1846. Medical Reference Works, 1679-1966: A Selected Bibliography. *(Publications no.3).* John B. Blake; Charles Roos. Chicago, IL: Medical Library Association, 1967. 343p.

This bibliography contains citations to medical books with arrangement by subject, author, and title and is an important reference work. Supplements began in 1970. It is good for historical information.

1847. Morton's Medical Bibliography. 5th. Brookfield, VT: Ashgate, 1992. 1,046p., index. $145.00. ISBN: 0-85967-897-0.

This bibliography previously called *Garrison and Morton's Medical Bibliography* is intended to document the most "important contributions to the literature of medicine and ancillary sciences." It is chronologically arranged by subject providing complete citations and brief annotations.

1848. Sickness and Wellness Publications. Janet R. Utts. Evanston, IL: J.G. Burke, 1989– , every 2 years with supplements in alternating years. v.1– , index. $50.00. ISBN: 0-934272-26-3v.2.

This bibliography/directory lists some 400 newsletters and magazines pertaining to sickness and wellness and aimed at the consumer or patient. It is arranged by subject providing names and addresses of organization or publisher and a complete description of the publication. An electronic version on disk is available.

Biographical Sources

1849. American Medical Directory. Chicago, IL: Press of the American Medical Association, 1906– , irregular. 1st– , index. $495.00. ISSN: 0065-9339.

Previously called the *American Medical Directory of Physicians* and published in 4 volumes each time, this directory provides a list of registered physicians in the United States and its territories. Doctors of osteopathy are included. It is available online and on CD-ROM.

1850. Bibliography of Medical and Biomedical Biography. Leslie T. Morton; Robert J. Moore. Brookfield, VT: Gower, 1989. 208p., bibliog., index. $69.95. ISBN: 0-85967-797-4.

This work is based on John L. Thornton's *Select Bibliography of Medical Biography* (Library Association, 1970), with some 1,600 entries.

1851. Biographical History of Medicine: Excerpts and Essays on the Men and Their Work. John H. Talbott. New York, NY: Grune & Stratton, 1970. 1,211p., illus., bibliog. out-of-print.

Some 550 medical scientists from 250 BC through the first half of the 20th century are included in this historical biographical work. Illustrations of the individuals are included.

1852. Directory of Medical Specialists. Chicago, IL: Marquis Who's Who, 1940– , irregular. 1st– , index. $295.00. ISSN: 0070-5829.

Previously called *Directory of Medical Specialists Holding Certification by American Boards*, this work provides current biographical information for over 400,000 specialists.

1853. International Medical Who's Who. Harlow, Great Britain: Longman, 1980– , irregular. v.1– , index. $310.00.

This biographical directory lists some 12,000 medical specialists from all fields of medicine as well as related disciplines. It is issued in two volumes each time with the first volume containing the biographies and the second being a listing of the experts by disciplines within each country.

1854. Medical Directory. Detroit, MI: Gale Research/St. James Press, 1845– , annual. v.1– , index. $150.00. ISSN: 0305-3342.

This directory provides an alphabetical listing of medical practitioners registered in Great Britain.

1855. Medical Sciences International Who's Who. 5th. Detroit, MI: Gale Research, 1992. 2v., index. $553.00. ISBN: 0-582-10104-2.

Some 8,000 biographies are included in this who's who. It covers over 90 countries and includes individuals for related biomedical fields.

Dictionaries, Glossaries, and Thesauri

1856. Aspen Dictionary of Health Care Administration. Arnold S. Goldstein. Frederick, MD: Aspen, 1989. 352p. $29.00. ISBN: 0-8342-0077-5.

This specialized dictionary covers some 1,400 terms associated with the administration of health care, including insurance, legal, and welfare terminology.

1857. Black's Medical Dictionary. 36th. C. Witt Havard. London, Great Britain: A & C Black, 1990. 750p., illus. $60.00. ISBN: 0-384-20901-5.

Having been published since 1906, Black's is a standard medical dictionary providing clear definitions as well as information on therapy and diagnosis. Two

other older but still well-respected dictionaries are *Blakiston's Gould Medical Dictionary* (McGraw-Hill, 1979) and *Butterworths Medical Dictionary* (Butterworth-Heinemann, 1980) previously known as the *British Medical Dictionary*.

1858. Dictionary of Biomedical Acronyms and Abbreviations. 2nd. Jacques Dupayrat. New York, NY: Wiley, 1990. 184p. $39.95. ISBN: 0-471-92649-3.

This dictionary covers medicine, biology, and biochemistry. Other useful dictionaries of this type include Kai Haber's *Common Abbreviations in Clinical Medicine* (Raven Press, 1988); Rolf Heister's *Dictionary of Abbreviations in Medical Sciences* (Springer-Verlag, 1989) and *Stedman's Abbreviations, Acronyms, and Symbols* (Williams & Wilkins, 1992).

1859. Dictionary of Medical Eponyms. Barry Firkin; J.A. Whitworth. Park Ridge, NJ: Parthenon Publishing Group, 1987. 591p., illus., bibliog. $55.00. ISBN: 1-85070-138-5.

Eponyms are terms that reflect the name of the person who developed the term, a location of where the disease can be found or an anatomical feature. Each medical eponym in this dictionary includes definition and history.

1860. Dictionary of Medical Syndromes. 3rd. Sergio I. Magalini; Sabina C. Magalini; Giovanni De Francisci. Philadelphia, PA: Lippincott, 1990. 1,042p., bibliog., index. $89.50. ISBN: 0-397-50882-4.

Also called *Magalini*, this classic work contains some 2,700 syndromes providing synonyms, symptoms and signs, etiology, pathology, diagnostic procedure, treatment, and prognosis. Another useful but less comprehensive work is Stanley Jablonski's *Illustrated Dictionary of Eponymic Syndromes, and Diseases and Their Syndromes* (Saunders, 1969).

1861. Dictionary of Medical Terms for the Nonmedical Person. 2nd. Mikel A. Rothenberg; Charles F. Chapman. New York, NY: Barron's, 1989. 490p., illus. $8.95. ISBN: 0-8120-4098-8.

Previously called *Medical Dictionary for the Nonprofessional*, this dictionary gives simple definitions for the layperson. Two other general dictionaries are *Faber Pocket Medical Dictionary* (Faber & Faber, 1989) and the *Bantam Medical Dictionary* (Bantam, 1982).

1862. Dorland's Illustrated Medical Dictionary. 27th. W.A. Newman Dorland. Philadelphia, PA: Saunders, 1988. 1,888p., illus. $31.95. ISBN: 0-7216-3154-1.

Also called *Illustrated Medical Dictionary* and first published in 1900, this work has become another standard medical dictionary. It is also available in a pocket edition.

1863. Elsevier's Encyclopedic Dictionary of Medicine. New York, NY: Elsevier, 1987-90. 4v., index. $314.50v.1; $233.00v.2; $237.00v.3; $180.00v.4. ISBN: 0-444-42823-2v.1; 0-444-42824-0v.2; 0-444-87293-0v.3; 0-444-42826-7v.4.

This multilingual dictionary (French, German, Italian and Spanish) provides definitions of terms as well as translations.

1864. Facts on File Dictionary of Health Care Management. Joseph C. Rhea; Steven Ott; Jay M. Shafritz. New York, NY: Facts on File, 1988. 692p., bibliog. $50.00. ISBN: 0-8160-1637-2.

Also called *Dictionary of Health Care Management*, this dictionary provides definitions to the terms encountered by health care managers including jargon and acronyms.

1865. HarperCollins Illustrated Medical Dictionary. New York, NY: HarperCollins, 1993. 534p., illus. (part in color). $19.00. ISBN: 0-06-273142-4.

Also called *Illustrated Medical Dictionary* and previously called *Melloni's Illustrated Medical Dictionary*, this work provides some 2,700 illustrations that help with the definition of the terms.

1866. International Dictionary of Medicine and Biology. E. Lovell Becker. New York, NY: Churchill Livingstone, 1986. 3v., index. $425.00. ISBN: 0-471-01849-X.

Some 150,000 terms are included in this very comprehensive medical dictionary. It also covers related terms from biology, anthropology, biomedical engineering, environmental health, and veterinary medicine. An abridged edition was published in 1989 as *Churchill's Illustrated Medical Dictionary*.

1867. Logan's Medical and Scientific Abbreviations. Carolyn M. Logan; M. Katherine Rice. Philadelphia, PA: Lippincott, 1987. 673p. $28.95. ISBN: 0-397-54589-4.

Some 20,000 abbreviations are identified in this dictionary. There are numerous other books of this type, each with some unique terms: Sheila B. Sloane's *Medical Abbreviations and Eponyms* (Saunders, 1985); Marilyn Fuller Delong's *Medical Acronyms and Abbreviations* (Medical Economics Books, 1989); *MASA: Medical Acronyms, Symbols and Abbreviations* (Neal-Schuman, 1988); Stanley Jablonski's *Dictionary of Medical Acronyms and Abbreviations* (Hanley & Belfus, 1992); and Neil M. Davis' *Medical Abbreviations* (Neil M. Davis, 1988).

1868. Medical Phrase Index: A One-Step Reference to the Terminology of Medicine. 2nd. Jean A. Lorenzini. Oradell, NJ: Medical Economics Books, 1989. 948p. $45.00. ISBN: 1-878487-26-4.

This book is intended for secretaries and medical transcriptionists. The terms, procedures, and phrases are listed alphabetically for identification purposes so that the context in which they are used can be outlined. Two other useful companions to this book are W. Joseph Garcia's *Medical Sign Language* (Thomas, 1983) and *Glossary of Medical Terminology for Health Professionals* (Springhouse, 1991).

1869. Medical Word Finder: A Reverse Medical Dictionary. Betty Hamilton; Barbara Guidos. New York, NY: Neal-Schuman, 1987. 177p. 445.00. ISBN: 1-55570-011-X.

This unique dictionary provides the medical term when a term or phrase is known giving synonyms, related terminology, and suffixes and prefixes.

1870. Merriam-Webster's Medical Desk Dictionary. Springfield, MA: Merriam-Webster, 1993. 790p. $24.95. ISBN: 0-87779-125-2.

Previously published as *Webster's Medical Desk Dictionary*, this reference is a very good general dictionary for the layperson. Another Webster-type reference is *Webster's New World Medical Word Finder* (Prentice-Hall, 1987).

1871. New American Medical Dictionary and Health Manual. 5th newly enlarged. Robert E. Rothenberg. New York, NY: New American Library, 1988. 555p., illus. $4.95. ISBN: 0-451-15152-6.

This general dictionary provides easy-to-understand definitions of some 9,800 terms. It also includes many tables of useful information such as calories, drugs, first aid, and common poisons.

1872. Quick Medical Terminology: A Self-Teaching Guide. 3rd. Genevieve Love Smith; Phyllis E. Davis; Shirley Soltery Steinen. New York, NY: Wiley, 1992. 288p., illus., index. $14.95. ISBN: 0-471-54267-9.

This dictionary provides the reader some 500 medical terms and how to use them. It explains the use of Greek and Latin prefixes and suffixes and explains word roots and forms. Two other books dealing with terminology are Sandra R. Patterson and Lawrence S. Thompson's *Medical Terminology from Greek and Latin* (Whitston, 1978) and *Brady's Introduction to Medical Terminology* (Appleton & Lange, 1990).

1873. Sloane-Dorland Annotated Medical-Legal Dictionary. Richard Sloane. St Paul, MN: West Publishing, 1987. 787p., illus. $99.00. ISBN: 0-314-93512-6.

This dictionary covers the terminology found in the medical-legal field. Many of the definitions are linked to judicial judgments.

1874. Stedman's Medical Dictionary. 25th. Thomas Lathrop Stedman. Baltimore, MD: Williams & Wilkins, 1990. 1,784p., illus. (part in color), index. $41.00. ISBN: 0-683-07916-6.

Stedman's is considered a classic medical dictionary. It includes pharmacy and dentistry terms and provides pronunciation and derivation. It contains numerous tables and appendixes. There is an abridged edition published as *Webster's New World/Stedman's Concise Medical Dictionary* (Webster, 1987).

1875. Taber's Cyclopedic Medical Dictionary. 15th. Clayton L. Thomas. Philadelphia, PA: Davis, 1985. 2,170p., illus. $27.95. ISBN: 0-8036-8309-X.

This standard medical dictionary includes terms on nursing and allied health. It contains over 56,000 terms. For just a list of the terms in this dictionary with pronunciation consult *Taber's Medical Word Book with Pronunciations* (Davis, 1990).

Directories

1876. Allied Health Education Directory. Chicago, IL: American Medical Association, 1968– , annual. 1st– , index. $36.00. ISSN: 0194-3766.

Previously called *Allied Medical Education Directory*, this important work provides information about medical education programs. Each program is described in detail.

1877. American Hospital Association Guide to the Health Care Field. Chicago, IL: American Hospital Association, 1945– , annual. v.1– , index. $195.00. ISSN: 0094-8969.

Also called *Guide to the Health Care Field* or *AHA Guide to the Health Care Field*, this directory provides a listing of registered hospitals including systems and organizations.

1878. Barron's Guide to Medical and Dental Schools. 5th. Saul Wischnitzer. New York, NY: Barron's, 1991. 380p., index. $13.95. ISBN: 0-8120-4645-5.

Also called *Guide to Medical and Dental Schools*, this well-known guide provides useful information for those considering medical or dental school. In-depth descriptions of the various schools are provided as well as numerous facts and statistics.

1879. Directory of Women's Health Care Centers. Phoenix, AZ: Oryx Press, 1989. 143p., index. $45.00. ISBN: 0-89774-525-6.

The National Association of Women's Health Professionals helped to compile this directory that describes the healthcare centers that emphasize women's health.

1880. Encyclopedia of Medical Organizations and Agencies. 4th. Karen Backus. Detroit, MI: Gale Research, 1992. 1,211p., index. $205.00. ISBN: 0-8103-6910-9.

Some 12,200 organizations and agencies are described in this directory providing complete directory information as well as information about their publications and a statement of the group's purpose.

1881. Federal Health Information Resources. Melvin S. Day. Arlington, VA: Information Resources Press, 1987. 246p., index. $29.50. ISBN: 0-87815-055-2.

This detailed directory lists some 187 federal agencies that collect and provide health information. Full descriptions of the agencies are provided including information about services, databases, and publications.

1882. Health Resource Builder: Free and Inexpensive Materials for Libraries and Teachers. Carol Smallwood. NC: McFarland, 1988. 251p., index. $18.95. ISBN: 0-89950-359-4.

Arranged by subject, this useful small work is a directory of organizations that can provide free or low-cost publications pertaining to physical health, mental health, and safety. Name, address, and telephone number are given for each entry but titles of publications are normally not listed.

1883. Medical and Health Information Directory. Anthony Thomas Kruzas. Detroit, MI: Gale Research, 1978– , irregular. 1st– , index. $585.00. ISSN: 0749-9973.

This comprehensive directory published in 3 volumes each time, provides a guide to organizations, agencies, institutions, services, and information sources in medicine and health-related fields. The 3 volumes cover v.1—Organizations, agencies, and institutions; v.2—Publications, libraries, and other information services; v.3—Health services.

1884. Medical Research Centres. 10th. Harlow, Great Britain: Longman/Gale Research, 1993. 2v., index. $470.00. ISBN: 0-582-06123-7.

Some 9,000 entries, arranged by country, describe the medical and biochemical research that is conducted in over 100 countries. It provides information on industrial enterprises, research labs, universities, societies, and professional associations. Another work covering societies is G. Zeitak and F. Berman's *Directory of International and National Medical and Related Societies* (Pergamon, 1990).

1885. National Health Directory. Frederick, MD: Aspen, 1992. 736p., index. $89.00. ISBN: 0-685-57168-8.

This directory provides information about individuals who influence the health industry including congressional committees and sub-committees, congressional delegations, federal agencies, and state, county, and city officials.

Encyclopedias

1886. American Medical Association Encyclopedia of Medicine. Charles B. Clayman. New York, NY: Random House, 1989. 1,184p., illus., index. $44.45. ISBN: 0-394-56528-2.

This encyclopedia of some 5,000 entries covers such topics as drugs, diseases, disorders and conditions, tests, procedures, and common medical terminology. A drug glossary of 2,500 generic drugs is also included. Other useful encyclopedias are the *Medical and Health Encyclopedia* (Ferguson, 1991) and *World Book Medical Encyclopedia* (World Book, 1988).

1887. Concise Encyclopedia of Medical and Dental Materials. *(Advances in Materials Science and Engineering).* David Williams; Robert W. Cahn; Michael B. Bever. New York, NY: Pergamon Press, 1990. 412p., illus., bibliog., index. $200.00. ISBN: 0-08-036194-3.

This comprehensive encyclopedia covers all of the materials that are used in the medical and dental professions. It describes the materials in detail and provides information on their uses.

1888. Encyclopedia of Alternative Health Care. Kristin Gottschalk Olsen. New York, NY: Pocket Books, 1989. 325p., index. $8.95. ISBN: 0-671-66256-2.

This encyclopedia of holistic medicine provides good discussions of the various holistic medical systems that have been developed.

1889. Encyclopedia of Bioethics. Warren T. Rich. New York, NY: Free Press, 1978. 4v., bibliog., index. $250.00. ISBN: 0-02-926060-4.

Although somewhat dated, this is still an excellent treatise/encyclopedia of bioethical problems related to medicine. Some topics covered include euthanasia, abortion, experimentation, and artificial insemination.

1890. Encyclopedia of Medical Devices and Instrumentation. John G. Webster. New York, NY: Wiley, 1988. 4v., illus., bibliog., index. $575.00. ISBN: 0-471-82936-6.

This highly technical encyclopedia provides detailed information on various medical devices and instrumentation. It covers both specific types of instruments as well as broad informational topics.

1891. Encyclopedia of the Human Body. Renato Dulbecco. San Diego, CA: Academic Press, 1991. 8v., illus. (part in color), bibliog., index. $1,950.00. ISBN: 0-1222-6751-6v.1.

Over 620 articles are included in this encyclopedia that covers the human body. Related materials from the fields of anthropology, behavior, biochemistry, biophysics, cytology, ecology, evolution, genetics, immunology, neurosciences, pharmacology, physiology, and toxicology are included. The subject index is thorough with over 50,000 entries.

1892. Medicine, Literature, and Eponyms: An Encyclopedia of Medical Eponyms Derived from Literary Characters. Alvin E. Rodin; Jack D. Key. Malabar, FL: Krieger, 1989. 345p., illus., bibliog., index. $42.50. ISBN: 0-89464-277-4.

This interesting encyclopedia provides explanations of why a particular medical malady is named after literary or cultural individual. It is arranged alphabetically with complete descriptions.

1893. Merck Manual of Diagnosis and Therapy. 15th. Robert Berkow; Andrew J. Fletcher. Rahway, NJ: Merck Sharpe and Dohme Research Labs, 1987. 2,696p., illus., index. $21.50. ISBN: 0-911910-06-9.

With the first edition published in 1899, the Merck Manual has become a standard encyclopedic source of information on the diagnosis and treatment of diseases. No physician is without this book.

1894. New A to Z of Women's Health: Concise Encyclopedia. revised. Christine Ammer. New York, NY: Facts on File, 1989. 472p., illus. $39.00. ISBN: 0-8095-6325-8.

Some 1,000 entries are included in this very useful encyclopedia that covers women's health. Each entry contains an overview of the topic being discussed. Two other similar works are Derek Llewelyn-Jones' *A-Z of Women's Health* (Oxford University Press, 1990) and Kenneth N. Anderson's *Signet/Mosby Medical Encyclopedia* (New American Library, 1987).

1895. Oxford Companion to Medicine. John Walton; Paul B. Beeson; Ronald Bodley Scott. New York, NY: Oxford University Press, 1986. 2v., illus., index. $150.00. ISBN: 0-19-261191-7.

This title is a comprehensive source of information on medicine in general. Some 150 topics in alphabetical order are covered in detail. Also included are some 5,000 shorter dictionary entries of medical terms and 1,000 biographical entries.

1896. Physics in Medicine and Biology Encyclopedia: Medical Physics, Bioengineering, and Biophysics. T.F. McAinsh. New York, NY: Pergamon Press, 1986. 2v., illus., bibliog., index. $420.00. ISBN: 0-08-026497-2.

Intended for the student who has a basic understanding of physics, this encyclopedia provides discussions of medical topics in terms of the physics theories that are used.

Guides to the Literature

1897. Finding The Sources of Medical Information: A Thesaurus-Index to the Reference Collection. Barbara Shearer; Geneva L. Bush. Westport, CT: Greenwood Press, 1985. 225p. $49.95. ISBN: 0-313-24094-9.

This title is a natural-language index to some 400 reference books and textbooks using the tables of contents as the source of information. The listed reference books are considered a core-collection.

1898. Guide to Information Sources in Alternative Therapy. Barbara Allan. Brookfield, VT: Gower, 1988. 216p., illus., index. $44.95. ISBN: 0-566-05611-9.

This book is a unique source of information about materials that pertain to alternative therapy such as acupuncture and holistic therapies. It lists reference materials, periodicals, general books, organizations, bookstores, nonprint materials, databases, and other useful information.

1899. Health Sciences Information Sources. Ching-Chih Chen. Cambridge, MA: MIT, 1981. 767p., bibliog., index. $80.00. ISBN: 0-262-03074-8.

Arranged by type of publication and then by subject, this excellent guide provides annotated entries for those medical resources that would be useful in a reference setting.

1900. Research Guide to the Health Sciences: Medical, Nutritional, and Environmental. *(Reference Sources for the Social Sciences and Humanities, no.4).* Kathleen J. Haselbauer. New York, NY: Greenwood Press, 1987. 655p., illus., bibliog., index. $65.00. ISBN: 0-313-23530-9.

Some 2,000 sources are included in this guide arranged into four categories of general, basic science, social aspects, and specialties. Full bibliographical information is given followed by a critical annotation.

Handbooks and Manuals

1901. American Medical Association Family Medical Guide. revised and updated. *(American Medical Association Home Health Library).* Jeffrey R. Kunz; Asher J. Finkel. New York, NY: Random House, 1987. 832p., illus. (part in color), index. $35.00. ISBN: 0-394-55582-1.

This AMA title is one of the better home medical guides that, among other topics, provides discussions on some 650 diseases. The disease portion is arranged by body system and gives symptoms, risks involved, patient response, and treatment.

1902. Author's Guide to Biomedical Journals: Complete Manuscript Submission Instructions for 185 Leading Biomedical Periodicals. New York, NY: Mary Ann Liebert, Inc., 1993. 600p., index. $175.00. ISBN: 0-913-113-61-1.

The complete unabridged instructions for submitting manuscripts are given for each of the 185 biomedical periodicals. Both U.S. and foreign titles are included.

1903. Complete Guide to Medical Tests. H. Winter Griffith. Tucson, AZ: Fisher Books, 1988. 948p., index. $19.95. ISBN: 1-55561-011-0.

This patient handbook provides a wealth of accurate information about the medical tests that are prescribed by physicians. It gives good advice on risks, benefits, and side effects.

1904. Complete Guide to Symptoms, Illness and Surgery: Where Does It Hurt? What Does It Mean?: A Doctor Answers Your Questions. H. Winter Griffith. Tucson, AZ: Body Press, 1992 (c1988). 896p., index. $29.95; $17.95pbk. ISBN: 0-685-56436-3; 0-399-51749-9pbk.

This handbook for the patient covers some 500 ailments and 160 common surgeries. The information is well-documented and is intended to help the physician in explaining the symptoms to the patient. For a handbook that covers 100 of the most common symptoms consult John Wasson's *Common Symptom Guide* (McGraw-Hill, 1984).

1905. Complete Medicare Handbook. Eugene Landay. Rocklin, CA: Prima Publishing and Communications, 1990. 200p., index. $8.95. ISBN: 1-55958-036-4.

This handbook is based on the *Medicare Handbook* (GPO, 1990) presenting the basic information that one needs to know in order to work with Medicare.

1906. Conn's Current Therapy: Latest Approved Methods of Treatment for the Practicing Physician. Philadelphia, PA: Saunders, 1992. 1,206p., illus., bibliog., index. $63.40. ISBN: 0-721-64269-1.

This annually revised handbook provides the latest treatment measures for diseases. It is arranged by disease and discusses the disorder with recommendations on treatment.

1907. Current Medical Diagnosis and Treatment. Norwalk, CT: Appleton & Lange, 1962– , annual. v.1– , illus., bibliog., index. price varies per year. ISSN: 0092-8682.

Previously called *Current Diagnosis and Treatment*, this annually revised handbook has become a Bible for diagnosing medical problems. For each disease or syndrome it provides diagnosis, treatment, prognosis, and references.

1908. Everywoman's Medical Handbook. Miriam Stoppard. New York, NY: Ballantine, 1989. 384p., index. $19.95. ISBN: 0-345-35721-3.

This title is a good general handbook that stresses medical diagnosis and treatment as they pertain to women.

1909. Handbook of Medical Library Practice. 4th. Louise Darling; David Bishop; Lois Ann Colaianni. Chicago, IL: Medical Library Association, 1982. 3v., illus., bibliog., index. $70.00. ISBN: 0-8108-2446-9.

This basic handbook for medical libraries provides detailed guidance on all aspects of medical librarianship. The 3 volumes cover v.1—Public services in health science libraries; v.2—Technical services in health sciences libraries; v.3—Health science librarianship and administration.

1910. Handbook of Medical Treatment. 18th. *(JMP Handbook Series).* William Skach; Charles L. Daley; Christopher E. Forsmark. Greenbrae, CA: Jones Medical Publications, 1988. 545p., illus., index. $19.95.

This good general handbook on the more common diseases is not as comprehensive as some other handbooks.

1911. Hospital Contracts Manual. Baker and Hostetler Law Firm. Frederick, MD: Aspen, 1982– , semiannual. v.1– , index. $375.00. ISBN: 0-89443-828-X.

This authoritative handbook provides hospital administrators information about legal issues and management issues. It covers such topics as contracts, negotiating, alternative language, compensation, and other legal matters.

1912. Industrial Medicine Desk Reference. David F. Tver; Kenneth A. Anderson. New York, NY: Chapman & Hall, 1986. 307p., illus., index. $39.95. ISBN: 0-412-01101-8.

This small handbook provides quick information about industrial hazards including chemicals. It is not intended to replace the much larger and more comprehensive works that are available.

1913. Laboratory Test Handbook with Key Word Index. 2nd. David S. Jacobs. Baltimore, MD: Williams & Wilkins, 1990. 1,244p., illus., bibliog., index. $39.95. ISBN: 0-683-04368-4.

This all-inclusive handbook contains a multitude of laboratory tests presented in a standardized format. It provides test name with synonyms, patient care recommendations, specimen requirements, reference ranges, interpretive information, and references. Also of use is a much shorter work of the more common tests, Solomon Garb's *Laboratory Tests in Common Use* (Springer Publishing, 1976).

1914. Physician's Handbook. 21st. *(Concise Medical Library for Practitioner and Student).* Marcus Krupp. Los Altos, CA: Appleton & Lange, 1985. 800p., illus., index. $19.00. ISBN: 0-87041-025-3.

This excellent handbook has proven to be an important part of the reference collection. It provides information on diagnosis of diseases and therapeutic procedures. Data on examinations, tests, and accepted procedures are provided.

Histories

1915. Bibliography of the History of Medicine. Bethesda, MD: National Library of Medicine, 1965– , irregular. no.1– , index. $25.00. ISSN: 0067-7280.

This bibliography contains those citations in the National Library of Medicine MEDLINE database that pertain to the history of medicine and related disciplines.

1916. Cambridge World History of Human Disease. Kenneth F. Kipl. New York, NY: Cambridge University Press, 1993. 1,176p., bibliog., index. $150.00. ISBN: 0-521-33286-9.

This title is a comprehensive history of human disease as documented geographically throughout the world. The first 4 parts give background information followed by 3 parts that describe the history of disease in major regions of the world. The last part is the largest and provides a history of each disease from AIDS to yellow fever.

1917. History of Medical Illustration, from Antiquity to A.D. 1600. Robert Herrlinger. London, Great Britain: Pitman Medical, 1970. 178p., illus. (part in color), bibliog., index. out-of-print.

Being a translation of *Geschichte der Medizinischen Abbildung*, this small book covers the fascinating field of medical illustration.

1918. History of Medicine. Lois N. Magner. New York, NY: Dekker, 1992. 393p., index. $55.00. ISBN: 0-8247-8673-4.

This well-written historical survey of medicine is for the student. Also of interest is Nancy Duin and Jenny Sutcliffe's *History of Medicine: From Prehistory to the Year 2020.*

1919. History of Medicine. *(Yale University School of Medicine Medical Library Publication 27).* Henry Ernest Sigerist. New York, NY: Oxford University Press, 1951-61. 2v., illus., bibliog., index. $22.50v.1; $19.95v.2. ISBN: 0-19-500739-5v.1; 0-19-505079-7v.2.

This work is a classic history of early medicine. The first volume covers primitive and archaic medicine and the second volume covers early Greek, Hindu, and Persian medicine. Two other well-known works are Arturo Castiglioni's *History of Medicine* (Aronson, 1975) and Charles Greene Cumston's *Introduction to the History of Medicine from the Times of the Pharos to the End of the XVIIIth Century* (Davisons, 1968).

1920. Source Book of Medical History. Logan Clendening. New York, NY: Dover, 1942. 685p., bibliog. $14.95. ISBN: 0-486-20621-1.

This classic history of medicine is still used as a textbook. Another useful work that compliments this one is Albert Lyons's *Medicine: An Illustrated History* (Abrams, 1987, c1978).

Periodicals

1921. American Family Physician. Kansas City, MO: American Academy of Family Physicians, 1950– , monthly. v.1– , index. $75.00. ISSN: 0002-838X.

1922. American Journal of Clinical Pathology. Philadelphia, PA: Lippincott/American Society of Clinical Pathologists, 1931– , monthly. v.1– , index. $140.00. ISSN: 0002-9173.

1923. American Journal of Medicine. New York, NY: Cahners, 1946– , monthly. v.1– , index. $100.00. ISSN: 0002-9343.

1924. American Journal of the Medical Sciences. Philadelphia, PA: Lippincott, 1820– , monthly. v.1– , index. $110.00. ISSN: 0002-9629.

1925. American Medical News. Chicago, IL: American Medical Association, 1958– , weekly. v.1– , index. $60.00. ISSN: 0001-1843.

1926. Annals of Internal Medicine. Philadelphia, PA: American College of Physicians, 1922– , semimonthly. v.1– , index. $79.00. ISSN: 0003-4819.

1927. Archives of Internal Medicine. Chicago, IL: American Medical Association, 1908– , monthly. v.1– , index. $65.00. ISSN: 0003-9926.

1928. British Medical Bulletin. Edinburgh, Great Britain: Churchill Livingstone, 1943– , 4/year. v.1– , index. $200.00. ISSN: 0007-1420.

1929. British Medical Journal. London, Great Britain: British Medical Journal, 1832– , weekly. v.1– , index. $246.00. ISSN: 0007-1447.

1930. Bulletin of the History of Medicine. Baltimore, MD: Johns Hopkins University Press/American Association for the History of Medicine, 1933– , quarterly. v.1– , index. $53.00. ISSN: 0007-5140.

1931. Bulletin of the World Health Organization. Geneva, Switzerland: World Health Organization, 1947– , 6/year. v.1– , index. $104.00. ISSN: 0042-9686.

1932. Hospital Practice. New York, NY: H.P. Publishing, 1966– , 18/year. v.1– , index. $54.00. ISSN: 8750-2836.

1933. JAMA: Journal of the American Medical Association. Chicago, IL: American Medical Association, 1848– , weekly. v.1– , index. $79.00. ISSN: 0098-7484.

1934. Journal of Family Practice. Norwalk, CT: Appleton & Lange, 1974– , monthly. v.1– , index. $96.00. ISSN: 0094-3509.

1935. Journal of Internal Medicine. Osney Mead, Great Britain: Blackwell, 1869– , monthly. v.1– , index. $255.00. ISSN: 0954-6820.

1936. Journal of the Canadian Medical Association. Ottawa, Ontario, Canada: Canadian Medical Association, 1911– , semimonthly. v.1– , index. $91.00. ISSN: 0008-4409.

1937. Journal of the Royal Society of Medicine. London, Great Britain: Royal Society of Medicine, 1907– , monthly. v.1– , index. $180.00. ISSN: 0141-0768.

1938. Lancet. London, Great Britain: Lancet, 1823– , weekly. v.1– , index. $95.00. ISSN: 0140-6736.

1939. Medical Science Research. Northwood, Great Britain: Science and Technology Letters, 1986– , 24/year. v.1– , index. $590.00. ISSN: 0269-8951.

1940. New England Journal of Medicine. Waltham, MA: Massachusetts Medical Society, 1812– , weekly. v.1– , index. $93.00. ISSN: 0028-4793.

1941. New York State Journal of Medicine. Lake Success, NY: Medical Society of the State of New York, 1901– , monthly. v.1– , index. $40.00. ISSN: 0028-7628.

1942. Quarterly Journal of Medicine. Eynsham, Great Britain: Oxford University Press, 1907– , monthly. v.1– , index. $210.00. ISSN: 0033-5622.

1943. Social Science and Medicine. Tarrytown, NY: Pergamon Press, 1978– , 24/year. v.1– , index. $1,320.00. ISSN: 0277-9536.

NURSING

Abstracts and Indexes

1944. Cumulative Index to Nursing and Allied Health Literature. Glendale Adventist Medical Center. Glendale, CA: CINHAL Information Systems, 1961– , bimonthly. v.1– , index. $220.00. ISSN: 0146-5554.

Previously called *Cumulative Index to Nursing Literature* and absorbing *Nursing and Allied Health Index*, this index, also called *CINAHL*, covers nursing and other allied health publications. It is also available online and on CD-ROM.

1945. International Nursing Index. New York, NY: American Journal of Nursing, 1966– , quarterly. v.1– , index. $250.00. ISSN: 0020-8124.

This international indexing publication indexes over 270 journals, providing subject and name access. It also lists dissertations, journals, serials, and major monographs. It is also available online and on CD-ROM.

1946. Nursing Studies Index, 1900-1959. Virginia Henderson. New York, NY: Garland, 1984 (reprint of 1972). 4v., index. $50.00. ISBN: 0-8240-6518-8.

This major index covers nursing literature for 1900-1959. It provides abstracts and covers the English language materials in periodicals, books, and pamphlets.

Bibliographies

1947. Bibliography of Nursing Literature: The Holdings of the Royal College of Nursing, 1976-1980. Frances Walsh; Alice W. Thompson. London, Great Britain: Library Association, 1986. 405p., index. $108.00. ISBN: 0-85365-746-7.

Also called *Nursing Bibliography*, this work is a continuation of the *Bibliography of Nursing Literature, 1859-1960; 1961-1970; 1971-1975*. These volumes provide an historical bibliography of nursing.

Biographical Sources

1948. American Nursing: A Biographical Dictionary. *(Garland Reference Library of Social Sciences, v.368).* Vern L. Bullough; Olga Maranjian Church; Alice P. Stein. New York, NY: Garland, 1988. 358p., illus., bibliog., index. $70.00. ISBN: 0-8240-8540-X.

This selective biographical dictionary covers 175 women and 2 men who were key individuals in the field of nursing. A detailed biography of each person provides an historical approach to the nursing profession.

1949. Dictionary of American Nursing Biography. Martin Kaufman; Joellen Watson Hawkins; Loretta P. Higgins; Alice Howell Friedman. New York, NY: Greenwood Press, 1989. 462p., bibliog., index. $55.00. ISBN: 0-313-24520-7.

Being a companion to *Dictionary of American Medical Biography*, this biographical dictionary focuses on people from early pioneer days to the mid-19th century. Detailed biographical information is given for each entry.

1950. Who's Who in American Nursing, 1988-1989. 3rd. Washington, DC: Society of Nursing Professionals/National Reference Press, 1989. 656p. $69.95. ISBN: 0-940863-14-6.

Entries in this biographical dictionary are determined by achievement. Alphabetically arranged, it provides standard personal, family, and educational information.

Dictionaries, Glossaries, and Thesauri

1951. Dictionary of Nursing Theory and Research. Bethel Ann Powers; Thomas R. Knapp. Newbury Park, CA: Sage, 1990. 180p., illus. $42.95; $21.95pbk. ISBN: 0-8039-3411-4; 0-8039-3412-2pbk.

This somewhat technical but still useful dictionary covers terms related to the theory and research of nursing practice and management.

1952. Duncan's Dictionary for Nurses. 2nd. Helen A. Duncan. New York, NY: Springer Publishing, 1989. 802p., illus., bibliog. $44.95; $24.95pbk. ISBN: 0-8261-6201-0; 0-8261-6200-2pbk.

Also called *Dictionary for Nurses*, this practical dictionary is prepared by a nurse for nurses, providing definitions of health science terms. Also useful is *Bailliere's Nurse's Dictionary* (Saunders, 1984). For a very specialized area consult *Bailliere's Midwives Dictionary* (Saunders, 1991).

1953. McGraw-Hill Nursing Dictionary. New York, NY: McGraw-Hill, 1979. 1,008p., illus. $23.95. ISBN: 0-07-045019-6.

Although dated, this work is still a good general dictionary for nursing.

1954. Mosby's Medical, Nursing, and Allied Health Dictionary. 3rd. Walter D. Glanze; Kenneth N. Anderson; Lois E. Anderson. St Louis, MO: Mosby, 1990. 1v. various paging, illus. (part in color). $25.95. ISBN: 0-8016-3227-7.

Previously called *Mosby's Medical and Nursing Dictionary*, this useful dictionary is aimed at the nursing profession including terms, eponyms, and abbreviations. A pocket edition was published in 1990 as *Mosby's Pocket Dictionary of Medicine, Nursing, and Allied Health*.

Directories

1955. Guide to Programs in Nursing in Four-Year Colleges and Universities: Baccalaureate and Graduate Programs in the United States and Canada. Barbara K. Redmany; Linda K. Amos; Ruth Lamothe. New York, NY: American Council of Education/Macmillan, 1987. 472p., index. $90.00. ISBN: 0-02-901490-5.

Although dated, the guide is still useful for address information.

Encyclopedias

1956. Encyclopedia and Dictionary of Medicine, Nursing, and Allied Health. 4th. Benjamin Frank Miller; Claire Brackman Keane. Philadelphia, PA: Saunders, 1989. 1,427p., illus. $20.20. ISBN: 0-7216-3202-5.

This encyclopedia for nurses, paramedics, and students provides information on all aspects of medicine. The explanations and definitions are brief and include numerous illustrations.

Guides to the Literature

1957. Core Collection in Nursing and the Allied Health Sciences: Books, Journals, Media. Annette Peretz; Aurelia Stephan; Edwin Terry. Phoenix, AZ: Oryx Press, 1990. 236p., index. $42.50. ISBN: 0-89774-464-0.

This work is an annotated guide to recommended books, journals, and media in nursing and allied health.

Handbooks and Manuals

1958. Diagnostic Tests Handbook. Regina D. Ford. Springhouse, PA: Springhouse, 1987. 703p., illus., bibliog., index. $21.95. ISBN: 0-87434-138-8.

This handbook contains various laboratory tests and other diagnostic procedures. Tests are arranged in alphabetical order within separate chapters on the designated category. Patient-teaching guidelines are included.

1959. Handbook of Drugs for Nursing Practice. Virginia Burke Karb; Sherry F. Queener; Julia B. Freeman. St Louis, MO: Mosby, 1989. 1,206p., illus., bibliog., index. $28.95. ISBN: 0-8016-2608-0.

More than 1,000 commonly administered drugs are listed providing descriptions, dosage, preparations, and interactions.

1960. Handbook of Nursing Diagnosis. 5th. Lynda Juall Carpenito. Philadelphia, PA: Lippincott, 1993. 513p., index. $17.95. ISBN: 0-397-55054-5.

This standard handbook for nurses provides information on diagnostic procedures.

1961. Lippincott Manual of Nursing Practice. 5th. Doris Smith Suddarth; Lillian Sholtis Brunner. Philadelphia, PA: Lippincott, 1991. 1,607p., illus., bibliog., index. $52.50. ISBN: 0-397-54787-0.

Also called *Manual of Nursing Practice* and *Lippincott Nursing Manual*, this is considered one of the major nursing handbooks. It covers medical and surgical practices, maternity, and pediatrics and includes full descriptions of ailments and their treatments.

1962. Lippincott's Nurse's Drug Manual. Jeanne C. Scherer. Philadelphia, PA: Lippincott, 1985. 1,166p., color illus., index. $26.50. ISBN: 0-397-54435-9.

Derived from *Drug Facts and Comparisons*, this handbook provides a good identification guide to some 1,000 drugs. The largest part is the alphabetical list of drugs that have detailed discussions about each drug listed.

1963. Mosby's Nursing Drug Reference, 1991. Linda Skidmore-Roth. St Louis, MO: Mosby Yearbook, 1992. 1,037p., illus., index. $32.00. ISBN: 0-8016-6198-6.

This comprehensive handbook of drugs provides complete descriptions and uses. Also, equally as important, is the *Nurse's Drug Handbook* (Saunders, 1993).

1964. Mosby's Pharmacology in Nursing. 18th. Leda M. McKenny; Evelyn Salerno. St Louis, MO: Mosby Yearbook, 1992. 1,220p., bibliog., index. $47.95. ISBN: 0-8016-63199-8.

Also called *Pharmacology in Nursing* , this classic handbook for nurses covers current concepts in nursing practice. A quick medication administration reference guide is included.

1965. Nurse's Almanac. 2nd. Howard S. Rowland; Beatrice L. Rowland. Gaithersburg, MD: Aspen, 1984. 849p., bibliog., index. $113.00. ISBN: 0-89443-599-X.

The *Nurses's Almanac* is a good source of quick information that nurses need in day-to-day work including patient problems and services and dying and the terminally ill.

1966. Nurse's Clinical Guide, Dosage Calculations. Belle Erickson; Catherine M. Todd. Springhouse, PA: Springhouse, 1991. 212p., illus., bibliog., index. $22.95. ISBN: 0-87434-318-6.

This handbook provides guidance in drug dosage calculations used in the clinical environment.

1967. Nurse's Quick Reference: An A to Z Guide to 1001 Professional Problems. Springhouse, PA: Springhouse, 1990. 373p., illus., index. $29.95. ISBN: 0-87434-194-9.

From *Nursing Magazine*, this general handbook provides alphabetically arranged discussions of topics that pertain to nursing, including legal matters, emergencies, and careers.

1968. Nursing Administration Handbook. 3rd. Howard S. Rowland; Beatrice L. Rowland. Gaithersburg, MD: Aspen, 1992. 624p., illus., bibliog., index. $69.00.

This very good handbook covers methods, procedures, checklists, and charts used in nursing management on a day-to-day basis.

1969. Nursing Drug Handbook. Springhouse, PA: Springhouse, 1981– , annual. v.1– , illus., bibliog., index. $23.95. ISSN: 0273-320X.

Also called *Drug Handbook* and revised on an annual basis, this standard handbook provides the latest drug information as well as general information on drug therapy, drug actions, reactions, and interactions.

Periodicals

1970. American Journal of Nursing. New York, NY: American Journal of Nursing/American Nurses' Association, 1900– , monthly. v.1– , index. $45.00. ISSN: 0002-936X.

1971. Canadian Journal of Nursing Research/Revue Canadienne de Recherche en Sciences Infirmieres. Montreal, Quebec, Canada: McGill University, 1969– , quarterly. v.1– , index. $48.00. ISSN: 0318-1006.

1972. Heart and Lung. St Louis, MO: Mosby Yearbook, 1972– , bimonthly. v.1– , index. $94.00. ISSN: 0147-9563.

1973. International Journal of Nursing Students. Tarrytown, NY: Pergamon Press, 1965– , quarterly. v.1– , index. $224.00. ISSN: 0020-7489.

1974. JEN: Journal of Emergency Nursing. St Louis, MO: Mosby Yearbook, 1975– , bimonthly. v.1– , index. $98.00. ISSN: 0099-1767.

1975. JOGNN: Journal of Obstetric, Gynecologic, and Neonatal Nursing. Philadelphia, PA: Lippincott, 1972– , bimonthly. v.1– , index. $65.00. ISSN: 0884-2175.

1976. Journal of Community Health Nursing. Hillsdale, NJ: Lawrence Erlbaum, 1984– , quarterly. v.1– , index. $120.00. ISSN: 0737-0016.

1977. Journal of Intravenous Nursing. Philadelphia, PA: Lippincott, 1978– , bimonthly. v.1– , index. $75.00. ISSN: 0896-5846.

1978. Journal of Nursing Administration.
Philadelphia, PA: Lippincott, 1971– , 11/year.
v.1– , index. $90.00. ISSN: 0002-0443.

1979. Journal of Nursing Education.
Thorofare, NJ: Slack, 1962– , 9/year. v.1– ,
index. $42.00. ISSN: 0022-3158.

1980. Journal of Pediatric Nursing.
Philadelphia, PA: Saunders, 1986– , bimonthly.
v.1– , index. $59.00. ISSN: 0882-5963.

1981. Journal of Practical Nursing. Silver
Spring, MD: National Association for Practical
Nurse Education and Service, 1951– ,
quarterly. v.1– , index. $15.00. ISSN:
0022-3867.

1982. Journal of Professional Nursing.
Philadelphia, PA: Saunders/American
Association of Colleges of Nursing, 1985– ,
bimonthly. v.1– , index. $112.00. ISSN:
8755-7223.

**1983. Journal of the American Association of
Occupational Health Nurses.** Thorofare, NJ:
American Association of Occupational Health
Nurses, 1953– , monthly. v.1– , index. $53.00.
ISSN: 0891-0162.

1984. Midwifery. Edinburgh, Scotland:
Churchill Livingstone, 1984– , 4/year. v.1– ,
index. $244.00. ISSN: 0266-6138.

1985. Nursing Management. Dundee, IL: S-N
Publications, 1970– , monthly. v.1– , index.
$25.00. ISSN: 0744-6314.

1986. Nursing Outlook. St Louis, MO: Mosby
Yearbook, 1953– , bimonthly. v.1– , index.
$35.00. ISSN: 0029-6554.

1987. Nursing Research. New York, NY:
American Journal of Nursing, 1952– ,
bimonthly. v.1– , index. $70.00. ISSN:
0029-6562.

1988. Orthopaedic Nursing Journal. Pitman,
NJ: Anthony J. Jannetti/National Association
of Orthopaedic Nurses, 1981– , bimonthly.
v.1– , index. $28.00. ISSN: 0744-6020.

1989. Pediatric Nursing. Pitman, NJ: Anthony
J. Jannetti, 1975– , bimonthly. v.1– , index.
$28.00. ISSN: 0097-9805.

1990. Rehabilitation Nursing. Skokie, IL:
Association of Rehabilitation Nurses, 1975– ,
bimonthly. v.1– , index. $50.00. ISSN:
0278-4807.

PHARMACY AND PHARMACOLOGY

Abstracts and Indexes

1991. American Drug Index. St Louis, MO:
Facts and Comparisons, 1950– , annual. 1st– ,
index. $34.50. ISSN: 0065-8111.
This index lists some 20,000 drugs alphabetically
by generic name with cross-indexing from brand and
chemical names. It provides proprietaries, dosage,
forms, and manufacturer's information.

**1992. International Pharmaceutical Ab-
stracts.** Washington, DC: American Society of
Hospital Pharmacists, 1964– , semimonthly.
v.1– , index. $425.00. ISSN: 0020-8264.
This subject arranged abstracting service provides
coverage of all international pharmaceutical periodicals. It is also available online and on CD-ROM.

**1993. Merck Index: An Encyclopedia of
Chemicals and Drugs.** 11th. Rahway, NJ:
Merck, 1989. 1v. various paging, illus., index.
$35.00. ISBN: 0-911970-28-X.
This work is a standard and indispensable listing of
chemicals, drugs, and related biological products, providing a description that includes structural forms,
chemical properties, toxicity, medical and veterinary
uses, and dosages. It is also available online.

Bibliographies

1994. Cocaine: An Annotated Bibliography.
Carlton E. Turner. Jackson, MS: Research
Institute of Pharmaceutical Sciences,
University of Mississippi, 1988. 2v. $125.00.
Cocaine is a comprehensive bibliography of arti-
cles, patents, books, and book chapters relating to all
aspects of cocaine, its uses, and addiction. Volume 1
covers 1855-1949 and volume 2 covers post-1950.

1995. Drug Abuse Bibliography. Troy, NY:
Whitston, 1970– , annual. v.1– , index. $85.00.
ISBN: 0-87875-412-1 1991.
This annual supplement to Joseph Menditto's
*Drugs of Addiction and Non-Addiction, Their Use and
Abuse: A Comprehensive Bibliography 1960-1969*
provides coverage of all the literature pertaining to
drug abuse.

Dictionaries, Glossaries, and Thesauri

**1996. Dictionary of Drug Abuse Terms and
Terminology.** Ernest L. Abel. Westport, CT:
Greenwood Press, 1984. 187p., bibliog. $49.95.
ISBN: 0-313-24095-7.

Some 3,000 terms are included in this dictionary. It focuses on hard drugs and street language but does have some terms relating to alcohol and tobacco. Also useful is an older, more general work, Richard R. Lingeman's *Drugs from A to Z: A Dictionary* (McGraw-Hill, 1974).

1997. Dictionary of Drugs: Chemical Data, Structures, and Bibliographies. J. Elks; C.R. Ganellin. New York, NY: Chapman & Hall, 1990. 2v., bibliog., index. $1,250.00. ISBN: 0-412-27300-4.

Over 6,000 drugs are included in this very comprehensive dictionary bringing together information found in several other sources including the *Dictionary of Organic Compounds*. Full descriptions of each drug are found in volume one while the second volume contains name, molecular formula, CAS registry number, type of compound, and structure indexes. For antibiotics, consult the *Dictionary of Antibiotics and Related Substances* (Chapman & Hall, 1988) and the 13-volume treatise/handbook *CRC Handbook of Antibiotic Compounds* (CRC, 1980-87).

1998. Dictionary of Pharmacy. Julian H. Fincher. Columbia, SC: University of South Carolina Press, 1986. 374p. $24.95. ISBN: 0-87249-444-6.

This very good dictionary covers the broad terminology in the field of pharmacy including medicinal chemistry, pharmacology, pharmacognosy, administration, practice, and history. Another useful smaller work is John Carpenter's *Pharmacology from A to Z* (Manchester University Press, 1988).

1999. Dictionary of Steroids. D.N. Kirk. New York, NY: Chapman & Hall, 1991. 2v., bibliog., index. $1,350.00. ISBN: 0-412-27060-9.

This detailed dictionary provides information on some 10,000 naturally occurring and synthetic steroids. It is alphabetically arranged and provides such data as chemical name, molecular weight and formula, CAS registry, diagrams showing stereochemistry, and bibiliographic references.

2000. Elsevier's Dictionary of Pharmaceutical Sciences and Techniques. A. Sliosberg. New York, NY: Elsevier, 1968-1980. 2v., index. $249.00/volume. ISBN: 0-444-40544-2 v.1; 0-444-41664-1 v.2.

This multilingual dictionary covers all areas of pharmacy. The 2 volumes cover v.1—Pharmaceutical Technology in English, French, Italian, Spanish, and German; v.2—Materia Medica in English, French, Italian, Spanish, German, and Latin.

2001. Pharmacological and Chemical Synonyms: A Collection of Names of Drugs, Pesticides and Other Compounds Drawn from the Medical Literature of the World. 9th. E.E.J. Marler. New York, NY: Elsevier, 1990. 562p. $179.00. ISBN: 0-444-90487-5.

This useful dictionary identifies synonyms of drugs, pesticides, and other compounds.

2002. Slang and Jargon of Drugs and Drink. Richard A. Spears. Metuchen, NJ: Scarecrow Press, 1986. 585p., bibliog. $42.50. ISBN: 0-8108-1864-7.

This historical dictionary covers slang and jargon of drugs and alcohol from 1700 to the present. Each entry provides definition, alternate spelling, part of speech, dates, geographic origin, and source of information. For a more general dictionary on just alcohol, consult Mark Keller's *Dictionary of Words about Alcohol* (Rutgers Center for Alcohol Studies, 1982).

2003. USAN and the USP Dictionary of Drug Names. Rockville, MD: U.S. Pharmacopeia Convention, 1961-71– , annual. no.10– , index. $130.00. ISSN: 0090-6816.

Previously called *United States Adopted Names* and cumulating from 1961 each year, this dictionary provides a list of established drug names for drugs in the U.S. and abroad. The United States Pharmacopeia Convention (USP) provides standards of strength, quality, purity, packaging, and labeling for drugs in the U.S.

Directories

2004. Pharmaceutical Marketers Directory. Boca Raton, FL: CPS Communications, 1977– , annual. v.1– , index. $155.00.

This directory lists some 1,500 pharmaceutical and healthcare manufacturers plus advertising agencies, healthcare journals, and alternative media. Each entry is described, giving standard directory information including names, titles, addresses and telephone and FAX numbers.

Encyclopedias

2005. Encyclopedia of Alcoholism. 2nd. Robert O'Brien; Morris Chafetz; Glen Evans. New York, NY: Facts on File, 1991. 346p., illus., bibliog., index. $45.00. ISBN: 0-8160-1955-X.

This work is a general encyclopedia on alcoholism with coverage including beverages, social implications with racial and ethnic groups, theories, and terminology associated with alcohol and its abuse.

2006. Encyclopedia of Drug Abuse. 2nd. Glen Evans. St Louis, MO: Facts on File, 1990. 370p., bibliog., index. $45.00. ISBN: 0-8160-1956-8.

This encyclopedia covers hard drugs and prescription drugs presenting information about their abuse, sociological implications, and legal ramifications.

2007. Encyclopedia of Pharmaceutical Technology. James Swarbrick; James C. Boylan. New York, NY: Dekker, 1988– , irregular. v.1– , bibliog., index. $180.00/volume. ISBN: 0-8247-2800-9v.1.

This treatise-like encyclopedia covers the discovery, development, regulation, manufacturing, and commercialization of drugs and dosage forms. It includes information on pharmaceutics, pharmacokinetics, analytical chemistry, quality assurance, toxicology, and manufacturing. Volume 6 was published in 1992.

2008. Pharmaceutical Manufacturing Encyclopedia. 2nd. Marshall Sittig. Park Ridge, NJ: Noyes, 1988. 2v., illus., bibliog., index. $225.00. ISBN: 0-8155-1144-2.

Some 1,300 pharmaceuticals are described in this 2-volume work providing therapeutic function, chemical name, common name, structure formula, CAS registry number, trade names, year introduced, manufacturing process, and references.

Guides to the Literature

2009. Drug Information: A Guide to Current Resources. Bonnie Snow. Chicago, IL: Medical Library Association, 1988. 243p., illus., bibliog., index. $22.40. ISBN: 0-8108-2430-2.

This self-study text is for learning about and identifying print and nonprint sources of information about drugs. Two useful guides to the more broad areas of pharmacy are Theodora Andrews's *Guide to the Literature of Pharmacy and Pharmaceutical Sciences* (Libraries Unlimited, 1986) and Barry Strickland-Hodge's *Keyguide to Information Sources in Pharmacy* (Mansell, 1989).

2010. How to Search the Medical Sources. *(Information Sources in the Medical Sciences Series).* Brian Livesey; Barry Strickland-Hodge. Brookfield, VT: Gower, 1989. 119p., bibliog., index. $38.95. ISBN: 0-566-03533-2.

This title is a basic introduction to searching the medical literature. It covers all types of materials providing good descriptions of the cited sources. It does have an European bias.

2011. Information Sources in the Medical Sciences. 4th. Leslie T. Morton; Shane Godbolt. Boston, MA: Bowker-Saur, 1992. 608p., index. $100.00. ISBN: 0-86291-596-1.

Previously called *Use of Medical Literature*, this guide provides access to reference sources in 16 medical fields. It is one of the better frequently updated guides.

2012. Introduction to Reference Sources in the Health Sciences. Fred W. Roper; Jo Anne Borkman. Chicago, IL: Medical Library Association, 1984. 302p., illus., bibliog., index. $27.20. ISBN: 0-8108-2429-9.

Arranged by type of reference source, this guide provides descriptions of the various materials that are used in health science libraries.

Handbooks and Manuals

2013. AHFS Drug Information. Bethesda, MD: American Society of Hospital Pharmacists, 1992. 2,363p., illus., index. $95.00. ISBN: 1-879907-07-0.

Previously called *American Hospital Formulary Service Drug Information* and kept up to date with quarterly supplements, this book provides evaluative drug information. It is arranged by pharmacologic-therapeutic use. Complete description of each drug includes formula, pharmacology, spectrum, cautions, toxicity, dosage, drug interactions, and other information.

2014. American Red Cross First Aid and Safety Handbook. New York, NY: Little, Brown & Co, 1992. 300p., illus., index. $29.95; $14.95pbk. ISBN: 0-316-73645-7; 0-316-73646-5pbk.

This standard first aid handbook is used worldwide. Another useful handbook is the *American Medical Association Handbook of First Aid and Emergency Care* (Random House, 1990).

2015. Complete Drug Reference 1993. Yonkers, NY: Consumer Reports Book, 1992. 1,640p., index. $39.95. ISBN: 0-89043-587-1.

Also called *USP DI: Advice for Patient*, this is a recognized source of information on drugs for patients, providing description, use, pronunciation, dosage, information needed before taking a drug, proper use, precautions, and side effects. A small useful handbook of drug side effects is Edward L. Stein's *Prescription Drugs and Their Side Effects* (Putnam, 1991).

2016. Complete Guide to Prescription and Non-Prescription Drugs. 1993. H. Winter Griffith. Los Angeles, CA: Body Press, 1992. 1,104p., index. $15.95. ISBN: 0-399-51766-9.

This guide is one of many handbooks providing quick information about drugs that are purchased as prescription or nonprescription. Brief descriptions are provided including dosage, contraindications, and precautions. Two other similar works are David R. Zimmerman's *Essential Guide to Nonprescription Drugs* (HarperCollins, 1983) and James W. Long's *Essential Guide to Prescription Drugs* (HarperCollins, 1991). *AARP Pharmacy Service Prescription Drug Handbook* (HarperPerennial, 1992) is also an excellent book for the lay person.

2017. CRC Handbook of Medicinal Herbs.
James A. Duke. Boca Raton, FL: CRC, 1985. 696p., illus., bibliog., index. $275.00. ISBN: 0-8493-3630-9.

Also called *Handbook of Medicinal Herbs*, this work covers 365 species of herbs having medicinal or folk medicinal uses. Each herb is described in detail scientifically and for use.

2018. Cutting's Handbook of Pharmacology: The Actions and Uses of Drugs.
7th. Windsor C. Cutting; T.Z. Csaky; Byron A. Barnes. Norwalk, CT: Appleton-Century-Crofts, 1984. 786p., illus., bibliog., index. $49.95. ISBN: 0-8385-1418-9.

This regularly revised handbook, also called *Handbook of Pharmacology*, has become a recommended source of information on drug actions and uses. It is arranged by therapeutic uses and provides data on chemistry, history, toxicity, structural formula, and drug mechanisms.

2019. Drug Facts and Comparisons.
45th. St Louis, MO: Facts and Comparisons, 1982. 1 looseleaf v., various paging, index. $165.00. ISBN: 0-932686-91-5.

Previously called *Facts and Comparisons*, this title has become a well-referenced source of drug information. It is published in looseleaf format with monthly updates and provides facts on some 12,000 products grouped by therapeutic use so quick comparisons can be made. An annual hardbound edition is also available that incorporates the previous year's monthly updates.

2020. Drug Interaction Facts, 1992.
St Louis, MO: Facts and Comparisons, 1992. 1 looseleaf v., index. $75.00. ISBN: 0-932686-41-9.

Being a companion to *Drug Facts and Comparisons* and published in the same format with a main volume and monthly updates, this work provides all available facts concerning the interactions of drugs. It is also available on diskette. Two other older but still useful works are Richard R. Harkness' *Drug Interactions Handbook* (Prentice-Hall, 1986) and Murray Weiner's *Drug Interaction Compendium* (Dekker, 1988).

2021. Essential Guide to Psychiatric Drugs.
updated. Jack M. Gorman. New York, NY: St Martin's Press, 1992. 416p., illus., bibliog., index. $14.95. ISBN: 0-312-06967-7.

This specialized handbook provides the user information about psychiatric drugs including a drug reference guide. The drugs are fully described. Also useful is Alan J. Gelenberg's *Practitioner's Guide to Psychoactive Drugs* (Plenum, 1991).

2022. Food and Drug Interaction Guide.
Brian L.G. Morgan. New York, NY: Simon & Schuster, 1986. 335p., bibliog., index. $10.95. ISBN: 0-671-52430-5.

Some 300 over-the-counter drugs are covered in this useful handbook. The emphasis is on the interactions of these drugs with the foods we eat including short- and long-term effects, treatment, and prevention.

2023. Generic Drug Identification Guide.
3rd. J.R. Swim. Abilene, TX: DISCo, 1990. 330p., index. $21.95. ISBN: 0-9626339-0-9.

This unique handbook provides the following information about each generic drug: product ID, generic name, strength, dosage form, shape, color, and drug company. Two sections provide this information either by ID code or generic name. There are also generic and brand cross-reference indexes.

2024. Handbook of Abusable Drugs.
Kenneth Blum. New York, NY: Gardner Press, 1992. 721p., illus., bibliog., index. $49.95. ISBN: 0-89876-196-4.

This very good handbook of social pharmacology provides an overview of the biochemical, pharmacologic, and sociological research related to drug abuse. Testing, diagnosis, treatment, and other information is provided in detail.

2025. Handbook of Non-Prescription Drugs.
9th. Washington, DC: American Pharmaceutical Association, 1990. 1,112p., index. $109.00. ISBN: 0-917330-60-9.

This handbook is a recognized source of information about over-the-counter drugs with descriptions. There are several tables, providing data on the most frequently used products.

2026. Handbook of Pediatric Drug Therapy.
Springhouse: Springhouse, PA. 693p., illus., bibliog., index. $24.95. ISBN: 0-87434-217-1.

The bulk of this handbook is an alphabetically arranged list of pediatric drugs by generic name providing trade names, properties, uses, dosage, indications, actions, contraindications, precautions, interactions, adverse actions, and related information. Also of use is Harry C. Shirkey's *Pediatric Dosage Handbook* (American Pharmaceutical Association, 1992). For a general family drug handbook, consult Allen J. Ellsworth's *Family Practice Drug Handbook* (Mosby Yearbook, 1991).

2027. Handbook of Poisoning: Prevention, Diagnosis, and Treatment. 12th. Robert H. Dreisbach; William O. Robertson. Norwalk, CT: Appleton & Lange, 1987. 589p., illus., bibliog., index. $16.50. ISBN: 0-8385-3643-3.

This well-written handbook provides a summary of poisons and poisoning. The first section discusses poisoning and its preventions, diagnosis and treatment while the second section covers specific poisons. Another more technical source of information on poisoning is Sidney Kaye's *Handbook of Emergency Toxicology: A Guide for the Identification, Diagnosis, and Treatment of Poisoning* (Thomas, 1988).

2028. Modell's Drugs in Current Use and New Drugs. 38th. Walter Modell; Daniel A. Hussar. New York, NY: Springer Publishing, 1992. 208p. $18.95. ISBN: 0-8261-7651-8.

Previously called *Drugs in Current Use and New Drugs* (1955-1987) and *Modell's Drugs*, this small handbook provides information on the description, preparation, and use of drugs. For evaluations of drugs consult Walter Modell's *Drugs of Choice* (Mosby, 1958/59-).

2029. Physician's 1992 Drug Handbook. Springhouse, PA: Springhouse, 1992. 1,174p., bibliog., index. $24.95. ISBN: 0-87434-411-5.

Also called *Drug Handbook*, this is a good handbook for the practicing physician providing quick drug information. It would supplement the *PDR*.

2030. Physicians' Desk Reference: PDR. 46th. Oradell, NJ: Medical Economics, 1992. 2,543p., color illus., index. $54.95. ISBN: 1-56363-003-6.

Also called *PDR*, this book is the drug Bible providing essential information about signs, symptoms, and treatments of overdose as well as other pertinent drug information. Two companion volumes are the *Physicians' Desk Reference for Nonprescription Drugs* (Medical Economics, 1991) and *Physicians' Desk Reference for Ophthalmology* (Medical Economics, 1991). All are also online and on CD-ROM.

2031. Physicians' Generix: The Official Drug Reference of FDA Prescribing Information and Therapeutic Equivalents: 1993. Smithtown, NY: Data Pharmaceutica, 1993. 1v., various paging, index. $68.00. ISBN: 1-880891-03-4.

This book provides complete descriptions of all FDA approved drugs. It also includes information on how the drug is supplied and its wholesale price.

2032. U.S. Pharmacopeia/National Formulary. 22nd/17th. Rockville, MD: U.S. Pharmacopeia, 1990. 1v. various paging, index. $300.00.

This title is the standard U.S. compendia of drug standards. It was, at one time, 2 different publications, now published together every 5 years with supplements issued each year. The *U.S. Pharmacopeia* includes some 3,000 monographs on drug substance and dosage forms while the *National Formulary* contains 250 monographs on inactive or excipients known as pharmaceutic ingredients. This publication is the official compendia for the Food, Drug, and Cosmetic Act. An older dispensing work is the *United States Dispensatory* (Lippincott, 1978).

2033. United States Pharmacopeia Dispensing Information: USP DI. Easton, PA: United States Pharmacopeial Convention, 1980– , annual. v.1– , (3v. per year), index. $195.00.

Also called *USP DI* or *USP Dispensing Information* and updated bimonthly by *USP DI Update*, this is the most authoritative source of information available that provides counseling information with clinically relevant drug information. The 3 volumes cover v.1—Drug information for the health care professional; v.1—Advice for the patient; v.3—Approved drug products and legal requirements review. The Consumers Union also reprints and publishes volume 2 as *United States Pharmacopeia Drug Information for the Consumer*.

Histories

2034. Dictionary of Protopharmacology: Therapeutic Practices, 1700-1850. J. Worth Estes. Canton, MA: Science History Publications, 1990. 215p., illus., bibliog. $39.95. ISBN: 0-88135-068-0.

This dictionary provides an interesting history of therapeutic practices.

2035. Pharmacy: An Illustrated History. David L. Cowen; William H. Helfand. St Louis, MO: Mosby Yearbook, 1988. 272p., illus., bibliog., index. $75.00. ISBN: 0-8709-1498-0.

This excellent history of pharmacy is easy to read. Its coverage is general, but the information given is authoritative.

Periodicals

2036. Agents and Actions. Basel, Switzerland: Birkhauser, 1969– , 12/year. v.1– , index. $585.00. ISSN: 0065-4299.

2037. American Druggist. New York, NY: American Druggist, 1871– , monthly. v.1– , index. $36.00. ISSN: 0190-5279.

2038. American Journal of Hospital Pharmacy. Bethesda, MD: American Society of Hospital Pharmacists, 1945– , monthly. v.1– , index. $105.00. ISSN: 0002-9289.

2039. American Journal of Pharmaceutical Education. Alexandria, VA: American Association of Colleges of Pharmacy, 1937– , 4/year. v.1– , index. $100.00. ISSN: 0002-9459.

2040. American Journal of Pharmacy. Philadelphia, PA: Philadelphia College of Pharmacy and Science, 1825– , quarterly. v.1– , index. price not available. ISSN: 0730-7780.

2041. American Pharmacy. Washington, DC: American Pharmaceutical Association, 1912– , monthly. v.1– , index. $50.00. ISSN: 0160-3450.

2042. Apothecary. Los Altos, CA: HCMS, 1888– , 6/year. v.1– , index. $18.00. ISSN: 0003-6560.

2043. Archives of Toxicology. Berlin, Germany: Springer-Verlag, 1930– , 10/year. v.1– , index. $850.00. ISSN: 0340-5761.

2044. Biochemical Pharmacology. Tarrytown, NY: Pergamon Press, 1958– , 24/year. v.1– , index. $2,256.00. ISSN: 0006-2952.

2045. British Journal of Pharmacology. Basingstoke, Great Britain: Macmillan, 1946– , monthly. v.1– , index. $664.00. ISSN: 0007-1188.

2046. Drug and Cosmetic Industry. Cleveland, OH: Avanstar Communications, 1914– , monthly. v.1– , index. $20.00. ISSN: 0012-6527.

2047. Drug Information Journal. Tarrytown, NY: Pergamon Press, 1966– , quarterly. v.1– , index. $290.00. ISSN: 0092-8615.

2048. Drug Topics. Montvale, NJ: Medical Economics, 1857– , monthly. v.1– , index. $58.00. ISSN: 0012-6616.

2049. European Journal of Clinical Pharmacology. Berlin, Germany: Springer-Verlag, 1968– , 12/year. v.1– , index. $627.00. ISSN: 0031-6970.

2050. European Journal of Pharmacology. Amsterdam, Netherlands: Elsevier, 1967– , 66/year. v.1– , index. $3,099.00. ISSN: 0014-2999.

2051. General Pharmacology. Tarrytown, NY: Pergamon Press, 1970– , bimonthly. v.1– , index. $888.00. ISSN: 0306-3623.

2052. Hospital Formulary. Cleveland, OH: Avanstar Communications, 1966– , monthly. v.1– , index. $35.00. ISSN: 0098-6909.

2053. Hospital Pharmacy. Philadelphia, PA: Lippincott, 1966– , monthly. v.1– , index. $80.00. ISSN: 0018-5787.

2054. International Journal of Clinical Pharmacology, Therapy and Toxicology. Deisenhofen, Germany: Dustri-Verlag Dr. Karl Feistle, 1967– , monthly. v.1– , index. $154.00. ISSN: 0174-4879.

2055. Journal of Clinical Pharmacology. Philadelphia, PA: Lippincott/American College of Clinical Pharmacology, 1961– , 12/year. v.1– , index. $120.00. ISSN: 0009-2700.

2056. Journal of Medicinal Chemistry. Washington, DC: American Chemical Society, 1958– , bimonthly. v.1– , index. $487.00. ISSN: 0022-2623.

2057. Journal of Natural Products. Downers Grove, IL: American Society of Pharmacognosy, 1938– , monthly. v.1– , index. $200.00. ISSN: 0163-3864.

2058. Journal of Pharmaceutical Sciences. Washington, DC: American Pharmaceutical Association, 1961– , monthly. v.50– , index. $195.00. ISSN: 0022-3549.

2059. Journal of Pharmacology and Experimental Therapeutics. Baltimore, MD: Williams & Wilkins/American Society of Pharmacology and Experimental Therapeutics, 1909– , monthly. v.1– , index. $285.00. ISSN: 0022-3565.

2060. Journal of Pharmacy and Pharmacology. London, Great Britain: Pharmaceutical Society of Great Britain, 1949– , monthly. v.1– , index. $315.00. ISSN: 0022-3573.

2061. Pharmaceutical Journal. London, Great Britain: Royal Pharmaceutical Society of Great Britain, 1841– , weekly. v.1– , index. $126.00. ISSN: 0031-6873.

2062. Pharmacological Reviews. Baltimore, MD: Williams & Wilkins/American Society for Pharmacology and Experimental Therapeutics, 1951– , quarterly. v.1– , index. $90.00. ISSN: 0031-6997.

2063. Pharmacologist. Bethesda, MD: American Society for Pharmacology and Experimental Therapeutics, 1959– , quarterly. v.1– , index. $20.00. ISSN: 0031-7004.

2064. Pharmacology. Basel, Switzerland: S. Karger, 1959– , monthly. v.1– , index. $293.00. ISSN: 0031-7012.

2065. Pharmacology and Therapeutics. Tarrytown, NY: Pergamon Press, 1975– , 12/year. v.1– , index. $1,552.00. ISSN: 0163-7258.

2066. Pharmacology and Toxicology. Copenhagen, Denmark: Munksgaard International, 1944– , 12/year. v.1– , index. $280.00. ISSN: 0901-9928.

2067. Pharmacy Times. Port Washington, NY: Romaine Pierson, 1935– , monthly. v.1– , index. $30.00. ISSN: 0003-0627.

2068. Research in Immunology. Paris, France: Editiones Scientifiques Elsevier, 1887– , 9/year. v.1– , index. $265.00. ISSN: 0923-2494.

2069. Toxicon. Tarrytown, NY: Pergamon Press, 1962– , 12/year. v.1– , index. $728.00. ISSN: 0041-0101.

2070. Trends in Pharmaceutical Sciences. Barking, Great Britain: Elsevier, 1979– , monthly. v.1– , index. $382.00. ISSN: 0165-604X.

2071. Vitamins and Hormones: Advances in Research and Applications. San Diego, CA: Academic Press, 1943– , irregular. v.1– , index. price per volume varies. ISSN: 0083-6729.

SPECIAL MEDICAL AREAS

Abstracts and Indexes

2072. Abstracts on Hygiene and Communicable Diseases. London: Bureau of Hygiene and Tropical Diseases, 1926– , monthly. v.1– , index. $150.00. ISSN: 0260-5511.

This abstracting service covers the broad areas of personal hygiene with an emphasis on communicable diseases including STDs. It is also available online.

2073. AIDS Book Review Journal. H. Robert Malinowsky. Chicago, IL: University of Illinois at Chicago, 1993 , irregular. no.1– , index. free over INTERNET. ISSN: 1068-4174.

This is an electronic reviewing journal that reviews books, videos, and journal titles that pertain to AIDS, safer sex, and sexually transmitted diseases. It can be subscribed to at no charge by using INTERNET: Tell Listerv@UICVM sub AIDSBKRV followed by your first and last name or send note to: Listserv@UICVM or Listserv@UICVM.UIC.EDU with note sub AIDSBKRV followed by your first and last name.

2074. CSA Neurosciences Abstracts: Incorporating Endocrinology Abstracts. Bethesda, MD: Cambridge Scientific Abstracts, 1982– , monthly. v.1– , index. $635.00. ISSN: 0141-7711.

This abstracting service covers neuroscience and endocrinology including such areas as aging, neuropharmacology, molecular microbiology, genetics, sleep, and immunology. It is also available online and on CD-ROM.

2075. Immunology Abstracts. Bethesda, MD: Cambridge Scientific Abstracts, 1976– , monthly. v.1– , index. $815.00. ISSN: 0307-112X.

This abstracting service includes some 13,200 abstracts a year covering cancer, vaccine research, t-cells, lymphokines, antigens, and other related topics. It is also available online and on CD-ROM.

2076. Index to Dental Literature. Chicago, IL: American Dental Association, 1839– , quarterly. v.1– , index. $175.00. ISSN: 0019-3992.

This work is an alphabetical author and subject index to dental literature. It is also available online and on CD-ROM.

2077. Virology and AIDS Abstracts. Bethesda, MD: Cambridge Scientific Abstracts, 1967– , monthly. v.1– , index. $715.00. ISSN: 0896-5919.

Previously called *Virology Abstacts*, this service covers viruses that affect humans, animals, and plants. AIDS is covered in detail for human viruses including immunological concerns, epidemiology, disease patterns, symptoms, diagnosis, treatment, and investigational drugs. It is also available online and on CD-ROM.

Bibliographies

2078. AIDS (Acquired Immune Deficiency Syndrome) for year. Troy, NY: Whitston, 1981/86– , irregular. v.1– , index. $55.00/volume. ISBN: 0-685-48693-1v.1.

Also called *AIDS Bibliography* , this very comprehensive ongoing bibliography covers AIDS literature—all types of publications.

2079. Annotated Bibliography of DSM-III. Andrew E. Skodol; Robert L. Spitzer. Washington, DC: American Psychiatric Press, 1987. 649p., illus., bibliog., index. $42.50. ISBN: 0-88048-257-5.

This bibliography pertains to the third edition of the *Diagnostic and Statistical Manual of Mental Disorders: DSM-III*, giving citations to the literature that covers this topic.

2080. Death, Grief, and Bereavement: A Bibliography, 1845-1975. Robert Lester Fulton. New York, NY: Ayer, 1977. 253p. $27.50. ISBN: 0-405-09570-8.

There are many bibliographies pertaining to death, grief and dying. This one is a retrospective listing. Two other useful titles are Albert Jay Miller and Michael James Acri's *Death: A Bibliographic Guide* (Scarecrow Press, 1977) and G. Howard Poteet and Joseph C. Santora's *Death and Dying: A Bibliography, 1974-1978* (Whitson, 1989).

Dictionaries, Glossaries, and Thesauri

2081. Descriptive Dictionary and Atlas of Sexology. Robert T. Francoeur. Westport, CT: Greenwood Press, 1991. 792p., illus. $95.00. ISBN: 0-313-25943-7.

This comprehensive dictionary covers the terms, phrases, and concepts that are associated with the study of sex.

2082. Dictionary of Epidemiology. 2nd. John M. Last; International Epidemiological Association. New York, NY: Oxford University Press, 1988. 141p., illus., bibliog. $29.95; $14.95pbk. ISBN: 0-19-505480-6; 0-19-505481-4pbk.

This small but useful dictionary defines terminology associated with epidemiology.

2083. Dictionary of Eye Terminology. 2nd. Barbara Cassin; Sheila Salomon; Melvin L. Rubin. Gainsville, FL: Triad, 1990. 285p., illus. $17.95. ISBN: 0-937404-33-0.

This very good, small dictionary for students and nonprofessionals provides definitions of terms, acronyms, drug names, and optical and optometric terms. Pronunciation is provided for difficult terms. For op-

tometry consult Michel Millodot's *Dictionary of Optometry* (Butterworth-Heinemann, 1990).

2084. Dictionary of Gerontology. Diana K. Harris. New York, NY: Greenwood Press, 1988. 201p., illus., index. $45.00. ISBN: 0-313-25287-4.

This brief dictionary lists some 800 terms found in the field of gerontology. Important drugs, key organizations, special techniques, and syndromes are included.

2085. Dictionary of Immunology. Fred S. Rosen; Lisa A. Steiner; Emil R. Unanue. New York, NY: Stockton Press, 1989. 223p., illus. $60.00. ISBN: 0-935859-58-6.

Some 1,000 terms are covered in this specialized dictionary including those pertaining to allergies, cellular immunology, and antibody research.

2086. Dictionary of Obstetrics and Gynecology. Christopher Zink. New York, NY: W. DeGruyter, 1988. 277p., illus. (part in color). $34.95. ISBN: 0-89925-533-7.

Being a translation of *Psychrembel Worterbuch Gynakologie und Geburtshilfe*, this small work is intended for the working professional. Terms used in English-speaking countries have been added.

2087. Dictionary of Speech Therapy. David W.H. Morris. New York, NY: Taylor & Francis, 1988. 189p. $27.00. ISBN: 0-85066-444-6.

This small dictionary contains definitions to terms associated with speech therapy. For the anatomical nomenclature consult Joseph F. Brown's *Dictionary of Speech and Hearing Anatomy and Physiology* (Speech and Hearing Service, 1975).

2088. Dictionary of the Sport and Exercise Science. Mark H. Anshel. Champaign, IL: Human Kinetics Books, 1991. 163p., illus. $27.00. ISBN: 0-87322-305-5.

Although not comprehensive, this small dictionary contains the more commonly encountered terms found in the literature pertaining to sports medicine and exercise. Also of use is David F. Tver and Howard F. Hunt's *Encyclopedic Dictionary of Sports Medicine* (Chapman & Hall, 1986).

2089. Dictionary of Toxicology. Ernest Hodgson; Ernest B. Mailman; Janice E. Chambers. New York, NY: Van Nostrand Reinhold, 1988. 395p., illus., bibliog. $86.95. ISBN: 0-442-31842-1.

This well-compiled dictionary of toxicological terms includes related terminology from anatomy, pathology, and physiology.

2090. Dictionary of Visual Science. 4th. David Cline. Radnor, PA: Chilton, 1989. 820p., illus. $55.00. ISBN: 0-8019-7862-9.

This dictionary includes terms and acronyms in all areas of visual science. Syndromes are included as well as pronunciation.

2091. Glossary of Genetics: Classical and Molecular. 5th. R. Rieger. New York, NY: Springer-Verlag, 1991. 553p. $39.00. ISBN: 0-387-52054-6.

This title is a standard dictionary of genetics terminology.

2092. Jablonski's Dictionary of Dentistry. Stanley Jablonski. Malabar, FL: Krieger, 1992. 938p. $119.50. ISBN: 0-89464-477-7.

Jablonski is an established medical dictionary compiler. This one covers in detail the field of dentistry and all its allied areas.

2093. Jablonski's Dictionary of Syndromes and Eponymic Diseases. 2nd. Stanley Jablonski. Malabar, FL: Krieger, 1991. 665p., illus. $99.50. ISBN: 0-89464-224-3.

Also called *Dictionary of Syndromes and Eponymic Diseases* and previously called *Illustrated Dictionary of Eponymic Syndromes and Diseases and Their Synonyms*, this work lists and defines the multitude of syndromes and eponymic diseases. Another larger and very useful work is Sergio I. Magalini's *Dictionary of Medical Syndromes* (Lippincott, 1990).

2094. Psychiatric Dictionary. 6th. Robert Jean Campbell. New York, NY: Oxford University Press, 1989. 811p. $55.00. ISBN: 0-19-505293-5.

This dictionary is based on the terminology and usage as established by the *Diagnostic and Statistical Manual of Mental Disorders: DSM-III-R*. It includes associated terms from neuropsychology, neuroanatomy, and neurometrics. Another smaller work is the American Psychiatric Association's *American Psychiatric Glossary* (American Psychiatric Press, 1988).

Directories

2095. AIDS Directory: An Essential Guide to the 1500 Leaders in Research, Services, Policy, Advocacy, and Funding. Washington, DC: Buraff, 1993. 814p., index. $250.00. ISBN: 1-882594-00-2.

This excellent directory contains some 1,500 national, regional, and international organizations that are concerned with AIDS. It is arranged alphabetically by name of the organization and includes complete directory information.

2096. AIDS Information Sourcebook. 3rd. H. Robert Malinowsky; Gerald J. Perry. Phoenix, AZ: Oryx Press, 1991. 276p., index. $39.95. ISBN: 0-89774-598-1.

Basically a directory of AIDS facilities, this sourcebook also includes a chronology, a bibliography, and a glossary.

2097. Allergy Products Directory. 2nd. American Allergy Association. Menlo Park, CA: Allergy Publications Group, 1987. 122p. $9.95. ISBN: 0-9616708-2-7.

This small compact directory lists allergy products. Another newer, more expensive, and larger directory is *Allergy Products Directory* (Gordon Press, 1992).

2098. American Dental Directory. Chicago, IL: American Dental Association, 1947– , annual. v.1– , index. $100.00. ISSN: 0065-8073.

This annual provides geographical listing of organizations, educational institutions, and dentists.

2099. Asthma Resources Directory. Carol Rudoff; Joann Blessing-Moore. Menlo Park, CA: Allergy Publications, 1990– , irregular. v.1– , index. $29.95. ISBN: 0-944569-01-3v.1.

This directory is a very good source of information on services and products. It is divided into 4 parts: asthma triggers, patient support, medical care, and information sources.

2100. Directory of Medical Rehabilitation Programs. Phoenix, AZ: Oryx Press, 1990. 357p., index. $95.00. ISBN: 0-89774-530-2.

Also called *Medical Rehabilitation Programs*, this directory describes some 1,150 programs in the United States that are provided by hospitals, private practices, or free-standing facilities.

2101. Directory of Pain Treatment Centers in the United States and Canada. Phoenix, AZ: Oryx Press, 1989. 207p., index. $65.00. ISBN: 0-89774-529-9.

Also called *Pain Treatment Centers in the U.S. and Canada* this directory provides information about pain centers. It is arranged alphabetically by state, then city with each entry providing a full range of directory information.

2102. Directory of Psychiatry Residency Training Programs. Washington, DC: American Association of Directors of Psychiatric Residency Training, 1982– , irregular. v.1– , index. $25.00. ISBN: 0-89042-703-8 4th ed.

This directory lists and describes various residency programs sponsored in the United States. The listings are provided by the American Association of Directors of Psychiatric Residency Training, American Medical

Student Association, American Psychiatric Association, and National Institute of Mental Health.

2103. Drug, Alcohol, and Other Addictions: A Directory of Treatment Centers and Prevention Programs Nationwide. 2nd. Phoenix, AZ: Oryx Press, 1993. 682p., index. $68.50. ISBN: 0-89774-623-6.

This comprehensive directory lists facilities that provide treatment for drug, alcohol, and other addictive abuses.

2104. National Directory of AIDS Care. 1991/92. Albuquerque, NM: NDAC, 1991. 608p., index. $75.00.

This detailed directory lists AIDS care facilities and people providing some 14,000 names, addresses, and telephone numbers. It includes national resources, state health departments, service oriented agencies and organizations, government agencies, health care providers, testing sites, hotlines, educational resources, and scientific/research facilities.

Encyclopedias

2105. Concise Encyclopedia of Psychology. Raymond J. Corsini. New York, NY: Wiley, 1987. 1,242p., illus., index. $110.00. ISBN: 0-471-01068-5.

This work is an abridged edition of the 4-volume *Encyclopedia of Psychology* (Wiley, 1984). It is a well-respected reference work containing most all of the information in the 4-volume work but greatly reduced in wordage.

2106. Diseases of the Nose, Throat, Ear, Head and Neck. 14th. John J. Ballenger. Philadelphia, PA: Lea & Febiger, 1991. 1,376p., illus., bibliog., index. $199.50. ISBN: 0-8121-1345-4.

Divided into several parts by region of the head and neck, this treatise-type book presents thorough coverage of all diseases that affect this area of the body. Extensive bibliographies and good illustrations are included.

2107. Encyclopedia of Aging and the Elderly. F. Hampton Ray; Charles Russell. New York, NY: Facts on File, 1992. 308p., illus., bibliog., index. $45.00. ISBN: 0-8160-1869-3.

This general encyclopedia for the layperson covers the processes of growing old. It is not comprehensive but does present a good overview.

2108. Encyclopedia of Blindness and Vision Impairment. Jill Sardegna; T. Otis Paul. New York, NY: Facts on File, 1991. 329p., bibliog., index. $45.00. ISBN: 0-8160-2153-8.

Some 500 general articles are included in this encyclopedia, covering all areas of blindness including

sociological issues, diseases, treatments, schools, and rehabilitation services.

2109. Encyclopedia of Deafness and Hearing Disorders. Carl Turkington. New York, NY: Facts on File, 1992. 278p., illus., index. $45.00. ISBN: 0-8160-2267-4.

This encyclopedia is a very good general, nontechnical source of information about deafness and hearing disorders.

2110. Encyclopedia of Death. Robert Kastenbaum; Beatrice Kastenbaum. Phoenix, AZ: Oryx Press, 1989. 295p., illus., bibliog. $74.50. ISBN: 0-89774-262-X.

This very comprehensive work covers death—historically and scientifically. It includes a great deal of folklore, customs, and myths that are associated with death.

2111. Encyclopedia of Immunology. Ivan M. Roitt; Peter J. Delves. San Diego, CA: Academic Press, 1992. 3v., illus., bibliog., index. $450.00. ISBN: 0-12-226760-5.

This encyclopedia of 596 signed articles covers both clinical and experimental immunology. Discussions are brief, contain references to related entries, and have bibliographies.

2112. Encyclopedia of Neuroscience. George Adelman. Boston, MA: Birkhauser, 1987. 2v., illus., bibliog., index. $165.00. ISBN: 0-8176-3335-9.

Articles from this are also published as *Comparative Neuroscience and Neurobiology*. Some 700 authored entries are included in this reference source covering all the neuroscience disciplines.

2113. Encyclopedia of Phobias, Fears, and Anxieties. Ronald M. Doctor; Ada P. Kahn. New York, NY: Facts on File, 1989. 487p., illus., index. $45.00. ISBN: 0-8160-1798-0.

This general encyclopedia provides nontechnical discussions of phobias, fear, and anxieties including theories, biographies, and some historical background.

2114. Family Mental Health Encyclopedia. Frank J. Bruno. New York, NY: Wiley, 1991. 422p., index. $24.95. ISBN: 0-471-63573-1.

This title is intended for the layperson who wants general nontechnical information about mental health. It includes concepts, biographies, schools of thought, and other topics all arranged alphabetically.

2115. Professional Guide to Diseases. 4th. Springhouse, PA: Springhouse, 1991. 1,311p., illus., bibliog. $32.95. ISBN: 0-87434-388-7.

This book is an excellent guide to the diseases of the human body. It is divided into two parts: diseases of the whole body and diseases of specific organs. It gives a complete description of the disease, including accepted forms of treatment.

Guides to the Literature

2116. The Consumer Health Information Source Book. 4th. Alan M. Rees. Phoenix, AZ: Oryx Press, 1994. 210p., bibliog., index. $42.50. ISBN: 0-89774-796-8.

The Consumer Health Information Source Book is an important guide to over 3,500 information sources including popular books, guides, handbooks, encyclopedias, magazines, journals, newsletters, pamphlets, booklets, brochures, leaflets, reports, core professional medical textbooks, consumer health information software, CD-ROM products, online databases, publishers, support groups, consumer advocacy organizations, health information clearinghouses, and toll-free hotlines.

2117. How to Find Information about AIDS. 2nd. Jeffrey T. Huber. New York, NY: Haworth Press, 1991. 288p., bibliog., index. $29.95; $14.95pbk. ISBN: 1-56024-140-3; 0-918393-99-Xpbk.

This good sourcebook explains where to look for information about AIDS. The largest part is a directory of organizations, health departments, and research institutes. This section is followed with chapters on hotlines, electronic sources, print sources, and audiovisual producers and distributors.

2118. Learning AIDS: An Information Resource Directory. 2nd. New York, NY: American Foundation for AIDS Research/Bowker, 1989. 280p., index. price not available. ISBN: 0-9620363-1-5.

Previously called *AIDS Information Resources Directory*, this title is a guide to books, pamphlets, posters, instructional materials, and audiovisuals that pertain to AIDS. Some entries are evaluated as to their quality.

Handbooks and Manuals

2119. AIDS Manual: A Guide for Health Care Administrators. Jack A. DeHovitz; Teresa J. Altimont. Owings Mills, MD: National Health Publishers, 1988. 1v. loose-leaf, illus., bibliog. price not available. ISBN: 0-932500-97-8.

The *AIDS Manual* is an excellent source of AIDS information with an emphasis on policies and procedures for hospitals, other medical facilities, home health and hospice, substance abuse treatment centers, family planning programs, and correctional facilities. Other information includes CDC publications on AIDS, legal aspects, state statutes, and state and national resources.

2120. Americans with Disabilities Act Handbook. 2nd. Henry H. Perritt. New York, NY: Wiley, 1991. 576p., illus., index. $125.00.

This handbook covers in detail the regulations that pertain to the Americans with Disabilities Act (ADA). It includes the full ADA text, definitions, unlawful discrimination, accommodation requirements, expense, hardship, and litigation procedures.

2121. Chemotherapy Resource Book. Michael C. Perry. Baltimore, MD: Williams & Wilkins, 1991. 1,190p., index. $135.00. ISBN: 0-683-06859-8.

Intended as a handbook for those using chemotherapy, this work covers the field in detail. It is a technical book and intended for the professional.

2122. Diagnostic and Statistical Manual of Mental Disorders: DSM-III-R. 3rd. American Psychiatric Association. Washington, DC: American Psychiatric Press, 1987. 576p., bibliog., index. $43.95; $32.95pbk. ISBN: 0-89042-018-1; 0-84042-019-Xpbk.

This book is the standard reference work for definitions, procedures, statistics, and diagnosis in the field of mental disorders. No mental health professional or library should be without this important work.

2123. Handbook of Clinical Dietetics. 2nd. American Dietetic Association. New Haven, CT: Yale University Press, 1992. 1v. various paging, bibliog., index. $50.00. ISBN: 0-300-05218-9.

Comprehensive coverage of all aspects of dietary management are included in this work, including specific diseases, general, and maintenance. For information on diets of older persons, consult Jeng M. Hsu and Robert L. Davis's *Handbook of Geriatric Nutrition* (Noyes, 1982).

2124. Handbook of Clinical Neurology. P.J. Vinken; G.W. Bruyn. New York, NY: Elsevier, 1968– , irregular. v.1– , illus., bibliog., index. price per volume varies. ISBN: 0-444-90420-4v.49.

This comprehensive treatise/handbook covers all areas of neurology. Each volume is unique and discusses a specific topic such as disturbance of nervous functions or injuries of the spine and spinal cord. There are extensive bibliographies making this a major reference work.

2125. Handbook of Experimental Immunology. 4th. D.M. Weir; Leonore A. Herzenberg; Caroline Blackwell. Boston, MA: Blackwell Scientific, 1986. 4v., illus., bibliog., index. price per volume varies.

This practical "how-to" handbook contains the major accepted techniques that are used in understanding and measuring the body's resistance to diseases. The 4 volumes cover v.1—Immunochemistry; v.2—Cellular immunology; v.3—Genetics and molecular immunology; v.4—Applications of immunological methods in biomedical science. A comprehensive work covering endocrinology is George H. Gass and Harold M. Kaplan's *CRC Handbook of Endocrinology* (CRC, 1982-87).

2126. Handbook of Laboratory Health and Safety Measures. 2nd. S.B. Pal. Boston, MA: Kluwer, 1990. 567p., illus., index. $144.50. ISBN: 0-85200-766-3.

Every facet of laboratory safety from preventing accidents to first aid is covered in this comprehensive handbook. This should be in all laboratories and made essential reading for researchers.

2127. Handbook of Medical Emergencies in the Dental Office. 3rd. Stanley Malamed; Kenneth S. Robbins. St Louis, MO: Mosby, 1987. 406p., illus., bibliog., index. $38.95. ISBN: 0-8016-3102-5.

This specialized handbook provides information on what to do if the following occurs in the dental office: unconsciousness, respiratory difficulty, convulsive seizures, local anesthetic reactions, drug reactions, and chest pains.

2128. Handbook of Medical Sociology. 4th. Howard E. Freeman; Sol Levine. Englewood Cliffs, NJ: Prentice-Hall, 1989. 548p., illus., bibliog., index. price not available. ISBN: 0-13-380305-8.

This specialized handbook of sociological concerns in the medical profession covers such topics as specific illness, education in socio-medicine, and the areas and methods of research in this growing field.

2129. Handbook of Neurochemistry. 2nd. Abel Laytha. New York, NY: Plenum Press, 1982-1985. 10v., illus., bibliog., index. $120.00/volume.

This treatise/handbook on neurochemistry covers in the 10 volumes: v.1—Chemical and cellular architecture; v.2—Experimental neurochemistry; v.3—Metabolism in the nervous system; v.4—Enzymes in the nervous system; v.5—Metabolic turnover in the nervous system; v.6—Receptors in the nervous system; v.7—Structural elements in the nervous system; v.8—Neurochemical systems; v.9—Alteration of metabolites in the nervous system; v.10—Pathological neurochemistry. Also useful as a companion volume is Lawrence Brass and Peter K. Stys's *Handbook of Neurological Lists* (Churchill Livingstone, 1991).

2130. Handbook of Occupational Safety and Health. Lawrence Slote. New York, NY: Wiley, 1987. 744p., illus., index. $110.00. ISBN: 0-471-81029-0.

This handbook is a good source for OSHA information, accident prevention, safety, and potential health hazard issues.

2131. Handbook of Orthodontics. 4th. Robert E. Mayers. Chicago, IL: Year Book Medical, 1988. 577p., illus., bibliog., index. $54.95. ISBN: 0-8151-6003-8.

This handbook is a standard for dentists and dental students as well as a good reference source for libraries. Although not detailed in all areas, it presents a good overview of all aspects of orthodontics.

2132. Handbook of Orthopaedic Surgery. 10th. H. Robert Brashear; R. Beverly Raney, Sr.; Alfred Rivers Shands. St Louis, MO: Mosby, 1986. 547p., illus., bibliog., index. $49.95. ISBN: 0-8016-4080-6.

Previously called *Shands' Handbook of Orthopaedic Surgery*, this title is the best handbook covering orthopaedics. It covers the research in the areas of arthritis, tumors, palsy-type diseases, deformities, and accidents.

2133. Handbook of Parkinson's Disease. 2nd. William C. Koller. New York, NY: Dekker, 1992. 618p., illus., index. $185.00. ISBN: 0-8247-8675-0.

Parkinson's Disease is a number-one concern in medical care for the elderly. This handbook provides the latest information about the disease as well as methods of health care for those with the disease.

2134. Handbook of Psychiatric Emergencies. 3rd. (*Emergency Handbook Series, v.12, no.3*). Andrew Edmund Slaby; Julian Lieb; Laurence R. Tancredi. New York, NY: Medical Examination, 1986. 489p., bibliog., index. $33.75. ISBN: 0-87488-363-6.

This general reference source outlining specific emergencies, their causes, course of treatment, and results is good for the professional.

2135. Handbook of Sexology. J. Money; H. Musaph. New York, NY: Elsevier, 1978. 5v., illus., bibliog., index. $80.00. ISBN: 0-685-05991-X.

Although somewhat dated, the facts presented in this book are still valid. The 5 volumes cover v.1—History and ideology; v.2—Genetics, hormones and behavior; v.3—Procreation and parenthood; v.4—Selected personal and social issues; v.5—Selected syndromes and therapy.

2136. Handbook of Surgery. 9th. (*JMP Handbook Series*). Theodore R. Schrock. Greenbrae, CA: Jones Medical, 1989. 586p., illus., index. $15.95. ISBN: 0-930010-10-8.

This frequently revised standard handbook provides basic information in a concise format for students and professionals. Good for its charts and tables.

2137. Handbook of Toxicologic Pathology.
Wanda M. Haschek-Hock; Colin G. Rousseaux. San Diego, CA: Academic Press, 1991. 1,080p., illus., bibliog., index. $199.00. ISBN: 0-12-330220-X.

This highly technical handbook covers the areas of toxicology as related to pathology. Poisoning is a serious public health concern. This up-to-date source of information is a needed work.

2138. Intensive Care Medicine. 2nd. New York, NY: Little, Brown & Co, 1991. 2,096p., illus., bibliog., index. $155.00.

This comprehensive handbook/textbook covers all aspects of intensive care medicine including pulmonary problems, coronary care, gastrointestinal diseases, infectious diseases, surgical problems, and immunological issues. Also covered are shock and trauma, pharmacokinetics, transplantation, psychiatric issues, and nutrition.

2139. International Handbook on Abortion.
Paul Sachdev. New York, NY: Greenwood Press, 1988. 520p., bibliog., index. $85.00. ISBN: 0-313-23463-9.

With the political focus on abortions, this handbook provides basic information about abortions for professionals.

2140. Krusen's Handbook of Physical Medicine and Rehabilitation. 4th. Frederic J. Kottke; Justus F. Lehmann; Frank Hammond Krusen. Philadelphia, PA: Saunders, 1990. 1,323p., illus., bibliog., index. $96.00. ISBN: 0-7216-2985-7.

Krusen's is an essential reference handbook on physical medicine and rehabilitation. It is comprehensive and contains many large bibliographies. It is also known as the *Handbook of Physical Medicine and Rehabilitation*. A related and useful handbook is Allan M. Ley's *Sports Injury Handbook* (Wiley, 1993).

2141. Manual of Geriatric Medicine. T.J.M. Van der Cammen; G.S. Rai; A.N. Exton-Smith. New York, NY: Churchill Livingstone, 1991. 298p., illus., bibliog., index. $39.95. ISBN: 0-443-03433-8.

This small handbook/manual highlights the areas that professionals should be concerned about in geriatric medicine. Also useful is Edward J. Masoro's specialized work, *CRC Handbook of Physiology in Aging* (CRC, 1981).

2142. Munro Kerr's Operative Obstetrics.
10th. J.M. Kerr; P.R. Myerscough. London, Great Britain: Baillere Tindall, 1982. 508p., illus., bibliog., index. $49.60. ISBN: 0-7020-0904-0.

Also called *Operative Obstetrics*, this is a standard British text. Although British in its approach, it is an important handbook for any medical collection. For a general handbook consult Ralph C. Benson's *Handbook of Obstetrics and Gynecology* (Appleton & Lange, 1983).

2143. Sexually Transmitted Diseases. 2nd.
King K. Holmes. New York, NY: McGraw-Hill, 1990. 1v. various paging, illus., bibliog., index. $98.00. ISBN: 0-07-029677-4.

There are many handbooks on STDs but this is an excellent comprehensive work. It covers all diseases, including AIDS, providing information about the disease and treatment. Also of use is L.C. Parish's *Sexually Transmitted Diseases: A Guide for Clinicians* (Springer-Verlag, 1988).

2144. Silver, Kempe, Bruyn and Fulginiti's Handbook of Pediatrics. 16th. Gerald B. Merenstein; David W. Kaplan; Adam A. Rosenberg; Henry K. Silver; C. Henry Kemp; Henry B. Bruyn; Vincent A. Fulginiti. Norwalk, CT: Appleton & Lange, 1991. 1,050p., illus., bibliog., index. $25.00. ISBN: 0-8785-3639-5.

Previously called *Handbook of Pediatrics*, this work is the Bible of pediatrics for physicians and students. It is pocket-size with concise but complete pediatric information.

Histories

2145. History of Cancer: An Annotated Bibliography. *(Bibliographies and Indexes in Medical Studies, no.3)*. James Stuart Olson. New York, NY: Greenwood Press, 1989. 426p., index. $65.00. ISBN: 0-313-25889-9.

History of Cancer is a good annotated bibliography covering the field of cancer.

2146. History of Pediatrics, 1850-1950. *(Nestle Nutrition Workshop Series, v.22)*. Buford L. Nichols; Angel Ballabriga; Norman Ketchmer. New York, NY: Raven Press, 1990. 295p., illus., bibliog., index. $59.00. ISBN: 0-88167-695-0.

This book is a brief but interesting history of pediatrics up to 1950.

Periodicals

2147. AIDS Alert. Atlanta, GA: American Health Consultants, 1986– , monthly. v.1– , index. $219.00. ISSN: 0887-0292.

2148. AIDS Policy and Law. Washington, DC: Buraff, 1986– , biweekly. v.1– , index. $487.00. ISSN: 0887-1493.

2149. American Heart Journal. St Louis, MO: Mosby Year Book, 1925– , monthly. v.1– , index. $160.00. ISSN: 0002-8703.

2150. American Journal of Cardiology. New York, NY: Cahners, 1958– , 24/year. v.1– , index. $95.00. ISSN: 0002-9149.

2151. American Journal of Obstetrics and Gynecology. St Louis, MO: Mosby/American Gynecological and Obstetrical Society, 1920– , monthly. v.1– , index. $169.00. ISSN: 0002-9378.

2152. American Journal of Ophthalmology. Chicago, IL: Ophthalmic Publishing, 1884– , monthly. v.1– , index. $55.00. ISSN: 0002-9394.

2153. American Journal of Psychiatry. Washington, DC: American Psychiatric Press/American Psychiatric Association, 1844– , monthly. v.1– , index. $56.00. ISSN: 0002-953X.

2154. American Journal of Sports Medicine. Waltham, MA: American Orthopaedic Society for Sports Medicine, 1972– , bimonthly. v.1– , index. $70.00. ISSN: 0363-5465.

2155. American Journal of Surgery. New York, NY: Cahners, 1891– , monthly. v.1– , index. $95.00. ISSN: 0002-9610.

2156. Anesthesiology. Philadelphia, PA: Lippincott/American Society of Anesthesiologists, 1940– , monthly. v.1– , index. $120.00. ISSN: 0003-3022.

2157. Annals of Allergy. Palatine, IL: American College of Allergists, 1943– , monthly. v.1– , index. $42.50. ISSN: 0003-4738.

2158. Annals of Otology, Rhinology and Laryngology. St Louis, MO: Annals Publishing, 1892– , monthly. v.1– , index. $92.00. ISSN: 0003-4894.

2159. Blood. Philadelphia, PA: W.B. Saunders, 1946– , monthly. v.1– , index. $210.00. ISSN: 0006-4971.

2160. Brain. Eynsham, Great Britain: Oxford University Press, 1878– , 6/year. v.1– , index. $195.00. ISSN: 0006-8950.

2161. British Journal of Cancer. Basingstoke, Great Britain: Macmillan, 1947– , monthly. v.1– , index. $497.00. ISSN: 0007-0920.

2162. British Journal of Radiology. Market Harborough, Great Britain: Allen Wells International/British Institute of Radiology, 1896– , monthly. v.1– , index. $224.00. ISSN: 0007-1285.

2163. British Journal of Surgery. Jordan Hill, Great Britain: Butterworth-Heinemann, 1913– , monthly. v.1– , index. $179.00. ISSN: 0007-1323.

2164. Cancer. Philadelphia, PA: Lippincott/American Cancer Society, 1948– , semimonthly. v.1– , index. $95.00. ISSN: 0008-543X.

2165. Cancer Research. Baltimore, MD: Williams & Wilkins/American Association for Cancer Research, 1941– , monthly. v.1– , index. $210.00. ISSN: 0008-5472.

2166. Dental Assistant Journal. Chicago, IL: American Dental Assistants Association, 1931– , quarterly. v.1– , index. $20.00. ISSN: 0011-8508.

2167. Ear, Nose and Throat Journal. Cleveland, OH: International Publishing, 1922– , monthly. v.1– , index. $70.00. ISSN: 0145-5613.

2168. Fertility and Sterility. Birmingham, AL: American Fertility Society, 1949– , monthly. v.1– , index. $140.00. ISSN: 0015-0282.

2169. Journal of Bone and Joint Surgery. Boston, MA: Journal of Bone and Joint Surgery, 1903– , 10/year. v.1– , index. $50.00. ISSN: 0021-9355.

2170. Journal of Clinical Psychiatry. Memphis, TN: Physicians Postgraduate Press, 1940– , monthly. v.1– , index. $54.00. ISSN: 0160-6689.

2171. Journal of Dental Research. Washington, DC: American Association for Dental Research, 1919– , monthly. v.1– , index. $240.00. ISSN: 0022-0345.

2172. Journal of Dentistry. Jordan Hill, Great Britain: Butterworth-Heinemann, 1972– , bimonthly. v.1– , index. $192.00. ISSN: 0300-5712.

2173. Journal of Endocrinology.
Almondsbury, Great Britain: Journal of
Endocrinology, 1939– , monthly. v.1– , index.
$410.00. ISSN: 0022-0795.

2174. Journal of Experimental Medicine.
New York, NY: Rockefeller University Press,
1896– , monthly. v.1– , index. $200.00. ISSN:
0022-1007.

2175. Journal of Immunology. Baltimore,
MD: American Association of Immunologists,
1916– , semimonthly. v.1– , index. $300.00.
ISSN: 0022-1767.

2176. Journal of Infectious Diseases.
Chicago, IL: University of Chicago
Press/Infectious Diseases Society of America,
1904– , monthly. v.1– , index. $186.00. ISSN:
0022-1899.

2177. Journal of Pediatrics. St Louis, MO:
Mosby Yearbook, 1932– , monthly. v.1– ,
index. $162.00. ISSN: 0022-3476.

2178. Journal of the American Dental Association. Chicago, IL: American Dental
Association, 1913– , monthly. v.1– , index.
$45.00. ISSN: 0002-8177.

2179. Journal of the National Cancer Institute. Bethesda, MD: U.S. National Cancer
Institute, 1940– , fortnightly. v.1– , index.
$51.00. ISSN: 0027-8874.

2180. Journal of Urology. Baltimore, MD:
Williams & Wilkins/American Urological
Association, 1917– , monthly. v.1– , index.
$150.00. ISSN: 0022-5347.

2181. Laboratory Animal Science. Cordova,
TN: American Association for Laboratory
Science, 1950– , bimonthly. v.1– , index.
$70.00. ISSN: 0023-6764.

2182. Laryngoscope. St Louis, MO:
Triological Foundation/American
Laryngological, Rhinological, and Otological
Society, 1896– , monthly. v.1– , index.
$125.00. ISSN: 0023-852X.

2183. Molecular and Cellular Endocrinology.
Limerick, Great Britain: Elsevier, 1974– ,
24/year. v.1– , index. $1,392.00. ISSN:
0303-7207.

2184. Pediatrics. Elk Grove Village, IL:
American Academy of Pediatrics, 1948– ,
monthly. v.1– , index. $115.00. ISSN:
0031-4005.

2185. Psychiatry. New York, NY: Guilford,
1937– , quarterly. v.1– , index. $88.00. ISSN:
0033-2747.

2186. Radiology. Oak Brook, IL: Radiological
Society of North America, 1915– , monthly.
v.1– , index. $185.00. ISSN: 0033-8419.

2187. Surgery. St Louis, MO: Mosby
Yearbook/Society of University Surgeons,
1937– , monthly. v.1– , index. $159.00. ISSN:
0039-6060.

Chapter 9: Agriculture

Agriculture is the science of raising crops and livestock for food. It is an old discipline with the word coming from the Latin *agar* meaning field and *cultura* meaning cultivation. Agriculture is an applied science using all of the physical sciences as well as some areas of engineering. In addition to being concerned with plant and animal production, it includes the machinery and materials needed to produce, process, manufacture, and market all of the plant and animal products.

In the area of plant production there are specialized subdivisions, including:

- Agronomy—the study of field crops.
- Floriculture—the production, marketing, and sale of bedding plants, cut flowers, potted plants, foliage plants, flower arrangements, and home gardening.
- Forestry—all aspects of maintaining forests.
- Horticulture—the science of growing flowers, vegetables, and fruits.
- Landscape Architecture—the study of the use of plants in garden architecture.
- Plant Breeding—the development of better plants.

Animal husbandry pertains to the raising of domestic animals and includes their care, breeding, and feeding. Originally veterinary medicine was used only for the medical care of domesticated animals. It is now much more comprehensive and includes the health of all livestock, including poultry, wild birds, pets, wildlife, fur-bearing animals, zoo animals, aquatic mammals, and fish. It also is concerned with the some 200 diseases of animals that can be transmitted to humans. The animal industry is large and highly technical and includes the raising of poultry, cattle, swine, goats, sheep, fur-bearing animals, fish, shellfish, and the wide array of domestic pets.

Until recently, the literature for the agricultural areas was spread among many reports published by a myriad of institutes. Most of this literature is now accessible through the *Bibliography of Agriculture Index*. *Medicus* and *Biological Abstracts* are also key sources of information. Handbooks and manuals are common, especially in areas of environmental concern, such as using pesticides and herbicides.

GENERAL AGRICULTURE

Abstracts and Indexes

2188. Agrindex: International Information System for the Agricultural Sciences and Technology. FAO. Lanham, MD: UNIPUB, 1975– , monthly. v.1– , index. $60.00/issue. ISSN: 0254-8801.

Also available online, this index documents agriculture and related materials from several information centers throughout the world, including the U.S. National Agricultural Library. It includes books, journal articles, atlases, and technical reports.

Bibliographies

2189. Agricultural Journal Titles and Abbreviations. 2nd. U.S. Department of Agriculture, National Agricultural Library. Phoenix, AZ: Oryx Press, 1983. 136p., bibliog., index. $45.00. ISBN: 0-89774-071-8.

This bibliography lists journal titles used by the U.S. National Agricultural Library plus abbreviations that are commonly utilized by the Library. Also of interest would be *Agricultural Terms: As Used in the Bibliography of Agriculture* (Oryx Press, 1978).

2190. Bibliography of Agriculture. U.S. Department of Agriculture, National Agricultural Library. Phoenix, AZ: Oryx Press, 1942– , monthly. v.1– , index. $650.00; $595.00 for annual cumulations. ISSN: 0006-1530.

This bibliography is compiled from the AGRICOLA database and is an index to the documents at the U.S. National Agricultural Library. It covers all aspects of agriculture. There is an annual cumulative index. It is also available online and on CD-ROM.

Biographical Sources

2191. Agricultural and Veterinary Sciences International Who's Who. 3rd. Harlow, Great Britain: Longman, 1987. 1,195p., in 2v. $450.00. ISBN: 0-582-90159-6.

Some 7,500 senior scientists from over 100 countries prominent in the agricultural and veterinary science fields are covered in this directory.

2192. Many Names of Country People: An Historical Dictionary from the Twelfth Century Onward. John T. Schlebecker. New York, NY: Greenwood Press, 1989. 325p., bibliog. $55.00. ISBN: 0-313-26417-1.

This dictionary contains some 1,750 names of people in agriculture from AD 1100 to 1985. It also includes definitions of early agricultural terms.

2193. Who's Who in World Agriculture: A Biographical Guide in the Agricultural and Veterinary Sciences. 2nd. Harlow, Great Britain: Longman, 1985. 2v., index. $295.00. ISBN: 0-582-90111-1.

Some 12,000 agricultural scientists and veterinarians are included in this directory. Full biographical information is given.

Dictionaries, Glossaries, and Thesauri

2194. Agricultural Handbook: A Guide to Terminology. M. Whitby; P. Rowlinson; M. Topham; A. Younger. Cambridge, MA: Blackwell Scientific, 1988. 236p. $24.95. ISBN: 0-632-01821-6.

This dictionary of agricultural terms covers economics, policies, institutions, animals and their products, management, and crops and their products.

2195. Agriculture Dictionary. Ray V. Herren; Roy L. Donahue. Albany, NY: Delmar, 1991. 553p., illus. $24.95; $17.95pbk. ISBN: 0-8273-4095-8; 0-8273-4097-4pbk.

This general agriculture dictionary has some 15,000 terms. Also of use would be Arthur W. Farrall's *Dictionary of Agricultural and Food Engineering* (Interprint Publishers, 1979).

2196. Black's Agricultural Dictionary. 2nd revised. London, Great Britain: A&C Black, 1985. 432p., illus., index. $42.50. ISBN: 0-389-20556-7.

Black's is a standard dictionary for the agricultural field. It does have a British slant, but it is very comprehensive.

2197. Dictionary of Agriculture: German, English, French, Spanish, Italian, Russian. 5th. Gunther Haensch; Gisela Haberkamp de Anton. Munich, Germany: BLV Verlagsgesellschaft, 1987. 1,264p., index. $350.00. ISBN: 0-8288-0036-7.

This very comprehensive multilingual dictionary covers all areas of agriculture and related disciplines.

2198. Dictionary of Terpenoids. J.D. Connolly; R.A. Hill. New York, NY: Chapman & Hall, 1992. 3v., index. $1,800.00. ISBN: 0-412-25770-X.

This dictionary lists over 22,000 terpenoid compounds giving structure diagrams, biological data, and complete physical descriptions and properties. There are name, molecular formula, CAS registry number, and species indexes. Terpenoids are important as flavorings, fragrances, anti-cancer agents, plant growth hormones, and insect sexual hormones.

2199. Vocabulary of Agriculture. (*Terminology Bulletin, v.197*). Ottawa, Ontario, Canada: Department of the Secretary of State of Canada, 1990. 1,213p. $64.75.

This English/French, French/English dictionary contains some 9,000 agricultural terms. Some entries include a short technical note, observation, or definition.

Directories

2200. Historical Directory of American Agricultural Fairs. Donald B. Marti. New York, NY: Greenwood Press, 1986. 300p., bibliog., index. $59.95. ISBN: 0-313-24188-0.

Some 200 state, regional, country and local fairs are included in this directory giving history, attendance, special events, and where to write for additional information.

2201. U.S. Agricultural Groups: Institutional Profiles. William Paul Browne; Allan J. Cigler. New York, NY: Greenwood Press, 1990. 274p., index. $55.00. ISBN: 0-313-25088-X.

Also called *United States Agricultural Groups*, this book describes some 100 private organizations that are concerned with agricultural policy making. It includes membership groups, trade, cooperatives, unions, public interest, think tanks, and policy research institutes.

Guides to the Literature

2202. Agricultural and Animal Sciences Journals and Serials: An Analytical Guide. *(Annotated Bibliographies of Serials: A Subject Approach, no.4).* Richard D. Jensen; Connie Lamb; Nathan M. Smith. Westport, CT: Greenwood Press, 1986. 211p., index. $49.95. ISBN: 0-313-24331-X.

Journals and serials with a research emphasis in agricultural economics, agronomy, animal science, fisheries, forestry, horticulture, and veterinary science are covered in this guide. Some popular and trade magazines are included. Each entry contains an evaluative annotation.

2203. Keyguide to Information Sources in Agricultural Engineering. Bryan Morgan. New York, NY: Mansell, 1985. 209p., index. $39.00. ISBN: 0-7201-1720-8.

This resource is a good general guide to sources of information for agricultural engineering. It includes a survey of the literature, annotated bibliography of sources of information, and a discussion on the organizational sources of information. Also of use would be J. Richard Blanchard and Lois Farrell's *Guide to Sources for Agricultural and Biological Research* (University of California Press, 1981).

Histories

2204. Agriculture in America, 1622-1860: Printed Works in the Collections of the American Philosophical Society, The Historical Society of Pennsylvania, the Library Company of Philadelphia. Andrea J. Tucher. New York, NY: Garland, 1984. 212p. out-of-print.

This scholarly bibliography covers early American books on agriculture. Also of use is John T. Schlebecker's *Bibliography of Books and Pamphlets on the History of Agriculture in the U.S. 1607-1967* (ABC-Clio, 1969).

2205. Encyclopedia of American Agricultural History. Edward L. Schapsmeier. Westport, CT: Greenwood Press, 1975. 467p., index. $55.00. ISBN: 0-8371-7958-0.

This brief encyclopedia details American agricultural history. Two other useful histories that have been reprinted are Percy W. Bidwell's *History of Agriculture in the Northern United States, 1620-1860* (Kelley, 1973, c1925) and Lewis C. Gray's *History of Agriculture in the Southern United States to 1860* (Kelley, 1973, c1933).

Tables

2206. World Crop and Livestock Statistics, 1948-1985: Area, Yield and Production of Crops; Production of Livestock Products. FAO. Lanham, MD: UNIPUB, 1987. 760p., index. $70.00. ISBN: 92-5-002530-0.

This title is another good statistical survey from the Food and Agriculture Organization with the information taken from the *FAO Production Yearbook*. Over 170 countries are represented, giving a variety of crop and livestock statistics.

Yearbooks, Annuals, and Almanacs

2207. FAO Production Yearbook. FAO. Lanham, MD: UNIPUB, 1948– , annual. v.1– , index. $30.00.

This yearbook is a good source of agricultural statistics including land usage, irrigation, agriculture population, crop production, livestock production, food supply, and means of production.

2208. Yearbook of Agriculture. Washington, DC: GPO, 1894– , annual. v.1– , index. price varies per year. ISSN: 0084-3628.

Through 1937 this yearbook was an annual report with statistics on all areas of agriculture. In 1938 the format changed with each year having a theme and reports pertaining only to that theme. Topics have included: Grass, 1948; Water, 1955; Land, 1958; Seeds, 1961; Outdoors, 1966; That We May Eat, 1975; Animal Health, 1984; Our American Land, 1987; America in Agriculture, 1990; and Agriculture and the Environment, 1991.

Periodicals

2209. Agricultural Education. Mechanicsville, VA: Agricultural Education Magazines, 1929– , monthly. v.1– , index. $7.00. ISSN: 0732-4677.

2210. Agricultural Engineer. Silsoe, Great Britain: Institution of Agricultural Engineers, 1944– , quarterly. v.1– , index. $46.00. ISSN: 0308-5732.

2211. Agricultural Engineering. St Joseph, MI: American Society of Agricultural Engineers, 1920– , bimonthly. v.1– , index. $38.50. ISSN: 0002-1458.

2212. Agricultural History. Berkeley, CA: University of California Press/Agricultural History Society, 1927– , quarterly. v.1– , index. $25.00. ISSN: 0002-1482.

2213. Agriculture International. Horley, Great Britain: Agraria Press, 1949– , 11/year. v.1– , index. $72.00. ISSN: 0269-2457.

2214. American Agriculturist. Orlando, FL: HBJ Farm Publications, 1842– , monthly. v.1– , index. $9.00. ISSN: 0161-8237.

2215. American Journal of Agricultural Economics. Ames, IA: Iowa State University/American Agricultural Economics Association, 1919– , 5/year. v.1– , index. $90.00. ISSN: 0002-9092.

2216. Applied Engineering in Agriculture. St Joseph, MI: American Society of Agricultural Engineers, 1985– , 6/year. v.1– , index. $59.00. ISSN: 0883-8542.

2217. ASAE Transactions. St Joseph, MI: American Society of Agricultural Engineers, 1958– , bimonthly. v.1– , index. $171.00. ISSN: 0001-2351.

2218. Experimental Agriculture. Cambridge, Great Britain: Cambridge University Press, 1965– , quarterly. v.1– , index. $149.00. ISSN: 0014-4797.

2219. Farm Journal. Philadelphia, PA: Farm Journal, Inc., 1877– , 14/year. v.1– , index. $14.00. ISSN: 0014-8008.

2220. Farmer's Digest. Brookfield, WI: No-Till Farmer, 1937– , 10/year. v.1– , index. $15.00. ISSN: 0046-3337.

2221. Journal of Agricultural Science. Cambridge, Great Britain: Cambridge University Press, 1905– , 6/year. v.1– , index. $341.00. ISSN: 0021-8596.

2222. NACTA Journal. Urbana, IL: National Association of Colleges and Teachers of Agriculture, 1957– , quarterly. v.1– , index. $25.00. ISSN: 0149-4910.

2223. Outlook on Agriculture. Wallingford, Great Britain: C.A.B. International, 1956– , quarterly. v.1– , index. $179.00. ISSN: 0030-7270.

2224. Successful Farming. Des Moines, IA: Meredith Corp, 1902– , 12/year. v.1– , index. $12.00. ISSN: 0039-4432.

2225. Tropical Agriculture. Jordan Hill, Great Britain: Butterworth-Heinemann, 1924– , quarterly. v.1– , index. $352.00. ISSN: 0041-3216.

2226. Tropical Science. London, Great Britain: Whurr Publishers, 1959– , quarterly. v.1– , index. $125.00. ISSN: 0041-3291.

ANIMAL AND VETERINARY SCIENCE

Abstracts and Indexes

2227. Animal Breeding Abstracts. Wallingford, Great Britain: C.A.B. International, 1933– , monthly. v.1– , index. $485.00. ISSN: 0003-3499.

This international abstracting journal covers animal breeding, genetics, reproduction, and production plus research on immunogenetics, genetic engineering, and fertility improvement. It is also available online and on CD-ROM.

2228. Nutrition Abstracts and Reviews: Section B—Livestock Feeds and Feeding. Wallingford, Great Britain: C.A.B. International, 1977– , monthly. v.1– , index. $409.00. ISSN: 0309-135X.

This abstracting service covers the literature pertaining to livestock feeds and feeding including the analysis, technology, and biochemistry of the feeds. It is also available online and on CD-ROM.

2229. Veterinary Bulletin: A Monthly Abstract Journal on Veterinary Science. Wallingford, Great Britain: C.A.B. International, 1931– , monthly. v.1– , index. $556.00. ISSN: 0042-4854.

Previously called *Tropical Veterinary Bulletin*, this abstracting journal covers all aspects of animal health, nutrition, diseases, reproduction, and related topics. It is also available online.

Biographical Sources

2230. American Veterinary Medical Association Directory. Chicago, IL: American Veterinary Medical Association, 1920– , semimonthly. v.1– , index. $60.00.

Also called the *AVMA Directory*, this directory lists veterinarians throughout the United States. It is updated on a regular basis and gives brief biographical and directory information for each entry.

Dictionaries, Glossaries, and Thesauri

2231. Black's Veterinary Dictionary. 16th. Geoffrey P. West. Totowa, NJ: Barnes & Noble, 1988. 703p., illus. $43.50. ISBN: 0-389-20777-2.

This work is the standard dictionary for veterinary science, covering anatomy, physiology, diseases, diagnosis, treatment, and first aid.

2232. Concise Veterinary Dictionary. New York, NY: Oxford University Press, 1988. 890p., illus. $37.50. ISBN: 0-19-854208-9.

This concise but well-written dictionary of veterinarian terms covers diseases, disease-causing organisms, physiology, biochemistry, anatomy, husbandry, surgery, and toxicology. It is not as comprehensive as *Black's Veterinary Dictionary*.

2233. Dictionary of Animal Health Terminology in English, French, Spanish, German, and Latin. Roy Mack. New York, NY: Elsevier, 1992. 426p., index. $157.00. ISBN: 0-444-88085-2.

Over 5,000 terms are included in this multilingual dictionary covering veterinary medicine in general; infectious, parasitic, and noninfectious disease; and anatomy and physiology of domestic animals. These terms originally appeared in the *Dictionary of Animal Production Terminology* (Elsevier, 1985).

2234. Elsevier's Dictionary of Fishery, Processing, Fish, and Shellfish Names of the World. R. Negedly. New York, NY: Elsevier, 1990. 623p., index. $179.50. ISBN: 0-444-88039-7.

This comprehensive multilingual dictionary lists terms and names in the fishery trade. Languages included are English, French, Spanish, German, and Latin.

Encyclopedias

2235. Aquarium Encyclopedia. Gunther Sterba. Cambridge, MA: MIT Press, 1983. 608p., illus. (part in color), bibliog., index. $45.00. ISBN: 0-262-19207-1.

This very comprehensive encyclopedia describes aquariums, their care and maintenance, and the life they contain.

2236. Atlas of Cats of the World: Domesticated and Wild. Dennis Kelsey-Wood. Neptune City, NJ: T.F.H, 1989. 384p., illus., bibliog., index. $59.95. ISBN: 0-86622-666-4.

Some 50 recognized cat breeds are described in this encyclopedia giving information on purchasing, nutrition, health care, history, psychology, genetics, and foreign travel with cats. Information on each cat breed includes origin, character, appearance, and faults. Also of use is the smaller book by Richard Gebhardt, *Complete Cat Book* (Howell Books, 1991).

2237. Atlas of Dog Breeds of the World. Bonnie Wilcox; Chris Walkowicz. Neptune City, NJ: T.F.H, 1989. 912p., color illus., bibliog., glossary, index. $100.00. ISBN: 0-86622-930-2.

This encyclopedic atlas describes some 400 worldwide dog breeds of which only a third are recognized by the American Kennel Club. It gives for each breed country, weight, height, coat, color, other names, registry, group, and photograph.

2238. Complete Book of the Dog. New York, NY: Holt, Rinehart, & Winston, 1985. 224p., illus. (part in color), index. $19.98. ISBN: 0-03-006019-2.

This handy little book covers such topics as evolution, genetics, dog/human relationships, training, anatomy, health, and nutrition. A listing of dog breeds is included. Also of use is David Taylor's *Ultimate Dog Book* (Simon & Schuster, 1990).

2239. Complete Dog Book: The Photograph, History and Official Standard of Every Breed Admitted to AKC Registration and the Selection, Training, Breeding, Care, and Feeding of Pure-Bred Dogs. 18th. American Kennel Club. New York, NY: Howell Books, 1992. 672p., illus., index. $22.95. ISBN: 0-87605-463-7.

This title is the Bible of dog books produced by the American Kennel Club. As the subtitle states, it is comprehensive and considered the authority on all AKC registered breeds. For coverage of breeds not recognized by AKC see the *Atlas of Dog Breeds of the World*.

2240. Completely Illustrated Atlas of Reptiles and Amphibians for the Terrarium. Fritz Jurgen Obst; Klaus Richter; Udo Jacob. Neptune City, NJ: T.F.H, 1988. 830p., illus. (part in color), index. $100.00. ISBN: 0-86622-958-2.

This encyclopedic atlas describes reptiles and amphibians that can be used in terrariums. For each entry information is given on common name, number of species, distribution, common characteristics, natural history, photograph, and terrarium care. There are sections on the care of the terrarium.

2241. Dr. Axelrod's Atlas of Freshwater Aquarium Fishes. 3rd. Herbert R. Axelrod. Neptune City, NJ: T.F.H, 1989. 797p., color illus., index. $29.95. ISBN: 0-86622-748-2.

This comprehensive encyclopedia covers all freshwater fishes that are used in aquariums. Each fish is fully described and includes recommended aquarium setups. There is a smaller version for the amateur called *Dr. Alexrod's Mini-Atlas of Freshwater Aquarium Fishes* (T.F.H., 1987) or Cliff Harrison's *Popular Tropical Fish for Your Aquarium* (TAB Books, 1982) would also be useful.

2242. Dr. Burgess's Atlas of Marine Aquarium Fishes. Warren E. Burgess. Neptune City, NJ: T.F.H, 1988. 736p., illus., index. $69.95. ISBN: 0-86622-896-9.

This comprehensive encyclopedia covers thousands of species of marine fish that can be used in aquariums. Complete descriptions are given along with recommended aquarium setups. A smaller but useful source would be Martyn Haywood's *Popular Marine Fish for Your Aquarium* (TAB Books, 1982).

2243. Harper's Illustrated Handbook of Cats: A Guide to Every Breed Recognized in America. Roger Caras. New York, NY: Harper & Row, 1988. 191p., illus. (part in color), index. $9.95. ISBN: 0-06-091199-9.

This handbook is an encyclopedic guide to the 39 cat breeds that are recognized in the United States. Each entry includes some history, personality, appearance, potential health problems, and care and grooming. Another useful and popular book is Michael Wright's *Book of the Cat* (Summit Books, 1981).

2244. Harper's Illustrated Handbook of Dogs. Roger Caras. New York, NY: Harper & Row, 1985. 319p., illus. (part in color), index. $9.95. ISBN: 0-06-091198-0.

This handbook is a good general encyclopedia of the dog breeds recognized by the American Kennel Club plus other pure breeds, mongrels, mixed-breeds, mutts, and random-breeds. Each entry gives information on personality, appearance, potential health problems, care, and exercise.

2245. Horse: A Complete Encyclopedia. Pam Cary. Toronto, Canada: Doubleday Canada, 1987. 224p., illus. (part in color), index. $24.95. ISBN: 0-7064-2869-2.

This general encyclopedia covers the history of the horse, horse care, sports, and descriptions of selected breeds. Another useful but older book describing horses and ponies is the *World Atlas of Horses and Ponies* (Crescent, 1980).

2246. International Encyclopedia of Horse Breeds. Jane Kidd. Tucson, AZ: HP Books, 1986. 208p., color illus., index. $14.95. ISBN: 0-89586-393-6.

Also known as the *Illustrated International Encyclopedia of Horse Breeds and Breeding* this encyclopedia describes 141 horse breeds. For each breed information given includes scale of height, country of origin, color, features, history, and present day uses.

2247. Simon and Schuster's Guide to Cats. Gino Pugnetti; Mordecai Siegal. New York, NY: Simon & Schuster, 1983. 255p., illus. (part in color), bibliog., index. $23.95; $10.95pbk. ISBN: 0-671-49167-9; 0-671-49170-9pbk.

The first section of this guide presents general information and history about cats. The second section gives detailed descriptions of 40 cat breeds. Also of use are the *Standard Guide to Cat Breeds* (Gallery Press, 1982) and David Taylor's *Ultimate Cat Book* (L.J. Kaplan, 1989).

Handbooks and Manuals

2248. A-Z of Horse Diseases and Health Problems: Signs, Diagnoses, Causes, Treatment. Tim Hawcroft. New York, NY: Howell Book House, 1990. 304p., illus., index. $19.95. ISBN: 0-87605-884-5.

This nontechnical handbook covers the diagnosis and treatment of ailments affecting horses. A list of ailments requiring immediate veterinarian attention is included. Also of use is Colin J. Vogel's *Stable Veterinary Handbook* (Trafalgar Square, 1990).

2249. All about Tropical Fish. 4th completely revised. Derek McInerny; Geoffrey Gerard; Chris Andrews. New York, NY: Facts on File, 1989. 480p., illus. (part in color), bibliog., index. $29.95. ISBN: 0-8160-2168-6.

All about Tropical Fish is a well-established handbook for those wishing to maintain an aquarium. It covers construction, setup, water, equipment, fish foods, snails, pests and diseases, plants, fish, and breeding. A large portion of the book is a description of the various species of aquarium fish including 18 species of tropical marine fish.

2250. Clinical Dissection Guide for Large Animals: Horse, Ox, Sheep, Goat, Pig. Gheorghe M. Constantinescu. St Louis, MO: Mosby, 1991. 461p., illus., index. price not available. ISBN: 0-80-162564-5.

This handbook/textbook covers those large animals that would normally be treated by a veterinarian. They include the horse, ox, sheep, goat, and pig. This is a detailed book covering the dissections in a step-by-step discussion.

2251. Complete Handbook of Approved New Animal Drug Applications in the United States. Dallas, TX: Shotwell & Carr, 1992. 1v., various paging, index. price not available.

As with drugs for humans, there are new drugs being approved on a regular basis for animals. This handbook covers those drugs in detail.

2252. Cornell Book of Cats: A Comprehensive Medical Reference for Every Cat and Kitten. Mordecai Siegal; Cornell Feline Health Center. New York, NY: Villard Books, 1989. 451p., illus., glossary, index. $24.95. ISBN: 0-394-56787-0.

This comprehensive handbook covers cat acquisition, behavior, nutrition and disorders, anatomy, physiology, and medical emergencies. One chapter is devoted to the descriptions of 41 breeds. Three appendixes cover disease transmittal by pets to humans, vaccinations, and diagnostic tests. Three other cat care books that are also useful include Katrin Behrend's *Complete Book of Cat Care* (Barron's, 1991); Delbert G. Carlson's *Cat Owner's Home Veterinary Handbook* (Howell Books, 1983); and William J. Kay's *Complete Book of Cat Health* (Macmillan, 1985).

2253. Current Techniques in Small Animal Surgery. 3rd. M. Joseph Bojrab; Stephen J. Birehard; James L. Tomlinson, Jr. Philadelphia, PA: Lea & Febiger, 1990. 950p., illus., bibliog., index. $98.50. ISBN: 0-8121-1193-1.

This detailed handbook for the animal surgeon covers diagnosis, pre-operation, risks, preparation, anaesthesia, surgery, and recovery. The step-by-step procedures are excellent.

2254. Handbook of Veterinary Anesthesia. William W. Muirr, III; John A.E. Hubbel. St Louis, MO: Mosby, 1989. 340p., illus., index. $33.95. ISBN: 0-8016-3583-7.

This handbook covers veterinary anesthesia, cardiopulmonary emergencies, and euthanasia. A list of commonly used drugs, apparatus, and manufacturers is included.

2255. Handbook of Veterinary Procedures and Emergency Treatment. 5th. Robert Warren Kirk; Stephen I. Bistner. Philadelphia, PA: Saunders, 1990. 1,016p., illus., bibliog., index. $45.95. ISBN: 0-7216-5464-9.

This comprehensive handbook covers everything from emergency care to examination procedures to laboratory tests. An emergency index is included.

2256. Horse Owner's Veterinary Handbook. James M. Giffin; Tom Gore. New York, NY: Howell Book House, 1989. 400p., illus., index. $29.95. ISBN: 0-87605-880-2.

This handbook for the horse owner helps in identifying an emergency and in describing symptoms to a veterinarian. It also covers general health and nutrition of the horse. Also of use is Chris May's *Horse Care Manual* (Barron's, 1989).

2257. Illustrated Veterinary Guide for Dogs, Cats, Birds, and Exotic Pets. Chris C. Pinney. Blue Ridge Summit, PA: TAB Books, 1992. 736p., illus., index. $29.95. ISBN: 0-8306-1986-0.

This comprehensive handbook for pet owners covers pet selection, housing, and training; health and dental care; immunizations; nutrition and diet; disease identification and treatment; emergency first aid; and breeding and reproduction. Exotic pets include guinea pigs, hamsters, gerbils, mice, rats, rabbits, ferrets, pot-bellied pigs, reptiles, and tropical fish.

2258. Merck Veterinary Manual: A Handbook of Diagnosis, Therapy, and Disease Prevention and Control for the Veterinarian. 6th. Clarence M. Fraser. Rahway, NJ: Merck, 1986. 1,677p., illus., index. $19.00. ISBN: 0-911910-53-0.

This handbook could be considered as the Bible for veterinarians giving information on diagnosis, therapy, disease prevention, and control of diseases. It is well-indexed with the information contained in 10 separate topical sections. Another very comprehensive handbook is Robert Warren Kirk's *Current Veterinary Therapy* (Saunders, 1989) which is frequently updated.

2259. Modern Livestock and Poultry Production. 4th. James R. Gillespie. Albany, NY: Delmar Publishers, 1992. 964p., illus., index. $43.95. ISBN: 0-8273-4087-7.

This well-known handbook/textbook on livestock and poultry covers breed identification, selecting and judging, feeding, management practices, diseases and parasites, housing and equipment, and marketing.

2260. Pet Owner's Guide to Dogs. Kay White. New York, NY: Howell Book House, 1986. 160p., illus. (part in color), index. $12.95. ISBN: 0-87605-769-5.

Information for dog owners is given in this handbook covering selecting, housing, and caring for dogs. Fifty-eight breeds are described. Another newer book for dog owner's from the same publisher is Delbert G. Carlson's *Dog Owner's Home Veterinary Handbook* (Howell Book House, 1992).

2261. Veterinary Pharmaceuticals and Biologicals 1991/92. 7th. Lenoxa, KS: Veterinary Medicine Publishing, 1990. 939p., illus. (part in color), index. $32.95. ISBN: 0-9350-7842-8.

This regularly published handbook covers all pharmaceuticals and biologicals used by veterinarians. Complete descriptions and uses are provided. Another veterinary drug source is Donald C. Plumb's *Veterinary Drug Handbook* (Pharmavet Publishing, 1991). A useful handbook/textbook of veterinary pharmacology is *Upson's Handbook of Clinical Veterinary Pharmacology* (Dan Upson Enterprises, 1988).

2262. Walthan Book of Dog and Cat Nutrition: A Handbook for Veterinarians and Students. 2nd. A.T.B. Edney. New York, NY: Pergamon, 1988. 137p., illus., bibliog., index. $44.00. ISBN: 0-08-035730-X.

This handbook is a good source of information on dog and cat nutrition covering balanced diet, feeding through life, clinical small animal nutrition, imbalanced feeding, and special diets.

Yearbooks, Annuals, and Almanacs

2263. Animal Health Yearbook. Rome, Italy: FAO, 1956– , annual. v.1– , index. $56.00. ISSN: 0066-1872.

This annual publication of the Food and Agriculture Organization (FAO) lists statistics on animal disease in tabular form.

2264. FAO Fisheries Series. Geneva, Switzerland: UNESCO, 1989– , irregular. v.1– , index. price per volume varies. ISSN: 0259-2509.

Previously called *Yearbook of Fishery Statistics* and *FAO Fisheries Studies*, this statistical book, with two volumes per year, gives information on a wide variety of topics such as catches of fish, fishing units, fish farming, commodities, and fish production.

Periodicals

2265. American Bee Journal. Hamilton, IL: Dadant & Sons, 1861– , monthly. v.1– , index. $14.96. ISSN: 0002-7626.

2266. American Journal of Veterinary Research. Schaumburg, IL: American Veterinary Medical Association, 1940– , monthly. v.1– , index. $105.00. ISSN: 0002-9645.

2267. Avian Diseases. Kennett Square, PA: American Association of Avian Pathologists, 1957– , quarterly. v.1– , index. $60.00. ISSN: 0005-2086.

2268. British Poultry Science. Oxford, Great Britain: Carfax, 1960– , 5/year. v.1– , index. $99.00. ISSN: 0007-1668.

2269. British Veterinary Journal. London, Great Britain: Bailiere Tindall, 1875– , bimonthly. v.1– , index. $166.00. ISSN: 0007-1935.

2270. Canadian Journal of Veterinary Research/Revue Canadienne de Recherche Veterinaire. Ottawa, Ontario, Canada: Canadian Veterinary Medical Association, 1937– , quarterly. v.1– , index. $85.00. ISSN: 0830-9000.

2271. Canadian Veterinary Journal/Revue Veterinaire Canadienne. Ottawa, Ontario, Canada: Canadian Veterinary Medical Association, 1960– , monthly. v.1– , index. $90.00. ISSN: 0008-5286.

2272. DVM Newsmagazine. Cleveland, OH: Avanstar Communications, 1970– , monthly. v.1– , index. $24.00. ISSN: 0012-7337.

2273. Journal of Animal Science. Champaign, IL: American Society of Animal Science, 1942– , monthly. v.1– , index. $160.00. ISSN: 0021-8812.

2274. Journal of Small Animal Practice. London, Great Britain: British Veterinary Association, 1960– , monthly. v.1– , index. $220.00. ISSN: 0022-4510.

2275. Journal of the American Animal Hospital Association. Denver, CO: American Animal Hospital Association, 1965– , bimonthly. v.1– , index. $97.00. ISSN: 0587-2871.

2276. Journal of the American Veterinary Medical Association. Schaumburg, IL: American Veterinary Medical Association, 1877– , semimonthly. v.1– , index. $70.00. ISSN: 0003-1488.

2277. Journal of Veterinary Medical Education. Blacksburg, VA: Association of American Veterinary Medical Colleges, 1974– , 2/year. v.1– , index. $20.00. ISSN: 0748-321X.

2278. Journal of Veterinary Medicine: Series A—Animal Physiology, Pathology and Clinical Veterinary Medicine; Series B—Infectious Diseases, Immunology, Fovel Hygiene, Veterinary, Public Health. Berlin, Germany: Paul Parey, 1953– , 10/year A; 10/year B. v.1– , index. $629.00 A; $629.00 B. ISSN: 0931-184X A; 0931-1793 B.

2279. Modern Veterinary Practice. Goleta, CA: American Veterinary Publications, 1920– , 12/year. v.1– , index. $42.00. ISSN: 0362-8140.

2280. Poultry Science. Champaign, IL: Poultry Science Association, 1908– , monthly. v.1– , index. $75.00. ISSN: 0032-5791.

2281. Veterinary Clinics of North America: Equine Practice; Food Animal Practice; Small Animal Practice. Philadelphia, PA: Saunders, 1971– , 12/year. v.1– , index. $188.00. ISSN: 0749-0739; 0749-0720; 0195-5615.

2282. Veterinary Medicine. Lenaxa, KS: Veterinary Medicine Publishing, 1905– , monthly. v.1– , index. $41.95. ISSN: 8750-7943.

2283. Veterinary Record. London, Great Britain: British Veterinary Association, 1888– , weekly. v.1– , index. $160.00. ISSN: 0042-4900.

FOOD AND NUTRITION

Abstracts and Indexes

2284. American Regional Cookery Index. Rhonda H. Kleiman. New York, NY: Neal-Schuman, 1989. 221p., index. $55.00. ISBN: 1-55570-029-2.

This index covers 25 English-language cookbooks that contain regional recipes that may be difficult to locate. It uses over 10,000 subject headings keyed to the specific recipes. See also the *Garland Recipe Index* which is a companion volume and the *International Cookery Index*.

2285. Consumer Health and Nutrition Index. Alan M. Rees. Phoenix, AZ: Oryx Press, 1985– , quarterly. v.1– , index. $135.00. ISSN: 0883-1963.

This index provides access to the top articles in health and general magazines and newsletters that are for the layperson. The articles from some 69 periodicals are arranged alphabetically by author or title under subject topics. It is also available on CD-ROM.

2286. Cooks Index: An Index of Cookery Periodicals and Cookbooks. John Gordon Burke. Evanston, IL: John Gordon Burke, 1989– , irregular. v.1– , index. $55.00. ISSN: 0731-8634.

This useful index covers cookbook and periodical articles but not of individual recipes. It is a useful collection development source for cookbooks. The actual indexing begins with 1975. It is also available online.

2287. Food Science and Technology Abstracts. Shinfield, Great Britain: International Food Information Service, 1969– , monthly. v.1– , index. $1,245.00. ISSN: 0015-6574.

This very comprehensive abstracting service covers food science and all associated disciplines including nutrition, crops, and technologies used in the food industries. It is also available online and on CD-ROM.

2288. Garland Recipe Index. *(Garland Reference Library of the Humanities, v.414).* Kathryn W. Torgeson; Sylvia J. Weinstein. New York, NY: Garland, 1989. 314p., bibliog., index. $51.00. ISBN: 0-8240-9124-8.

This work is an index to the recipes in 48 well-known cookbooks. It is indexed by name, principal food ingredients, and cooking style.

2289. International Cookery Index. *(Neal-Schuman Cookery Index Series, no.1).* Rhonda H. Kleinman; Allan M. Kleinman. New York, NY: Neal-Schuman, 1987. 230p., index. $65.00. ISBN: 0-918212-87-1.

This index provides access to some 25,000 recipes from 51 English-language cookbooks. See also the *American Regional Cookery Index* and the *Garland Recipe Index*.

2290. Nutrition Abstracts and Reviews: Section A—Human and Experimental. Farnham, Great Britain: C.A.B. International, 1977– , monthly. v.1– , index. $610.00. ISSN: 0309-1295.

Previously this abstracting journal was not split into two parts. This part continues the coverage of the original journal, indexing and abstracting all research materials pertaining to nutrition in humans. This service is also available online and on CD-ROM.

Bibliographies

2291. English Language Cookbooks, 1600-1973. Lavonne Axford. Detroit, MI: Gale Research, 1976. 675p., index. $98.00. ISBN: 0-8103-0534-8.

This historical bibliography covers cookbooks for the years 1600-1973.

2292. Nutrition and Disease: An Annotated Bibliography. Karen Lieberman-Nissen. New York, NY: Garland Press, 1991. 192p., index. $25.00. ISSN: 0-8240-7977-9.

This annotated bibliography lists by disease some 400 English-language sources focusing on current research in nutrition for major diseases.

Dictionaries, Glossaries, and Thesauri

2293. Chef's Companion: A Concise Dictionary of Culinary Terms. Elizabeth Riely. New York, NY: Van Nostrand Reinhold, 1986. 215p., illus., bibliog. $29.95. ISBN: 0-442-27846-2.

This small dictionary with concise definitions covers food, food-related, and other terms associated with the food industry.

2294. Complete Beverage Dictionary. Robert A. Lipinski. New York, NY: Van Nostrand Reinhold, 1992. 425p. $34.95. ISBN: 0-442-23987-4.

This very comprehensive dictionary covers terms relating to beverages as well as the beverages themselves.

2295. Consumer's Dictionary of Food Additives. 3rd. Ruth Winter. New York, NY: Crown, 1989. 352p., bibliog. $10.95. ISBN: 0-517-57262-1.

This dictionary defines the multitude of food-additive terms for the consumer. It indicates whether they are beneficial or potentially toxic. A smaller, older, but still useful dictionary is Melvin A. Bernarde's *Food Additive Dicitionary* (Wallaby Books, 1981).

2296. Cooking A to Z. Jane Horn. San Ramon, CA: Ortho Books, 1988. 640p., illus., index. $32.95. ISBN: 0-89721-147-2.

This beautifully illustrated dictionary contains more than 600 recipes plus 400 defined terms covering cooking techniques, ingredients, and equipment.

2297. Dictionary of Food and Nutrition. Jean Adrian; Gilberte Legrand; Regine Frange. New York, NY: VCH, 1988. 233p., illus. $47.00. ISBN: 0-89473-404-4.

This small translation of *Dictionaire de Biochimie Alimentaire et de nutrition* emphasizes the biochemistry of foods but also covers general material on food science and technology. Also of interest would be Arnold E. Bender's *Dictionary of Nutrition and Food Technology* (Butterworths, 1990), now in its 6th edition and the *Prentice-Hall Dictionary of Nutrition and Health* (Prentice-Hall, 1985).

2298. Dictionary of Food Ingredients. 2nd. Robert S. Igoe. New York, NY: Van Nostrand Reinhold, 1989. 225p. $33.95. ISBN: 0-442-31927-4.

The main part of this dictionary covers some 1,000 approved food ingredients giving chemical properties and their uses. Another part groups the ingredients by function such as colors, sweeteners, spices, etc.

2299. Dictionary of Food, Nutrition, and Cookery. Erich Luck. New York, NY: French and European Publications, 1983. 392p. $175.00. ISBN: 0-8288-0842-2.

This English and German dictionary covers food terminology. Also of interest to translators would be *Elsevier's Dictionary of Food Science and Technology* (Elsevier, 1977) in English, French, Spanish, German, and Italian.

2300. Food Lover's Companion: Comprehensive Definitions of over 3,000 Food, Wine, and Culinary Terms. Sharon Tyler Herbst. New York, NY: Barron's, 1990. 582p., illus., bibliog. $10.95. ISBN: 0-8120-4156-9.

This excellent dictionary covers terms related to foods, dishes, sauces, equipment, techniques, names of drinks, foreign food, menus, and brand names. Etymology is included for some terms.

2301. Knight's Foodservice Dictionary. John B. Knight; Charles A. Satter. New York, NY: Van Nostrand Reinhold, 1987. 393p. $39.95. ISBN: 0-442-24666-8.

This specialized dictionary covers the terms used in the foodservice industry including basic terms, ingredients, cost controls, culinary arts, equipment, management information systems, menus, nutrition, sanitation, safety, bars, and service and merchandising. A useful, but brief, dictionary would be Wilbur A. Gould's *Glossary for the Food Industries* (CTI Publications, 1990).

2302. Longman Illustrated Dictionary of Food Service: Food, Its Components, Nutrition, Preparation, and Preservation. Nicholas Light. Chicago, IL: Longman Trade, 1989. 184p., illus., index. $8.95. ISBN: 0-582-02162-6.

Close to 1,250 definitions are included in this small dictionary covering all areas of food. Useful appendices include vitamins, minerals, proteins, food poisoning bacteria, and food additives.

2303. Master Dictionary of Food and Wine. Joyce Rubash. New York, NY: Van Nostrand Reinhold, 1990. 372p. $27.95. ISBN: 0-442-23465-1.

Some 8,000 terms are covered in this culinary dictionary covering ingredients, cooking styles, techniques of preparing, and utensils. A separate area covers wine.

2304. Nutrition and Diet Therapy Dictionary. 3rd. Virginia S. Claudio; Rosalinda T. Lagua. New York, NY: Van Nostrand Reinhold, 1991. 420p., illus. $49.95. ISBN: 0-442-00465-6.

Over 4,000 terms stressing nutrition, diet therapy, and diet in disease are included in this dictionary. Also covered are sports nutrition, genetics and nutrition, and nutrition through the life-cycle. Two special features are a collection of different diets and a listing of treatments of nutritional principles in various physiological and pathological conditions.

Directories

2305. ACCIS Guide to UN Information Sources on Food and Agriculture. *(ACCIS Guide to United Nations Information Sources, no.1).* FAO. Lanham, MD: UNIPUB, 1987. 124p., index. price per volume varies. ISBN: 92-5-102604-1.

From the Advisory Committee for the Co-Ordination of Information Systems (ACCIS), this directory includes libraries, documentation centers, special units, databases, and selected publications concerned with food and nutrition.

2306. Cooksource: An Indispensable Guide to the Best Mailorder Sources for Specialty Foods, Ethnics, and Regional Ingredients and Other Kitchen Supplies. Isabelle Tourneau. New York, NY: Doubleday, 1990. 256p., index. $15.95. ISBN: 0-385-41092-1.

The *Cooksource* is a good directory of where to buy various materials pertaining to cooking through mail-order suppliers. It is divided into three parts covering quality provisions and foods, ethnic food suppliers, and cook's materials such as books and equipment.

2307. Directory of Food and Nutrition Information for Professionals and Consumers. 2nd. Robyn Frank; Holly Berry Irving. Phoenix, AZ: Oryx Press, 1992. 400p., index. $55.00. ISBN: 0-89774-689-9.

This directory lists 550 organizations in Part I that provide information services on nutrition education, food science, food service management, and related aspects of applied nutrition. Complete directory information is given for each entry. Part II contains information resources including reference materials, abstracts and indexing services, journals, museums, books, audiovisual materials, cookbooks, consumer magazines, hotlines, and organizations.

2308. Food, Hunger, Agribusiness: A Directory of Resources. Thomas P. Fenton; Mary J. Heffrom. Maryknoll, NY: Orbis Books, 1987. 131p., illus., index. $19.50. ISBN: 0-933595-21-2.

This directory covers food and hunger and includes entries for organizations, books, periodicals, pamphlets, articles, audiovisuals, and other sources relating to food and hunger.

Encyclopedias

2309. Alexis Lichine's New Encyclopedia of Wines and Spirits. 5th. Alexis Lichine. New York, NY: Knopf, 1987. 771p., illus., bibliog., index. $45.00. ISBN: 0-394-56262-3.

Also called *New Encyclopedia of Wines and Spirits*, this is the standard encyclopedia for wines and spirits. The largest part of the book is the alphabetically arranged articles covering wine, wine terms, wine-growing regions, and wine-producing nations. See also *Sotheby's World Wine Encyclopedia*. Two other good sources are *Hugh Johnson's Modern Encyclopedia of Wines* (Simon & Schuster, 1983) and his *World Atlas of Wine* (Simon & Schuster, 1985).

2310. Columbia Encyclopedia of Nutrition. Myron Winick; Brian L.G. Morgan; James Rozovski; Robin Marks-Kaufman. New York, NY: Putnam, 1989 (c1988). 349p., index. $12.95. ISBN: 0-399-51573-9.

There are 127 alphabetically arranged topics pertaining to nutrition in this small encyclopedia covering diseases, vitamins and minerals, techniques, and conditions. Current research is evaluated.

2311. Complete Book of Herbs, Spices, and Condiments. Carol A. Rinzler. New York, NY: Facts on File, 1990. 199p., illus., bibliog., index. $19.95. ISBN: 0-8160-2008-6.

This colorful and very informative encyclopedia covers the various herbs, spices, and condiments that are used in cooking.

2312. Doctor's Vitamin and Mineral Encyclopedia. Sheldon Saul Hendler. New York, NY: Simon & Schuster, 1991 (c1990). 496p., bibliog., index. $11.95. ISBN: 0-671-74092-X.

This small but well-written encyclopedia presents information about vitamins and minerals. It is intended for the physician but is equally as useful for general reference.

2313. Encyclopedia of Common Natural Ingredients Used in Food, Drugs, and Cosmetics. Albert Y. Leung. New York, NY: Wiley, 1980. 409p., bibliog., index. $100.00. ISBN: 0-471-04954-9.

This is an excellent overview of those ingredients that occur naturally and are used in the preparation of foods, drugs, or cosmetics.

2314. Encyclopedia of Food Engineering. 2nd. Carl W. Hall; Arthur W. Farrall; A.L. Rippen. Westport, CT: Avi, 1986. 882p., illus., index. $135.00. ISBN: 0-87055-451-4.

This alphabetically arranged encyclopedia covers the areas of food engineering (science of food, marketing, storage, and transportation) and food technology (composition of foods, microbiology, nutrition, quality control, and preservation of food crops and animal products). Also of interest would be Douglas M. Considine's *Foods and Food Production Encyclopedia* (Van Nostrand Reinhold, 1982).

2315. Encyclopedia of Food Science and Technology. Y.H. Hui. New York, NY: Wiley, 1992. 4v., illus., index. $595.00. ISBN: 0-471-50541-2.

This comprehensive encyclopedia covers physical and biological properties of food, enhancement of food quality, food preservation, new foods, food processing, food storage, and food distribution. It is international in coverage. Smaller but older one-volume works include Patrick Coyle's *World Encyclopedia of Food* (Facts on File, 1982) and the *McGraw-Hill Encyclopedia of Food, Agriculture, and Nutrition* (McGraw-Hill, 1977).

2316. Encyclopedia of Food Science, Food Technology, and Nutrition. San Diego, CA: Academic Press, 1993. 8v., illus., bibliog., index. $2,100.00. ISBN: 0-12-226850-4.

This comprehensive multi-volume encyclopedia provides a wide range of information on foods and nutrition. It covers such topics as commodities, microbiology, toxicology, food storage and distribution, food industry, diet, nutrition and disease, and clinical nutrition as well as numerous other topics in the 1,030 articles.

2317. Foods and Nutrition Encyclopedia. Clovis, CA: Pegus Press, 1983. 2v., illus., index. $79.95. ISBN: 0-685-09845-1.

The articles in this encyclopedia cover food and its relation to health. The food articles give history, kinds, chemical composition, processing, selection, preparation, and nutritional values. A condensed version was published as *Food and Health: A Nutrition Encyclopedia* (Pegus Press, 1986).

2318. New Frank Schoomaker Encyclopedia of Wines. revised. Alexis Bespaloff. New York, NY: Morrow, 1988. 624p., maps, index. $422.45. ISBN: 0-688-05749-7.

This general encyclopedia covers wines and wine terminology. It has good coverage of the world's wine producing regions. Another source is the *Illustrated Guide to Wines, Brews, and Spirits* (W.C. Brown, 1983). For U.S. wines and wineries consult Anthony D. Blue's *Buyer's Guide to American Wines* (Harper-Perennial, 1992) which lists wineries and gives descriptions of their wines.

2319. Nutrition and Health Encyclopedia. 2nd. David F. Tver; Percy Russell. New York, NY: Van Nostrand Reinhold, 1989. 639p., illus., bibliog. $44.95. ISBN: 0-442-23397-3.

This general nutrition and health encyclopedia covers such areas as body chemistry and composition, major foods, food additives, food toxins, nutrition-related diseases, metabolic functions, and food and drug interactions.

2320. Penguin Encyclopedia of Nutrition. John Yudkin. New York, NY: Viking Penguin, 1986. 431p., illus., index. $7.95. ISBN: 0-14-008563-7.

This very good small encyclopedia stresses the relationship of food and people by covering such topics as food supplies and the population, distribution, and preservation. Foods are basically those found in Western diets either regularly or infrequently. Also useful is Annette B. Natow's *Pocket Encyclopedia of Nutrition* (Pocket Books, 1986).

2321. Sotheby's World Wine Encyclopedia: A Comprehensive Reference Guide to the Wines of the World. Tom Stevenson. Boston, MA: Little, Brown, 1988. 480p., illus. (part in color), maps, index. $40.00. ISBN: 0-8212-1690-2.

This excellent encyclopedic survey lists the wines of the world with beautiful illustrations and numerous tables and maps. See also *Alexis Lichine's New Encyclopedia of Wines and Spirits.* For just the United States consult Leon D. Adams's *Wines of America* (McGraw-Hill, 1990).

2322. Terry Robard's New Book of Wine: The Ultimate Guide to Wines Throughout the World. Terry Robard. New York, NY: Putnam, 1984. 527p., illus., index. $19.95. ISBN: 0-399-12909-X.

Previously called the *New York Times Book of Wine*, this book covers the wines of the world and includes wine tasting and making, tasting parties, serving wine, aging and storage, labels, wine laws, and glassware, as well as the specific wines.

Guides to the Literature

2323. Food and Nutrition Information Guide. Paula Szilard. Littleton, CO: Libraries Unlimited, 1987. 358p., bibliog., index. $45.00. ISBN: 0-87287-457-5.

This guide to materials published in the 10 years prior to 1987 covers food and human nutrition, dietetics, food science and technology, and related areas. Relevant indexing/abstracting services and online databases are also discussed.

2324. Information Sources in Agriculture and Horticulture. George P. Lilley. New Providence, NJ: K.G. Saur, 1992. 580p., index. $110.00. ISBN: 0-408-30101-5.

This work is a very good guide to sources of information in the fields of agriculture and horticulture plus related areas.

2325. Keyguide to Information Sources in Food Science and Technology. Syd Green. New York, NY: Mansell, 1985. 231p., index. $50.00. ISBN: 0-7201-1748-8.

This title is a guide to the literature of materials associated with food sciences. The first part discusses the types of sources while the second part is an annotated bibliography of sources in specific areas of food science such as dairy or food additives. The third part is a directory of food science related organizations throughout the world.

Handbooks and Manuals

2326. AACC Approved Methods. 8th complete. St Paul, MN: American Association of Cereal Chemists, 1991. 1v. with supplements through 1991. $280.00. ISBN: 0-913250-31-7.

This work is the standard handbook for food science methodology. It includes complete preparation and set-up information, easy-to-follow procedures, appropriate precautions, and pertinent references.

2327. Bowes and Church's Food Values of Portions Commonly Used. 15th. Anna De Planter Bowes; Jean A. Thompson Pennington; Charles Frederick Church. New York, NY: HarperCollins, 1989. 328p., bibliog., index. $24.95; $12.95pbk. ISBN: 0-06-055157-7; 0-06-096364-6pbk.

Also called *Food Values of Portions Commonly Used*, this is an authoritative handbook for dieticians listing the food values of the recommended portions of hundreds of commonly used foods. For detailed scientific coverage of the nutritive values of processed foods consult Miloslav Rechcigl's 2-volume *CRC Handbook of Nutritive Value of Processed Food* (CRC, 1982). The *Recommended Dietary Allowances* published by the National Research Council is the standard source for dieticians (National Academy Press, 1989).

2328. Complete Book of Food: A Nutritional, Medical and Culinary Guide. Carol A. Rinzler. New York, NY: World Almanac, 1987. 488p., index. $24.95; $14.95pbk. ISBN: 0-88687-320-7; 0-88687-436-Xpbk.

This handbook aids the user in preparing foods for their best nutritional value. It also indicates the medical aspects of good nutrition.

2329. Elements of Food Engineering. 2nd. Ernest L. Watson; John C. Harper. New York, NY: Van Nostrand Reinhold, 1988. 308p., illus., bibliog., index. $51.95. ISBN: 0-442-22677-2.

This handbook covers the basic engineering fundamentals, including thermodynamics, fluid flow, heat transfer, mixtures of gases and vapors, refrigeration, and dehydration, plus their applications to food processing.

2330. Food Additives Handbook. Richard J. Lewis, Sr. New York, NY: Van Nostrand Reinhold, 1989. 592p., bibliog., index. $78.95. ISBN: 0-442-20508-2.

The main part of this handbook contains a listing of over 1,300 alphabetically arranged food additives giving identifiers (codes and chemical names), properties, food-related uses, occupational restrictions, and toxicological data. It is well-indexed. For more comprehensive coverage of food additives consult Thomas E. Furia's 2-volume *CRC Handbook of Food Additives* (CRC, 1983). Another useful book is M. Fonder's *Food Additives Tables* (Elsevier, 1989).

2331. Food and Culture in America: A Nutrition Handbook. Pamela Gayan Kittler; Kathryn Sucher. New York, NY: Van Nostrand Reinhold, 1989. 384p., illus., bibliog., index. $39.95. ISBN: 0-442-28322-9.

This handbook is intended to help nutritionists and dieticians in their work with ethnic groups. It covers

religion, cultural perspectives, traditions, therapeutic use, food habits, and nutrition, to name a few topics.

2332. Food Chemicals Codex. 3rd. Washington, DC: National Academy Press, 1981. 735p., illus., index. $75.00. ISBN: 0-309-03090-0.

This work is the standard source of chemical information on foods. A supplement was issued in 1992.

2333. Food Handbook. C.M.E. Catsberg; G.J.M. Kemper-Van Dommelen. New York, NY: Ellis Horwood, 1990. 382p., illus., bibliog., index. $74.95. ISBN: 0-7476-0054-6.

This handbook is a translation of *Levensmiddelenleer Produklinformatie over Voedings en Gemotmiddelin*. It covers food production, preservation, and distribution with special chapters on the various classes of food. Three other useful sources are June Gates' *Basic Foods* (Holt, Rinehart & Winston, 1987); Margaret McWilliams' *Food Fundamentals* (Wiley, 1985); and Dennis R. Heldman's *Handbook of Food Engineering* (Dekker, 1992).

2334. Food Industries Manual. 22nd. M.D. Ranken. New York, NY: Van Nostrand Reinhold, 1988. 350p., illus., index. $199.00. ISBN: 0-317-67261-4.

This concise handbook/manual is for those working in the food industries. The information is brief but very well written.

2335. Food Sanitation. 3rd. Rufus K. Guthrie. New York, NY: Van Nostrand Reinhold, 1988. 330p., illus., bibliog., index. $51.95. ISBN: 0-442-20544-9.

This handbook covers all aspects of food handling and sanitation in the food processing industries from harvesting, to processing, to marketing.

2336. Food Science Sourcebook. 2nd revised enlarged. Herbert Ockerman. New York, NY: Van Nostrand Reinhold, 1991. 2v., illus., index. $199.95. ISBN: 0-442-23388-4.

Previously called *Source Book for Food Scientists*, this comprehensive handbook is still a good source of information on food technology. It contains a dictionary of terms including related terms for plants, animals, vitamins, spices, and additives. The handbook portion is called "Food Composition, Properties and General Data," containing numerous charts, tables, and government statistics and data. Another useful sourcebook is Ioannis S. Scarpe's *Sourcebook on Food and Nutrition* (Marquis Academic Media, 1982).

2337. Gary Null's Nutrition Sourcebook for the 80s. Gary Null. New York, NY: Macmillan, 1983. 328p., index. $7.95. ISBN: 0-02-059500-X.

This consumer's handbook covers food nutrition for those on a restricted diet. Lists of foods with their nutritional values are included plus information on harmful effects, sources, and food preparations.

2338. Handbook of Diet Therapy. 5th.
Dorothea Turner. Chicago, IL: University of Chicago Press, 1970. 260p., bibliog., index. $17.50. ISBN: 0-226-81718-0.

This handbook for the dietician outlines the needs for good diet therapy in disease prevention and good body maintenance. Diets are described as well as the therapies.

2339. Handbook of Tropical Foods. *(Foods Science Series, no.9)*. Harvey T. Chan, Jr. New York, NY: Dekker, 1983. 656p., illus., bibliog., index. $165.00. ISBN: 0-8247-1880-1.

This specialized handbook covers the exotic foods that are available for the consumer giving information on where found, values, and uses.

2340. Handbook of Vitamins. 2nd revised and enlarged. *(Food Science and Technology, v.40)*. Lawrence J. Machlin. New York, NY: Dekker, 1991. 595p., illus., bibliog., index. $125.00. ISBN: 0-8247-8351-4.

Information on all aspects of vitamins is included in this comprehensive handbook. Source, uses, hazards, and other areas are stressed.

2341. Modern Nutrition in Health and Disease. 7th. Maurice E. Shils; Vernon R. Young. Philadelphia, PA: Lea & Febiger, 1987. 1,694p., illus., bibliog., index. $84.95. ISBN: 0-8121-0984-8.

This work is a standard textbook/handbook on nutrition. It is considered the source of information on nutrition and its application to proper health and use in combating disease.

2342. Nutrition Almanac. 3rd. John D. Kirschmann; L.J. Dunne. New York, NY: McGraw-Hill, 1990. 340p., bibliog., index. $19.95; $15.95pbk. ISBN: 0-07-034906-1; 0-07-034912-6pbk.

This small handbook discusses food, nutrition, and health. Its main use as a reference source is its table of over 600 foods with their nutrional values and a chart that indicates individual nutrient needs of individuals based on size, metabolism, and caloric requirements.

2343. Nutrition Desk Reference: NDR.
Robert H. Garrison; Elizabeth Somer. New Canaan, CT: Keats Publishing, 1985. 245p., illus., bibliog., index. $34.95. ISBN: 0-87983-523-0.

This general handbook presents information on diet, vitamins and minerals, nutrition and cancer, nutrition and cardiovascular diseases, and nutrition and drugs.

2344. Practical Nutrition: A Quick Reference for the Health Care Practitioner. Margaret D. Simko; Catherine Cowell; Maureen S. Hreha. Rockville, MD: Aspen, 1989. 352p., illus., bibliog., index. $38.00. ISBN: 0-8342-0048-1.

This handbook covers a wide range of topics on practical nutrition including pregnancy and lactation, the infant, the young child, school-aged child, adolescent, the adult, the elderly, and AIDS patients. Other nutrition handbooks from Aspen include Annalynn Skipper's *Dietitian's Handbook of Enteral and Parenteral Nutrition* (1989); Rosita Schiller's *Handbook for Clinical Nutrition Services Management* (1991); Ronni Chernoff's *Geriatric Nutrition* (1991); and Patricia M. Queen's *Handbook of Pediatric Nutrition* (1992).

2345. Source Book of Flavors. *(Avi Sourcebook and Handbook Series, v.2)*. Henry B. Heath. Westport, CT: Avi, 1981. 863p., illus., bibliog., index. $126.95. ISBN: 0-87055-370-4.

This handbook is thorough and complete covering the research and development of flavor industries, descriptions of flavor laboratories, and the standard methods of analysis used in the flavor industries. Information is presented on plants, essential oils, and flavor agents.

Periodicals

2346. British Food Journal. Bradford, Great Britain: MCB University Press, 1899– , 9/year. v.1– , index. $1,159.00. ISSN: 0007-070X.

2347. Chilton's Food Engineering. Radnor, PA: Chilton Co, 1928– , monthly. v.1– , index. $50.00. ISSN: 0193-323X.

2348. Dairy Foods. Chicago, IL: Delta Communications, 1900– , 13/year. v.1– , index. $82.00. ISSN: 0888-0050.

2349. Food and Wine. New York, NY: American Express, 1978– , monthly. v.1– , index. $26.00. ISSN: 0279-6740.

2350. Food Research International. Barking, Great Britain: Elsevier, 1968– , 6/year. v.1– , index. $320.00. ISSN: 0963-9969.

2351. Food Technology. Chicago, IL: Institute of Food Technologists, 1947– , monthly. v.1– , index. $72.00. ISSN: 0015-6639.

2352. Gourmet. New York, NY: Conde Mast Publications, 1941– , monthly. v.1– , index. $18.00. ISSN: 0017-2553.

2353. Journal of Dairy Research. Cambridge, Great Britain: Cambridge University Press, 1929– , 4/year. v.1– , index. $245.00. ISSN: 0022-0299.

2354. Journal of Dairy Science. Champaign, IL: American Dairy Science Association, 1917– , monthly. v.1– , index. $140.00.

2355. Journal of Food Engineering. Barking, Great Britain: Elsevier, 1982– , 12/year. v.1– , index. $456.00. ISSN: 0260-8774.

2356. Journal of the Science of Food and Agriculture. Barking, Great Britain: Elsevier, 1950– , 12/year. v.1– , index. $606.00. ISSN: 0022-5142.

2357. Nutrition Action Healthletter. Washington, DC: Center for Science in the Public Interest, 1974– , 10/year. v.1– , index. $19.95. ISSN: 0199-5510.

2358. Nutrition Reviews. New York, NY, Germany: Springer-Verlag, 1942– , 12/year. v.1– , index. $66.00. ISSN: 0029-6643.

2359. Nutrition Week. Washington, DC: Community Nutrition Institute, 1970– , weekly. v.1– , index. $75.00. ISSN: 0736-0096.

2360. Prepared Foods. Chicago, IL: Delta Communications, 1895– , 13/year. v.1– , index. $84.00. ISSN: 0747-2536.

2361. Proceedings of the Nutrition Society. Cambridge, Great Britain: Cambridge University Press, 1941– , 3/year. v.1– , index. $190.00. ISSN: 0029-6651.

PLANT SCIENCE, AGRONOMY, AND HORTICULTURE

Abstracts and Indexes

2362. Forestry Abstracts. Wallingford, Great Britain: C.A.B. International/Forestry Bureau, 1939– , monthly. v.1– , index. $485.00. ISSN: 0015-7538.

This major abstracting journal covers the world's literature on forestry including land use and conservation. It is also available online.

2363. Herbage Abstracts: Monthly Abstract Journal on Grassland Husbandry and Fodder Crop Production. Wallingford, Great Britain: C.A.B. International, 1931– , monthly. v.1– , index. $360.00. ISSN: 0018-0602.

This specialized abstracting journal covers the management, productivity, and economics of grasslands and fodder crops; species and cultivar description; fodder conservation; composition and nutrition value; botany; plant physiology; grassland ecology; and seed production, testing and storage. It is also available online.

2364. Horticultural Abstracts: Compiled from World Literature on Temperate and Tropical Fruits, Vegetables, Ornamentals, Plantation Crops. Wallingford, Great Britain: C.A.B. International, 1931– , monthly. v.1– , index. $671.00. ISSN: 0018-5280.

This major abstracting journal covers all aspects of horticulture. It is also available online.

2365. Pesticide Index. London, Great Britain: Royal Society of Chemistry, 1988. 258p., index. $49.95. ISSN: 0-85186-339-X.

This work is an identification index to pesticides used in the agricultural industry.

2366. Weed Abstracts. Wallingford, Great Britain: C.A.B. International, 1954– , monthly. v.1– , index. $305.00. ISSN: 0043-1729.

This specialized abstracting journal covers weeds, weed control, and allied topics. It is also available online.

Atlases

2367. Atlas of United States Trees. *(Miscellaneous Publications of the U.S. Department of Agriculture, no.1145).* U.S. Forest Service. Washington, DC: GPO, 1971-81. 6v., maps, bibliog. out-of-print.

This detailed atlas covers the various species of trees that grow in the United States.

2368. Geographical Atlas of World Weeds. LeRoy G. Holm. Melbourne, FL: Krieger, 1991 (c1979). 391p., index. $67.50. ISBN: 0-89464-357-6.

This reprint of a classic atlas shows the distribution of major weeds in the world and their impact on the agricultural economy.

Dictionaries, Glossaries, and Thesauri

2369. Color Dictionary of Flowers and Plants for Home and Garden. Roy Hay; Patrick M. Synge. New York, NY: Crown Books, 1982. 584p., color illus. $17.00. ISBN: 0-517-52456-2.

This dictionary contains well-written and illustrated descriptions of flowers and plants that would be appropriate for home and garden. Two other useful but older dictionaries are Ben Healey's *Gardener's Guide to Plant Names* (Scribner's, 1972) and *Gardener's Dictionary of Plant Names* (Cassell, 1972).

2370. Dictionary of Cultivated Plants and Their Regions of Diversity: Excluding Most Ornamentals, Forest Trees, and Lower Plants. 2nd. A.C. Zeven; J.M.J. DeWet. Lanham, MD: UNIPUB, 1983. 263p. $50.00. ISBN: 90-220-0785-5.

This dictionary has brief listings and descriptions of worldwide cultivated plants indicating where they are located.

2371. Dictionary of Landscape. George A. Goulty. Brookfield, VT: Gower, 1991. 309p. $59.95. ISBN: 0-85967-845-8.

All areas of landscape gardening are included in this specialized dictionary.

2372. Dictionary of Useful and Everyday Plants and Their Common Names. Frank Norman Hawes; John Christopher Willis. New York, NY: Cambridge University Press, 1974. 290p., bibliog. $49.95. ISBN: 0-521-08520-9.

Based on John Christopher Willis' *Dictionary of the Flowering Plants and Ferns*, this dictionary contains terminology associated with those plants that are considered useful or commercial. Two other good sources are Nelson Coon's *Dictionary of Useful Plants* (Rodale Press, 1974) and George Usher's *Dictionary of Plants Used by Man* (Constable, 1974).

2373. Glossary for Horticultural Crops. James Soule. New York, NY: Wiley, 1985. 898p., bibliog., index. $54.95. ISBN: 0-471-88499-5.

This glossary of horticultural terms includes fruit crops, ornamentals, floriculture, and vegetables.

2374. Hillier Colour Dictionary of Trees and Shrubs. H.G. Hillier. North Pomfret, VT: Trafalgar Square, 1981. 323p., color illus. $34.95. ISBN: 0-7153-8192-X.

A good descriptive dictionary, this book has excellent color illustrations of trees and shrubs.

2375. Hortus Third: A Concise Dictionary of Plants Cultivated in the United States and Canada. L.H. Bailey; Ethel Zoe Bailey; Liberty Hyde Bailey Hortorium. New York, NY: Macmillan, 1976. 1,290p., illus., index. $150.00. ISBN: 0-02-505470-8.

This book is an essential reference work for those working with cultivated plants. It includes an index to some 10,400 common plant names. Also useful is P.H. Davis' *Identification of Flowering Plant Families Including Key to Those Native and Cultivated in North Temperate Regions* (Cambridge University Press, 1989).

2376. New Gardener's Dictionary. Jack Kramer. New York, NY: Wiley, 1992. 480p., illus., index. $35.00. ISBN: 0-471-52090-X.

This dictionary contains close to 2,000 garden plants, trees, shrubs, houseplants, annuals, perennials, vines, bulbs, and herbs. For each entry a description, use, and growing instructions are given.

2377. New Royal Horticultural Society Dictionary of Gardening. Anthony Huxley; Mark Griffiths; Margot Levy. New York, NY: Stockton Press, 1992. 4v., illus., index. $795.00. ISBN: 1-56159-001-0.

Also called the *New RHS Dictionary of Gardening*, this extensive dictionary covers some 50,000 plants, including every plant in cultivation in North America. It provides descriptions of each plus practical guidelines for growing each. Also included are essays on the craft, science, art, and history of gardening. Another 4-volume set useful for historical purposes would be the *Dictionary of Gardening* (Oxford University Press, 1956).

2378. Thesaurus of Agricultural Organisms: Pests, Weeds, and Diseases. New York, NY: Chapman & Hall, 1990. 2v., illus., index. $400.00. ISBN: 0-442-30422-6.

This very comprehensive dictionary covers agricultural pests, weeds, and diseases, giving descriptions of each and control measures.

2379. Weeds and Words: The Etymology of the Scientific Names of Weeds and Crops. Robert L. Zimdahl. Ames, IA: Iowa State University Press, 1989. 125p., illus., index. $19.95. ISBN: 0-8138-0128-1.

This small dictionary covers 228 weed species and 35 crops, giving etymology, names, description, and a brief discussion of why that name was chosen.

Directories

2380. Agricultural Research Centres. London, Great Britain: Longman, 1990. 987p., index. $470.00. ISBN: 0-582-06122-9.

This directory covers 130 countries and provides some 8,000 profiles of agricultural and technological laboratories doing research in agriculture, fisheries, food, forestry, horticulture, and veterinary science. Complete directory information and descriptions are given.

2381. European Directory of Agrochemical Products. 2nd. Hamish Kidd; Douglas Hartley; John M. Kennedy. Nottinghham, Great Britain: Royal Society of Chemistry, 1986. 4v., index. $249.00/volume. ISBN: 0-85186-673-5v.1.

This comprehensive directory/index of agrochemical products covers in 4 volumes: v.1—Fungicides; v.2—Herbicides; v.3—Insecticides and Acaricides; v.4—Plant growth regulators, etc.

2382. Field Guide to U.S. National Forests: Region by Region, State by State. Robert H. Mohlenbrock. Chicago, IL: Congdon & Weed, 1984. 304p., index. $11.95. ISBN: 0-312-92206-X.

This field guide provides descriptions of the national forests in the United States.

2383. Gardening by Mail 1: A Source Book. Barbara J. Barton. Sebastopol, CA: Tusker Press, 1987. 320p., index. $16.00. ISBN: 0-937633-02-X.

Although somewhat dated, this directory gives sources of information for seeds, supplies, and other gardening needs.

2384. Horticultural Research International: Directory of Horticultural Research Institutes and Their Activities in 63 Countries. 4th. International Society for Horticultural Science. Lanham, MD: UNIPUB, 1986. 903p., index. $175.00. ISBN: 90-6605-332-1.

Some 16,650 horticultural scientists at 1,250 institutes in 63 countries are included in this directory. Complete descriptions of each country and its institutes are given with names of prominent personnel.

2385. World Directory of Pesticide Control Organizations. George Ekstrom; Hamish Kidd. Boca Raton, FL: CRC, 1989. 311p., index. $79.95. ISBN: 0-85186-723-5.

This specialized directory lists organizations doing research and providing services in the area of pesticide control.

Encyclopedias

2386. American Horticultural Society Encyclopedia of Garden Plants. Christopher Brickell. New York, NY: Macmillan, 1989. 608p., illus., index. $49.95. ISBN: 0-02-557920-7.

The first part of this encyclopedia is a plant catalog containing descriptions of more than 4,000 garden plants. The second part contains advice on propagation, pruning, and pest or disease control of some 8,000 plants. Also of use would be the *Reader's Digest Encyclopedia of Garden Plants and Flowers* (Reader's Digest, 1987).

2387. Complete Vegetable Gardener's Sourcebook. revised. Duane Newcomb; Karen Newcomb. New York, NY: Prentice-Hall, 1989. 408p., illus., index. $14.95. ISBN: 0-13-612110-1.

This sourcebook is a good encyclopedia for vegetable gardeners giving descriptions, cultivation, and harvesting information.

2388. Concise Encyclopedia of Wood and Wood-Based Materials. Arno P. Schniewind; Robert W. Cahn; Michael B. Bever. New York, NY: Pergamon Press, 1989. 354p., illus., bibliog., index. $125.00. ISBN: 0-262-19289-6.

This title is a spin-off from the 1988 edition of the *Encyclopedia of Materials Science and Engineering.* It is intended to be a comprehensive encyclopedia covering all aspects of wood and wood-based materials. Also of use would be H.A. Core's *Wood Structures and Identification* (Syracuse University Press, 1985).

2389. Encyclopedia of Natural Insect and Disease Control: The Most Comprehensive Guide to Protecting Plants. Roger B. Yepsen. Emmaus, PA: Rodale Press, 1984. 490p., illus., index. $24.95. ISBN: 0-87857-488-3.

Previously called *Organic Plant Protection*, this is an encyclopedic guide to protecting plants from bugs, diseases, and the environment at large. For just ornamental plants consult Pascal Pompey Pirone's *Diseases and Pests of Ornamental Plants* (Wiley, 1978).

2390. Encyclopedia of Wood. revised. Forest Products Laboratory. New York, NY: Sterling, 1989. 464p., illus., bibliog., index. $19.95. ISBN: 0-8069-6994-6.

Originally published in 1930 by the U.S. government as the *Agriculture Handbook*, this useful book gives information on the physical and mechanical properties of wood and how these properties are affected by variations in the wood itself. For a worldwide identification of timber consult the 3-volume set *World Timbers* (University of Toronto Press, 1969).

2391. Larousse Gardens and Gardening. New York, NY: Facts on File, 1990. 624p., illus., index. $35.00. ISBN: 0-8160-2242-9.

This translation of *Larousse Jardins et Jardinage* covers history, garden types, techniques, and a descriptive list of ornamental plants. Also of use is *Rodale's Illustrated Encyclopedia of Gardening and Landscaping Techniques* (Rodale Press, 1990).

2392. New York Botanical Garden Illustrated Encyclopedia of Horticulture. Thomas H. Everett. New York, NY: Garland, 1980. 10v., illus. (part in color), bibliog, index. $1,070.00. ISBN: 0-8153-0256-8.

Also called *Encyclopedia of Horticulture*, this work is the ultimate source of information on gardening and horticulture. It is comprehensive in its 10 volumes covering everything from indoor gardening, plants, and organic gardening to pest control, economical aspects, and greenhouses.

2393. Oxford Companion to Gardens. Patrick Goode; Michael Lancaster. New York, NY: Oxford University Press, 1986. 635p., illus. (part in color), bibliog., index. $49.95; $25.00pbk. ISBN: 0-19-866123-1; 0-19-286138-7pbk.

This work is an encyclopedia of gardens as an art form, giving descriptions of notable gardens and the people who developed them.

2394. RHS Encyclopedia of House Plants: Including Greenhouse Plants. Kenneth A. Beckett. Topsfield, MA: Salem House, 1987. 492p., color illus., glossary, index. 434.95. ISBN: 0-88162-285-0.

For each entry in this encyclopedia a statement of the plant's origin is given followed with information on environment, temperature requirements, and plant shape. Also of interest would be *Rodale's Encyclopedia of Indoor Gardening* (Rodale Press, 1980).

2395. Rodale's All New Encyclopedia of Organic Gardening: The Indispensable Resource for Every Gardener. Fern Marshall Bradley; Barbara W. Ellis. Emmaus, PA: Rodale Press, 1992. 704p., illus., index. $29.95. ISBN: 0-87857-999-0.

This encyclopedia of 420 entries covers garden designs, landscape ideas, and techniques for growing flowers, fruits, and vegetables. The fruit and vegetable entries give information on growing, harvesting, fertilizing, pest control, freezing, and more; all within the range of organic gardening. Another related book for organic gardeners is Barbara W. Ellis's *Organic Gardener's Handbook of Natural Insect and Disease Control* (Rodale Press, 1992).

2396. Wise Garden Encyclopedia. New York, NY: HarperCollins, 1990. 1,043p., illus. $45.00. ISBN: 0-06-016114-0.

This encyclopedia of garden terms includes specific garden plants, processes, tools, vegetables, and other gardening information. An older but still useful book is Martin Stangl's *Chilton's Encyclopedia of Gardening* (Chilton, 1975).

2397. Wyman's Gardening Encyclopedia. 2nd. Donald Wyman. New York, NY: Macmillan, 1986. 1,221p., illus. $50.00. ISBN: 0-02-632070-3.

This book is one of the most widely recognized encyclopedias of gardening available covering everything from the plants to pesticide control to quarantining. For a brief amateur approach consult the *Time-Life Encyclopedia of Gardening* (Time-Life, 1980).

Guides to the Literature

2398. Gardening: A Guide to the Literature. Richard T. Isaacson. New York, NY: Garland, 1985. 198p., index. $22.00. ISBN: 0-8210-9019-5.

Gardening is a recommended and annotated list of some 700 books on all aspects of gardening

2399. Keyguide to Information Sources in Aquaculture. Deborah A. Turnbull. London, Great Britain: Mansell, 1989. 137p., index. $55.00. ISBN: 0-7201-1853-0.

This title is a very good guide to the primary reference sources covering aquaculture, including databases, newsletters, and annuals.

2400. North American Horticulture: A Reference Guide. 2nd. Thomas M. Barrett; American Horticultural Society. New York, NY: Macmillan, 1991. 427p., illus., index. price not available. ISBN: 0-02-897001-2.

Published by the foremost horticultural society in the country, this reference guide is comprehensive and up to date.

Handbooks and Manuals

2401. Agrochemicals Handbook. 3rd. Douglas Hartley; Hamish Kidd. London, Great Britain: Royal Society of Chemistry, 1991. 1v., various paging, index. $425.00. ISBN: 0-85186-416-3.

Over 750 pesticide active ingredients used in the agriculture industry are included in this handbook. Complete descriptions, uses, and warnings are given as well as prices. Biyearly updates are issued.

2402. Commercial Timbers of the World. 5th. Douglas Patterson; F.H. Titmuss. Brookfield, VT: Gower, 1988. 339p., illus., bibliog., index. $74.95. ISBN: 0-291-39718-2.

Previously called *Concise Encyclopedia of World Timbers*, this handbook covers the architectural and engineering aspects of timber as well as timber identification, properties, and processing. Also of use would be *Timbers of the World* (Construction Press, 1979-80).

2403. Complete Handbook of Garden Plants.
Michael Wright; Sue Minter; Brian Carter.
New York, NY: Facts on File, 1984. 544p.,
color illus., index. $24.95. ISBN:
0-87196-632-8.

Over 9,000 garden plants of the temperate zones are covered in this handbook, excluding fruits and vegetables. It is arranged in alphabetical order by botanical name, giving a complete description.

2404. Complete Vegetable Gardener's Sourcebook. new and revised. Duane Newcomb;
Karen Newcomb. New York, NY:
Prentice-Hall, 1989. 408p., illus., index.
$14.95. ISBN: 0-13-612110-1.

This handy little handbook covers topics such as soil types, organic gardening, and pest management. The largest and most useful part of the book is "vegetable varieties" which is an alphabetical listing of vegetables with descriptions.

**2405. CRC Handbook of Natural Pesticides:
Methods.** Bhushan N. Mandava. Boca Raton,
FL: CRC, 1985– , irregular. v.1– , bibliog.,
index. price per volume varies. ISBN:
0-8493-3651-1v.1.

Also called *Handbook of Natural Pesticides*, this is a comprehensive treatise/handbook covering all aspects of natural pesticides. The 6 volumes thus far published are v.1—Theory, practice, and detection; v.2—Isolation and identification; v.3—Insect growth regulators; v.4—Pheromones; v.5—Microbial insecticides; v.6—Attractants.

2406. Crop Protection Chemicals Reference.
7th. New York, NY: Wiley, 1991. 2,170p.,
index. $105.00. ISBN: 0-471-53282-7.

Over 500 agricultural chemicals are covered in this handbook giving content, patent number, EPA registry number, and trademarks, as well as safety and storage information.

**2407. European Garden Flora: A Manual for
the Identification of Plants Cultivated in
Europe, Both Out-of-Doors and Under Glass.**
S.M. Walters. New York, NY: Cambridge
University Press, 1984– , irregular. v.1– , illus.,
bibliog., index. price per volume varies. ISBN:
0-5212-4859-0v.1.

This comprehensive handbook describes all plants cultivated in Europe giving detailed descriptions for identification. The first 3 volumes cover v.1—Pteridophyta, Gymnospermae, Angiospermae-Monocotyledons; v.2—Monocotyledons; v.3—Picotyledons.

2408. Field Crop Diseases Handbook. 2nd.
Robert F. Nyvall. New York, NY: Van
Nostrand Reinhold, 1989. 817p., index. $99.95.
ISBN: 0-442-26722-3.

Some 1,200 diseases of 25 field crops are covered in this handbook giving cause, distribution, symptoms, and control.

2409. Forestry Handbook. 2nd. Karl F.
Wenger. New York, NY: Wiley, 1984. 1,335p.,
illus., bibliog., index. $75.00. ISBN:
0-471-06227-8.

This handbook is intended for the forester giving detailed information on all aspects of forestry including economy, harvesting, replanting, diseases, and recreational use of forests.

**2410. Garden Trees Handbook: A Complete
Guide to Choosing, Planting, and Caring for
Trees.** Alan Toogood. New York, NY: Facts
on File, 1990. 223p., illus. (part in color),
index. $19.95. ISBN: 0-8160-2275-5.

This publication is a good small handbook with excellent illustrations on the common trees found in gardens.

2411. Handbook of Edible Weeds. James A.
Duke. Boca Raton, FL: CRC, 1992. 246p.,
illus., index. $24.95. ISBN: 0-8493-34225-2.

Detailed descriptions of 100 edible weeds are given in this book.

2412. Insect Pests of Farm, Garden, and Orchard. 8th. Ralph H. Davidson; William F.
Lyon. New York, NY: Wiley, 1987. 640p.,
illus., bibliog., index. $46.95. ISBN:
0-471-01124-X.

Detailed descriptions are provided of all insect pests that farmers, gardeners, and fruit growers encounter. Control measures are also given. A smaller and more colorful handbook is *Rodale's Color Handbook of Garden Insects* (Rodale, 1983).

2413. Insects that Feed on Trees and Shrubs.
2nd revised. Warren T. Johnson; Howard H.
Lyon. Ithaca, NY: Comstock/Cornell, 1991.
528p., illus., bibliog., index. $52.50. ISBN:
0-8014-2602-2.

This authoritative handbook describes insects that feed on cultivated trees and shrubs. Complete descriptions for identification are given as well as methods of control.

2414. Introduction to Floriculture. 2nd. Roy
A. Larson. New York, NY: Academic Press,
1992. 636p., illus., bibliog., index. $54.50.
ISBN: 0-12-437651-7.

This textbook/handbook is on the specialized area of floriculture.

2415. Knott's Handbook for Vegetable Growers. 3rd. Oscar A. Lorenz; Donald N. Maynard.
New York, NY: Wiley, 1988. 456p., illus.,
index. $42.95. ISBN: 0-471-85240-6.

This useful handbook covers such topics as botanical and foreign names of vegetables, transplant and crop production, row covers, soils, fertilizers, irrigation, and weed control. Also of interest would be the *Organic Gardener's Complete Guide to Vegetables and Fruits* (Rodale, 1982).

2416. Manual of Cultivated Broad-Leafed Trees and Shrubs. Gerd Krussmann. London, Great Britain: Batsford, 1984-86. 3v., illus., bibliog., index. $65.00/volume. ISBN: 0-917304-78-1v.1; 0-88192-005-3v.2; 0-88192-006-1v.3.

Being a translation of *Handbuch der Laubgeholze*, this 3-volume treatise/handbook covers only broad-leafed trees and shrubs of the world. It has excellent descriptions to help in identification.

2417. Pesticide Handbook-Entoma. College Park, MD: Entomological Society of America, 1965– , irregular. v.1– , index. $7.50/issue. ISSN: 0553-8521.

Formed from the combination of *Pesticide Handbook* and *Entoma*, this ongoing handbook, published by the Entomological Society of America, describes the various pesticides that are currently in use.

2418. Pesticide Manual: A World Compendium. 9th. Charles R. Worthing; Raymond J. Hance. Cambridge, MA: Blackwell Scientific, 1991. 1,141p., index. $155.00. ISBN: 0-948404-42-6.

This general authority on pesticides gives details for over 650 compounds and microbial agents used as active ingredients of products for the control of crop pests and diseases, animal ectoparasites, and pests in public health. One section also lists superseded compounds.

2419. Plant Diseases of International Importance. A.N. Mukhopadhyay; U.S. Singh; J. Kuman; H.S. Chaube. New York, NY: Prentice-Hall, 1992. 4v., illus., index. $328.00. ISBN: 0-13-678582-4v.1; 0-13-678558-1v.2; 0-13-678566-2v.3; 0-13-67857-3v.4.

Over 80 of the most important crop diseases around the world are covered in detail in this 4-volume handbook. It presents historical background information, distribution and economic importance, symptoms, organisms or agents, disease cycle, inoculation and disease rating, epidemiology, and management of the disease. The 4 volumes cover v.1—Diseases of cereals and pulses; v.2—Diseases of vegetables and oil seed crops; v.3—Diseases of fruit crops; v.4—Diseases of sugar, forest, and plantation crops.

2420. Principles of Gardening. Hugh Johnson. New York, NY: Simon & Schuster, 1984. 272p., illus. (part in color), bibliog., index. $17.95. ISBN: 0-671-50805-9.

This small guide covers amateur gardening.

2421. Rodale's Garden Insect, Disease and Weed Identification Guide. Miranda Smith; Anna Carr. Emmaus, PA: Rodale Press, 1985. 328p., illus. (part in color), bibliog., glossary, index. $21.95; $15.95pbk. ISBN: 0-87857-758-0; 0-87857-759-9pbk.

This is not a book on how to control insects, diseases, and weeds with insecticides and pesticides but rather an identification handbook that helps to educate farmers and gardeners in recognizing life cycles, growth habits, and the ecological role of all three.

2422. Vegetable Growing Handbook: Organic and Traditional Methods. 3rd. Walter E. Splittstoesser. New York, NY: Van Nostrand Reinhold, 1990. 362p., illus., bibliog., index. $42.95. ISBN: 0-442-23971-8.

The first half of this well-known handbook deals with vegetable production, while the second half covers in encyclopedic format individual vegetables with descriptions about growing. Also of use would be Mas Yamaguchi's *World Vegetables* (Avi, 1983).

2423. Weed Control Handbook. 8th. Raymond J. Hance; K. Holly. Cambridge, MA: Blackwell Scientific, 1990. 582p., illus., index. $94.00. ISBN: 0-632-02459-3.

This handbook gives information about weeds, herbicides, and the principles governing weed control and vegetation management. The formulation and application of herbicides is treated as a separate chapter.

2424. Why and How of Home Horticulture. D.R. Bienz. San Francisco, CA: W.H. Freeman, 1980. 513p., illus., bibliog., index. $34.95. ISBN: 0-7167-1078-1.

This textbook-style handbook explains how to be an amateur horticulturist.

Histories

2425. Encyclopedia of American Forests and Conservation History. Richard C. Davis. New York, NY: Macmillan, 1983. 2v., illus., index. $200.00. ISBN: 0-02-907350-2.

This encyclopedia is an excellent history of the growth of the forestry industry in the United States. Articles are well-documented. For a bibliography of American forest history consult Ronald J. Fahl's *North American Forest and Conservation History* (Duke University Press, 1977).

2426. Historical Dictionary of Forestry and Woodland Terms. N.D.G. James. New York, NY: Blackwell, 1991. 235p. $49.95. ISBN: 0-63-117636-5.

Historical terms associated with forestry are included in this dictionary.

Yearbooks, Annuals, and Almanacs

2427. FAO Fertilizer Yearbook. Lanham, MD: FAO, 1951– , annual. v.1– , index. $39.00. ISSN: 0251-1525.

Previously called *Annual Fertilizer Review, Fertilizers: An Annual Review of World Production, Consumption and Trade*, and *Annual Review of World Production, Consumption, and Trade of Fertlizers*, this yearbook presents statistical information on all aspects of fertilizers and their uses.

2428. FAO Yearbook: Forest Products. Lanham, MD: FAO, 1946– , annual. v.1– , index. $36.00. ISBN: 92-5-002892-X 1990.

This annual provides tabular statistics on forest production and the import and export of forest products. Statistics are provided for the previous 12 years.

Periodicals

2429. Agronomy Journal. Madison, WI: American Society of Agronomy, 1907– , bimonthly. v.1– , index. $85.00. ISSN: 0002-1962.

2430. American Nurseryman. Chicago, IL: American Nurseryman, 1904– , semimonthly. v.1– , index. $45.00. ISSN: 0003-0198.

2431. American Potato Journal. Orono, ME: Potato Association of America, 1913– , monthly. v.1– , index. $40.00. ISSN: 0003-0589.

2432. Canadian Journal of Forest Research. Ottawa, Ontario: National Research Council of Canada, 1971– , monthly. v.1– , index. $91.00. ISSN: 0045-5067.

2433. Canadian Journal of Soil Science. Ottawa, Ontario: Agricultural Institute of Canada, 1921– , quarterly. v.1– , index. $107.00. ISSN: 0008-4271.

2434. Cereal Chemistry. St Paul, MN: American Association of Cereal Chemists, 1924– , bimonthly. v.1– , index. $120.00. ISSN: 0009-0352.

2435. Cereal Foods World. St Paul, MN: American Association of Cereal Chemists, 1956– , monthly. v.1– , index. $70.00. ISSN: 0146-6283.

2436. Crop Science. Madison, WI: Crop Science Society of America, 1961– , bimonthly. v.1– , index. $65.00. ISSN: 0011-183X.

2437. Fertilizer Research. Doredrecht, Netherlands: Kluwer, 1980– , monthly. v.1– , index. $860.00. ISSN: 0167-1731.

2438. Fine Gardening. Newton, CT: Taunton Press, 1988– , bimonthly. v.1– , index. $24.00. ISSN: 0896-6281.

2439. Florists' Review. Topeka, KS: Florists' Review, 1897– , monthly. v.1– , index. $36.00. ISSN: 0015-4423.

2440. Flower and Garden. Kansas City, MO: KC Publishing, 1957– , bimonthly. v.1– , index. $12.95. ISSN: 0162-3249.

2441. Forest Ecology and Management. Amsterdam, Netherlands: Elsevier, 1978– , 32/year. v.1– , index. $1,176.00. ISSN: 0378-1127.

2442. Forest Products Journal. Madison, WI: Forest Products Research Society, 1947– , 10/year. v.1– , index. $115.00. ISSN: 0015-7473.

2443. Forest Sciences. Bethesda, MD: Society of American Foresters, 1955– , quarterly. v.1– , index. $45.00. ISSN: 0015-749X.

2444. Grass and Forage Science. Oxford, Great Britain: Blackwell, 1946– , quarterly. v.1– , index. $142.00. ISSN: 0142-5242.

2445. Horticulture. Boston, MA: Horticulture Limited Partnership, 1904– , monthly. v.1– , index. $20.00. ISSN: 0018-5329.

2446. Journal of Forestry. Bethesda, MD: Society of American Foresters, 1902– , monthly. v.1– , index. $50.00. ISSN: 0022-1201.

2447. Journal of Horticultural Science. Ashford, Great Britain: Headley Brother/Horticultural and Agricultural Research Station, 1919– , bimonthly. v.1– , index. $195.00. ISSN: 0022-1589.

2448. Journal of Soil Science. Osney Mead, Great Britain: Blackwell, 1950– , quarterly. v.1– , index. $126.00. ISSN: 0022-4588.

2449. Journal of the American Society for Horticultural Science. Alexandria, VA: American Society for Horticultural Science, 1903– , bimonthly. v.1– , index. $165.00. ISSN: 0003-1062.

2450. Journal of the Soil Science of America.
Madison, WI: Soil Science of America, 1936– ,
bimonthly. v.1– , index. $85.00. ISSN:
0361-5995.

2451. Pest Control. Cleveland, OH: Avanstar
Communications, 1933– , monthly. v.1– ,
index. $22.00. ISSN: 0031-6121.

2452. Pesticide Biochemistry and Physiology.
San Diego, CA: Academic Press, 1971– ,
9/year. v.1– , index. $342.00. ISSN: 0048-3575.

2453. Pesticide Science. Barking, Great
Britain: Elsevier, 1970– , 12/year. v.1– , index.
$526.00. ISSN: 0031-613X.

2454. Plant Disease. St Paul, MN: APS
Press/American Phytopathological Society,
1917– , monthly. v.1– , index. $210.00. ISSN:
0191-1917.

2455. Science of Food and Agriculture.
Ames, IA: Council for Agricultural Science
and Technology, 1983– , semiannual. v.1– ,
index. $10.00. ISSN: 0738-9310.

2456. Seed World. Des Plaines, IL: Scranton
Gillette Communications, 1915– , monthly.
v.1– , index. $18.00. ISSN: 0037-0797.

2457. Soil Science. Baltimore, MD: Williams
& Wilkins, 1916– , monthly. v.1– , index.
$105.00. ISSN: 0038-075X.

2458. Weed Research. Oxford, Great Britain:
Blackwell, 1961– , bimonthly. v.1– , index.
$168.00. ISSN: 0043-1737.

2459. Weed Science. Champaign, IL: Weed
Science Society of America, 1952– , quarterly.
v.1– , index. $80.00. ISSN: 0043-1745.

PART 3
Indexes

Title Index

Author Index

Subject Index

Brain

Building

Ecology

Econometrics

Economic Geology

Edible Plants

Electric Lighting

Electric Motors

Electrical Engineering

Fairs

Historical Directory of American Agricultural Fairs, **2200**

Fastening

Standard Handbook of Fastening and Joining, **1711**

Ferns

Encyclopedia of Ferns, **352**

Ferns and Allied Plants: With Special Reference to Tropical America, **354**

Peterson Field Guide Series, **254**

Fertilizers

FAO Fertilizer Yearbook, **2427**

Fiber Optics

Fiber Optics Standard Dictionary, **1340**

Film Production

Computer Animation Dictionary: Including Related Terms Used in Computer Graphics, Film and Video, Production, and Desktop Publishing, **533**

Filters

Electronic Filter Design Handbook: LC Active, and Digital Filters, **1368**

First Aid

American Red Cross First Aid and Safety Handbook, **2014**

First Aid Manual for Chemical Accidents, **468**

Fish Diseases

Handbook of Fish Diseases, **981**

Fisheries

Agricultural and Animal Sciences Journals and Serials: An Analytical Guide, **2202**

Agricultural Research Centres, **2380**

Aquatic Sciences and Fisheries Abstracts, **914**

Elsevier's Dictionary of Fishery, Processing, Fish, and Shellfish Names of the World, **2234**

FAO Fisheries Series, **2264**

Fishes

All about Tropical Fish, **2249**

Aquarium Encyclopedia, **2235**

Audubon Society Field Guides, **253**

Birds: A Guide to the Literature, **971**

Dr. Axelrod's Atlas of Freshwater Aquarium Fishes, **2241**

Dr. Burgess's Atlas of Marine Aquarium Fishes, **2242**

Encyclopedia of Aquatic Life, **946**

Fish Physiology, **1001**

Fishes of the World, **979**

Handbook of Fish Diseases, **981**

Handbook of Tropical Aquarium Fishes, **986**

History of Fishes, **999**

World Encyclopedia of Fishes, **963**

Flavorings

Rodale's Illustrated Encyclopedia of Herbs, **358**

Flavors

Source Book of Flavors, **2345**

Floriculture

Glossary for Horticultural Crops, **2373**

Introduction to Floriculture, **2414**

Flowering Plants

Flowering Plant Index of Illustration and Information, **324**

Flowering Plants of the World, **355**

Index Kewensis: Plantarum Phanerogamarum Nomina et Synonyma Omnium Generum et Specierum a Linnaeo Usque ad Annum MDCCCLXXXV Complectens, **326**

Flowers

Audubon Society Field Guides, **253**

Color Dictionary of Flowers and Plants for Home and Garden, **2369**

Peterson Field Guide Series, **254**

Flowmeters

Flow Measurement Engineering Handbook, **1693**

Fluid Mechanics

Encyclopedia of Fluid Mechanics, **1689**

Fluid Power

Fluid Abstracts, **1219**

Fluids

Fluid Flow Measurement Abstracts, **1683**

Fluid Mechanics Source Book, **1694**

Fluid Power Design Handbook, **1695**

Food Additives

Consumer's Dictionary of Food Additives, **2295**

Food Additives Handbook, **2330**

Food Science

AACC Approved Methods, **2326**

ACCIS Guide to UN Information Sources on Food and Agriculture, **2305**

Agricultural Research Centres, **2380**

Alexis Lichine's New Encyclopedia of Wines and Spirits, **2309**

American Regional Cookery Index, **2284**

Bowes and Church's Food Values of Portions Commonly Used, **2327**

British Food Journal, **2346**

Chef's Companion: A Concise Dictionary of Culinary Terms, **2293**

Chilton's Food Engineering, **2347**

Columbia Encyclopedia of Nutrition, **2310**

Complete Beverage Dictionary, **2294**

Complete Book of Food: A Nutritional, Medical and Culinary Guide, **2328**

Complete Book of Herbs, Spices, and Condiments, **2311**

Consumer Health and Nutrition Index, **2285**

Consumer's Dictionary of Food Additives, **2295**

Cooking A to Z, **2296**

Cooks Index: An Index of Cookery Periodicals and Cookbooks, **2286**

Cooksource: An Indispensable Guide to the Best Mailorder Sources for Specialty Foods, Ethnics, and Regional Ingredients and Other Kitchen Supplies, **2306**

Dairy Foods, **2348**

Dictionary of Food and Nutrition, **2297**

Dictionary of Food Ingredients, **2298**

Mental Disorders